W9-CZI-897

AFRICAN AMERICAN
WRITERS

AFRICAN AMERICAN WRITERS

SECOND EDITION

VALERIE SMITH

EDITOR IN CHIEF

VOLUME 1

JAMES BALDWIN TO GAYL JONES

Charles Scribner's Sons
an imprint of the Gale Group
New York • Detroit • San Francisco • London • Boston • Woodbridge, CT

Charles Scribner's Sons
1633 Broadway
New York, NY 10019

Gale Group
27500 Drake Rd.
Farmington Hills, MI 48331

1 2 3 4 5 6 7 8 9 10

Printed in the United States of America

Library of Congress Cataloging-in-Publication Data

African American Writers / Valerie Smith, editor.   Rev. ed.
      p. cm.
      Includes bibliographical references and index.
      ISBN 0-684-80638-X (set)   ISBN 0-684-80639-8 (vol. 1)   ISBN 0-684-80640-1 (vol. 2)
      1. American literature—Afro-American authors—Dictionaries. 2. Afro-American authors—Biography—Dictionaries. 3. Afro-Americans in literature—Dictionaries. I. Smith, Valerie, 1956–
PS153.N5 A344   2000
810.9′896073′03   dc21
00-058371

CONTENTS

Volume I

CONTENTS

Volume II

INTRODUCTION

*A*FRICAN AMERICAN WRITERS, second edition, is designed as a work of reference to complement both *American Writers*, the multi-volume set of literary biographies of authors past and present, which was first published in 1974, and *African American Writers*, first edition, which first appeared in 1991.

The articles in this work are intended to appeal to a wide readership, including students in secondary and advanced education, teachers, librarians, scholars, editors, and critics, as well as the general public. Their purpose is to provide an introduction to the work of African American writers who have made a significant contribution to African American, American, and world letters, culture, and history; to stimulate the reader's enjoyment of the texts produced by these authors; and to give students the means to pursue further study of specific writers or the field in general. The articles do not conform to a fixed pattern, but speaking generally, each contains a biographical overview, a survey of the subject's principal writings, and an assessment of the work as a whole. Each article is equipped with a selected bibliography that records the subject's writings in chronological order, in the form both of collected editions and of separate works, including modern and paperback editions. When relevant, the bibliography lists film adaptations and the author's work in other media. The bibliography concludes with a list of biographical and critical publications, including both books and articles, to guide the reader who is interested in further research.

African American Writers is not conceived as an encyclopedia of literature by African Americans, nor is it a series of articles planned so comprehensively as to include every African American writer of historical importance. It is rather more a critical anthology possessing both the virtues and the limitations of such a grouping. It offers neither the schematized form of the encyclopedia nor the ostensible completeness of design of the literary history. On the other hand, it is limited neither by the impersonality of the one nor the uniformity of the other. Since each contributor speaks with only one voice out of many, she or he is principally concerned with explaining her or his subject as fully as possible rather than with establishing an order of merit or making "placing" comparisons (since each contributor might well "place" differently). The prime task is one of presentation and exposition rather than of assigning critical praise or censure. The contributors consist of established as well as emerging literary scholars and critics; each writes enthusiastically about her or his subject and sets out to explain the author's significance.

This edition was initially conceived as a text that would expand the range of the first edition of *African American Writers*, which was developed in response to the increased critical and popular attention African American literature has received since the 1960s and to compensate for the underrepresentation of African American writers in the earlier *American Writers* volumes. To reflect important, recent developments in Afro-Americanist literary criticism and theory, the first edition included entries on slave narrators, playwrights, and a range of black feminist writers. However, given practical considerations, such as the necessity for uniform page counts, the anthology could not pretend to absolute comprehensiveness. Generally speaking, younger, contemporary writers who have published fewer than three texts or who have published only during the previous five years were absent from that volume. For the most part, the writers included had produced a substantial body of work that reflected the diversity of African American literary and intellectual work.

The second edition of *African American Writers* differs substantially from its predecessor. Twenty-one new subjects have been added, so that the text includes more essays on African American literary figures and topics that have gained in importance during the last decade. For example, the essays on Lucille Clifton, Countee Cullen, Michael Harper, Yusef Komunyakaa, Jay Wright, and the Black Arts movement respond to a much-needed, heightened interest in African American poetry. The articles on Toni Cade Bambara, Octavia Butler, Samuel Delany, Leon Forrest, Charles Johnson, Adrienne Kennedy, Jamaica Kincaid, Clarence Major, John A. Williams, Sherley Anne Williams, and August Wilson reflect the impact of these authors' contributions during the last decade and suggest the complexity of black postmodernist writing. Earlier writers—such as Jessie Fauset, Chester Himes, and Pauline Hopkins—have been added in recognition of their influential contributions as prose writers and cultural critics. And a new essay on spiritual autobiography has been included to raise the reader's awareness of the significance of this genre to the history of African American letters. In addition, essays from the first edition have all been either updated or substantially revised, to reflect either developments in the critical assessment of the subject, or to incorporate discussions of the writer's recent work. Finally, the look of the anthology has been changed in favor of a more attractive, two-volume glossy format.

Because of the specific set of historical conditions under which the first African Americans were brought to this country and the various forms of oppression they have endured subsequently, African American writers have confronted complex issues of influence and reception. As is the case with all writers, African American authors have sought literary models whose work they might engage as they produce their own texts. Yet the ideological, critical, and aesthetic assumptions of their American and European models, rooted in a Western humanist tradition that has denied the full humanity of blacks, women, and other marginalized communities, often confront them with im-

INTRODUCTION

ages and narrative strategies that subvert the purposes of their own literary endeavors.

In addition, as Henry Louis Gates Jr. and others have argued, African American literature was long read for its documentary, rather than its aesthetic value. Early intellectuals were initially interested in the poetry of Phillis Wheatley, for example, because it exemplified the rational capacities, and thereby the humanity of people of African descent. During the antebellum period, slave narratives were read largely as evidence of the atrocities slaves endured. Well into the twentieth century, critiques of literature by African Americans continue to address the authenticity of its representations.

All literature might be said to be ideological, shaped as it is by the social and political circumstances under which it is produced. The political nature of African American literature is especially pronounced, given these issues of influence and reception as well as the larger fact that it is created by people who represent a population that has historically been oppressed. Nevertheless, as one considers the relation between African American literature and the contexts within which it is produced, one must also acknowledge that the works are not mere polemic. The authors undertake various stylistic and generic experiments; their work must be read to assess its aesthetic as well as its political achievements.

The contributors to this work employ a range of strategies to address the complicated status of black texts as, simultaneously, aesthetic objects and political responses. Critics historically viewed the poetry of Phillis Wheatley, the first African American to publish a book, as being both imitative of Neoclassical verse by such figures as Alexander Pope and Samuel Pepys, and detached from the exigencies of the experience of slavery. More recent scholarship on Wheatley's work has revealed the subversive impulse beneath the restrained surface of her poems.

John C. Shields shows in his essay on Wheatley that not only does the content of her poetry address subtly the issue of slavery, but her use of imagery displays an awareness of her African heritage and articulates a revolutionary poetics. Shields' close readings of several of Wheatley's lyrics reveal the striking complexity of her language. He explores the nature of her oft-cited debt to a number of sixteenth- and seventeenth-century English poets. Yet Shields also argues that Wheatley is able to challenge some of the assumptions of her literary models by introducing and manipulating metaphors and strategies of address derived from African cultural traditions and practice.

The narratives written by freed and fugitive slaves more clearly and directly exemplify the links between literary production and historical circumstances for African American writers. The earliest genre in which substantial numbers of African American writers published, slave narratives were generally commissioned by Northern white abolitionists in order to generate anti-slavery sentiment. With their vivid accounts of the kinds of atrocities to which slaves were submitted and their poignant descriptions of slave suffering, these texts served their polemic purpose well. Yet their political agenda is linked subtly to their personal function. By writing the story of their lives in slavery and their achievement of freedom, the slave narrators claimed their right to their subjectivity, no mean feat for a people who by law were counted as only three-fifths human.

INTRODUCTION

In his essay on the slave narratives, Mason Lowance Jr. describes the complex aims of these works. Testimonies of personal experience, the narratives were intended also to analyze and criticize the inhumane system of slavery. Moreover, even as they are constructed out of the creative and imaginative processes of memory, they were required to bear the burden of facticity. To prove their veracity most incorporate the text of actual documents from slavery, such as bills of sale from slave auctions.

Lowance explores ways in which several specific narrators experiment with oral and written expressive forms in order to construct frameworks for the stories of their lives. For example, the formulaic structure of many of the narratives reflects both their origin in African oral traditions and the demands and restrictions placed upon their content by the abolitionist movement. The narrators treated here employ the structure and certain metaphors found in Puritan spiritual autobiographies, yet they generally focus more on the achievements of an individual self, or that self in relation to a community of fellow slaves, than on the experience of divine guidance. Additionally, they draw on conventions of the American Indian captivity narratives; for the slave narrators, however, the white, ostensibly Christian, and civilized characters are generally the villains.

The end of the Civil War and Emancipation did not mean the end of the racist oppression of African Americans; their exploitation simply assumed other forms. Economic and political claims of newly freed blacks fanned pervasive racial fears and hatred, spawning a segregated Southern, Jim Crow culture with lynching, vigilante justice, and limited educational opportunities. Late nineteenth- and early twentieth-century African American writers took on these subjects in hopes of contributing to a social revolution. These writers' commitments to the political implications of their creative work are all the more apparent when we note that several of them maintained careers simultaneously as activists and literary figures.

Frances Ellen Watkins Harper's long life spanned most of the nineteenth century as well as the first decade of the twentieth. During her career she lectured professionally for the anti-slavery cause as well as the movement for equal rights after the Civil War. Indeed, as Frances Smith Foster demonstrates in her essay, Harper was one of the first African American women to support herself primarily through her political work, speaking widely in support of abolition, temperance, civil rights, and peace. Moreover, like many of her contemporaries, she sought ways of unifying her aesthetic and political impulses: her poetry and fiction alike reveal her attempts to use familiar literary forms to proffer penetrating social critiques and articulate bold programs for social change.

In her essay, Daphne Brooks explores how Pauline Hopkins, "the single most productive black woman writer at the turn of the century," worked in a range of genres in order to contribute to contemporaneous social movements and struggles for racial autonomy and self-definition. Drawing on feminist performance theory as well as the intellectual history of the period, she suggests subtle connections within Hopkins' diverse body of work and points to her enduring impact on future generations of writers.

During his lifetime, Charles Waddell Chesnutt supported himself alternatively as an attorney and a writer. As William L. Andrews argues, Chesnutt believed that literature might lead Americans to a vision of racial equality; in his early fiction he drew on characters and dialect his readers would recognize from the "plantation tradition" novels to convey his social message. In the hands of southern apologists, including Thomas Nelson Page and Thomas Dixon, such stories of the Old South lamented the passing of the slavery period. Chesnutt manipulated these conventional settings to describe the nature of folk life and rituals in the antebellum period and to critique exploitative practices during slavery and Reconstruction.

Chesnutt enjoyed a widespread readership so long as he wrote in this mode. As his career evolved, however, he was drawn increasingly to writing novels that addressed the political and racial situation of his day more directly. His 1901 novel, *The Marrow of Tradition,* for instance, offers a fictionalized account of the 1898 Wilmington, North Carolina, riots. As his writing became more politically engaged, Chesnutt's readership declined; he was viewed by his contemporary white readership as focusing too directly on volatile subject matter.

Educator, publisher and editor, attorney, lyricist, diplomat, journalist, poet, novelist, and secretary of the National Association for the Advancement of Colored People, James Weldon Johnson played a major role in the political and literary traditions of African Americans. As Joseph T. Skerrett Jr. demonstrates, throughout much of his life, Johnson too sought to reconcile his political and artistic ideas. His was a prominent and insistent voice in the struggle for national anti-lynching legislation. In his various literary pursuits he sought to reveal the indigenous power as well as the expressive potentialities of so-called Negro music and verse.

All of these writers sustained varied and diverse careers. Yet in her or his own way, each made substantial contributions to the development of an African American literary tradition. Not only did Harper, Hopkins, Chesnutt, and Johnson provide models for ways in which subsequent generations of writers might represent issues of racial and sexual difference and programs for social change in fictional and poetic forms, but they also explored the literary possibilities of the dialect that had come to be associated with the culture of African Americans. Their efforts to mine the expressive power of colloquial speech inspired much of the experimentation with the vernacular that has characterized the work of later African American writers.

As Esther Nettles Rauch remarks, historians consider the 1890s to be the nadir of post-Civil War United States history. During this time, separate schools, churches, modes of transportation and other public services sprung up for black and white Americans. The tyranny of Jim Crow, lynching, low pay, and increasing numbers of race riots led to an exodus from the South to northern cities such as East St. Louis, Chicago, Baltimore, Philadelphia, and New York City.

New cultural and political energy developed in these urban centers; cultural historians and literary critics have called the period from 1917 to 1929, characterized by a substantial volume of intellectual and creative work, the Harlem Renaissance. Bruce Kellner identifies 1917 as the pivotal year in this era for three reasons. During this year the first Silent Protest Parade (a mass demonstration against racial violence nationwide) occurred; Claude McKay published three poems in a journal with a largely white circulation; and three plays about black Americans opened on Broadway. James Weldon Johnson, W. E. B. Du Bois, and Marcus Garvey ranked among the key political and intellectual figures of the era.

The burgeoning population of Harlem during this era reflected the diversity of African American life. Concentrated in this small community were working-class families and individuals as well as middle-class professionals, literary figures, and entertainers. It proved to be the center for significant political organizations, such as Garvey's Universal Negro Improvement Association. In Harlem, musical and literary forms developed; authors such as Jean Toomer, Jessie Redmon Fauset, Nella Larsen, Langston Hughes, Countee Cullen, Zora Neale Hurston, Johnson, and McKay figured centrally in this world. Not surprisingly, Harlem was a cultural center for blacks in New York City. It also appealed to cosmopolitan whites who considered the lives and culture of people of color to be exotic.

In their work, the authors of the period respond to the challenges and concerns raised by their antecedents, and to the sociological, political, and aesthetic issues sparked by the complexity of the contemporary scene. As the black middle class in general and the black middle class readership in particular expanded, complex questions emerged as to what topics black arts and letters ought to address. Many outspoken intellectuals believed that black artists should take the more affluent and educated members of their race as their subjects to provide models for other African Americans and evidence for whites of black abilities and talents. To their minds, blacks who represented the comic, profligate, or primitive aspects of their culture capitulated to the tastes of the white readers to the detriment of blacks. On the other hand, many black artists defended their right to select their subjects as they saw fit; they believed that the essence and power of black culture was to be found among its poor, working class, and rural folk.

W. E. B. Du Bois—novelist, poet, essayist, sociologist, political theorist, activist, editor, and one of the most influential figures this country has produced—figured centrally in the political and intellectual life of black America during this period and throughout the twentieth century. As a founding member of the all-black radical Niagara movement and the integrated NAACP, as well as the first editor-in-chief of *The Crisis*, the NAACP journal, Du Bois helped set the agenda for African American social change. Throughout his career he explored questions about the nature and potentialities of human, specifically black leadership.

George Cunningham notes that in *The Souls of Black Folk*, Du Bois critiques the materialism, accommodation, and ignorance he associates with Booker T. Washington, the premier black leader in the late nineteenth century. Returning to a notion he had considered earlier, that individuals ought to strive to embody the most distinguished characteristics of their society and culture, Du Bois contrasts the figure of Washington with those of other nineteenth-century leaders possessed of idealism, intelligence, and a willingness to struggle. Moreover, in *Souls*, Du Bois constructs a notion of African America that is rooted in the spirit of the folk derived from Africa.

Du Bois' vision of human idealism and the redemptive power of the black folk explains his lack of sympathy with some of the kinds of writing his contemporaries produced. While he approved of Jean Toomer's *Cane*, wishing only that Toomer had written in a less self-consciously lyrical manner, he had little patience for works that focused on the urban environment and its potential for sensual expression. He remained concerned that black writers represent the most admirable qualities of the race to their white readers.

In texts that focus primarily on the black elite, Nella Larsen and Jessie Fauset explored the complex interactions of race and class in their writing. Jacquelyn Y. McClendon describes Larsen's exploration of the psychological effects of racial dualism and marginality on the burgeoning urban black middle class in her novels *Quicksand* and *Passing*. Her fictions of the color line recall the questions of racial and sexual difference raised by Johnson and Chesnutt.

A highly educated and well-traveled woman, Fauset taught high school and worked as an influential journalist and editor in addition to publishing several novels, poems, and works of short fiction. Lois Leveen reads her novels as texts that reveal both the opportunities available to and the limitations imposed upon working- and middle-class African Americans in the early decades of the twentieth century. Moreover, the essay provides a sense of her varied contributions to African American intellectual life during and after the Harlem Renaissance.

According to Nathan Grant, Countee Cullen embodied many of the contradictions and complications associated with the Renaissance. Most notably, he was educated in the classic literatures and cultures of the west, yet sought to articulate the struggles of black people in the United States and throughout the world. Although he wrote a novel and some literature for children, Cullen is perhaps best known for his sonnets and lyric poems.

Claude McKay, Langston Hughes, and Zora Neale Hurston, on the other hand, all drew their inspiration from black vernacular culture. McKay, a cosmopolitan intellectual who lived in Jamaica, the United States, Europe, and North Africa, mined the cultural traditions of black common people for his poetic inspiration. Wayne Cooper demonstrates the variety of ways in which McKay experimented with the possibilities of Jamaican dialect poetry. Working within models derived from Elizabethan and Romantic verse, McKay developed a vision of personal and racial past and present condition.

Hughes' voluminous output makes him one of the most important African American artists of his era and of the twentieth century. As Arnold Rampersad argues, throughout his career, Hughes sought to capture the cadences of common American speech both in poetry and in prose. In his early verse, Hughes tried to preserve the content of the blues within traditional European verse forms. He later developed the forms of blues poetry.

Zora Neale Hurston, trained as an anthropologist, spent years documenting the speech of African Americans throughout the South. This research led to the publication of her collections of African American folktales; moreover, it informed the language of her fiction, including her best-known and most influential novel, *Their Eyes Were Watching God*. As Cheryl Wall shows, Hurston's contemporaries considered her story of rural black folk to be politically retrograde, palatable primarily to the white taste for nonthreatening black characters and situations. So thorough was black disapproval of her work, that throughout much her life, Hurston's writings were out of print. Only after her death, and with the rise of black feminism, has her work begun to achieve its rightful place in the canon of black letters.

INTRODUCTION

The debate over the appropriate content and styles for black writers was played out in highly publicized differences among three central figures in the evolution of African American fiction: Richard Wright, Ralph Ellison, and James Baldwin. Wright was first able to find an outlet for his creativity and his political energy through the Communist Party's John Reed Clubs and Franklin D. Roosevelt's Federal Writers' Project in Chicago during the Great Depression. When he moved to New York in the mid 1930s he articulated and defined his ideas about the work that black writing should perform. Best known for his experiments with literary naturalism, Wright sought to represent the conditions that circumscribed the lives of the black underclass. Joyce Ann Joyce points out that notwithstanding his ideological commitments, Wright was also committed to perfecting his craft.

However, Wright rejected African American writing that, to his mind, reproduced stereotypes of the rural folk or celebrated the achievements of the black middle class. The arbitrariness of this kind of ideologically based judgment is evident in his assessment of a complex work such as Hurston's *Their Eyes Were Watching God*. In his *New Masses* review he argues that the book capitulated to white people's stereotyped fantasies about black lives, calling it a novel with "no theme, no message, no thought."

Robert G. O'Meally describes the time when Wright and Ralph Ellison first met in Harlem during the 1930s. Although both were relative newcomers to the urban literary scene, Wright was older and on the verge of his first major success. The two men admired each other's talents and shared common political beliefs; Wright encouraged Ellison to continue writing. By the 1940s, however, Ellison's career began to follow a different direction from Wright's. For him, characters such as Wright's Bigger Thomas (in *Native Son*) were less than human, constructed primarily as indictments of white oppression. Throughout his writing he eschews narrowly defined ideological agendas in favor of meditative fictions and essays that seek to illuminate the complexities and paradoxes of the human condition.

The subtleties of *Invisible Man* made it a critical and popular success when it was published in 1953. However, by the time of the Black Nationalist movement of the late 1960s, Ellison was looked upon with some skepticism by African American radical intellectuals. They accused him and his work of an accommodationist impulse, a charge with which Ellison may have at least partly agreed, since, as O'Meally notes, for Ellison the imagination is integrative.

Wright served also as an enthusiastic mentor for James Baldwin, first in Harlem and later in Europe during the 1940s. That relationship, too, broke down over disagreements about the ideological work of black literature. Baldwin publically criticized *Native Son*. His attacks on the book separated him from Wright and alienated him from a number of the key figures in the black intellectual and literary community. Yet, David Van Leer shows that Baldwin's political affinities shifted throughout his career. The aestheticized distancing in his earlier work over time becomes replaced by a more prophetic and politicized conception of the meaning of blackness in America by the mid sixties.

Although this account of major developments in African American literature privileges the achievements of three canonized, male fiction writers, the range of authors represented in this edition makes clear that poets and women writers made substantial contributions to black and American letters during the middle decades of the twentieth century. In his discussion of the work of Melvin Tolson, Wilburn Williams shows that this poet defies the familiar categorizations of African American literary history. Tolson was born in the late nineteenth century, a contemporary of writers such as Jean Toomer. His career trajectory is atypical, for he published the poetry for which he is best known late in life. So too are the subjects and forms of his poetry unusual. While the content of his poetry reflects his immersion in African American history and culture, he displays a complex relationship to modernism, Marxism, and canonical white British and American writers.

According to Alan M. Wald, the work of Chester Himes only began to receive the critical attention it deserves in recent decades. A prolific and important midcentury writer, Himes is perhaps best known for his early radical fiction and the series of detective novels he wrote after emigrating first to France and then to Spain. His concern with such issues as the construction of black masculinities, social history, the politics of labor, and the meaning of national identity put his work in important dialog with both his contemporaries and subsequent generations of writers.

A contemporary of Richard Wright and Chester Himes, Ann Petry is perhaps best known for her naturalist novel, *The Street,* which some critics underestimate, considering it a feminist version of *Native Son.* The novel is much more complex than that formulation suggests, however; its subtle representation of the ways in which race, class, and gender inform and transform each other in the lives of urban black men and women have made it a profoundly influential text in its own right. Marilyn Mobley McKenzie's essay provides an intensive discussion of Petry's other works—short stories, novels, and children's fiction—to indicate the range of topics the writer addressed throughout her career.

The work of Gwendolyn Brooks—novelist, autobiographer, and Pulitzer Prize–winning poet—reflects many of the intellectual and political developments of the twentieth century. Strikingly attentive to the nuances of poetic language as well as its ideological subtext, throughout her career Brooks manipulates imagery and structure to articulate the circumstances of the struggles and joys of so-called ordinary people and to critique the paradoxes of American culture.

Jacquelyn Y. McLendon shows that the political changes of the late sixties defined Brooks' long-standing commitments to black people even more acutely. Her poetic voice became more explicitly ideological; she determined that her work would appear only under the imprint of black-owned publishing houses. Moreover, she committed herself to supporting the creative talents of younger black writers; in that role she contributed much to the development of the poets associated with the Black Arts movement.

Although her career was brief, Lorraine Hansberry also responded to the political and cultural developments that swept the nation during the late fifties and the sixties. A major playwright, Hansberry was deeply committed both to the perfection of her craft and to the movement for social change. *A Raisin in the Sun,* Hansberry's play about the triumph of a black family over racism and the divisions wrought by their class aspirations, was a striking success because it struck a chord within Americans at a critical moment in our national history. Yet, as Margaret Wilkerson indicates, much of the enduring value of the play may be found in the layers of meaning that contemporary critics have over-looked. A play that addresses issues of gender, class difference, and international black politics, *Raisin* anticipates many of the complexities that shape and trouble life in the late twentieth century. Hansberry's presience is played out in her later, more unruly work, none of which enjoyed the kind of critical acclaim that met her celebrated first play.

Throughout the nineteenth and early to mid twentieth centuries, African American authors have addressed a wide range of topics, although the specter of racism recurs as an issue in their work. The florescence of black writers on the contemporary scene has led to a significant broadening of the sorts of topics and styles that might be said to characterize African American literature at the present time. As Harryette Mullen shows in her essay on the Black Arts movement, renewed interest in cultural origins as a result of the civil rights and Black Nationalist movements, changes in immigration patterns, the globalization of the world economy, and other factors might explain some writers' attempts to represent through their language and narratives the connections between African American, African, and Afro-Caribbean cultural practices. Further, a variety of poets, novelists, and playwrights explore the possibilities of literature to reclaim and revise the silences and misapprehensions surrounding the lives of black Americans throughout history. Some writers, such as Samuel Delany, Charles Johnson, Adrienne Kennedy, and John Edgar Wideman, construct elaborate interplays between tropes associated with African American expressive culture and the self-reflexive, verbal play of post-modernism. The rise of black feminist writing has clarified the significance to African American literature of questions regarding the constructions of gender and sexuality.

In his essay on Amiri Baraka, William J. Harris shows how the author's work responds to stages in his own personal growth in relation to a succession of literary, cultural, and political movements. His education in classical poetic forms, the styles of black music, and the power of the black vernacular, as well as his connections with the Beat poets, all inflect the voice and structure of his early work. In response to the racial violence of the sixties, Baraka's poetry of that period expresses positions associated with Black Nationalism in a language that captures the texture of jazz and the blues. Moreover, his performance style reveals the deep connection between black music and poetry. Baraka now identifies himself more fully with global Marxism than Black Nationalism, although he does acknowledge some connections between the two affiliations. His work continues to explore the ways in which the political conditions that shape human life inflect various modes of cultural production.

In her essay, Thadious Davis describes Ernest Gaines' explorations of the resonances of place in his fictions of Louisiana. In the tradition of writers such as Toomer, Hurston, and others, Gaines understands the richness of the vernacular speech of the southern rural black folk. However, the enclaves he describes operate as sites where broad economic and political issues may be felt.

Essayist, novelist, poet, and editor, Ishmael Reed is clearly influenced by the kinds of forces that inflect the work of writers such as Baraka and Gaines, and then some. Henry Louis Gates Jr. counts Reed among the premier artists of his time, and shows how his parodies of literary conventions and cultural tropes

CHRONOLOGY

1441	Portuguese slave trade begins.
1441–1863	12–15 million Africans transported to North and South America as slaves; 10–20 percent die on shipboard; each slave allotted about 3½ feet of space.
1526	First slaves to be brought to an American colony revolt in the Carolinas and flee to live with Native Americans in the interior.
1619	Twenty African slaves brought to Jamestown, Virginia, as indentured servants.
1670	Institution of slavery legally recognized in all colonies.
1688	Quakers in Germantown, Pennsylvania, make the first formal protest against slavery to be made in the western hemisphere.
1700	New England shippers begin to import slaves directly from Africa as part of the so-called Triangle Trade; slaves number 28,000 in North America, with 23,000 in the South.
1712	South Carolina passes its Act for the Better Ordering and Governing of Negroes and Slaves, which serves as a model for slave codes in other colonies. Major slave insurrection in New York City, in which nine whites are killed; twenty-one blacks are executed, and nine commit suicide.
1739	Extensive slave revolts around Charlestown, South Carolina; fifty-one whites and many more slaves are killed.
1745–1797	Olaudah Equiano
1753–1784	**Phillis Wheatley**
1754	Antislavery pamphlet, *Some Considerations on the Keeping of Negroes*, by Quaker John Woolman, is distributed throughout the colonies and abroad.
1770	The Boston Massacre, in which British soldiers fire into a crowd, killing five, including African American Crispus Attucks, an escaped slave, who is given a hero's burial. Led by Anthony Benezet, Quakers open a school for African Americans in Philadelphia.
1773–1774	African Americans in Boston petition for right to purchase their own freedom.
1774	Continental Congress calls for an end to the slave trade and an embargo on all countries that participate in it.
1775	African Americans are excluded from service in the Continental Army because George Washington, Benjamin Franklin, and others fear that arming slaves would lead to insurrection.
1775–1783	Eight to ten thousand African Americans serve in the Revolutionary forces, five thousand as soldiers. Thousands of slaves escape during the Revolution; South Carolina lost more than a fifth of its slave population.
1776	First emancipationist society organized in Philadelphia. To counteract Virginia Governor Lord Dunmore's offer to free all male slaves who join the British forces, Continental Congress approves the enlistment of free African Americans.

In the original draft of the Declaration of Independence, Thomas Jefferson speaks strongly against slavery, accusing George III not only of supporting this "execrable commerce," but also of inciting the slaves "to rise in arms among us"; the entire passage is struck at the insistence of South Carolina, Georgia, and some slave-trading New England states.

1777   Vermont is the first state to abolish slavery.

1780   Pennsylvania passes a gradual abolition law.

1783   Massachusetts abolishes slavery. The Treaty of Paris, ending the American Revolution, provides for the return of slaves captured by the British, but the ships leaving New York and Charleston carry almost 10,000 fugitive slaves.

1784   Connecticut and Rhode Island pass gradual abolition acts.

1784–1790   Many state and local antislavery societies formed.

1786   Importation of slaves ends in all states but South Carolina and Georgia.

1787   African Free School founded by the New York Manumission Society.
In the Northwest Ordinance, Continental Congress excludes slavery from the Northwest Territory.
Free African Society founded by preachers Richard Allen and Absalom Jones in Philadelphia, providing a political voice for African Americans.
All states ratify the U.S. Constitution, containing provisions for the return of fugitive slaves, counting a slave as three-fifths of a person for purposes of taxation and representation, and sanctioning the slave trade until at least 1808.
The first census counts 757,363 African Americans in the United States, comprising 19 percent of the total population; 9 percent are free.
A law of Congress limits naturalization to white aliens.

1791   The Bill of Rights passed.
Six state abolition societies petition Congress to end the slave trade.

1793   Fugitive Slave Act makes it criminal to harbor a fugitive slave or prevent his or her arrest.
Eli Whitney invents the cotton gin, which, by making it possible to separate the fiber from the seed, greatly increases the profitability of cotton growing.

1797–1883   Sojourner Truth, an abolitionist orator.

1803   In violent uprising African American protestors burn parts of New York City.

1804   New Jersey passes a gradual abolition law.
All states north of the Mason-Dixon line have antislavery laws.

1807   Great Britain abolishes slave trade.
Federal law bans African slave trade; law goes into effect one year later but is widely violated.

1808–1860   250,000–300,000 African slaves brought into the South illegally.

1812   African Americans make up one-sixth of the U.S. Navy force during the War of 1812.

1813–1897   Harriet Jacobs

1815   Two regiments of free African Americans fight under General Andrew x-Jackson against the British in the Battle of New Orleans.
First migration of African Americans from the South to the Northwest Territory.

1816   American Colonization Society founded in Washington to transport free blacks to Africa; at the organizational meeting Henry Clay praises the society's aim to "rid our country of a useless and pernicious, if not dangerous, portion of its population."
African Methodist Episcopal Church organized.

1816–1884   William Wells Brown, author of the first African American novel, *Clotel, or the President's Daughter* (1853), and other novels, plays, and works of history.

1817   New York passes a gradual abolition act.

1818   Andrew Jackson defeats a force of Native Americans and African Americans at the Battle of Suwanee, ending the First Seminole War.

CHRONOLOGY

1818–1895	Frederick Douglass
1820	According to the Missouri Compromise, Maine is admitted to the Union as a free state and Missouri is admitted as a slave state—making twelve slave states and twelve free states—and slavery is prohibited in the Louisiana Purchase north of the 36° 30′ latitude. Army disallowed to accept African Americans.
1821	The first all-black acting troupe, the African Company, begins performances in New York City; Ira Aldridge, later acclaimed throughout Europe, makes his start here.
1821–1913	Harriet Tubman, leader of the Underground Railroad.
1822	Liberia founded by American Colonization Society. The Denmark Vesey slave conspiracy is betrayed in Charleston, South Carolina.
1825–1911	**Frances Ellen Watkins Harper**
1827	Slavery abolished in New York; 10,000 slaves freed on July 4th.
1828	Thomas D. Rice introduces the character of "Jim Crow" in Louisville, Kentucky.
1830	Under the Indian Removal Act, Native Americans are relocated across the Mississippi River to make way for the cotton kingdom. Nat Turner leads seventy slaves in a rebellion in Virginia; sixty whites massacred by twenty or thirty slaves; the South thrown into a panic; Turner captured and hung. Convention movement, addressing public issues affecting African Americans, begins with a national meeting in Philadelphia.
1831	*The Liberator*, an abolitionist newspaper, begun by William Lloyd Garrison. First Annual Convention of the People of Color is held in Philadelphia.
1831–1861	75,000 slaves escape to freedom by way of the Underground Railroad.
1832	New England Anti-Slavery Society founded in Boston.
1833	Slavery abolished in the British empire.
	Oberlin founded as the first integrated college in the Unites States. American Anti-Slavery Society founded in Philadelphia.
1836	The so-called "gag rule" is passed by the House of Representatives, providing for the laying aside of all antislavery petitions: "gag rule" is not rescinded until 1845, principally in response to agitation by John Quincy Adams.
1838	Calhoun's Resolutions, stating that Congress is not to interfere with slavery in the states, the District of Columbia, or the territories, passes in the Senate.
1839	Theodore Dwight Weld's antislavery book, *American Slavery As It Is*, published; 100,000 copies sold. Liberty Party, first antislavery political party, organizes. A group of Africans led by Cinque, who revolted against their captors and seized the slave ship *L'Amistad* off the coast of Cuba, are defended by John Quincy Adams before the Supreme Court and win their freedom.
1840	American and Foreign Antislavery Society founded in New York.
1841	Frederick Douglass, three years after he escaped slavery in Maryland, joins the abolition movement, lecturing with the Massachusetts Antislavery Society.
1842	In the case of *Prigg v. Pennsylvania* the Supreme Court rules that states have no power over cases under the Fugitive Slave Act, thus preventing states from either helping or hindering fugitive slaves; the ruling establishes a precedent for the so-called "personal liberty" laws.
1845	Texas admitted to the Union as a slave state.
1847	Dred Scott files suit for his freedom with his master's widow on the grounds that he had lived with his master on free soil.
1848	Bill passed to extend restrictions on slavery to Oregon territory.
1849	Harriet Tubman escapes from slavery; she returns to the South nine-

teen more times in her life to bring more than 300 slaves out of slavery. In the case of *Roberts v. City of Boston* Massachusetts Supreme Court enunciates the doctrine of "separate but equal" educational facilities.

1850   The Compromise of 1850 provides for the admission of California as a free state, New Mexico and Utah with or without slavery, a broader Fugitive Slave Act, and the abolition of the slave trade in the District of Columbia.

1852   Harriet Beecher Stowe's antislavery novel *Uncle Tom's Cabin* is published, selling over 300,000 copies in its first year.
Sojourner Truth delivers her "Ain't I a Woman" speech at the Second National Women's Suffrage Convention in Akron, Ohio.

1854   First African American college, Lincoln University, founded as Ashmun Institute by Presbyterians in Oxford, Pennsylvania.
Kansas-Nebraska Act, proposed by Stephen Douglas of Illinois, provides for the organization of the territories of Kansas and Nebraska with or without slavery and the repeal of the Missouri Compromise's prohibition of slavery north of 36° 30' line.

1855   Massachusetts legislature passes an act desegregating schools.

1856   The Republican Party is formally organized to support a free-soil policy in the West.

1856–1915   Booker T. Washington, the founder of the Tuskegee Institute.

1857   In its decision on the *Dred Scott v. Sanford* case, the Supreme Court declares that slaves are not citizens, that Congress had no power to outlaw slavery in the territories.

1858   Accepting the nomination for Senator from Illinois, Abraham Lincoln delivers his "House Divided" speech. In the Lincoln-Douglas debates, Lincoln advocates the continuance of the Fugitive Slave Act, the gradual abolition of slavery in the District of Columbia, the prohibition of slavery in the territories, and the gradual ab-

olition of slavery in the United States; Douglas wins the election.

1858–1932   **Charles W. Chesnutt**

1859   *Afro-American Magazine*, a library magazine, begins publication in New York.

1859–1930   **Pauline Hopkins**

1860   Lincoln is elected president.
Senate adopts Jefferson Davis' Resolutions that all attacks on slavery violate the Constitution, that the national government should protect slavery in the territories, and that state laws interfering with the recovery of runaway slaves are unconstitutional.

1861   Jefferson Davis is declared the President of the Confederate States of America.
Civil War declared with the Confederate attack on Fort Sumter, South Carolina.

1862   The National Freedmen's Relief Association is founded in New York to assist slaves in making the transition to freedom.
Congress authorizes President Lincoln to accept African Americans for military service.
Congress declares that the United States should cooperate with any state that adopts gradual abolition by paying for the slaves.

1863   Lincoln signs the Emancipation Proclamation on January 1, freeing all slaves except those in states not in rebellion.
During the draft riots in New York City—incited by poor immigrants protesting the 1863 Conscription Act that allowed a man to buy his way out of the draft by paying $300—white immigrants attack African Americans and their property; 1,200 people, mostly black, are killed.

1864   Two African American brigades participate in a decisive Union victory in Nashville.

1865   Jefferson Davis signs a bill authorizing use of slaves as soldiers in the Confederate Army.
Thirteenth Amendment to the Constitution, abolishing slavery in the

United States, goes to the states for ratification.
Confederacy surrenders at Appomattox, Virginia.
Abraham Lincoln assassinated.
All reconstructed states write black codes into state constitutions, stripping African Americans of social, civil, political, and economic rights.
Congress establishes Freedmen's Bureau as part of the War Department to aid refugees and freedmen.
Ku Klux Klan founded in Tennessee to defeat radical reconstruction and establish white supremacy by violence in the South.

1866 — Over President Johnson's veto, Congress passes Civil Rights Act declaring freedmen to be U.S. citizens.
Major race riots in Memphis and New Orleans.

1867 — Reconstruction Acts, providing for new state constitutions and military supervision of voter enrollment in the South, passes over President Johnson's veto; enforcement of these acts provides blacks with the majority of votes in most Southern states.

1868 — Fourteenth Amendment, introduced in 1866, is ratified, guaranteeing citizenship and equal rights to freedmen.

1868–1963 — **W. E. B. Du Bois**

1869 — The 41st Congress includes two African American representatives and one African American senator; between 1870 and 1900 twenty-two blacks, including thirteen ex-slaves, serve in Congress.

1870 — Fifteenth Amendment, passed by Congress in 1868, is ratified, banning voter discrimination on the basis of race, color, or previous condition of servitude.
Klan violence contributes to the Democrats' regaining control of Southern states.
Nineteen percent of African Americans are literate, according to U.S. census.

1871–1930 — Northern migration and segregation result in the development of African American ghettos in northern cities.

1871–1938 — **James Weldon Johnson**

1872–1906 — **Paul Laurence Dunbar**

1873–1875 — Increasing racial violence in southern states with massacres of African Americans in Louisiana, Tennessee, and Mississippi.

1875 — Civil Rights Act prohibits discrimination in public accommodations, conveyances, theaters, and juries.

1877 — Under the Compromise of 1877 southern congressmen agree to the election of Rutherford Hayes as president if Republicans promise to withdraw federal troops from the South.

1878 — Democrats are now in control of Congress and impede presidential power to use troops to guarantee fair elections.
Beginning of the darkest period of African American history, marked by persistent violence from whites in the North and South.

1879 — Exodus of some 50,000 African Americans to the North.
Colored Farmer's Alliance founded as a brother organization to all-white Farmer's Alliance with a membership of 1,250,000.

1881 — Tuskegee Institute founded in Alabama by Booker T. Washington.

1881–1907 — Tennessee begins modern segregation with a "Jim Crow" law segregating railroad cars; Florida, Mississippi, Texas, Louisiana, Alabama, Kentucky, Arkansas, Georgia, South Carolina, North Carolina, Virginia, Maryland, and Oklahoma follow suit.

1882–1947 — 3,426 African Americans lynched.

1882–1961 — **Jessie Redmon Fauset**

1883 — Civil Rights Act of 1875 held unconstitutional.
National Convention of Colored Men called in Louisville to assert political independence from the Republican Party.

1884–1885 — Eleven states enact civil rights laws.

1887 — Formation of first African American baseball team, the Union Grants, in Chicago.

1887–1940 — Marcus Garvey, nationalist leader of the "Back to Africa" movement.

1890 — Mississippi Constitutional Convention begins the systematic exclusion of African Americans from political franchise in the South using literacy and "understanding" tests later adapted by South Carolina, Louisiana, North Carolina, Alabama, Virginia, Georgia, and Oklahoma.
First Afro-American National League convention.
Forty-three percent of African Americans literate, according to U.S. census.

1890–1948 — **Claude McKay**

1891–1960 — **Zora Neale Hurston**

1891–1964 — **Nella Larsen**

1894–1967 — **Jean Toomer**

1895 — Booker T. Washington delivers his "Atlanta Compromise" address at the Cotton Exposition in Atlanta, advocating education as a way to earn equality.

1896 — In the case of *Plessy v. Ferguson* the Supreme Court upholds the doctrine of "separate but equal" civil rights for African Americans.
National Association of Colored Women founded in Washington, D.C.

1898–1966 — **Melvin Tolson**

1900 — Du Bois first uses the line, "The problem of the twentieth century is the problem of the color line, " at a conference in London.

1901 — After George White says farewell to the House of Representatives, there is no black in Congress again until 1928.

1901–1989 — **Sterling Brown**

1902–1967 — **Langston Hughes**

1903–1946 — **Countee Cullen**

1904 — Race riots in Springfield, Ohio, and Savannah, Georgia.

1905 — W. E. B. Du Bois founds the Niagara Movement at a conference of African American leaders in Fort Erie, New York, to demand abolition of racial discrimination and oppose the conciliatory policies of Booker T. Washington.

1906 — In the so-called Brownsville Raid, African American soldiers raid a Texas town in retaliation for racial insults, and President Roosevelt orders dishonorable discharge of three companies.

1908 — Race riot in Springfield, Illinois; militia is called in.

1908–1960 — **Richard Wright**

1908–1997 — **Ann Petry**

1909 — Founding of the National Association for the Advancement of Colored People (NAACP).

1909–1984 — **Chester Himes**

1910 — First edition of the *Crisis* magazine sells 1,000 copies; by 1918 the magazine has a circulation of 100,000.

1911 — National Urban League founded.
Marcus Garvey organizes black nationalist Universal Negro Improvement Association (UNIA) in Jamaica.

1913–1980 — **Robert Hayden**

1914 — Sam Lucas is the first black actor to play Uncle Tom on screen in the World Pictures version of the novel.

1914–1994 — **Ralph Ellison**

1915 — In the NAACP's first major court victory, Oklahoma's "grandfather clause" is declared unconstitutional.
NAACP tries to prevent the showing of D. W. Griffith's *Birth of a Nation*.
Northern migration follows racial violence and boll weevil devastation in South; 350,000 African Americans migrate in a year and a half.

1915–1920 — Ku Klux Klan is revived; in 1920 the Klan has 100,000 members in twenty-seven states.

1915–1934 — U.S. Marines occupy Haiti.

1915– — **Margaret Walker**

1916–1924 — United States occupies Dominican Republic.

1917 — United States purchases the Virgin Islands.
Ten thousand African Americans march in New York City to protest lynching and discrimination.
Marcus Garvey founds the newspaper *Negro World* in New York and, on a speaking tour of the United

States, gains wide support for the UNIA.

1917–1918　365,000 African Americans return from World War I, demanding equal rights and opportunities; African Americans made up 11 percent of the overseas troops.

1917–　Gwendolyn Brooks

1919　Twenty-seven major race riots in northern and southern cities, the worst in Chicago and Washington, during what becomes known as the "Red Summer."
W. E. B. Du Bois organizes the first Pan-African Congress in Paris aimed at influencing postwar negotiations to extend self-determination to Africa.
AFL votes to abolish discrimination in union membership.

1919–1924　Congressional effort to frame anti-lynching legislation fails.

1920　Organization of National Negro Baseball League.
UNIA holds national convention in Liberty Hall, Harlem, and establishes African government-in-exile with Marcus Garvey as provisional president.

1920–1930　Development of the Negro Renaissance and Harlem Renaissance.

1923　500,000 African Americans migrate to the North.

1924　Ku Klux Klan has 4.5 million members.

1924–1987　James Baldwin

1925　New York Public Library buys Arthur Schomburg's private collection of African American history and literature.
Alain Locke edits *The New Negro* anthology, hailing the coming of a "new spirit" for African Americans.

1925–1965　Malcolm X

1925–　John A. Williams

1929　Great Depression begins; African American unemployment rate rises to 40–60 percent in northern cities.
American Communist Party recruits in northern cities and rural South.

1929–1968　Martin Luther King, Jr.

1929–　Paule Marshall

1930–1965　Lorraine Hansberry

1931　Scottsboro Trials, in which nine African American youths are framed for rape in Alabama, becomes a worldwide scandal; proceedings go on for twenty years.

**1931–　Adrienne Kennedy
Toni Morrison**

1933　NAACP initiates court attacks on segregation and discrimination in education.

1933–　Ernest Gaines

**1934–　Audre Lorde
Amiri Baraka
Jay Wright**

1936　Jesse Owens wins four gold medals in 100- and 200-meter dash at Berlin in Olympics.

**1936–　Lucille Clifton
June Jordan
Clarence Major**

1937–1997　Leon Forrest

**1938–　Michael Harper
Ishmael Reed**

1939–1995　Toni Cade Bambara

1941　March on Washington to protest military segregation planned but canceled when President Franklin D. Roosevelt establishes Fair Employment Practices Commission to prohibit discrimination in defense industries because of race, color, creed, or national origin.

1941–　John Edgar Wideman

1942　Margaret Walker's *For My People* wins Yale Series of Younger Poets competition.
Founding of pacifist Congress of Racial Equality (CORE) in Chicago.

1942–　Samuel R. Delany

1943　Race riots in Detroit; Los Angeles; Harlem; Beaumont, Texas; and Mobile, Alabama.
Membership denied to African Americans by thirty AFL unions.

1944　War Department abolishes segregation in recreation and transportation facilities on Army posts.
Texas primary elections excluding

African Americans held unconstitutional by the Supreme Court.
United Negro College Fund chartered.

1944–1999   Sherley Anne Williams

1944–   Alice Walker

1945–   August Wilson

1946   Race riots in Columbia, Tennessee; Athens, Georgia; and Philadelphia. Supreme Court bans segregated interstate bus travel.

1947   NAACP presents petition on racial injustice in America to United Nations; no action taken. Southern Regional Council study reveals that only 12 percent of African Americans in South meet voting requirements.
CORE begins first Freedom Ride to integrate transportation facilities in the South.
Jackie Robinson becomes the first black to play for a major league baseball team, the Brooklyn Dodgers.

1947–   Octavia Butler
Yusef Komunyakaa

1948   President Truman bans discrimination in the Armed Forces.
States' Rights Party, founded on platform based on racial segregation, nominates Strom Thurmond of South Carolina for President.

1948–   Charles Johnson
Ntozake Shange

1949–   Gayl Jones
Jamaica Kincaid

1950   Ralph J. Bunche awarded Nobel Peace Prize for his Palestinian peace efforts.
Gwendolyn Brooks wins Pulitzer Prize (poetry) for *Annie Allen*.

1950–   Gloria Naylor

1952   Ralph Ellison's *Invisible Man* wins National Book Award.

1953   In the case of *Terry v. Adams*, the Supreme Court holds that segregated primary elections violate the Fourteenth Amendment.

1954   In the case of *Brown v. Board of Education*, the Supreme Court rules racial segregation in public schools unconstitutional.

1955   Interstate Commerce Commission bans segregation in buses, waiting rooms, and travel coaches involved in interstate travel.
Rosa Parks refuses to give up her seat to a white man on a city bus in Montgomery, Alabama.
Fourteen-year-old Emmett Till is lynched in Mississippi; two white male suspects are acquitted by an all-white, all-male jury.

1956   One hundred senators and congressmen issue a manifesto promising to use "all lawful means" to overthrow the *Brown v. Board of Education* decision of 1954.
Bus boycott in Montgomery, Alabama, led by Martin Luther King, Jr. Supreme Court rules bus segregation unconstitutional.

1957   Southern Christian Leadership Conference organized with Martin Luther King, Jr. as president.
One thousand federal troops sent to Little Rock, Arkansas, to assist integration of public schools.
Federal Civil Rights Commission created.

1959   Lorraine Hansberry's *A Raisin in the Sun* becomes the first play by an African American to win Best Play of the Year Award of the New York Drama Critics.

1960   Sit-in movement begins in Greensboro, North Carolina, with a demonstration against segregation at lunch counters.
Student Nonviolent Coordinating Committee (SNCC) organized in Atlanta.
President Dwight Eisenhower signs Civil Rights Act of 1960.
Black Nationalist leader Elijah Muhammad calls for creation of a separate state for African Americans.

1960–1963   Over 20,000 people arrested for participation in nonviolent demonstrations in the South.

1961   Committee on Equal Employment Opportunity established.

CORE begins Freedom Rides through the South to test compliance with bus desegregation orders.

1962 Citizens in large northern cities begin suits claiming de facto segregation in northern schools.

Twenty-fourth Amendment banning the poll tax in federal elections sent to states for ratification.

Twelve thousand federal troops sent to University of Mississippi to prevent riot over admission of James H. Meredith, its first African American student.

Executive order bans discrimination in federally assisted housing.

1963 Martin Luther King, Jr. leads mass demonstrations in Birmingham, Alabama, to desegregate the city. Voter registration drives held in the South. NAACP leader Medgar W. Evers assassinated in Jackson, Mississippi. Four African American girls die in a church bombing, in Birmingham, Alabama.

In the largest project in the nation's history, 200,000 join the March on Washington for Jobs and Freedom; Martin Luther King, Jr. delivers his "I Have a Dream" speech.

1964 Resigning from the Black Muslim movement, Malcolm X founds Organization of Afro-American Unity.

Harlem Youth Opportunities Unlimited (HARYOU) publishes *Youth in the Ghetto: A Study of the Consequences of Powerlessness.*

Riots in Harlem, Jersey City, Philadelphia, Rochester, and Chicago.

During the Freedom Summer hundreds of black and white college students converge on Mississippi to focus national attention on civil rights violations.

Three civil rights workers murdered near Philadelphia, Mississippi; charges against the nineteen suspects, including a local sheriff, are dismissed by February 1965.

Martin Luther King, Jr. awarded Nobel Peace Prize.

Congress passes Civil Rights bill with strong public accommodations and fair employment sections.

1965 Malcolm X assassinated in New York City.

President Johnson creates cabinet-level Council on Equal Opportunity. Martin Luther King, Jr. leads thousands of civil rights activists on a five-day march from Selma to Montgomery, Alabama.

Voting Rights Bill passed by Senate, 77–19.

Six-day race riot in Watts, Los Angeles; 35 dead, 883 injured.

1966 Stokely Carmichael of SNCC introduces the concept of "Black Power," later endorsed by CORE and rejected by NAACP.

Race riots in Cleveland and Chicago. Civil Rights bill aimed at ending housing discrimination fails in Congress.

Huey Newton and Bobby Seale found the Black Panthers in Oakland, California.

1967 New renaissance of African American arts begins in Harlem.

Martin Luther King, Jr. leads thousands in a peace march to the U.N. Thurgood Marshall becomes the first African American Supreme Court Justice.

Riots in Newark and Detroit.

1968 Martin Luther King, Jr. assassinated in Memphis, Tennessee.

Congress passes open housing law, and Supreme Court decision prohibits discrimination in sale and rental of housing.

Reverend Ralph Abernathy and Coretta Scott King lead Poor People's Campaign on Washington, D.C.; shanty town set up near Capitol.

1970 Two African American students killed by National Guard during Vietnam War protest at Jackson State College in Mississippi.

1971 Inmates revolt at Attica Correctional Facility, and thirty-two inmates and eleven guards are killed.

U.S. Commission on Civil Rights accuses Nixon administration of failing to carry out civil rights laws.

Peaceful and violent protests against African Americans throughout the South; ten black activists arrested in Wilmington, North Carolina.

Jesse Jackson forms People United to Save Humanity (PUSH)

1972 Black Congressional Caucus accuses Nixon administration of abandoning efforts for racial equality.
President Nixon states opposition to busing for school integration.
Wilmington 10 convicted of fire-bombing.
National Black Political Convention meets and prepares a political agenda.
Shirley Chisholm runs for President of the United States.

1973 National Black Feminist Organization founded.
U.S. Census Bureau reports the erosion of some of the economic gains made by African Americans in the previous decade.

1973–1977 Newly released documents reveal FBI interference with civil rights activities in the 1960s.

1974 Supreme Court invalidates Detroit's school busing plan.
Amiri Baraka urges Congress of African Peoples to change directions, emphasizing class struggle rather than racial differences.

1975 Violence breaks out in Louisville, Kentucky, at start of court-ordered busing to integrate schools.

1977 Alex Haley wins Pulitzer Prize for *Roots*.

1979 In the case of *United Steelworkers of America v. Brian Weber* Supreme Court rules that employers can give preference to African Americans to eliminate "manifest racial imbalance."
Resurgence of Ku Klux Klan in South.

1979–1981 Serial murders of African American children in Atlanta.

1980 Racial violence erupts in Miami; nine dead, 163 injured.
NAACP holds emergency meeting to deal with "near hysteria" in African American communities following the election of Ronald Reagan as President.
U.S. Census shows millions of middle-class African Americans are returning to the South.

1981 Reagan administration's budget cuts disproportionately affect African Americans.

1982 Leadership Conference on Civil Rights charges Justice Department with attacking civil rights laws.

1983 Alice Walker wins the American Book Award and Pulitzer Prize (fiction) for *The Color Purple*.
Gloria Naylor wins The American Book Award for her first novel, *The Women of Brewster Place*.
Reagan's reconstituted Civil Rights Commission opposes affirmative action.

1984 Jesse Jackson runs for president and delivers his "Rainbow Coalition" speech at the Democratic Convention.

1985 Police bomb house in Philadelphia claimed to be headquarters of black radical group MOVE, killing eleven people, four of these children, and destroying two blocks of homes.

1986 *Ebony* devotes a special issue to crisis in the African American family.
Dr. Martin Luther King, Jr.'s birthday observed as a federal holiday for the first time.

1987 Rita Dove wins Pulitzer Prize (poetry) for *Thomas and Beulah*.
Civil rights demonstration in all-white Cumming, Georgia.

1988 Toni Morrison wins Pulitzer Prize (fiction) for *Beloved*.
Jesse Jackson runs for president a second time.

1989 Minor exodus of African Americans from large inner cities to suburbs and small towns.
Jesse Jackson leads movement to replace "black" with "African American."

1990 1965 civil rights march from Selma to Montgomery, Alabama, reenacted.
Nelson Mandela, newly released from prison, tours North America. Millions turn out to see him.

1991 President Bush nominates Clarence Thomas, a conservative, to replace Thurgood Marshall on the Supreme Court.

Four Los Angeles police officers are indicted on charges, including assault with a deadly weapon, for beating Rodney King.
An African American burial ground is discovered in Manhattan.
The National Civil Rights Museum opens at the Lorraine Motel in Memphis, the site of the assassination of Martin Luther King, Jr.
Riots break out between blacks and Jews in Crown Heights, Brooklyn, when a young black boy is killed by a car driven by a Jewish driver.

1992   Carol Mosely-Braun becomes the first black woman to hold a seat in the U.S. Senate.
Riots break out in Los Angeles after the four white police officers who had beaten Rodney King are acquitted.
The Federal Reserve issues its second annual report on lending discrimination, stating that mortgage applications from blacks and Hispanic Americans are rejected about twice as often as those from whites and Asian Americans.

1993   President Clinton appoints Hazel Rollins O'Leary as secretary of energy, Clifton R. Wharton, Jr. as Deputy Secretary of State, Mike Espy as head of the Agriculture Department, Ron Brown as Secretary of Commerce, Jesse Brown as Veterans Affairs Secretary, and Joycelyn Elders as Surgeon General.
Police Sergeant Stacey C. Koon and Officer Laurence M. Powell are found guilty of violating Rodney King's civil rights after being tried again in federal court.
Toni Morrison becomes the first African American to win a Nobel Prize for literature.

1994   The Florida legislature agrees to pay up to $150,000 to each survivor of the Rosewood Massacre.
Joycelyn Elders resigns as U.S. Surgeon General after making controversial statements on sex education and drug use.
Benjamin Franklin Chavis joins the Nation of Islam as an organizer and close adviser to Minister Louis Farrakhan after resigning from the NAACP.

Stanley Crouch wins the prestigious Guggenheim "genius" award.

1995   Bob Watson is hired to be the General Manager of the New York Yankees. He is the first African American to hold this position.
Colin Powell publishes his memoir *My American Journey.*
Louis Farrakhan of the Nation of Islam organizes the Million Man March.
Eubie Blake is featured on a U.S. postage stamp.

1996   Arthur Ashe is honored in his native Richmond by the erection of a statue on Monument Avenue, the city's central thoroughfare.
Ron Brown and his party are killed in an airplane crash while on a trip to Croatia.
Kweisi Mfume is sworn in as the head of the NAACP.

1997   Tiger Woods wins the Masters Tournament at age twenty-one.
Betty Shabazz is badly burned in a fire set by her grandson; she dies three weeks later.
Lee Brown is elected mayor of Houston.

1998   Julian Bond is elected Chair of the Board of the NAACP.
James Byrd, Jr. is beaten and dragged to his death in Jasper, Texas, by two white supremacists.
Kwame Tuore (Stokely Carmichael) dies of prostate cancer.
Richard Pryor becomes the first recipient of the Kennedy Center's Mark Twain prize for humor.

1999   Michael Jordan retires from basketball after leading the Chicago Bulls to their sixth NBA championship.
A long-lost poem by Phillis Wheatley, "Ocean" is read publicly for the first time in 226 years.
President Clinton grants Henry O. Flipper a presidential pardon fifty-nine years after his death. Flipper was court-martialed in 1881 on thievery charges.
Amadou Diallo, a young African immigrant, is shot and killed by four New York City policemen in the doorway of his Bronx apartment building.

The federal government investigates the New Jersey State Police and New York City Police department for their policies of "racial profiling."

A protest led by the relatives of victims of police brutality from across the country is held in Washington, D.C.

Lincoln Center celebrates Duke Ellington's 100th birthday with a centennial year tribute honoring his contributions to jazz and classical music.

2000 South Carolina is the last state in the nation to recognize Martin Luther King, Jr.'s birthday as a state holiday.

Tennis player Venus Williams wins the Women's singles in Wimbledom, making her the second African American to do so.

Tiger Woods becomes the youngest player to win all four major golf championships—the British Open, the Masters, the PGA Championship, and the U.S. Open.

Gustavas A. McLeod becomes the first man to pilot an open-cockpit plane to the North Pole.

Christopher Paul Curtis wins the Newbery Medal and the Coretta Scott King Author award for his book, *Bud, Not Buddy*; this marks the first time that one book has won both awards.

The South Carolina Senate votes to remove the Confederate flag from the dome of the State Capitol Building.

JAMES BALDWIN
(1924–1987)

DAVID VAN LEER

AFTER JAMES BALDWIN'S death at St.-Paul-de-Vence, France, on 1 December 1987, more than five thousand mourners attended a memorial service at New York's Cathedral of St. John the Divine. The eulogies were delivered by such respected writers as Maya Angelou, Amiri Baraka, and Toni Morrison. Yet the reverential character of the occasion might have surprised an outsider, for Baldwin's final years were not ones of unequivocal triumph. As a celebrity, Baldwin was regularly quoted in the media on issues of race, but by the 1980s his literary reputation seemed less secure than it had been in his early days of promise in the late 1940s and early 1950s or in the fiery fulfillment of that promise in the 1960s. His last works were not popular with critics or readers. After having had two projects rejected, Baldwin broke with Dial Press, his publishers for almost thirty years, and when—under another publisher's imprint—he issued his collected essays, *The Price of the Ticket* (1985), the *New York Times* gave the volume only a brief mention on an inside page of its Sunday book review section.

Before the revival of interest following his death, Baldwin might have seemed an author whose time had passed. Indeed, his literary values, forged as they were in the 1940s and 1950s, can strike modern readers as old-fashioned. His plots display little of the fractured narration or abrupt time shifts characteristic of experimental fiction since the 1960s. His characters are complex but consistent, becoming in the 1970s more realistic and commonplace just when those of his fellow writers were becoming more magical and fantastic. Even his elegant language, modeled on the syntactical balance and moral intensity of black sermon rhetoric and of Henry James, can seem too controlled compared to the frenetic prose of the postmodernists, and verbose compared to the spare language currently favored by the literary descendants of minimalist short-story writer Raymond Carver.

Recent objections to Baldwin's style indicate more general reservations about his literary achievement. First, next to the small but uniformly skillful body of work by his contemporary Ralph Ellison, Baldwin's output looks unwieldy. It is often said of his more than twenty books and countless uncollected pieces that the essays surpass the novels, which are in turn better than the plays. The fiction is occasionally rejected wholesale as too autobiographical and insufficiently plotted, and in later years as downright propagandistic. Baldwin's characteristic themes also cause difficulty. Some readers recoil from his religious settings and "come to Jesus" rhetoric. Others regret his "integrationist" preoccupation with the relations between blacks and whites, heterosexuals and homosexuals. Finally, his Jamesian emphasis on the figure of the artist and on the redemptive power of love displeases those looking for more practical solutions to social injustice.

Comparable objections have been made to much American writing of the 1950s, which some modern readers find too conservative. Especially interesting in Baldwin's case, however, are the political (and racial) assumptions that underlie these apparently objective literary judgments—about the static character of literary genres, the universal appeal of masterful literature, and the politics of prose style. Many of these assumptions have been challenged by literary critics in the 1970s and 1980s. If in one sense, then, literary fashion has passed Baldwin by, in another sense it is just catching up to him. And the emotional afterglow surrounding his death affords the opportunity not simply to reaffirm Baldwin's importance to African American culture but to reevaluate the very character of his whole literary project.

James Arthur Baldwin was born (perhaps out of wedlock) in Harlem on 2 August 1924. Three years later his mother, Emma Berdis Jones, married David Baldwin, the man whom he called "Father," but who (as James Baldwin discovered in his teens) was actually his stepfather. A factory worker during the week and storefront preacher on the weekends, David Baldwin was a strict parent embittered by the tyranny of "white devils." Baldwin escaped from his home life through schoolwork, his writing, and occasional movies and less frequent plays. At his junior high school he met the celebrated black poet Countee Cullen, to whom he showed some of his early literary attempts.

In 1938, when he was fourteen, he joined the church of Mount Calvary of the Pentecostal Faith and soon became a preacher. In later years, Baldwin cynically described his period in "the church racket" as a "gimmick" designed to lift him out of the ghetto, an experience comparable to the "criminal careers" by means of which other blacks triumphed over their environment. Whatever the true motivation for his ministerial career, at De Witt Clinton High School (from 1938 to 1942) he downplayed his religious activities and, with friends, started visiting Greenwich Village, where he met the

gay black artist Beauford Delaney. The contradictions between his secular and religious interests were intensified at this time by an extended homosexual relationship with a Harlem racketeer.

After three years as a preacher Baldwin broke away from the church—and subsequently from his home in Harlem—to take a series of menial jobs in New Jersey. When David Baldwin was hospitalized with tuberculosis, Baldwin returned to New York to care for the family. Upon the father's death, Baldwin moved to Greenwich Village, both to work on a novel based on his family experiences and to profit from the greater sexual permissiveness downtown. In 1944 he met Richard Wright, one of his literary idols, who read Baldwin's writing and in 1945 secured for him Harper & Brothers' Eugene F. Saxton fellowship, including a grant of five hundred dollars and a promised reading of the finished work. When a hastily completed draft of the family novel was rejected by two presses, Baldwin in embarrassment began to distance himself from Wright, some months before the older writer's emigration to France in 1946.

While still trying to solve the problems of his novel, Baldwin began in 1947 to attract attention for his book reviews in the *Nation* and the *New Leader*. These reviews culminated in the celebrated (and controversial) essay "The Harlem Ghetto," published in *Commentary* in 1948. This earliest of Baldwin's famous essays took a bleak but clear-sighted view of Harlem, focusing especially on the problems of black newspapers, politicians, churches, and anti-Semitism. Later in the year he won a Rosenwald Foundation Fellowship grant (but again no book contract) for his text accompanying a series of photographs of storefront churches. Supported by this money, he began to outline a new, bohemian narrative that would later be seen as a preliminary version of his second and third novels. Yet although he continued to publish articles and some short fiction, Baldwin increasingly felt trapped in New York. In November 1948, he applied his remaining grant funds toward a ticket to Paris.

In Europe, Baldwin associated with such French writers as Jean-Paul Sartre, Simone de

Beauvoir, and Jean Genet, as well as a group of American expatriates including Saul Bellow, Truman Capote, Terry Southern, Herbert Gold, and, of course, Richard Wright. Early on during this Paris stay, Baldwin wrote two essays that solidified his reputation as a controversial critic of black culture. The first, "Everybody's Protest Novel," published in 1949 by *Partisan Review*, surveyed the limitations of Harriet Beecher Stowe's *Uncle Tom's Cabin*, an abolitionist novel that according to Baldwin's title was the prototype for American fiction of "protest." In the final pages of the essay, Baldwin coupled Mrs. Stowe's novel with Wright's most famous work, *Native Son*, claiming that Wright's murderous Bigger Thomas was the inverse of Stowe's martyred Uncle Tom. The passage was brief and not explicitly critical, but Wright took the comparison badly. So did many of Wright's supporters, who felt that Baldwin was being ungenerous to the reigning master of black fiction and, given Wright's well-known sensitivity, disingenuous in his surprise at Wright's reaction. Baldwin's later, more direct critique of *Native Son*—"Many Thousand Gone," published by *Partisan Review* in November–December 1951—ensured that the break with Wright would be permanent.

Some readers saw these two essays as oedipal attacks on Wright as the younger author's literary father, comparable to Baldwin's later negative comments on his stepfather, David. Yet whatever the psychological motives behind the essays, the political assumptions beneath his aesthetic decisions would remain central throughout Baldwin's work: that an individual sense of identity and self-worth must accompany any social reform, and that any criticism directed toward individual instances of racism can simply reinforce the conceptual framework that permits discrimination. According to the earlier essay, "protest" fiction supports the structures of oppression: "The oppressed and the oppressor are bound together within the same society; they accept the same criteria, they share the same beliefs." In the second essay, Baldwin argued that by representing, in the character of Bigger Thomas, white society's worst fears about black violence, Wright had

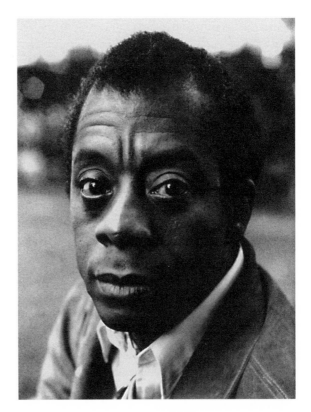

James Baldwin

implicitly denied the humanity of blacks and had suggested instead that "Negro life is in fact as debased and impoverished" as white racists claim. While acknowledging Bigger's rage to be real and universal, Baldwin felt that Wright had underestimated the importance of the ironic adjustment by which every black made peace with "the 'nigger' who surrounds him and the 'nigger' in himself."

Although the *Partisan Review* essays confirmed Baldwin's reputation as a rising author, he continued to have trouble finishing the long-awaited family novel. In 1951, his lifelong friend the painter Lucien Happersberger suggested that Baldwin retreat to his own hometown in Switzerland to complete the novel. Although the retreat was not entirely relaxing—Baldwin later described the town's racism in "Stranger in the Village," published in *Harper's Magazine* (1953)—it was there in 1952 that he finished his first novel, revised and published in 1953 as *Go Tell It on the Mountain*. This novel, his most fully crafted piece of fiction and by many accounts his best, draws loosely on Baldwin's family experiences to recount the conversion of John Grimes on his fourteenth birthday. Using Jamesian indirect discourse to represent in an apparently objective manner the subjective thoughts of his characters, Baldwin also imitates the rhetoric of pentecostal preaching both explicitly, in the sermons delivered throughout the text, and implicitly, in the more religious moments of the characters' private thoughts. A long middle section intersperses throughout John's soul-searching the recollections of his bitter aunt Florence, his resigned mother, Elizabeth, and—most important—his stepfather, Gabriel, a former profligate and now a strict preacher with a waning congregation and an angry relation to his son Roy and stepson John. These flashbacks allow the novel to treat simultaneously the contemporary religious awakening of a young man in Harlem and the sexual and racial tensions experienced by the previous generation down South and in the subsequent "great migration" north.

The formal control of the novel, however, belies the emotional turmoil it depicts. All the characters are tested in terms of their ability to love; most fail the test. Florence's confrontation with death is clouded by her ambition, envy, and finally hatred of her brother Gabriel. Elizabeth's love for John's father is admirable, but is not strong enough to survive the social pressures of white racism; nor can she protect John from the wrath of his stepfather. Gabriel is the most passionate figure, but also the most reprehensible. Contemptuous of all women and rejected by his two sons (both named Royal), Gabriel has allowed his religious fervor to evolve into a form of hypocrisy directed especially at his stepson John. Even John's own final conversion offers little hope for redemption. The "irony" that he overcomes in his religious experience may be the very irony he needs to develop a sense of self in white society. As the novel's final sentences imply, his conversion is as much an act of aggression against his stepfather as an acceptance of his own identity.

The ambiguity of conversion in *Go Tell It on the Mountain* suggests more general tensions in the text. In many ways the book is unlike any of Baldwin's later works. Concentrated on a few central figures, the narrative is relatively unconcerned with the social origins of black oppression that later become Baldwin's primary focus. In emphasizing the centrality of the family and especially of the father figure, Baldwin implicitly criticizes those more political works that, like Wright's *Native Son,* place society over the family and often depict the latter as weak and fatherless. By locating tension entirely within the family unit, Baldwin's novel almost absolves the white community of its responsibility. Finally, the book is ambiguous about the possibility of self-affirmation. John's conversion experience is both an act of hate and of love. And Baldwin's very language pulls simultaneously in two directions. Beginning with its title, the book uses religious formulations to criticize religious assumptions. Yet, as Baldwin's own case against Wright suggests, this imitative form of "protest" may leave unchallenged the real structures of oppression.

Go Tell It on the Mountain is a powerful and moving story whose very personal dimension—its reduction of the problem of race relations to the familial problem of stepfathers and sons—made it acceptable to a wide readership. But is it Baldwin's masterpiece? Baldwin's subsequent fiction, though less brilliantly structured, was also more uncompromising. While waiting for *Go Tell It on the Mountain* to appear in print, Baldwin drafted his first play, *The Amen Corner,* based loosely on the crisis that ended his religious career (just as *Go Tell It on the Mountain* was based on that which began it). Not commercially viable in the theater world of the 1950s, the play was presented by Howard University in 1955 but did not appear on Broadway until 1965.

Having won a Guggenheim grant on the strength of *Go Tell It on the Mountain,* Baldwin now worked on a second novel, drawing on some of the material from the earlier projected bohemian plot. Around the same time, he collected some of his essays—including the Harlem piece and the two Wright critiques—in *Notes of a Native Son* (1955). The collection's title essay marked a new complexity in his nonfiction. An elegant mixture of autobiography and political analysis, alluding in its title both to Henry James's *Notes of a Son and Brother* and to Wright's novel, the piece juxtaposes Baldwin's account of his troubled relationship to David Baldwin, that of his personal experience of racism in New Jersey, and his description of a Harlem riot following the alleged murder of a black soldier by a white policeman. The essay's resolution addresses directly the contradiction at the heart of *Go Tell It on the Mountain:* that the acceptance of personal differences that is necessary for people to develop independent identities is directly at odds with the denial of political differences that is necessary in order for people to obtain equal power.

The paradox of "difference" implicit in the conclusion to "Notes" is even more central to Baldwin's second novel, *Giovanni's Room* (1956), which was published in the United States only after being turned down by several prestigious presses. At the end of *Go Tell It on the Mountain,* John turned to the sympathetic young saint Elisha to "tell him . . . something for which he found no words." This implicit homosexual dimension of John's relation to Elisha, de-emphasized in the published version of *Go Tell It on the Mountain,* became the focus of Baldwin's next novel. Just as *Go Tell It on the Mountain* is a variation on *Native Son,* so *Giovanni's Room* looks back to a whole range of white American novels, including Fitzgerald's *The Great Gatsby* and James's *Daisy Miller* and *The Ambassadors.* But primarily it is a sexually honest reworking of Hemingway's vision in *The Sun Also Rises* of sterility and anomie among "lost" expatriates. The spare plot developed out of Baldwin's projected bohemian novel: on the eve of his male lover's execution, a gay narrator, David, recalls his sexual dishonesty with his fiancé, Hella, and his failure to confess openly his homosexual passion for the doomed Giovanni.

One of the first contemporary novels to deal overtly with homosexuality, *Giovanni's Room* shocked readers most for its total disinterest in shocking them. The Hemingwayesque prose is as chilly as Baldwin's earlier religious rhetoric was overheated. The depiction of homosexual sex, though discreet, is matter-of-fact in tone:

Baldwin's model is not the florid prose style of Oscar Wilde or Thomas Mann but the dispassionate tone of André Gide, Jean Genet, or, as always, Henry James. Nor, in fact, is homosexuality finally the subject of *Giovanni's Room,* any more than religion was the subject of *Go Tell It on the Mountain.* David's inability to confront his sexuality does not arise from the forbidden quality of that love. More basic is the difficulty all people have and the danger they feel in expressing any emotion, whether normative or unconventional.

Nevertheless, the treatment of sexual identity in Baldwin's new novel troubled readers and critics. Overemphasizing the importance of the theme of homosexuality, straight critics misread the work as an autobiographical plea for the privileged status of gay love. Baldwin repeatedly protested this reading: though himself unashamedly gay, he thought homosexual and heterosexual love merely two versions of the same emotional experience. In his most elegant formulation, he remarked that the word *homosexual* might be an adjective, perhaps even a verb; it was not, however, a noun. Gay readers in turn were disturbed by Baldwin's aestheticization of homosexuality. Giovanni was seen as too passive, a sentimental portrait of the gay man as innocent; and by making David's failure rest so heavily on his emotional dishonesty, Baldwin made sexual preference a question of self-identity—a position as politically naive as that which reduced racial to familial strife.

Go Tell It on the Mountain and *Giovanni's Room* are in some senses paired novels. Both are tightly organized brief works with few characters and relatively simple plots and settings; both hold the individual responsible for his social condition. For his third novel, Baldwin returned to the sprawling bohemian story from which he had extracted *Giovanni's Room.* The resulting work, *Another Country,* which took six years to complete, was longer than the two first novels put together and treated at least eight major characters, male and female, representing various races, regions, nationalities, and sexual preferences. Although not favorably reviewed when it appeared in 1962, the novel eventually sold four million copies and became Baldwin's most popular work. The book's notoriety, both positive and negative, probably resulted from its frank depiction of bisexuality and interraciality in a manner more graphic than was customary in the early 1960s.

In one sense *Another Country* combines elements from both earlier books; it reaffirms Baldwin's belief in love and in individual self-realization, with perhaps greater optimism than had been displayed in the first two novels. Responding to the suicide of Rufus Scott, a black jazz musician, his sister and various white friends work out their feelings of guilt through an intricate cycle of relations and infidelities that ultimately leads to a rediscovery of traditional human virtues, though in untraditional pairings. Despite the novel's familiar themes, however, the language is more expansive and free of the studied lyricism of the earlier novels. What is more important, Baldwin's argumentation strategy was beginning to change. Still highly crafted, the narrative borrows from the Beats a structural looseness and sexual candor that can make the plot seem a string of capricious couplings. There is, of course, none of the Beats' willful spontaneity, for all the characters recommit to their original partners in the novel's final pages. The intermixing of races, regions, and sexual preferences is not arbitrary but polemical, situating individual crises within the context of the specific sociopolitical conditions that aggravate and even create them. Unlike the earlier novels, *Another Country* conceived the problem of self-identity as at least in part a social issue: racism and to a lesser extent homophobia mark the failure of the white, straight society within which they occur. The absence of the aesthetic distance that had protected readers of the first two novels made this third more threatening, for all its apparent optimism.

At the center of Baldwin's new political emphasis is his brief but powerful characterization of Rufus Scott, who dies in the first fifth of the novel but remains present in the thoughts of the other characters. He is the giant on whose shoulders the others, like pygmies, stand to look—in one reading of the ambiguous title—

into another country. Moreover, his anger and violence in the opening pages are never fully eradicated by the reconciliations of the remaining characters. He is caught in an abusive relationship with a southern white woman whom he loves but brutalizes. Yet his irrational response to white oppression is perceived sympathetically; discrimination explains his brutality, indeed almost excuses it. Incorporating into the novel the cultural detail previously reserved for his essays, Baldwin presents through Rufus's eyes the sociology of the Harlem essay as well as the psychology of black self-hatred associated with his father in *Notes of a Native Son*. When Rufus jumps off the bridge "built to honor the father of his country," he becomes a symbol of racial anger, more a black Ahab than Gabriel Grimes: "He thought, You bastard, you motherfucking bastard. Ain't I your baby, too? *. . . all right, you motherfucking Godalmighty bastard, I'm coming to you.*"

The growing political undercurrent in Baldwin's fiction was perhaps even more evident in the essays he published while writing *Another Country*—essays that were collected, shortly before the novel appeared, in *Nobody Knows My Name* (1961). Like the novel, these pieces focus primarily on the role of the black in white society, often in terms of Baldwin's own personal relation to crucial movements or figures. Reporting on the Sorbonne's Conference of Negro-African Writers and Artists in "Princes and Powers" (*Encounter*, 1957), Baldwin questions the validity of an international black culture and was even more suspicious of the African delegates' desire to define that culture in terms of their own antagonism to Europe. Yet his skepticism derives not from an essential "integrationist" antipathy to the notion of black solidarity and separatism. Instead he challenges the participants' very definition of "culture." Was there a transnational black culture, and if so, of what would it consist beyond a "history of oppression," entirely negative and reinscribing within itself the discriminatory practices it sought to transcend? On the other hand, white imperialism, bad as it was, had become after the fact part of the history of certain black cultures. To claim that the culture of

American blacks was simply "given" them by the whites who robbed them of their African heritage is to ignore what blacks had subsequently made of that "gift."

A similar desire to attend to both individual responsibility and political oppression informed Baldwin's final account of Wright, in the three-part essay "Alas, Poor Richard" (1961). It is perhaps not surprising that in trying to understand the limitations of his own aesthetic distancing, Baldwin reconsidered with even less generosity than before a writer whose "protest" he had earlier criticized for its lack of distance. In these postmortems, Wright becomes one of the "most illustrious victims" in the war between blackness and whiteness, despising American Negroes and despised as one by the Africans. Yet—as the title's Shakespearan allusion implies—the essay is not about Wright. Just as Hamlet confronts his mortality on the occasion of discovering Yorick's skull, so does Baldwin examine after Wright's death the difficulties of his own position as black artist and expatriate: "For who has not hated his black brother? Simply *because* he is black, *because* he is brother. And who has not dreamed of violence? . . . Which of us has overcome his past?" Acknowledging the Bigger within himself, Baldwin recognizes in his attacks on Wright not the killing of the father but the skirmishes between different aspects of his own divided self. Whatever Wright's real role in Europe as mediator between American and African blacks, Baldwin confesses in this last farewell to Wright his own need to work out a political identity as a black within American culture.

At the center of the essays in *Nobody Knows My Name* and implicit in the multiraciality of *Another Country* lay Baldwin's psychological need to confront white America. Baldwin had, of course, never completely deserted his homeland. He returned to America regularly throughout the 1950s for professional and personal reasons. Nor would he ever completely return. The last twenty years of his life were spent largely abroad: in Paris, Istanbul, even Africa; and finally in St.-Paul-de-Vençe in the south of France. Yet after 1954, when the Supreme Court ruled that segregation in schools was unconstitutional, Baldwin increasingly defined himself in terms of American society, and especially as witness of and participant in the racial changes effected by the civil rights movement. In 1957 he visited the South for the first time, reporting on the integration of schools and meeting with Martin Luther King, Jr., who was just then becoming a national figure in civil rights. The celebrity that attended *Nobody Knows My Name* increased Baldwin's value for the movement, not only as a speaker for King but as a spokesman for the somewhat more radical programs of the Congress on Racial Equality (CORE) and the Student Nonviolent Coordinating Committee (SNCC). Baldwin's ambiguous position is probably best represented by the fiery but ineffectual meeting he arranged in 1963 between Robert Kennedy, then attorney general, and various celebrities, including Harry Belafonte, Lena Horne, Lorraine Hansberry, and Rip Torn.

Baldwin's role in the civil rights movement is still debated; the effect of political activism on his work, however, is fairly clear. Although he never denied the importance of individual self-realization, he increasingly argued that society determined the means and limits of that realization. The vaguely existential aestheticism of the early works gave way to the tensions between individual responsibility and racial oppression that mark the transitional works *Nobody Knows My Name* and *Another Country*. Baldwin's full commitment to a political reading of the black self did not emerge until the mid 1960s in the works *The Fire Next Time* and *Blues for Mister Charlie*. Like his previous nonfiction, *The Fire Next Time* (1963) was drawn from Baldwin's magazine publications. Yet this "collection" contained only two writings—the brief essay "My Dungeon Shook: Letter to My Nephew on the One Hundredth Anniversary of the Emancipation" and the lengthy piece "Down at the Cross: Letter from a Region in My Mind." In the first, Baldwin's earlier charge against Wright's Bigger Thomas is redirected against himself through two alter egos—his stepfather and a nephew bearing his own name. David Baldwin was defeated long before he died because, at the bottom of his heart, he really believed what white people said about him. . . . You [James the nephew, but also

James the novelist] can only be destroyed by believing that you really are what the white world calls a *nigger.*" The addition of the adjective *white* to a familiar point suggests Baldwin's new emphasis: "The details and symbols of your life have been deliberately constructed to make you believe what white people say about you." The necessary personal reorientation that Baldwin had called for since *Go Tell It on the Mountain* now takes place within social revolution, not apart from it.

The second essay is more complex. This work, too, begins traditionally, with yet another autobiographical account of the period treated in *Go Tell It in the Mountain* and *The Amen Corner.* Previously Baldwin had considered religious enthusiasm as symptomatic of familial and sexual tensions and hence as something that would pass when the tensions passed. In "Down at the Cross," however, it is an active agent in oppression: the issue is not autobiographical, a question of what Baldwin had personally found in religion, but political: what society had placed there for him to find. In light of the policing role of Christianity, Baldwin considers, remotely but sympathetically, the parallel place of the Black Muslim movement within black culture: "The dream, the sentiment is old; only the color is new." As always in Baldwin's work, "protest" reinforces the structures of oppression; the sole alternative is interracial cooperation and love. Yet "love" here is meant on a social, not a personal level: for blacks "love" means accepting a history of oppression; for whites, it means confessing that history. Nor does integration remain the model of community: "Do I really *want* to be integrated into a burning house?" The final word is one not of hope but of threat. A bill will soon be presented. If America is unwilling to pay, the result will be conflagration. For, as the book's final lines explicate the essay's title (taken from a slave song), God is no longer apologetic: though his rainbow promises never again to destroy the world with water, he still commands fire.

Critics unanimously recognized the power of Baldwin's formulations, but many were puzzled by his prophetic stance. Although apocalyptic rhetoric had often served Baldwin as a

stylistic tool, it had never been used to address the reader directly, divorced from the context of a dramatic scene. Even in the essays, social criticism had all been circumscribed by the subject under discussion—Baldwin's fights with his stepfather, or Richard Wright, or the African Congress. Now, however, for all the essay's autobiographical trappings, Baldwin was not speaking about himself, as artist or as black man; instead it was the reader's self that must be realized. The "Negro problem," redefined as the "Negro's tyrannical power," arises from a white myth about the black character, especially its inferiority. And the solution involves a social realignment in which whites must take an active, even dominant, role. After an initial flurry of enthusiasm (in which *The Fire Next Time,* like *Nobody Knows My Name* and *Another Country* before it, sold over a million copies), critics began to question Baldwin's argument for its alleged timidity, stylistic imprecision, and curiously passive view of blacks.

Growing reservations about Baldwin were even more evident in the critical response to his next work. *Blues for Mister Charlie* (1964) offered a fictionalized account of Emmett Till, a black youth murdered for supposedly whistling at a white woman. The play was too long, political, and bleak to find a commercial audience. Its dramatic texture was inconsistent: after two relatively realistic acts, the final act interrupted the trial proceedings with passionate soliloquies, in an experimental mode recalling the conservative surrealism of Thornton Wilder's *Our Town.* Yet critics attacked the play less for its form than for the anger it directed at southern white racists. Baldwin, who had earlier invested each of his characters with an individual richness, now was accused of reducing them to slogan-spouting stereotypes, writing what Philip Roth (in the *New York Review of Books*) called "soap opera" for "a Black Muslim nation."

Although the critics' call for a more sympathetic depiction of an unjustly acquitted murderer today sounds self-serving, their evaluation should not be rejected outright as "Mister Charlie's" unwillingness to hear of his own injustice. In *Blues for Mister Charlie* Baldwin does treat characters differently than he had in his early novels. There is little here of the Jamesian subtlety with which Baldwin once represented emotions. Although the play's characters do not seem to have complex motives, however, complexity is not so much absent as it is silenced. The relationships between the murdered man and his father, between the murderer and his white friend, and between the white friend and blacks in general, especially the murdered man's father and girlfriend: all are highly ambiguous, and find their antecedents in earlier works, especially *Go Tell It on the Mountain* and *Another Country.* Yet as the plot develops, the social system of southern racism overwhelms individual initiative. Rituals of racial discrimination come to control individual intentions (a process reflected technically in the third act, where symbolism overshadows narration). As a result, racism as a form of cultural solidarity impedes justice. The resulting flattening of the characters is less a dramatic failure on Baldwin's part than a deliberate political point: whatever the complexity, even innocence, of everyone's motives, the oppressive structure of racial inequality does not permit anyone to act except as a stereotype.

Some critics have suggested that the works after *Blues for Mister Charlie* betray a waning vitality. Baldwin himself invited this interpretation when he spoke in *No Name in the Street* (1972) of his disenchantment with the failure of civil rights after the assassination of King. "Since Martin's death, in Memphis, and that tremendous [funeral] day in Atlanta, something has altered in me, something has gone away.... One could scarcely be deluded by Americans anymore, one scarcely dared expect anything from the great, vast, blank generality." Yet the signs of exhaustion and repetition in the works after 1968 need not read as failures of imagination, any more than the propagandistic elements of *Blues for Mister Charlie* must be interpreted as failures of craft.

Some of the hostility directed against Baldwin after the publication of *The Fire Next Time* and *Blues for Mister Charlie* arose simply from white fear in the turbulent 1960s of any argument that seemed to condone black violence.

Yet the more interesting and long-lasting objection involved not Baldwin's political radicalism but the moral conservativism that supported it. The argument was formulated in *Advertisements for Myself* by Norman Mailer, Baldwin's major competitor in the 1950s for the title of leading literary hipster. In "Evaluations—Quick and Expensive Comments on the Talent in the Room" (1961), Mailer judged Baldwin "too charming" to be truly confrontive, his prose too "sprayed with perfume" ever to tell the reader "Fuck you." Baldwin gently exposed the racism and homophobia underlying Mailer's self-serving attack in "The Black Boy Looks at the White Boy" (*Esquire*, 1961; collected in *Nobody Knows My Name*).

Mailer's charge resurfaced, more cogently formulated, in Eldridge Cleaver's 1968 polemic, *Soul on Ice.* Cleaver stigmatized Baldwin as an "Uncle Tom" for his criticisms of Wright, his reservations about African nationalism, and his lack of masculinity. The essay betrays the limitations of 1960s bombast in both its sexism and its homophobia (Cleaver compares homosexuality to "baby-rape"). Yet formally the argument is an echo of Baldwin's own critique of Wright: in both cases a younger writer rejects an older man's depiction of black rage as unintentionally reinforcing the racist assumptions of white culture. Baldwin saw Bigger Thomas's violence as an internalization of whites' dehumanization of blacks; Cleaver attacks Rufus Scott's suicide as an internalization of their hatred. Cleaver concludes regarding Baldwin, much as Baldwin had regarding Wright, that his work betrays a fundamental self-contempt that paralyzes him politically.

It is unlikely that Baldwin took Cleaver's diatribe very seriously. His brief reference to it in *No Name in the Street* is surprisingly free of rancor. For, apart from his rejection of certain formulations as politically inexpedient, Cleaver had merely identified a general problem that Baldwin himself had begun to confront in *Blues for Mister Charlie:* the difficulty of depicting victimization without robbing the victims of their individuality. Blame automatically empowers villains: their culpability measures the force of their actions. Those who suffer seem more passive. The problem had always plagued Baldwin's narratives, especially in the more symbolic characters like Giovanni or Rufus Scott. Even the tormented John Grimes is literarily less compelling than his persecuting stepfather. Nor, as Cleaver cruelly pointed out, does Baldwin's hollow language about "manhood" really enrich his characterizations.

As Baldwin's works became more political, then, he found himself facing the same dilemma that he claimed had crippled Richard Wright. Not only was Baldwin now the target of oedipal attacks from a new generation of black writers; in voicing his own form of "protest," he robbed his characters of the very self-determination he had found missing in Bigger. Thus while other writers like Truman Capote and Norman Mailer turned increasingly to nonfiction, Baldwin in the 1970s and 1980s in some senses turned away from it. Already established as the finest essayist of his generation, Baldwin continued, of course, to produce impressive cultural criticism. *No Name in the Street* (1972) is a sophisticated account of race relations in the 1950s and 1960s, a wide-ranging sequel to *The Fire Next Time.* Deftly intertwining his public memories of Martin Luther King, Jr., Malcolm X, and school desegregation in Charlotte and Little Rock with his more private experiences in Germany, Hollywood, New York, and France, Baldwin reviewed the closely reasoned arguments of *Nobody Knows My Name* in an impressionistic, fragmented style. *The Devil Finds Work* (1976) is a brief but suggestive reading of American racial stereotypes as Baldwin experienced them in his life of moviegoing. His final work, *The Evidence of Things Seen* (1985), exposes the racial and sexual implications of a widely publicized series of child murder trials in Atlanta in 1985, arguing that in such a situation philosophical assumptions and sociological realities create evidence rather than discover or examine it.

This late nonfiction displays Baldwin's verbal felicity and moral integrity. At its best, in *No Name in the Street,* it is also intricately constructed, using postmodern techniques of discontinuity and juxtaposition to portray the diversity of experience—and of racism. Yet these

works lack the passion of the angry pieces of the 1960s, as if Baldwin knew he was preaching to a dwindling congregation. The strategy that had failed in *The Fire Next Time* to win over the heightened liberal conscience of the 1960s was unlikely to awaken more apathetic readers to the neoracist sensibility of the 1980s. Baldwin himself had become typed as the voice of black rage, and readers absorbed his apocalyptic cadences without attending to his arguments.

Having proven his worth as an essayist, in his final years Baldwin paradoxically made his more challenging assessments of American culture in a series of flawed novels. For if readers took his nonfiction for granted, in fiction he still had the ability to shock, unsettle, and confuse. After *Blues for Mister Charlie,* Baldwin went to work on a long novel, publishing in the interim only a single collection of short stories, *Going to Meet the Man* (1965). When *Tell Me How Long the Train's Been Gone* appeared in 1968, the huge work seemed less an advance than a regression. The tensions between Leo and Caleb Proudhammer recall similar relationships between brothers in *Go Tell It on the Mountain* and even more in the short story "Sonny's Blues" (*Partisan Review,* 1957). Leo's bisexuality looks back to both *Giovanni's Room* and *Another Country,* while the uncharacteristic use of a first-person narrator echoes David's role in the earlier gay novel. Yet the psychological subtlety and stylistic elegance of the earlier period are not evident in Leo's wordy narrative. Caleb's abrupt conversion from rebellious youth to persecuting minister seems unmotivated. And the sections dealing with Leo's acting career satirize too obviously the limitations of Lee Strasberg, whose Actors' Studio had mounted an inadequate production of *Blues for Mister Charlie.*

Yet like that play, the novel *Tell Me How Long the Train's Been Gone* may deliberately avoid literary richness in characterization and plot in order more clearly to dramatize the incompatibility of personal self-fulfillment and social conscience. Baldwin's intention to disorient is clearest in his use of the figure of Black Christopher, the bisexual black militant whose love affair with Leo ends the story. Although he is the titular hero of the last third of the book as well as the novel's most striking character, Christopher has a relatively small role in the plot. A shadowy figure for most of the book, in the final pages he abruptly exposes the paradox at the heart of this sentimental novel of black education: the discovery of a black self distances that self from black culture, a culture that Baldwin has defined in terms of its denial of selfhood. The problem of the black in America is not knowledge but power: Christopher concludes quite simply, "We need guns." Leo's very achievements as an individual place him outside any culture, "under surveillance" by whites and blacks alike. And what for 350 pages seems an account of personal fulfillment shifts suddenly in the final pages to become a denial of its possibility.

The contradictions of *Tell Me How Long the Train's Been Gone* are matched in the uncertain focus of Baldwin's next novel, *If Beale Street Could Talk* (1974). This comparatively short work, superficially more unified than the previous novels, represents an apparent return to the earlier lyrical style and the themes of salvation through art and love. The idealized story of pure love between the narrator, Clementine Rivers (Tish), and her artist boyfriend, Alfonzo Hunt (Fonny), is played against the harsh realities of white oppression, represented by Fonny's unfair imprisonment on a spurious charge of rape. Yet here too the simplicity may be illusory. The very tension between the romance plot and the naturalistic setting makes resolution impossible: the crying of Tish and Fonny's child in the book's final sentence suggests simultaneously the hope for future life and the inhospitable character of the present.

Moreover, the narrative ambiguities, often read as flaws, may further suggest the complexity of Baldwin's theme. Baldwin seems intentionally to undermine his own simplistic dichotomy between the nobility of the blacks and the oppression of the system. The plot remains in fact unresolved—Fonny is never brought to trial. The black characters' own guilt is regularly exposed. The suicide of Fonny's father, Frank, at the novel's end not only depicts the annihilation of black selfhood by the white legal system: it inscribes within the novel Cleaver's attack on the passivity of Baldwin's suffering blacks. Unlike the heroic Rufus, Frank is implicitly criticized for giving in to defeat and despair. Baldwin similarly undercuts the even more admirable character of Tish's mother, Sharon. The awkward episode in which Sharon travels to Puerto Rico to convince the rape victim to change her testimony may be illogical and undermotivated. It is also the most unsettling sequence in the book, one in which racial hierarchies are inverted as blacks oppress Hispanics. Like Frank's cowardly suicide, Sharon's ineffectual attempt to strong-arm the Latina calls into question the self-righteous assumptions of the book's depiction of injustice. Complicity and reciprocity—not oppression and victimization—are the novel's true models for interracial exchange.

Baldwin's final novel, *Just Above My Head* (1979), is in some senses an autumnal reconsideration of his own literary beginnings. Intertwining the stories of Arthur Montana, a gay male Gospel singer, and Julia Miller, a child evangelist who later becomes a fashion model, the plot recalls the early religious works in its settings and the novel *Another Country* in its sexual preoccupations and scope. Yet the conciliatory tone of the work only underscores the bleakness of some of its conclusions. The integrationism of *Another Country* is replaced by an implicit separatism: white society is rejected as irretrievably racist, and the characters work out their salvation wholly within the black community. The book's treatment of personal relationships is similarly pessimistic. Homosexuality is, even more than before, a viable option for many of the characters, but neither as a panacea nor as a prelude to pansexuality. The self-contempt and homophobia that can accompany it are fully explored. Further, Baldwin reaffirms the importance of the family as the model for community, but only after depicting the incestuous emotions it can generate.

Although the story—like those of the previous two novels—is told in the first person, *Just Above My Head* blurs the effect of such direct narration by shifting from a central to a peripheral character: to Hall, Arthur's brother and Julie's lover. The key to Baldwin's mixed tone is in fact Hall's ambiguous voice. While his personal commitment to his brother and lover shows in his moving praise of both, his distance from the protagonists adds an element of uncertainty to his evaluations: his own emotions are insufficiently examined ever to be fully credited. This odd mix of closeness and distance reaches its peak in the crucial pages of the protagonists' sexual initiations—Arthur with a fellow male singer, Julia with her father. In both cases Hall's sympathetic account is qualified by the simple fact that he cannot know what actually happened at these very private moments. Throughout the book, feelings of hopefulness are thus undercut by the desperation of Hall's need to justify the inescapable realities of life and death.

Baldwin's late works are perplexing. The narratives can feel too autobiographical, as Baldwin relentlessly examines the same issues of race, sexual preference, and familial tensions. The prose and plotting can seem erratic. Yet the difficulties that critics experience with these late products merely highlight the degree to which we may need to reconsider Baldwin's whole literary output. As Baldwin became a celebrity, his importance as a public symbol at times overshadowed his work as a writer. In the years since his death it has become possible to divorce his personality from the racial, political, and sexual stereotypes others imposed on him—to see him clearly as a person.

It is time now to effect a similar divorce of those stereotypes (and that personality) from the literature he wrote—to see him clearly as an author. In the 1950s Baldwin's importance lay in his realistic depiction of the psychological effects of racism within the black community in America. Throughout the later 1950s and early 1960s he continued to explore in his nonfiction the role of both blacks and whites in fostering racial tensions. In his fiction and theater, however, Baldwin increasingly examined the limitations of simplistic accounts of victimization—whether of racial minorities or of homosexuals—focusing as much on the complicity of the victim as on the culpability of the oppressor. These late works are difficult pieces in both their stylistic irregularities and their political implications. But only when we understand where Baldwin's writing was going in the troubled final years of his life can we begin to gauge accurately the nature of his literary and political projects as a whole.

Selected Bibliography

PRIMARY WORKS

NOVELS AND SHORT STORIES

Go Tell It on the Mountain. New York: Knopf, 1953.
Giovanni's Room. New York: Dial Press, 1956.
Another Country. New York: Dial Press, 1962.
Going to Meet the Man. New York: Dial Press, 1965.
Tell Me How Long the Train's Been Gone. New York: Dial Press, 1968.
If Beale Street Could Talk. New York: Dial Press, 1974.
Little Man, Little Man: A Story of Childhood. New York: Dial Press, 1976.
Just Above My Head. New York: Dial Press, 1979.

DRAMA

Blues for Mister Charlie: A Play. New York: Dial Press, 1964.
The Amen Corner: A Play. New York: Dial Press, 1968.
One Day, When I Was Lost: A Scenario Based on Alex Haley's "The Autobiography of Malcolm X." London: Michael Joseph, 1972.

NONFICTION

Notes of a Native Son. Boston: Beacon Press, 1955.
Nobody Knows My Name: More Notes of a Native Son. New York: Dial Press, 1961.
The Fire Next Time. New York: Dial Press, 1963.
Nothing Personal. Photographs by Richard Avedon. New York: Atheneum, 1964.
No Name in the Street. New York: Dial Press, 1972.
A Dialogue: James Baldwin and Nikki Giovanni. Philadelphia: Lippincott, 1973.
A Rap on Race. With Margaret Mead. Philadelphia: Lippincott, 1973.
The Devil Finds Work: An Essay. New York: Dial Press, 1976.
Jimmy's Blues: Selected Poems. London: Michael Joseph, 1983.
The Price of the Ticket: Collected Nonfiction. New York: St. Martin's/Marek, 1985.
The Evidence of Things Not Seen: An Essay. New York: Holt, Rinehart and Winston, 1985.

SECONDARY WORKS

BIOGRAPHICAL AND CRITICAL STUDIES

Baker, Houston A., Jr. *The Journey Back: Issues in Black Literature and Criticism.* Chicago: University of Chicago Press, 1980.

———. *Blues, Ideology, and Afro-American Literature, a Vernacular Theory.* Chicago: University of Chicago Press, 1984.

Beam, Joseph, ed. *In the Life: A Black Gay Anthology.* Boston: Alyson Publications, 1986.

Bloom, Harold, ed. *James Baldwin.* New York: Chelsea House, 1986.

Bone, Robert. *The Negro Novel in America.* Rev. ed. New Haven: Yale University Press, 1965.

Campbell, James. *Talking at the Gates: A Life of James Baldwin.* New York: Penguin, 1992.

Chametzky, Jules, ed. *Black Writers Redefine the Struggle: A Tribute to James Baldwin.* Amherst, N.Y.: Institute for Advanced Study in the Humanities/ University of Massachusetts Press, 1989.

Cleaver, Eldridge. *Soul on Ice.* New York: McGraw-Hill, 1968.

Davis, Arthur P., and J. Saunders Redding. *Cavalcade: Negro American Writing from 1760 to the Present.* Boston: Houghton Mifflin, 1971.

Dixon, Melvin. *Ride Out the Wilderness: Geography and Identity in Afro-American Literature.* Urbana: University of Illinois Press, 1987.

Eckman, Fern Marja. *The Furious Passage of James Baldwin.* New York: M. Evans, 1966.

Fabre, Michel. *The Unfinished Quest of Richard Wright.* Translated by Isabel Barzun. New York: William Morrow, 1973.

Gates, Henry Louis, Jr. "The Welcome Table: Essays from the Fiftieth Anniversary of the English Institute." In *English Inside and Out: The Places of Literary Criticism.* Edited by Susan Guber and Jonathan Kamholtz. New York: Routledge, 1993. Pp. 47–60.

Gibson, Donald B., ed., *Five Black Writers: Essays on Wright, Ellison, Baldwin, Hughes, and LeRoi Jones.* New York: New York University Press, 1970.

Harper, Philip Brian. *Are We Not Men?: Masculine Anxiety and the Problem of African-American Identity.* New York: Oxford University Press, 1996.

Harris, Trudier. *Black Women in the Fiction of James Baldwin.* Knoxville: University of Tennessee Press, 1985.

———, ed. *New Essays on "Go Tell It on the Mountain."* New York: Cambridge University Press, 1996.

Howe, Irving. *A World More Attractive: A View of Modern Literature and Politics.* New York: Horizon, 1963.

Kinnamon, Keneth, ed. *James Baldwin: A Collection of Critical Essays.* Englewood Cliffs, N.J.: Prentice-Hall, 1974.

Kollhöfer, Jacob, ed. *James Baldwin: His Place in American Literary History and His Reception in Europe.* New York: P. Lang, 1991.

Lee, Robert A. *James Baldwin: Climbing to the Light.* New York: St. Martin's Press, 1991.

Leeming, David Adams. "An Interview with James Baldwin on Henry James." *Henry James Review* 8:47–56 (Fall 1986).

———. *James Baldwin: A Biography.* New York: Alfred A. Knopf, 1994.

Levin, David. "Baldwin's Autobiographical Essays: The Problem of Negro Identity." *Massachusetts Review* 5:239–47 (1964).

Macebuh, Stanley. *James Baldwin: A Critical Study.* New York: Third Press/Joseph Okpaku, 1973.

Major, Clarence. *The Dark and Feeling: Black American Writers and Their Work.* New York: Third Press/ Joseph Okpaku, 1974.

McBride, Dwight A, ed. *James Baldwin Now.* New York: New York University Press, 1999.

Nelson, Emmanuel S. "The Novels of James Baldwin: Struggles of Self-Acceptance." *Journal of American Culture* 8:11–16 (Winter 1985).

———. "Critical Deviance: Homophobia and the Reception of James Baldwin's Fiction." *Journal of American Culture* 14:91–96 (Fall 1991).

Nobel, David W. *The Eternal Adam and the New World Garden.* New York: George Braziller, 1968.

O'Daniel, Therman B., ed. *James Baldwin: A Critical Evaluation.* Washington D.C.: Howard University Press, 1977.

Porter, Horace A. *Stealing the Fire: The Art and Protest of James Baldwin.* Middletown, Conn.: Wesleyan University Press, 1989.

Pratt, Louis. *James Baldwin.* Boston: Twayne, 1978.

Rohy, Valerie. "Displacing Desire: Passing, Nostalgia, and *Giovanni's Room.*" In *Passing and the Fictions of Identity.* Edited by Elaine K. Ginsberg. Durham, N.C.: Duke University Press, 1996. Pp. 218–33.

Sarotte, Georges Michel. *Like a Brother, Like a Lover: Male Homosexuality in the American Novel and Theatre from Herman Melville to James Baldwin.* New York: Doubleday, 1978.

Standley, Fred L., and Nancy V. Burt, eds. *Critical Essays on James Baldwin.* Boston: G. K. Hall, 1988.

Standley, Fred L., and Louis H. Pratt, eds. *Conversations with James Baldwin.* Jackson: University Press of Mississippi, 1989.

Standley, Fred L., and Nancy V. Standley. *James Baldwin: A Reference Guide.* Boston: G. K. Hall, 1980.

Sylvander, Carolyn Wedin. *James Baldwin.* New York: Ungar, 1980.

Thomas, Kendall. " 'Ain't Nothin' Like the Real Thing': Black Masculinity, Gay Sexuality, and the Jargon of Authenticity." In *Representing Black Men.* Edited by Marcellus Blount and George Cunningham. New York: Routledge, 1996. Pp. 55–69.

Troupe, Quincy, ed. *James Baldwin: The Legacy.* New York: Simon & Schuster, 1989.

Weatherby, W. J. *James Baldwin: Artist on Fire.* New York: Donald I. Fine, 1989.

BIBLIOGRAPHY

Stanley, Fred L., and Nancy V. Stanley, *James Baldwin: A Reference Guide.* Boston: G. K. Hall, 1980.

TONI CADE BAMBARA

(1939–1995)

MADHU DUBEY

IN THE EARLY 1970s, when Toni Morrison was working as an editor at Random House and actively looking to publish black women authors, Toni Cade Bambara strode into her office and engaged her in witty conversation. Morrison later recalled that soon after this first encounter Bambara submitted some short stories that were "beautifully political without being pedestrian." Like Morrison, Bambara found her voice as a writer during the 1960s, a decade marked by an upsurge in African American political and literary expression. The Black Arts movement that dominated this era of black literary production called for a politically committed art that would directly serve the black community. In keeping with the temper of this period, Bambara described her writing (in her essay "What It Is I Think I'm Doing Anyhow") as an "attempt to celebrate the tradition of resistance, . . . to tap Black potential, and . . . to join the chorus of voices that argues that exploitation and misery are neither inevitable nor necessary." What distinguishes Bambara's multifaceted career as a writer, activist, educator, and later as a film-maker, is her enduring preoccupation with the political dimensions of writing and other forms of cultural expression.

Although Bambara did not acknowledge to herself that she was a writer until 1973, even as a child she would write voraciously on any surface she could find, including strips from her father's newspapers and the cardboard squares around which her mother's stockings came wrapped. Toni Cade Bambara was born in New York City on March 25, 1939, to Helen Brent Henderson Cade and Walter Cade II. She was named Miltona Mirkin Cade, after her father's employer, Milton Mirkin. At the age of five, she announced that she was changing her first name to Toni, and in 1970, while pregnant with her daughter Karma Bene, she added Bambara to her name in honor of a signature she found among her great-grandmother's papers. (Bambara is the name of a West-African tribe near the Niger region.) Bambara dedicated her award-winning novel *The Salt Eaters* to her mother, "who in 1948, having come upon me daydreaming in the middle of the kitchen floor, mopped around me." An outspoken woman with passionate intellectual interests, Helen Cade instilled in her daughter and her son (Walter Cade III, who grew up to be an artist) an abiding respect for the life of the imagination, and recognized their daydreaming as "important work." She took great pride in her collection of books, which first introduced her children to the work of African American writers such as Gwendolyn Brooks and Langston Hughes. Helen Cade also seems to have passed on to her daughter her powerful sense of justice as well as her courage in speaking out against injustice. In interviews, Bambara often recalled her mother's angry visits to her school to tell off her teachers about some unfair act or word reported to her by her daughter. An active member of the Women's League of Voters, Helen Cade contributed (under the name Helen Cade Brehon) to Toni Cade's first book, *The Black Woman: An Anthology* (1970).

Encouraged by her mother, Toni Cade wrote plays on African American public figures like Frederick Douglass and George Washington Carver for elementary school programs and frequently contributed to her high school literary journal. Quite early in her life Cade's writing began to receive public recognition. In 1959, the year Cade received her undergraduate degree in theatre arts and English literature from Queens College in Queens, New York, she was awarded the John Golden Award for Fiction. During that same eventful year, she received the Pauper Press Award for nonfiction from *The Long Island Star*, for which she had been a freelance writer, and published her first short story, "Sweet Town," in *Vendome* magazine. From then onward, Cade's stories, articles, and reviews began appearing in numerous anthologies and journals.

Cade spent the decade of the 1960s, which was formative of her political and literary sensibility, involved in a wide range of educational, professional, and community-service pursuits. Following her bachelor's degree, she studied theatre, dance, and film at various institutions in New York City (including New York University, the New School of Social Research, and the Studio Museum of Harlem Film Institute) and abroad, at the University of Florence, the Commedia del'Arte in Milan, and the Ecole de Mime Etienne Decroux in Paris. In 1965 Cade took on a position as lecturer in English at City College of New York, where she had completed her master's degree in American literature the previous year. In 1969 she became assistant professor in English at Livingston College of Rutgers University in New Brunswick, New Jersey, where she was eventually promoted to associate professor. Over the course of the decade, Bambara performed community work in numerous capacities, including advisor for the City College SEEK program for minority stu-

dents, social investigator at Harlem Welfare Center, director of recreation in the psychiatric department of Metropolitan Hospital, program director at Colony House Community Center in Brooklyn, and coordinator of various other neighborhood programs.

The Black Woman

Cade's first book, *The Black Woman*, published in 1970 under the name Toni Cade, clearly attests to her intellectual and political commitment to the black community. Cade opens her preface to this book by declaring, "We are involved in a struggle for liberation . . . What typifies the current spirit is an embrace . . . of the community and a hardheaded attempt to get basic with one another." This attempt to get basic involved, in Cade's view, an acknowledgment of the gender inequalities in the black liberation movement, and a consideration of what "liberation for ourselves [i.e., black women] means." In the preface, Cade states that the book "grew out of an impatience" with the fact that existing scholarship "directly relevant to [black women] wouldn't fill a page." A landmark effort to fill this gap, *The Black Woman* contains writings by black women from diverse class, educational, and occupational backgrounds on a range of issues "directly relevant" to their lives, including politics, family, education, housing, sexuality, and culture. The volume was widely acclaimed as a first of its kind in the United States, and it helped open the door to several anthologies by and about black women that were to be published over the course of the decade.

The Black Woman contains poems, short stories, and autobiographical as well as analytical essays on various facets of black women's experience. Contributors include some well-known writers—such as Nikki Giovanni, Audre Lorde, Paule Marshall, and Alice Walker—and others who had never previously been published. The volume did not aim to present any one ideological position as representative of the black woman; instead, its authors voiced diverse and often conflicting opinions on black

Toni Cade Bambara

this emphasis on female self-determination, "On the Issue of Roles" calls into question the rigidly polarized definitions of masculine and feminine roles that hold sway in American capitalist society and denounces the perpetuation of these gender divisions within the black liberation movement. Cade examines alternate conceptions of gender identity in non-Western societies in order to establish a truth that would be repeatedly reinforced by her fiction—that human nature is a historically changeable and "pretty malleable quality."

Tales and Stories for Black Folks

If Cade's first published anthology provided black women a public arena for self-expression, her second anthology, *Tales and Stories for Black Folks*, published the following year under the name Toni Cade Bambara, sought to transmit to black youth the eloquent powers of African American oral expression. This collection, named outstanding book of 1972 in juvenile literature by the *New York Times Book Review*, was intended to teach young African Americans "how to listen, to be proud of our oral tradition, our elders who tell their tales in the kitchen." Like *The Black Woman*, *Tales and Stories* features famous authors, including Ernest Gaines, Langston Hughes, and Alice Walker, as well as lesser-known writers and students from Bambara's composition course at Livingston College. In addition to reprinting some previously published fiction, Bambara contributed a political fable to the collection, coauthored with Geneva Powell, a community worker from Newark. "The Three Little Panthers" criticized attempts at social assimilation by bourgeois, suburban African Americans and affirmed the cultural resources of black inner-city life.

women's roles within the family, community, the black liberation movement, and the nation. Cade herself contributed three essays to the collection (two of them reprints of earlier publications) that address some of the pressing questions facing black nationalist and feminist politics during this period. In "The Great White Hope," Cade's review of a white theatrical production broadens into a discussion of the nature and function of art in the black liberation movement. "The Pill: Genocide or Liberation?" criticizes the anti–birthcontrol policy taken by many male leaders of the black liberation movement. In a measured feminist analysis, Cade refuses to celebrate the pill as a means of sexual liberation for women, but at the same time she insists that the pill is valuable insofar as it increases a woman's ability to control her life and to make her own choices. Seconding

Bambara's message about the rich potential of black urban life was drawn from her own personal experience of growing up in Harlem during the 1940s and 1950s. In an interview with Zala Chandler decades later, Bambara described the Harlem of these times as "a community

17

where African genius was very much in evidence." In addition to various "community meeting places" such as the Apollo, the Schomburg Library, and several black bookstores, Harlem also contained Speaker's Corner, the informal institution that proved to be vital to Bambara's education as an intellectual, writer, and political activist. Located at 125th Street and Seventh Avenue, this street corner functioned as a public forum where all sorts of people—including women from sanctified churches, women from the Ida B. Wells clubs, Muslims, Rastafarians, trade unionists, political party members, and members of the National Negro Congress—would speak about current public issues that impinged on the community. Bambara recalls in her essay, "Salvation Is the Issue," that these accomplished orators first made her aware of "the power of the word, the importance of the resistance tradition, and the high standards our community has regarding verbal performance." The valuable lessons Bambara learned here about language as a medium of resistance bore fruit in her first volume of short stories, *Gorilla, My Love*, published in 1972.

Gorilla, My Love

Bambara's first published book of fiction reaped the highest critical praise. Reviewers hailed *Gorilla, My Love* for its realistic depiction of black urban life from the point of view of streetwise and sensitive young girls and for its unerring ear for the vernacular language spoken by these girl-narrators and their communities. In "Salvation Is the Issue," Bambara ranks Zora Neale Hurston very highly among her "critical foremothers," primarily for her use of African American "folkways as the basis of 'art.' " If Hurston decisively established the voice of rural southern black folk as a literary language, Bambara achieved something comparable with the vernacular language of northern urban folk. The stories in *Gorilla, My Love* were also very much in tune with the spirit of the nationalist Black Arts movement, which encouraged literary uses of urban vernacular language as the

source of a new and authentic black voice. In an obituary tribute, one of the foremost spokesmen for the Black Arts movement, Amiri Baraka, gave Bambara the richly deserved title of an "uptown Griot." Perhaps Bambara's most remarkable achievement in *Gorilla, My Love* is that she nowhere relies on a standard English narrative frame to mediate the vernacular speech of her characters to a reading audience imagined as outsiders to the community. Instead, her first-person narrators speak as linguistic and cultural insiders, and Bambara lets their vernacular expression stand as a self-sufficient literary language in its own right, opening the way for future black women novelists such as Gayl Jones, Alice Walker, and Sapphire.

The vernacular idiom used by the girl narrators of *Gorilla, My Love* emerges as a language not only remarkably resilient in emotional range and nuance, but also as a fine-tuned instrument of social critique. Most of the stories in this volume are initiation tales about young girls growing into an awareness of their own sexuality as well as of their expected roles in the family, community, and wider society. It is by listening to the speech of peers and older women that many of the narrators discover their own place within a community of black women and acquire the vernacular knowledge that equips them to make the transition from girlhood into womanhood. Critical studies of these stories have highlighted the oral expressive practices that transmit female folk wisdom within and across the generations, such as signifying in "Basement" and "The Survivor," or the cautionary tales, secular sermons, and call-and-response conversations that school the protagonist of "The Johnson Girls" into a shrewd awareness of the ways of men.

The initiation tale offered Bambara an ideal vehicle for examining socially prescribed definitions of femininity, and the vernacular voice of the young girls serves as a perfect medium for defamiliarizing narrow social expectations of women. In her essay, "On the Issue of Roles," Bambara called for the creation of "new" and "perhaps . . . androgynous" identities as crucial first steps toward political transformation.

18

Readers of *Gorilla, My Love* are given glimpses into the resistant possibilities of androgynous identity through the often tomboyish girl narrators who inhabit liminal gender spaces not yet fully captured by social convention. An excellent example of this is Squeaky in "Raymond's Run." A track runner as well as a fearlessly self-determined girl, Squeaky is pressured by her mother to wear organdy dresses with satin sashes and to participate in more traditionally feminine activities such as dancing. Squeaky's blunt narrative voice exposes the incongruity between delicate feminine ideals and the hard realities of her own experience as a poor black girl, as she rails against the idea of "trying to act like a fairy or a flower or whatever you're supposed to be when you should be trying to be yourself, whatever that is, which is, as far as I'm concerned, a poor Black girl who really can't afford to buy shoes and a new dress you only wear once a lifetime."

Similarly, the unnamed narrator of "The Hammer Man" struggles to make the transition from tomboy to her mother's model of femininity, which involves switching from shorts to skirts and participating in fashion shows, even as she knows that "Dick and Jane was full of crap from the get-go." Her received notions of femininity are thrown into crisis in the story's climactic scene, as she watches the police randomly brutalize a young black boy, Manny, for nothing but playing basketball in a park that is supposedly closed. Watching this scene, the narrator tests the truisms she has been taught in school (such as the image of kind and protective police) against the reality of black urban life, and is ultimately compelled to repudiate socially imposed feminine roles as she fiercely confronts the policemen in defense of Manny. In the justly celebrated title story of the collection, Hazel displays the same bold spirit of defiance, as she burns down a candy stand to protest the false advertising of a theatre that screens a movie about Jesus Christ billed as "Gorilla, My Love." Hazel's display of anger and disappointment at adult duplicity is all the more effective for its forthright expression: "Cause if you say Gorilla, My Love, you suppose to mean it. . . . I mean even gangsters in the movies say

The cover of Bambara's short story collection
Gorilla, My Love.

My word is my bond. So don't nobody get away with nothin far as I'm concerned."

The stories in *Gorilla, My Love* starkly depict the multiple forms of inequality that confront black children living in poor urban neighborhoods. The child's voice in these stories functions as the sharpest possible linguistic weapon, allowing Bambara to attack social injustice without heavy-handed didacticism. As Susan Willis has observed, the child who is not yet fully socialized into the ways of her world is able to perceive social contradictions with startling freshness, thereby stimulating a heightened consciousness in the reader. For example, in one of Bambara's most frequently anthologized stories, "The Lesson," the racialized economic inequities of capitalist society are made vividly real through a child's discovery that the price of a single toy sold in F.A.O. Schwarz could feed an entire family. What ultimately makes these stories so memorable is the complex stance taken by the girl narrators to various forms of injustice, combining clear-eyed disenchantment with humor, and warm compassion with streetwise scorn for sentimentality.

Although the stories featuring girl narrators undoubtedly form the centerpiece of *Gorilla, My Love*, Bambara's achievement as a writer is equally evident in other stories with adult protagonists and narrators. Two such stories, "My Man Bovanne" and "Mississippi Ham Rider," are unique for their subtle portrayal of "the folk," whether from the urban north or rural south. "My Man Bovanne" focuses on an older urban woman named Miss Hazel attending a benefit for a black political party. Miss Hazel's children are ashamed to find their mother dancing sensuously with a blind man named Bovanne. The youngsters in the neighborhood used to appreciate Bovanne for his ability to "fix things," that is, until "Black Power got hold their minds and mess em around till they can't be civil to ole folks." Narrated in Miss Hazel's voice, the story humorously reveals the hypocrisy of a nationalist ideology that embraces the folk as a political abstraction but has little tolerance for actual members of the folk. Aware that she and Bovanne have been invited to the benefit because "we grass roots," Miss Hazel satirizes the notion of grass roots subscribed to by the younger and politically militant generation: "And I ain't never been souther than Brooklyn Battery and no more country than the window box on my fire escape. And just yesterday my kids tellin me to take them countrified rags off my head and be cool. And now can't get Black enough to suit em." Whereas her children dismiss Bovanne as a Tom, Miss Hazel not only treats him with affection but also insists on his centrality to any viable conception of black nationalism—"Cause old folks is the nation" too. Through the generosity and specificity of Miss Hazel's vernacular voice, the story suggests that any conception of black political community must be capacious and founded on respect for the variegated humanity of the folk.

"Mississippi Ham Rider" is narrated by Inez Williams, an educated black woman who is down south trying to persuade an old blues singer to travel north to record his songs. Described by Inez as "Mr. Ethnic-Authentic," Ham Rider is wanted by record companies up north to satiate the hunger of "folkway-starved sophisticates." At the same time as Inez values his cultural currency, she also sees the bluesman as a primitive and simple-minded figure residing in a timeless folk realm. Deftly exposing the contradictions of the "heritage business," which turned the folk into fetishes precisely by locating them outside politics and history, Bambara has her narrator describe Ham Rider as "impressive, the way a good demolition site can be." Inez considers asking the bluesman about his perception of the Civil Rights movement that was then overhauling the rural south, but decides not to, because "he had already taken on a legendary air and was simply not of these times."

Like Miss Hazel, however, Mississippi Ham Rider is ultimately revealed to be a willful and self-determined individual with a shrewd grasp "of these times," as he tries to negotiate the best financial deal for himself and his family in a situation he knows to be exploitative. Similar to Miss Hazel's dismissal of condescending notions of grassroots, the bluesman provides an account of himself that mocks the stereotype of backward country folk: " 'I don't sing no cotton songs, sister . . . And I ain't never worked in the fields or shucked corn. And I don't sing no nappy-head church songs neither. And no sad numbers about losing my woman and losing my mind.' " "Mississippi Ham Rider," along with "My Man Bovanne," imbues the folk with canny acuity and linguistic sophistication, refusing to romanticize them as emblems of cultural authenticity. What these stories share with other stories in the collection that feature child narrators is Bambara's use of a black vernacular language that never strains to demonstrate, for it simply assumes, the complex humanity of the folk. The language of the folk in these stories effortlessly renders their autonomy and independent will, and above all, their incisive critical understanding of their own positions in society and history.

The Sea Birds Are Still Alive

The years following the publication of *Gorilla, My Love* were among the most eventful in Bambara's life. In 1974 Bambara moved with her daughter to Atlanta, where she continued her involvement in various cultural, educational, and community programs and institutions. To give a selective example of her multifarious activities at this time, Bambara served as artist-in-residence at Spelman College; founder and director of the Pomoja Writers Collective; founding member and officer of the Conference Committee on Black South Literature and Art; associate and aide of the Institute of the Black World; program coordinator for the Arts-in-the-Schools Project sponsored by the Atlanta Public School System; production artist-in-residence for the Neighborhood Arts Center in Atlanta; consultant in Women's Studies at Atlanta and Emory Universities; and research mentor at the School of Social Work in Atlanta.

During the five years between *Gorilla, My Love* and the publication of her second collection of short stories, Bambara's sense of the value and purpose of her writing underwent radical transformation. In 1973, the year before her move to Atlanta, Bambara visited Cuba as a guest of the Federation of Cuban Women. In "Salvation Is the Issue," Bambara recalls that she did not see herself primarily as a writer until her return from Cuba, when she realized the truth of what the Black Arts movement "had been teaching for years—that writing is a legitimate way, an important way, to participate in the empowerment of the community." Two years later, in 1975, Bambara went to Vietnam as a member of a delegation called The North American Academic Marxist-Leninist Anti-Imperialist Feminist Women. The profound impact of these two visits is visible everywhere in *The Sea Birds Are Still Alive,* published in 1977. Not only is the title story about the struggle against U.S. imperialism in Vietnam, but virtually all the stories draw connections be-

tween antiracist politics within the United States and anti-imperialist political movements in Asia and Africa.

As Bambara recounts in "What It Is I Think I'm Doing Anyhow," during her Atlanta years she also came to realize more forcefully than ever before the pragmatic value of writing. She had always preached that "A writer, . . . like any other member of the community, ought to try to put her/his skills in the service of the community" but it was not until she lived in Atlanta that Bambara found herself practicing this in the most literal sense. After her picture was published in a local newspaper, her neighbors would knock on her door and ask her whether she was the "writin lady." And before she knew it, Bambara had embarked on a new career as the "neighborhood scribe," using her skills to serve the immediate, practical needs of her community. In exchange for writing "letters to relatives, snarling letters to the traffic chief about the promised stop sign, nasty letters to the utilities, angry letters to the principal about the confederate flag hanging in front of the school," Bambara was rewarded with "sweet potato dumplings, herb teas, hair braiding" and occasional complaints about her poor penmanship. The question of the writer's practical accountability to his or her community is always at the forefront of the stories collected in *The Sea Birds Are Still Alive.*

In some respects, *Sea Birds* is a very different book from *Gorilla, My Love.* The stories in the second volume are more overtly political in content and wider in geographical scope than the first collection. Critical reception of *Sea Birds* was mixed. Some reviewers were disappointed that Bambara did not rely on vernacular language as consistently as she had in her first collection, and others objected to the didacticism of the stories. Much of the critical discomfort with *Sea Birds* was rooted in the widely held assumption that art and politics do not mix well, that explicit political messages compromise artistic quality. But, as Toni Morrison remarked of Bambara in *Deep Sightings and Rescue Missions* (1996), any "hint that art was over there and politics over here would break her up into tears of laughter." And indeed, the strength of the stories in Bambara's second collection is their seamless fusion of art and politics. It is clear that these stories could only have been written by someone who was engaged in political struggle and community service on a daily basis and at an intensely personal level. Bambara examines here the many self-doubts and emotional conflicts that any individual dedicated to revolutionary action must necessarily confront. The militant vision Bambara advocates is all the more persuasive because the stories render so palpably the traumatic psychological processes by which individuals transform themselves into political activists.

Four of the five overtly political stories in *Sea Birds* present female protagonists who question the purity and singularity of their commitment to revolutionary action. All four stories are narrated in a first-person voice that gives the reader intimate access to the conflicts experienced by their protagonists. The narrator of "The Apprentice" struggles to overcome her physical exhaustion and her defeatist spirit, fearful that she is not up to being a revolutionary. Lacey in "Broken Field Running," overwhelmed by rage and despair, longs for the return of the 1960s, for "The energy of the seventies just don't do me nuthin." The unnamed narrator of "The Long Night" questions her own strength of will: faced with the probability of police torture, she wonders whether she will be able to maintain silence about the radical organization to which she belongs. Virginia in "The Organizer's Wife" oscillates between her personal desire to escape the co-op farm that forms the story's site of political action and her sense of obligation to her husband's political goals. All these women ultimately arrive at a renewed commitment to revolutionary politics that does not, however, decisively resolve or banish their emotional uncertainties. The stories in *Sea Birds* suggest that revolution is slow, arduous, and forever incomplete, and that personal upheaval is a prerequisite for durable political change.

Bambara's rare achievement in these first-person stories of the process of politicization is that she communicates the desire for change at the most visceral level. In addition to seam-lessly fusing concrete personal experience and abstract political principles, the stories in *Sea Birds* exquisitely blend laughter and outrage, the two qualities that Bambara liked most in her own writing. In "Salvation Is the Issue" Bambara writes that while her "heart is a laughing gland . . . , near that chamber is a blast furnace where a rifle pokes from the ribs. The combination makes for a desperado kind of writing sometimes." She mentions as an example "Broken Field Running," initially written in a state of "poker-hot rage" and later revised to incorporate humor to temper the outrage. It is her gift for laughter, Bambara notes, that always alerts her to the fact that her "polemical slip is showing," but she is also very careful not to use laughter to "screen" or "dodge" an "uncomfortable reality." The end result is stories that maintain a very fine balance between unflinching realism and visionary hope, honest recognition of grim social conditions and optimism about the possibility of improvement.

Although *Sea Birds* bristles with the conviction that political change is just around the corner, the stories never provide quick recipes for revolution. In her essay "On the Issue of Roles" Bambara criticized the black nationalist leaders of the 1960s for assuming that revolution could be made like "instant coffee." Like other African American women writers of the time, Bambara maintained an alternate vision of political change as a hard-won process that must always be rooted in past traditions and in the everyday activities of ordinary people. In the title story of *Sea Birds*, for example, the revolutionary overthrow of U.S. imperial order is brought about by the "rear guard," personified here in the figure of an elderly widow who serves young rebels as "a walking manual" of age-old indigenous practices of rebellion. Similarly, in "The Long Night" and "Broken Field Running," ancestral memories and expectations help nourish the younger generation's desire for political change. Yet Bambara is always wary of the false comfort offered by nostalgia for the past. In "Broken Field Running," when faced with the bleak conditions of the contemporary ghetto, Lacey harks back to a golden era when elders like Pop Johnson and Miss Gladys kept the black community "a sovereign place," but she soon abandons this nostalgic impulse, "knowing there's no refuge . . . in the highly selective fiction I've made of the past."

Despite their obvious differences, the stories in *Gorilla, My Love* and *Sea Birds* share an unsentimental approach to black folk tradition as a source of emotional sustenance and social opposition for young girls and women. The second volume contains some coming-of-age tales reminiscent of those found in *Gorilla, My Love,* which present young girls grappling with the question of what kind of women they are going to become. But in the later stories this question is more overtly infused with political overtones. In "A Girl's Story" the ancestral figure, Dada Bibi, helps young girls at the neighborhood community center come to terms with their emergent womanhood by recounting stories about an African warrior-princess that fuse feminist and cultural nationalist values into a folk medium. Incorporating the girls' occasionally skeptical questions and comments in later retellings, Dada Bibi's stories exhibit the interactivity of black folk tradition as well as its adaptability to current demands. For the adult narrators of "Medley" and "Witchbird," folk tradition proffers inspiring models of independent womanhood. The rhythms and sensibility of blues and jazz music permeate these stories, shaping their improvisational structures as well as their explorations of feminine sexuality and identity. In "Medley" Sweet Pea is the prototype of a blues woman, with her frank enjoyment of her sexuality, her tough and tender sensibility, her pragmatic opportunism, and her matter-of-fact refusal to assume a nurturing feminine role. "Witchbird," after a scathing exposition of the mammy roles imposed on black women in their domestic and public lives, similarly affirms the blues as a medium that allowed black women freedom and fullness of expression.

Developing in fictional form many of the issues raised by Bambara's contributions to *The Black Woman*, the stories in *Sea Birds* insist that sexual and familial matters are every bit as political as the more public racial concerns

highlighted by the black liberation movement of the 1960s. "A Tender Man," the only story in the collection to focus on a male character, implies that the political transformation of the black community will remain unfinished until black men as well as women work to redefine existing gender divisions. The most topical story in the volume, "A Tender Man" also dramatizes the mutual antagonism between men and women over domestic matters and sexual politics that seems to have stymied the black liberation movement by the 1970s. The main character, Cliff, is known to be highly principled in the public sphere of campus politics, but is reluctant to exercise full responsibility as a father. When called on this by a black woman, Cliff defensively summons up grotesque mental images of black women disrupting political meetings with their feminist demands: "sisters shouting from the podiums, the rooftops, the bedrooms, telling warriors dirty diapers was revolutionary work." However, Cliff struggles to surmount his strong animosity toward "aggressive" and "assertive" black women, and by the end he promises to reform himself into a tender man and a responsible father. Like most of the stories in *Sea Birds*, "A Tender Man" boldly confronts the existing tensions between black nationalist and feminist politics, but ends with the hope that a rapprochement between these adversarial positions is possible in the not-too-distant future.

In interviews and essays, Bambara often expressed her preference for the short story as the form best suited to her own imaginative aims and abilities. A "brazenly 'message' writer" (as she described herself in "What It Is I Think I'm Doing Anyhow"), Bambara found that the short story served her didactic intentions better than longer narrative forms: It "makes a modest appeal for attention, allowing me to slip up alongside the reader on her/his blind side and grab'm." Moreover, Bambara appreciated the "fairly portable" nature of the short story, which could be composed in bits and snatches and therefore easily integrated with domestic and professional activities. Yet, after the publication of *The Sea Birds Are Still Alive*, Bambara felt compelled to try her hand at writing a novel because, as she wrote in "Salvation Is the Issue," the genre was favored by the "publishing industry, the academic establishment, reviewers, and critics."

The Salt Eaters

Bambara's first novel, *The Salt Eaters* (1980), was published only four years after *The Sea Birds Are Still Alive,* yet it captures a wholly different political mood and reality. The novel shows that the black political unity of the 1960s has splintered by the late 1970s into a "Babel of paths, of plans," and presents a host of political movements pulling in conflicting directions. This loss of political purpose is compounded by sharp rifts between various camps, including materialists and spiritualists, political activists and cultural workers. The disintegration of black community is reflected in the very structure of the novel, which switches abruptly from one locale, time frame, and point of view to another without providing readers any cues for synthesizing all its disjunctive story lines into a coherent narrative. Adding to these difficulties is the novel's casual blending of multiple planes of reality. Living characters converse with those who have died, but are nevertheless present, and crucial scenes in the novel project events and discoveries that may occur in the future.

The Salt Eaters won the American Book Award in 1981, although it received mixed critical attention. Reviewers admired the novel's ambitious scope and complex design, but expressed frustration with its confusing plot and narration. One way of gaining access to the difficult form of *The Salt Eaters* is to approach it as "a kind of jazz suite," as Bambara described the novel in an interview with Kalamu ya Salaam. The novel's sudden shifts in time and space as well as its disorienting juxtapositions of the actual and the imaginary begin to make sense when viewed as essential aspects of a jazz mode that seeks an inclusive ordering of past and future, reality and possibility, individual and communal experience. The novel focuses on the story of Velma Henry, who has suffered

a psychological breakdown resulting from her failure to juggle the competing demands of being a wife, mother, cultural worker, and political activist. The narration ripples outward to present numerous variations on the central theme of Velma's recovery, with the subsidiary stories of other characters amplifying the collective implications of Velma's crisis.

At once cause and effect of Velma's illness is her dissociation from the regenerative potential of her past; consequently, her healing takes the form of a re-connection made possible through the medium of music. As faith healer Minnie Ransom performs the ritual ceremony of laying on of hands, Velma wonders, "what was this anyway, a healing or a jam session?" And indeed, as Bambara's favorite critic of her novel, Eleanor Traylor, has shown, the improvisational and synthetic mode of jazz music gives form to the seemingly chaotic structure of *The Salt Eaters*. Velma sits immobilized within the present tense of the novel's action (which only covers a few hours in a single day), but her mind roams across different moments of her life. In a supplementary movement, the narrative voice (which is not always identified with Velma's) ranges over the recent and distant past of Claybourne, the town in Georgia in which the novel's action takes place. Personal and communal experience, historical memory and mythology coalesce throughout the novel. What lends coherence to all these diverse levels of time and reality is not linear chronology but the question of what past traditions can offer the individual in a moment of present danger and crisis.

The answer to this question is developed through the paradoxical symbolism of mud and salt. As Velma's mind goes wandering, she repeatedly recalls and suppresses an image of mud mothers in a cave. This mythical image of ancient feminine power both seduces and terrifies Velma, for it simultaneously symbolizes the fertilizing potential of the past, the invasion of the conscious mind by primal and unconscious memories, and a collective maternal presence that threatens to blur the boundaries of her individual self. Just as the mud mothers can be both smothering and regenerative, so, too, does salt symbolize paralyzing as well as nourishing uses of the past. Salt functions as an antidote to the sting of the serpent, which in the novel represents the lure of assimilation into Western culture. Salt-eaters are those who draw on the past in order to "stay centered in the best of [their] people's traditions." However, too much salt, or rigid conformity to past ways, can obstruct people's readiness for change. As suggested by the novel's allusions to the Biblical story of Lot's wife, who turned into a pillar of salt because she could not resist looking back, excessive "loyalty to old things, a fear of the new, a fear of change" result in ossification of the self. Like jazz music, *The Salt Eaters* resumes traditions that can be adapted to meet the changing needs of the present and the future, and this dynamic approach to the past is dramatized by the fluid structure of the novel.

The jazz mode perfectly served Bambara's ambition in *The Salt Eaters* to find a form that would encompass multiple dimensions of reality and experience. Jazz exemplifies through its improvisational techniques an expansive and flexible approach to reality. In "What It Is I Think I'm Doing Anyhow" Bambara remembers that she came to the writing of *The Salt Eaters* "with the belief that everything is possible." Part of the complexity of *The Salt Eaters* arises from Bambara's effort to validate possible realities discredited by modern Western standards of rational and scientific knowledge. Bambara houses these alternate forms of knowledge in the Southwest Community Infirmary, described as a "seat of knowing" committed to maintaining "the ancient wisdoms, the real, the actual, the sho-nuff original folk stuff behind them Greek impostors." This institute for alternative medicine perpetuates the folk knowledge and practices of a variety of marginalized cultural traditions. Velma's healing is completed only when she is able to move without any sense of dissonance between actual and imagined, secular and sacred, historical and mythical levels of reality. The reader, too, is nudged toward an inclusive grasp of reality by the novel's intermingling of actual events that are occurring in the present with dreams, fantasies, and visions of future possibility. The end of the novel employs the innovative technique of flash-forward to integrate future potentialities into the fabric of everyday existence. In fact, the novel's climax and resolution hinge on various characters' receptivity to transformations that might happen in the future.

The associative mode of jazz enabled Bambara to resist what she called in her preface to *Daughters of the Dust* (1992) the "great American afflictions, amnesia and disconnectedness." The main problem that ails Velma as well as the black liberation movement in the novel is the failure to make connections between different political goals, cultural traditions, and systems of knowledge. In "Salvation Is the Issue" Bambara suggested that one avenue out of the political impasse of the late 1970s was available through the African American "faculty for synthesis" evident in cultural forms such as jazz. *The Salt Eaters* contains many moments and models of cultural synthesis, the most critically acclaimed of these being the Seven Sisters, a traveling multimedia troupe of women of color who effectively bridge the differences between political activists and cultural workers, and among various communities of color. A similarly synthetic vision is realized through the character Campbell's versatile ability to incorporate diverse frames of reference (including the myth of the vodoun serpent-deity Damballah, scientific laws of thermodynamics, the principles of billiards, and Biblical tales) into a holistic vision of "universal knowledge." As Gloria Hull has demonstrated in her valuable elucidation of the novel, *The Salt Eaters* "challenges the way to the future" through its elaboration of a "dialectic of connectedness which is both meaning and structure of the book."

This way to the future requires respect for social differences as much as an ability to forge cultural connections and political coalitions. Critics disagree on whether the novel succeeds in projecting this kind of multifarious yet coherent vision, with most arguing that the novel's fragmented narrative form overwhelms its quest for wholeness. Yet, like Bambara's other fiction, *The Salt Eaters* evinces a powerful desire for psychic and political change along with the conviction that such a change is just within our reach. At the end of the novel, Velma rises off her stool like a "burst cocoon." The town of Claybourne is awash in a baptismal thunderstorm that seems to realign the very physical coordinates of time and space. The spring carnival, with its planned enactment of a slave insurrection, is just about to begin, and the many characters of the novel are poised on the verge of momentous personal and political transformations. In the closing scene of the novel, "Choices [are] being tossed into the street like dice, like shells, like kola nuts, like jackstones." Robust optimism about the open-ended promise of human agency suffuses all of Bambara's writings, including her fiction, cultural criticism, and political essays.

Film and Video Career

While working on her novel, Bambara had found that she had to contort the very language itself in order to convey her synthetic vision in writing. Her search for a pliable medium prompted her turn to a new genre she considered more amenable to experimentation—film. In 1986 Bambara joined the Scribe Video Center in Philadelphia, where she remained until her death from colon cancer in December 1995. Here, she taught script-writing and served as production facilitator for the Community Visions project designed to aid community organizations to "explore video as an instrument of social change," as recorded in *Deep Sightings and Rescue Missions*. During her Philadelphia years, Bambara collaborated in writing screenplays for several documentary videos, all of which demonstrate her unflagging commitment to art that can raise critical consciousness about racial issues. The most highly acclaimed of these include two documentary videos produced by Louis Massiah, to which Bambara contributed as scriptwriter and narrator. "The Bombing of Osage Avenue," which examined the deadly police bombing of the headquarters of MOVE, an Afrocentric back-to-nature organization, in West Philadelphia in 1985, was awarded two best documentary awards (from

the Pennsylvania Association of Broadcasters and the National Black Programming Consortium) in 1986, the year of its release. In 1995 Massiah produced a documentary video for PBS television, "W. E. B. Du Bois: A Biography in Four Voices," comprised of four sections each written, directed, and narrated by well-known African American writers Toni Cade Bambara, Amiri Baraka, Wesley Brown, and Thulani Davis.

The depth, range, and rigor of Bambara's interest in film is amply displayed in her most eclectic collection of writing, *Deep Sightings and Rescue Missions*, published posthumously in 1996. In her preface to this collection of short stories, interviews, cultural criticism, and political essays, Toni Morrison remarks that Bambara's work on the Du Bois and MOVE documentaries exemplifies her "determination to help rescue a genre from its powerful social irrelevancy." Bambara's brilliant essays on film in this volume consider from various angles the question of the social value of film. In "School Daze," a feminist evaluation of Spike Lee's film, and "Reading the Signs, Empowering the Eye," an appreciation of Julie Dash's *Daughters of the Dust*, Bambara considers how mainstream and independent African American films might work as means of "reconstructing cultural memory, of revitalizing usable traditions of cultural practices, and of resisting the wholesale and unacknowledged appropriation of cultural items" originally produced by communities of color. Bambara's hope that cinema can help usher in a "pluralistic" and "transcultural" national consciousness is grounded in a wealth of information about the burgeoning independent film movements among people of color in the United States as well as in the Third World. These essays represent exemplary models of film criticism, combining political discussion, film history, thematic discussion, and minutely detailed frame-by-frame analyses.

Deep Sightings and Rescue Missions offers a dazzling exhibition of Bambara's versatile interests and talents. In addition to an interview with Louis Massiah and five previously unpublished short stories that extend the themes explored in Bambara's earlier fiction, the book also contains a poignant nonfictional piece on an elderly neighbor who taught Bambara when she was an aspiring writer that her art should "be grounded in cultural specificity and shaped by the modes of Black art practice." In the title essay, Bambara contemplates tensions between assimilationist and independent black politics during the 1980s and 1990s. Spanning various genres (including literary and film criticism, social and political analysis, autobiographical remembrances of political debates in her family, dialogues with African American and immigrant acquaintances on the street), "Deep Sight and Rescue Missions" reveals clear continuities between the multiple facets of Toni Cade Bambara the fiction writer, film-maker, teacher, political analyst, and community activist. Confronted with "the system's monstrous ability to absorb, co-opt, deny, marginalize, deflect, defuse, or silence," the essay suggests the same remedies as did the symbols of salt and of the Seven Sisters in *The Salt Eaters*. By working tirelessly to "maintain a deep connection with the briar patch" (or with the particularity of one's own cultural traditions), while at the same time forging alliances with other marginalized communities, artists and activists of color can help bring about a "reconceptualization of 'America.'"

Those Bones Are Not My Child

In 1999, four years after Bambara's death, her friend and editor Toni Morrison and her daughter Karma Bene Bambara helped bring to publication an epic novel, *Those Bones Are Not My Child*, which Bambara had researched and written over a period of twelve years. In an interview with Valerie Boyd, Morrison confesses that when she found the manuscript, it was complete but for a missing first page. As documented in "Writing Atlanta's Nightmare," Morrison finally found the page after an eight-month long search, but she still faced the daunting task of shortening the 1800-page manuscript to commercially saleable proportions. Morrison found the novel "very, very intricate, almost cunning" in its structure, and

had to read it over a dozen times before finally cutting it down by more than half its original length. *Those Bones* deals with the nightmarish case of at least eighteen (and perhaps up to forty) African American children who were murdered in Atlanta between 1979 and 1981. In June 1981 a black man, Wayne Williams, was arrested as the leading suspect in the child murders. Although Williams was convicted on two counts of murder the following year, questions still remain about whether the murders were racially motivated hate crimes covered up by the police and the city administration. *Those Bones* seeks to commit to history a vernacular version of these events that was eclipsed by the mass media. The child murders deeply affected Bambara, prompting her to remark in her interview with Zala Chandler that: "even if I were not a writer, I would have been compelled to become a writer in order to document what was going on in Atlanta. I felt an obligation to provide a forum for the version that was so different from the official one."

The novel opens with the disappearance of a teenage boy, Sundiata Spencer. As his mother Marzala and her estranged husband begin a frenzied search for their son, Bambara depicts in harrowing and precise detail the emotional repercussions of the child murders on the Spencer family, their web of friends and acquaintances, and the local black community. Most of the novel alternates between the point of view of Marzala and her husband, and the slim plot of their search shuttles constantly between an uncertain present and a remembered past when their family was still intact. Whereas the first third of the novel steeps the reader in the psychological trauma of the Spencer family, the middle section broadens to cover the public investigation of the murders. Bambara lays bare in exhaustive detail the conflict between the city administration and STOP, a group of activist parents and community members demanding a more committed inquiry into the murders. The long middle section of the novel is often difficult to follow, because Bambara accumulates documentary evidence about the investigation, brings in a host of characters who are sketchily developed, and extensively explores various possible interpretations of the murders advanced by different characters. The density of documentary detail slows down the narrative momentum, the more so because the compelling story of the Spencer family is relegated to the background. In the final section of the novel, however, narrative pace quickens and psychological interest in the characters intensifies as the Spencers find their son and struggle to coax out of him a coherent narrative about what exactly happened to him while he was missing.

Those Bones Are Not My Child expertly interlaces the private drama of the Spencer family with an in-depth public account of African American urban life in the late-twentieth century. Bambara paints a complex portrait of the racial and class conflicts plaguing Atlanta, the much-vaunted "Black Mecca" of the new South and the "City Too Busy to Hate." On the one hand, readers see the tourist-guide version of Atlanta, with its first black mayor Maynard Jackson's boosterist administration, its gleaming and futuristic convention centers, and its prosperous black middle class. But on the other hand, we are also shown an Atlanta of widening economic and racial disparities, of bureaucratic corruption and inhumanity. One of Bambara's aims in this novel was to make sure that readers would not dismiss the Atlanta child murders as isolated freak events, but would instead view them in "the context of what is happening nationally to Black people—physically, economically, and politically." *Those Bones* delineates this wider context with an impressive sense of scale and nuance, linking the murders not only to the ascendancy of right-wing politics and the proliferation of white supremacist organizations at the national level, but also to racialized terrorism in Britain and South Africa. Bambara's comprehensive and synthetic political vision (glimpsed in her earlier fiction) is in full evidence here, as she nudges the reader to make connections among local, national, and international political trends.

In common with *The Salt Eaters*, Bambara's second novel insists on the urgent need for holistic vision, as a way of resisting the atomized and disjointed vision inculcated by the media.

At one level, *Those Bones* can be read as a detective novel that seeks to reconstruct a violent and dimly understood past into a causally interlinked narrative order. The prologue sets out for readers several possible interpretations of the child murders—"Klan-type slaughter, cult-type ritual murder, child-porn thrill killing, drug-related vengeance, commando/mercenary training, and overlapping combinations." The middle section of the novel pursues each of these ordering possibilities, as the characters struggle to fit a welter of clues into a coherent pattern. As we make our way through a maze of competing narratives and counternarratives, readers are pressed into self-conscious awareness of the processes of reading signs and making meaning. We are urged to draw connections among the events construed as random in official versions, but at the same time alerted to the temptations of overreading and imposing patterns unsupported by facts. Although the novel ultimately leaves the case unresolved (as it remains in reality), denying its own impetus for narrative order and meaning, it does nevertheless impress upon its readers the ethical responsibility involved in storytelling and fiction-writing. In order to "be told right, lest it dishonor those who'd lived through it," the story of the child murders must be recounted such that "the teller would not distance himself or herself from communal disaster." Bambara's novel certainly succeeds in thoroughly immersing the reader into the personal and public crises in the black community sparked by the child murders.

In contrast to the vigorous optimism of Bambara's other work, *Those Bones Are Not My Child* is a grim book. Whereas *The Salt Eaters* ultimately affirms the possibility of achieving expansive, transcendent vision, her second novel is relentlessly realistic, mired in the limiting conditions of the here and now. However, the novel is not without its own modest affirmations—of the Spencer family's emotional resilience, of neighborly support and communal concern for the Spencers, and, above all, of the desire for public truth that galvanizes segments of black Atlanta into collective political action. Although readers do not come away from *Those*

Bones Are Not My Child with a definitive version of the truth, they are left with a strong sense of the value of historical and narrative understanding. Bambara's novel shows us that this kind of understanding is increasingly at risk in the information society of the late-twentieth century. In the future-driven Atlanta presented in the novel, the "oracle" takes the form of Aquarius, a supercomputer that can tabulate and cross-reference data at unimaginable speed. *Those Bones* lays bare the fallacious vision of a society in which "We are informed about everything, . . . so we understand nothing." In her article, "Morrison Brings Friend's 'Bones' to Print," Valerie Boyd cites Toni Morrison's comment that she felt committed to publishing Bambara's novel because "the history of the world was incomplete if this book wasn't published." As an attempt to resist the public amnesia fostered by the mass media and a testament to the difficulty of sustaining historical narratives in an information society, Bambara's final published work will undoubtedly reverberate powerfully into the twenty-first century.

Selected Bibliography

PRIMARY WORKS

NOVELS AND SHORT STORIES

Gorilla, My Love. New York: Random House, 1970.
The Sea Birds Are Still Alive: Collected Stories. New York: Random House, 1977.
The Salt Eaters. New York: Random House, 1980.
Those Bones Are Not My Child. New York: Pantheon Books, 1999.

OTHER WORKS

The Black Woman: An Anthology. Edited by Toni Cade. New York: Signet, 1970.
Tales and Stories for Black Folks. Edited by Toni Cade Bambara. Garden City, N.Y.: Zenith, 1971.
Southern Exposure: Southern Black Utterances Today. Edited by Toni Cade Bambara and Leah Wise. Atlanta: Institute for Southern Studies, 1975.
Deep Sightings and Rescue Missions: Fiction, Essays, and Conversations. Edited and with a preface by Toni Morrison. New York: Pantheon Books, 1996.

SELECTED ESSAYS

"Black Theater." In *Black Expression: Essays by and about Black Americans in the Creative Arts*. Edited by Addison Gayle Jr. New York: Weybright and Talley. Pp. 134–43.
"Thinking About My Mother." *Redbook*, September 1973, pp. 73, 155–56.
"What It Is I Think I'm Doing Anyhow." In *The Writer on Her Work*. Edited and with an introduction by Janet Sternberg. New York: Norton, 1980. Pp.153–68.
"Salvation Is the Issue." In *Black Women Writers (1950–1980): A Critical Evaluation*. Edited by Mari Evans. Garden City, N.Y.: Doubleday, 1984. Pp. 41–47.
Preface to *Daughters of the Dust: The Making of an African American Woman's Film*, by Julie Dash. New York: New Press, 1992. Pp. xi–xvi.

SCREENPLAYS

"Zora." WGBH-TV, 1971.
"Transactions." Produced by the School of Social Work, Atlanta University, 1979.
"Epitaph for Willie." K. Heran Productions, 1982.
"Tar Baby." Sanger/Brooks Film Productions, 1984. (Based on the novel by Toni Morrison.)
"The Bombing of Osage Avenue." WHYY-TV, Philadelphia, 1986.
"Cecil B. Moore: Master Tactician of Direct Action." WHYY-TV, Philadelphia, 1987.
"W. E. B. Du Bois: A Biography in Four Voices." San Francisco: California Newsreel, 1995.

SECONDARY WORKS

BIOGRAPHICAL AND CRITICAL STUDIES

Aiken, Susan Hardy. "Telling the Other('s) Story, or, the Blues in Two Languages." In *Dialogues/Dialogi: Literary and Cultural Exchanges Between (Ex)Soviet and American Women*. Edited by Susan Hardy Aiken et al. Durham: Duke University Press, 1994. Pp. 206–23.
Alwes, Derek. "The Burden of Liberty: Choice in Toni Morrison's *Jazz* and Toni Cade Bambara's *The Salt Eaters*." *African American Review* 30:353–65 (September 1996).
Baraka, Amiri. "Toni." In *Eulogies*. New York: Marsilio, 1996. Pp. 180–85. (Originally published as "Toni—a Tribute." In *The New York Amsterdam News*, May 4, 1996, pp. 13, 30.)
Barrett, Lindon. "Identities and Identity Studies: Reading Toni Cade Bambara's 'The Hammer Man.' " *Cultural Critique* 39:5–29 (Spring 1998).
Boyd, Valerie. "Morrison Brings Friend's 'Bones' to Print." *The Atlanta Journal and Constitution*, October 17, 1999, p. 1L.
———. "Writing Atlanta's Nightmare." *The Atlanta Journal and Constitution*, October 17, 1999, p. 3L.
Burks, Ruth Elizabeth. "From Baptism to Resurrection: Toni Cade Bambara and the Incongruity of Language." In *Black Women Writers (1950–80): A Criti-*

cal Evaluation. Edited by Mari Evans. Garden City, N.Y.: Doubleday, 1984. Pp. 48–57.

Butler-Evans, Elliott. *Race, Gender, and Desire: Narrative Strategies in the Fiction of Toni Cade Bambara, Toni Morrison, and Alice Walker.* Philadelphia: Temple University Press, 1989.

Byerman, Keith Eldon. *Fingering the Jagged Grain: Tradition and Form in Recent Black Fiction.* Athens: University of Georgia Press, 1985.

———. "Healing Arts: Folklore and the Female Self in Toni Cade Bambara's *The Salt Eaters.*" *Postscript* 5:37–43 (1988).

Collins, Janelle. "Generating Power: Fission, Fusion, and Postmodern Politics in Bambara's *The Salt Eaters.*" *MELUS* 21, no. 2:35–47 (Summer 1996).

Comfort, Mary. "Liberating Figures in Toni Cade Bambara's *Gorilla, My Love.*" *Studies in American Humor* 3, no. 5:76–96 (1998).

Dance, Daryl Cumber. "Go Eena Kumbla: A Comparison of Erna Brodber's *Jane and Louisa Will Soon Come Home* and Toni Cade Bambara's *The Salt Eaters.*" In *Caribbean Women Writers.* Edited by Selwyn R. Cudjoe. Wellesley, Mass.: Calaloux Publications, 1990. Pp. 169–84.

Deck, Alice A. "Toni Cade Bambara." In *Dictionary of Literary Biography.* Vol. 38, *Afro-American Writers after 1955.* Detroit: Gale Research, 1985. Pp. 12–22.

Ensslen, Klaus. "Toni Cade Bambara: *Gorilla, My Love.*" In *The African American Short Story 1970 to 1990: A Collection of Critical Essays.* Edited by Wolfgang Karrer and Barbara Puschmann-Nalenz. Trier: Wissenschaftlicher Verlag Trier, 1993. Pp. 41–57.

Frye, Charles A., et al. "How to Think Black: A Symposium on Toni Cade Bambara's *The Salt Eaters.*" *Contributions in Black Studies* 6:33–48 (1983–1984).

Griffin, Farah Jasmine. "Toni Cade Bambara: Free to Be Anywhere in the Universe." *Callaloo* 19, no. 2:229–31 (Spring 1996).

Hargrove, Nancy D. "Youth in Toni Cade Bambara's *Gorilla, My Love.*" *Southern Quarterly* 22, no. 1:81–99 (Fall 1983).

Hull, Gloria. " 'What It Is I Think She's Doing Anyhow': A Reading of Toni Cade Bambara's *The Salt Eaters.*" In *Home Girls: A Black Feminist Anthology.* Edited by Barbara Smith. New York: Women of Color Press, 1983. Pp. 124–42.

Kelley, Margot Anne. " 'Damballah is the first law of thermodynamics': Modes of Access to Toni Cade Bambara's *The Salt Eaters.*" *African American Review* 27:479–93 (Fall 1993).

Koreneva, Maya. "Children of the Sixties." In *Dialogues/ Dialogi: Literary and Cultural Exchanges Between (Ex)Soviet and American Women.* Edited by Susan Hardy Aiken et al. Durham: Duke University Press, 1994. Pp. 191–205.

Korenman, Joan S. "African-American Women Writers, Black Nationalism, and the Matrilineal Heritage." *College Language Association Journal* 38, no. 2:143–61 (December 1994).

Lyles, Lois F. "Time, Motion, Sound and Fury in *The Sea Birds Are Still Alive.*" *College Language Association Journal* 36, no. 2:134–44 (December 1992).

Morrison, Toni. "Vigilance and Heart-Cling." *The Nation*, October 28, 1996, pp. 66–67.

Onesto, Li. "In Memory: Toni Cade Bambara: Passing on the Story." *Race and Class* 38, no. 1:79–87 (July–September 1996).

Rosenberg, Ruth. " 'You Took a Name that Made You Amiable to the Music': Toni Cade Bambara's *The Salt Eaters.*" *Literary Onomastics Studies* 12:165–94 (1985).

Traylor, Eleanor W. "Music as Theme: The Jazz Mode in the Works of Toni Cade Bambara." In *Black Women Writers (1950–1980): A Critical Evaluation.* Edited by Mari Evans. Garden City, N.Y.: Doubleday, 1984. Pp. 58–70.

Vertreace, Martha M. "Toni Cade Bambara: The Dance of Character and Community." In *American Women Writing Fiction.* Edited by Mickey Pearlman. Lexington: University Press of Kentucky, 1989. Pp. 155–66.

Washington, Mary Helen. "Blues Women of the Seventies." *Ms.*, July 1977, pp. 36–38.

Wideman, John. "The Healing of Velma Henry." *New York Times Book Review*, June 1, 1980, p. 14.

Willis, Susan. *Specifying: Black Women Writing the American Experience.* Madison: University of Wisconsin Press, 1987.

INTERVIEWS

Bonetti, Kay. " 'The Organizer's Wife': A Reading By and Interview with Toni Cade Bambara." Columbia, Mo.: American Audio Prose Library, 1982.

Bowser, Pearl, and Louis Massiah. "The Micheaux Legacy." *Black Film Review* 7, no. 4:10–15 (1993).

Chandler, Zala. "Voices beyond the Veil: An Interview with Toni Cade Bambara and Sonia Sanchez." In *Wild Women in the Whirlwind: Afra-American Culture and The Contemporary Literary Renaissance.* Edited by Joanne M. Braxton and Andrée Nicola McLaughlin. New Brunswick, N.J.: Rutgers University Press, 1990. Pp. 342–62.

Guy-Sheftall, Beverly. "Commitment: Toni Cade Bambara Speaks." In *Sturdy Black Bridges: Visions of Black Women in Literature.* Edited by Roseann P. Bell, Bettye J. Parker, and Beverly Guy-Sheftall. Garden City, N.Y.: Doubleday, 1979. Pp. 230–49.

Jackson, Deborah. "Interview with Toni Cade Bambara." *Drum Magazine*, Spring 1982, pp. 43–44.

Salaam, Kalamuya. "Searching for the Mother Tongue." *First World* 2:48–52 (1980).

Tate, Claudia. "Toni Cade Bambara." In *Black Women Writers at Work.* Edited by Claudia Tate. New York: Continuum, 1983. Pp. 12–38.

Tally, Justine. "Not About to Play It Safe: An Interview with Toni Cade Bambara." *Revista Canaria de dios Ingleses* 11:141–53 (November 1985).

BIBLIOGRAPHIES

Hargrove, Nancy D. "Toni Cade Bambara." In *Contemporary Fiction Writers of the South: A Bio-Bibliographical Sourcebook*. Edited by Robert Bain and Joseph M. Flora. Westport, Conn.: Greenwood Press, 1993. Pp. 32–45.

Morton, Nanette. "Toni Cade Bambara." In *Contemporary African American Novelists*. Edited by Emmanuel S. Nelson. Westport, Conn.: Greenwood Press, 1999. Pp. 22–28.

Vertreace, Martha M. "Toni Cade Bambara: The Dance of Character and Community." In *American Women Writing Fiction: Memory, Identity, Family, Space*. Edited by Mickey Pearlman. Lexington: University Press of Kentucky, 1989. Pp. 166–71.

FILMS BASED ON THE WORKS OF TONI CADE BAMBARA

"The Johnson Girls," The Soul Show. WNET-TV, 1972.
"The Long Night," ABC-TV, 1981.
"Raymond's Run," For Learning in Focus. American Short Story Series, PBS-TV, 1985.

AMIRI BARAKA
(1934–)

WILLIAM J. HARRIS

AMIRI BARAKA'S UNIQUE contributions to American letters have confirmed his place among American writers of lasting significance and influence. For students of African American literature, Baraka's importance is augmented by the close parallels between his personal history and the development of African American aesthetics since the 1940s. As a poet, dramatist, novelist, and social critic, Baraka has addressed his audience both as a singularly powerful advocate of individual expression and as an outraged spokesman for all black artists. In tracing the evolution of Baraka's thought, we can read the history of the literary revolution that has shaped his work and in turn has been shaped by his participation.

Watershed points in Baraka's career have coincided with his several name changes. At his birth in Newark, New Jersey, on October 7, 1934, his parents, Coyt LeRoy Jones and Anna Lois Russ Jones, named him Everett LeRoy. Shortly before entering college, Baraka adopted the French spelling LeRoi. While involved in the militant Black Nationalist movement in the 1960s, he rejected his own imitation of white affectation, adopting the Bantuized Muslim name Imamu ("spiritual leader") Ameer (later respelled Amiri, "blessed one") Baraka ("prince"). In the 1970s Baraka, like many other black writers, found the tightly focused Black Nationalist project confining; he began to ex-plore the possibilities of global revolution through his study of Marxist doctrine. He came to view Black Nationalism as tainted with the narrowly provincial bourgeois values of the white society it opposed. Repudiating both, he registered this political metamorphosis by dropping the name Imamu sometime between late 1974 and early 1975. As Amiri Baraka, he continues to search for literary forms of expression that will encompass both his commitment to Marxist politics and his insistence on the individual's right to forge a personal identity through language and action.

Early Life and Education

Baraka began writing while he was growing up in the industrial city of Newark. He was a gifted young student whose academic achievements were encouraged by his father, a postal supervisor, and his mother, a social worker. He first attended the Central Avenue Elementary School, a predominantly black school, and then went on to graduate with honors from Barringer High School, a college preparatory institution, which, he recalls in "Philistinism and the Negro Writer," "was mainly attended by children of Italian parentage. It was about 98 percent white. At first there were only six Negroes, then twelve Negroes in the entire school." In seventh grade he began writing a comic strip, "The Crime Wave"; during his high school years he wrote short stories.

All his juvenile works are apparently now lost, but Baraka gives an account of this period in a biographical note in *New American Story* (1965), edited by Donald M. Allen, in which he remembers attending Barringer High School in the guise of a "skinny prim middle class Negro, i.e., lower middle-class American." Also in the same note he stated that during his free time he "drifted about the Third Ward slum to meet junkies, whores, drugs, general dissolution," and learned to "protect" himself from the "shabbiness of 'black bourgeois' projected social progress." As he said in *Home*, his association with the Third Ward's "Hillside Place bads" did not disrupt his studies at this point: "I was 'saved' from them by my parents' determination and the cool scholarship game which turns stone killers pure alabaster by graduation time."

Baraka played the middle-class game long enough to win a science scholarship to the Newark branch of Rutgers University in 1951, but left in 1952 to immerse himself in the black academic world at Howard University in Washington, D.C. At Howard, Baraka was fortunate in encountering three scholars whose influence he would draw upon repeatedly in future years: Nathan A. Scott Jr., the renowned professor of theology and literature; E. Franklin Frazier, who has been called the most distinguished black sociologist of the first half of the twentieth century; and, perhaps Baraka's most profoundly inspiring early role model, Sterling A. Brown, a poet, literary scholar, and gifted teacher who has attained almost legendary stature in the black academic community.

Scott introduced Baraka to the work of Dante, whose poetry has continued to influence Baraka's writing throughout his career, most explicitly in his novel *The System of Dante's Hell* (1965). Frazier's highly critical view of the black middle class, discussed at length in his book *Black Bourgeoisie* (1957), profoundly influenced Baraka's own views. In an interview with Theodore R. Hudson, Baraka says Brown en-

couraged Baraka's interest in blues and jazz: "He taught classes in black music. Unofficial classes. A. B. Spellman and I both developed in his class." Spellman went on to become a poet and jazz critic; Baraka has continued to explore the aesthetic potential of black music throughout his career in both his fiction and his nonfiction writings, extolling black music as both the most authentic and original creation of African American culture.

Impressed as he was with the scholars at Howard, however, Baraka found the conservative political atmosphere inimical to him. He wrote in "Philistinism and the Negro Writer," "Howard University shocked me into realizing how desperately sick the Negro could be, how he could be led into self-destruction and how he would not realize that it was the society that had forced him into a great sickness." This realization increasingly distracted Baraka, and his academic work suffered. In 1954, in the fall of his senior year, he flunked out.

That same year, he joined the Air Force, attaining the rank of sergeant before his discharge. After basic training in Geneva, New York, he received meteorological schooling at Chanute Field near Rantoul, a town in central Illinois. In his autobiography he describes a life-changing epiphany that occurred during a weekend trip to Chicago:

One time I was drifting around the South Side, near the University of Chicago, feeling alone, as usual, isolated, as usual, my usual emotional stock in trade, and I bump into this bookstore called the Green Door. It had a green door, and kind of orange plastic in the window so the sun wouldn't ruin the books. I came to rest staring into the window. There were books there I didn't recognize, a few I did. Like we'd had *Portrait of the Artist* my first year at Rutgers and I'd looked at it, but it was a *school* book and for that reason I didn't take it seriously. Though parts of it vaguely fascinated me even then. A copy of this was in the window, and next to it *Ulysses*, the book opened to the first page so you could see the words "Stately plump Buck Mulligan . . ." I stared at the words and tried to read them. I saw other books, Pound, Eliot, Thomas, philosophy books, art books, statistics, and poetry. Something dawned on me, like a big light bulb over my noggin. The comic-strip *Idea* lit up my mind at that moment as I stared at the books. I suddenly understood that I didn't know a hell of a lot about anything. What it was that seemed to move me then was that learning was *important.* I'd never thought that before. The employment agency I'd last gone to college at, the employment agency approach of most schools I guess, does not emphasize the *beauties* and the absolute *joy* of learning. . . . I vowed, right then, to learn something new every day. It was a deep revelation, something I felt throughout my whole self. I was going to learn something every day. That's what I would do. Not just as a pastime, something to do in the service, but as a life commitment.

While he was stationed in Puerto Rico, this commitment transformed Baraka's military service into a literary apprenticeship. He read voraciously, sometimes two books a day, kept a journal, and wrote poetry, which he submitted to both major and small magazines. During this period he experienced a second revelation of his exclusion from the white literary tradition, which he describes in his autobiography:

> I had been reading one of the carefully put together exercises *The New Yorker* publishes constantly as big poetic art, and gradually I could feel my eyes fill up with tears, and my cheeks were wet and I was crying, quietly softly but like it was the end of the world. . . . I was crying because I realized that I could never write like that writer. Not that I had any real desire to, but I knew even if I had had the desire I could not do it. I realized that there was something in me so *out,* so unconnected with what this writer was and what that magazine was that what was in me that wanted to come out as poetry could never come out like that and be *my* poetry.

The poetics of the *New Yorker* could not accommodate the poetry that grew from Baraka's

Amiri Baraka

lived experience. Convinced that genuine poetry must be founded in experience, and that the white literary establishment offered no linguistic medium for genuine expressions of the black experience, Baraka began his long and continuing search for a black poetics, for an authentic language and appropriate mode of expression.

Simultaneous with his recognition of white literary forms as arbitrary impositions, rather than eternal verities, was his recognition of other forms of oppression so ubiquitous and traditional that they had been invisible to him. His tenure in the Air Force gave him ample opportunity to examine the mechanics of power and its abuse, as he records in his essay "Philistinism and the Negro Writer":

> When I went into the Army [*sic*] it shocked me into realizing the hysterical sickness of the oppressors and the suffering of my own

people. When I went into the Army [*sic*] I saw how the oppressors suffered by virtue of their oppressions—by having to oppress, by having to make believe that the weird, hopeless fantasy that they had about the world was actually true.

His alienation from the military power structure drove Baraka further into his studies. His unorthodox library and his great literary appetite made him appear suspect to those who did not share his tastes; although he was not politically active at this time, he was anonymously accused of communist sympathies. This, combined with his less than enthusiastic regard for military discipline, resulted in his dishonorable discharge in 1957.

Beat Period:
Preface to a Twenty Volume Suicide Note . . .

For the next several years, Baraka lived in New York's Greenwich Village, where he met Allen Ginsberg and Charles Olson, became involved in the literary circles of the Beat generation, and received increasingly positive responses to his writing. In 1958 he cofounded *Yugen* (with Hettie Cohen, whom he had married in the same year), an influential little magazine devoted to the new poetry of the postwar avant-garde, publishing works by Olson, Frank O'Hara, and William Burroughs. The journal continued until 1963. Baraka's own work began appearing in an array of little magazines, such as the *Naked Ear, Big Table, Evergreen Review,* and *Kulchur.* One of his poems caught the eye of Langston Hughes. Baraka remembers his astonishment: "He sent me a letter, and I'd never talked to him before in my life. He sent me a letter and said he liked the poem!" With Hughes's recommendation, Baraka was awarded the John Hay Whitney Fellowship for Creative Writing in 1961. He was the only black poet included in Donald Allen's groundbreaking anthology, *The New American Poetry: 1945–1960* (1960), which contained works by the most important poets of the young generation: Olson, Robert Creeley,

Edward Dorn, Ginsberg, and O'Hara. Looking back on his involvement with the Beat avant-garde, Baraka remembers its populist goals in *Beat Vision:*

One of its strongest moments was redefining what poetry was, redefining what art in general was. Questioning those things that had been put out, traditional values and academic values and, trying to put forward a more mass-oriented kind of art, a more people-oriented kind of art. For instance, during the whole Beat period readings became more important. People wanted to actually read poetry and the whole oral tradition was sort of reinvoked, to get poetry off the pages; because largely academic poetry is to be read in books and never heard at all.

William Carlos Williams, one of the spiritual fathers of the New American Poetry, had a particularly important effect on Baraka's approach to poetry. While Baraka was searching for a new means of expression, his reading of Williams suggested to him that he already possessed such a means in the vernacular idioms of the black community. In an interview in 1979, with Richard W. Bruner, he echoed the lesson he had found in Williams's *Paterson:* "I have my own language . . . we can use our language and rhythms to recreate these experiences."

Other major influences during this period were Olson, Ginsberg, and O'Hara. Olson furnished Baraka with the open-form poem, maintaining that contemporary poets are obliged not to revitalize preconceived poetic forms but rather to capture the living flux of reality. From Ginsberg, Baraka gained an appreciation of poetic candor and adventure, and a conviction that poetry should concern itself with the real world rather than with the artifices of academe or the self-delusions of the middle class. O'Hara gave him a sense of the poem as a personal utterance vocalizing the events of everyday experience. Baraka synthesized all these influences with his own increasingly idiosyncratic voice. He crafted a personalized version of the avant-garde style that in turn influenced an entire generation of black writers by providing a basis for the creation of a distinctly black literature.

Baraka published the products of his years with the Beats in his first volume of poetry, *Preface to a Twenty Volume Suicide Note . . .* (1961). He dedicated several of the poems to prominent Beat and avant-garde figures. The extraordinary candor of this book reflects the lasting influence of Ginsberg and O'Hara. As in all of Baraka's poetry, the speakers of these very personal poems can be identified with the poet without violating his art.

Baraka speaks in three voices in *Preface:* the hip Beat poet, the pop vernacular rhetorician, and the blues singer. The most autobiographical speaker is the hip Beat in the title poem:

Lately, I've become accustomed to the way
The ground opens up and envelops me
Each time I go out to walk the dog.

The speaker finds the contemporary world without foundation. Without grounds for moral certainty, there can be no meaningful religious rituals:

And then last night, I tiptoed up
To my daughter's room and heard her
Talking to someone, and when I opened
The door, there was no one there . . .
Only she on her knees, peeking into

Her own clasped hands.

Baraka began searching for a justifiable ethical system early in his career. At Howard University he was attracted to Dante's monumental faith in his own position; in Greenwich Village he was attracted to the Beats in part by their pained nostalgia for a clear moral vision. When Jack Kerouac cried out, "God. I want God to show me His face," he spoke not only for himself but for the entire Beat generation.

Baraka's pop vernacular voice speaks in the poem "In Memory of Radio":

Who has ever stopped to think of the
    divinity of Lamont Cranston?
(Only Jack Kerouac, that I know of: & me.

The rest of you probably had on WCBS and
    Kate Smith,
Or something equally unattractive.)

Lamont Cranston was The Shadow, a fictional crime fighter, and a hip hero of the imagination; Kate Smith, a singer, was a conventional square. The Beat poets affirmed popular art like Lamont Cranston's radio show as a particularly American wellspring of vernacular diction and secular iconography. The pop world encompassed both the present and the past, expressing a mad dada anarchy that was reworked into avant-garde poems such as Ginsberg's "Howl," and yet reassuringly addressing the Beats in native voices from their childhoods. Kerouac lists among the most popular resources of the Beat generation the "completely senseless babble of the Three Stooges" and the "ravings of the Marx brothers." Baraka's pop vernacular narrator mines his childhood memories of radio as sources of artistic imagery:

Saturday mornings we listened to *Red
    Lantern* & his undersea folk.
At 11, *Let's Pretend*
& we did
& I, the poet, still do, Thank God!

Yet to imagine is not enough—to pretend is not enough—to provide moral authority for action:

Am I a sage or something?
Mandrake's hypnotic gesture of the week?
(Remember, I do not have the healing
    powers of Oral Roberts . . .
I cannot, like F. J. Sheen, tell you how to
    get saved & *rich!*
I cannot even order you to gaschamber
    satori like Hitler or Goody Knight

& Love is an evil word.
            . . .
.   .   .   .   .   . & besides
who understands it?
I certainly wouldn't like to go out on that
    kind of limb.

Magicians, religious leaders, and charismatic dictators may elect themselves to ethical authority by chicanery and force of will, but Baraka's resolute commitment of authenticity and candor precludes moral exhortation based on bad faith. His poetic persona is morally paralyzed; even more debilitatingly, he is cut off from the poet's traditional source of power, love.

Baraka's blues voice enters into "Look for You Yesterday, Here You Come Today," with reminiscences of a Jimmy Rushing song, and the brief appearance of the great blues singer Bessie Smith: "& Tonto way off in the hills / moaning like Bessie Smith." Tonto's cries in the hills meld with Smith's ethnic music in a fusion of American voices. But, again, Baraka finds no possibility for action in this poem; imagination fails and the Lone Ranger remains a distanced, romantic figure from Baraka's past:

> O, God . . . I must have a belt that glows
> green
> in the dark. Where is my Captain Midnight
> decoder??
> I can't understand what Superman is
> saying!

THERE MUST BE A LONE RANGER!!!

In "Look for You Yesterday," the certitudes of childhood remain ultimately irretrievable; in "Notes for a Speech," we hear Baraka lamenting the African past that he felt, in 1960, he could not reclaim: "African blues / does not know me. . . . / You are / as any other sad man here / american." During an interview published in the *Sullen Art* (1963), Baraka articulated his feelings about race and art at the time he wrote *Preface:*

> I'm fully conscious all the time that I am an American Negro, because it's part of my life. But I know also that if I want to say, "I see a bus full of people," I don't have to say, "I am a Negro seeing a bus full of people." I would deal with it when it has to do directly with

the poem, and not as a kind of broad generalization that doesn't have much to do with a lot of young writers today who are Negroes.

Preface is a book of irony, nostalgia, and inaction. The Beat stance excludes the possibility of the heroic moral exemplar; the poet has no active models in the real world. He can retreat temporarily into the imagination, but the imaginary is inevitably defeated by the real. As in Ginsberg's "Howl," the poet can be a victim of American society, but he cannot change it.

In 1961, with the poet Diane di Prima, Baraka launched the *Floating Bear*, which showcased the same authors as *Yugen* but was intended to be a faster and more flexible publication. Also in 1961 Baraka and di Prima and others established the New York Poets Theatre which produced one-act plays by the contemporary avant-garde, including Baraka's play version of "The System of Dante's Hell." In 1962 di Prima and Baraka had a child together, Dominique. Over the years, di Prima has become a writer in her own right, producing over thirty books, such as *Memoirs of a Beatnik* (1969), the epic poem *The Loba As Eve* (1977), and *Pieces of a Song* (1990).

In 1963 Baraka published *The Moderns*, an anthology of contemporary avant-grade fiction including work by Burroughs, Kerouac, Creeley, Dorn, and di Prima. Baraka has edited three anthologies to date; each has stood as a manifesto of his current aesthetic position. In *The Moderns* he argues for an avant-garde prose based on the principles developed by the New American Poetry and a restoration of the modernist tradition embodied by Joyce, Williams, Pound, and the imagists.

Politicization, *The Dead Lecturer*, and the Move to Black Aesthetics

At this point in his career, Baraka was not writing a poetry of political protest; he was enmeshed in the "integrationist poetics" practiced by black writers in the 1940s and 1950s. Houston A. Baker coined this term in his seminal essay "Generational Shifts and the Recent Criticism of Afro-American Literature" (1981). During the "integrationist" period, black authors still emphasized the distinctly American aspects of their work rather than the distinctly African American qualities. Baker outlines two succeeding epochs in the history of African American literature: the period dominated by the black aesthetic (1960s to 1970), which accentuated the black experience rather than the American, and the era of the new Aristotelians (1970s to 1980), when black artists concentrated on the development of indigenous forms. At the end of the integrationist decades, after Baraka's 1958 marriage to Hettie Cohen, whom he has described as a "middle class Jewish lady," and during his association with the largely white Beat poets, Baraka was poised on the threshold of the next phase of his career, the turbulent years when he was the key architect of the militantly separatist black aesthetic.

Visiting Cuba in 1960 radically altered Baraka's view of his role as a black artist; the effects were not visible until several years later, but in *The Autobiography* he has called the trip "a turning point" in his life. The Latin American writers he met there showed him the importance of politically engaged art. In a letter to Rubi Betancourt, a Mexican intellectual housed at Syracuse University, he said that "Cuba split me open." And in his 1960 essay "Cuba Libre," collected in *Home: Social Essays* (1966), he adds, "I tried to defend myself, 'Look, why jump on me? I understand what you're saying. I'm in complete agreement with you. I'm a poet . . . what can I do? I write, that's all, I'm not even interested in politics.'" The Mexican poet Jaime Shelley screamed at him: "You want to cultivate your soul? In that ugliness you live in, you want to cultivate your soul? Well, we've got millions of starving people to feed, and that moves me enough to make poems out of." This personal and highly emotional encounter with Third World political poets eventually turned Baraka away from the poetics and philosophies of the Beat generation; in the following years his energies were directed toward political art. He deplored his own complacency after returning from Cuba:

The rebels among us have become merely people like myself who grow beards and will not participate in politics. Drugs, juvenile delinquency, complete isolation from the vapid mores of the country, a few current ways out.

The bohemians offered no real political alternatives; since 1960, Baraka has been a committed humanist poet, seeking not merely new ways of expressing himself but also new ways to change the world.

Baraka discussed his disillusionment with the moral vacuity of Beat poetry in an October 1961 letter to the poet Edward Dorn, housed at the Lilly Library, Indiana University. He says:

If my letter re your poem sounded crusadery and contentious I'm sorry. But I have gone deep, and gotten caught with images of the world, that exists, or that will be here even after we go. I have not the exquisite objectivity of circumstance. The calm precise mind of Luxury. Only we, on this earth, can talk of material existence as just another philosophical problem. . . . "Moral earnestness" (if there be such a thing!) ought be transformed into action. (You name it.) I know we think that to write a poem, and be Aristotle's God is sufficient. But I can't sleep. And I do not believe in all this relative shit. There is a right and a wrong. A good and a bad. And it's up to me, you, all of the so-called minds, to find out. It is only knowledge of things that will bring this "moral earnestness."

The beginnings of his divorce from the Beat generation are evident in Baraka's poems collected in *The Dead Lecturer*, which was published in 1964 but contains work from several years earlier. In *Beat Vision* Baraka observes:

[Even] though some of these poems are somewhat derivative, I began to get my own tone. My own voice begins to emerge more. . . . The *Dead Lecturer* is much more coming to grips with my own concerns, the key one of which was the question of estrangement, of being, say, a schizophrenic, being concerned internally with one group of ideas but at the same time, seeing other people's concerns were different. And being linked to other people's concerns by your being linked to other people, but at the same time having your own group concerns.

In *The Dead Lecturer* Baraka begins casting off white linguistic forms, and thereby rejecting the passive white stance of the Beats; he begins searching in earnest for an authentic black voice that will allow him to act in the world. In "An Agony. As Now," the protagonist cries out:

> I am inside someone
> who hates me. I look
> out from his eyes. Smell
> what fouled tunes come in
> to his breath.

The poem shows the divided plight of the black man trapped in a white world, yet feeling a growing allegiance centered elsewhere.

The political events of the 1960s severed Baraka from his apolitical white friends, who felt the only legitimate political action was disengagement from the "square" world. The Beats could offer Baraka no heroes, but he found one in Robert F. Williams, who advocated armed self-defense for blacks against the Ku Klux Klan. In 1960 four black students sat in at a whites-only lunch counter in Greensboro, North Carolina. The Congress of Racial Equality's Freedom Riders took to the southern roads in 1961 to confront segregation on interstate buses. The year 1963 saw the murders of John F. Kennedy in Texas, Medgar Evers in Mississippi, and four young black girls in a church in Birmingham, Alabama.

As these events unfolded, Baraka responded with the first stirrings of Black Nationalist sentiment in his work. Before he could create an alternative black poetics, it was necessary that he free himself of the powerful influence of his white friends. To paraphrase Harold Bloom, Baraka had to clear an imaginative space for himself. The violence of his poetic diction during this transition is an index of the difficulty of his task. In "BLACK DADA NIHILISMUS," the poet calls up the powers of blackness to

> Rape the white girls. Rape
> their fathers. Cut the mothers' throats.
> Black dada nihilismus, choke my friends.

To forge an entirely original black poetic form, Baraka focused on the structures and tones of blues and jazz, translating them into a poetic equivalent of black music that would allow him to cast off the imposed forms of the white tradition. In "Rhythm & Blues" he mocks his efforts among the Beats to preserve the white modernist tradition through pop art:

> This is the man who saved us
> Spared us from the disappearance of the
>   sixteenth note, the
> destruction
> of the scale. This is the man who against
>   the black pits of despairing genius
> cried, "Save the Popular Song."

Here, the sixteenth note and the scale represent white Western art. Baraka no longer wanted to be the "fair-haired boy" who saved the West. The best the Beats could offer him was the opportunity to be a great artist of a dying order:

> I am deaf and blind and lost and will not
>   again sing your quiet
> verse. I have lost even the act of poetry, and
>   writhe now for cool horizonless dawn.
>   The
> shake and chant, bulled electric motion,
>   figure of what there will
> be as it sits beside me waiting to live past
>   my own meekness.

In *The Dead Lecturer* we see Baraka leaving the cul-de-sac of "quiet" white verse. He is striving to overcome his meekness, his fear of giving up his old self and sensibility and to take on the new black forms, the shake and the chant, that will permit the birth of a new and more active art and self.

Dutchman and *The Slave*

In 1963 Baraka published the first of his meditations on black music, *Blues People*, a full-length narrative history of American blues and jazz. This social-aesthetic study begins with the slave lyric and ends with the contemporary avant-garde. Baraka concentrates on the blues form as a coupling of the American and African experiences: "Undoubtedly, none of the African prisoners broke out into *St. James Infirmary* the minute the first of them was herded off the ship."

Baraka's renewed appreciation for the aesthetic potential of black music informs his two-scene play *Dutchman*, which opened Off-Broadway in New York on March 24, 1964. *Dutchman* won the 1964 Obie Award, and Baraka suddenly was nationally renowned. *Dutchman's* protagonist, Clay, is a young, middle-class black who has not learned to fuse the roles of poet and revolutionary. He has failed to become an apolitical European poet, a black Baudelaire. On the subway he meets a beautiful and mysterious white woman, Lula. As a secret agent of white society, Lula seeks out the repressed murderer-revolutionary in the middle-class black. Once the black reveals his true revolutionary self, Lula's job is to kill him. She pushes Clay to the exploding point:

Shit, you don't have any sense, Lula, nor feelings either. I could murder you now. . . . And all these weak-faced ofays squatting around here, staring over their papers at me. Murder them too.

His mistake in the face of the enemy is his failure to act. He only speaks, discarding his protective mask:

Ahhh. Shit. But who needs it? I'd rather be a fool. Insane. Safe with my words, and no deaths, and clean, hard thoughts, urging me to new conquests.

Before Lula stabs him at the end of his outburst, however, he has outlined a framework for an aesthetics based on black music. His examples

are the great black musicians Charlie Parker, a jazz saxophonist, and Bessie Smith:

Charlie Parker? Charlie Parker. All the hip white boys scream for Bird. And Bird saying, "Up your ass, feeble-minded ofay! Up your ass." And they sit there talking about the tortured genius of Charlie Parker. Bird would've played not a note of music if he just walked up to East Sixty-seventh Street and killed the first ten white people he saw. Not a note! And I'm the great would-be poet. Yes. That's right! Poet. Some kind of bastard literature . . . all it needs is a simple knife thrust. Just let me bleed you, you loud whore, and one poem vanished. A whole people of neurotics, struggling to keep from being sane. And the only thing that would cure the neurosis would be your murder. Simple as that. I mean if I murdered you, then other white people would begin to understand me. You understand? No. I guess not. If Bessie Smith had killed some white people she wouldn't have needed that music. She could have talked very straight and plain about the world. No metaphors. No grunts. No wiggles in the dark of her soul. Just straight two and two are four. Money. Power. Luxury. Like that. All of them. Crazy niggers turning their backs on sanity. When all it needs is that simple act. Murder. Just murder! Would make us all sane.

For Baraka, as well as for Clay, black art had been an art of sublimation, one that permits the artist to ignore the world while he busies himself with the disinterested creation of beauty. Clay recognizes the artist's responsibility to construct a new art of agitation. Interestingly, Lula herself is an artist of agitation, bringing the black man to the boiling point not for revolution but for exposure.

In the context of Baraka's oeuvre, *Dutchman* is a liberal, not a radical, work. His purpose in depicting Bessie Smith as a murderer was not to bring about revolution but to promote understanding. James Baldwin's *Blues for Mister Charlie*, which opened on Broadway in April 1964, resembled *Dutchman* in that it was more

The cover for the mimeographed script of "Slave Ship."

political than Baldwin's earlier work but not yet a clear call for violence. In the summer of 1964, however, race riots across the country retrospectively conferred a new militancy upon both plays. In *The Autobiography* Baraka recalls:

> There had been a couple rebellions in other cities just before Harlem went up, in Jacksonville and then in a suburb of Chicago. But Harlem had the media coverage. It was like the proof that the ticking inside our heads had a real source. . . . It made *Blues for Mister Charlie* and *Dutchman* seem dangerously prophetic.

The Slave, Baraka's next play, opened off Broadway in December 1964 and was prophetic in a more personal sense. As the play opens, Walker Vessels arrives at the home of his white ex-wife, Grace Easley, to retrieve his two mulatto daughters. Baraka, father to "two beauti-

ful mulatto girls," Kellie Elisabeth and Lisa Victoria Jones, would divorce his white wife, Hettie, in 1965. Kelly has become a curator and art historian interested in Latin American and contemporary African art. Lisa has become a writer-journalist who is the author of the essay collection *Bulletproof Diva: Tales of Race, Sex, and Hair* (1994), and the screenwriter for the television movie of Dorothy West's *The Wedding* (1998). She has also collaborated with director Spike Lee on a number of books on black film.

Vessels is a former poet turned revolutionary. In 1964 Baraka was still struggling to conceive a character that could combine both roles. To become a true black revolutionary, Vessels must renounce white poetry, must kill his love for it. The white tradition in this play is represented by Grace's new husband, Easley, a white college professor. Easley epitomizes both the failure of white liberalism and the dying white Western literary tradition that Vessels must escape to become a new man devoted to a new black moral system. Learning the white language has turned Vessels from his natural mission—the liberation of his people. Vessels confides to his ex-wife:

> I swear to you, Grace, I did come into the world pointed in the right direction. Oh, shit, I learned so many words for what I've wanted to say. They all come down on me at once. But almost none of them are mine.

In this play, the war between blacks and whites breaks out in the physical action denied to Clay in *Dutchman.* Walker has not yet found a black vocabulary, but he replaces the rejected white words with violent acts. After slapping Easley as hard as he can, Walker exclaims: "Bastard! A poem for your mother!" He sees his assault as the only form of authentic poetry available to him. But, with his reference to Easley's mother, he has inadvertently fallen into a form of authentic black diction, the vernacular insult form of "playing the dozens." Thus, Baraka moves in this play toward a successful fusion of poetic diction and revolutionary action. *The Slave* is less dramatic than *Dutchman,* but may be the more interesting of the two plays. Both have grown in complexity over the years. The summer after *The Slave* opened, the Watts riots in Los Angeles exploded into five days of destructive violence, making *The Slave* look more realistic than its subtitle, *A Fable in a Prologue and Two Acts,* would suggest.

In 1965 Baraka published his only novel, *The System of Dante's Hell.* Although he modeled the book on Dante's *Inferno,* he altered Dante's design, particularly in "The Heretics," the longest section of the novel, to reflect his own judgments of the various degrees of sin:

> I put the Heretics in the deepest part of hell, though Dante had them spared, on higher ground.
>
> It is heresy, against one's own sources, running in terror, from one's deepest responses and insights . . . the denial of feeling . . . that I see as basest evil.

Baraka's protagonist in "The Heretics" is an "imitation white boy," culturally assimilated in the North, who returns to his spiritual home, the black South. There he meets Peaches, a black woman who wants him to settle with her. In her company, he feels that "things had come to an order." She offers him a "real world, of flesh, of smells, of soft black harmonies and color." But the heretic runs away, secretly convinced that he is Stephen Dedalus: "My soul is white, pure white, and soars."

The Black Arts Movement

As racist violence escalated in the 1960s, Baraka became increasingly convinced that the evil infecting heretic blacks was inherent in white society. The assassination of Malcolm X in 1965 was shocking proof of the incompatibility of black and white cultures and marked a definitive end to Baraka's "integrationist" period. Baraka left the Village and Hettie Cohen and moved uptown to Harlem to become a cultural nationalist. Hettie Cohen Jones has become a writer herself, producing several children's books, such as *Big Star Fallin' Mama, Five Women in Black Music* (1974) and her beat memoir of self-discovery, *How I Became Hettie Jones* (1990), which, in large part, reflects her years with Baraka. In his new role Baraka proclaimed that "Black People are a race, a culture, a Nation." He received a Guggenheim Fellowship in 1965 and founded Black Arts Repertory Theater School, a prototype for the black militant theater of the late 1960s. In *Visions of a Liberated Future* Baraka recalled:

> It was part of our commitment to the black revolutionary democratic struggle that we collaborated to create the Black Arts Repertory Theater School (BARTS) in Harlem. Both Larry [Neal] and Askia [Muhammad Toure] were among the chief catalysts for that blazing and progressive, though short-lived, institution. . . .
>
> We wanted an art that was as black as our music.
>
> . . . We wanted the oral tradition in our work, we wanted the sound, the pumping rhythm of black music.

In his autobiography, Baraka looks back over twenty years at the reactionary fervor of the Black Nationalist movement and concludes that "we hated white people so publicly, for one reason, because we had been so publicly tied up with them before."

In late 1965 Baraka returned to Newark, where he established Spirit House, a black cultural center. In 1966 he published his first nonfiction collection, *Home: Social Essays.* These chronologically ordered articles show him becoming "blacker" with each page. In the preface, he boasts: "By the time this book appears, I will be even blacker." The book is an invaluable compendium of Baraka's evolving nationalist ideas on race, art, politics, and culture. In August of that year, he married a black woman, Sylvia Robinson (later renamed Amina Baraka), who would bear him five children: Obalaji Malik Ali, Ras Jua Al-Aziz, Shani Isis Makeda, Amiri Seku Musa, and Ahi Mwenge.

Tales, Baraka's only collection of short stories, appeared in 1967. It includes "The Screamers," in which rhythm and blues saxophonist Lynn Hope incites a street riot merely by playing wild black music, and "Words," which chronicles Baraka's homecoming to Harlem:

> When I walk in the streets, the streets don't yet claim me, and people look at me, knowing the strangeness of my manner, and the objective stance from which I attempt to "love" them.
>   . . . In the closed circle I have fashioned. In the alien language of another tribe. I make these documents for some heart who will recognize me truthfully.

It was in renunciation of the alien language of another tribe that Baraka assumed his Bantuized Muslim name. Paradoxically, he received additional support from the white establishment during this militant year. The National Endowment for the Arts awarded him a grant in 1966, and he was a visiting lecturer at San Francisco State College in 1967. During his stay there, he met the cultural nationalist Ron Karenga, whose revolutionary aesthetics were influential in Baraka's developing thought.

During the 1967 Newark riots, Baraka was arrested on charges of illegal firearms possession and resisting arrest. The judge presiding at his trial found occasion to read to the all-white jury Baraka's poem "Black People!" Baraka was convicted of a misdemeanor, sentenced to a two-year jail term, and fined one hundred dollars. He responded: "I'm being sentenced for the poem. Is that what you are saying?" The conviction was overturned on appeal.

His second anthology, *Black Fire*—the manifesto defining his political position during his black aesthetic period—appeared in 1968. It included Larry Neal's central statement of the black aesthetic:

> What all this has been leading us to say is that the poet must become a performer, the way James Brown is a performer—loud, gaudy and racy. He must take his work where his people are: Harlem, Watts, Philadelphia, Chicago and the rural South. He must learn to embellish the context in which the work is executed; and, where possible, link the work to all usable aspects of the music. . . .
>   The artist and the political activist are one. They are both shapers of the future reality. Both understand and manipulate the collective myths of the race. Both are warriors, priests, lovers and destroyers.

Baraka's concurrence is evident in his own performance style, which is a great treat to watch: he sings, preaches, scats, and performs as engagingly as any soul singer. He considers the political value of performance in his second musical study, *Black Music* (1968), where he analyzes the style of the great tenor saxophonist John Coltrane:

> Trane is a mature swan whose wing span was a whole new world. But he also showed us how to murder the popular song. To do away with weak Western forms. He is a beautiful philosopher.

For Baraka, Coltrane typifies the ideal black artist because he destroyed white Western forms of art and created new black ones to replace the white ones.

In 1969 Baraka published *Black Magic,* a collection of his poetry written between 1961 and 1967. These poems record Baraka's escape from moral paralysis into a confrontation with issues of language and action. In "A POEM SOME PEOPLE WILL HAVE TO UNDERSTAND," Baraka has abandoned the ornate flourishes characterizing the poems in *The Dead Lecturer:*

> We have awaited the coming of a natural
> phenomenon. Mystics and romantics,
>   knowledgeable
> workers
> of the land.
>
> But none has come.
> (*Repeat.*)
>   but none has come.
> Will the machinegunners please step
>   forward?

The "mystics and romantics," the white liberals, all of good will, have failed to improve the world; it is time to move to the more extreme measures of the machinegunners. In "A Poem for Black Hearts," the poet announces Malcolm X as the new black hero of action and reformation:

> black man, quit stuttering and shuffling,
>   look up
> black man, quit whining and stooping, for
>   all of him,
> For Great Malcolm a prince of the earth, let
>   nothing in us rest
> until we avenge ourselves for his death.

In "Black Art," Baraka emphasizes the need for poems that are made up of real things in this world: "Poems are bullshit unless they are / teeth or trees or lemons piled / on a step." Only poems composed of real things can effect real social change: "We want 'poems that kill.'"

In "For Tom Postell, Dead Black Poet," Baraka chillingly turns on the Jews who have befriended him and with whom he has identified: "I got the extermination blues, jewboys." He

explains in "Black Art" that there can be "no love poems written / until love can exist freely and / cleanly." But in "For Tom Postell," the manufactured hatred expressed in his brutal and repugnant effort to extricate himself from his old friends' influence seems a dangerous and ignoble avenue to new love. Yet when he writes of his return to Harlem, he realizes that "The World Is Full of Remarkable Things," including love: "Quick night / easy warmth / The girlmother lies next to me."

Marxism

In 1970 Baraka campaigned for the black candidate Kenneth Gibson in his successful bid for the office of mayor of Newark. For the next three years he continued publishing and speaking as a Black Nationalist. In 1971 he published *Raise Race Rays Raze,* a collection of essays on Black Nationalism and black theater, including "7 Principles of US: Maulana Karenga & the Need for a Black Value System." Karenga's thought permeates the entire volume. Karenga taught Baraka the importance of black cultural revolution, that is, that culture and the arts were central for the transformation of the black masses and therefore, black art, to be effective, had to be collective, Afrocentric, and politically committed. In short, before there could be a black revolution, the minds and values of the black masses had to be changed and the arts would be the primary instrument of this change.

By 1974, however, Karenga's principles had become counterproductive for Baraka, just as the white literary tradition had a decade earlier. He categorically rejected Black Nationalism and became a black Third World socialist. In a *New York Times* article of December 27, 1974, written by Joseph F. Sullivan, he asserted:

> It is a narrow nationalism that says the white man is the enemy. . . .
>
>   Nationalism, so-called, when it says "all non-blacks are our enemies," is sickness or criminality, in fact, a form of fascism.

However, in a more recent interview included in *The Poetry and Poetics of Amiri Baraka*, Baraka relates his Marxist and his Black Nationalist revolutionary stages:

> I think fundamentally my intentions are similar to those I had when I was a Nationalist. That might seem contradictory, but they were similar in the sense I see art as a weapon of revolution. It's just now that I define revolution in Marxist terms. But I came to my Marxist view as a result of having struggled as a Nationalist and found certain dead-ends theoretically and ideologically, as far as Nationalism was concerned, and had to reach out for a communist ideology.

His first slim volume of Marxist-Leninist poetry, *Hard Facts*, appeared in 1975, and was followed in 1978 by his collection of Marxist plays, *The Motion of History*.

The year 1978 also saw the stage production of one of Baraka's most imaginative Marxist works of that early stage, *What Was the Relationship of the Lone Ranger to the Means of Production?* This neo-surrealist update of the proletarian drama of the depression era somewhat resembles Clifford Odet's *Waiting for Lefty* (1935). The central character, MM (the Masked Man), is a capitalist exploiter who enters a factory to teach the workers the basic tenets of capitalism. A dead worker is unceremoniously dumped from a wheelbarrow; the lesson for the workers here is "Don't fuck with God!" When the workers discover a bandit behind the mask, rather than a superhero, they strike. Baraka revitalizes this 1930s theatrical formula by introducing the pop culture figures of the Lone Ranger and Tonto (here named Tuffy). He challenges the American myth of the Western hero, exposing the Lone Ranger not as the idealist fighting for truth and justice but as the "collective spirit of capitalism" who manufactures lies to keep the workers in their places.

Selected Plays and Prose and *Selected Poetry*, including the new Marxist poems of *Poetry for the Advanced*, were both published in 1979. Not surprisingly, Baraka's Marxist theater and art have met a warmer reception from

Third World critics than from the American press. E. San Juan, an exiled Filipino leftist intellectual, discussing *Lone Ranger* in *Amiri Baraka: The Kaleidoscopic Torch*, finds it "the most significant theatrical achievement of 1978 in the Western hemisphere." But Baraka had not at that point found a truly contemporary Marxist form.

In 1980 Baraka published "In the Tradition" (reprinted in *The Baraka Reader*), his most mature completed Marxist work to that date. In this poem, Baraka celebrates the jazz alto saxophonist Arthur Blythe's recording *In the Tradition,* and the entire black musical canon Blythe's recording represents. He sees the entire history of American blacks inscribed in the black musical tradition, a tradition "of love and suffering truth over lies," a tradition of black heroes, victims, and poets as well as musicians. Blythe's recording itself celebrates the musical artists John Coltrane, Duke Ellington, and Fats Waller, whose work, Baraka insists, "says plainly to us fight." Baraka's final line, "DEATH TO THE CLAN!," is more convincing than the conclusions to some of his other Marxist poems because, in this instance, his hortatory passion grows out of the emotional intensity of the poem. With this work, Baraka moves beyond his imitation of 1930s artistic forms to create new ones combining Marxist doctrine with the black oral and musical traditions. This is a Marxist jazz poem, drawing on jazz rhythms and scat sounds mimicking the sounds of musical instruments. When reading the poem in performance, Baraka actually sings some lines. His reading of this and other poems can be heard on the excellent 1981 recording, *New Music–New Poetry*, with David Murray on tenor saxophone and Steve McCall on bass clarinet.

Black Nationalism and Later Works

In 1979, not long after Baraka had joined the Africana studies department at the State University of New York at Stony Brook, he was arrested in Greenwich Village after an alleged dispute with his wife over the price of children's shoes. His original sentence following this incident was three months on Riker's Island, but this was commuted to forty-eight consecutive weekends in a Harlem halfway house. During his incarceration in 1982 and 1983, he wrote his brilliant memoir, *The Autobiography of LeRoi Jones/Amiri Baraka* (1984; 1997), which recounts the years from his boyhood in Newark through his Black Nationalist period.

One of the more controversial features of the Black Nationalist platform was the unabashedly sexist precept requiring that black women submit to the wishes of their men. A prime example of Baraka's own sexism can be found in his play *Madheart* (1966), in which Black Man repeatedly beats Black Woman until she agrees to submit to his domination. While he was writing his autobiography, Baraka was also working on a project that illustrates his growth beyond Black Nationalist chauvinism. In 1983 he collaborated with his wife, Amina, on his third anthology, *Confirmation: An Anthology of African American Women*.

Since 1983 Baraka has been active in many different areas. His socialist essays on art, culture, and politics collected in *Daggers and Javelins* (1984) provide valuable insights into his materialist aesthetic and deserve more attention than they have received. In 1987 he published *The Music*, which includes poems as well as music criticism in the Marxist mode on such artists as Miles Davis, Woody Shaw, and Chico Freeman. In 1988 he worked in Jesse Jackson's presidential campaign because he felt Jackson represented "Black and progressive political desire." In 1989 the Before Columbus Foundation's American Books, the California multicultural book prize, gave Baraka and Edward Dorn the Life Achievement Award. As a full professor Baraka continued to teach at Stony Brook in the 1980s and the early 1990s; however, in 1994 he partially retired from the university, becoming an adjunct professor.

In 1995 Baraka published *Wise, Why's, Y's*, a poem in the epic tradition of Walt Whitman and Ezra Pound. In his introduction, Baraka observes, "*Why's/Wise* is a long poem in the tra-

dition of the Djali (Griots) but this is about African American (*American*) History. It is also like [Melvin] Tolson's *Liberia*, WCW's [William Carlos Williams's] *Patterson [sic]*, [Langston] Hughes' *Ask Yr Mama*, [Charles] Olson's *Maximus* in that it tries to tell the history / life like an ongoing Tale." He defines "griots" as "the African Singer-Poet-Historians who carried word from bird, mouth to ear, and who are the root of our own African-American Oral Tradition." It is a poem about African American slavery, both actual and spiritual, before and after the Civil War. Baraka's concerns regarding authentic black language and black music are a thematic focus in the work; each of the forty poems begins with a title of an African American song—either jazz, blues, or spiritual—and a specific performer. This suggests that the music and the performer embody the "ongoing Tale" of the tradition that Baraka is decoding, unfolding, in lyric language. Furthermore, it is an epistemological poem that wants to reveal the "stone reality" of African American experience in the New World. In fact, Baraka ironically demands that the reader: "Think of Slavery / as / Educational!" With its scope, dark humor, complexity, wisdom, and linguistic inventiveness, *Wise* is one of Baraka's greatest poetic achievements.

In 1996 Baraka published *Funk Lore*, a selection of recent poems, which lacks the unity of *Wise*. Yet in this collection he continues to strive to bring the complexity of musical expression to the written word. When in "Monk's World" the poet says:

That street where midnight
Is round, the moon flat
& blue, where fire engines solo
& cats stand around & look
is Monk's world

He is endeavoring to create in words an effect similar to the great jazz pianist and composer Thelonious Monk's jagged-edged music and slipping rhythms, in essence, he is seeking to reinvent Monk's world in written language. Baraka wants to write the blues in words because he feels that "We are the blues / ourselves," that is, the blues is the profoundest articulation of the spirit of the African American people. From his first book, *Preface to a Twenty Volume Suicide Note* to the present, Baraka has been venturing to find the verbal equivalent to black music to express the spiritual history of the African American people.

Also in 1996 he published *Eulogies,* a moving collection of leftist political celebrations of important figures who have died over the past thirty years. In his preface Baraka says of these figures: "These are my maximum cultural/political heroes and my extended community and human family. These are the ones I grew up with, loved, and was/am influenced by. They are the fighters, the advanced, the artists, the intellectuals—people discontent with things as they are. Not all of them are well known, but all represent a developed and advanced way of living in the world." Some of the eulogized are Malcolm X, John Colrane, Larry Neal, Kimako Baraka—his sister—Bob Kaufman, James Baldwin, "Dizzy" Gillespie, Toni Cade Bambara, and William Kunstler. It is an inspiring work in which Baraka declares "whoever loved these brothers must pick up their gauntlet, accept the swift baton. We must celebrate our fallen by word and by deed!"

On October 7, 1999, his sixty-fifth birthday, Baraka fully retired from Stony Brook, becoming professor emeritus. In retirement he continues to be quite active, appearing around the country, lecturing, and giving poetry readings. In fact, he has a number of new book-length manuscripts ready for publication, including *Unity & Struggle: Political Essays* and *RAZOR: Essays on Revolutionary Art for Cultural Revolution* and numerous shorter works on such individuals as Malcolm X, John Coltrane, Sun Ra, and Miles Davis.

As in the Beat days, Baraka has returned to the small presses, and they staunchly support him, publishing him in the three most important avant-garde anthologies of the times—*From the Other Side of the Century: A New American Poetry 1960–1990* (1994), edited by Douglas Messerli; *Postmodern American Poetry* (1994), edited by Paul Hoover; and *Poems for the Millennium* (1995; both volumes, 1998), edited by Jerome Rothenberg and Pierre Jorie—and in numerous magazines, such as *New American Writing, Long Shot, Hambone,* and *Sulfur.* Significantly, Baraka has not been reviewed in the mainstream *The New Times Book Review* since 1987 and has not appeared in any edition of the middle-of-the-road annual, *The Best American Poetry,* which began publication in 1988.

Over the course of Baraka's career, critics have learned to intelligently discuss Baraka's Beat and Black Nationalist work. Two recent studies, *Taking It to the Streets: The Social Protest Theater of Luis Valdez and Amiri Baraka* by Harry J. Elam (1997) and *A Nation within a Nation: Amiri Baraka (LeRoi Jones) and Black Power Politics* by Komozi Woodard (1999), are especially successful with the Black Nationalist period. Elam admirably presents Baraka's political aesthetics, while Woodard succeeds in situating Baraka within Black National politics. Yet discussion of the Marxist work, which Baraka has produced since the mid-1970s, has barely begun. This is an area ripe for future scholarship.

In 1987 Baraka, along with Toni Morrison and Maya Angelou, eulogized James Baldwin during a funeral service at the Cathedral of St. John the Divine in New York. In *Eulogies* he called Baldwin "God's black revolutionary mouth"; surely this description is as applicable to Baraka himself as it is to Baldwin. Baraka's entire career has been devoted to bringing the revolution to the word. In his sixties, Baraka has become a senior maverick of African American literature. He is a major avant-garde artist who has helped turn black art from other-directed to ethnically centered. His art, like that of fellow New Jersey poet William Carlos Williams, proves that the universal is found in the particular. Both writing out of their particular worlds tell the human story. He is more than the most brilliant writer of the Black Arts movement of the 1960s—that momentary fame has undercut his greater importance—he is simply a great twentieth-century American writer.

Selected Bibliography

PRIMARY WORKS

PLAYS AND FICTION

Dutchman and The Slave. New York: William Morrow, 1964.

The System of Dante's Hell. New York: Grove Press, 1965.

The Baptism & The Toilet. New York: Grove Press, 1967.

Tales. New York: Grove Press, 1967.

Four Black Revolutionary Plays: All Praises to the Black Man. Indianapolis: Bobbs-Merrill, 1969.

J-E-L-L-O. Chicago: Third World Press, 1970.

The Motion of History, and Other Plays. New York: William Morrow, 1978.

Selected Plays and Prose of Amiri Baraka/Leroi Jones. New York: William Morrow, 1979.

The Fiction of LeRoi Jones/Amiri Baraka. Chicago: Lawrence Hill Books, 2000.

POETRY

Preface to a Twenty Volume Suicide Note . . . . New York: Totem Press, 1961.

The Dead Lecturer. New York: Grove Press, 1964.

Black Magic: Target Study, Black Art, Collected Poetry. Indianapolis: Bobbs-Merrill, 1969.

In Our Terribleness. With Fundi (Bill Abernathy). Indianapolis: Bobbs-Merrill, 1970.

It's Nation Time. Chicago: Third World Press, 1970.

Spirit Reach. Newark, N.J.: Jihad Productions, 1972.

Hard Facts. Newark, N.J.: People's War, 1975.

Selected Poetry of Amiri Baraka/Leroi Jones. New York: William Morrow, 1979.

The Sidney Poet Heroical. New York: I. Reed Books, 1979.

New Music—New Poetry. With David Murray and Steve McCall. India Navigation, 1981. (A disk.)

reggae or not! New York: Contact II, 1981.

From the Other Side of the Century: A New American Poetry 1960–1999. Edited by Douglas Messerli. Los Angeles: Sun and Moon Press, 1994. (A recent anthology including poems by Baraka.)

Postmodern American Poetry. Edited by Paul Hoover. New York: Norton, 1994. (A recent anthology including poems by Baraka.)

Poems for the Millennium. Edited by Jerome Rothenberg and Pierre Jorie. Berkeley: University of California Press, 1995, vol. 1; 1998, both volumes. (An anthology including poems by Baraka.)

Transbluesency: Selected Poems of Amiri Baraka/Leroi Jones. New York: Marsilio, 1995.

Wise, Why's, Y's. Chicago: Third World Press, 1995.

Funk Lore. Los Angeles: Littoral Books, 1996.

NONFICTION

Blues People: Negro Music in White America. New York: William Morrow, 1963.

Home: Social Essays. New York: William Morrow, 1966; reprinted: Hopewell, N.J.: Ecco Press, 1998.

Black Music. New York: William Morrow, 1968; reprinted: Westport, Conn.: Greenwood Press, 1980.

Raise Race Rays Raze: Essays Since 1965. New York: Random House, 1971.

The Autobiography of LeRoi Jones/Amiri Baraka. New York: Freundlich, 1984; amended and expanded edition: Chicago: Lawrence Hill Books, 1997.

Daggers and Javelins. Essays, 1974–1979. New York: William Morrow, 1984.

The Music: Reflections on Jazz and Blues. New York: William Morrow, 1987.

Eulogies. New York: Marsilio Publishers, 1996.

ANTHOLOGIES EDITED BY BARAKA

The Moderns: An Anthology of New Writing in America. Edited and with an introduction by Leroi Jones. New York: Corinth, 1963.

Black Fire: An Anthology of Afro-American Writing. Edited and with an introduction by Leroi Jones and Larry Neal. New York: William Morrow, 1968.

Confirmation: An Anthology of African American Women. Edited by Amiri and Amina Baraka. New York: William Morrow, 1983.

READERS AND INTERVIEWS

The LeRoi Jones/Amiri Baraka Reader. Edited by William J. Harris. New York: Thunder's Mouth Press, 1991; second edition, 2000.

Conversations with Amiri Baraka. Edited by Charlie Reilly. Jackson: University Press of Mississippi, 1994.

UNCOLLECTED ESSAYS

"Philistinism and the Negro Writer." In *Anger, and Beyond: The Negro Writer in the United States.* Edited by Herbert Hill. New York: Perennial Library, Harper & Row, 1968. Pp. 51–61.

"Confessions of a Former Anti-Semite." *The Village Voice* 17, no. 23:1, 19–23 (December 1980).

SECONDARY WORKS

BIOGRAPHICAL AND CRITICAL STUDIES

Allen, Donald, ed. *The New American Poetry: 1945–1960.* New York: Grove Press, 1960.

Allen, Donald, and Robert Creeley, eds. *New American Story.* With an introduction by Warren Tallman. New York: Grove Press, 1965.

Baker, Houston A. " 'These Are Songs If You Have the/ Music': An Essay on Imamu Baraka." *Minority Voices* 1, no. 1:1–18 (Spring 1977).

———. "Generational Shifts and the Recent Criticism of Afro-American Literature." *Black American Literature Forum* 15, no. 1:3–21 (Spring 1981).

Benston, Kimberly. *Baraka: The Renegade and the Mask.* New Haven: Yale University Press, 1976.

———. *Imamu Amiri Baraka (LeRoi Jones): A Collection of Critical Essays.* Englewood Cliffs, N.J.: Prentice-Hall, 1978.

Brown, Lloyd W. *Amiri Baraka.* Boston: Twayne, 1980.

Bruner, Richard W. "Interview with Amiri Baraka." 1970. (Housed at the Schomberg Center of Oral History, New York.)

Elam, Harry J. *Taking It to the Streets: The Social Protest Theater of Luis Valdez and Amiri Baraka.* Ann Arbor: University of Michigan Press, 1997.

Fischer, William C. "Amiri Baraka." In *American Writers* Supp. 2, part 1. Edited by A. Walton Litz. New York: Scribners, 1981. Pp. 29–63.

Fox, Robert Elliot. *Conscientious Sorcerers: The Black Postmodernist Fiction of LeRoi Jones/Amiri Baraka, Ishmael Reed, and Samuel R. Delany.* New York: Greenwood Press, 1987.

Gibson, Donald B., ed. *Five Black Writers.* New York: New York University Press, 1970.

———. *Modern Black Poets: A Collection of Critical Essays.* Englewood Cliffs, N.J.: Prentice-Hall, 1973.

Gwynne, James B., ed. *Amiri Baraka: The Kaleidoscopic Torch.* New York: Steppingstones Press, 1985.

Harris, William J. *The Poetry and Poetics of Amiri Baraka: The Jazz Aesthetic.* Columbia: University of Missouri, 1985.

Hudson, Theodore R. *From LeRoi Jones to Amiri Baraka: The Literary Works.* Durham, N.C.: Duke University Press, 1973.

Jones, Hettie. *How I Became Hettie Jones.* New York: Dutton, 1990.

Klinkowitz, Jerome. *Literary Disruptions: The Making of a Post-Contemporary American Fiction.* Second edition. Urbana: University of Illinois Press, 1980.

Knight, Arthur, and Kit Knight, eds. *The Beat Vision: A Primary Sourcebook.* New York: Paragon House, 1987.

Kofsky, Frank. *Black Nationalism and the Revolution in Music.* New York: Pathfinder Press, 1970.

Lacey, Henry C. *To Raise, Destroy, and Create: The Poetry, Drama, and Fiction of Imamu Amiri Baraka (LeRoi Jones).* Troy, N.Y.: Whitson, 1981.

Melhem, D. H. "Revolution: The Constancy of Change: An Interview with Amiri Baraka." *Black American Literature Forum* 16, no. 3:87–103. (Fall 1982).

Neal, Larry. *Visions of a Liberated Future: Black Arts Movement Writing.* Edited by Michael Schwartz. New York: Thunder's Mouth Press, 1989.

Nielsen, Aldon L. *Writing Between the Lines: Race and Intertextuality.* Athens: University of Georgia Press, 1994.

Ossman, David, ed. *The Sullen Art.* New York: Corinth, 1963.

Pickney, Darryl. "The Changes of Amiri Baraka." *New York Times Book Review,* December 16, 1979, pp. 9, 29.

Rampersad, Arnold. *The Life of Langston Hughes.* Vol. 2, *1941–1967, I Dream a World.* New York: Oxford University Press, 1988.

Rosenthal, M. L. *The New Poets: American and British Poetry Since World War II.* New York: Oxford University Press, 1967.

———. "American Poetry Today." *Salmagundi* no. 22–23:57–70, esp. 61–64 (Spring–Summer 1973).

Sollors, Werner. *Amiri Baraka/LeRoi Jones: The Quest for a "Populist Modernism."* New York: Columbia University Press, 1978.

Sullivan, Joseph F. "Baraka Abandons 'Racism.'" *The New York Times,* December 27, 1974, p. 35.

Woodard, Komozi. *A Nation within a Nation: Amiri Baraka (LeRoi Jones) and Black Power Politics.* Chapel Hill: University of North Carolina Press, 1999.

BIBLIOGRAPHIES

Dace, Letitia. *LeRoi Jones (Imamu Amiri Baraka): A Checklist of Works by and about Him.* London: Nether Press, 1971.

———. "Amiri Baraka (LeRoi Jones)." In *Black American Writers: Bibliographical Essays.* Vol. 2, *Richard Wright, Ralph Ellison, James Baldwin, and Amiri Baraka.* Edited by Thomas M. Inge et. al. New York: St. Martin's Press, 1978. Pp. 121–78.

Harris, William J. *The Poetry and Poetics of Amiri Baraka: The Jazz Aesthetic.* Columbia: University of Missouri Press, 1985.

Hudson, Theodore. *From LeRoi Jones to Amiri Baraka: The Literary Works.* Durham, N.C.: Duke University Press, 1973.

Sollors, Werner. *Amiri Baraka/Leroi Jones: The Quest for a "Populist Modernism."* New York: Columbia University Press, 1978.

THE BLACK ARTS MOVEMENT
Poetry and Drama from the 1960s to the 1970s

HARRYETTE MULLEN

POLITICS, CULTURE, AND aesthetics came together in the Black Arts movement, a catalytic influence on the poetry and drama of African Americans during the latter half of the 1960s and the first half of the 1970s. Poets and playwrights, including Amiri Baraka, Larry Neal, Askia Muhammad Touré, Sonia Sanchez, Etheridge Knight, Mari Evans, Carolyn Rodgers, Julia Fields, Nikki Giovanni, Haki Madhubuti, June Jordan, Ed Bullins, Ben Caldwell, Woodie King, and Ron Milner, were inspired by the radical politics and incendiary rhetoric of the Black Power movement, which itself had been inspired by the Afrocentric message and stirring oratorical style of the well-known former Nation of Islam spokesman Malcolm X as well as the writings and speeches of Third World anticolonialists, revolutionists, and theorists, such as Kwame Nkrumah, Julius Nyerere, Patrice Lumumba, Jomo Kenyatta, Mao Tse-tung, Fidel Castro, Amilcar Cabral, Che Guevara, and Frantz Fanon.

The Black Power movement was profoundly influenced by the struggle for self-determination of so-called Third World nations in Africa, Asia, and Latin America, as they fought to free themselves from colonialism—the exploitation of nations with "undeveloped" resources by more politically and economically powerful industrial nations—and as they considered alternatives to international capitalism, which thrives on the exploitation of working people by privileged elites. Third World leaders frequently sought and found support from the Soviet Union, which, along with the United States, had emerged after World War II as a global power. Locked together in a cold war, with "mutually assured nuclear destruction" a possible outcome, the totalitarian Communist system of the Soviet Union and the democratic capitalist system of the United States competed to influence the political and economic development of the Third World. Communism had scored a major victory when Mao Tse-tung's Cultural Revolution swept through China, alarming the Western democracies while inspiring other Marxist-led revolutionary movements in the Third World. The U.S. intervention in Vietnam raised the political consciousness of many African Americans, whether they were veterans of that war, activists and critics protesting the war, or "everyday people" who grasped the contradiction of ostensibly defending democracy in a distant foreign country when the full benefits of democracy had yet to be extended to black Americans.

The presence of exiled South African poets, such as Keorapetse Kgositsile and Dennis Brutus, also influenced the Black Arts movement. Their experience protesting *apartheid* resembled the struggle to end *de jure* racial segregation in the American South. Their poetry drew

Malcolm X addresses a rally in Harlem in 1963.

on images of oppression common to black South Africans confined to poor townships and Bantustans, unable to travel in their own country without passes, as well as black Americans ghettoized in the urban North, unable to vote in the South without risking their lives. An example of the intersection of African and African American politics is Kgositsile's poem "When Brown Is Black," dedicated to H. Rap Brown, who became a Black Power leader after breaking with the traditional Civil Rights movement as a member of the Student Nonviolent Coordinating Committee (SNCC). The following excerpt from the poem underscores the correspondence of injustice that brings Africans and African Americans together, as the poet pledges solidarity with a brotherhood of common cause.

> For Malcolm,
> for the brothers in Robben Island
> for every drop of Black blood
> from every white whip
> from every white gun and bomb
> for us and again for us
> we shall burn
> and beat the drum

> resounding the bloodsong
> from Sharpeville to Watts

Linking Malcolm X to black South African political prisoners, such as Nelson Mandela, who as leaders of the banned African National Congress (ANC) were confined on Robben Island, and connecting the 1965 Watts riot against the policing of the black community in Los Angeles to the 1960 Sharpeville massacre of South African demonstrators protesting pass laws, the poem refers to a diaspora of black liberation struggle, in which the poet and the poem's dedicatee were participants.

Radical black thinkers viewed the historical relationship of the dominant white culture to the nonwhite minorities within the United States as consistent with America's intervention in the economies and politics of the Third World. As the exploited nations won political independence from European colonizers and began to confront American "imperialists," the aspirations of Third World political leaders provided models and established the agenda of the black liberation struggle in the United States. The rhetorical strategies, philosophical justifications, cultural values, and political concerns of that struggle are echoed in the writing of the Black Arts movement. The following excerpt from A. B. Spellman's "The Beautiful Day #9 *for rob't mcnamara*" exemplifies the explicit parallel that leaders of the Black Power movement and writers associated with the Black Arts movement drew between America's racial politics and its dealings with emerging Third World nations, from Vietnam to Congo.

the beast's backing up. his ass
is grass. have him. in hue
they say taylor can be had
with a gallon of gas. in the congo
they say tshombe leaning
on the beast is leaning on air.

stateside shades
watching the beast in his jungle
biting blackness from the sides of
ibo, shinto, navajo, say
no mo, charlie.

by biting i mean standing before
all that is human
ripping the shadow from a man's back
throwing it in his face
& calling it him.

but what if that shadow was the beast
gray as the grave, hanging on?
what if his mirror was blackness
the knife of the shadow
the thaw of the times?

The poet demonstrates a passionate engagement with global politics, condemning men who represented U.S. interests or collaborated with European colonialists in Third World countries: Maxwell Davenport Taylor, U.S. Ambassador to South Vietnam; and Moise Tshombe who, as Prime Minister of Congo after the assassination of Patrice Lumumba, used white mercenaries to crush political rebels. With its dedication to Robert S. McNamara, the U.S. Secretary of Defense who "escalated" the war in Vietnam during the Kennedy and Johnson administrations, and with its references to "charlie," a colloquial black in-group term for a

white male, and "the beast," a pejorative term borrowed from Elijah Muhammad's Nation of Islam to refer to white oppressors, Spellman's poem boldly interprets U.S. domestic and foreign policy through the lens of racial antagonism, as it predicts the imminent decline of white domination.

Some black writers of the 1960s who participated in the diverse activities of the Black Arts movement also were influenced by innovative and oppositional aesthetic movements that challenged mainstream artistic traditions and literary canons. Before his political affiliation with Black Power as a founder of the Black Arts movement, Amiri Baraka (LeRoi Jones) had been associated with the Black Mountain poets as well as the Beat movement, which also included African Americans Bob Kaufman and Ted Joans. Avant-garde music was a common interest of several writers associated with the Black Arts movement. Both Baraka and A. B. Spellman wrote jazz reviews and liner notes. Clarence Major was associated with visual artists and experimental poets and fiction writers. Members of the early 1960s writers' workshop, Umbra, including Tom Dent, Ishmael Reed, Lorenzo Thomas, David Henderson, Calvin Hernton, Oliver Pitcher, Lloyd Addison, and Norman Pritchard, also had connections to avant-garde aesthetic movements in music, literature, and visual arts.

After the 1965 assassination of Malcolm X, which many felt was orchestrated by the FBI, a number of black writers felt a need to link their artistic expression more directly to the collective political activity that would hasten social change. The influence of the Black Arts movement was felt in virtually every major U.S. city with a significant African American population. The movement tended to be associated most strongly with cities where activist artists and intellectuals founded political organizations, workshops, theaters, literary journals, and independent presses that offered alternative venues for the development and proliferation of the socially conscious black art and culture that movement leaders advocated. New York and New Jersey were centers of activity with the Black Arts Repertory Theatre/School

(BARTS) and Spirit House founded by Baraka and his associates, including former Umbra members Askia Muhammad Touré (Roland Snellings) and Charles and William Patterson. Baraka found other politically active poets, including Larry Neal, with whom he joined forces as he moved from his bohemian life on the Lower East Side to the black community of Harlem, later returning to his birthplace, Newark. The Midwest was another stronghold of the Black Arts movement. Chicago was the home of a number of vital institutions, including the Organization of Black American Culture (OBAC), Haki Madhubuti's Third World Press, and *Black World*, the nationally distributed magazine edited by Hoyt Fuller. Third World, along with two important presses located in Detroit, Dudley Randall's Broadside Press and Naomi Long Madgett's Lotus Press, published many of the emerging poets of the movement, as well as more established poets, such as Gwendolyn Brooks, whose political consciousness had been raised by the movement. Detroit was also the home of director Woodie King and playwright Ron Milner. Karamu House, originally founded as a multicultural neighborhood center, included a historically significant regional black theater that became a hub of Black Arts activity in Cleveland. In Indianapolis, poet Mari Evans produced and directed a television program, *The Black Experience*, which lasted from the late 1960s to the early 1970s. The influence of the Black Arts movement also reached into the South and Southwest, with the activity of writers including Tom Dent, John O'Neal, Gilbert Moses, Jerry Ward, and Kalamu ya Salaam (Val Ferdinand) in organizations such as the Free Southern Theater, Blkartsouth, and the Southern Black Cultural Alliance. In the early 1970s, former Umbra members Tom Dent and Lorenzo Thomas moved from New York to New Orleans, Louisiana, and Houston, Texas, respectively. The Black Arts movement stretched to the West Coast with the participation of poets including Quincy Troupe and Kamau Daa'ood in the Watts Writers Workshop, the presence of the Watts Repertory The-

atre Company directed by Jayne Cortez, and the Watts Prophets in Los Angeles; as well as the association of playwright Ed Bullins with the Black Arts Alliance, Black Arts/West, and Black House, in the San Francisco Bay Area.

The performative aspects of poetry and drama were useful in attracting audiences for the movement's political messages, and emerging poets and dramatists found that they could express their revolutionary ideas and develop alternative, community-based projects independently of mainstream institutional support, given the relatively inexpensive production of poetry broadsides, chapbooks, pamphlets, posters, and one-act plays featuring small casts with minimal theatrical staging. Further encouraged by unprecedented access to mainstream media, which sought out black speakers to explain their political movement, activists, poets, and dramatists explored radical ideas that have profoundly altered American culture and politics. Emphasizing the oral and performance traditions of African Americans, particularly such vernacular practices as "rapping," "signifying," "sounding," and "running it down," the Black Arts movement created a public cultural space for the later emergence of "hip-hop" and "spoken word" poetry.

In some quarters, the movement's emphasis on vernacular orality and performance challenged the literary pedigree of poetry, persistently equating poetry with speech, music, and dance, while frequently expressing ambivalence about the relationship of the writing of the Black Arts movement to prior or contemporary literary movements and traditions. However, it is perhaps most accurate to say that the writers who constituted what is known as the Black Arts movement, as well as the many others who were energized and influenced by their activity, used "any means necessary" to foment a cultural revolution, including the usual means by which literary movements gain attention, such as publishing periodicals, anthologies, manifestos, and critical theories that served to define the movement and its aesthetic. Representative anthologies and critical texts of the period include *Black Fire*, edited by Amiri Baraka and Larry Neal; *The New Black Poetry*, edited by Clarence Major; *SoulScript*, edited by June Jordan; *The Poetry of Black America*, edited by Arnold Adoff; *Understanding the New Black Poetry*, edited by Stephen Henderson; and *The Black Aesthetic*, edited by Addison Gayle.

The more politically oriented representatives among contemporary rap artists have inherited the attitudes and styles of movement-influenced ensemble performers such as the Last Poets and the Watts Prophets, as well as individuals such as Nikki Giovanni and Gil Scott-Heron, who attracted popular audiences by recording their poetry with polyrhythmic African drumming, or with gospel, blues, or jazz musical accompaniment. Scott-Heron's albums included poems about racially motivated police brutality in the United States and the fight to end apartheid in South Africa. His work, including *The Revolution Will Not Be Televised*, received significant air play on radio stations across the country. Scott-Heron's title poem insisted that mainstream mass media were irrelevant to the black struggle even as his record label took advantage of the media's interest in the movement in order to distribute the recording of his performance poetry. Notwithstanding Scott-Heron's disclaimer, the graphic images broadcast on television news programs heightened viewers' awareness of national protest movements and international liberation struggles. Several of Giovanni's most popular poems, including the widely anthologized "Ego Trippin' (There May Be a Reason Why)," were distributed in both printed texts and electronic recording media, with some audiences encountering the recordings before (or instead of) reading her poetry in a book. A poem with broad popular appeal, "Ego Trippin' " combines hyperbole and humor with populist Afrocentric history, heroic myth, feminist self-assertion, and a celebration of black pride.

More controversial are poems for which the Black Arts movement remains notorious, such as Giovanni's "The True Import of Present Dialogue: Black vs. Negro," a scornful taunt containing the shocking lines:

Nigger
Can you kill
Can you kill
Can a nigger kill
Can a nigger kill a honkie
Can a nigger kill the Man
Can you kill nigger
Huh? nigger can you
kill
Do you know how to draw blood
Can you poison
Can you stab-a-jew
. . .
Can you piss on a blond head
Can you cut it off
. . .
Can you kill a white man
Can you kill the nigger
in you
Can you make your nigger mind
die
Can you kill your nigger mind
And free your black hands to
strangle
Can you kill
Can a nigger kill
Can you shoot straight ahead and
Fire for good measure
Can you splatter their brains in the street
. . .
Can we learn to kill WHITE for BLACK
Learn to kill niggers
Learn to be Black men

The elevated diction of Giovanni's title frames a jarring street-wise explication of contemporary discussions among black activists.

For many black Americans, such deliberately provocative poems as this one, inspired by Baraka's influential manifesto-poems "Black Art" and "Black Dada Nihilismus," struck a responsive chord in the often extreme dialogue of the late 1960s, given the prevalence of racial strife and televised violence. Such poems record the trauma and mark the transition from the integrationist goals of the nonviolent Civil Rights movement to the militant stance of the Black Power movement, as African Americans became enraged by the impunity of racist murderers, assassins, and terrorists whose aim was to kill the hopes and dreams of black people. Like similar works of the period, Giovanni's poem oscillates between a literal call for retaliatory violence, urging revolutionary blacks to murder racist whites, and a wish for the metaphorical death of the oppressive "honkie" and the submissive "nigger." The most generous reading of such works is that they insist on the destruction of a social order that dehumanizes the oppressor as well as the oppressed.

While Giovanni, Scott-Heron, and others tended to appeal to broad popular tastes, Amiri Baraka and Jayne Cortez showed that audiences could also relate to poetry that was stylistically complex as well as uncompromisingly political, performed in collaboration with musicians no less sophisticated. Baraka often tried to capture in writing and performance the syncopated rhythms and improvisational brilliance of black music. His collaborations with jazz musicians were in keeping with his theory that black music could connect the writing of the movement to a more intrinsically African expressive tradition. In practice, Baraka, Cortez, and others found that audiences responded enthusiastically when poetry and music were combined, and readings became emotionally charged performances. A writer influenced by the Francophone surrealism of African and Caribbean poets of the Negritude movement, as well as by close association with avant-garde jazz composers and visual artists, Cortez frequently performed and recorded with the most innovative players. Ntozake Shange followed a similar path, performing her poetry with respected musicians, and attracting even larger audiences to see her theatrically staged "choreopoem" *for colored girls who have considered suicide/ when the rainbow is enuf,* a feminist work that broke through many spoken and unspoken proscriptions on black women's writing.

Cortez and Shange, as well as Sonia Sanchez, June Jordan, and other feminist poets influenced by the Black Arts movement, discarding the genteel reticence of previous generations, often employed black vernacular and "street talk," along with the searing rhetoric of racial

politics and images of global struggle, in poems that examined the personal and political significance of gender and sexuality as well as race and class. Dudley Randall defended the raw language of fiery women poets like Sanchez, explaining that "she hurls obscenities at things obscene." While the Black Arts movement contributed to the emergence of many prominent women writers, including lesbian feminists such as Audre Lorde, African American women committed to fighting both racial and gender inequality were sometimes seen as a threat to the solidarity of black struggle, particularly when they exposed to public scrutiny the "dirty secret" of sexual violence within black families and communities. Heterosexist norms and homophobic rhetoric also contributed to an inhospitable climate for gay men and lesbians within the movement, as homosexuality was frequently deplored in Black Arts writing as a pathology of European origin, and even as a form of genocide.

Nevertheless, the political, social, and cultural upheaval of the 1960s, of which the Black Power and Black Arts movements were a part, led to widespread interest in "marginal" identities and exploration of "minority" experience, resulting in the emergence of new American writers and literatures under the banner of cultural diversity or multiculturalism, as the "mainstream" culture of the United States has come to acknowledge the significance of its constituent subcultures and their evolving relations with the culture of middle-class white Anglo-Saxon Protestant heterosexuals. Contemporary manifestations of black cultural nationalism, Afrocentrism, and the appropriation by mass media of the urban vernacular styles of African American youth through the spread of hip-hop culture are phenomena that were influenced by the Black Arts movement's synthesis and transformation of ideas inherited from previous nationalistic and pan-Africanist black movements.

Incorporating elements of both avant-garde and populist movements, the Black Arts movement challenged several basic assumptions of modern Western culture, including the idea that art should have universal significance, and the association of great works of art with individual genius. Many African American writers questioned the universality of works that, they argued, were produced by and for members of a white intellectual elite. They frequently disparaged the privileged individual voice associated with Western traditions of lyric poetry and argued in favor of alternative criteria for creating and judging their own work. Does the work address and engage the black audience? Is the language comprehensible and are the ideas accessible to the audience? Does the work encourage the audience to change themselves and transform their reality in a positive direction? These were considered to be the relevant criteria for evaluating Black Art.

Rather than cultivating the persona of a uniquely gifted and sensitive individual expressing intimate emotions through finely crafted images, many black poets and dramatists saw their task as exhorting and inciting their audience to political action, forging a powerfully assertive collective voice for African Americans, validating the vernacular speech of the black proletariat, and celebrating the beauty and humanity of black people. The ritual of call and response from the black folk tradition became a model for the interaction of audiences and performers as dramatists, perhaps seeing the insurgent black theater as a secular substitute for the emotional catharsis of the black church, wrote plays that addressed issues of particular interest to black audiences and staged revolutionary "rituals" that questioned the relevance of Christianity to African Americans and urged black audiences to move from the role of spectators to activists. Taking poetry and drama out of the library and theater and into the streets, and attracting audiences usually ignored in established literary and theatrical circles, African American writers experimented with ways of representing an oppositional black voice that was more a collective shout than the refined murmur or awed silence associated with Western traditions of literature.

The political activity of the decade sparked an explosion of black expressiveness in arts and culture as artists and writers responded to, participated in, and were inspired by progressive and radical movements from Civil Rights and

Sonia Sanchez

Black Power to antiwar, feminist, and gay liberation struggles. The positive aspirations of the Black Arts movement were often indiscriminately mixed with the masculine bias, homophobia, anti-Semitism, violent imagery, simplistic racial dichotomies, and inflexible aesthetics and politics of several writers and theorists associated with the Black Arts movement. Such internal contradictions provoked spirited dialogue and critique, as artists were challenged to define their political and aesthetic principles in response to the urgent manifestos of the Black Arts movement. Ishmael Reed and Al Young, cofounders of the journal *Yardbird Reader*, were among those who disagreed with the prescriptive black aesthetic associated with proponents of the Black Arts movement. Young created a pseudonymous spoken word poet, O. O. Gabugah, whose writings were parodies of Black Arts style, while Reed countered the manifestos of Baraka and others with the syllogisms of "The Reactionary Poet," which reads in part:

If you are a revolutionary
Then I must be a reactionary
For if you stand for the future
I have no choice but to
Be with the past
. . .
In your world of
Tomorrow Humor
Will be locked up and
The key thrown away
The public address system
Will pound out headaches
All day
Everybody will wear the same
Funny caps
And the same funny jackets
Enchantment will be found
Expendable, charm, a
Luxury
Love and kisses
A crime against the state
Duke Ellington will be
Ordered to write more marches

"For the people," naturally
If you are what's coming
I must be what's going

Make it by steamboat
I likes to take it real slow.

The critic Phillip Brian Harper has argued that the movement produced works that called for black unity, yet were ultimately divisive since the terms used to attack the dominant white culture could also be read as simultaneously condemning and silencing elements within the black communities that the movement hoped to organize. Harper suggests that the ambivalence he detects in the messages of the Black Arts movement arises from the divided intentions of writers whose aim was not only to inform, instruct, and incite the black audience to whom the work is explicitly addressed, but also to disturb and frighten the white reader or spectator to whom the work refers obliquely.

Ultimately, political and aesthetic disagreements—including disagreements about the proper interaction of aesthetics and politics—

divided the Black Arts movement. Some participants, including Kalamu ya Salaam, have noted that internal disagreements were aggravated by external pressures, including the government's surveillance, infiltration, and ultimate destruction of radical organizations that advocated the political, economic, and cultural self-determination of African Americans. Paradoxically, the government was also a source of funding for community-based arts and cultural centers, Artists in Schools Programs, and fellowships from the National Endowment for the Arts, contributing to the development of black artists as African American communities began to claim their share of federal entitlement programs. Some have argued that the apparent benevolence of such government interventions eroded the collective spirit of the movement, co-opting artists and creating a competitive environment in which individuals vied for the limited number of jobs, grants, and fellowships that became available to artists of color.

Like the Harlem Renaissance of the 1920s, the Black Arts movement resulted in an outpouring of music, art, and literature and inspired many educated and middle-class African Americans to reevaluate and to identify themselves more closely with the vernacular culture associated with the black proletariat. At its best, the Black Arts movement stimulated a creative exploration of the folk, popular, and fine art traditions of a community in which diversity and unity, innovation and preservation, are interactive forces. At worst, some critics and theorists, in their eagerness to purge black identity of all traces of Europe, proposed narrow prescriptions for black creativity that resulted in formulaic expression from some artists. Even this served to provoke others to question and transgress the limits, while the thorough exploration of blackness not only contributed to the collective self-knowledge of African Americans, but also helped to redefine the culture of the United States as a multicultural hybrid rather than a white monocultural melting pot.

Paradoxically, as much as it was concerned with defining the cultural distinctiveness of African Americans, the Black Arts movement also helped to create unprecedented opportunities for the creative expression of African Americans to enter and influence "mainstream" American culture. Sometimes the more "black rage" was vented in the work, the more the writer was celebrated in the mainstream culture. In addition to the interesting tension of political, aesthetic, and commercial impulses, another contradiction that the Black Arts movement posed for writers was the idea that black Americans possessed no authentic literature or language of their own. Writers wrestled with the concept that they were severed from the spoken languages and orature of their African ancestors, with no intrinsic connection to the language and literature of their historical oppressors. The English language itself was perceived by some as a tool of oppression, as writers stressed the historical fact that captive Africans had been forced to abandon their native languages.

The more fluent in standard English, the more immersed in established literary culture, the more likely one might be accused of having abandoned one's own traditions, or abandoning the black community by writing works that it could not comprehend, or enjoy, or draw upon for inspiration in the coming revolution. Such accusations in fact were launched by younger writers associated with the Black Arts movement, including Amiri Baraka and Haki Madhubuti, against their elders such as Robert Hayden, Melvin Tolson, and Gwendolyn Brooks, whose works had been praised by white mainstream critics.

Amiri Baraka and Ntozake Shange were among the writers who confessed discomfort or frustration with written literature and with the English language itself as vehicles unsuitable for black expression. In part they were uncomfortable with a perceptible tension in their roles as black artists of middle-class background, and a conflict between the functions of art and political protest. Many writers experimented with ways to make the language of their texts express the "authentic" blackness called for by the leaders of the Black Arts movement. In some experiments, writers including Baraka, Shange, Sonia Sanchez, and others attempted to recode black vernacular as a politically conscious, culturally authentic, aesthetically

eloquent form of expression for African Americans. Other writers, including Adrienne Kennedy, Ishmael Reed, Jayne Cortez, Clarence Major, Steve Cannon, and Lorenzo Thomas, were more concerned with transgressing boundaries in order to expand in every dimension the expressive possibilities for African American writers interested in a full spectrum of discursive practice. However, the movement influenced the thinking of even these dissenting writers, as suggested by this excerpt from Clarence Major's essay, "The Black Criterion":

> The black poet confronted with western culture and civilization must isolate and define himself in as bold a relief as he can. He must chop away at the white criterion and destroy its hold on his black mind because seeing the world through white eyes from a black soul causes death. The true energy of black art must be brought fully into the possession of the black creator.

For the movement leader Amiri Baraka, black literature is compromised by the necessity of using the oppressor's language. Baraka insists in *Black Music,* a collection of his critical essays on blues and jazz, that only music comes close to a pure expression of black sensibility and African cultural memory, as Leslie Catherine Sanders argues in *The Development of Black Theater in America:*

> Jones's insistence that black music is the only truly indigenous aspect of Afro-American culture is tied to his idea that the music constitutes the only language solely developed by Afro-Americans, and is the only language that is validly descriptive of their experience. When used by black people, white language and other aspects of white culture, because imposed, create a rupture between things and their representations [resulting in profound personal and cultural alienation].

Rather than resign himself to the disturbing rift between words and things, or the split within the self between the desire for what "whiteness" signifies and the desire for what "blackness" signifies, or the African Ameri-

can's double consciousness, or the artist's alienation from the community, as complexities
characteristic of the modern or postmodern
condition, Baraka confronts the sense of internal division in this excerpt from his poem "An
Agony. As now."

> I am inside someone
> who hates me. I look
> out from his eyes. Smell
> what fouled tunes come in
> to his breath. Love his
> wretched women.

Far from accepting the agonizing rupture that
creates and intensifies the black artist's sense
of alienation, Baraka admonishes himself and
others for failure to be wholly and consistently
black in thought, word, and action. Through
political affiliation with the Black Power movement, Baraka and others were persuaded that
the African American's double consciousness
was a disease that could be cured, if the correct
prescription were supplied.

Audre Lorde looks for the roots of divided
consciousness in the intersection of language
and subjectivity, focusing specifically on the
black writer's (and more generally, any African
American's) relation to language and literacy in
"Learning to Write." Here the childhood experience of learning the alphabet is accompanied
by physical as well as psychological violence,
calling to mind Ntozake Shange's statement
that as a writer her commitment is to subverting "the language in which I learned to hate
myself."

> Is the alphabet responsible
> for the book
> in which it is written
> that makes me peevish and nasty
> and wish I were dumb   again?

> We practiced drawing our letters
> digging into the top of the desk
> and old Sister Eymard
> rapped our knuckles
> until they bled
> she was the meanest of all
> but none of the grownups

> would listen to us
> until she died in a madhouse.

> I am a bleak heroism of words
> that refuse
> to be buried alive
> with the liars.

Like Toni Morrison's indictment of the "Dick
and Jane" elementary reading primer in her
novel *The Bluest Eye*, Lorde's poem critically
examines the black student's acquisition of
literacy in English, a language tainted by its European origin, its role in institutionalizing racism, and its use as an instrument of domination. By extension, the poem addresses the
African American's compulsory immersion in
Western culture as transmitted by a Eurocen-
tric curriculum. In this case, the young student's painful introduction to the dominant
culture is compounded by the fact that the abusive primary teacher is presumably a white nun
in a parochial school. Thus the poem possibly
implies that the cruel instructor sees herself as
a missionary bringing enlightenment to unfortunate black children.

The poem offers critical insight into what
Paulo Freire, the radical philosopher of education, called the "pedagogy of the oppressed."
The poet recalls a childhood memory and offers
a retrospective critique of a representative ped-
agogical encounter that can be read as both an
individual and a collective experience of African American double consciousness. On the
one hand, the child acquires education and literacy in a coercive system that denigrates or
ignores black experience as it inculcates the
ideology of white supremacy. On the other
hand, education and literacy are tools that allow black speakers and writers to articulate
their sense of alienation and oppression, and
empower them to resist and critically attack
their oppressors. In this case, the students use
their newly acquired literacy to deface the
school's property by carving the alphabet into
the wooden desks of the classroom, perhaps in-
scribing their names or initials, as if that were
the only way of leaving their own mark on the
educational institution.

Such concerns led some African Americans

to establish black schools with Afrocentric curricula. Others demanded that schools, colleges, and universities include the study of African languages and cultures, that they expand literature canons and curricula to include works by black authors, that they establish Black Studies programs, and that historically white educational institutions of higher learning recruit black faculty as well as students. Although Lorde coined the aphorism that the master's tools will never dismantle the master's house, nevertheless she continued, like others influenced by the Black Arts movement, to criticize oppression while writing in "the oppressor's language."

As an alternative to a language that is blamed for distorting black people's perceptions of themselves and the world, Baraka's poem "Ka' Ba" proposes that African Americans might one day speak a different language of "sacred words."

A closed window looks down
on a dirty courtyard, and black people
call across or scream across or walk across
defying physics in the stream of their will

Our world is full of sound
Our world is more lovely than anyone's
tho we suffer, and kill each other
and sometimes fail to walk the air

We are beautiful people
with african imaginations
full of masks and dances and swelling
 chants
with african eyes, and noses, and arms,
though we sprawl in grey chains in a place
full of winters, when what we want is sun.

We have been captured,
brothers. And we labor
to make our getaway, into
the ancient image, into a new

correspondence with ourselves
and our black family. We need magic
now we need the spells, to raise up
return, destroy, and create. What will be

the sacred words?

The poem refers to a present reality, in which African Americans live in a state of degradation, and their healthiest response is to resist oppression. Baraka contrasts this scene with some possible future in which liberated black people, no longer reacting to oppression, can put their creative energy to better use. Perhaps hoping that as a poet he might be the one to create, speak, and write the language that would bring about such a visionary future, Baraka imagines "sacred words" wielded as magic spells to transform the present reality of degradation and destruction into the imagined future of dignity and creativity. Baraka calls for what Quentin Hill advocates in a statement on poetics collected in *The New Black Poets:* "The ritual of transubstantiation . . . the changing of white words to black ones." A possible example of serendipitous word magic is the inclusion of the poem's title in the syllables of the poet's name: "Ka' Ba," a holy place in Mecca housing an ancient black stone, is also the end and the beginning of "Baraka."

Rather than prophesying a visionary language of sacred words and magic spells that would heal the split black consciousness and conjure the hidden power of black creativity, like Baraka in "Ka' Ba," Sonia Sanchez often takes a different approach to language. Although in some poems she responds to Baraka's prophetic call to create a new language or recover an ancient one—punctuating her text with refrains in African languages, or experimenting with nonverbal vocalizations intended to represent voices of ancestors, or incorporating extralinguistic cries, yells, whoops, and hollers to express intense emotion—Sanchez frequently shows how black speakers have always already altered the European language, so that English acquires subversive connotations other than those associated with its usage as a language of oppressors. Sanchez's book, *We A BaddDDD People,* was published by Broadside Press in 1970, the same year that Clarence Major published a *Dictionary of Afro-American Slang,* a standard reference work as "Black English" became a subject for serious scholarship.

In the following excerpt from her title poem "We a BaddDDD People," Sanchez employs nonstandard grammar, spelling, punctuation, and slang, transforming "bad English" into witty African American colloquialism transliterated from speech to text, while demonstrating how black vernacular, deployed as stylistic opposition to standard English, can reverse the meaning of words, so that "bad" is understood as "good, excellent, beautiful, wonderful." Similarly, the poet reinterprets often stigmatized physical features and behavior attributed to African Americans, reversing their signification as well. In form as well as content, the poem validates black aesthetic preferences and affirms blackness.

<pre>
    i mean.
      we bees real
    bad.
      we gots bad songs
    sung on every station
    we gots some bad   NATURALS
    on our heads
      and brothers gots
    some bad loud (fo real)
      dashiki threads
        on them.
                  i mean when
    we dance   u know we be doooen it
                    when we talk
                    we be doooen it
          when we rap
          we be doooen it
              and
    when we love. well. yeh. u be knowen
    bout that too.   (un-huh!)
                  we got some BAAADDD
    thots and actions
          like off those white mothafuckers
          and rip it off if it ain't nailed
          down and surround those wite/
          knee/ grow / pigs & don't let them
          live to come back again into
          our neighborhoods
</pre>

Both Baraka and Sanchez turn negation into affirmation as they imply that a perhaps inchoate political consciousness of and unsystematic resistance to oppression may underlie "negative" aspects of black people and black communities. In "We a BaddDDD People," Sanchez differs in her ability to embrace the possibilities of the present, while Baraka's imagination travels to the distant past and visionary future in "Ka' Ba." Sanchez also speaks as a prophet urging her people to match revolutionary practice to the fiery language and political theory of the movement, in her poem "blk/ rhetoric," which begins with the rhetorical question:

<pre>
    who's gonna make all
    that beautiful blk/ rhetoric
    mean something.
</pre>

The ideology and rhetoric of the Black Power and Black Arts movements encouraged African Americans to resolve their double consciousness through psychic dissociation from white America, complete identification with their black selves, and solidarity with the black nations of Africa and other Third World nations struggling to assert their freedom. As Larry Neal and Amiri Baraka acknowledged, the figure of Malcolm X was crucial to connecting the internal racial politics of the United States to international liberation movements. The compelling force of the rhetoric of Malcolm X, whose speeches and television appearances gained him popularity with black audiences, succeeded in encouraging many black Americans to consider their own interests as separate from and opposed to those of white Americans, as indicated in the following poem by Ted Joans, a surrealist poet who, like LeRoi Jones/ Amiri Baraka, was active before the Black Arts movement as an artist associated with the Beat movement.

My Ace of Spades
MALCOLM X SPOKE TO ME and sounded
    you
Malcolm X said this to me & THEN TOLD
    you that!
Malcolm X whispered in my ears but
    SCREAMED on you!
Malcolm X praised me & condemned you
Malcolm X smiled at me & sneered at you
Malcolm X made me proud & so you got
    scared
Malcolm X told me to HURRY & you
    began to worry

Malcolm X sang to me but GROWLED AT
   YOU !!
Malcolm X words freed me & they
   frightened you
Malcolm X tol' it lak it DAMN SHO IS
Malcolm X said that everybody will be
   F R E E !!
Malcolm X said that everybody will be
   F R E E !!
Malcolm X told both of us the T R U T H.
. . . .
         now didn't he?

The insistent anaphora of Joans's chantlike poem reiterates the experience of many black Americans, and particularly the writers of the Black Arts movement, for whom the words of Malcolm X were a catalyst for change and a litmus test of radical black identity. The committed black consciousness proposed by Malcolm X seemed to offer the prescription to heal the internal split of a double consciousness divided between identification with cultural "blackness" and identification with cultural "whiteness." Choosing black over white was the prescription for unity and solidarity in a black struggle for self-awareness, self-definition, and self-determination. As Joans suggests, a person's attitude toward Malcolm X placed him or her clearly on one side or the other, identified either with the oppressors of black people or with those who were fighting for freedom. For African American writers of various political and aesthetic tendencies, the words of Malcolm X focused the attention of disparate groups and individuals, helping to consolidate a collective black consciousness in a brief moment of clarity before the politics of the late 1960s and 1970s became more diffuse, less starkly clear-cut.

As another black Beat poet, Bob Kaufman, reminded himself and others, poetry exists in the rupture between language and reality. The socially conscious artist wants neither to suffer oppression nor to perpetuate a culture of oppression, but to perceive what is and imagine what might be. Here, opposition to the dominant culture expresses itself in a litany of affirmative negation that keeps open the possibility of another existence. Surrealistic images of violence and banality convey both awareness and estrangement in the following lines excerpted from Kaufman's poem "I, Too, Know What I Am Not":

No, I am not death wishes of sacred rapists,
   singing
  on candy gallows.
No, I am not spoor of Creole murderers
   hiding
  in crepe-paper bayous.
. . .
No, I am not Indian-summer fruit of Negro
   piano tuners,
  with muslin gloves.
No, I am not noise of two-gun senators, in
   hallowed
  peppermint hall.
No, I am not pipe-smoke hopes of cynical
   chiropractors,
  traffickers in illegal bone.
No, I am not pitchblende curse of Indian
   suicides,
  in bonnets of flaming water.
. . .
No, I am not kisses of tubercular sun
   addicts, smiling
  through rayon lips.
No, I am not chipped philosopher's tattered
   ideas sunk
  in his granite brain.
No, I am not report of silenced guns,
   helpless
  in the pacifist hands.
. . .
No, I am not peal of muted bell, clapperless
  in the faded glory.
No, I am not the whistle of Havana whores
   with cribs
  of Cuban death.
No, I am not shriek of Bantu children, bent
  under pennywhistle whips.
No, I am not whisper of African trees,
  leafy Congo telephones.
No, I am not Leadbelly of blues, escaped
  from guitar jails.
No, I am not anything that is anything I am
  not.

Perhaps Kaufman's answer to the divided consciousness that so troubled fellow Beat poet LeRoi Jones might be found in the final line of this poem: "I am not anything that is anything I am not," a self-evident yet intriguing statement, a linguistic Mobius strip, offered to the reader like an elusive Zen Buddhist koan. Although we can infer from the text that the poet is aware of political realities, the poem defies reduction to a straightforward didactic message, never presuming to solve the perplexity of identity or assuage the anxiety of double consciousness. The poet remains singular in his individuality and multiple in his ability to imagine the experience of others.

Selected Bibliography

Adoff, Arnold, ed. *The Poetry of Black America: Anthology of the 20th Century.* New York: Harper & Row, 1973.

Baker, Houston. *Blues, Ideology, and Afro-American Literature.* Chicago: University of Chicago Press, 1984.

Baraka, Amiri. *The Autobiography of LeRoi Jones.* New York: Lawrence Hill, 1997.

Benston, Kimberly. *Baraka: The Renegade and the Mask.* New Haven, Conn.: Yale University Press, 1976.

Brooks, Gwendolyn, ed. *A Broadside Treasury.* Detroit: Broadside Press, 1971.

Chapman, Abraham. *Black Voices.* New York: Mentor/ New American Library, 1968.

Dent, Thomas, Gilbert Moses, and Richard Schechner. *The Free Southern Theater.* Indianapolis: Bobbs-Merrill, 1969.

Dershowitz, Alan, Archie Epps, and Malcolm X. "The African Revolution and Its Impact on the American Negro." *Harvard Law School Forum* (December 16, 1964). http://www.law.harvard.edu/studorgs/forum/40s.html

Freire, Paulo. *Pedagogy of the Oppressed.* Translated by Myra Bergman. New York: Continuum, 1970.

Gates, Henry L. *Black Literature and Literary Theory.* New York: Methuen, 1984.

Gates, Henry L., and Nellie McKay, eds. *Norton Anthology of African American Literature.* New York: W. W. Norton, 1997.

Gayle, Addison. *The Black Aesthetic.* Garden City, N.Y.: Doubleday, 1972.

Harper, Phillip Brian. "Nationalism and Social Division in Black Arts Poetry of the 1960s." *Critical Inquiry* 192 (Winter 1993).

Hatch, James, and Ted Shine. *Black Theater, USA: Forty-Five Plays by Black Americans 1847–1974.* New York: The Free Press/ Macmillan, 1974.

Henderson, Stephen. *Understanding the New Black Poetry.* New York: William Morrow, 1973.

Jones, LeRoi (Amiri Baraka). *Black Music.* New York: William Morrow, 1970.

Jones, LeRoi (Amiri Baraka), and Larry Neal. *Black Fire: An Anthology of Afro-American Writing.* New York: William Morrow, 1968.

Jordan, June. *Soulscript: Afro-American Poetry.* Garden City, N.Y.: Zenith Books/Doubleday, 1970.

King, Woodie, ed. *BlackSpirits: A Festival of New Black Poetry in America.* New York: Random House, 1972.

———. *New Plays for the Black Theatre.* Chicago: Third World Press, 1989.

Lee, Don L. (Haki Madhubuti). *Dynamite Voices: Black Poets of the 1960s.* Detroit: Broadside Press, 1971.

Major, Clarence, ed. *The New Black Poetry.* New York: International Publishers, 1969.

———. *The Garden Thrives: Twentieth-Century African-American Poetry.* New York: HarperCollins, 1996.

Neal, Larry. *Visions of a Liberated Future: Black Arts Movement Writings.* New York: Thunder's Mouth Press, 1989.

Nielsen, Aldon. *Black Chant: Languages of African-American Postmodernism.* Cambridge: University of Cambridge Press, 1997.

Oyewole, Abiodun, and Umar Bin Hassan, with Kim Green. *Last Poets on a Mission: Selected Poetry and History of the Last Poets.* New York: Henry Holt, 1996.

Patterson, Lindsay. *Black Theater: A 20th Century Collection of the Work of Its Best Playwrights.* New York: Dodd, Mead, 1971.

Randall, Dudley, ed. *The Black Poets.* New York: Bantam Books, 1971.

Salaam, Kalamu ya. *The Magic of Juju: An Appreciation of the Black Arts Movement.* Chicago: Third World Press, 2000.

Sanchez, Sonia. *We A BaddDDD People.* Detroit: Broadside Press, 1970.

Sanders, Leslie Catherine. *The Development of Black Theater in America: From Shadows to Selves.* Baton Rouge: Louisiana State University Press, 1988.

Smitherman, Geneva. *Talkin and Testifyin: The Language of Black America.* New York: Houghton Mifflin, 1977.

Thomas, Lorenzo. *Extraordinary Measures: Afrocentric Modernism and 20th-Century American Poetry.* Tuscaloosa: University of Alabama Press, 2000.

Thompson, Julius. *Dudley Randall, Broadside Press, and the Black Arts Movement in Detroit, 1960–1995.* Jefferson, N.C.: McFarland, 1999.

Wilentz, Ted, and Tom Weatherly, eds. *Natural Process: An Anthology of New Black Poetry.* New York: Hill & Wang, 1970.

GWENDOLYN BROOKS
(1917–   )

JACQUELYN Y. MCLENDON

GWENDOLYN BROOKS'S POETRY and fiction focuses, for the most part, on ordinary people—from "The Bean Eaters" to "Jessie Mitchell's Mother" to a "Bronzeville Woman in a Red Hat"—and ordinary events—like "feeding a wife [and] satisfying a man." Brooks discovered early in life that "what was common could also be a flower," a notion that was to become a kind of Gwendolyn Brooks aesthetic and serve as a description of what the poet herself called a "G. B. voice." Although she believes in the power of the ordinary to be both significant and beautiful, her motivation is not to mythologize or to romanticize her characters. She simply writes about black people as people, not as curios.

Brooks's choice of character and theme reflects, then, her belief that "a poet should write out of his own milieu" and her desire to speak to her race:

My aim . . . is to write poems that will somehow successfully "call" . . . all black people; black people in taverns, black people in alleys, black people in gutters, schools, offices, factories, prisons, the consulate; I wish to reach black people in pulpits, black people in mines, on farms, on thrones; not always to "teach"—I shall wish often to entertain, to illumine. My newish voice will not be an imitation of the contemporary young black voice, which I so admire, but an extending adaptation of today's G. B. voice.

(*Report from Part One*, p. 183)

When Brooks made this statement, she knew that in order to accomplish such a task, she could not write "Ezra Pound poetry," but she believed the kind of poetry she did write could also be "good" poetry.

Brooks's belief in the beauty and power of the ordinary, the commonplace, has been significant in her personal life as well. She has said often and in a variety of ways that she thinks of herself as "ordinary. But beautiful." To emerge from the times in which she was born and raised with such an attitude shows great strength of character—the world was not particularly kind to dark-skinned children. It was a world in which she was "rechristened . . . Ol' Black Gal" by the other children. In her autobiography, *Report from Part One* (1972), Brooks recalls that she learned very early in school that "to be socially successful, a little girl must be Bright (of skin)." It is a wonder, then, that she ever acquired, not to mention maintained, the attitude that her black skin was "beautiful," "charming!" and even "convenient." It is a wonder, too, that she became confident enough, as Haki Madhubuti (Don L. Lee) suggests, to do the unexpected, for the general and prevailing feeling was that "Negroes" did not write poetry.

Certainly her parents, David Anderson Brooks and Keziah Corine (Wims) Brooks, were responsible for much of her attitude, even at an early age, that she was somehow, in her words, "beyond the pale." For one thing, they both valued learning and passed that attitude on to their children. Her father attended Fisk University for a year, hoping to pursue a medical career, a plan he had to eventually forgo. Her mother, after finishing Emporia State Normal School, taught fifth grade at Monroe School in Topeka, Kansas, where she had been born and raised, and where she gave birth to Gwendolyn Elizabeth on 7 June 1917.

David and Keziah Brooks also gave to Gwendolyn and her brother, Raymond, born when Brooks was sixteen months old, a good sense of home. Brooks lovingly describes home as a warm place that "meant a . . . Duty-Loving Mother, who played the piano [and] made fudge," among other things, and that also "meant . . . father, with kind eyes [and] songs. . . ." She dispels the myth that because one is poor, one has to be unhappy.

Both parents encouraged Brooks's writing. Her mother saw to it that she had the time to write by relieving her of most household chores. She also encouraged Brooks to write plays to be performed by a group of young people for special church programs. Keziah Brooks had no doubt that her daughter would be "the *lady* Paul Laurence Dunbar." Her father saw to it that she had the space to write and provided her with a desk that had compartments, drawers, and a shelf for books.

Brooks received encouragement and help from other quarters as well. She wrote to James Weldon Johnson at age sixteen, sending him some of her poems. She received letters from Johnson, telling her she had talent, that she should read the modern poets, and that she should not be "afraid to use the extra syllable." She felt a good deal encouraged by Johnson's advice and praise even though on meeting him in person, he seemed cold and did not remember having received her poems or having written to her.

Langston Hughes, on the other hand, impressed her quite differently. She met him, soon after meeting Johnson, when Hughes gave a reading at the Metropolitan Community Church in Chicago, which she attended with her mother. Keziah Brooks gave Hughes "a whole pack of [her daughter's] stuff," which "he read . . . right there." Like Johnson, he told her she was talented and to keep writing. Little did she know at that time that she would one day be on intimate enough terms with Hughes to entertain him in her home. During what she called the "party era" of her life (1941–1949), she and her husband were involved with all kinds of artists and gave a party for Hughes in their two-room apartment, into which they "squeezed perhaps a hundred people." Brooks also looks fondly back on a time when Hughes "dropp[ed] in unexpectedly" and, when invited to share a humble dinner of "mustard greens, ham hocks and candied sweet potatoes," exclaimed, "Just what I want!"

Hughes's unpretentiousness added to the respect Brooks already had for him, particularly because of his own admiration of "the word 'black' when that word was less than a darling flag." According to Brooks, Hughes also "loved the young" and helped her, as he did many young writers, by "devot[ing] his column to [her] work . . . before and after [her] books were published."

Brooks's deep respect for Hughes as "the noble poet, the efficient essayist, the adventurous dramatist," as well as a fine man whose "words and deeds . . . were rooted in kindness, and in pride" is important to note because his poetry and his attitude about race are more telling influences on her poetic career than the poetry of someone like Ezra Pound, whom she says she didn't admire, but with whom she is more often compared. From reading Hughes she realized and appreciated the importance of writing about the ordinary aspects of black life.

At age twenty-three, Brooks received help and encouragement in a practical way when she was given the opportunity to take part in a poetry class at the Southside Community Art Center in Chicago. The class was opened to young black people by Inez Cunningham Stark amid objections that since she was white and wealthy, she would be raped, robbed, contamiwaitnated, or killed by those "savages" in "the very *buckle* of the Black Belt," where she proposed to hold the workshop. Stark, whom Brooks described as a rebel, took on the class anyway, a class in which Brooks learned much about modern poetry and had the opportunity to discuss her work seriously. She also saw for the first time the life-style of the white and wealthy when she visited Stark's apartment on Chicago's Gold Coast. The whole experience was "several kinds of eye-opener."

Although she received a good deal of help and encouragement, Brooks seems to have decided the subject matter of her poetry for herself, again taking her cue from writers like Langston Hughes. Even though her earliest poetry was, she confesses, of the lofty type, she later subscribed to the belief that it was best to write about what one knew. Moreover, her own family members and their histories could have provided grist for the mill even if Brooks had never met another person outside the Brooks/Wims clan. Her paternal grandfather, Lucas Brooks, was a slave who escaped to freedom, fought in the Civil War. He and his wife Elizabeth raised twelve children, instilling in them the importance of family ties. Of others on her father's side of the family, she knew very little, but the "Bits. Pieces. Wisps" she did know were all that were necessary for such an imaginative girl. Most of her poetry was taken from real life and "twisted," as she says of *Maud Martha*, "highlighted or dulled, dressed up or down."

As for her maternal relatives, she recalls Aunt Eppie Wims Small, whose husband, Joe Small of Kalamazoo, was pensioned off at twenty-five dollars a week for life by the wealthy white family for whom he had worked. She recalls as well Aunt Gertrude Robinson, who danced the Charleston (and taught it to young Gwendolyn), laughed a lot, and was married to Uncle Paul Robinson, who told jokes and once played piano in a nightclub. Aunt Beulah, "The Queen," taught sewing as a young girl and rose to become head of the sewing department at a high school in Tulsa. She never married, took care of her parents, dressed stylishly, and lived very comfortably.

Gwendolyn Brooks

Also on her mother's side, there were Uncle Willie of Milwaukee, a chiropractor; Uncle Tommy of Topeka; and her Uncle Ernest (married to her mother's sister Ella), on whom, Brooks says, the character "Tim" in *Maud Martha* was based. These were the people Brooks knew or heard stories of as she was growing up, and thus became likely subjects for her lyrics.

Of course, Brooks's dreams and imaginings were not limited to subjects for her poetry; she also dreamed—like many young girls—of boys. She did not have many boyfriends because she was shy and dark. Thus, most of her early experiences with romance were in the form of dreams in which she was adored, got married, and had children. She eventually began to date, not just dream about dating, and at age twenty-one met Henry Blakely, a "fella who wrote" and who, the following year, became her husband.

Gwendolyn and Henry had two children, Nora and Henry, Jr. They were poor but happy: "We . . . had a deal of fun, sharing our growth." She speaks fondly of "friends, movies, children, picnics," and with pride of the "formidable strength of Henry Lowington Blakely the Second." On the whole, those who knew them felt their marriage was successful and a model for others.

In the early years of her marriage, Brooks's career as a writer began to take off. Her first collection of poetry, *A Street in Bronzeville,* was published in 1945. Five years later she won the Pulitzer Prize for *Annie Allen* (1949). During this period, she also wrote reviews for the *Daily News,* the *Sun-Times,* and the *Tribune,* Chicago's newspapers, and for *Black World* (then the *Negro Digest*), the *New York Times,* and the *New York Herald Tribune.* Brooks also began teaching while continuing to write. In 1963 she was asked to start a poetry workshop at Chicago's Columbia College. She also taught at Elmhurst College in Illinois, Northeastern Illinois State College, the University of Wisconsin at Madison, and briefly at the City College of New York.

Brooks and her husband separated in December 1969 and were reconciled in 1973. Although Brooks does not elaborate on the causes of the separation from her husband, except that it was not caused by any extramarital affairs, it is quite obvious that at least part of the problem had to do not only with her success as a poet but also with the time and effort she of necessity put into writing and teaching. She explained in an interview with Ida Lewis of *Essence* magazine:

> He [Henry] was very pleased when any good thing happened to me, though I know that, being a man, he did have problems adjusting to what I was doing. . . . Part of it was due to the fact that we both wrote. It's hard on the man's ego to be married to a woman who happens to get some attention before he does.

Brooks did not fall apart or fall silent after her separation. Nor does her poetry reflect any excessive bitterness about marriage, men, and motherhood. She does realize, however, that "marriage is a hard, demanding state," that "if you're a woman, you have to set yourself aside constantly," and that she could not and would not make those sacrifices again: "What is right for me [is] to be able to control my life."

Thus, Brooks learned through personal experience what it means to be black and female. Even though she has been severely criticized for her various attitudes about both—for example, for her one-time belief in integration as a solution to racism and for what seemed to some a lack of feminist sympathies—she has always been aware of her own blackness and femaleness. As she charts her growth and development as artist and (black) woman in *Report from Part One,* it becomes clear that the awareness had always been there and only needed to be nurtured. What may appear to have sprung full-blown into her poetics and her lifestyle under the influence of the "contemporary young black voice" of the 1960s was actually a gradual blossoming into poetic maturity and into womanhood from the seedlings of her own youth.

Undeniably the Black Arts movement and its practitioners had their influence on Brooks, but as Hortense J. Spillers asserts in "Gwendolyn the Terrible: Propositions on Eleven Poems": "Black and female are basic and inherent in her poetry. The critical question is *how* they are said." The "how" of Brooks's poetry has been its most debated aspect. That is, critical attention has focused on what is often called her dual commitment, the alleged white style and black content of her poetry. This criticism, in its double-consciousness frame of reference alone, does not consider the full complexity of Brooks's poetics—for example, her frequent use of parody—and the interplay of voices in her texts that are not merely echoes of other (white) writers and traditions. Indeed, in the very act of appropriating conventional forms for unconventional subjects—by consciously subverting the dominant genres and their often repressive discourse—Brooks makes both the forms and the language her own. Further, the differences, more so than the echoes, are significant in Brooks's texts because in her differences lies an implicit criticism not only of contemporary society but also of literary form.

The subversion of form and the critique of American society are everywhere apparent in

Brooks's first collection, *A Street in Bronzeville,* and the last piece in the collection, "Gay Chaps at the Bar," is a perfect case in point. A sequence consisting of twelve sonnets based on reflections about World War II by the men who fought it, it is dedicated to her brother, "Staff Sergeant Raymond Brooks and every other soldier." D. H. Melham, whose *Gwendolyn Brooks: Poetry and the Heroic Voice* (1987) is a comprehensive, full-length study of Brooks's work, categorizes the sonnets by characteristics she identifies as Petrarchan, Shakespearean, some combination of the two, or variants on both. Yet these poems are at such variance with both the Petrarchan and Shakespearean traditions as to be scarcely definable as such.

Indeed, Brooks parodies the sonnet, both its form and its content. First, the poems that make up this sequence are all slant rhymed, a technique Brooks calls off-rhyme. She explains that she used "off-rhyme" because she felt "it was an off-rhyme situation." Further, many of the lines defy scansion. Others vary between pentameter and hexameter (even one heptameter), with stresses that vary primarily between iambs and trochees. Thus, while we are to be reminded of tradition, Brooks's poetry, in contradistinction, becomes a medium for the creation and expression of a new voice.

Although the sonnet long ago ceased to be used simply to express love, the sonnet sequence has seldom been used other than as a means to record a speaker's unrequited love or secret admiration of another. Brooks's sequence, on the other hand, passionately describes the thoughts and feelings of servicemen—especially black servicemen—who were once "gay chaps at the bar" but who "return from the front crying and trembling." While love is one subject upon which they meditate, it does not assume the centrality of, say, death, which is a natural preoccupation in time of war.

Brooks's description of these men's chaotic lives is all the more effective for its juxtaposition with descriptions of the strict regimentation and alleged orderliness of the armed forces. Moreover, since the sonnet form in all its rigidity is the perfect shape of order, Brooks is able to demonstrate through parody the futility of attempting to achieve order. The first sonnet in the sequence exemplifies the point:

> We knew how to order. Just the dash
> Necessary. The length of gaiety in good
>   taste.

In the first line "order" is stressed—is literally punctuated—by the full stop of the period, and the line at least resembles the conventional iambic pentameter line. The second line, however, immediately subverts the notion of order in the sonnet by breaking away from iambic pentameter; at the same time it subverts the notion of order in the soldier's life through the distorted speech pattern. As the poem continues, so does the juxtaposition of order and disorder, the lines moving back and forth between five and six metrical feet. The soldier, too, moves from the order described in the first lines and a life of gaiety, women, and love, to a chaotic world in which he must learn to "chat with death" and "to holler down the lions in this air."

Although Brooks has often been criticized for being difficult and obscure, she is not intentionally so. Rather, she relies on the vertiginous power of the imagination and, through evocative language and imagery, celebrates the "Negro hero" at the same time that she deplores war—that "cry of bitter dead men who will never / Attend a gentle maker of musical joy"—and racism, "those / Congenital iniquities that cause / Disfavor of the darkness." Further, while she is, as always, conscious of every word, in the fourth sonnet she explores the inadequacies of words, especially those spoken to a soldier going off to war—words like "goodby," "come back," or "careful."

Other poems in the sequence lament the hopes and dreams that must wait "till I return from hell" and emphasize the need to keep "allegiances . . . to the dead." Finally, in the last poem of the sequence, "the progress," Brooks returns to the ironies of attempting to achieve order. Despite all the evils caused by the war that the soldiers decry, they "still . . . wear [their] uniforms" and "remark on patriotism, sing, / Salute the flag." Likewise, after breaking form so radically throughout the sequence, the poet adheres more strictly than in any of the other sonnets to conventional sonnet form. In effect, like the soldiers, the sonnet wears its "uniform."

Yet, the lines "But inward grows a soberness, an awe / A fear, a deepening hollow through the cold," which describe the reality of the soldiers' lives after war, might easily refer to the poet's medium of expression—the sonnet—as it conforms to the rigidity but recognizes the inadequacies of tradition. Thus, at the very end of the sonnet, when uniform, patriotism, salutes to the flag—tradition—have failed the soldiers and they wonder simply "how shall we smile . . . / Settle in Chairs" the poem breaks again from tradition both metrically and in its visible shape:

> . . . . The step
> Of iron feet again. And again   wild.

The unusually wide space between "again" and "wild" emphatically reminds us of the tension—the conflict, if you will—between chaos and order.

Not all the poems in the collection deal with so somber a subject as war, but all reflect the impact of poverty and oppression on the lives of black people. From "the old-marrieds," who are constrained to be silent in the "crowding darkness" of their lives, to the occupants of the "kitchenette building," who are "Grayed in, and gray," to "chocolate Mabbie," doomed to loneliness because of her dark skin, and to the infamous Satin-Legs Smith, whose aspirations surpass his possibilities, in *A Street in Bronzeville* Brooks paints portraits of the common man in his infinite variety.

Quite different from *A Street in Bronzeville* is the Pulitzer Prize-winning *Annie Allen*, Brooks's second collection, published by Harper's in 1949. It is made up of four parts: "Notes from the Childhood and the Girlhood," "The Anniad," "Appendix to the Anniad," and "The Womanhood." The first section describes the heroine's birth and the people and events that shape her growth into young womanhood. The second chronicles her journey as a young

woman in search of self through a simultaneous search for romantic love. The third returns to the subject of war touched on in "The Anniad," and the fourth, "The Womanhood," chronicles the life of a more mature Annie as she reflects on problems beyond self and community that affect, whether directly or indirectly, herself and her children. Langston Hughes, in a review for *Voices*, dated 14 November 1949 (published in the winter of 1950), cites "The Womanhood" as the "most effective" section of the collection because, among other reasons, it is "movingly expressed."

Included in the collection is Brooks's invention, the sonnet-ballad, in a poem by that title and one entitled "the rites for Cousin Vit." It also includes a sonnet sequence, "the children of the poor." But the central piece is the mock-heroic "The Anniad." The use of the mock-heroic mode is another instance in which Brooks appropriates a traditional form for her own uses. Alluding to Homer's *The Iliad* and Virgil's *The Aeneid*, she uses the conventions of the epic for commonplace characters, events, and situations. The poetic meter is more suitable to ballads—tetrameter and, for the most part, trochaic—and, of course, ballads are more often thought of as the lyric of the folk. Thus, in parodying form, Brooks is able to present the quest in a modern-day perspective and to invert the traditional image of the white, male hero. These ironic inversions become a way for both Brooks and Annie to gain power and voice.

Annie begins her search for love as a fanciful young girl, hoping for a "paladin / Which no woman ever had." When she meets Tan Man, she is not quite a woman. She is yet "ripe and rompabout, / All her harvest buttoned in, / All her ornaments untried." She feels a desire to experience and celebrate this approaching phase of her life.

Tan Man, however, takes advantage of her youth and eagerness and seduces her. Shortly afterward, he goes off to war and returns an embittered man, having discovered his powerlessness in an arena where power means being white and male. He attempts to (re)gain power through his "random passion," which manifests itself in affairs with various women—"a

GWENDOLYN BROOKS

gorgeous and gold shriek," a "maple banshee," "a sleek slit-eyed gypsy"—anyone but Annie, whom he finds "limpid and meek." Finally, the "smallness that [he] had to spend, / Spent," Tan Man returns to Annie, only to die from the "overseas disease" he contracted during the war.

Thus, by the end of the poem Annie is alone; she is "tweaked and twenty-four" and "almost thoroughly, / Derelict and dim and done." Yet she still has dreams to fall back on, a testament to Brooks's belief that even the "grimmest of [lives] is likely to have a streak or two streaks of sun." It is interesting to note how often critics disregard the "almost" when quoting the above lines, the omission suggesting perhaps a death-in-life existence for Annie. However, Annie is not defeated or doomed to death-in-life existence, for she is, as Brooks describes her, only "temporarily overwhelmed by grief." She makes a comeback in "The Womanhood," emerging as a mature woman who has learned a lesson in self-esteem and self-reliance, that in fact "There are no magics or elves / Or timely godmothers," which is quite a change from the "thaumaturgic lass" we meet at the outset of "The Anniad."

In the decade or so following the publication of *Annie Allen*, Brooks published several volumes of poetry and her one novel, *Maud Martha* (1953). The most widely known of the poetry collections is *The Bean Eaters* (1960), and certainly one of the most compelling poems in the collection is the title poem. "The Bean Eaters" is about an aging, poor couple whose lives have grown monotonous. What keeps them going, however, is "Remembering, with twinklings and twinges, / As they lean over the beans in their rented back room that / is full of beads and receipts and dolls and cloths / tobacco crumbs, vases and fringes." The inextricability of form and content is apparent here in the monotony of the couple's lives conveyed by the conventional line lengths and rhyme scheme, and by the prosaic language of the first two stanzas. Yet when the couple's memories are described, Brooks moves into free verse, the cluttered lines emphasizing the cluttered back room and at the same time working as a kind

of catalog of both the niceties ("twinklings") and the disappointments ("twinges") of their lives.

"The Bean Eaters," along with several other poems, continues themes found in Brooks's earlier poetry, especially the notion of the tiny, cramped physical and emotional space of the poor, which can be redeemed by the power of memory or the imagination to provide "a streak or two streaks of sun." Other themes taken up in this collection include the inevitable ill fate of the high school dropout that Brooks lyricizes in one of her most frequently anthologized poems, "We Real Cool." She also explores racism and violence in such poems as "A Bronzeville Mother Loiters in Mississippi. Meanwhile, a Mississippi Mother Burns Bacon"; "The Last Quatrain of the Ballad of Emmet Till"; and "The Chicago *Defender* Sends a Man to Little Rock." In "A Bronzeville Mother," Brooks vividly depicts the hatred that rears its ugly head against "a blackish child / Of fourteen" accused of making unseemly advances to a white woman but whom Brooks describes as having "eyes still too young to be dirty, / And a mouth too young to have lost every reminder / Of its infant softness." In "The Last Quatrain" she describes his mother, "a pretty-faced thing," who sorrowfully "kisses her killed boy." She recreates the violence in Little Rock, the "hurling [of] spittle, rock, / Garbage and fruit," the "scythe / Of men harassing brownish girls," and the "bleeding brownish boy. . . ."

For the most part, though, the poems in *The Bean Eaters* are about ordinary people, like the title couple, whom Brooks portrays sometimes with sympathy and humor, always with honesty and love. "Mrs. Small," for example, is about a women whose name is indicative of her life, but Brooks suggests that in performing her menial chores she is "continuing her part / Of the world's business." "Jessie Mitchell's Mother" returns to another theme that predominates in Brooks's poetry—light skin versus dark—in its depiction of an old woman's contempt for her dark-skinned daughter and the mother's belief that because her daughter is black, "her way will be black." She clings, even on her deathbed, to the received notions about the superi-

71

ority of light skin and dreams, although she is now a "stretched yellow rag," of "her exquisite yellow youth." The poem's ending with these thoughts is all the more ironic in view of the way the old woman actually looks while she lies dying. Both the daughter's description of her mother and the title that places the mother in a subordinate role indicate that the older woman's views are outmoded. She is "jelly-hearted and she has a brain of jelly." She is "not essential. / Only a habit would cry if she should die."

The daughter, Jessie Mitchell, though dark-skinned and held in contempt by her mother, represents a newer way of thinking that promises to outlive, as Jessie herself will outlive, the mother and her way of thinking. Jessie has dignity and strength that even the mother recognizes, though she doesn't value them: "Young, and so thin, and so straight. / So straight! as if nothing could ever bend her." Jessie Mitchell is like many of the women in the collection—like Mrs. Small, described earlier, or the title character in the poem "Bronzeville Woman in a Red Hat," who wears her red hat proudly despite her "extraordinary blackness" and who walks boldly into the kitchen of her white "wage-paying mistress" and kisses the woman's child "square on the mouth!"

The collection does not neglect the stories of black men, and Brooks shows that she has understanding and sympathy for their difficulties as well. In "The Ballad of Rudolph Reed," she treats the indignities and violence a man suffers trying to protect himself, "his dark little wife, / And his dark little children three" as they attempt to integrate a white neighborhood. Rudolph Reed is killed for wanting more for his family than nights listening to "plaster / Stir as if in pain," as the rats try to scratch their way through, or listening to "roaches / Falling like fat rain." "Bronzeville Man with a Belt in the Back" also treats, although metaphorically and in a less dramatic way, the physical as well as emotional dangers black men face in a racist society. "A Man of the Middle Class" is about a man who has lost his blackness, and therefore his identity, by taking on the values of and trying to assimilate into the dominant culture.

These themes, Brooks's concern for men, women, and children who are poor and oppressed, are dramatized even more extensively in *In the Mecca* (1968). Conceived of and begun as a novel, *In the Mecca* evolved, for various reasons, into a book-length poem based on life in Chicago's old Mecca Building. The title poem's meaning turns on the search Mrs. Sallie Smith undertakes for Pepita, one of her nine children, in that the search for Pepita also becomes a spiritual search for self, and the central question, "WHERE PEPITA BE"' resounds throughout the poem as a constant reminder of the human need for self-discovery. The difficulty of accomplishing such a task is made apparent through the insistent repetition of the answer given by Mrs. Sallie's other children— "*Ain seener I ain seen er I ain seen er* / Ain seen er I ain seen er I ain seen er"—and the variety of ways this answer is echoed by other characters throughout the poem. By the end of the poem, we realize that in a community such as the Mecca perhaps self-discovery is not simply difficult but impossible. Indeed, the question and answer have been reduced to "Pepita? No." In fact, Pepita has been murdered.

What is most striking about this poem is its embodiment of elements of the grotesque, as if Brooks felt she must shock the reader into a recognition of man's inhumanity. The poem is fragmented, filled with ironic inversions—indeed, perversions—and exaggerations of speech so that everything familiar is called into question and reduced to absurdity. For example, Brooks suggests at one point in the poem that a perverted version of the Twenty-third Psalm is more appropriate in the Mecca. The changes are apparent at the very beginning in the lines "The Lord was their shepherd. / Yet did they want." The phrase "green pastures" becomes "jungles or pastures"; and "Their gaunt / Souls were not restored, their souls were banished." The poem continues with a line-for-line distortion of the original. And, unlike the original, the end offers no comfort, in that "goodness and mercy should follow them / all the days of their death," not life.

Another example of the kind of perversion that occurs is the narrator's description of Mrs.

Sallie's children and their hates. In essence, they hate everything that suggests material comfort for those more fortunate than themselves, and they hate the people who possess such comforts. In short, "Lace handkerchief owners are enemies of Smithkind." Juxtaposed against this description of hates are the lines "Melodie Mary likes roaches, / and pities the gray rat." In this reversal of the expected, Brooks demonstrates the debilitating effects of poverty and oppression.

The entire poem is a distortion not only of content but also of form. It is for the most part free verse. Stanza and line lengths vary, and there is no discernible organizational pattern. However, interpolated throughout are ballads like "The ballad of Edie Barrow" or passages resembling ballads, like the passage in which "Emmet and Cap and Casey / yield visions of vice and veal." Highly alliterative, these sections have definite rhyme schemes and fairly regular trimeter or tetrameter lines. The extremity to which Brooks carries repetition suggests that language fails just as everything else fails "in the Mecca." Even the opening line—"Sit where the light corrupts your face"—is proleptic of the subsequent distortions.

"In the Mecca" represents a "newish voice" for Brooks, for in this poem the calm and rational tones of the earlier poetry have all but disappeared. She is Gwendolyn the iconoclast, the blasphemer—indeed, to borrow from Hortense Spillers, she is "Gwendolyn the terrible."

The four collections discussed above—*A Street in Bronzeville, Annie Allen, The Bean Eaters,* and *In The Mecca*—represent the bulk of Brooks's poetry published during the first twenty-five years of her poetic career. In addition, she published *Bronzeville Boys and Girls* (1956) and *Selected Poems* (1963), the latter containing selections from the above volumes and a group of poems under the title "New Poems."

The volumes that constitute the next stage of her career show Brooks still intent upon her aim to "call" black people. Some of the poems in *Riot* (1969), *Family Pictures* (1970), and *Beckonings* (1975), reprinted in *To Disembark* (1981), are continuations of themes found in *In*

the Mecca. However, the poems in *Family Pictures* are more optimistic, in that Brooks depicts the achievement of selfhood or, at the very least, reveals a belief that self-definition is attainable. Even Lincoln West, in "The Life of Lincoln West," who suffers because he does not fit the received standards of good looks, because he is hated by his father and mother and called "black, ugly, and odd" by a racist white man, by the end of the poem finds comfort in knowing that he is "the real thing." The poem celebrates on a lesser scale what other poems—especially "Young Heroes" I, II, and III—celebrate grandly: blackness and self-discovery. The volume entitled *Blacks* (1987) contains, like *The World of Gwendolyn Brooks,* poems from all of the individual collections; to them are added poems from *To Disembark* and selections from *The Near-Johannesburg Boy and Other Poems* (1986).

The publication of these later collections, from *Riot* on, marks what Brooks considered a big change in her life, her decision to use black publishers. Although *The World of Gwendolyn Brooks* (1971) was published by Harper & Row, her publisher since 1945, the bulk of her work during this period was published by Broadside Press and Third World Press. Brooks saw this as a positive change in her life and as much a part of her "newish voice" as the poetry itself.

A discussion of Brooks's work must focus on the poetry since she is primarily a poet. However, it is essential to consider her major prose works, including *Maud Martha* (1953) and the unconventional autobiography *Report from Part One* (1972). Ostensibly a novel, *Maud Martha* resembles a book-length poem that seems to be divided into poetic sketches (chapters), some of which are extremely short. Unlike *In the Mecca,* however, *Maud Martha* was conceived of as a novel and remained so. An autobiographical bildungsroman of sorts, it details the simultaneous physical and spiritual growth of its protagonist from age seven to adulthood: Maud's days at school, her life with her family, her early romantic interests, her marriage to Paul Phillips, the birth of their first child, and their life together. The novel ends after the war with Maud Martha pregnant again.

Maud Martha's content is also reminiscent of Brooks's poetry. In it we find a parade of characters who bear a striking resemblance to types found in her earlier poetry and who will appear again in her later poetry. With the same deft strokes used to paint the characters in her poems—the same compression and yet the same warmth—she describes "Mrs. Teenie Thompson. Fifty-three"; "Coo" and "Coopie" Whitestripe, who were involved in a "truly great love"; and Madame Snow, "the color of soured milk . . . and very superior to her surroundings." Then there's poor Oberto, whose wife, Marie, sorely neglects the domestic chores and is "a woman of affairs"; Oberto, whom the neighbors pity but who thinks he is the "happiest man . . . in his community."

In addition, many of the same themes that predominate in the poetry are given voice in *Maud Martha.* One of the most noticeable is the light skin versus dark skin theme, commonly called the "black and tan motif." Clearly, Maud Martha experiences some difficulties because she is dark-skinned. She is conscious of her color as a factor in how others perceive her, especially her husband, Paul. In a chapter with the telling title "if you're light and have long hair," Paul is invited to the Annual Foxy Cats Dawn Ball, and Maud Martha believes he will take her only because she has seen the invitation, because she is pregnant, and because he is too kind to injure her feelings. At the dance, although she claims not to feel inferior, she is much concerned by Paul's dancing "with someone red-haired and curved, and white as white."

In the next chapter, when Maud Martha is in labor, Paul is sickened by her whimpers and screams, preferring to think of a fair woman he'd met at the Dawn Ball a few months before. Her mother's amazement that Maud has given birth to "a handsome child" is another instance in which we are made aware of the negative construction put on color. Since the novel's point of view is clearly Maud's, however, these thoughts seem more self-recriminations than revelations of Paul's and her mother's attitudes. Although at various points Maud denies feelings of inferiority because of her skin color or her sex, the fact that she feels she is perceived by others only in terms of her color undercuts her moments of self-assurance.

Maud Martha ends with a chapter entitled "back from the wars!" in which Maud is feeling full of life and contemplating "What, *what,* am I to do with all this life"' Despite all the difficulties she has experienced, this is a relatively optimistic ending. The fact that some have survived the war gives her the hope that mankind, specifically her kind, "the least and commonest flower . . . would . . . come up again in the spring." Indeed, at the very end of the novel, as Brooks writes, "in the meantime [Maud Martha] was going to have another baby." The novel ends on the obvious and familiar theme of rebirth and affirmation of life that come with spring.

At the end little has been resolved of the tensions—familial, marital, racial—that have been the crux of the novel. Thus, the novel's ending with Maud's feelings of abundant life and promise might seem somewhat contrived, especially coming just after the sketch in which her little girl is slighted by a white Santa Claus. Brooks's explanation that the first passage she wrote of this novel was not used until the opening of the last chapter rather confirms both this notion of a contrived ending and the feeling one gets while reading the novel that abundant life and promise are the exact final impressions Brooks felt appropriate.

Perhaps such an ending is not so disturbing in light of the fact that much in the story was taken out of her own life, that "there's fact-meat in the soup among the chunks of fancy." The belief, then, in the survival of her kind perhaps gives Maud Martha, as it does Brooks, the strength she needs to face life and the incentive she needs to celebrate it. An explanation for both women's attitudes may be youth and naïveté for as Brooks says, during the 1950s and 1960s, although she was aware of injustices, she was ignorant of what lay behind them; she believed in integration; and she relied heavily on Christianity. In the novel, Maud Martha expresses similar views through her actions and, in fact, the penultimate chapter ends with her addressing a presumably superior being who might be able to protect Maud's daughter, little Paulette, from life's ills and disillusionments.

Brooks's true autobiography, entitled *Report from Part One*, is again a departure from convention. Its several parts include reminiscences of her life, photographs, interviews, and sketches of some of her poems and of *Maud Martha*. This, then, is no straightforward chronology of Brooks's life even though the substance is there. She presents a picture of her early life through her own recollections of home and school. However, part of the picture is created by her presentation of her mother's "memories of early Gwendolynian life," in the form of a narrative in which her mother pretends that Brooks is speaking. When she comes to an account of her paternal relatives, she admits that she knows little about them but presents a narrative account, much in the manner of a short story, of what she does know and has heard from her father.

The most striking aspect of the autobiography is its conformance to an oral tradition, through storytelling, through interviews in which one hears dialogue between Brooks and the interviewers, and finally through the parts of the book that resemble journal or diary entries. The orality of *Report from Part One* draws it closer to the poetic quality of the rest of Brooks's writings.

These gifts of her poetry and prose are immeasurable, but they are not the only gifts Brooks has shared and continues to share with others. She has, as Haki Madhubuti and others acknowledge, shared her wealth, often paying the prize money to winners of poetry contests out of her own pocket. She has conducted poetry workshops for the young, including at one time a workshop for a teenage gang in Chicago, the Blackstone Rangers.

Brooks's contributions have not been meanly rewarded. In addition to the Pulitzer, she has received numerous honorary degrees from American colleges and universities. She was Library of Congress consultant in poetry (1985–1986) and became Illinois's poet laureate, succeeding Carl Sandburg, in 1968. She received Guggenheim fellowships (1946, 1947) and grants from the American Academy of Arts and Letters and the National Institute of Arts and Letters (both in 1946). There is the Gwendolyn Brooks Cultural Center at Western Illinois University and the Gwendolyn Brooks Junior High School in Harvey, Illinois. And anthologies have been dedicated to her: *To Gwen with Love: An Anthology Dedicated to Gwendolyn Brooks* (1971) and *Say That the River Turns: The Impact of Gwendolyn Brooks* (1987).

Expressed in *Say That the River Turns* are the love and recognition of some of the people who know Brooks best. Henry Blakely, for instance, remembers the first time he met her at an NAACP meeting at which she had to give a report. He recognized her inner beauty and "felt warm in that shining." Her daughter, Nora Brooks Blakely, describes Brooks as not only a wonderful mother but also a woman who "opens places for people—new doorways and mindpaths." Along with the essays are poems written by both well- and less-known poets, one of the most eloquent of them by Sonia Sanchez, "Gwendolyn Brooks at Temple University." In this poem Sanchez describes Brooks's poetry as "ellingtonian nocturnes [that] saturate us with / jewels and magic," and she describes Brooks herself as a "woman. whose color of life is / like sun. whose laughter is prayer."

Through it all, Brooks has continued in her quiet and unassuming way to make a conscious effort to change and to grow, especially as a writer. Her later writings are not, as has been said of them, more socially aware than the earlier ones. Rather, all of her writings together reflect her belief that a writer must "respond to his climate," must "write about what is in the world." In so doing, Brooks lives up to her promise not to compromise her work; that is, without forsaking her "duty to words," she writes poems that are meaningful to her people—to black people. She is her own best example that "true black writers speak *as* blacks, *about* blacks, to blacks."

Selected Bibliography

PRIMARY WORKS

POETRY

A Street in Bronzeville. New York: Harper & Brothers, 1945.
Annie Allen. New York: Harper & Brothers, 1949.

Bronzeville Boys and Girls. New York: Harper & Brothers, 1956.

The Bean Eaters. New York: Harper & Row, 1960.

Selected Poems. New York: Harper & Row, 1963.

The Wall: For Edward Christmas. Detroit: Broadside Press, 1967.

In the Mecca. New York: Harper & Row, 1968.

Riot. Detroit: Broadside Press, 1969.

Family Pictures. Detroit: Broadside Press, 1970.

Aloneness. Detroit: Broadside Press, 1971.

A Broadside Treasury. Detroit: Broadside Press, 1971.

Jump Bad: A New Chicago Anthology. Detroit: Broadside Press, 1971.

The World of Gwendolyn Brooks. New York: Harper & Row, 1971.

The Tiger Who Wore White Gloves. Chicago: Third World Press, 1974.

Beckonings. Detroit: Broadside Press, 1975.

Primer for Blacks. Chicago: Black Position Press, 1980.

To Disembark. Chicago: Third World Press, 1981.

The Near-Johannesburg Boy and Other Poems. Chicago: The David Company, 1986.

Blacks. Chicago: The David Company, 1987.

Gottschalk and the Grande Tarantelle. Chicago: The David Company, 1988.

Winnie. Chicago: The David Company, 1988.

Children Coming Home. Chicago: The David Company, 1991.

PROSE

Maud Martha. New York: Harper & Brothers, 1953.

The Black Position. Detroit: Broadside Press, 1971–. (Brooks is editor of this annual volume.)

Report from Part One. Detroit: Broadside Press, 1972.

A Capsule Course in Black Poetry Writing. Detroit: Broadside Press, 1975.

Young Poet's Primer. Chicago: Brooks Press, 1980.

Report from Part Two. Chicago: Third World Press, 1996.

SECONDARY WORKS

BIOGRAPHICAL AND CRITICAL STUDIES

Bloom, Harold, ed. *Gwendolyn Brooks.* Philadelphia: Chelsea House Publishers, 2000.

Bolden, B. J. *Urban Rage in Bronzeville: Social Commentary in the Poetry of Gwendolyn Brooks, 1945–1960.* Chicago: Third World Press, 1999.

Brown, Patricia L., Don L. Lee, and Francis Ward, eds. *To Gwen with Love: An Anthology Dedicated to Gwendolyn Brooks.* Chicago: Johnson Publishing, 1971.

Christian, Barbara. *Black Feminist Criticism: Perspectives on Black Women Writers.* New York: Pergamon Press, 1985.

Davis, Arthur P. "The Black-and-Tan Motif in the Poetry of Gwendolyn Brooks." *CLA Journal* 6:90–97 (1962).

———. "Gwendolyn Brooks: Poet of the Unheroic." *CLA Journal* 7:114–25 (1963).

———. *From the Dark Tower: Major Afro-American Writers, 1900–1960.* Washington, D.C.: Howard University Press, 1974.

Evans, Mari, ed. *Black Women Writers (1950–1980): A Critical Evaluation.* Garden City, N.Y.: Anchor/Doubleday, 1984.

Hull, Gloria T. "A Note on the Poetic Technique of Gwendolyn Brooks." *CLA Journal* 19:280–85 (1975).

Kent, George E. *A Life of Gwendolyn Brooks.* Lexington: University Press of Kentucky, 1990.

Madhubuti, Haki R., ed. *Say That the River Turns: The Impact of Gwendolyn Brooks.* Chicago: Third World Press, 1987.

Melhem, D. H. *Gwendolyn Brooks: Poetry and the Heroic Voice.* Lexington: University Press of Kentucky, 1987.

Mootry, Maria K., and Gary Smith, eds. *A Life Distilled: Gwendolyn Brooks, Her Poetry and Fiction.* Urbana and Chicago: University of Illinois Press, 1987.

Shaw, Harry B. *Gwendolyn Brooks.* Boston: Twayne, 1980.

Spillers, Hortense J. "Gwendolyn the Terrible: Propositions on Eleven Poems." In *Shakespeare's Sisters: Feminist Essays on Women Poets.* Edited by Sandra M. Gilbert and Susan Gubar. Bloomington: Indiana University Press, 1979. Pp. 233–44.

Wade-Gayles, Gloria. *No Crystal Stair: Visions of Race and Sex in Black Women's Fiction.* New York: Pilgrim Press, 1984.

Washington, Mary Helen. " 'Taming All That Anger Down': Rage and Silence in Gwendolyn Brooks' *Maud Martha.*" In *Black Literature and Literary Theory.* Edited by Henry Louis Gates, Jr. New York: Methuen, 1984.

Wright, Stephen Caldwell, ed. *On Gwendolyn Brooks: Reliant Contemplation.* Ann Arbor: University of Michigan Press, 1996.

INTERVIEWS

Brooks, Gwendolyn. "Interview." *Triquarterly* 60: 405–10 (Spring/Summer 1984).

Brown, Martha H. "Interview with Gwendolyn Brooks." *Great Lakes Review* 6:48–55 (Summer 1979).

Garland, Phyl. "Gwendolyn Brooks: Poet Laureate." *Ebony,* July 1968, pp. 48–49.

Hull, Gloria T., and Posey Gallagher. "Update on Part One: An Interview with Gwendolyn Brooks." *CLA Journal* 21:19–40 (September 1977).

"Interview with Gwendolyn Brooks." *Black Books Bulletin* 2, no. 1:28–35 (Spring 1974).

Kufrin, Joan. "Our Miss Brooks." *Chicago Tribune Magazine* 28 (March 1982).

Stavros, George. "An Interview with Gwendolyn Brooks." *Contemporary Literature* 2:1–20 (Winter 1970).

Tate, Claudia, ed. *Black Women Writers at Work.* New York: Continuum, 1983.

BIBLIOGRAPHY

Miller, R. Baxter. *Langston Hughes and Gwendolyn Brooks: A Reference Guide.* Boston: G. K. Hall, 1978.

STERLING BROWN
(1901 – 1989)

STEPHEN E. HENDERSON
WITH NEW SCHOLARSHIP BY MARK A. SANDERS

STERLING ALLEN BROWN, a pioneering and gifted poet, a seminal scholar, a brilliant critic, a master teacher, and mentor to hundreds, is generally acknowledged as the dean of African American literature. He was born in Washington, D.C., on 1 May 1901, the youngest of the six children (and the only son) of Rev. Sterling Nelson Brown, minister of Lincoln Temple Congregational Church and professor of religion at Howard University, and of Adelaide Allen Brown, who had been valedictorian of her class at Fisk University.

Brown received an excellent education both in the classroom and outside it. He heard learned discourse in his father's church and at home, where he was awakened to the love of poetry by his mother. He attended Lucretia Mott School and later distinguished himself at Dunbar High School, where Angelina Weld Grimke taught him English and Jessie Redmon Fauset taught him French, and where his classmates included Allison Davis, Montague Cobb, William Hastie, and Charles Drew. Brown received a scholarship to Williams College, from which he graduated in 1922 as a member of Phi Beta Kappa and with a scholarship to Harvard, where he received a master's degree in 1923. At Williams, inspired by George Dutton, he became deeply involved in the new realistic poetry of Edwin Arlington Robinson, Carl Sandburg, and Robert Frost. The example of the Irish

writers Sean O'Casey and J. M. Synge led him to resolve to write about black life as it truly was, without resorting to stereotypes or gloss. Education in black culture came while he was teaching in Virginia. This resolve gradually became his life's mission.

After graduation from Harvard, spurred on by his father and the historian and educator Carter G. Woodson, Brown took a teaching post at Virginia Theological Seminary and College at Lynchburg, Virginia (1923–1926). Although he acquired a reputation for stringent grading, he was a popular teacher who was both admired and respected by his students. And from them Brown learned the great life lessons of racial strength and cultural resiliency. He admired his students' dedication, their faith, and their wonderful speech, which he studied and winnowed and incorporated into his poetry. His students also introduced him to the "songster" Calvin "Big Boy" Davis, from whom he acquired ballads, spirituals, and blues. Brown made Davis the subject of three of his earliest poems: "When de Saints Go Ma'ching Home," "Odyssey of Big Boy," and "Long Gone." He also devoted two poems, "Virginia Portrait" and "Sister Lou," to Mrs. Bibby, the mother of one of his students. To Brown she signified a kind of wisdom and, in effect, offered a lesson that he never forgot and that provided a resonant awareness throughout his poetry and his life. It was also in Lynchburg in December, 1927, that Brown married Daisy Turnbull. The couple later adopted a son.

Although Brown called himself an "amateur folklorist," since he was seeking artistic and philosophical (not scientific) truth, he is held in high esteem by folklorists, especially for the accuracy of his investigation of folk forms such as blues, ballads, and folktales. Indeed, the hallmark of Brown's poetry is its exploration of the bitter dimension of the blues, which he links with a view of humankind that he shares with Sandburg, Frost, Robinson, and Edgar Lee Masters. Their influence helped to catalyze Brown's work without diluting it, and he extended the literary range of the blues without losing their authenticity. When he employed other folk forms, such as the ballad, the "folk epic," the "lie," and the song-sermon, he did so with complete confidence, not only in his skill but also in his models, both the literary (Sandburg, Frost, James Weldon Johnson, and Robinson) and the folk (blues, ballads, and the people who created them).

Brown, a complex man of enormous energy and a masterful talent, gained the admiration and respect of professionals and authorities in the fields of sociology, history, education, and government. Among his earliest and closest friends were the sociologists Charles S. Johnson and E. Franklin Frazier, who inscribed a copy of *Black Bourgeoisie* "To my favorite literary sociologist." In the mid 1930s Brown was consultant to Gunnar Myrdal while the latter was preparing his encyclopedic study of black life, *An American Dilemma* (published in 1944). For this project Brown produced a monumental study of black theater and culture that has served generations of scholars as an introduction to the subject. Although this study was left unpublished, it remains indispensable to a knowledge of the subject.

Among Brown's oldest friends—those who called him "Dutch"—were men and women destined for historical distinction: Ralph Bunche, statesman; Rayford W. Logan, historian; Mercer Cook, linguist and mentor to the Negritude movement; and William Hastie, judge. However, not all of his friends were from the intel-

lectual elite, for Brown always went where the people were, refusing to disown them (as many black intellectuals did). Instead, he stood up for them, and the dignity and wisdom that they embodied. In a moving statement on his relationship to Brown, anthropologist Alan Lomax said in 1975:

I saw Sterling not in classrooms but standing up for the right of his people's culture in governmental and scholarly circles. I saw the inspiring work that he did on the WPA Writers' Project and in the American Council of Learned Societies; I appeared on platforms with him when he spoke with passion and with double-edged laughter about the things he knew and loved. One of America's greatest poets and one of America's authentically original and beautiful people.

Brown was a teacher for over fifty years (including forty years at Howard, 1929–1969), and teaching was his greatest source of pride. In an interview with Genevieve Ekaete in 1974, Brown stated, "My legacy is my students." Although he retired in 1969, by 1973 he was placing his battered briefcase on the desk and arranging a small library in front of a new class. His former students were as excited as the new ones. One of the latter, Michael Winston, then director of the Moorland-Spingarn Research Center and later Howard University's vice-president for academic affairs, mused, "This great man thought that I could *be* somebody." Among the many other students who became his lifelong friends were Clyde Taylor, Eugenia Collier, Bernard Bell, the Dasein poets (among them Percy Johnston, Al Frazier, Ozzie Govan, Joseph White, Nate Richardson, and Leroy Stone), Eloise Spicer, Amiri Baraka, Sherley Anne Williams, Oscar Brown Jr., and Ossie Davis.

As a writer, Brown produced important work both as a critic and scholar and as a poet. As a scholar he was instrumental in defining and critiquing the African American literary canon. His work in this area, self-assured and reliable, converges in *Negro Poetry and Drama* and *The Negro in American Fiction* (both 1937); *The Ne-*

gro *Caravan,* edited with Arthur P. Davis and
Ulysses Lee (1941); and *Outline for the Study
of the Poetry of American Negroes* (1931). In
addition, he produced for the Myrdal project the
previously mentioned study of blacks in the
American culture, which, though incomplete,
is invaluable. Darwin Turner, distinguished
scholar of American and African American literature, sums up the scholarly achievement of
Brown in these words:

Sterling Brown

I had completed research in Afro-American
fiction and drama and had known of Brown's
work. But, as I probed further, I discovered
that all trails led, at some point, to Sterling
Brown. His *Negro Caravan* was *the* anthology
of Afro-American literature. His unpublished
study of Afro-American theatre was *the* major
work in the field. His study of images of Afro-
Americans in American literature was a pioneer work. His essays on folk literature and
folklore were preeminent. He was not always
the best critic (I still have a fondness for Saunders Redding's *To Make a Poet Black*), but
Brown was and is the literary historian who
wrote the Bible for the study of Afro-
American literature. Moreover, he seemed to
enjoy and respect all Afro-American writers,
the folk as well as the elite.

For the study of African American poetry,
Brown's 1937 book is still valuable, still fresh.
It is comprehensive and challenging, full of insights into the texts. Especially noteworthy is
the inclusion of "Negro" poetry in the tradition
of American poetry. This was a crucial position,
shared by many, to which Brown clung throughout his career. There was no sufferance of double standards, no confusion of a "racial bunt
with an Aryan home-run," as it sometimes
seemed in the 1960s, but neither was there any
sufferance of prejudice or any hesitation in
pointing to the limitations of the cultural mainstream. Brown believed in one standard—excellence—and one of his chief discoveries was
that excellence was found in cultural tributar-
ies, if one understood the connections and history of the literature and the people who produced it.

Brown argued the uniqueness of the folk
forms and demonstrated their power, especially
when contrasted with the contemporary romantic poetry in standard English produced by
black poets who patterned their work on traditional European forms and themes. His discussion of "Negro folk poetry" encompasses
crucial issues of theme, structure, and propriety
that still confront black writers and critics.
Thus he took up the debate on the originality
of spirituals and the opposition of African and
Euro-American models to the form, concluding
that there are elements of both in the songs.
The ultimate creators, however, were the slaves,
he stated, and even Southern white scholars admitted that "The words of the best White spirituals cannot compare as poetry with the words
of the best Negro spirituals." To which Brown
added: "It remains to be said that for the best
Negro spirituals, camp-meeting models remain
to be discovered."

Brown discussed the philosophy of the spirituals and refuted the notion that they were
merely escapist in nature. They reflected real
suffering and real longing for freedom, both
earthly and spiritual. He singled out "He Never
Said a Mumbling Word" and "Were You There,"
which tell of Jesus' suffering on the cross, and
saw them as "among the most lyrical cries of
all literature." From this we see Brown's emotional and philosophical kinship not only with

the "black and unknown bards" who created this moving expression but also with the scholars and poets who preceded him in their spiritual and aesthetic discovery: Thomas Wentworth Higginson, W. E. B. Du Bois, and James Weldon Johnson, whom Brown called "mentor." Understanding this kind of faith in the folk creators of the spiritual, we begin to observe the origin and evolution of Brown's aesthetic and philosophy.

The other side of the coin is the social realism expressed in secular rhymes, ballads, work songs, and blues. "At times they belong with the best of folk poetry," Brown said, "and the people who create them at their best cannot be dismissed as clowns." Indeed, these people (designated blues people by LeRoi Jones, one of Brown's protégés) would become the subjects of Brown's portraiture in *Southern Road* and other poems. Still, as James Weldon Johnson notes in his introduction to that volume, Brown does not make mere transcriptions of this vital speech but deepens its meanings.

Like Johnson before him, Brown takes up the hard question posed by the use of dialect, with its associated vilification of black people. He considers the compromises that Paul Laurence Dunbar had to make as he sought to straddle two differing poetry traditions. And with acerbic wit he considers the "contemporary" poetry scene (1914–1936). He dismisses those poets who ignore the real world for one of romantic escape. Their own personalities and struggles should have been recorded: "They refused to look into their own hearts and write." Interestingly, Brown's discussion of dialect and European models is still relevant, for the clash of opposing factions is still to be heard in the arena of the black aesthetic. Also implied in Brown's discussion is the still debated question of identification or identity—What is a "black" poem? Poets of the recent Black Arts movement contend that a criterion of the black poem is black authorship, whereas Brown has always acknowledged the skill and craftsmanship of such writers as Vachel Lindsay and Carl Sandburg, their usefulness as models, and their influence upon his own work. For Brown, the standard of measurement is realism, fidelity to the spirit and objective reality of his subjects. This honesty is consistent in Brown and is the cornerstone of all of his achievement.

In his discussions of blacks in the area of drama, Brown provides the reader with a fact-filled history of American drama and the roles played by blacks both as subjects and as writers. His informed and subtle judgments still provide a valuable introduction to the subject, and scholars and critics of blacks in the cinema also find Brown's pioneering studies relevant to their efforts. He discusses stereotypes; blackface minstrelsy; early black actors such as Ira Aldridge, who played Othello to Edmund Kean's Iago; and The African Company, dating from 1821, which specialized in Shakespeare. The historical popularity of stage versions of Harriet Beecher Stowe's *Uncle Tom's Cabin* and other abolitionist propaganda, the emergence of the comic black stereotypes, and the evolution of blackface minstrelsy in the "Negro Show" contributed to the climate in which the latter emerged.

According to Brown, however, serious comprehensive treatment and the important relation of black life and character were left waiting for the advent of realism. Contributing to this development was the sympathetic, understanding treatment of folk life, as in the Irish theater, and "the careful study of the Negro's social experience." The ultimate appearance of the realism that Brown speaks of intersects his own work at Howard University, where he served as director of the Howard Players. The theater remained an integral part of Brown's artistic and educational interests. One sees this in his lectures and in his poetry readings—his diction is precise; his timing, perfect.

If Sterling Brown had created nothing else, the anthology *The Negro Caravan* (1941) would have accorded him a secure place in literary history. This book was not the first anthology of African American writing, but it was the most comprehensive and the best until then. It is still the best. As the editors point out, earlier anthologies were more narrowly literary, sometimes focusing on a single genre, such as poetry, or on a particular period, as did Benjamin Brawley's *Early Negro American Writers*. According to the preface of *Negro Caravan:*

80

This anthology of the writings of American Negroes has three purposes: (1) to present a body of artistically valid writings by American Negro authors, (2) to present a truthful mosaic of Negro character and experience in America, and (3) to collect in one volume certain key literary works that have greatly influenced the thinking of American Negroes, and to a lesser degree, that of Americans as a whole.

To achieve their purposes, the editors covered the whole range of black writing—from Phillis Wheatley and Jupiter Hammon to Richard Wright. The selections are arranged in eight sections according to type, with selections arranged chronologically. Each author's work is preceded by a brief biographical and bibliographical note. Among the selections are speeches, pamphlets, letters, biography and autobiography, and essays classified into historical, social, cultural, and personal types. There is also a generous representation of folk literature, the direct influence of Brown, preceded by a brilliant essay on the literary and social importance of the texts. Finally, there is a useful chronology of historical and cultural events in America as a whole, and in black America. The book is a classic, and its influence has been fundamental.

Brown's first published poem was "When de Saints Go Ma'ching Home" (*Opportunity* 5:48 [July 1927]). Other poems appearing before the publication of his first volume include "Challenge," "Odyssey of Big Boy," "Return," "Salutamus," and "To a Certain Lady, in Her Garden" (all in *Caroling Dusk*, edited by Countee Cullen [1927]). Additional poems are "Thoughts of Death" (*Opportunity* 6:242 [6 August 1928]); "Riverbank Blues" (*Opportunity* 7:148 [May 1929]); "Effie" (*Opportunity* 7:304 [October 1929]); "Long Gone," "Memphis Blues," "Slim Greer," "Southern Road," "Strong Men" (in *The Book of American Negro Poetry*, edited by James Weldon Johnson [1931]); "Convict," "New St. Louis Blues," "Old King Cotton," "Pardners," "Revelations," "Slow Coon" (later "Slim Lands a Job?"), and "Tin Roof Blues" (in *Folk-Say* edited by Benjamin A. Botkin [1931]).

Although the above listing tells us nothing about the order of composition, it does imply something about order of publication and the configuration that this group of poems makes: for example, the sonnet "Salutamus" and the poems "Challenge" and "Return" from the "Vestiges" section of *Southern Road*, as well as the contrasting poem "Odyssey of Big Boy," which represents a turning away from the genteel and the lyrical to the folk model. We can see how the poet selects and melds these different styles in a process everywhere evident in *Southern Road*. One must marvel at the skill, the ear, the touch by which this mosaic of black life becomes a book, an organic entity that over the years has achieved legendary, at times archetypal, character.

Brown chooses the road, one of the central metaphors of the black experience—indeed, of the human experience—as the unifying motif of his book. Many critics have commented on the felicity of that choice, reflecting as it does powerful connections in the history and culture of the group. Among the forms that the road has taken are the creeks and the rivers, the railroad, the Underground Railroad, the gospel train, the way of survival, the slippery path to hell, the lonesome valley, the Big Road of Life. Immersed as he was in folklore, Brown could ring many changes on the "lonesome road," the junction "where the Southern cross the Yellow Dog," John Henry, the poor wayfaring traveler, and the restless spirit that drives the blues man with a hell hound on his trail. Joanne Gabbin emphasizes the road as "a path of knowledge and experience" epitomized in the words of an old spiritual:

O de ole sheep dey knows de road,
Young lambs gotta find de way.

This communication between the old and the young establishes a bond and a continuity between the generations that give "credence to the idea that the Black literary tradition is one continuous line of development issuing from the earliest folk thought and utterance." In several respects the organization of *Southern Road* implies the dynamics of the social and moral forces whose struggle the poems amplify and illumine.

Southern Road is divided into four parts, each preceded by an epigraph and a dedication, as follows:

> Part One: Road So Rocky. "Road May be Rocky / Won't Be Rocky Long . . ." (spiritual), for Anne Spencer
> Part Two: On Restless River. "O, de Mississippi River, so deep an' wide . . ." (blues), for Allison Davis
> Part Three: Tin Roof Blues. "I'm got de tin roof blues, / Got dese sidewalks on my mind." ("Tin Roof Blues"), for Poodle Williams
> Part Four: Vestiges. "When I was one-and-twenty: I heard a wise man say:" (A. E. Housman), for Rose Anne.

With his talent for architectonics Brown sets up a controlled field, a kind of grid, on which to situate our responses. Each of the "pylons" that link the book can also be recognized as chords, each chord consisting of four terms or tones, from the enumeration to the title to the quotation to the dedication. Each level builds to the final nomination, and each element affects us on a different level, though the levels overlap and converge. The last, the deepest level, is the personal, the level of friendship and love. With the passing of time that level becomes a de facto monument against the day when nothing remains of the specific identity but the "sounds of our names."

That movement of names through present time to future time, I submit, is a movement toward a final object that is expressed thus in the dedication of *Collected Poems:* "To Rose Anne [Brown's wife, Daisy], as ever." Characteristically, the epigraphs and dedications move from the literary to the folk to the vernacular, and this practice continues elsewhere in the *Collected Poems,* where the poet moves from his circle of recent friends in *No Hiding Place* to those of his youth, friends of Dunbar days who called him Dutch. They appear in dedications of *The Last Ride of Wild Bill.* The dedication reads: "To the Dunbar Independents

(who prodded my tall tales) Axe/Bill/Forty-Five/Flap/Ike/Lancess/Sam/In memory of Charlie and Ralph." The last two names are those of the medical scientist Charles Drew and of the statesman Ralph Bunche.

The opening poem of *Southern Road,* "Odyssey of Big Boy," is one of Brown's best and most popular. It also sets the tone for the collection. A delightful ballad, the poem is characterized by humor, stoicism and endurance, racial pride, and technical virtuosity. The hero of the poem, Calvin "Big Boy" Davis, is the "songster" Brown met while at Virginia Seminary. His identification with Davis extends beyond personal friendship to an absorption of the qualities that the man, as the epitome of a culture and a tradition, embodied. And at the end of the poem Big Boy identifies not only with the legendary John Henry but also with the prototypical blues wanderer, "the po' boy a long ways from home," the Original Brother, "old Jazzbo." It is not accidental that the SNCC (Student Nonviolent Coordination Committee) Freedom Fighters in the deep South in the 1960s occasionally signed their names as "Junebug Jazzbo Jones"—they, in effect, led that life. In this poem a full life has been recorded. A life marked by good times and bad, but one that, with all of its dangers and hardships, was eagerly embraced. It is a quality occasionally heard in the blues: "I have had my fun, if I don't get well no mo'." But, like the singer in the blues, Big Boy is in the prime of a life that he, for all his good timing, has lived to the fullest.

> Done took my livin' as it came,
>   Done grabbed my joy, done risked my
>   life;
> Train done caught me on de trestle,
>   Man done caught me wid his wife,
>   His doggone purty wife. . . .

Another poem inspired by "Big Boy" brings an intimate touch to the portrait of the itinerant musician. In "Long Gone," the wanderlust seizes Big Boy's mind as he lies on his pallet listening to the lonely sounds of the trains. He remembers the woman at his side:

82

When I oughta be quiet,
 I is got a itch
Fo' to hear de whistle blow
 Fo' de crossin' or de switch,

An' I knows de time's a nearin'
 When I got to ride,
Though it's homelike and happy
 At yo' side.
. . . .
Ain't no call at all, sweet woman,
 Fo' to carry on—
Jes' my name and jes' my habit
 To be Long Gone. . . .

There are hundreds of blues songs that sound these feelings of restlessness and nameless dissatisfaction, but Brown captures the mood in his ballad form before it is shaped by the bitter sensuality of the blues. As it stands, it retains a certain lyricism that one associates with youth and the passing of time.

Brown develops these feelings into a spacious composition that enables him to comment on the final leaving as adumbrated in a homely but powerful vision of the Last Judgment, as it were. Appropriately, "When de Saints Go Ma'ching Home" opens with the following dedication:

(To Big Boy Davis, Friend.
In Memories of Days Before He Was
Chased Out of Town for Vagrancy.)

There is an effective interplay of memory, mutability, and imagination that forces the seminarians, the professor, and, indeed, the readers to understand more fully the meaning of their association with Big Boy—he is a repository and a guardian of their past, their culture, and somehow they will not let that die. The poem begins ". . . his chant of saints, / "When de saints go ma'chin home. . . . " / and that would end his concert for the day." Brown's handling of the narrative elements is excellent, especially the shifting perspectives. First there is the close-up of the tuning of the guitar:

He would forget
The quieted bunch, his dimming cigarette

Stuck into a splintered edge of the
 guitar;
Sorrow deep hidden in his voice, a far
And soft light in his strange brown eyes;
Alone with his masterchords, his
 memories. . . .
  Lawd I wanna be one in nummer
  When de saints go ma'chin' home.

Seemingly transfixed, Davis was absorbed by the vision of a Beulah Land created by the mingling of faith, imagination, and music. In that vision, there follows a processing "Of saints— his friends—'a-climbin' fo' deir wings,' " created again out of faith and incorruptible song.

Section two of the poem presents the saints, including asthmatic Deacon Zachary, "A-puffin' an' a-wheezin' / up de golden stair." There is "ole Sis Joe / In huh big straw hat, / An' huh wrapper flappin' . . . in de heavenly win'. . . ." There's "Ole Elder Peter Johnson" puffing on his corncob pipe, and the "little brown-skinned chillen" dancing to the heavenly band. There is "Maumee Annie," with her washing done, and old Grandpa Eli, puzzling on a question to ask St. Peter.

In this poem, the procession melds several literary traditions—the classical, the romantic, and the folk minstrel (including the dialect poems of Paul Laurence Dunbar). In the classical, there is the roll call of heroes as in the *Iliad*, the procession of negative characters in *Lycidas*; in the romantic, the procession of mourners in *Ad-onais*; in the folk minstrel, the revelers in Dunbar's "The Party," and its descendants in black popular song, such as Little Richard's "Long Tall Sally," who is "built for speed," who has "everything Uncle Tom needs." After the concert is over, Big Boy would go where "we / Never could follow him—to Sophie probably, / Or to his dances in old Tinbridge flat." After one such concert Davis never came back. Before he disappeared, however, he had allowed Brown to take his picture and had taught him about John Henry, the ballads, the work songs, and the blues.

Just as he had developed friendships and had virtually soaked up black folk culture during his years at Virginia Seminary, Brown in his next two teaching jobs continued his self-education: at Lincoln University in Missouri (1926–1928) and at Fisk University (1928–1929). At both places he got to know the hotels, the barber shops, the shoeshine parlors, and other black businesses that were special gathering places for local wits and raconteurs. He visited rural communities and learned their ways first hand. At Jefferson City, Missouri, he spent long hours listening to tall tales told by a waiter named Slim who kept everyone in stitches and was the prototype for the character Slim Greer, one of Brown's best-known creations. At Fisk, Brown met "the best liar I ever ran across." This was Will Gilchrist, the master yarn spinner, the immortal "Gillie," who probably influenced Brown's performance style as much as anyone other than Calvin "Big Boy" Davis. To a degree, Gilchrist and Davis were co-creators with the poet, as Brown himself would readily concede. Later, Brown would playfully refer to himself as Slim and would, in turn, be called "Slim" by friends. In fact, the identification at times is so amazing that Edward A. Jones, a colleague from Atlanta, called Slim "Brown's poetic alter ego."

There are five Slim Greer poems: three in "On Restless River" and two, "Slim Hears the Call" and "Slim in Hell," omitted from *The Collected Poems*. Briefly these poems exploit the racial, male, unself-conscious lore that never appears in Paul Laurence Dunbar or James Weldon Johnson. This is the dimension of the vernacular that Johnson calls "the common, racy, living speech of the Negro in certain phases of real life." In "Slim Lands a Job?" the hero goes to Big Pete's Cafe, looking for a job. Pete warns Slim that he has a "slow nigger" whom he's going to fire. Then:

> A noise rung out
>   In rush a man
> Wid a tray on his head
>   An' one on each han'
>
> Wid de silver in his mouf
>   An' de soup plates in his vest
> Pullin' a red wagon
>   Wid all de rest. . . .

De man's said, "Dere's
  Dat slow coon now
Dat wuthless lazy waiter!"
  An' Slim says, "How?"

An' Slim threw his gears in
  Put it in high,
An' kissed his hand to Arkansaw,
  Sweetheart . . . good-bye!

There are other stunning portraits throughout Brown's poems, a number of them in *Southern Road*. In "Virginia Portrait" a formal rendering of Mrs. Bibby, the wise mother of one of his students, is presented with monumental dignity and grace:

> Even when winter settles on her heart,
> She keeps a wonted, quiet nonchalance,
> A courtly dignity of speech and carriage,
> Unlooked for in these distant rural ways.

There is the tragic Johnny Thomas (in the poem bearing his name), taken by everyone for a "consarned fool." He gets hooked on gambling and a "fancy woman":

> De jack run low
> De gal run out
> Johnny didn't know
> What 'twas all about.

He then commits murder and is executed:

> Dropped him in de hole
> Threw de slack lime on,
> Oughta had mo' sense
> Dan to evah git born.

A similar fate dogs the convict in "Southern Road." Aside from the drama and the metaphoric extensions of the poem, especially noteworthy is the manner in which the poet takes a three-line blues stanza and transforms it into a work song. The lines are punctuated by the convict's breath, which also regulates the rhythm of his swing. This practice in the oral tradition—in black preaching—is still widely employed even by urban ministers. The virtuoso handling of rhetorical devices, especially those which are endemic to the black tradition, undergirds many aspects of literary performance, from folk rhymes to sermons to contemporary "rap" songs. A kind of revival of these practices has taken place since the early 1970s, not only in poetry but also in fiction. Brown (with "Strong Men" and "Ma Rainey" in *Southern Road*, "The Last Ride of Wild Bill" in the collection of that title, and "Old Lem" in *No Hiding Place*), Zora Neale Hurston, James Weldon Johnson, and Langston Hughes were forerunners in their use of this style.

Brown's rhetoric—the rhetoric of the black tradition—is greatly influenced by music in both obvious and subtle ways. A good deal of this word play still remains in the black community; even when it appears to be on the wane, it reappears somewhere else. The golden solemnity of Martin Luther King Jr., and the fire darts of Malcolm X's wit are fused and subsumed in the torrential talent of Jesse Jackson. In similar manner the apocalyptic be-bop of Larry Neal and Amiri Baraka, the popular prophecy of Nikki Giovanni and Sonia Sanchez—all poets of the 1960s—have been reborn in "rap" music. Larry Neal, poet and theorist of the Black Arts movement, called for a poet who had the drive and skill of James Brown: "Did you ever hear a poet scream like that?" The poets arrived with the Last Poets (among them Felipe Luciano and Gylan Kain), whose kinetic chanting provided a generational link with the "rappers" of the 1980s and 1990s, and with other performer "poets." The point is that the pattern had already been established by Brown and Langston Hughes; and before them, James Weldon Johnson; and before him, Frances Ellen Watkins Harper, whose animated delivery style was geared to maximum audience impact.

It is virtually impossible to read Brown's poetry aloud and not realize his masterful skills. His effects are not accidental, and he doesn't have to scream. When he wants it to, the poem screams, as in "The Ballad of Joe Meek." In poem after poem he never falters and always delights. In a live reading by the poet, one would note his powerful and sonorous voice, capable of myriad shadings and inflections. In "Sister Lou," for example, which fuses the

poem's images with its rhythms and musicality, the voice of an old woman speaking softly to a dying friend becomes the overwhelming presence:

Jesus will find yo' bed fo' you
Won't no servant evah bother wid yo' room.
Jesus will lead you
To a room wid windows
Openin' on cherry trees an' plum trees
Bloomin' everlastin'
An' dat will be yours
Fo' keeps.
Den take yo' time. . . .
Honey, take yo' bressed time.

Fascination with music is not confined, of course, to Brown. It is a feature of African American writing in general, especially the poetry, and it would be strange indeed if the poets neglected so prominent a part of their heritage. In Brown's "Ma Rainey" the Mother of the Blues performs to an audience of poor working people. The laughing, cackling crowd quiets down when Ma comes on stage. In his famous description Brown suggests her role of healer, consoler, and priestess:

O Ma Rainey,
Sing yo' song;
Now you's back
Whah you belong,
Get way inside us,
Keep us strong. . . .

O Ma Rainey,
Lil' an' low;
Sing us 'bout de hard luck
Roun' our do';
Sing us 'bout de lonesome road
We mus' go. . . .

Ma's rendering of "Backwater Blues" brings comfort and solace to the weeping audience. The delineation of the spirit is precise, pure, and presented with economy. It answers all of the questions regarding the use of dialect that James Weldon Johnson raises.

Another example of Brown's incorporating music into his rhetoric is found in "Strong Men." Like powerful hammer blows, the accusatory rhythm is driven by the syntax. Rewritten, the framing lines read: "They dragged you . . . They chained you . . . They huddled you . . . They sold you. . . . They broke you. . . . They scourged you. . . . They branded you. . . ." This pattern is a kind of call and response, although the "call" is more an attack or command. But there's no doubting the response: "You sang. . . . You sang. . . . You sang. . . . You sang. . . . You sang."

Again comes the negative call to despair: "They cooped you. . . . They penned you. . . . And you sang, and they were afraid. And what did you sing" Spirituals, work songs, ragtime and jazz.

> You sang:
> Me an' muh baby gonna shine, shine
> Me and muh baby gonna shine.

The Charleston set to poetry.

In "Cabaret," a truly remarkable poem, Brown shows how the economic and political power of the "overlords" exploits and perverts African American creativity, as a complex stream of consciousness is juxtaposed to recollection of the disastrous floods of 1927, which the poet had addressed earlier in "Ma Rainey" and "Children of the Mississippi."

"Vestiges," Part Four of *Southern Road*, is quite different from the others and poses certain problems for the reader. Anticipating its difficulty, Brown smoothly works this section into the design of the book. First, according to Brown himself, the title "Vestiges" signifies an earlier group of writings in traditional Euro-American forms from which he had turned away. It also implies that those works and lines were not being renounced, but superseded by the new realism. So he is salvaging the best work of his youth with full knowledge that he would not pass that way again.

Mechanically, "Vestiges" is connected to the other three parts of *Southern Road* by the dedication to "Rose Anne" (his wife, Daisy) and by the poem "To a Certain Lady, in Her Garden" which bears a parenthetical dedication to Anne Spencer—to whom Part One was dedicated. Thematically, "Vestiges" addresses the perennial concerns of the young artist: romantic love, mutability, fame, and the passing of youth. Stylistically, the poems are written in sonnet form ("Challenge"), in iambic pentameter quatrains ("To a Certain Lady"), iambic tetrameter quatrains ("Against That Day"), in free verse ("Thoughts of Death"), and in a blank verse reminiscent of James Thompson and William Cooper ("Mill Mountain"). These connections are indicative of Brown's poetic range and the kinds of literary options available to him before he chose his realistic models.

Between the publication of *Southern Road* in 1932 and its republication in 1974, there is a strange and disturbing lapse. Certainly Brown was not silent, for in 1937 he had scheduled *No Hiding Place*, his second book of poems, for publication. The book was rejected for reasons that are unclear, and Brown became bitter. In the 1960s Brown's popularity soared, buoyed by the discovery of his work by a larger audience, some of whom were stirred by the Black Consciousness movement of the 1960s and 1970s. In 1975, Brown was persuaded to publish *The Last Ride of Wild Bill and Eleven Narrative Poems*. In the title poem the headlong, rhythmic rush of the poem is driven by a witty, audacious "skeletonic" verse in which Brown is fluent.

In 1980 *The Collected Poems of Sterling A. Brown* appeared. *No Hiding Place*, published as a section of *Collected Poems*, lacks the symmetry and range of *Southern Road* but is nonetheless a worthy effort. Its eight parts, when considered together, create a kind of personal odyssey (or travelogue): Part One: Harlem Stopover; Part Two: The Cotton South; Part Three: Down in Atlanta; Part Four: "Rocks Cried Out"; Part Five: Road to the Left; Part Six: Frilot Cove; Part Seven: Washington, D.C.; Part Eight: Remembrances. As in *Southern Road*, the last part is devoted to memories.

Although frequent reprinting had made a few of the poems fairly well known—"Old Lem," "An Old Woman Remembers," "Remembering Nat Turner," "Puttin' on Dog," and "Long Track Blues"—most of them were hardly known and others, such as the Cajun poems of "Frilot Cove," were total surprises to most readers. In a few cases one senses directions and leads that the poet briefly followed and then, apparently, dropped. There is a satirical critique of self-appointed race leaders in "The Temple," "The New Congo," and "Memo: For the Race Orators" (on black traitors); there are perversions of history through excess racial zeal in "The Temple," and through prejudice in "Remembering Nat Turner." In these poems Brown is rather close in tone to Melvin Tolson and Frank Marshall Davis. Class struggle and dignity and unity among the working classes are themes of the "Road to the Left" section. Class, not race, is the unifying factor. In "Raise a Song," music functions as a mask and ironic bandage to physical and spiritual injuries of the poor and the homeless. "Colloquy" is a satire on the "solidarity" of black worker and white worker. The touchstone is the wisdom of the black folk tradition:

But dere's hard times comin'—wuss'n hard
    times now.
An' in de hard times dat I recollec'
De whites stood together on top of our
    shoulders
An' give it to us square in de neck.

In "Street Car Gang"—a litany of social and economic woes, the urban parallel to "Old Lem" in its description of the oppression of black manhood by the whites in power—a younger worker calls for revolutionary change of the entire system:

By Gawd we do the work
What come from it is ours.

Although not much is known about why *No Hiding Place* was not published earlier, some suggest that Brown was simply involved with too many projects during this period. A glance at his publications list is thus revealing. In addition, Brown taught a full course load of fifteen hours at Howard, served as director and adviser to the Federal Writers' Project and similar efforts, and was involved in academic politics.

Brown himself felt that the sharp social threats and reactions to the militancy of the period made him politically suspect. There were also difficult professional and personal decisions to be made. For example, his acceptance of a position at Vassar College in 1945 received national attention and promised the kind of recognition he wanted. But the returning veterans of World War II needed him, too. And Howard University needed him, and his people needed him, so he remained there. Brown had touched many lives, and when he came out of retirement in 1973–1975, he helped to energize a new generation of scholars and artists at the Howard University Institute for the Arts and the Humanities. During this time he was becoming more widely known, for his lectures and poetry readings. A new generation had thus discovered him, and at long last some of the symbols of acceptance and appreciation were bestowed upon him. He received honorary doctorates from Howard University, Williams College, Boston University, Harvard, Vassar, and Brown, and other academic institutions. He also was elected to the Academy of American Poets and proclaimed poet laureate of the District of Columbia.

A personal subtext to Brown's poetry, especially as it is shaped by *Southern Road* and *No Hiding Place*, is his love for "Rose Anne" (actually Daisy, his wife of more than fifty years), and his abhorrence of pomposity and fakery. His courtship and youth speak in a variety of voices, one of which appears in "Honey Mah Love":

Dear child
Someday there will be truce from
    quarreling.
And someday all our silly fears will cease.
Someday there will be ways that we shall
    learn
To bilk old clandestine Time, and to return
His cheats, with one on him. Oh we shall
    bring
Someday to our ecstatic worshipping
More than our fretting fervor; something
    nearer peace,
Something near the surety we have been
    dreaming of.

Happy at last. . . . Oh happy! Honey, mah
love. . . .

Brown died in Washington, D.C. on 17 January 1989.

Selected Bibliography

PRIMARY WORKS

BOOKS

Outline for the Study of the Poetry of American Negroes. New York: Harcourt, Brace, 1931. Supplement to *Book of American Negro Poetry,* edited by James Weldon Johnson.
Southern Road. New York: Harcourt, Brace, 1932. Reprinted Boston: Beacon Press, 1974.
The Negro in American Fiction. Washington, D.C.: Associates in Negro Folk Education, 1937. Reprinted with *Negro Poetry and Drama.* New York: Atheneum, 1969.
Negro Poetry and Drama. Washington, D.C.: Associates in Negro Folk Education, 1937. Reprinted with *The Negro in American Fiction.* New York: Atheneum, 1969.
The Negro Caravan. Edited by Brown with Arthur P. Davis and Ulysses Lee. New York: Dryden Press, 1941. Reprinted New York: Arno Press, 1970.
The Last Ride of Wild Bill and Eleven Narrative Poems. Detroit: Broadside Press, 1975.
The Collected Poems of Sterling A. Brown. Selected by Michael S. Harper. New York: Harper & Row, 1980.

ESSAYS ON HISTORY

"The Negro in Washington." In *Washington: City and Capital,* by the Federal Writers Project. Washington, D.C.: U.S. Government Printing Office, 1937.
"The Negro in American Culture." Unpublished memoranda in Carnegie/Myrdal Study of Blacks in America. New York: Schomburg Library.
"Saving the Cargo (Sidelights on the Underground Railroad)." *Negro History Bulletin* 4:151–54 (April 1941).
"The Negro in the American Theatre." In *Oxford Companion to the Theatre.* Edited by Phyllis Harnoll. London: Oxford University Press, 1950. Pp. 672–79.
"Negro American," by Brown with John Hope Franklin and Rayford Logan. In *Encyclopaedia Britannica.* 1967 ed. Vol. 16.

ESSAYS ON LITERATURE AND FOLKLORE

"The Blues as Folk Poetry." In *Folk-Say.* Vol. I. Edited by Benjamin A. Botkin. Norman: University of Oklahoma Press, 1930. Pp. 324–39.
"The Negro Character as Seen by White Authors." *Journal of Negro Education* 2:179–203 (April 1933).
"The American Race Problem as Reflected in American Literature." *Journal of Negro Education* 8:275–90 (July 1939).

"A Century of Negro Portraiture in American Literature." *Massachusetts Review* 7:73–96 (Winter 1966).

MISCELLANEOUS ESSAYS

The Reader's Companion to World Literature. Edited by Lillian H. Hornstein and G. D. Percy. New York: Dryden Press, 1956. (Brown contributed nineteen articles.)
"A Son's Return: Oh Didn't He Ramble." *Kujichaqulia,* November 1973, pp. 4–6. (An autobiographical essay.)

SECONDARY WORKS

BIOGRAPHICAL AND CRITICAL STUDIES

Benston, Kimberly W. "Sterling Brown's After-Song: 'When de Saints Go Ma'ching Home' and the Performance of Afro-American Voice." *Callaloo* 5:33–42 (February–May 1982).
Callahan, John F. "In the Afro-American Grain." *The New Republic,* December 20, 1982, pp. 25–28.
Ekaete, Genevieve. "Sterling Brown: A Living Legend." *New Directions: The Howard University Magazine* 1:5–11 (Winter 1974).
Gabbin, Joanne V. *Sterling A. Brown: Building the Black Aesthetic Tradition.* Westport, Conn.: Greenwood Press, 1985.
Gates, Henry Louis. "Songs of a Racial Self: On Sterling A. Brown." In his *Figures in Black: Words, Signs and the Racial Self.* New York: Oxford University Press, 1987.
Henderson, Stephen E. "The Heavy Blues of Sterling Brown: A Study of Craft and Tradition." *Black American Literature Forum* 14:32–44 (1980).
Lomax, Alan. "American Folklorist Alan Lomax's Comments on Sterling Brown." In *Sterling A. Brown: A UMUM Tribute,* by the Black History Museum Committee. Philadelphia: Black History Museum, 1976.
Rowell, Charles H. "Sterling A. Brown and the Afro-American Folk Tradition." *Studies in the Literary Imagination* 7:131–52 (Fall 1974).
Stuckey, Sterling. Introduction to *Southern Road,* by Sterling A. Brown. Boston: Beacon Press, 1974. Pp. xiii–xxxiv.
Turner, Darwin T. "For Sterling Brown: A Remembrance." In *Sterling A. Brown: A UMUM Tribute,* Vol. 4, by the Black History Museum Committee. Philadelphia: Black History Museum, 1976.

BIBLIOGRAPHIES

"Bibliography of Works by and About Sterling A. Brown." In *Sterling A. Brown: A UMUM Tribute,* by the Black History Museum Committee. Philadelphia: Black History Museum, 1976.
O'Meally, Robert G. "An Annotated Bibliography of the Works of Sterling A. Brown." *CLA Journal* 19:268–79 (December 1975). Enlarged in *Callaloo* 5:90–105 (February–May 1982); and in Brown's *Collected Poems,* pp. 243–55.

New Scholarship

In his comprehensive review of Sterling A. Brown's career, Stephen Henderson accurately frames Brown's literary and critical work in terms of its pursuit of democratic and egalitarian ideals for African Americans. Throughout his career, Sterling Brown unflinchingly celebrated the full humanity of African Americans; he fought tirelessly for full political and social citizenship, and in doing so investigated—through poetry, cultural and literary criticism, and through the making of anthologies—the importance of more accurate and more complex representation of blacks in American letters. In a special edition of the journal *Callaloo* dedicated to Sterling Brown in 1998, Deborah H. Barnes discusses the way Brown simultaneously counters racist stereotypes while offering broader and more complex portraits of black life, which in effect reformulate the paradigms used to perceive and understand African American culture:

> Brown's contention [is] that the Negro's historic oppression is closely linked to his discursive distortion by whites—that is, the malign way Blacks are inscribed in American narratives. Seemingly, legions of "blind men," either intentionally or ignorantly, have misconstrued the Negro's character and history to "justify his exploiters" as well as his exploitation.

Barnes reports Brown's observation that American writers are "blinded" by timeworn racist stereotypes, which obscure the "complete, complex humanity" that is denied to American blacks.

Critical attention in the 1990s largely focused on Brown's poetry, reading the way in which it pursues this larger project of accurate representation. Reexamining the political and artistic contexts in which Brown conceived and executed his work, such criticism has looked at Brown's poetry within the context of interracial political, and artistic movements, including the cultural setting of the Harlem Renaissance, in order to account for the various artistic and political alliances Brown maintained and used during much of his career. It has been well documented that he rejected the label "Harlem Renaissance" in favor of "New Negro Renaissance," a term that more overtly asserts the politics of full citizenship for African Americans. By referring to himself as a New Negro, Brown places his poetry and prose in relation to political figures such as W. E. B Du Bois, Ida B. Wells-Barnett, Allison Davis, Charles Hamilton Houston, and others. So too, his self-ascribed label linked his work with institutions such as the National Association for the Advancement of Colored People (NAACP) and the Urban League, both of which defined themselves in terms of the African American struggle for full citizenship.

Equally as important as the term's ability to affiliate Brown's work with black politics, the label "New Negro Renaissance" also served to lay claim to yet a broader cultural and artistic context, that is, a tradition of modernism largely defined in relation to democratic ideals and progressive politics. Critics and creative writers throughout the twentieth century fashioned a more visible brand of modernism, one that was resistant to political claims and largely preoccupied with cultural exhaustion, entropy, ennui, and fragmentation. Figures such as T. S. Eliot, Ezra Pound, and particularly for Brown, the Agrarians (a group that included John Crowe Ransom, Allen Tate, and Robert Penn Warren among others) attempted to restrict literature and literary criticism to a very narrow definition of aesthetics, necessarily restricting the possibility of political advocacy and self-consciously reducing the Negro to caricature and stereotype.

Yet when Brown writes in *Negro Poetry and Drama* (1937), "what it means to be a Negro in the modern world is a revelation much needed in poetry," he lays claim to an alternative, competing strand of modernism, one that can convey the meaning and value of black life, in all its complexity and in its modern context. Looking back to Walt Whitman as progenitor, influenced by John Dewey and William James's versions of pragmatism, and largely energized by second-generation European immigrant writers and publishers, a "pluralist" or "nativist" brand of modernism sought to celebrate American cultural and ethnic diversity and thus American egalitarianism. Consequently, as Jewish, Irish, Italian, and Native, and other Americans asserted their ethnically specific identity within a larger cultural and political context of plurality they created an alternative conception of American modernism, one invoking democratic possibilities inherent in cultural diversity.

Along with Alain Locke, Langston Hughes, Jean Toomer, and Zora Neale Hurston, Brown conceived his artistry largely in concert with this nativist-pluralist strain of modernism. Insisting on African Americans as historical beings (rather than as ahistorical types), perpetually in the act of crafting their own realities, their own future, Brown reconceives folk ways, idioms, and culture, not as static artifact but as dynamic process—constantly subject to change, ever adapting. Thus the personas represented in many of Brown's most successful poems are captured in the act of articulation, in the process of calling forth folk idioms and forms (and their attending mythologies) as these personas struggle to rationalize their condition and so begin to reconceive the future.

"Odyssey of Big Boy"

"Odyssey of Big Boy," one of Brown's earliest and most successful poems, well illustrates his sense of black modernism. A portrait of a blues singer and roustabout whom he met while teaching at Virginia Seminary in Lynchburg, "Odyssey" portrays Calvin "Big Boy" Davis in the ongoing process of self-re-creation, in the act of imagining immortality. The title itself—a reference to Homeric travel and worldly experience—suggests the way that both persona and poem move back and forth between folk and Western epic literary traditions as both marshal all available cultural references. (In a similar sense, Brown said of himself, in a 1980 speech at the Library of Congress, "I'm also a 4-H Man: Homer, Heine, Hardy, and Houseman; if you want four or five more, you can put Langston Hughes and few other 'H's' in there"—forthrightly claiming the widest and most eclectic set of literary and artistic tradi-

tions for his own poetic project. Also, Brown's riffing on the 4-H Club, an organization that introduces young people to agricultural skills, Brown makes the reference literary rather than agricultural.) As the poem announces itself as folk epic, in dialect no less, it also presents folk forms reworked, bent to the highly personal purposes of Davis's biography. More specifically, Davis's ballad is not the traditional third-person narrative rehearsing the deeds of a cultural hero; instead, as he faces his own mortality, Davis begins a highly personal and incomplete journey into an uncertain future. The poem begins and ends not with a statement about the past, but with a plea for what the future might be. The first stanza reads:

> Lemme be wid Casey Jones,
> Lemme be wid Stagolee,
> Lemme be wid such like men
> When Death takes hol' on me,
> When Death takes hol' on me.

And the final stanza:

> An' all dat Big Boy axes
> When times comes fo' to go,
> Lemme be wid John Henry, steel drivin'
>   man,
> Lemme be wid old Jazzbo,
> Lemme be wid old Jazzbo . . .

Within this frame, Davis delivers his autobiography, a history of jobs, travel, and love that presents a figure embodying the transcendent values of folk cultural heroes such as John Henry, Stagolee, and Casey Jones. Thus, having "seen what dey is to see," Davis's life should serve as evidence that he deserves entry into that pantheon of folk cultural gods.

But as Davis's odyssey toward myth and immortality depends upon the content of the autobiography, it also depends upon the form through which the autobiography is delivered. Davis's choice of poetic form for his oration is not arbitrary by any means; indeed the form of "Odyssey" is almost identical to the folk ballad "John Henry," which Brown anthologized in *The Negro Caravan* (1941). With only a slight variation in length of line, Davis adopts for himself the folk ballad form that has carried John Henry into immortality; Davis's gesture is historical, reaching into the past to claim a form and voice that will help him to construct his future. Or put another way, Davis grafts his biography onto a cultural continuum; we see him in the process of self-creation in concert with folk forms equally adaptive, and also in the process of becoming.

Furthermore, even as the poem plays on the perpetual tension between past and future, "Odyssey" invests itself fully in the perpetual present moment of articulation. Using the past as evidence and the future as possibility, the entire poem consists of the voice in the perpetually open gesture of creation. As Kimberly Benston, (writing in *Callaloo*, 1982), puts it:

> Brown's poems inscribe the past not as a nostalgic after-thought but as a process engendering unlimited visions, not as a feeble gesture toward an unrealizable ideal but as a dynamic proposition, and *after-song* that is both petition and re-petition.

Thus the poem serves as vocal epic, presenting Big Boy Davis—improvisationalist, wordsmith, student of tradition, and blues hero—as the sign of the modernity of folk culture. In essence, a poem concerned with black subjectivity as it operates in and through history, "Odyssey" presents its subject and the very process of creation within a modernist context, rather than separate from it.

Southern Road

In a similar vein, "Southern Road," the poem which provides the title for Brown's most celebrated collection, repositions folk culture and artistic creation within this larger conceptual context and so begins to reveal how the entire collection (if not all of Brown's poetry) comments on modernism and effectively appropriates some of its features in the service of more accurate African American representation. In this poem, Brown adapts a work song—a form evolved from field hollers and slave work

songs—preserves its blues-inflected characteristics, and yet reconstructs the form for his unique poetic purpose. In original folk form, work songs usually consist of clusters of verses often describing working conditions, and formally punctuated by a visceral accent, "hunh," necessary for coordinating group work, often on chain gangs. In Brown's famous essay, "Negro Folk Expression: Spirituals, Seculars, Ballads and Work Songs," (in *A Son's Return: Selected Essays of Sterling Brown*, 1996) he describes the work song:

> More widely spread and know are the Negro work songs whose rhythm is times with the swing back and down and the blow of broadaxe, pick, hammer, or tamper. The short lines are punctuated by a grunt as the axe bites into the wood, or the hammer finds the spike head.
>
> Dis ole hammer—hunh
> Ring like silver—hunh (3)
> Shine like gold, baby—hunh
> Shine like gold—hunh.

These highly improvisational songs usually moved randomly from stanza to stanza as the "caller" makes up the lyrics, sustaining a regular rhythm but seldom sustaining thematic or narrative development from stanza to stanza. Brown takes the form and blues ethos of work songs and reconstructs the idiom to convey narrative content. Thus "Southern Road" presents a persona, incarcerated and doomed to a life of hard labor, yet able to narrate the circumstances of his life, and thus exercising a modicum of control over them:

> Chain gang nevah—hunh—
> Let me go;
> Chain gang nevah—hunh-
> Let me go;
> Po' los' boy, bebby,
> Evahmo' . . .

At first glance, this title piece depicts an all too common sight on the southern landscape of Brown's time: a black man working on a chain gang. In this sense, the poem suggests both incarceration and stasis, both for the persona within the poem and for all black men struggling under southern racial oppression. But the poem, with its blues implications, also suggests the ritualized ways which blacks resist such stifling circumstances. Ralph Ellison, in his essay "Richard Wright's Blues" (in *The Collected Essays of Ralph Ellison,* 1995), defines the blues in a way that sheds considerable light on the recuperative potential in the form and the poem:

> The blues is an impulse to keep the painful details and episode of a brutal experience alive in one's aching consciousness, to finger its jagged grain, and to transcend it, not by the consolation of philosophy but by squeezing from it a near-tragic, near-comic lyricism. As a form, the blues is an autobiographical chronicle of personal catastrophe expressed lyrically.

By imposing artistic form on the chaotic circumstances of a life, and by singing out one's oppression and psychic pain, the poem's persona and the poem itself enact a ritual of resistance and recovery, not defeat. The poem suggests the power of folk idioms and rituals as tools for African Americans to exercise some sense of control over their conditions rather than always being subject to them. Furthermore, the poem "Southern Road" (like the poem "Odyssey") celebrates the moment of vocalization, and thus the process of artistic creation. Like Calvin "Big Boy" Davis, the persona whose voice we hear in "Southern Road" exists in the perpetual present, in a subjective moment of self-assertion and of self-articulation, essential elements of agency.

Thus, as the poem reconfigures folk form, it emphasizes the subjective and temporal, and ultimately presents the blues and folk idioms as modern and adaptive tools for African American individual and collective responses to social conditions. "Southern Road" begins to expand in order to encompass the larger modernist implications of "the road," the central metaphor for the entire collection *Southern Road.* Echoing Walt Whitman's "Song of the Open Road" (a poet and a poem that are also cited by Langston Hughes, Carl Sandburg, and many others in the pluralist tradition), Brown invokes a progenitor for his book and his overarching poetic vision. For Whitman, the open road promises expansive possibilities for the realization of the self and, in turn, for the power of poetry. In a similar sense, the road for Brown serves as an open possibility for the poet-chronicler traversing the southern landscape and noting the teeming multiplicity of African American life on either side. If the road represents access to the southern milieu for the poet, it also offers—through mobility—greater possibilities for black folk themselves. It makes available the ability to travel, to change location, and thus to change one's prospects. Furthermore, if the road serves as access to geographical alternatives, then it also incorporates the idioms, rituals, forms, and voices used to create and inhabit alternative psychic spaces necessary for survival; in short, as we have seen in "Odyssey" and "Southern Road," the road can serve as a means of self-recreation. If this is the case, then the "southern road" of the book's title also points toward the artist, not simply reconstructing folk voices and forms, but in pursuit of his own technical and conceptual mastery. Thus, the road is as much about language, craft, and prosody—the tools of artistic inspiration—as it is concerned with the content of the poem and the representation of the southern milieu. Indeed the metaphor doesn't observe the distinction between form and content, but insists upon eclectic literary traditions and formal mastery as content-filled enterprises in and of themselves.

Finally, the road, for Brown, is not simply a representation of limitless possibility. As an entity that exists in both the physical and metaphysical senses, the road also presents (and represents) tragedy, setbacks, and failure. As a thing divided, often lined with the trappings of commerce on either side, the road entertains duality, ambiguity, and ambivalence. Indeed, the road is never perpetually "open," and it is richly complicated—mythic, tragic, ordinary, and promising, just as modern black life tends to be.

Ultimately, Brown's multilayered metaphor suggests the various ways his poetic project insists upon a larger modernist context. As Kimberly Benston puts it, "Brown's profoundly modernist consciousness of poetry's radical historicity, its desire to be both original and related to what precedes it," compels him to present historicized figures, black personas and voices, not in a static representation of the ahistorical folk, but as historical actors in the process of their own becoming. By the same token, folk cultural forms are not a product of the past, but comprise an ultimately modern culture fully equipped to respond to its rapidly changing milieu. So too, Brown remains in conversation with a pluralist tradition in modernism, one celebrating the full participation of African American culture and one supporting Brown's claim to the widest, most eclectic array of artistic traditions.

No Hiding Place

In addition to reading Brown's poetry in a larger modernist context, critics have begun to examine his artistic connections to the American Communist Party (CPUSA) and more generally the Communist Left. Along with Langston Hughes and Frank Marshall Davis, and a growing number of white writers, Brown wrote poetry in a social realist vein (what he often called "critical realism"), a mode of representation focussed on the vicissitudes of working-class life during the Depression. Brown referred to his own approach, his depiction of overtly racist and economically deprived conditions under which working-class blacks, both urban and rural, toil, as "critical realism." That he illustrates conditions directly, without romanticism or false optimism, and that this depiction works toward a criticism of the larger condition producing local hardships, makes his aesthetic project critically real.

Linking Brown's approach more directly with American Communist Party platforms, the critic James E. Smethurst reads Brown's poetry as a positive response to a 1928 article by the African American Communist William L. Patter-

son titled "Awake Negro Poets." According to Smethurst,

> Patterson's call in *New Masses* for African-American revolutionary poets who could articulate the conditions and concerns of the "Negro Masses" from a racial stance that was realistic, heroic, and sympathetic in ways that would be familiar to African Americans, and that would constitute a break from the earlier New Negro movement, was one that was answered by Brown with *Southern Road.*

Indeed, in both *Southern Road* and his 1937 collection *No Hiding Place*, Brown seeks to represent African American folk life and culture, not to "elevate" the forms into high art (essentially James Weldon Johnson's project in his 1927 volume *God's Trombones*); Brown works to reveal the folk as they represent themselves, and thus to execute an artistic approach very much in keeping with CPUSA agendas. Smethurst further asserts:

> What Brown seems to be interested in is closer to the slogan of the CPUSA-led League of Struggle for Negro Rights, "Promote Negro Culture in Its Original Form with Proletarian Content." In other words, rather than attempting to transmogrify the form of the folk expression into something "higher," Brown proposed to approach this expression on something like its own formal terms, but with a different, and presumably higher, consciousness.

Thus Brown identifies himself with the "vanguard party," particularly its politicized consciousness, insisting upon a sense of nationalism for African Americans and emphasizing interracial working-class solidarity. Perhaps "Road to the Left" in part 5 of *No Hiding Place* best illustrates this approach, championing interracial cooperation while celebrating African American folk forms.

In addition to affirmation, Brown pursues critical realism and its CPUSA associations through pointed criticism of institutions and trends that tend to threaten African American life. For example, Brown is consistently critical of the African American clergy and is often skeptical of institutionalized Christianity. The CPUSA's sense of religion essentially being "accommodationist," "Maumee Ruth," for example, sharply depicts the impotency of Christianity to rationalize a tragic life and an equally tragic death. So too, "Memphis Blues" seems to supplant a religious vision of the end of time with a thoroughly secular one, thus questioning the Christian notion of apocalypse. But most obviously, "Slim Hears the Call" spoofs the African American clergy as a group largely given to money-making and self-aggrandizement, rather than to believers and Christ's teachings.

Although Brown does celebrate black Christianity, most notably in "Sister Lou," "Strong Men," and "New Steps," Smethurst points out that he consistently chooses spirituals rather than more contemporary and largely urban-based gospel. This emphasis on spirituals begins to reveal a critique of urbanization for African Americans and the general assumption of "progress" associated with black migration to urban centers. Again, the CPUSA's emphasis on folk authenticity (and thus criticism of the corrosive effects of urban life), Brown often "characterizes life in the cities of the North, especially New York City, as fraudulent, pretentious, and downright delusionary and the black immigrants there as similarly pretentious and deluded, if not immoral." "Mecca," the first section of "New St. Louis Blues," and "The New Congo," to name only a few, well illustrate a vapidness, superficiality, or meaninglessness of black life in hostile urban centers. Ultimately for Brown, movement to the city does not necessarily signal progress or greater opportunity. But more often than not, migration results in individuals cut off from the sustaining vitality of folk culture, and thus subject to debased commercialism, inauthenticity, and both cultural and psychic paralysis.

Finally, when his work is read within the larger context of social realism and viewed as more closely associated with CPUSA aesthetics and political agendas, Brown emerges more ac-curately as the aesthetic and conceptual eclectic willing and able to marshal all available resources for his poetic projects. A voracious reader with an encyclopedic memory, Brown continued throughout his career to synthesize the most useful elements of his artistic and political surroundings. Fusing aesthetics and the politics of black representation, Brown wages war on racist stereotyping and caricature, ultimately replacing them with the richly complex humanity found at the heart of modern black life.

Amendment to the Selected Bibliography

PRIMARY SOURCES

Negro Poetry and Drama. Washington, D.C.: The Associates in Negro Folk Education, 1937.
The Collected Poems of Sterling A. Brown. Edited by Michael S. Harper. New York: Harper & Row, 1980. Reprinted Chicago: TriQuarterly Books, 1987.
A Son's Return: Selected Essays of Sterling A. Brown. Edited by Mark A. Sanders. Boston: Northeastern University Press, 1996.

SECONDARY SOURCES

Barnes, Deborah H. " 'The Elephant and the Race Problem': Sterling A. Brown and Arthur P. Davis as Cultural Conservators." *Callaloo* 21, no. 4:985–97 (Fall 1998).
Benston, Kimberly. "Sterling A. Brown's After Son 'When de Saints Go Ma'ching Home' and the Performance of Afro-American Voice." *Callaloo*, nos. 14–15:33–42 (February–May 1982).
Ellison, Ralph. "Richard Wright's Blues." In *The Collected Essays of Ralph Ellison.* Edited by John F. Callahan. New York: Modern Library, 1995. Pp. 128–44.
Jones, Gayl. *Liberating Voices: Oral Tradition in African American Literature.* Cambridge: Harvard University Press, 1991.
Sanders, Mark A. *Afro-Modernist Aesthetics and the Poetry of Sterling A. Brown.* Athens, Ga.: University of Georgia Press, 1999.
Smethurst, James Edward. *The New Red Negro: The Literary Left and African American Poetry, 1930–1946.* New York: Oxford University Press, 1999.

LITERARY JOURNALS

African American Review 31, no. 3 (1997). (Issue includes ten essays on Brown.)
Callaloo 21, no. 4 (Fall 1998). (Issue devoted to Brown.)

OCTAVIA BUTLER
(1947 –)

LISBETH GANT-BRITTON

OCTAVIA BUTLER IS the only African American female to date to have written a substantial body of futuristic fiction. She entered a field dominated for decades almost exclusively by Anglo American males. By introducing female characters of color into the genre commonly known as science fiction, Butler has helped widen it, making it more meaningful to a range of new readers. As meaningful as her work may be, however, it is not gratuitously optimistic. In fact, to read Butler is often to take a deep breath and confront extrapolations about the future that some readers might rather not face.

After receiving largely good reviews but laboring in relative obscurity for years, Butler finally became a member of the science-fiction canon, winning that genre's most prestigious honors, the Hugo Award (which she won in 1983 for "Speech Sounds" and 1985 for "Bloodchild") and the Nebula Award (1984 for "Bloodchild"; *Parable of the Sower* was a finalist in 1994). In 1995, Butler was also awarded a MacArthur Foundation Fellowship for her body of work. Butler's rise to widespread literary recognition for her eleven pithy novels and five terse short stories mirrors many of her own stalwart heroines' quests.

Publishers generally describe Butler's books as science fiction. In some respects, her work fits well within the category. They often demonstrate both the tremendous potential as well as terrifying possible danger of science, and medicine in particular. In the Xenogenesis trilogy, for example, cancer becomes a genetic tool; in the Patternmaster series, some humans become rampaging mutants. Yet Butler is more preoccupied with human development and interaction on a sociocultural plane than with technological innovations such as robots and computers. In her 1979 novel *Kindred*, for example, she provides no technical description at all of how the contemporary protagonist is mysteriously sent back into slavery. (That novel was published as mainstream fiction.) The 1993 *Parable of the Sower* and 1998 *Parable of the Talents* focus on the social and cultural effects of failed technology and politics on individuals, families, and communities in the United States. Butler explores possible ideological responses to these potential crises, such as organized religion and alternative life philosophies.

In considering Butler's overall oeuvre, therefore, it may be more appropriate to use the broader term "speculative fiction" to describe her narrative project. This larger category not only includes science fiction but also encompasses the subgenres of fantasy and contemporary nonrealistic fiction (often known by Robert Scholes's term "fabulation"). However, Butler's response to the genre issue is dismissive. In a 1997 interview, she told Joan Fry, "I would say

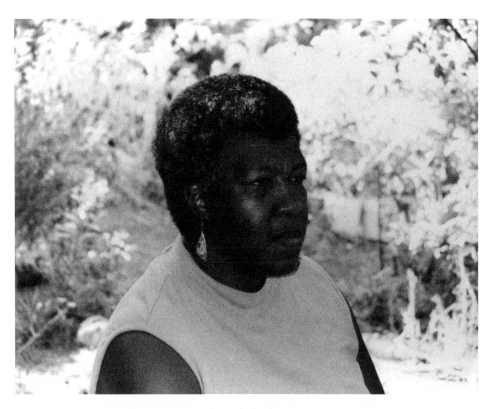

Octavia Butler

that speculative fiction is *any* kind of nonconventional fiction, from Borges to Isaac Asimov. But I don't make any distinction." Later, she explained, "I write about people who do extraordinary things. It just turned out that it was called science fiction."

Butler's no-nonsense approach to genre is typical of her lean, wry prose, which although fantastic and futuristic, has a gritty, down-to-earth feel. Her work may be more specifically categorized as feminist speculative fiction, according to Marleen Barr's broad definition of the genre in the 1987 *Alien to Femininity: Speculative Fiction and Feminist Theory.* Barr includes "feminist utopias, science fiction, fantasy, and sword and sorcery" literature in feminist speculative fiction. Butler, whose protagonists are primarily women, calls herself "a feminist always," although her equal concern with non-gender-specific oppression resonates with Alice Walker's idea of "womanism," in which works highlight modes of domination for males as well as females. In a 1979 interview

with Veronica Mixon, Butler declared, "Where is there a society in which men and women are honestly considered equal? What would it be like to live in such a society? Where do people not despise each other because of race or religion, class or ethnic origin?"

Butler's body of work spans multiple genres of science, speculative, and feminist fiction and examines a host of interrelating themes. She addresses science fiction's concern with the implications of technology—both its destructive and beneficial potential—often envisioning the America of the future as a postindustrial wasteland. Her works frequently critique the assumptive equation of the future with "progress." Butler's speculation about humanity in the twenty-first century and beyond examines humans' relationship to disease, genetics, and medicine and the impact advances in these fields could have on the evolution of the human race. In light of these phenomena, she further considers the tenuous position of people of color in the social landscape of centuries to

96

OCTAVIA BUTLER

come and how the lives of individuals are affected by the clash of competing political and economic forces and ideologies. Butler is especially interested in the role played by all women in the future, most especially women of color. Her feminist concerns include the exercise of agency by independent women of color, as well as shifting definitions of the family and sexuality in an increasingly posthuman society.

On a metathematic level, Butler helps define a futuristic tradition that has had few African American participants, male or female, until the 1990s. One of the exceptions is Pauline Hopkins, who as early as 1902 wrote visionary works containing elements that today one would describe as science fiction. Hopkins' novel about the past and the future, *Of One Blood or, the Hidden Self*, was serialized in the esteemed middle-class magazine *The Colored American*. After an interval of many years, several African American males began to publish science fiction and fantasy. In 1931, George Schuyler wrote *Black No More: Being an Account of the Strange and Wonderful Workings of Science in the Land of the Free, A.D. 1933–1940*, and in 1933–1939, he published *Black Empire*. But it was not until the 1960s, when Samuel R. Delany began publishing, that African American science fiction began to take off. Delany produced a range of material including fiction such as the 1966 *Babel-17* and his postmodern opus *Dhalgren* in 1974. He was also a major black theorist on issues of race, feminism, and sexuality in speculative fiction. Other African American male writers include Steven Barnes, who published *The Descent of Anansi* (with Larry Niven) in 1982, and Charles R. Saunders, who wrote the first of his African-inspired adventure fantasies, the Imaro trilogy, in 1961. Today, African American females who have published speculative fiction include Jewelle Gomez, with her 1991 futuristic vampire work *The Gilda Stories*, and more recently, Afro-Canadian Nalo Hopkinson, with the 1998 novel *Brown Girl in the Ring*.

Until the rise of feminism, most women of any race who wanted to publish speculative or science fiction tended to do so under male pseudonyms. For example, "James Tiptree" was discovered to be Alice Sheldon. Ursula Le Guin focused on male heroes in many of her novels, as in her 1969 novel *The Left Hand of Darkness*. In 1975, Joanna Russ caused controversy with her feminist utopia, *The Female Man*. By 1971, Butler had already set out on these uncertain waters, publishing her first short story, "Crossover" in the Clarion Science Fiction and Fantasy Writers' Workshop anthology in that same year. Five years later, her first novel, *Patternmaster*, finally appeared. With "a lot of ideas stored up," she wrote a book a year for the next five years, interspersed with short fiction. The effort eventually resulted in her 1993 novel, *Parable of the Sower*, being named a *New York Times* Notable Book of the Year in 1994. That same year, the novel was also cited as one of the New York Public Library's Top seventy-five Books of the Year.

Biography

Octavia Estelle Butler was born on June 22, 1947, in Pasadena, California, an only child. Her mother, Octavia Margaret Guy, had been pregnant with four boys before Octavia was born; three were miscarried, one was stillborn. Her father, Laurice James Butler, died when she was seven, primarily from overindulgence in food and drink. Butler's family on her maternal side is from southern Louisiana, a site that inspired her 1980 novel *Wild Seed*. As eldest daughter, the mother Octavia had to be taken out of school to help the family eke out a living on the plantation where they worked. Later in California, and by then a widow, the mother briefly considered remarriage but eventually chose against it. Young Octavia grew up in the shadow of her late maternal grandfather, a strict fundamentalist Baptist, who had forbidden dancing, makeup, and movies. These restrictions, coupled with young Octavia's height (she grew to be almost six feet tall), resulted in her becoming "painfully shy" as a teenager. "I believed I was ugly and stupid," she recalled. "I hid out in a big pink notebook—one that would hold a whole ream of paper. I made myself a universe in it. There could be a magic horse, a

Martian, a telepath. . . . There I could be any-where but here, any time but now, with any people but these."

Yet Butler also remembers being revivified at being able to "look up and see the stars and re-alizing there are parts of the world that human beings don't dominate" while visiting her ma-ternal grandmother's small chicken ranch in 1960 in the high desert near Barstow. The doz-ens of discarded books her mother brought home from the families for whom she did do-mestic work also kindled young Octavia's vivid imagination. In part to compensate for her own scant education, Mrs. Butler continually sought to help her daughter learn more. Reading to her until she was six, her mother enthusiastically secured a library card for Octavia as soon as she asked for one.

Her mother also encouraged Octavia to write. By her tenth birthday, the youngster was al-ready "pecking out stories two-fingered" on an ancient Remington typewriter her mother had scrimped to purchase. Butler credits her mother's unadulterated concern with causing her first epiphany about writing: "I was age ten. I was working on a story, and in a very natural way, my mother said, 'So, you might become a writer.' I thought, 'What? You mean people can be writers for a living?' "

By her twelfth birthday in 1959, Butler was eagerly writing complete stories, deciding she could do better than a science-fiction movie she saw called *Devil Girl from Mars*. She adopted the motto she learned in her archery class, "to aim high." Fortunately, she took this advice over that of a well-meaning aunt, who assured her that "Negroes can't be writers." A kindly science teacher helped thirteen-year-old Octa-via type her first efforts. After graduating from Pasadena's John Muir High School, she went on to take writing courses in addition to regular classes at Pasadena City College. Normally a two-year program, Butler took three years since she had to work. After graduating with a His-tory degree in 1968, she continued taking as-sorted courses at California State University, Los Angeles, but did not receive a degree. She took more writing classes at the Extension and Writers' Guild West at the University of Cali-fornia, Los Angeles, where she studied under Harlan Ellison. Later, he would mentor her at the Clarion Writers' Workshop, which would be the real starting point toward her goal of be-ing a professional writer.

At age eighteen, Butler received her first re-muneration for writing, all of fifteen dollars, winning a collegewide writing competition. It was enough to keep her going despite the fact that she would not publish her first short story until 1971. After college, she worked at a series of "terrible little jobs," everything from factory and warehouse work to food processing, clean-ing, clerical employment, and literacy tutoring. During that time, she developed the habit of rising at three o'clock in the morning to write (a habit she later changed to seven o'clock), de-scribing her dogged persistence as a "positive obsession." She elaborated in her 1993 essay, "Furor Scribendi," insisting that positive obses-sion is "a rage for writing . . . [a] burning need to write. . . . Call it anything you like; it's a use-ful emotion."

Butler was twenty-three before she sold her first two short stories at Clarion. One of them, "Crossover," was published in the workshop's paperback anthology in 1971. The other, al-though purchased by Harlan Ellison for possible inclusion in one of his anthologies, was never published. Unfortunately, Butler would have to endure "five more years of rejection slips and horrible little jobs . . . before [she] sold another word."

Butler's young adulthood was an amalgam of misery and motivation. Tall, statuesque, and writing constantly, she perplexed most of her young male contemporaries:

> I was miserable and worried that I was never going to do any better. I was the odd person, always writing or reading. People thought I was strange. They'd ask me, 'if you're not in school, why are you reading a book?' It was rough. Of course, at the time, I didn't know if I was going to succeed. I kept giving up writing like people give up cigarettes. A few days would go by and there I'd be, writing again. Writing was all that mattered. I kept going because I had to.

Eventually Butler realized that writing mattered to her even more than marriage: "I contemplated getting married once. But I discovered that the man in question thought writing was something silly I would get over when I started having kids. The relationship didn't go well after that. Eventually, we wandered away from each other. So, I got married to the writing."

Butler has described herself as being content to produce literature rather than children, calling herself "a hermit" at heart. After living almost exclusively in California, she moved in 1999 to a comfortable house in Seattle, Washington, not long after her mother died. Butler's mother, whom circumstances had forced away from intellectual pursuits, did live to see her offspring receive science fiction's highest literary accolades. For a daughter who painstakingly scribbled her first stories in the "cast-off notebooks" her mother brought home, Butler's oeuvre seems a fitting progeny indeed.

Patternmaster Series

Butler spent the years from 1971 to 1976 unsuccessfully imitating male pulp science fiction. She finally found her own voice in her first published novels, the Patternmaster series. The five books include *Patternmaster* (1976), *Mind of My Mind* (1977), *Survivor* (1978), *Wild Seed* (1980), and *Clay's Ark* (1984). In them, Butler takes the ostensibly gruesome and brutal subject matter of plague and resultant mutation, as well as eugenics, and fashions a complex inquiry into issues of power and domination, utopia and anti-utopia. In 1984, she wrote to Sandra Govan, "I began writing about power because I had so little."

Butler did not write the series in chronological order; *Wild Seed* begins the historic story line. The main male character in *Wild Seed* is a four-thousand-year-old Nubian named Doro, a vampire-like creature who continues to live by inhabiting one host body after another. Doro has heightened psychic powers that enable him to find others with potentially paranormal abilities. He decides to breed a superior species in

a network of extended families and communities that eventually take him into the nineteenth and twentieth centuries and to the United States.

Doro's main adversary is Anyanwu, a three-hundred-year-old Igbo (Onitsha) priestess and healer, whom he covets for his omnivorous project: "She was wild seed of the best kind. She would strengthen any line he bred her into, strengthen it immeasurably." However, Anyanwu, who is more beneficent, is repulsed and uses her ability as a shape-shifter to elude him. As Govan has observed, "In each of the published novels, the implicit struggle for power revolves around explicit conflicts of will and the contests of survival a heroine endures."

Anyanwu is a prime example of the kind of heroines Butler depicts. Strong-willed, physically capable, and usually endowed with some extra mental or emotional ability such as empathy, they nonetheless must often endure brutally harsh conditions as they attempt to exercise some degree of agency. It is also important to note that the female protagonists never come out unscathed. They must always compromise in some way, physically or emotionally, in their attempt to negotiate and somehow overcome systems of domination. After one hundred years of the chase, Anyanwu finally decides that suicide is her only escape. Doro, who does not want to face eternity alone, finally compromises, but only slightly. He agrees not to use her close relations as fodder for his new bodies. In making Doro bend to her will in the name of love, even begrudgingly, Anyanwu achieves a degree of victory. It is this kind of shading of implicit and explicit power that interests Butler.

The idea of such control in the hands of a group of superhuman people, some of whom might be black, becomes the intriguing basis for the series as a whole. In *Patternmaster*, Doro has fathered a line of telepaths with paranormal powers. The members of this group grapple with one another as they plan to take over the United States. In both *Patternmaster* and *Mind of My Mind*, Doro and his descendants are able to communicate in a giant "mental universe," or "pattern" of psionic or paranormal energy. In *Patternmaster*, Rayal, one of Doro's many sons and feudal lord of his own fiefdom, ruthlessly tests his sons, Teray and Coransee, by pitting one against the other for succession. However, it is Amber, Teray's lover and a healer, who uses her own abilities as a "terrifyingly efficient killer" and compassionate woman to help destroy his arrogant brother. Only through her intervention does Teray win. Amber, an example of Butler's feminist and humanist narrative project, intervenes because she discovers Teray has latent healing power himself. Thus, the text suggests that even though the male character may be flawed and violent, a strong but humanistic female may force him to change. When Teray offers Amber marriage as a prize, she reminds him that she plans to rule her own feudal domain: "What if I asked you to be my lead husband?"

As Frances Smith Foster has observed, "Butler makes it clear that these women, powerful and purposeful in their own right, need not rely upon eroticism to gain their ends. . . . Butler's females are usually healers, teachers, artists, mothers. Yet they are not the traditional literary Earth Mothers or Culture Bearers. They exercise direct authority." In Amber's case, she refuses to marry Teray, relying instead on her own political power. She also informs him that she prefers her own power as a female: "When I meet a woman who attracts me, I prefer women. . . . And when I meet a man who attracts me, I prefer men." (Bisexuality as an emblem of female independence is featured in Butler's *Parable of the Talents* as well.)

In *Patternmaster*'s equally violent sequel, *Mind of My Mind,* Butler juxtaposes another extremely strong-willed, independent female with a potentially dominating male. Mary, a young black woman from a poor neighborhood and with latent paranormal ability, must match wits with and eventually overcome her Patternist father/lover, the nearly immortal Doro. Mary demonstrates in this novel that being a loner and survivor can enable a female character to move from objectification to a more independent subject position. Similarly, Alanna, the Afro-Asian protagonist in *Survivor,* although not a paranormal, has many of Mary's powerful survivor attributes. On Earth, as one of the Mutes, she has to live off the land, fighting and killing to survive in the warlike conditions there. But she escapes with a group of missionaries who seek to get away from the warring Patternists and Clayarks. Like the protagonist in the Xenogenesis trilogy that follows, Alanna's is a struggle of interiority versus exteriority. She is the only human who risks getting to know the new planet's indigenous species intimately. An ostensibly marginalized Other like them, she is the only human open to more than superficial change, and to humane coexistence with the humanlike Kohn and Garkohn who already inhabit the planet. Unlike the missionaries, she eventually compromises her definition of what constitutes "humanity" and mates with one of the intelligent blue fur-covered species on the new planet.

In *Clay's Ark,* the series' final novel, Butler returns to earth to extend her unsettling scenario of a planet on the brink of chaos and destruction. Fascinated with disease as both a positive and negative agent of change, she posits a scenario in which a powerful parasite uses an astronaut's body as a host when he returns home after a failed space mission. The parasite threatens to turn the entire United States into a population of highly evolved mutants. The setting is the Mojave Desert, just at the California border. Walled, gated enclaves and armored passenger vehicles have become the order of the day in large cities. The lone astronaut has survived an emergency crash landing in the desert. He is aware of, but helpless to combat, a microorganism that is now directing his life. Under its influence, he develops heightened sensory and physical powers and eventually controls a small isolated enclave of desert dwellers. Driven by the tiny "alien" within, he directs mating among them, including two young Palos Verdes twins (early prototypes of "Valley Girl" vacuity) who happen by with their father.

As the macabre tale twists, most of the females in the desert group give birth not to humans but to a new mutant species. While the transformation includes biological enhancements (one person's leukemia begins to heal), it also creates half-humans, half-quadrupeds described as resembling Sphinxes. They come to be known as "Clayarks." Butler uses plague imagery (noting she had rabies in mind), so that a single scratch is sufficient to contaminate other humans. One of the hapless carriers remarks, "In a few months we'll be one of the few sane enclaves left in the country—maybe in the world." The novel concludes with the Clayarks running rampant, soon to begin their mindless attacks on the Mutes and Patternists. The carnage foreshadows the devastated urban landscape that eventually appears in *Parable of the Sower*. That novel's future inhabitants are terrorized not by physical mutants but by drug-induced "crazies":

> San Francisco is burning. . . . Maybe uninfected people are sterilizing the city in the only way they can think of. Or maybe it's infected people crazy with their symptoms. . . . In Louisiana there's a group that has decided the disease was brought in by foreigners—so they're shooting anyone who seems a little odd to them. Mostly Asians, blacks, and browns. . . . It will be chaos. Then a new order. Hell, a new species.

This passage exemplifies Hoda Zaki's observation that Butler's views on human nature and politics "serve as a critique of the contemporary social order and as the foundation for her utopian and dystopian vision." As Zaki notes, the microorganism only completes the destruction begun by humans.

When *Patternmaster* and *Mind of My Mind* begin, an active war is already raging between rampaging hordes of Clayarks, who exist amid the ruins of long-devastated cities, and the Mutes, closest to today's humans, who possess no extrasensory powers and who serve as slaves to the third group, the mentally superior Patternists. The narrative structure of blood feuds is a futuristic version of the romantic adventure stories and fantasies on which Butler cut her teeth. They feature familiar tropes of hierarchical familial and social structures including feudal lords and ladies with great houses whose lineage must be maintained, and battles among descendants, including horses, hunting, guns, and coming-of-age quests.

"Bloodchild"

After the Patternmaster series, Butler embarked on a very different kind of planetary saga in her subsequent Xenogenesis trilogy. But before she did, she explored similar ideas in her most powerful short story to date, "Bloodchild" (1984), which contains some of the same thematic elements as the Xenogenesis series and could be considered as a prelude to it. The frightening futuristic dilemma in "Bloodchild" involves humans who have had to escape to another planet for survival. Butler skillfully reverses the trope of animal captivity and breeding to make humans the Other. The captive humans stand in for people of color and other oppressed people who throughout history were kept in bondage and forced to serve those in power. By placing the animal-like creatures in control but also making them dependent on the earthlings, Butler also destabilizes the self-other binary of power and domination.

In "Bloodchild," Butler crafts a relationship between a Terran family and the Tlics, beings whom the earthlings offer a specialized service in exchange for protection and shelter in the Preserve allowed them. Through intimate dialogue between T'Gatoi, one of the high officials who has had a long relationship with the family, and Gan, raised to serve her, the reader discovers the eerie truth about the nature of this service. The Tlic are huge serpent-caterpillars who use warm-blooded human bodies as sites in which to lay their eggs. Thus "impregnated," the humans carry the Tlic larvae to term. Once the "grubs" are mature, a female Tlic cuts open the host with one of her sharp limbs in a painful, near-lethal "blood ceremony." The reader then discovers that Gan is a boy and that human males, not females, have this dangerous duty so that women are free to carry fetuses, more human fodder for further Tlic breeding.

Regarding Butler's human-animal trope, Elyce Rae Helford has observed that "through this destabilizing metaphorization, the complexity of human-alien relations allows us to see the degree to which species, like gender and race, is primarily a matter of who has the power to construct and label whom." Critics such as Helford and Larry McCaffery highlight the slavery metaphors in this narrative. Yet in a 1990 interview, Butler insisted to McCaffery, "I don't agree [with the slavery metaphor], although this may depend on what we mean by 'slavery.' . . . What I'm really talking about is symbiosis." She elaborated on this in her 1995 afterword to the story. Besides wanting to write a story to ease her fear of parasitic insects like the botfly, she wondered what it would really be like if humans had to move to an already inhabited planet: "I tried to write a story about paying the rent. . . . It wouldn't be the British Empire in space, and it wouldn't be *Star Trek*. Sooner or later the humans would have to make some kind of accommodation with their . . . hosts." In either case, as Helford has suggested, we learn from this disturbing story that "power relations ultimately determine the construction of identity." Who indeed are the "aliens"?

The Xenogenesis Trilogy

Alienism is also one of the dominant themes in Butler's 1987 *Dawn*, the first novel of her Xenogenesis trilogy. ("Xenogenesis" means production of offspring permanently unlike the parent.) This text asks the reader to rethink gender and race from the standpoint of the construction of difference, by positing yet another drastic situation in which humans must interact with a species from another world in order to survive. In *Dawn*, Earth is no longer habitable after a final nuclear holocaust. The Oankali, who travel in a spaceship nearly as large as a planet, gather up as many still-living humans as they can find. The Oankali are interested in the humans because they need to "trade" genes every so many generations in order to survive. They place most of the humans in suspended animation while they repair the earth. After 250 years, Lilith Iyapu, a black woman, is "Awakened" (Butler's capitalization). Because of her genetic makeup and stable personality, she is named leader of the first group of humans who will be allowed to return to the nearly restored planet. Butler calls her protagonist the

new "first mother" of the restored Earth. Lilith is the name of the woman said to have been excised from portions of the biblical account of the world's origins. She is also reputed to have given birth to monsters after being banished. Butler, therefore, seems to be making a statement about the exclusion of nonprivileged people, in particular women, from official sanction and recognition in the world, in spite of any crucial role they may play in it.

On a broader scale, the Xenogenesis trilogy severely critiques present-day systems of domination on Earth in general. Butler uses the "alien" species to decry what she sees as a problematic inborn human trait: a hierarchical tendency, which, linked with human aggression, results in what she considers to be disastrously self-destructive consequences for humanity. When the trilogy opens, this will to hierarchize and dominate has already resulted in Earth's destruction by nuclear disaster. The texts suggest that these tendencies toward power contribute to the inability of many of the survivors to believe that a species that looks deformed could be their equal. This arrogance nearly sabotages their chances of returning to the restored planet at all. Furthermore, the unwillingness of some to accept a black woman as leader rekindles tendencies toward racialism. Feminist theorist Donna Haraway devotes almost half a chapter of *Primate Visions* to *Dawn* and refers in "A Cyborg Manifesto" to Butler as one of her "theorists for cyborgs."

The 1988 *Adulthood Rites* and 1989 *Imago* continue to be concerned with the problematics of predatory and prideful tendencies as they affect human evolution. The Oankali finally relent in their seemingly inexorable pursuit of gene trading and allow a small band of human "resistors" to set up a colony on Mars. In trying to re-create familial and social structures away from the Oankali, however, the humans retreat to the same violent and hierarchical structures that put them there in the first place. Their situation is exacerbated by the fact that the Oankali have sterilized them, ostensibly for their own good. At one point, the rebellious humans steal Lilith's "construct" human-Oankali child, Akin, and attempt to hack off his Medusa-like

OCTAVIA BUTLER

sensory tentacles in an unfeeling effort to render his appearance more "human." Despite this danger, Akin studies the resistors and eventually comes to understand them. He goes on to mediate between the humans and Oankalis.

In *Imago*, the Oankali continue their gene experiments from Lilith's cancer cells, with unpredictable results. Lilith gives birth to Jodahs, another of her many "construct" hybrid children. This time, however, it is neither male nor female but a combination of human and ooloi, the third-sex creature with whom earthlings and Oankali mate. It has powers even the Oankali do not possess: it shape-shifts, can heal wounds and even regenerate limbs, and most important, may alter DNA with a touch. The youngster Jodahs must learn to heal or kill, give life or destroy it; otherwise the shape-shifter could mutate others and its environment accidentally. Eric White reads such transformation as empowering: "The advent of shapeshifters able to transform themselves at will enables maximally flexible and innovative responsiveness to heterogeneous situations." AnnLouise Keating, on the other hand, sees Jodahs as "the first of a new, potentially deadly species. . . . Jodahs represents a form of difference that even the Oankali fear."

There is a clear subtext regarding the perils of ignoring the troubling aspects of genetic engineering. Yet the creation of a third species—one potentially more powerful than either the humans or the Oankalis—invites the reader to reconsider what we traditionally think of as creation. The implication is that identity formation, as it is known today, is a mere fraction of what it may become. Furthermore, by juxtaposing Jodahs' seemingly unlimited potential with Lilith's relatively limited reproductive role, the trilogy also asks the reader to remember that a breakthrough in one aspect of society does not necessarily mean change in all others.

In that regard, Eva Cherniavsky is concerned with *Dawn* as a demonstration of "Lilith's sexual and reproductive agency" as a subaltern woman, in effect cast back into slavery whereby once again the black woman's body is "coded as breeder. . . . She [Cherniavsky] argues that by aligning elite reproductive practices with the

body of the female subaltern, Butler effects a strategic refiguration of the [contemporary] fertility clinic (and its ethos of voluntarism) as captive breeding zone." In Xenogenesis and other texts, Butler explores the psychic and physical stress of the continual silent threat to many people of color in America. Even though seemingly far-fetched, the threat is a potential for reactionary forces suddenly to snatch them back into a servile state. Butler's novel *Kindred* illustrates this concern.

Kindred

In *Kindred*, first published in 1979, protagonist Dana Franklin is startlingly and mysteriously transported back and forth from California in 1976 to antebellum Maryland in 1815. During these encounters, she experiences actual slavery and finds herself on the very plantation where her forebears had to toil. There she will have to save the life of Rufus Weylin, a young white slave owner who will eventually, through rape, become her own great-grandfather. In the contemporary portion of *Kindred*, Butler uses the convention of the fictional memoir. But when her narrator time travels into the past, the style resembles that of a slave narrative. On both levels of narration, Butler's didactic project as a science-fiction writer involves critiquing the present along with the past.

Dana is yanked back allegorically into the past and into an era in which she is stripped of her authority as an individual. This text implies that this may happen to anyone. The so-called gains of progress may be more illusory for people of color than one thinks, Butler suggests. As plantation owner Tom Weylin remarks, "Educated don't mean smart." Later in the novel, Dana comments to her contemporary husband, Kevin, that even though she has returned to modern times, "she no longer feels safe." (This comment is further complicated by the fact that Kevin is white.) Dana's observations, combined with her subsequent reading about the atrocities of Nazi Germany, lead her to perceive herself as living at an anxiety-provoking intersection of past, present, and future.

103

The painful reality of an African American woman's struggle for authority is an especially powerful theme in *Kindred*, although it appears in all of Butler's works. Dana's experience of being thrust back in time, and into the role of having to "mother" her own forebears so that she may eventually be born herself, leads to a direct challenge to many of her most-cherished contemporary beliefs about social equality and personal freedom. Like many of the readers, she has glibly contended that if she were a slave, she would never put up with its humiliations. But when she is hurtled back in time, beaten, threatened with sexual abuse, and frightened out of her wits, she must confront the painful specter of compromise for her survival. As noted previously, many of Butler's heroines must compromise in order to stay alive. Practical realists, often with children and other family or community members dependent on them for survival, they must do so. From the standpoint of conventional western science-fiction adventures, these female protagonists are decidedly antiheroic. Yet they seem in line with the hard-headed pragmatists Butler describes her mother and grandmother as having been.

The Parable Novels

The theme of pragmatic compromise for survival also underlies Butler's Parable novels, in which the main character, Lauren Olamina, struggles to create a new community, even a new world, amid the perilous breakdown of mid-twenty-first-century America. In *Parable of the Sower*, which takes place in the year 2025, America's entire West Coast is barely livable. A few wealthy communities outside of Los Angeles continue to prosper within heavily guarded walled compounds, virtual fortresses. But many members of the middle class, which barely exists in any ethnicity, are increasingly forced to become virtual slaves to the few remaining multinational corporations. Most of them work for subsistence incomes and vie to be hired by completely privatized "company towns," even though they know that they will be subsumed eventually by their debts to the corporation, much like debt slaves or sharecroppers.

The elder Olaminas, parents of the protagonist Lauren, an eighteen-year-old African American woman, represent the marginalized middle class. Lauren's father and his second wife, Corazon, a Latina, both have doctorates, but the university, barely alive itself, can only employ the father one day per week. For this, he must brave leaving their walled community for a long bicycle ride with a pistol strapped to his side, beneath his book bag. The family, like others in their neighborhood, survives by growing food in their backyard and harvesting local fruit trees. This depiction of the Olaminas demonstrates the result of a narrowly focused denial toward society's ills. There is nothing to be done about the larger problems of the world, the couple insists. The world outside of the Olamina's walls is the enemy; the most important thing is to hold on to one's own. Father Olamina has harsh advice for his loved ones: "There's nobody to help us but God and ourselves. I protect Moss's place in spite of what I think of him, and he protects mine, no matter what he thinks of me. We all look out for one another." The elder Olaminas, owners of their home and possessors of graduate degrees, represent the last generation of twentieth-century Americans to have been socialized to aspire to and at least partially fulfill some measure of the American Dream. But their version of coping does not suffice for daughter Lauren. Arguing to herself, she insists: "But God exists to be shaped. It isn't enough for us to just survive, limping along, playing business as usual while things get worse and worse. . . . There has to be more that we can do, a better destiny that we can shape. Another place. Another way. Something!" In contrast to Lauren's more radical reactions, the Olaminas find themselves located at the intersection of a conservative worldview, which focuses narrowly on the past and present, and their daughter's newly emerging, more radical one, which embraces change as necessary, even though threatening.

Butler seeks to dramatize the creative power inherent in the exploration of symbolic systems. Like other female characters of Butler,

Lauren struggles to create a new liberating meaning from an oppressive situation. She personifies the battle to overcome mental and physical subalternization by developing a new creed that she memorializes in "Earthseed: The Books of the Living." It is a combination predominantly of Christianity and Buddhism, which accepts "change as . . . the only lasting truth." In one passage from "Earthseed," Lauren observes:

> When apparent stability disintegrates,
> As it must—
> God is Change—
> People tend to give in
> To fear and depression. . . .
> They remember old hates and generate new
>   ones,
> They create chaos and nurture it.
> They kill and kill and kill . . .
> Until they are exhausted or destroyed . . .
> Or until one of them becomes
> A leader
> Most will follow,
> Or a tyrant
> Most fear.

With this belief as her basis, even when her family is eventually murdered by the looting homeless, Lauren escapes and leads another makeshift "family" north to freedom. She and her Earthseed comrades search for a location where they may found a new community. Eventually, the group sets up a homestead, which they dub Acorn. They choose that name because of the acorn bread they have learned to eat to survive. ("My mother and grandmother were survivors," Butler reminisced to Mixon in 1979.) Harvesting acorns also refers to the biblical "parable of the sower," about a man who went to sow his seed in a troubled land. Some of it fell by the wayside; some fell upon a rock. But some fell on good ground "and sprang up and bore fruit an hundredfold" (Luke 8:5–8). This religious imagery is picked up in Butler's sequel, *Parable of the Talents,* as is the quest motif.

The first novel ends with Lauren hoping eventually to escape the dying civilization on earth altogether and found a new colony on another planet, possibly Mars. Butler does not reveal whether Lauren successfully completes her quest until the end of *Parable of the Talents.* In the sequel, Lauren becomes simply Olamina. Here, as in most of Butler's novels, naming is significant. In this case, the single name is a signal of Lauren's developing maturity and her eventual status as Earthseed matriarch by the end of the second book. By the conclusion, her initial ragtag group has grown into a wealthy, influential, and nationally recognized organization, members of which do finally set off for Mars.

The central conflict in the second book centers on Olamina and her estranged daughter, originally named Larkin but who later renames herself Ashe Vere ("truth" or "righteousness"). The young woman does not know her mother because they were separated ever since she, as an infant, was kidnapped by radical Christians called Crusaders, bent on returning the country to fundamentalist values. In the confused mid–twenty-first century of this novel, many ideologies compete for the population's attention as the country attempts to return from the brink of complete societal collapse brought on by a string of inept presidents and megalomaniacal transnational corporations.

Butler employs a form of double narration to demonstrate the crumbling ideologies' unhealthy impact on families and communities throughout the country. The narration shifts back and forth spatiotemporally between the now-deceased Olamina (depicted by her journal entries, which form the core narrative) and daughter Ashe Vere's point of view, which forms the frame narrative. Ashe Vere serves as skeptical observer of her mother's Earthseed ideology and difficult but dedicated life. Filtered through the young woman's critical gaze, the reader learns about her mother's efforts to spread Earthseed widely and to foster change, in spite of Olamina's own brother Marc, a converted Christian. The mother-daughter duo teaches us as much from their losses as from their gains. They become metaphors of motion, embodying the essence of black women's efforts to simultaneously envision incremental changes and radical transformations not only within black communities but throughout the world as well.

The mother-daughter-uncle separation is emblematic. Not only does it reveal ways in which ideology may put further pressure on already-fragmented familial units, but the family's final, somewhat conditional, reconciliation also prompts the reader to reflect on how the basic definition and function of the family unit may change radically during the twenty-first century. In her work, Butler experiments with various intersubjective affiliations in conceptualizing familial units. These range from interracial combinations (as in *Kindred*) to relationships that span generations (as in the youthful/older Olamina/Bankole marriage in the Parable novels) to interspecies couplings (as in *Survivor* and *Dawn*). Only occasionally and in passing does Butler touch on issues of bisexuality or androgyny in her books. *Parable of the Talents* contains a brief and ultimately noneventful scene in which Olamina momentarily considers, then reconsiders, a homosexual encounter. With the exception of passing references (such as a brief comment by Amber in *Patternmaster*), relationships in Butler's fiction almost invariably concern the trope of heterosexual mating, and marriage involves a variation on the conventional familial unit.

Butler continues to problematize the benefits and threats of medicine by pointing to its powerful effect on humanity's mental and emotional as well as physical health. In *Parable of the Sower*, Lauren is born hyperempathetic because her mother took a "genius" drug meant to enhance intelligence. The drug's side effect does not become apparent until the second generation. In the novel's present time, daughter Lauren cannot control her feelings: she shares others' pain and pleasure even when she does not want to do so. For instance, in *Parable of the Sower*, she bleeds when her brother only pretends to be injured. Here the novel seems to take up where Philip K. Dick left off in his 1968 *Do Androids Dream of Electric Sheep?* (which was later adapted into the 1982 film *Blade Runner*, directed by Ridley Scott). In *Parable of the Sower*'s nearly defunct mid–twenty-first-

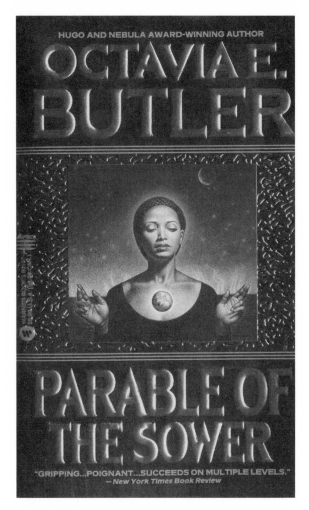

The cover for Butler's 1993 novel
Parable of the Sower.

century United States, empathy, the quality that helps people treat each other in a humane manner and not like objects, has all but disappeared. As Dick highlights in his novel, so too does Butler point out in *Parable of the Sower* that it may be difficult to continue life as we know it if American society does not have this important glue to hold it together. In many of her texts, Butler offers empathetic female protagonists willing to risk what little safety they have to help others through the mental and emotional trauma of dysfunctional conditions. These women range from the urban character Valerie in the short story "Speech Sounds" to the more primeval Anyanwu in *Wild Seed.*

Short Stories

Butler's unconventionality derives more from her often shocking extrapolations of how future relationships might develop amid the pressures of unpredictable future circumstances. One example occurs in Butler's experimental short story "The Evening and the Morning and the Night" (first published in *Bloodchild and Other Stories* in 1984), which focuses (as does *Clay's Ark*) on a pandemic brought about by human foibles. Scientists develop Hedeonco, a profitable "magic-bullet" cancer cure. The catch is that they find that the next generation of those treated develops a horrible genetic dysfunction known as Duryea-Gode disease (DGD). The gruesome side effect involves a brain disorder that causes adult sufferers to believe they are suffocating in their own skin, at which point, if not caught, they mutilate themselves terribly. Butler depicts a young man and woman who attempt a relationship even though both are carriers of this potentially horrific disease. Do they give up on life and each other because the medical odds seem stacked against them, or do they construct a reality, however limited, that allows them some modicum of a life?

Besides the thematic of interpersonal relations, "The Evening and the Morning and the Night" also calls attention to the problem of "personal responsibility" between the medical community and citizens at large. On the one hand, it signals the devastation that may be wrought in the name of "progress." On the other, it continues Butler's fascination with the ironic possibility that even a disease may have beneficial effects. In "The Evening and the Morning and the Night," DGD sufferers develop tremendous concentration and can perform brilliantly but narrowly, like idiot savants. The trope of medical benefit/medical threat is part of Butler's metatextual argument that neither absolute utopia nor dystopia is probable in American society. Butler problematizes even seemingly beneficial side effects. In *Clay's Ark*, those who are "contaminated" find themselves physically enhanced; in the Xenogenesis series, Lilith's cancer provides a breakthrough for the Oankali's genetic manipulations.

Butler's early short stories such as the 1971 "Crossover" and 1979 "Near of Kin" also display a concern with the risk of mental and emotional illness. Both take place in an indefinite present rather than in the future, but they do contain a glimmer of the emotional reaction to social tension that Butler develops in later futuristic societal characterizations. "Near of Kin" concerns a lonely young single woman who suspects, then finally discovers, that her birth is the result of an incestuous union between her mother and uncle. In typical Butlerean fashion, the text does not moralize; rather, it explores the social and emotional impetus that has led two lonely people to commit such an act. Similarly, "Crossover" treats a lonely young female factory worker whose "grindingly dull job" finally leads her to hallucination and alcoholism. The short story's nihilistic tone echoes Butler's self-assertion that she is "a pessimist if I'm not careful, a feminist always, a Black, a quiet egoist, a former Baptist, and an oil-and-water combination of ambition, laziness, insecurity, certainty, and drive."

The 1983 "Speech Sounds" is another early example of Butler's concern with possible societal degradation in a near-future America that she would fully develop in the Parable novels. Inspired by the growing tendency toward violence (and an actual fight on a Los Angeles bus Butler witnessed), "Speech Sounds" looks at a future world in which all but a few inhabits have literally lost the ability to speak. They revert to animal-like grunts and behavior, including violent gestures and territorial battles. Valerie Rye, a Los Angeles widow left on her own after her family succumbs to the mysterious disease, must cope with this disaster and the growing danger among ordinary people who attempt to continue to survive: "The illness, if it was an illness, had cut even the living off from one another."

In many of Butler's works, the very ordinariness of her characters and their landscape proves the most chilling. She presents people one sees at the corner store every morning; she extrapolates frightening scenarios straight from the daily news. Thus, readers often feel implicated, asking themselves classic "what if" questions. If current conditions escalated, would they act as the main characters do? In "Speech Sounds," despite the danger, the two main characters overcome their own violent impulses and finally help others. The male, Obsidian, dies for his efforts. Rye stumbles upon two orphaned children who can speak and promises to nurture them. The story's potentially tragic ending is thus tempered by a hopeful tone. But as in *Parable of the Talents* and other of Butler's novels, that hope is rendered as being tenuous at best. Nothing is guaranteed.

During an October 1995 telephone interview with Lisbeth Gant-Britton, Octavia Butler described her books as "cautionary tales." Her texts demonstrate the complex interrelationship between past, present, and future. Matter-of-factly and head-on, Butler presents both the marginalization as well as the pivotal importance of African Americans and other people of color. She demonstrates, on the one hand, that many people of color have been and continue to be buffeted by societal forces seemingly beyond their control. Yet she also shows that one exploited person determined to survive may in fact determine a new course of events for herself and indeed for an entire community or world.

Selected Bibliography

PRIMARY WORKS

NOVELS

Patternmaster Series (five novels)
Patternmaster. Garden City, N.Y.: Doubleday, 1976.
Mind of My Mind. Garden City, N.Y.: Doubleday, 1977.
Survivor. Garden City, N.Y.: Doubleday, 1978.
Wild Seed. Garden City, N.Y.: Doubleday, 1980.
Clay's Ark. New York: St. Martin's Press, 1984.

Single Novel
Kindred. Garden City, N.Y.: Doubleday, 1979. Reprint, with an introduction by Robert Crossley, Boston: Beacon Press, 1988.

Xenogenesis Trilogy
Dawn: Xenogenesis. New York: Warner Books, 1987.
Adulthood Rites: Xenogenesis. New York: Warner Books, 1988.
Imago: Xenogenesis. New York: Warner Books, 1989.
Trilogy reprinted as *Lilith's Brood.* New York: Aspect, Warner Books, 2000.

Parable Diptych
Parable of the Sower. New York: Four Walls Eight Windows Press, 1993.
Parable of the Talents. New York: Seven Stories Press, 1998.

SHORT STORIES

"Bloodchild." *Isaac Asimov's Science Fiction Magazine.* Worcester: Davis Publications, 1984.
"Crossover." In *Clarion: An Anthology of Speculative xFiction and Criticism from the Clarion Writers' Workshop.* Edited by Robin Scott Wilson. New York: New American Library, 1971. Pp. 140–44.
"Near of Kin." In *Chrysalis 4.* Edited by Roy Torgeson. New York: Zebra Books, 1979. Pp. 163–75.
"Speech Sounds." *Isaac Asimov's Science Fiction Magazine* 7:26–40 (December 1983).
L. Ron Hubbard Presents Writers of the Future, Vol. IX: The Year's 17 Best Titles. Edited by Algis Budrys and L. Ron Hubbard. Los Angeles: Bridge Publications, 1993.
Bloodchild and Other Stories. New York: Four Walls Eight Windows Press, 1995.

SECONDARY WORKS

BIOGRAPHICAL AND CRITICAL STUDIES

Allison, Dorothy. "The Future of Female: Octavia Butler's Mother Lode." In *Reading Black, Reading Feminist.* Edited by Henry Louis Gates Jr. New York: Penguin, 1990. Pp. 471–78.
Antczak, Janice. "Octavia E. Butler: New Designs for a Challenging Future." In *African-American Voices in Young Adult Literature: Tradition, Transition, Transformation.* Edited by Karen Patricia Smith. Metuchen, N.J.: Scarecrow Press, 1994. Pp. 311–36.
Barr, Marleen. *Alien to Femininity: Speculative Fiction and Feminist Theory.* New York: Greenwood Press, 1987.
Cherniavsky, Eva. "Subaltern Studies in a U.S. Frame." *Boundary 2* 23:85–110 (Summer 1996).
Dubey, Madhu. "Folk and Urban Communities in African-American Women's Fiction: Octavia Butler's *Parable of the Sower.*" *Studies in American Fiction* 27:103–28 (Spring 1999).
Foster, Frances Smith. "Octavia Butler's Black Female Future Fiction." *Extrapolation* 23:37–49 (Spring 1982).
Friend, Beverly. "Time Travel as a Feminist Didactic in Works by Phillis Einsenstein, Maryls Millhiser, and Octavia Butler." *Extrapolation* 23:50–55 (Spring 1982).
Gant-Britton, Lisbeth. "Octavia Butler's *Parable of the Sower:* One Alternative to a Futureless Future." In *Women of Other Worlds: Excursions through Science Fiction and Feminism.* Edited by Helen Merrick and Tess Williams. Nedlands: University of Western Australia Press, 1999. Pp. 278–94.
Govan Sandra Y. "Connections, Links, and Extended Networks: Patterns in Octavia Butler's Science Fiction." *Black American Literature Forum* 18:82–87 (Summer 1984).

————. "Homage to Tradition: Octavia Butler Renovates the Historical Novel." *MELUS* 13:79–96 (Spring–Summer 1986).

Green, Michelle Erica. " 'There Goes the Neighborhood': Octavia Butler's Demand for Diversity in Utopias." In *Utopian and Science Fiction by Women: Worlds of Difference.* Edited by Jane L. Donawerth and Carol A. Kolmerten. Syracuse, N.Y.: Syracuse University Press, 1994. Pp. 166–89.

Harris, Trudier. "This Disease Called Strength: Some Observations on the Compensating Construction of Black Female Character." *Literature and Medicine* 14, no. 1:109–26 (1995).

Helford, Elyce Rae. " 'Would You Really Rather Die Than Bear My Young?': The Construction of Gender, Race, and Species in Octavia E. Butler's 'Bloodchild.' " *African American Review* 28:259–71 (Summer 1994).

Keating, AnnLouise. "Octavia Butler." In *Contemporary African American Novelists: A Bio-Bibliographical Critical Sourcebook.* Edited by Emmanuel S. Nelson. Westport, Conn.: Greenwood Press, 1999. Pp. 69–75.

Kubitschek, Missy Dehn. "What Would a Writer Be Doing Working out of a Slave Market?" In her *Claiming the Heritage: African-American Women Novelists and History.* Jackson: University Press of Mississippi, 1991. Pp. 24–51.

McHenry, Susan, and Mali Michelle Fleming. "Octavia's Mind Trip into the Near Future." *Black Issues Book Review* 1:14–16, 18 (January–February 1999).

McKible, Adam. " 'These Are the Facts of the Darky's History': Thinking History and Reading Names in Four African American Texts." *African American Review* 28:223–35 (Summer 1994).

Miller, Jim. "Post-Apocalyptic Hoping: Octavia Butler's Dystopian/Utopian Vision." *Science-Fiction Studies* 25:336–60 (July 1998).

Mixon, Veronica. "Futurist Woman: Octavia Butler." *Essence,* April 1979, pp. 12, 15.

Peppers, Cathy. "Dialogic Origins and Alien Identities in Butler's *Xenogenesis.*" *Science-Fiction Studies* 22:47–62 (March 1995).

Phillips, Julie. "Feminist Sci-Fi: A Brave New World." *Ms.,* November–December 1994, pp. 70–73.

Raffel, Burton. "Genre to the Rear, Race and Gender to the Fore: The Novels of Octavia E. Butler." *Literary Review* 38:454–62 (Spring 1995).

Rushdy, Ashraf H. A. "Families of Orphans: Relation and Disrelation in Octavia Butler's *Kindred.*" *College English* 55:135–57 (February 1993).

Salvaggio, Ruth. "Octavia Butler and the Black Science-Fiction Heroine." *Black American Literature Forum* 18:78–81 (Summer 1984).

Shinn, Thelma J. "The Wise Witches: Black Women Mentors in the Fiction of Octavia E. Butler." In *Conjuring: Black Women, Fiction, and Literary Tradition.* Edited by Marjorie Pryse and Hortense J. Spillers. Bloomington: Indiana University Press, 1985. Pp. 203–15.

Weixlmann, Joe. "An Octavia E. Butler Bibliography." *Black American Literature Forum* 18:88–89 (Summer 1984).

White, Eric. "The Erotics of Becoming: *Xenogenesis* and *The Thing.*" *Science-Fiction Studies* 20:394–408 (November 1993).

Zaki, Hoda. "Utopia, Dystopia, and Ideology in the Science Fiction of Octavia Butler." *Science-Fiction Studies* 17:239–51 (July 1990).

INTERVIEWS

Beal, Frences M. "Black Women and the Science Fiction Genre: Interview with Octavia Butler." *Black Scholar* 17:14–18 (March–April 1986).

Fry, Joan. "An Interview with Octavia Butler." *Poets and Writers Magazine,* March–April, 1997, pp. 58–69.

Harrison, Rosalie G. "Sci Fi Visions: An Interview with Octavia Butler." *Equal Opportunity Forum Magazine* 8, no. 2:30–34 (1980).

Jackson, Jerome H. "Sci-Fi Tales from Octavia Butler." *Crisis* 101:4–7 (April 1994).

Kenan, Randall. "An Interview with Octavia Butler." *Callaloo* 14:485–504 (Spring 1991).

McCaffery, Larry. "An Interview with Octavia E. Butler." In *Across the Wounded Galaxies: Interviews with Contemporary American Science Fiction Writers.* Edited by Larry McCaffery. Urbana: University of Illinois Press, 1990. Pp. 54–70.

Potts, Stephen W. " 'We Keep Playing the Same Record': A Conversation with Octavia E. Butler." *Science-Fiction Studies* 23:331–38 (November 1996).

Rowell, Charles H. "An Interview with Octavia E. Butler." *Callaloo* 20:47–66 (Winter 1997).

See, Lisa. "Octavia E. Butler." *Publishers Weekly,* December 13, 1993, pp. 50–51.

RELATED WORKS

Barnes, Steven, with Larry Niven. *The Descent of Anansi.* New York: Tor, 1982; distributed by Pinnacle Books.

Delany, Samuel R. *Babel-17.* New York: Ace Books, 1966.

————. *Dhalgren.* New York: Bantam Books, 1974.

Dick, Philip K. *Do Androids Dream of Electric Sheep?* New York: Random House, 1968.

Gomez, Jewelle. *The Gilda Stories: A Novel.* Ithaca, NY: Firebrand Books, 1991.

Haraway, Donna. "A Cyborg Manifesto: Science, Technology, and Socialist-Feminism in the Late Twentieth Century." In her *Simians, Cyborgs, and Women: The Reinvention of Nature.* New York: Routledge, 1991. Pp. 149–81.

————. *Primate Visions.* New York: Routledge, 1989.

Hopkins, Pauline. "Of One Blood or, the Hidden Self." In her *The Magazine Novels of Pauline Hopkins.* New York and Oxford: Oxford University Press, 1988.

Hopkinson, Nalo. *Brown Girl in the Ring.* New York: Warner Books, 1998.

Le Guin, Ursula. *The Left Hand of Darkness.* New York: Ace Books, 1969.

Russ, Joanna. *The Female Man.* New York: Bantam Books, 1975.

Saunders, Charles R. *Imaro.* New York: Daw Books, 1981.

Schuyler, George [Samuel I. Brooks, pseud.]. *Black Empire.* Edited by Robert A. Hill and R. Kent Rasmussen. Boston: Northeastern University Press, 1991.

(Originally published in the Pittsburgh *Courier,* October 1937 through April 1938.)

————. *Black No More: Being an Account of the Strange and Wonderful Workings of Science in the Land of the Free, A.D. 1933–1940.* College Park, Md.: McGrath, 1969. (Originally published by Macaulay Co., 1931.)

Walker, Alice. *In Search of Our Mothers' Gardens: Womanist Prose.* San Diego: Harcourt Brace Jovanovich, 1983.

CHARLES W. CHESNUTT
(1858–1932)

WILLIAM L. ANDREWS

"I THINK I must write a book," Charles W. Chesnutt wrote in his journal on 29 May 1880 after a long day of teaching in the Colored Normal School of Fayetteville, North Carolina. "It has been my cherished dream," the young man continued, "and I feel an influence that I cannot resist calling me to the task." Few aspiring writers have predicted as accurately as Chesnutt what the thematic crux of their mature work would be:

> The object of my writings would be not so much the elevation of the colored people as the elevation of the whites—for I consider the unjust spirit of caste which is so insidious as to pervade a whole nation, and so powerful as to subject a whole race and all connected with it to scorn and social ostracism—I consider this a barrier to the moral progress of the American people; and I would be one of the first to head a determined, organized crusade against it.
>
> (Helen Chesnutt, p. 21)

The role of literature in such a crusade, Chesnutt decided, should be to "lead people out, imperceptibly, unconsciously, step by step" to the point at which the public mind would be ready to accept the idea of black equality and opportunity.

With these guidelines and goals in mind, Charles W. Chesnutt became the most widely respected African American fiction writer of his era. His work was issued by some of the most prestigious publishers in the United States; it was reviewed more extensively and more thoughtfully than any fiction previously published by a black American. Chesnutt's writing, which appeared during the nadir of African American sociopolitical fortunes, proved him an advocate for the interests of those African Americans with whom he most identified: middle-class mixed-race persons like himself. But he also championed the working-class blacks of the small-town South, whom he had come to know from his youth in North Carolina. Ambitious for national recognition and the financial rewards of literary success, Chesnutt tried his best to create popular novels that would be taken seriously as thoughtful examinations of current social problems. In his own time he failed to win an audience sizable enough to support his attempt to become a full-time, self-supporting man of letters. However, he is now recognized as a literary innovator whose mastery of his craft, particularly in the short story, enabled him to place a distinctive personal signature on his public message.

Charles Waddell Chesnutt was born in Cleveland, Ohio, on 20 June 1858. His parents, Andrew Jackson and Ann Maria Sampson Chesnutt, came from antebellum North Carolina's free black class. After serving in the Union

Army as a teamster, Chesnutt's father took his family back to his home state in 1866 and set up a grocery store in Fayetteville. Charles worked in the family business and attended school until his mother's death in 1871. To help with family expenses, he began teaching, first in Fayetteville (where he was a pupil-teacher at age fourteen) and later in rural schools around Charlotte, North Carolina, while studying on his own, particularly the classics of English and European literature. In 1877 Chesnutt returned to Fayetteville to teach in a normal school for black teachers recently established by the state of North Carolina. Three years later he was appointed principal of that school. In the meantime he had married Susan Perry (1878), the daughter of a prosperous Fayetteville barber, and they had begun a family. Yet Chesnutt was not satisfied. Although he was an African American with features barely distinguishable from those of whites, the young principal knew that his mixed racial heritage was a social liability for him as long as he stayed in the South. In the North, he hoped, a man would be judged by his ability alone, and any prejudice against him could be defeated by hard work and perseverance.

In the spring of 1883 Chesnutt resigned as principal of the normal school and set out for New York City to find employment "in some literary avocation, or something leading in that direction," as he confided to his journal. He was satisfied temporarily with the work he found as a stenographer and reporter, but his long-range goal was loftier. Ever since the publication of Albion Tourgée's *A Fool's Errand* (1879), a best-selling novel about Reconstruction in North Carolina, Chesnutt had been convinced that he, too, could make a name for himself as an author. He reasoned that if a Yankee carpetbagger with a limited knowledge of southern blacks and racial conditions could achieve such literary notoriety, then a black man like himself, who had an insider's view of the same subjects, could write at least as good a book about the South. As he looked to the future, Chesnutt concluded that success in literature offered the most likely means of satisfying his personal ambitions and his sense of moral responsibility

to people of color in America. Chesnutt moved to Cleveland early in 1884, and by May had settled his wife and their three children in comfortable quarters. He started to work in the legal department of the Nickel Plate Railroad, and he made his first mature attempts to break into print.

Beginning in 1885, with a sketch entitled "Uncle Peter's House," Chesnutt's name appeared on works distributed by the S. S. McClure newspaper syndicate, which published most of the humorous sketches and mildly sentimental or didactic squibs that Chesnutt wrote during the late 1880s. Through a friendship with George Washington Cable, the most liberal southern literary figure of the time, Chesnutt began writing for the Open Letter Club, a group of progressive southerners who were interested in constructive solutions to the South's problems. Cable was instrumental in the publication of his protégé's first essay, "What Is a White Man?," an indictment of the South's arbitrary and contradictory laws governing the definition of race, in the *Independent* in 1889. When Cable asked him to become his secretary, Chesnutt was flattered, but the court reporting business he had set up in 1887 seemed too promising to abandon. Besides, he had begun to taste real success as a short-story writer for some of the best magazines in America.

In August 1887, the *Atlantic Monthly* printed Chesnutt's "The Goophered Grapevine," his first important work of fiction. Set in North Carolina and featuring an ex-slave raconteur who could spin wonderful tales about antebellum southern life, "The Goophered Grapevine" appeared to be part of the "plantation tradition" of contemporary southern literature, typified in the work of Joel Chandler Harris and Thomas Nelson Page, who had made their fame writing nostalgic tales of the Old South in black dialect. But Chesnutt's story was singular in two respects: It presented the lore of "conjuration," African American hoodoo beliefs and practices, to a white reading public largely ignorant of black folk culture, and it introduced a new kind of black storytelling protagonist, Uncle Julius McAdoo, who shrewdly adapted his recollections of the past to secure his economic advantage in the present, sometimes at the expense of his white employer. Thomas Bailey Aldrich, editor of the *Atlantic Monthly*, was sufficiently impressed with Chesnutt's Uncle Julius stories to print two more of them in the next two years.

Chesnutt was pleased with Uncle Julius as his entrée into the literary world, but he did not want to be known as just a local color writer. "The Sheriff's Children," which appeared in the *Independent* in 1889, signaled a new direction in which Chesnutt planned to move. In its emphasis on the consequences of miscegenation, racial hatred, mob violence, and moral compromise in the postwar South, this story was the germ of much of Chesnutt's later fiction. "The Sheriff's Children" and a story called "Rena Walden," which Chesnutt tried unsuccessfully to publish in the *Century*, indicate his desire to write frankly about the origins, aspirations, and social and psychological dilemmas of persons of mixed racial heritage in the South.

But the chilly response of the *Century* to "Rena Walden" told Chesnutt that it would not be easy to place honest fictional portrayals of life along the color line in genteel literary magazines. Consequently he devoted himself during the 1890s to building a body of short fiction from which a salable book might be taken. In 1898, after reviewing Chesnutt's work, Walter Hines Page, a senior member of Houghton Mifflin in Boston, committed his company to publishing a collection of Chesnutt's conjure stories. In March 1899 *The Conjure Woman*, a volume of seven stories centered on Uncle Julius McAdoo, came out under Houghton, Mifflin's prestigious imprint.

The Conjure Woman was favorably received as a dialect book with a difference. Although the vogue of this kind of regional writing was waning, the character of Uncle Julius, the peculiar blend of realism and fantasy in his reminiscences, and the byplay between himself and the whites who hear, judge, and record his tales pleased the reviewers. Unlike most plantation fiction, which romanticized slavery and the slaveholders of the Old South, *The Conjure Woman* evoked a world of mean-spirited, penny-pinching masters so preoccupied with profit that they care nothing for the welfare or feel-

Charles W. Chesnutt

ings of their slaves. Through the magic of conjuration, slaves in several stories in the volume successfully resist the power wielded by their would-be exploiters. But whether they win or lose these contests, the slaves' sometimes comic, at other times tragic, humanity constitutes a triumph for Chesnutt as a portrayer of black people.

Employing universal folk motifs such as metamorphosis and the trickster figure (Uncle Julius), Chesnutt added a depth to his literary adaptations of black folklore not found in the work of more famous writers such as Joel Chandler Harris. By pitting the white narrator of *The Conjure Woman*, a literal-minded rationalist to whom Julius is merely a reciter of quaint fairy tales, against the narrator's wife, who realizes the deeper truths that lie beneath Julius's marvelous stories, Chesnutt's first book challenged the social and aesthetic premises on which genteel literary realism had been established.

Soon after *The Conjure Woman* came out, word began to spread that this new voice of realism belonged to an African American. Chesnutt had asked his publishers to omit this fact in their advertising, not because he wished to hide anything but because he wanted his work to be judged on its literary merits alone. Public curiosity about Chesnutt, along with the promising sales of his first book and the admiration expressed by several literary figures for his story "The Wife of His Youth," which the *Atlantic* published several months before *The Conjure Woman*, convinced Houghton Mifflin to bring out a second collection of Chesnutt's stories in 1899, just in time for the Christmas trade. This book was entitled *The Wife of His Youth and Other Stories of the Color Line*.

The fundamental social issue, as well as the unifying theme, in most of the stories of *The Wife of His Youth* is miscegenation in the United States. The title story of the volume, the tale "A Matter of Principle," and, to a lesser extent, "Her Virginia Mammy," analyze with both irony and pathos the racial prejudices of light-skinned, middle-class African Americans in "Groveland," Ohio. Many of Chesnutt's fictional models in these stories were people he knew through his membership in the Cleveland Social Circle, an exclusive society of upwardly mobile mulattoes who were reputed to discriminate against anyone with complexions darker than their own.

"The Wife of His Youth" tells how a leader of the "Blue Vein Society" triumphs over his class and color prejudices by acknowledging, after decades of separation, his dark-skinned plantation wife. In a less pathetic and more satirical case, Chesnutt deflates the racial pretensions of Cicero Clayton, the protagonist of "A Matter of Principle," by showing how this mulatto's "principle" of dissociation from dark-skinned blacks spoils his daughter's chance to marry a congressman. In "Her Virginia Mammy," Chesnutt broke with American social mores and literary tradition in his unhysterical depiction of the betrothal of a Boston Brahmin to a woman unaware of her black ancestry.

Chesnutt's objective and often sympathetic treatment of mixed-race persons was greeted by his less perceptive readers as a brief for intermarriage. However, more than one story in *The Wife of His Youth* makes it clear that while Chesnutt was in favor of the assimilation of people of color into the socioeconomic mainstream of American life, he believed that the most reliable means of accomplishing this was through black dedication to the middle-class work ethic. Nevertheless, Chesnutt did not ignore the fact that in the South there were racial problems that resisted his faith in the ameliorative powers of traditional rugged individualism.

In "The Web of Circumstance," a former slave tries to pull himself up by his bootstraps, but a combination of adverse circumstances, racism, and betrayal leave him broken and degraded at the end of the story. In this story and in "The Sheriff's Children," Chesnutt's pessimistic reaction to the rise of white supremacist attitudes and the eclipse of black opportunity in the "New South" of the 1890s became manifest. When the North Carolina expatriate surveyed the cancerous racism that threatened the entire social organism of the South, he could not adopt the pose of the urbane ironist that had let him write with comic imperturbability about the color consciousness of mulattoes of his own class. The problems of the South demanded a strong rhetorical reaction. Chesnutt would sentimentalize, sensationalize, even sermonize to force his readers to consider contemporary racial realities in the clarifying light of purely ethical considerations, unrefracted by custom, prejudice, or past traditions.

The Wife of His Youth did not sit particularly well with its reviewers or the public. Some critics, such as William Dean Howells, called Chesnutt a literary realist of the first order. Others were troubled by his concentration on such cheerless topics as segregation, mob violence, and, most obviously, miscegenation. Although his publishers were disappointed by the immediate sales of his second book, Chesnutt refused to look back. In the fall of 1899, with *The Wife of His Youth* on the verge of publication, he closed his prosperous court-reporting business to pursue his lifelong dream—a career as a full-time author. With a comfortable middle-class style of life to maintain and two daughters enrolled at Smith College, Chesnutt did not take this step lightly. But by living frugally on his savings and his modest royalties, he felt he could afford to test the literary waters for two years to see if writing would keep him and his family afloat financially. The reputation that his short-story collections had earned was starting to pay dividends in the form of readings and lectures. Moreover, Small, Maynard, and Company of Boston had asked Chesnutt to write a biography of Frederick Douglass for high schools, which appeared in that publisher's Beacon Biographies series in 1900. None of his first three books would make much money, Chesnutt knew, but he thought them all useful in creating an audience for the novels he hoped to publish soon.

In late 1899 Chesnutt put a novel-length version of his "Rena Walden" story in the hands of his editors at Houghton Mifflin. The product of ten years of thinking, revising, and expanding, "Rena Walden" was probably closer to Chesnutt's heart than anything else he would ever write. Houghton Mifflin accepted the novel in March 1900, asking that it be published under the title *The House Behind the Cedars*. Chesnutt hoped that his first novel would identify him as a writer whose perspective on the color line allowed his readers to see through abstract social problems to what he called "the element of human interest involved." In a letter to his publishers, he stated the plot of *The House Behind the Cedars* succinctly: it is "a story of a colored girl who passed for white."

The first half of the novel describes the attempt of Rena Walden, product of an illicit union between an antebellum southern gentleman and his free mulatto concubine, to assimilate into white upper-class society in a South Carolina town. Her brother, John, who has changed his surname to Warwick and has successfully passed into the white world, introduces his demure sister to George Tryon, a Carolina blue blood, who courts her fervently. In the second half of the novel, after Tryon learns of her background, Rena returns to the black community of her hometown to become a country schoolteacher. Harassed by Tryon

and a lecherous mulatto principal, Rena tries to return to the safety of her lodgings but dies as a result of fatigue and exposure.

The prospect of racial intermixing as a consequence of the putative freedom extended to blacks by the fourteenth and fifteenth amendments of the Constitution was discussed by many late-nineteenth-century fiction writers, pundits, and politicians. Chesnutt was virtually alone among novelists of his time in treating racially mixed characters like John and Rena Walden as having a morally and socially defensible argument, if not a natural right, to be accepted as white. People like the Waldens, who were, like Chesnutt, seven-eighths white, were black only by a "social fiction," Chesnutt declared in a series of articles he wrote for the *Boston Transcript* in the late summer of 1900. As long as white bigotry barred deserving people of color from access to the American Dream, persons like the Waldens would be forced to take a clandestine route to dignity and opportunity across the color line.

Chesnutt did not write *The House Behind the Cedars* to advocate miscegenation. He depicted in conventional fashion the tragic consequences of his heroine's attempt to pass for white. Nevertheless, he wanted to make his white readers aware of and responsive to the social, economic, and psychological rationale for mulatto assimilation into mainstream American life. In pursuit of this aim, Chesnutt dispassionately detailed the antebellum conditions that created the liaison between Molly Walden and her white lover as well as the alien status of the "bright mulatto" class in postwar "Patesville" (Fayetteville), the town in which the Waldens grow up.

Chesnutt went on to suggest reasons why traditional racial stereotypes do not fit the Waldens and standard moral categories cannot be applied to their actions. He did not try to idealize John Walden, but he made sure that Rena's brother was no degenerate, as popular mythology judged the mixed-blood to be. As a result, John Walden became one of the few convincingly portrayed mulattoes in late-nineteenth-century American fiction. His sister departs less from the literary convention of the "tragic mulatta," but in Chesnutt's attempt to arouse sympathy for his heroine, he never let Rena indulge in self-hatred over what too many whites would have judged facilely as her "tainted" blood.

Chesnutt personally detested the implication of most fiction dealing with mixed-race persons: that people like himself wanted to become white out of a poverty of self-respect owing to their shame at having a mixed ancestry. Many years earlier, Chesnutt had decided not to pass for white, though he could have done so, because he was unwilling to deny his family or his past. Yet he knew other mixed-bloods who had chosen the white world, and he could sympathize with their choice. *The House Behind the Cedars* was his literary memorial to these people, to what he termed their courage as well as the often tragic outcome of their strivings.

Chesnutt's first novel had only modest sales, but critics and reviewers were generally satisfied with its restrained and judicious treatment of an often-sensationalized social question. As a novel of purpose, the book was remarkably subdued and unpolemical. Its artfulness lay primarily in the disarming way mulattoes and their social options were characterized. Perhaps the novel's concessions to literary clichés and popular sentiment, as well as to the convention of the "tragic mulatta," were a price that Chesnutt felt he had to pay to present his favorite literary child to the American reading public.

Whatever faults may be attributed to the novel today, it was sufficiently well received in its own day to encourage both Houghton Mifflin and Harper's to solicit a second novel from Chesnutt. He was ready to oblige, convinced that the time was ripe for a problem novel on a major racial issue of immediate concern. For two years Chesnutt had been gathering information about an incident in Wilmington, North Carolina, in November 1898, when more than a score of black people had been killed during the overthrow of the town's government by a cadre of white supremacists. In February 1901 Chesnutt went to Wilmington and the Cape Fear region of North Carolina on a fact-finding mission. When he returned, he felt he had enough material to write the *Uncle Tom's Cabin* of his generation.

In the fall of 1901 Houghton Mifflin published Chesnutt's magnum opus, *The Marrow of Tradition*. It incorporates his most probing analysis of the causes and effects of the racial and social conditions pervasive in the New South. The novel contains the largest and most diverse cast of characters, the most complicated plotting, and the most problematic themes to be found in a single work in Chesnutt's corpus. The main thread of action knits together the lives of two families in "Wellington," North Carolina: the Carterets, who represent the New South aristocracy, and the Millers, a mixed-race couple who embody Chesnutt's idea of the progressive New Negro. As editor of Wellington's white newspaper, Major Carteret pursues a policy of defaming blacks while conspiring with other reactionaries to take over the town's government. Eventually his machinations lead to a race riot in which Dr. William Miller's son is killed. When Carteret goes to Miller to request aid for his critically ill son, the black doctor at first refuses. He changes his mind, however, after his wife, Janet, intercedes on behalf of her half sister, Olivia Carteret. At the end of the novel, Miller puts vengeance aside and sets out to save the Carterets' child, affirming in the process his centrality to the healing of the wounds of Wellington.

Several subplots and a dozen significant characters enable Chesnutt to present a wide spectrum of southern racial opinion and class identity. Appearing in the novel are an old-fashioned black mammy, a fawning "white man's nigger," an idealized old aristocrat and his loyal black retainer, a degenerate young aristocrat, a former Klan leader from the poor white trash, a beautiful southern belle, a vengeful black resistance fighter, and a young, Quaker-born southern liberal. All play rather predictable parts in demonstrating ideas that Chesnutt wished to bring out about the Southern social scene. Balancing types and anti-types within his cast of characters, Chesnutt dramatized his perception of the turn-of-the-century South as poised on a historical watershed.

An optimist, Chesnutt liked to think that the wave of discriminatory legislation that had swept the South in the 1890s would soon subside as whites and blacks evolved toward a higher level of civilization and a finer ideal of citizenship. But he could not ignore daily evidence suggesting that the post-Reconstruction South was sliding steadily backward toward its discredited traditions. In the writing of southern apologists like Thomas Nelson Page and Thomas Dixon, these old traditions—especially white supremacy and the aristocratic monopoly of power—were given a literary facelift, so that unreconstructed Dixie could pose as the "redeemed" and "reconciled" New South.

One of the major goals of Chesnutt's second novel was to tear away the New South's mask of progressivism in order to reveal the corruptness of its guiding traditions and principles. In an atmosphere of intimidation and violence, naked power politics, and ever-widening racial polarization, the South had little chance of reforming itself, Chesnutt believed, unless the national conscience could be galvanized in support of the region's embattled progressive forces. These forces are epitomized in Dr. Miller. "There's time enough, but none to spare," Miller is told at the close of the novel as he enters the Carteret house, from which he had previously been barred, on his mission of mercy. This remark sums up *The Marrow of Tradition's* urgent plea for moral action from white America.

Hoping for sales of twenty to thirty thousand, Chesnutt was disappointed to learn from his publisher that, despite an energetic advertising campaign, *The Marrow of Tradition* had sold fewer than five thousand copies in its first two months. Chesnutt had expected an outcry from southern reviewers, but he did not anticipate the split opinion among their northern counterparts, who could not agree on whether Chesnutt had been fair to the South. Some hailed him for his social realism, but others dismissed him as a bitter pessimist. Even the previously supportive William Dean Howells was disturbed and ambivalent about the book. The fact that few complained about the novel's workmanship or the power of its message led

Chesnutt to conclude that his subject matter and moral thesis were what had doomed the book. "I am beginning to suspect," he told his publisher (28 December 1901), "that the public as a rule does not care for books in which the principal characters are colored people, or written with a striking sympathy with that race as contrasted with the white race." Heeding the advice of his friends that he should withdraw temporarily from the field of racial problem novels, Chesnutt decided in 1902 that it was time to reopen his court-reporting business.

As he rebuilt his financial base, Chesnutt continued to write in his spare time. His public comments on racial conditions were confined to essays, the most important of which was "The Disfranchisement of the Negro," published in *The Negro Problem: A Series of Articles by Representative American Negroes of To-day* (1903). In this important volume Booker T. Washington and W. E. B. Du Bois argued their opposing solutions to "the Negro problem": the Tuskegee plan of industrial education for the masses versus the Du Bois program of higher education for the African American "talented tenth." Refusing to endorse either of these positions to the exclusion of the other, Chesnutt focused on suffrage as the only lasting guarantee of black advancement.

In 1903 Chesnutt wrote a novel of entertainment centering on a love triangle among a group of white, upper-class Bostonians. "Evelyn's Husband" seems to have been motivated by its author's frank desire for commercial success in a vein completely removed from that of his earlier race problem novels. But the editors who read the manuscript found it jejune and uninteresting. This put Chesnutt in a dilemma. He had been able to publish serious problem novels about the southern racial situation, but they had not appealed to the public at large. When he tried to write noncontroversial, mass-market fiction about white people in the North, however, he had not been able to attract a publisher. In the winter of 1903–1904, therefore, Chesnutt decided to return to the short story, a form he knew well and one that had brought him his first recognition. The result was "Baxter's Procrustes" (1904), the last story the author published in the *Atlantic* and his best-crafted work of short fiction.

Although "Baxter's Procrustes" is another of Chesnutt's nonracial stories, it has much in common with his earlier conjure and color line stories. Like Uncle Julius McAdoo, the enigmatic, dilettantish sometime writer known only as Baxter is a con artist and a trickster. His victims are the members of the Bodleian Club, an all-male organization of well-heeled bibliophiles whose ostensible love of literary classics is rooted in the consciousness that fine books make a wise investment. Baxter contrives a brilliant stratagem that exposes the misplaced priorities of his fellow Bodleians. In the process, Chesnutt satirizes the Bodleians' self-delusions as he had satirized the social pretensions of another exclusive society, the Groveland Blue Veins. Like the Blue Veins, the Bodleians were patterned on a social club in Cleveland to which Chesnutt belonged, though he was aware of the excesses and prejudices of its membership.

Cleveland's Rowfant Club, an all-white fraternity of upper-class book collectors, undoubtedly recognized themselves when they read "Baxter's Procrustes" in the June 1904 issue of the *Atlantic*. Two years earlier they had denied Chesnutt membership in their club because of the racial prejudice of a few of the Rowfanters. Chesnutt created Baxter to expose those who claimed to respect culture and humane letters but who actually cared much more for appearances. The tone of the story and its deft ironies show that it was conceived as a literary riposte, not an exercise in revenge. In 1910 Chesnutt was again nominated, and this time elected, a member of the Rowfant Club, and he took an active part in it in subsequent years.

In the spring of 1904 Chesnutt began to work with Walter Hines Page, a senior partner in the newly formed publishing house of Doubleday, Page, on a race problem novel called *The Colonel's Dream*. With the advice and guidance of Page, a liberal white North Carolinian and a southern expatriate like himself, Chesnutt hoped to write a novel about the New South that might accomplish something positive on the social front while restoring his literary reputa-tion. In this new book Chesnutt tried to enhance the identification of the majority of his readership with his protagonist by making him a white man, an enlightened ex-Confederate officer who has made himself rich in northern industry without losing his southern sense of noblesse oblige.

Colonel Henry French's return to his native North Carolina for health reasons reveals to him the land of his birth languishing in a social and economic depression. Like many heroes of economic novels from the Progressive era, French optimistically sets about reforming the archaic, often exploitative systems of education and production in his region. Resistance mounts steadily from Bill Fetters, a corrupt power broker and economic kingpin whose control over blacks and poor whites has reduced both classes to virtual servitude. Ultimately, in despair, the colonel gives up his dream of reform after violent acts of racist intimidation—including a lynching and the disinterring of a black man from a white cemetery—convince him that the people of his region are not yet civilized enough to accept the opportunities he would give them. He returns to the North alone, joined soon thereafter by a handful of other forward-looking southerners, black as well as white, at the end of the novel.

The Colonel's Dream is the final volume in what might be termed Chesnutt's New South trilogy. Each of the previously published novels tests out a means of alleviating the caste consciousness and social injustice that Chesnutt believed were endemic in the South. In *The House Behind the Cedars*, the strategies of the Waldens are shown to be risky, often self-defeating ways of gaining social rights and opportunities for African Americans. In *The Marrow of Tradition*, both violent resistance and diplomatic accommodation are weighed as alternatives for southern blacks. At the end of the novel, neither alternative proves itself capable of halting the spread of institutionalized racial repression in the postwar South. *The Colonel's Dream* asks whether white philanthropy, cooperative enterprise, and the pursuit of enlightened self-interest between blacks and whites could raise the socioeconomic prospects of everyone in the New South, thus creating a climate in which racial justice might thrive.

In articles, speeches, and letters, Chesnutt had subscribed to several of the colonel's programs for combating the social and economic ills of the New South. French sponsors an industrial school on the Tuskegee model, employs blacks in the rebuilding of a textile mill, attacks black peonage in the courts, and tries to soothe white suspicions and fears with reasoned appeals to fair play and business pragmatism. Yet, despite his moderate, well-intentioned progressivism, French ends up a loser, mainly because he realizes too late that his piecemeal reforms in education, economics, and civil rights have not addressed the fundamental moral and intellectual blight of racism in the small-town South.

"The very standards of right and wrong had been confused by the race issue," French concludes; in response, nothing less than "a new body of thought must be built up" to counter the massive mythology of racism that has permeated southern thought and institutions for centuries. Unfortunately, French does not know how to create this new thinking, nor does Chesnutt seem to have had a clear idea about how to do this, except by writing novels like *The Colonel's Dream*. Nevertheless, this novel's analysis of the problems facing the New South has been borne out by subsequent historical investigation, which in turn helps us to see Chesnutt as a dedicated muckraker, one of the precursors of twentieth-century southern realism. It is unlikely, however, that he took much comfort from the few reviewers who praised him for his honesty in recording the ugly facts of southern mill-town life. Most of the critics who bothered to comment on the novel at all felt it was too unpleasant and pessimistic to recommend it to their readers. Consequently, like Colonel French, Chesnutt in 1905 took his leave of the New South in literature as he had done some twenty years before in life.

After *The Colonel's Dream*, Chesnutt became involved in social and political activities that drew his attention and energy away from literature. He joined the Committee of Twelve for the Advancement of the Interests of the Ne-

gro Race, founded by Booker T. Washington for the purpose of preparing speeches and circulating materials designed to correct public misinterpretations of the African American cause. This alliance with Washington did not prevent Chesnutt from serving on the central committee of the rival Niagara Movement. He continued to stress both publicly and privately the necessity of predicating the reform of southern racial conditions on the restoration of the suffrage to blacks of that region. In several articles and speeches he foresaw the ultimate solution to the American race problem in the amalgamation of blacks and whites into one undifferentiated race. Toward this end, he fought caste consciousness and color barriers wherever he found them, whether in anti-intermarriage laws, Cleveland settlement houses, army training practices in the South, or popular films such as *The Birth of a Nation* (1915).

In the decade that followed the publication of *The Colonel's Dream*, Chesnutt became an established civic leader in Cleveland. He joined the Chamber of Commerce and the City Club; he presided over the Cleveland Council of Sociology and served on the General Committee of the National Association for the Advancement of Colored People. His court-reporting business flourished, enabling him to live affluently, travel abroad, and provide a college education for all four of his children. A mild stroke in June 1910 reduced his stamina for literary work, which by this time had become an intellectual hobby. Only three negligible short stories published locally in Cleveland and in the African American periodical press attest to Chesnutt's interest in belletristic writing during the decade following *The Colonel's Dream*.

The 1920s saw a revival of Chesnutt's enthusiasm for writing and some belated recognition for his pioneering literary labors at the turn of the century. In 1923 the black filmmaker Oscar Micheaux made *The House Behind the Cedars* into a film that played for black theater audiences around the country during the decade. The *Chicago Defender* serialized Chesnutt's first novel in 1922, putting it back into print for the first time in over fifteen years. Chesnutt kept his eye on the rise of the new Harlem school of writers, whom he welcomed in theory but often scolded in practice.

When W. E. B. Du Bois, editor of *The Crisis* and an admirer of Chesnutt's fiction, asked him to respond to the question "The Negro in Art: How Shall He Be Portrayed?" the dean of African American writers responded that there should be no limitation on the matter or manner of race literature. But when Chesnutt read books like Claude McKay's *Home to Harlem* (1928) and Wallace Thurman's *The Blacker the Berry* (1929), he found much to condemn in their failure to portray what he called "the real romance, the worthy ambition, the broad humanity" of black folk in all social classes. Along with Du Bois and the poet William Stanley Braithwaite, Chesnutt fought a rearguard action in the late 1920s against the aesthetic and social iconoclasts of the Harlem Renaissance, failing to see the ways in which his writing had anticipated theirs.

At the beginning and the end of the 1920s, Chesnutt created novels extolling the virtues of ostensibly mixed-blood heroes who, on discovering they are actually white, choose to remain "Negroes" rather than compromise themselves morally by accepting wealth and position in the more favored caste. The publishers who rejected "Paul Marchand, F. M. C." in 1921 judged this historical novel set in old New Orleans foreign in tone and theme to the social concerns and literary interests of Jazz Age America. By 1930 Chesnutt had an updated version of the same basic story, this time entitled "The Quarry," ready for Houghton, Mifflin, but the firm rejected it (as did Knopf), believing that "The Quarry" sounded too much like an old-fashioned thesis novel whose hero was so bloodless and high-minded that few contemporary readers would find him attractive.

Viewing Chesnutt's career from the perspective of these late manuscripts, one can see that the clear-sighted, often ironic analyst of the embryonic black middle class at the turn of the century had evolved into a somewhat tunnel-visioned literary apologist for the entrenched black bourgeoisie in the late 1920s. Chesnutt could not seem to get beyond his well-worn themes—the "tainted" past, the stolen birth-

right, the undeservedly wronged mulatto, and the moral problem of a divided racial heritage and loyalties—in the writing he attempted after *The Colonel's Dream*. His failure to reach an artistic resolution of the mixed-blood's cultural and racial ambivalences, except through exercises in literary avoidance and wish fulfillment, lends support to an estimate of Chesnutt as a frustrated and in some ways unfulfilled writer.

Chesnutt's literary triumphs were real, however, and not inconsiderable. In 1928 the NAACP awarded him its Spingarn Medal for his "pioneer work as a literary artist depicting the life and struggles of Americans of Negro descent, and for his long and useful career as scholar, worker, and freeman of one of America's greatest cities." The next year Houghton Mifflin reprinted *The Conjure Woman* in a handsome deluxe edition that put Chesnutt back in print thirty years after he had first become an author. When he died of arteriosclerosis on 15 November 1932, he was a neglected but by no means forgotten literary figure, especially in black America, where his books had become classics.

A year before his death, Chesnutt reckoned some of the gains and losses of his artistic career in "PostBellum—Pre-Harlem," an essay in literary autobiography. He accepted the fact that literary fashions had passed him by, but he took pride in pointing out how far African American literature and the attitude of the white literary world toward it had come since the days when he broke into print. Although he was too modest to do so, Chesnutt could have claimed an important role in preparing the public mind in America for the advent of the New Negro author of the 1920s, for in a basic sense, the new movement followed his precedent in unmasking the false poses and images of its era in order to refocus attention on racial realities in its America.

Almost single-handedly, Chesnutt established a truly African American literary tradition in the short story, if not in the novel. He was the first to make the broad range of African American experience his artistic bailiwick and to consider practically everything therein to be worthy of treatment. Chesnutt not only surveyed the literary topography of African American life; he also assayed some of its richest social and psychological veins. Because he was concerned with finding literary modes appropriate to his materials, he left to his successors examples of the uses of ironic distance in an African American fiction of manners, a precedent for a black magical realism, a concept of tragedy for a people once regarded as merely grotesque or pitiable, and a sense of the comic potential of the trickster figure from African American folklore. This was a rich artistic legacy that influenced such twentieth-century black writers as James Weldon Johnson and Nella Larsen. In his own era Chesnutt's achievement can be summed up succinctly: it was he who taught white America to respect a black fiction writer as a critical realist, even if it could not embrace him as a literary native son.

Selected Bibliography

PRIMARY WORKS

BOOKS

The Conjure Woman. Boston: Houghton Mifflin, 1899.

The Wife of His Youth and Other Stories of the Color Line. Boston: Houghton Mifflin, 1899.

Frederick Douglass. Boston: Small, Maynard, 1899.

The House Behind the Cedars. Boston: Houghton Mifflin, 1900.

The Marrow of Tradition. Boston: Houghton Mifflin, 1901.

The Colonel's Dream. New York: Doubleday, Page, 1905.

SHORT STORIES AND ARTICLES

"Dave's Neckliss." *Atlantic Monthly* 64:500–08 (1889).

"The Disfranchisement of the Negro." In *The Negro Problem: A Series of Articles by Representative American Negroes of To-day.* New York: James Pott, 1903. Pp. 79–124.

"Baxter's Procrustes." *Atlantic Monthly* 93:823–830 (1904).

"Race Prejudice; Its Causes and Its Cure." *Alexander's Magazine* 1:21–26 (1905).

"The Negro in Art: How Shall He Be Portrayed?" *The Crisis* 33:28–29 (1926).

"Post-Bellum—Pre-Harlem." *Colophon* 2, n.p. (1931). Reprinted in *The Crisis* 38:193–94 (1931); and in *Breaking into Print.* Edited by Elmer Adler. New York: Books for Libraries, 1968. Pp. 49–56.

MODERN EDITIONS AND ANTHOLOGIES

The Wife of His Youth. Introduction by Earl Schenck Miers. Ann Arbor: University of Michigan Press, 1968.

The Conjure Woman. Introduction by Robert M. Farnsworth. Ann Arbor: University of Michigan Press, 1969.

The Marrow of Tradition. Introduction by Robert M. Farnsworth. Ann Arbor: University of Michigan Press, 1969.

The Colonel's Dream. Miami, Fla.: Mnemosyne, 1969.

Frederick Douglass. New York: Johnson Reprints, 1970.

The Short Fiction of Charles W. Chesnutt. Edited by Sylvia Lyons Render. Washington, D.C.: Howard University Press, 1974.

The House Behind the Cedars. Introduction by William L. Andrews. Athens: University of Georgia Press, 1988.

Collected Stories of Charles W. Chesnutt. Edited by William L. Andrews. New York: Penguin, 1992.

The Conjure Woman and Other Conjure Tales. Edited by Richard H. Brodhead. Durham, NC: Duke University Press, 1993.

The House Behind the Cedars. Introduction by Donald Gibson. New York: Penguin, 1993.

The Journals of Charles W. Chesnutt. Edited by Richard H. Brodhead. Durham: Duke University Press, 1993.

The Marrow of Tradition. Introduction by Eric J. Sundquist. New York: Penguin, 1993.

Mandy Oxendine. Edited by Charles Hackenberry. Urbana: University of Illinois Press, 1997.

"To Be an Author": Letters of Charles W. Chesnutt, 1889–1905. Edited by Joseph R. McElrath Jr. and Robert C. Leitz, III. Princeton: Princeton University Press, 1996.

Paul Marchand, F.M.C. Introduction by Matthew Wilson. Jackson: University Press of Mississippi, 1998.

Charles W. Chesnutt: Essays and Speeches. Edited by Joseph R. McElrath Jr., Robert C. Leitz III, and Jesse S. Crisler. Stanford: Stanford University Press, 1999.

MANUSCRIPTS AND PAPERS

The Charles Waddell Chesnutt Collection of the Erastus Milo Cravath Memorial Library, Fisk University, contains Chesnutt's unpublished journals, letters, and novels, as well as a wealth of other memorabilia. The Library of the Western Reserve Historical Society in Cleveland, Ohio, also holds a significant collection of Chesnutt manuscripts and letters.

SECONDARY WORKS

BIOGRAPHICAL AND CRITICAL STUDIES

Andrews, William L. *The Literary Career of Charles W. Chesnutt.* Baton Rouge: Louisiana State University Press, 1980.

———. "William Dean Howells and Charles W. Chesnutt: Criticism and Race Fiction in the Age of Booker T. Washington." *American Literature* 48:327–339 (1976).

Baldwin, Richard E. "The Art of *The Conjure Woman.*" *American Literature* 43:385–98 (1971).

Bone, Robert A. *Down Home: A History of Afro-American Short Fiction from Its Beginnings to the End of the Harlem Renaissance.* New York: Putnam's, 1975.

Bruce, Dickson D., Jr. *Black American Writing from the Nadir: The Evolution of a Literary Tradition, 1877–1915.* Baton Rouge: Louisiana State University Press, 1989.

Burnette, Ricardo V. "Charles W. Chesnutt's *The Conjure Woman* Revisited." *CLA Journal* 30:438–53 (June 1987).

Chesnutt, Helen M. *Charles Waddell Chesnutt: Pioneer of the Color Line.* Chapel Hill: University of North Carolina Press, 1952.

Duncan, Charles. *The Absent Man: The Narrative Craft of Charles W. Chesnutt.* Athens: Ohio University Press, 1998.

Ferguson, Sally Ann. "Rena Walden: Chesnutt's Failed 'Future American.' " *Southern Literary Journal* 15: 74–82 (1982).

Gibson, Donald B. "Charles W. Chesnutt: The Anatomy of a Dream." In *Politics of Literary Expression: A Study of Major Black Writers.* Westport, Conn.: Greenwood, 1981. Pp. 124–54.

Hemenway, Robert. " 'Baxter's Procrustes': Irony and Protest." *CLA Journal* 18:172–185 (1974).

———. "The Functions of Folklore in Charles Chesnutt's *The Conjure Woman.*" *Journal of the Folklore Institute* 13:283–309 (1976).

Howells, William Dean. "Mr. Charles W. Chesnutt's Stories." *Atlantic Monthly* 85:699–701 (1900).

Keller, Frances Richardson. *An American Crusade: The Life of Charles W. Chesnutt.* Provo, Utah: Brigham Young University Press, 1978.

Mason, Julian D. "Charles W. Chesnutt as Southern Author." *Mississippi Quarterly* 20:77–89 (Spring 1967).

McElrath, Joseph R., Jr. "Collaborative Authorship: The Charles W. Chesnutt–Walter Hines Page Relationship." In *The Professions of Authorship: Essays in Honor of Matthew J. Bruccoli.* Edited by Richard Layman and Joel Myerson. Columbia: University of South Carolina Press, 1996. Pp. 150–68.

———. *Critical Essays on Charles W. Chesnutt.* New York: G. K. Hall, 1999.

Pickens, Ernestine Williams. *Charles W. Chesnutt and the Progressive Movement.* New York: Pace University Press, 1994.

Render, Sylvia Lyons. *Charles W. Chesnutt.* Boston: Twayne, 1980.

Sedlack, Robert P. "The Evolution of Charles Chesnutt's *The House Behind the Cedars.*" *CLA Journal* 19: 125–35 (1975).

Stepto, Robert B. " 'The Simple but Intensely Human Inner Life of Slavery': Storytelling, Fiction and the Revision of History in Charles W. Chesnutt's 'Uncle Julius Stories.' " In *History and Tradition in Afro-American Literature.* Edited by Gunther H. Lenz. Frankfurt: Campus, 1984. Pp. 29–55.

Sundquist, Eric. J. *To Wake the Nations: Race in the Making of American Literature.* Cambridge, Mass.: Harvard University Press, 1993.

Terry, Eugene. "Charles W. Chesnutt: A Victim of the Color Line." *Contributions to Black Studies* 1:15–44 (1977).

Wideman, John Edgar. "Charles Chesnutt and the WPA Narratives: The Oral and Literate Roots of Afro-American Literature." In *The Slave's Narrative.* Edited by Charles T. Davis and Henry Louis Gates Jr. New York: Oxford University Press, 1985. Pp. 59–78.

———. "Charles W. Chesnutt: *The Marrow of Tradition.*" *American Scholar* 42:128–34 (Winter 1972–1973).

BIBLIOGRAPHIES

Andrews, William L. "Charles W. Chesnutt: An Essay in Bibliography." *Resources for American Literary Study* 6:3–22 (Spring 1976).

Ellison, Curtis W., and E. W. Metcalf Jr. *Charles W. Chesnutt: A Reference Guide.* Boston: G. K. Hall, 1977.

LUCILLE CLIFTON
(1936–   )

DIANNE JOHNSON

IN A 1984 essay entitled "A Simple Language" Lucille Clifton described her writing this way:

> I use a simple language. I have never believed that for anything to be valid or true or intellectual or "deep" it had to first be complex. I deliberately use the language that I use. Sometimes people have asked me when I was going to try something hard or difficult, as if my work sprang from my ignorance. I like to think that I write from my knowledge not my lack, from my strength not my weakness. I am not interested if anyone knows whether or not I am familiar with big words, I am interested in trying to render big ideas in a simple way. I am interested in being understood not admired. I wish to celebrate and not be celebrated (though a little celebration is a lot of fun).

This is a useful description and explains her career in many ways. Perhaps most important, her writing is very accessible, and it is profound in its simplicity whether directed at adults or children. Regardless of the audience, Clifton is respectful of the reader. Because she celebrates life in all its beauty and all its potential for evil, she is now being celebrated more widely (though not yet in a full-length study) by critics who understand her importance in American liter-

ary history. And Clifton is clear about the fact that she has a place in this history. She is a black writer and an American, always, not just a writer who happens to be black. From Clifton's perspective, it is the poetry written by people of a variety of backgrounds that constitutes American poetry.

Clifton's writing does not fit neatly into periods. If there is any chronology to her writing, it is the chronology of the life of an ordinary woman, from the knowledge and strength of a person who lives an examined life. Just as there are no clear periods in her development as a writer, there is no clear distinction between the different genres that she is engaged in writing. Certainly it is easy to categorize the autobiography or to group together illustrated children's books, for example. But from another perspective, all her work is part of one whole project. Her formal autobiography, the poetry, the children's books, essays, and interviews are of a piece. For she is steadfast in her preoccupations and steadfast in her honesty.

Perhaps first and foremost, Clifton's writing is autobiographical. She writes about her own family and about black communities and histories. She writes about them in very intimate ways and in very political ways, informed by an African diasporic consciousness. Clifton is concerned not only with human beings but with the natural environment as well, communicating a respect for the earth and acknowledging the human responsibility to protect it. Clifton's poetry explores the individual human body in health and in sickness and examines both religion and spirituality as part of her ubiquitous concern with the inner lives of her readers, the ancestors, and herself.

In concert with the intimate and clear language that she uses, Clifton's subject matter, regardless of its smallness or immensity, creates for her readers a feeling of being at home in any Clifton book that they might open. The opening poem in Clifton's first published book, *Good Times* (1969) is, in fact, about the meaning of home, as defined by the particular people who live in a particular place. She declares that "we hang on to our no place/ happy to be alive/ and in the inner city/ or/ like we call it/ home." This untitled poem is simultaneously intensely personal, intensely political, and ultimately, full of faith in human beings—descriptions that can be applied to most of her writing, whether for adults or for children. In her children's books, as well as in her other work, she suggests powerfully that in its broadest context, home is synonymous with community. For example, in *The Black BC's* (1970) she writes: "G is for Ghetto/ a place where we can be at home/ loved and free"—equating home and community with the ghetto, and by extension, with Harlem—"the capital of urban black culture in America is New York City. It is called Harlem . . . , it is the one long identified as the spiritual home of the Black American . . . and it is home, a love-filled home, to millions."

The same year that she published *The Black BC's* she began the seven-volume children's book series centered around the indomitable character named Everett Anderson. (She last published a children's book in 1983.) Through Everett's experiences, Clifton explores the meaning of place and home in a more personal, detailed way than she can represent Harlem on one page of an alphabet book. Everett's place, Apartment 14A, is virtually personified and has a character all its own. It is "a blessing," as described in Everett's words in *Everett Anderson's Christmas Coming* (1971). In some ways, 14A is the grandmother who is identified, tra-

ditionally, with the African American extended family. It is the comforter and the refuge, a point of stability and permanence. From 14A Everett can watch the pretty part of snow, before it becomes slush. From 14A he can pretend that the noise of sirens is only other boys and girls playing, and not a sign of trouble. And he imagines in *Some of the Days of Everett Anderson*, high up in 14A, "that the stars are where apartments end."

The import of 14A is also evident on another level, more socially than individually based. In *Everett Anderson's 1-2-3* (1976), when his mother decides to remarry, Everett decides that "Three [people] can work and sing and dance/ and not make a crowd in 14A." And most significant in terms of the steadfastness of 14A in Everett's life is the announcement in *Everett Anderson's Nine Month Long* (1978) that "Something is growing in 14A." The apartment is placed on an almost equal level with Everett's mother as a place of nourishment for a new life. Not only does place have an enveloping and familiar quality (as with Everett and his new family members), but it also connotes a quality of expandability. Whether in a physical or psychological sense, it expands to encompass in turn new friends, a community, and a sense of relatedness to the world at large. This quality of almost palpable life is not at all separate from Clifton's writing about femaleness and family in her poetry for adults.

Lucille Clifton has made homes in many places around the country. But her first home, where she was born and named Thelma Lucille Sayles on June 27, 1936, was in Depew, New York. Her parents, Thelma Moore Sayles and Samuel L. Sayles Jr., were not formally educated but loved the spoken and the written word and loved family and emphasized the necessity of passing down family stories. Clifton's entire family lived in this small steel town outside of Buffalo, New York, where her grandfather and other male family members had gone from Georgia. She mentions in *Generations* the interesting little fact that her maternal grandfather "had come on the same train as my Daddy, in the strikebreaking." Lucille Clifton's home within this family of her birth and their ancestors and progeny is the home in which her writing lives, from which it departs, and to which it always returns.

Clifton entered Howard University at the age of seventeen and majored in drama and acted in the first performance of James Baldwin's *The Amen Corner.* Though she held a full scholarship, she remained there for only two years (1953–1955). She subsequently attended Fredonia State Teachers College in New York. Through her participation in a Buffalo group of black intellectuals interested in literature, drama, and philosophy, she met poet/novelist Ishmael Reed who shared her poetry with the acclaimed poet Langston Hughes. Hughes admired what he saw and published a number of her pieces in the anthology *Poetry of the Negro.* According to James Draper, she gives credit, as well, to Robert Hayden and Carolyn Kizer for helping her to begin her writing career. Fortuitously, she met her husband, Fred Clifton, through the same group. It was with him that she created the family that so tangibly inhabits her writing. When Clifton began her writing career she was the mother of six children under age ten: Sidney, Fredrica, Channing, Gillian, Graham, and Alexia. They are part and parcel of all her work. In some ways, the most touching of her children's books is *Everett Anderson's Goodbye* (1983), written during the time her husband was dying. In these verses, structured according to the formal stages of mourning, Everett says goodbye to his father.

Clifton's mother was central to her conceptualization of "home" until her untimely death at age forty-four, a fact that surfaces over and again in Clifton's poems. A fact that is just as important as her mother's age at her death is the extremely personal information that she did not have sexual relations with her husband, or anyone, else for the last twenty years of her life, after the birth of her son, Sammy. In her 1976 memoir, *Generations,* Clifton connects this fact with her mother's telling her repeatedly, "Get away, get away. I have not had a normal life. I want you to have a natural life. I want you to get away." In this context, Clifton's "poem on my fortieth birthday to my mother who died young," appearing in *Two-Headed*

Lucille Clifton

Woman (1980), makes perfect sense. Here she professes that she has "decided to keep running" and promises "I'm trying for the long one mama,/ running like hell and if i fall/ i fall." But Clifton does not fall, in artistic terms.

She began her working life as a claims clerk for the New York State Division of Employment in Buffalo (1958–1960) but also worked in the field of education early on as a literature assistant for the U.S. Office of Education in Washington, D.C. (1969–1971). Her first book, *Good Times,* was named by the *New York Times* as one of the best books of the year in 1969. That same year she received the Young Men's and Young Women's Hebrew Association (YM-YWHA) Poetry Center (New York City) Discovery Award. *An Ordinary Woman* received the University of Massachusetts Press Juniper Prize for original poetry. Clifton was a finalist for the Pulitzer Prize in poetry in 1980 and 1988. She was the poet laureate of Maryland from 1979 through 1982 and is the recipient of many other prizes, grants, and honors. These include several National Endowment for the Arts grants, the Shelley Memorial Award, a Lannan Literary Award, the Coretta Scott King Honor Award from the American Library Association, and an Emmy Award from the American Academy of Television Arts and Sciences. In 1999 she was elected Chancellor of the Academy of American Poets. In "the message of thelma sayles" in *Next*, Clifton recounts her mother's admonition to "turn the blood that clots on your tongue/ into poems. poems." And she has done this. Her career has flourished, at least in part, because she has kept running–growing intellectually, spiritually, and geographically to some extent—in response to her mother's own life story, writing about her home within her own body, her family, her community, and world, both in social and environmental terms.

Lucille Clifton is comfortable in her body. In "Where the Soul Lives," the last part of Bill Moyers' 1989 PBS series *Power of the Word*, she introduced her poem "homage to my hips" this way: "I write a lot about body parts. The reason for that is that I'm thrilled with my body parts. . . . So I like to celebrate the wonderfulness that I am." *Two-Headed Woman* (1980), for example, includes poems entitled "homage to my hair" and "homage to my hips." In the former she exclaims, "I'm talking about my nappy hair!" And though she didn't write a children's book specifically about hair, "homage to my hair" anticipates the 1999 controversy over Carolivia Herron's children's book *Nappy Hair* predated by such classics as Camille Yarbrough's *Cornrows* and followed by bell hooks' *Happy to Be Nappy* and others. In many poems, such as one particular tribute to Angela Davis in *Good News About the Earth* (1972), black hair takes on political ramifications. The same is true of the hips in "homage" in which the speaker is adamant that "these hips have never been enslaved." Certainly, the poem also alludes to the sexual allure of the hips, the fact that men appreciate hips. So on a deeper level, too, this poem is about an aesthetics of the body.

It is an aesthetics concerned on a basic level with skin color, specifically, with black skin. According to Dianne Johnson-Feelings, when

W. E. B. Du Bois and Jessie Fauset began conceptualizing the black children's magazine *The Brownies' Book* in 1919, they listed as one of their objectives "to make colored children realize that being colored is a normal beautiful thing." Indeed, Clifton responds over half a century later to the same kinds of implied concerns. In *Some of the Days of Everett Anderson* (1970), comprised of one poem for each day of the week, several of the poems are meditations upon blackness. At bedtime, Everett admits that it is silly to be afraid of the dark because by extension, that would amount to harboring fear of the darkness of his skin and that of his relatives: " 'afraid of the dark/ is afraid of me!'/ Says ebony/ Everett/ Anderson." In Wednesday's poem in the same book, Clifton starts each stanza with the line "Who's black?" though on the surface the question has nothing to do with the adventures that Everett is having. But rather than being gratuitous, the question, posed literally in this case, signifies the way in which the question is, in fact, present in a spiritual and fundamental way in much of Clifton's writing. The point is that Everett is black, as are many of his fellow characters. They are. It is a condition of their being that is simultaneously neither remarkable or ignorable. It is largely for this reason that these characters share a brotherhood. When their blackness deserves or demands special attention, it is accorded that attention. When it requires no particular attention, it is left so. The maturation process of Clifton's young characters consists partly of learning how to mediate between the two levels of consciousness.

But the blackness is always there and blackness fascinates Clifton, in a way, and always informs her writing. In *Good News About the Earth* (1972), for example, when she writes about "Solomon," she is actually writing about Delilah, she of black skin and black sound in the black night. In "after kent state" in the same volume, she draws connections between "white ways" and death and urges readers to "come into the/ Black/ and live." And she writes often about the Hindu goddess Kali, who interests her partly because she is depicted as being black and because she represents both creation and destruction. She says in the Mullany interview that she, that anyone, also represents both: "I tell my students all the time that 'both/and' is an African-American tradition, not 'either-or'." This is one of the many messages she communicates in her children's books as well.

Clearly, Clifton's writing for young people is as multilayered as her writing for adults. In *The Times They Used to Be* (1974), the body is linked, among other things, to religion. It is, in part, the story of Tassie—Tallahassie May Scott—who wasn't saved. Tassie's grandmother, evocative of Clifton's mother, a member of the sanctified church, admonishes her granddaughter: "You thirteen years old now, old enough to know sin/. . . . Come to God/ before your body is made all unclean." As it turns out, Tassie thinks that she has become a sinner because her period has started and she doesn't understand what is happening. Tassie's best friend is Sooky, the story's narrator. Sooky's family is at the center of the story. In particular, Sooky's Uncle Sunny deserves mention. Inspired at least in part by Clifton's maternal Uncle Buddy, Sunny was a member of the all-black 92nd division in the Jim Crow army and suffered mental consequences of being a war veteran. Sunny attended Tuskegee Institute. And "he could see spirits and things/ 'cause he was born with a veil over his face." By the end of the story he is dead, and the girls have learned something about life and death and the role of the body not in procreation in a narrow sense, but in the generation of generations.

Sooky and Tassie might be the child manifestations of the grownup Lucille Clifton who goes on to write "poem to my uterus," "poem in praise of menstruation," and "to my last period" in *Quilting: Poems 1987–1990* (1991). These poems were written following her hysterectomy in 1988, after her years of childbearing and after her husband's death, at age forty-nine, in 1984. Her poems on his life and death, her own life and her vulnerable body, and the lives of her children, all demonstrate her respect for the physical dimensions of human experience, which in many ways precede all other experience. In "poem to my uterus" she won-

ders "where can i go/ barefoot/ without you/ where can you go/ without me." She forces the reader to deal with the reality of the black body, barefoot (in pregnancy or otherwise) and bare. In "poem in praise of menstruation," Clifton raises the issue not only of human body and human procreation, but of the maternal in all of nature: "if there is in/ the universe such a river If/ there is some where water/ more powerful than this wild/ water/ pray that it flows also/ through animals/ beautiful and faithful and ancient/ and female and brave." Sooky and Tassie, as child alter egos, might indeed grow up to be the kind of poet who writes "the killing of the trees," reflecting upon moving into a subdivision built upon bulldozed land, or "telling our stories," the story of a fox who regularly visits the poet. The poet finally realizes, as stated in *The Terrible Stories* (1996), that "it was not/ the animal blood i was hiding from,/ it was the poet in her, the poet and/ the terrible stories she could tell."

The poet in the fox is the poet in the earth, is the poet in the human being, is the poet in Lucille Clifton. And she does tell, in *The Terrible Stories*, some stories that are terrible, stories of "how dangerous it is/ to be born with breasts" and "how dangerous it is to wear dark skin." In the same volume, she includes a poem, for instance, that talks about the appearance of Medgar Evers' son in the courtroom in 1994 when Byron de la Beckwith was finally being tried for the death of his father in 1963: "he came he says/ to show in this courtroom/ medgar's face." This mission to humanize black people is ubiquitous in her body of what is, ultimately, political writing. In the 1989 Bill Moyers piece, Clifton addresses this issue of politics and art in this way: "If I write out of my own life, I have to write out of the life of a black woman who is the child of slaves in America. I have to do that because I am honest, artistically. Some of my students say to me sometimes that . . . I seem to talk about race a lot and why couldn't we just talk about art. And art is beyond this sort of thing. Also as a student told me, 'I'm so tired of hearing about race.' Well, the student wasn't tireder than I am. I assure you; I'm tireder than that student. But this exists and I have to talk about it." So she tells the terrible stories.

One of the terrible stories Lucille Clifton recounts is the story of a letter written to W. E. B. Du Bois in 1905 by a Clark University researcher, investigating the relationship between crying and emotions. He questions Du Bois about a series of things including whether or not Negroes shed tears. Clifton's response to this incident, in *Quilting*, "reply" is an assurance that black people love and tire and fight and bleed and mourn, and weep, and more. Such a poem demonstrates Clifton's desire to communicate with the ignorant or the unthinking or even the malicious. However, she also writes a poem such as "note to myself," also in *Quilting*, with the epigram "it's a black thing you wouldn't understand" and Amiri Baraka's statement, "i refuse to be judged by white men." In this poem she questions "even the best," who might be interpreted to be the "best" white people who don't understand white privilege and white arrogance and history and who would still claim the right to define black people rather than have black people define themselves. And like Du Bois, Clifton's concern is to define and redefine black experience. While the poem laments that "the merely human/ is denied me still" she shows her humanity by declaring that she will continue to reach "across our history to touch,/ to soothe on more than one/ occasion/ and will again."

But Lucille Clifton does not merely reach across history. She delves into history, both African American and others, because of the conviction she articulates in Janet Mullaney's collection of interviews, *Truthtellers of the Times*, that "to trivialize history, including the stories and practices of other cultures, is a great mistake." To that end, she writes about Nagasaki, about Jamestown, about Lebanon, about South Africa, and more. But in particular, she is interested in the history of black people in the United States. Her 1972 volume, *Good News About the Earth*, for example, is dedicated to "the dead of Jackson and Orangeburg and so on and so on." The "so on" in this book and others includes civil rights activists and revolutionaries such as Harriet Tubman, Eldridge Cleaver,

Bobby Seale, Angela Davis, Clifton's father, her husband, Winnie Mandela, Nelson Mandela, the survivors of the Philadelphia MOVE tragedy, and Malcolm X.

In the Mullany interview, Clifton reflected on her inclusion of Malcolm X in her children's literature as well. Speaking about *The Black BC's*, she said, "I like that book because of my X ; in those days X in the alphabet was for xylophone. My X is for Malcolm. I was pleased to have thought of that in 1970!" Like Malcolm, Clifton has a concern with the many meanings of whiteness. In "my dream about being white" in a series of dream poems in *Next*, the speaker finds that she is "wearing white history/ but there's no future in those clothes." Rather, for Clifton, the future rests at least in part in knowing one's personal and communal history. This is quite apparent in her children's books, too. In September of *Everett Anderson's Year* (1974), it is plain that for Everett and his mother that knowledge of Africa is just as fundamental as the skill of counting. He asks, very seriously, why he needs to go to school if he already knows how to count and already knows about Africa!

The issue of identity and the African diaspora is explored dramatically and powerfully in Clifton's 1973 children's title *All Us Come Cross the Water*. An extended look at this book is useful because of its representativeness in terms of her entire oeuvre. Its most obvious message is that black peoples in the Americas all arrived together on slave ships. To some degree, Clifton acknowledges a bond between them based solely on their common place of origin in Africa. This assumption, at once simplistic and problematic, instigates the story's movement. The main character and narrator, Ujamaa (or Jim), describes the opening episode in this way: "I got this teacher name Miss Wills. This day she come asking everybody to tell where they people come from. Everybody from over in the same place suppose to stand up by theirselves." When Ujamaa neither says anything nor stands up, the teacher reproaches him: " 'We must not be ashamed of ourselves, Jim,' she say. 'You are from a great heritage. . . . Now you know you are from Africa, don't you?' " Ujamaa gives the polite retort "Yes, mam" and walks out in disgust stemming from the fact that he knows Africa is a continent rather than a country. As throughout Clifton's canon, there is no recoiling here from situations of conflict and disharmony—the teacher and student (perhaps identified more accurately as elder and youth) are at a complete impasse. The teacher lacks any insight into the source of Ujamaa's distress and the factors that motivate his behavior. His actions stem from the fact that he is indeed proud of his heritage rather than ashamed. And though he is not completely knowledgeable about his origins, he is appalled and disappointed that his elder is even less informed. Thus, Ujamaa's quest becomes one of search for information and education; he assumes the role of researcher and teacher.

Ujamaa's investigation into his past begins by questioning his sister, Rose, a nursing student much older than himself. Her reply is that their deceased mother was from Rome, Georgia, and their father from Birmingham. "Before that," Ujamaa implores. She answers that their grandfather was from Georgia also. When Ujamaa presses the question, she laughs, "They wasn't no way back before that. Before that we was a slave." Thinking that Rose sickens him, he walks away to try with his next informant, his father, who dismisses him, using his fatigue as an excuse, and tells him to "ask Big Mama them questions."

Big Mama is Ujamaa's "Mama's Mama's Mama. She real old and she don't say much, but she see things cause she was born with a veil over her face." Not surprisingly, it is she who gives Ujamaa the most penetrating yet most elusive reply. First, she tells him that her mother and grandmother came from Dahomey in Whydah in 1855. When Ujamaa responds too quickly with "That mean I'm from Whydah?" she continues on telling him that his father's people look like the Ashanti people who come from southern Ghana. When he continues questioning her, she responds with a question of her own, asking him who he is. While he replies verbally with his name, he thinks, "Shoot, she know who I am, it was her give me my name." Satisfied with his answer, she dismisses him

with, "Go on now then. I'm through." Making a much more complex statement than the brevity of her words suggests, in a manner akin to the West African proverbial tradition to which she is heir, Big Mama is confident in her clarity. Ujamaa, though, is not quite sure about the implications of what she has said to him.

The one part of the reply he does identify as being significant is her focus on name as a crucial and telling point. When he approaches his next informant his interest, too, is on naming, asking Tweezer what his real name is. Tweezer is one of Ujamaa's adult neighborhood friends whose constant advice to Ujamaa is that he be a good brother. Tweezer's response to this particular question is that he does not know his real name because it was left in Africa. The ensuing conversation deals with the fact that when Tweezer's enslaved forefather was brought to this country he was not asked his real name and did not volunteer it because of the belief that the name is the person; he is not completely enslaved if they do not know his name. At this point Ujamaa interjects that he was named by Big Mama and that the meaning of his name is "Unity." Tweezer is pleased and continues talking about the importance of self naming. This part of the conversation segues into a discussion of the difficulty of identifying what specific countries in Africa African Americans come from. Tweezer's reply is that African American and Caribbean people and others from various parts of the diaspora are from all of those countries: "All us crossed the water. We one people, Ujamaa. Boy got that name oughta know that. All us crossed the water."

The book culminates back in the classroom with Ujamaa demonstrating his newfound understanding of the meaning of unity and brotherhood, leading his classmates in standing up to the African American teacher in protest of her ignorance, lack of intellectual curiosity, and lack of guidance. Ujamaa's friends, Bo and Malik, don't understand all that Ujamaa understands, but they do understand and act upon, on some level, the intangible, unspoken, and unconditional aspect of what might be called brotherhood.

Perhaps most important, *All Us Come Cross the Water*, like several of Clifton's children's books, suggests the importance of asking questions. In a poignant piece entitled "Robert" in *Good Times*, the reader sees the pitiful consequences of not asking questions. Robert "was born obedient/ without questions" and ends up being mastered by those who control his mind and so "until he died/ the color of his life/ was nigger." Commenting further on the idea of thoughtful interrogation, Clifton said in the Moyers interview: "Poems are about questions. They're not about answers. When you write poems, you try to figure something out. You don't know. We know very little."

But in fact, Lucille Clifton knows a lot. If nothing else, she knows her own family history, including, of necessity, white ancestry. Harvey Nichols, her great-grandfather, who was eventually shot by Lucy, Clifton's great-grandmother and namesake, appears throughout her writing, sometimes named and sometimes as a nameless "whiteman." And even when referring to that complex interracial relationship, Clifton's sense of humor is always evident. In *Generations*, for example, she recalls herself and her siblings, as youngsters, dancing and singing. When her brother Sammy made any misstep, he would exclaim " 'Damn Harvey Nichols.' And we would laugh." She knows that name and naming are important. In fact, she often writes about the name Lucille and its derivation from "light." (In particular, see the section in *Two-Headed Woman* called "the light that came to Lucille Clifton" as well as the poem with the same first line in that same volume.) Light is ubiquitous in her writing for young adults as well. The one activity that Sooky and Tassie engage in over and over again in *The Times They Used To Be* is waiting for the streetlights to come on each evening. It is significant that the day Tassie becomes convinced that she is a sinner because she has begun to menstruate (and while she is in a state of total ignorance), she "didn't even stop/ to get first light." Neglecting to stop for first light is neglecting to take time to gain information or to cultivate personal or communal growth. Clifton invites both child and adult to always remember to stop for first light.

Like Ujamaa, Clifton knows that her African ancestry is integral to her being. She refers constantly to Africa as home. And in her autobiography and elsewhere she discusses in detail her line of descent. To Clifton, her name is an Afrikan name because she is named after strong women of African descent. Not surprisingly, her people, the models for Ujamaa's family, come from Whydah in Dahomey. As she mentions in *Generations*, her parents, particularly her father, Samuel "Gene" Sayles, always remind her that "You named for Dahomey women, Lue." And Clifton knows that her "tribe" is magical, indicated by the extra finger on each hand that they are born with. When Clifton, as narrator in *Next*, looks forward to the coming of her progeny in "if our grandchild be a girl," she is clear that the grandchild will inherit the fingers and the magic "remembered from dahomean women." In "the mississippi river empties into the gulf" in *The Terrible Stories*, she warns that it is a mistake for people to think of human and natural experience in terms of "only here. only now." She knows who her family was, is, and will be.

In part, this knowledge is due to Clifton's spirituality, biographical information commented upon by most of the scholars who write on her work. Akasha (Gloria) Hull suggests that Clifton "negotiate[s] the world as a two-headed woman, that is, one who possesses magical power, who can see what is here and visible as well as that which is beyond ordinary vision." And Clifton has spoken plainly in various interviews and statements about this way of negotiating the world and about her "religious" writing, sometimes in the voices of biblical figures. But one of her major contributions is that she explores religion, spirituality, and the syncretism between folk and religious beliefs in her children's books, perhaps most clearly in *The Lucky Stone* (1979).

One telling scene takes place at Sunday meeting when "a mighty man of God," an itinerant preacher, makes a rare visit to the community. Vashti wears around her neck a pouch holding the stone that proved lucky for her mother, an escaped slave. When the string holding the pouch breaks and the stone falls to the ground, Vashti scrambles to retrieve it, thus avoiding a bolt of lightning that strikes the spot where she had been standing and starts a fire. The saving power of the stone is praised as much as the saving power of Jesus.

Clifton's work is revisionist and refreshing in the context of the ways in which the religious practices and "superstitions" of African Americans have been stereotyped and distorted in American children's literature. In historical terms, black people were portrayed as primitive; after 1947, books about black people tended to eliminate superstition as a characteristic while continuing to portray them as religious, according to Johnson's *Telling Tales*. What Clifton's canon demonstrates, in contrast, is a kind of progression away from embarrassment in relation to certain portrayals. Unlike white (liberal) writers of children's books, Clifton sees no reason to avoid that which might be labeled, negatively, superstitious or primitive or to deny the overlay of the superstitious with the religious. Clifton's exploration of these motifs, in the late sixties, could indicate various things. But at least in part, her perpetuation of superstitious images can be viewed not as a resignation to stereotype but as acceptance of a world. It is a view that recognizes the power of the veil over the face and the attendant second sight as well as the power of the god worshiped by her sanctified grandmother.

Taking on one of the central historical moments dealing with superstition and magic in America, Clifton begins her section on sisters in *An Ordinary Woman* with a poem about the Salem witch trials. More accurately, the poem is about the black witches' understanding that what is terrifying is not the things they are accused of, but "the plain face of the white woman watching us." "To Ms. Ann" in the same volume is a brutally honest poem about white women abdicating their responsibilities for home making and child rearing to black women and never considering them sisters. This is only one of several poems throughout her work that confront the tensions between

black and white women in this society, partly because they do not always share the same experience or worldview. At the same time, Clifton is clear in the Moyers' interview that "American literature has to reflect the American people. It has to. Nothing else makes sense." And her work genuinely reflects that philosophy.

Clifton's fellow writer Maxine Kumin (who is white) first urged her to try writing children's books in the late sixties. And though those books are populated largely by black characters, they also include white and Latino characters as well as those representing other American ethnic communities, characters of different religious faiths, different class positions and speech styles, different levels of social consciousness, different genders and ages, and even varying intellectual abilities. *My Friend Jacob* (1980), for example, is the unusual story of a younger black boy who befriends the older, white, mentally slow Jacob.

Not only is Clifton's writing inclusive, but as suggested by the many epigrams to her poems, her literary influences are many and varied, ranging from Walt Whitman to Galway Kinnell to Emily Dickinson. In this connection, she recounts in the Mullany interview the humorous but ultimately disgusting story of a student who assumes that Clifton is not familiar with the entire range of American poetry and thus had the gall to try to pass off a Dickinson poem as her own work! In *Next*, Clifton writes a very interesting series of poems entitled "in white america." Together, they recount her thoughts upon visiting what was formerly an all-white women's school to give a reading. Her feelings are complex, and the visit invokes in her mind images of the black women who cleaned the chapel and the halls of the college. Ultimately, though, Clifton's feeling is that she loves those in the audience; they are humans. At the same time, however, she feels that as a black poet she has a message to proclaim; she is "a black cat/ in the belfry/ hanging/ and/ ringing." The allusion to lynching embedded here speaks volumes and reverberates with the work of others she first came to know during her Howard University years, Sterling Brown,

A. B. Spelman, LeRoi Jones, and Chloe Wofford (Toni Morrison), who later edited her work for Random House.

But as obvious as it might be that Clifton knows American history and American literature, what is just as impressive is the way in which, through her poetry, she writes herself into African American literary history in both subtle and more straightforward ways. "the lost baby poem" in *Good News About the Earth*, for example, brings to mind Gwendolyn Brooks' "Abortions Will Not Let You Forget." And in "amazons" in *The Terrible Stories*, the women who "swooped in a circle dance" following Clifton's breast cancer diagnosis include audre, who can be assumed to be black writer/activist Audre Lorde who died of breast cancer in 1992.

But no matter how many literary sisters Lucille Clifton might have, she always returns home to her family of origin and her family made with Fred; critics often comment on the extent to which her work is openly autobiographical. Her readers know, for instance, that her father had four children, including three girls by three different mothers, all of whom knew each well. "Sisters," from *An Ordinary Woman*, was written on the occasion of her sister Elaine Philip's birthday. Its major message is that they "be the same." The poem chronicles their running down Purdy Street, a location that shows up in her children's books. It chronicles other activities from their childhoods, their becoming mothers, their fears, their self love, and more. Clifton identifies this poem as a cultural poem, perhaps because of the embedded details that might be specific to African American culture: girls greasing their legs and touching up (straightening) the edges of their hair—again the nappy hair of black women's literature. (Haki Madhubuti discusses her work as cultural writing in his essay "Lucille Clifton: Warm Water, Greased Legs and Dangerous Poetry.") Her many poems for and to her daughters, her "almost me," embody this kind of cultural detail and, like her sister poems, are very personal at the same time. Like her own mother's urging her to get away, she commands her girls "to be/ good runners." And it goes without question that they inspire her to con-

tinue running, her journey through this life as a daughter, parent, teacher, writer, and member of varied but related communities of fellow human beings.

In the poem "My Boys" in *Ordinary Woman*, Clifton talks about her sons in a way that males are not always spoken about in African American literature—with tenderness, with adoration. But not surprisingly, this is the way she talks about many of the men in her life. And just as she is interested in female experience, she is interested in male experience and manhood. In a particularly memorable poem in *Good News About the Earth*, entitled #26, about the man known as Little Richard, Clifton tells something of his experience raising his twelve siblings after his parent's deaths, only to have his manhood questioned later by outsiders. She sees the same kind of beauty and more in her own sons. She imagines people stunned by their beauty questioning the meaning of this beauty. But fortunately for her readers, Lucille Clifton knows the meaning of their beauty. For her it is the reason for her celebration of life in its simplicity and in its complexity, its horror and its majesty, its tangibleness and its mysticism. Their beauty is the foundation for her message to all of the community's children whom she is certain possess wisdom that black adults can grow from.

Clifton remains a teacher as well as a writer. She has taught at numerous institutions, including Coppin State College, Goucher College, American University, Columbia University, and the University of California at Santa Cruz. This list continues with appointments at numerous other colleges and universities; among the many, she served as the Woodrow Wilson Scholar at Fisk University, one of the most historically significant of the historically black colleges. Currently, Clifton is Distinguished Professor of Humanities at St. Mary's College in Maryland. She participates regularly in the discovering and mentoring of young writers in programs such as the Cave Canem poetry retreat. For Clifton, finally, it is always about the generations. She reminds her progeny and all progeny of mother Africa of this in one of her most famous (untitled) poems in *Good News*

About the Earth; she lovingly invites their attention with the call "listen children" and goes on to remind them that we have always and in all ways loved each other. She tells them to pass this on—as she has done in her extraordinary body of writing that questions everything from the pedestrian to the sublime.

Lucille Clifton presents herself as an ordinary woman. But her readers know that she is an extraordinary ordinary woman. Just as important, they know that she thinks most women and men, raising children or going to work or engaged in other daily activities of life, of homemaking, are extraordinary women and men, too. In an untitled poem in *Quilting*, (the first line reads: "somewhere"), Clifton describes a woman just like herself caring for her home and for her children but who, upon finding a pen stuck between the couch cushions, "sits down and writes the words/ Good Times." The poem concludes: "i think of her as i begin to teach/ the lives of the poets/ about her space at the table/ and my own inexplicable life." The world of American children's literature and the worlds of poetry and memoir and the academy are all enriched by Lucille Clifton's presence at the table, by her writing about her extraordinary ordinary life.

Selected Bibliography

PRIMARY WORKS

POETRY

Good Times. New York: Random House, 1969; Toronto: Random House of Canada, 1969.
Good News About the Earth. New York: Random House, 1972; Toronto: Random House of Canada, 1972.
An Ordinary Woman. New York: Random House, 1974; Toronto: Random House of Canada, 1974.
Two-Headed Woman. Amherst: University of Massachusetts Press, 1980.
Next: New Poems. Brockport, N.Y.: BOA Editions, 1987.
Quilting: Poems. Brockport, N.Y.: BOA Editions, 1991.
The Book of Light. Washington, D.C.: Copper Canyon Press, 1993.
The Terrible Stories: Poems. Brockport, N.Y.: BOA Editions, 1996.
Blessing the Boats: New and Selected Poems 1988–2000. New York: BOA Editions, 2000.

CHILDREN'S BOOKS

Some of the Days of Everett Anderson. Illustrated by Evaline Ness. New York: Holt, Rinehart, 1970.
The Black BC's. Illustrated by Don Miller. New York: E. P. Dutton, 1970.
Everett Anderson's Christmas Coming. Illustrated by Evaline Ness. New York: Holt, Rinehart, 1971.
All Us Come Cross the Water. Illustrated by John Steptoe. New York: Holt, Rinehart, 1973.
The Boy Who Didn't Believe in Spring. Illustrated by Brinton Turkle. New York: E. P. Dutton, 1973.
Don't You Remember? Illustrated by Evaline Ness. New York: E. P. Dutton, 1973.
Good, Says Jerome. Illustrated by Stephanie Douglas. New York: E. P. Dutton, 1973.
Everett Anderson's Year. Illustrated by Ann Grifalconi. New York: Holt, Rinehart, 1974.
The Times They Used to Be. Illustrated by Susan Jeschke. New York: Holt, Rinehart, 1974.
My Brother Fine With Me. Illustrated by Moneta Barnett. New York: Holt, Rinehart, 1975.
Everett Anderson's Friend. Illustrated by Ann Grifalconi. New York: Holt, Rinehart, 1976.
Everett Anderson's 123. Illustrated by Ann Grifalconi. New York: Holt, Rinehart, 1976.
The Three Wishes. Illustrated by Stephanie Douglas. New York: Viking Press, 1976.
Amifika. Illustrated by Thomas DiGrazia. New York: E. P. Dutton, 1977.
Everett Anderson's Nine Month Long. Illustrated by Ann Grifalconi. New York: Holt, Rinehart, 1978.
The Lucky Stone. Illustrated by Dale Payson. New York: Delacorte Press, 1979.
My Friend Jacob. Illustrated by Thomas DiGrazia. New York: E. P. Dutton, 1980.
Sonora Beautiful. Illustrated by Michael Garland. New York: E. P. Dutton, 1981.
Everett Anderson's Goodbye. Illustrated by Ann Grifalconi. New York: Holt, Rinehart, 1983.

PERIODICAL PUBLICATIONS

Fiction
"It's All in the Game." *Negro Digest* 15:18–19 (August 1966).
"The Magic Mama." *Redbook* 134:88–89 (November 1969).
"Christmas Is Something Else." *House and Garden* 136:70–71 (December 1969).
"The End of Love Is Death, The End of Death Is Love." *Atlantic* 227:65–67 (March 1971).

Nonfiction
"We Know This Place." *Essence* 7 (July 1976).
"If I Don't Know My Last Name, What Is the Meaning of My First?: Roots, The Saga of an American Family." *Ms.* 5:45 (February 1977).

OTHER WORKS

Generations: A Memoir. New York: Random House, 1976; Toronto: Random House of Canada, 1976.

Good Woman: Poems and a Memoir 1969–1980. Brockport, N.Y.: BOA Editions, 1987.

"A Simple Language." In *Black Women Writers (1950–1980): A Critical Evaluation.* Edited by Mari Evans, 137–38. New York: Anchor/Doubleday, 1984.

SECONDARY WORKS

BIOGRAPHICAL AND CRITICAL STUDIES

Anaporte-Easton, Jean. "Healing Our Wounds: The Direction of Difference in the Poetry of Lucille Clifton and Judith Johnson." *Mid-American Review* 14(2): 78–87 (1994).

Bauer, Denise. "The Representation of the Female Subject by Three American Women Artists: Painter Alice Neel, Poet Lucille Clifton, and Filmmaker Claudia Weill, 1970–1980." *Dissertation Abstracts International* 59:5 (November 1998).

Blain, Virginia, Patricia Clements, and Isobel Grundy, eds. *The Feminist Companion to Literature in English: Women Writers from the Middle Ages to the Present* New Haven, CT: Yale University Press (1990).

Chevalier, T., ed. *Twentieth-Century Children's Writers.* Chicago: St. James, 1983.

Draper, James P., ed. *Black Literature Criticism: Excerpts from Criticism of the Most Significant Works of Black Authors over the Past 200 Years.* Detroit: Gale Research, 1992.

Edson, Russell, et al. "Worcester Poetry Festival: Statements by Poets, 1974–76." *Worcester Review* 4:38–46 (1981).

Evans, Mari, ed. *Black Women Writers (1950–1980): A Critical Evaluation.* Garden City, NY: Anchor/Doubleday, 1984.

Fink, Thomas. "Poets against Marginalization." *The Minnesota Review* 43–44:264–71 (fall 1994/spring 1995).

Holze, Sally Holmes, ed. *Fifth Book of Junior Authors and Illustrators.* Chicago: St. James, 1988.

Hull, Akasha. "In Her Own Images: Lucille Clifton and the Bible," in *Dwelling in Possibility: Women Poets and Critics on Poetry,* (Y. Prins and M. Schreiber, eds.) Ithaca, N.Y.: Cornell University Press, 1997 pp. 273–95.

———. "Channeling the Ancestral Muse: Lucille Clifton and Dolores Kendrick," in *Feminist Measures: Soundings in Poetry and Theory,* (Lynn Keller and Christianne Miller, eds.) Ann Arbor: University of Michigan Press, 1994, pp. 96–116.

Johnson, Dianne. *Telling Tales: The Pedagogy and Promise of African American Literature for Youth.* New York: Greenwood, 1990.

Johnson-Feelings, Dianne. *The Best of the Brownies' Book.* New York: Oxford University Press, 1996.

Johnson, Joyce. "The Theme of Celebration in Lucille Clifton's Poetry." *Pacific Coast Philology* 18:59–69 (1983).

Madhubuti, Haki. "Lucille Clifton: Warm Water, Greased Legs, and Dangerous Poetry." In *Black Women Writers (1950–1980) A Critical Evaluation,* edited by Mari Evans, 150. Garden City, NY: Anchor/Doubleday, 1984.

McClusky, Audrey T. "Tell the Good News: A View of the Good Works of Lucille Clifton." In *Black Women Writers (1950–1980): A Critical Evaluation,* edited by Mari Evans, 139–49. New York: Anchor/Doubleday, 1984.

Mullaney, Janet Palmer, ed. *Truthtellers of the Times: Interviews with Contemporary Women Poets.* Ann Arbor: University of Michigan Press, 1998.

Ostriker, Alicia. " 'Kin and Kin': The Poetry of Lucille Clifton." *Literary Influence and African-American Writers.* New York: Garland, 1996.

White, Mark Bernard. "Sharing the Living Light: Rhetorical, Poetic, and Social Identity in Lucille Clifton." *College Language Association Journal* 40, no. 3:288–304 (March 1997).

Worsham, Fabian Clements. "The Poetics of Matrilineage: Mothers and Daughters in the Poetry of African-American Women, 1965–1985." In *Women of Color; Mother–Daughter Relationships in 20th-Century Literature.* Edited by Elizabeth Brown-Guillory. Austin: University of Texas Press, 1996, pp. 117–31.

INTERVIEWS

Moyers, Bill. *Power of the Word.* "Where the Soul Lives." PBS, 1989.

Thiers, Naomi. In *Truthtellers of the Times: Interviews with Contemporary Women Poets.* Edited by Janet Palmer Mullaney. Ann Arbor: The University of Michigan Press, 1998.

Holladay, Hilary. "An Interview With Lucille Clifton: No Ordinary Woman." *Poets & Writers* (special issue on poetry in America), April 1999, pp. 30–35.

COUNTEE CULLEN
(1903–1946)

NATHAN GRANT

COUNTEE CULLEN REMAINS one of the great controversial—and contradictory—figures of the Harlem Renaissance, the sudden and significant flowering of African American art and letters in the 1920s and 1930s. That Cullen might well have had these attributes in nearly any period is arguable, for there is a specific doubleness that permeates his character. His temperament, however, was perhaps best suited to the Renaissance, lending much to its background; the era of the New Negro was itself a period of great ambivalence, from which arose its often marvelous ambiguity. The very tension between elements of Cullen's poetry and Cullen's own struggle toward artistic and political identity in the new, consciously pluralistic America of the young twentieth century are themselves representative of the Renaissance, a period of dualisms, and thus for many a period whose very name "Renaissance" misleads.

Background

In *Caroling Dusk* (1927), a book edited by Cullen that became one of the twentieth century's most important anthologies of African American verse, the brief biographical information he supplies is an invitation to intrigue. Born May 30, 1903, in New York City and "reared in the conservative atmosphere of a Methodist parsonage," Cullen cites his "chief problem" as being "that of reconciling a Christian upbringing with a pagan inclination." Ambiguity and a puckish sensibility begin here, as he continues by telling his readership that "his life so far has not convinced him that the problem is insoluble." Both the facts of his early life and his efforts to conceal these would seem to give him much to ponder in that regard. It was perhaps in 1918, when the poet was fourteen, that Cullen became the adopted son of the Reverend Frederick Asbury Cullen of the Salem Methodist Episcopal Church in Harlem, and his wife Carolyn Belle Mitchell Cullen. The adoption, apparently never having been formalized, may have taken place even sooner. As if it were not enough that this issue remains unsettled, the identities of his biological parents are less clear. It is most likely that shortly after his birth in Louisville, Kentucky, his mother, Elizabeth Lucas, left the child in the care of Elizabeth Porter, who may have been Cullen's paternal grandmother. But as Jean Wagner states in his influential study of black male poets of the period, *Black Poets of the United States* (1973), it also seems clear that Cullen painstakingly cultivated the mystery surrounding his early years, insisting that he was in fact the biological son of Frederick and Carolyn Mitchell Cullen. Yet even this curiosity seems not altogether unusual when one considers this period. Other African American writers from the 1920s, notably Nella Larsen, Jean Toomer, and Zora Neale Hurston, displayed—and continuously deployed—confusing identities. It is a safe observation that in many respects, Cullen's behavior mirrors that of several of his black contemporaries. At a time when the African American visage and voice were being examined, debated, and celebrated for virtually the first time, it is perhaps not difficult to imagine a concomitant discomfiture regarding origins and futures.

Cullen undertook his first attempts at poetry during his high school years. Already in 1918, while at the DeWitt Clinton High School in the Bronx, he wrote poetry that won awards in local competitions; notable among these was "Life's Rendezvous," collected in *My Soul's High Song.* This poem is a recasting of "I Have a Rendezvous with Death," a poem by an earlier New York poet, Alan Seeger. In the first half of Cullen's poem, the youthful and optimistic narrator is "betrothed to Beauty"; he can, in the second half, envision no time when his

> . . . impassioned flesh . . .
> Shall less desire its bread and wine
> All longing lost in primal clay.

This youthful exuberance, nourished by Christian faith, also foreshadows what would later be Cullen's tempestuous struggle with Christ and Christian symbolism, reaching its apex in his longest poem, "The Black Christ" (1929). A complication of this development, ironically, was his continuing academic success: he was elected to the honor society; he became vice-president of his graduating class; he became editor of the school newspaper, the *Clinton News;* and he served as associate editor of the school literary magazine, the *Magpie,* in which "Life's Rendezvous" was first published—in short, honors became quite familiar to the talented young Cullen. The daily ride from Harlem to school in the Bronx was Cullen's initiation to a perceived whiteness, to modes of expression the mastery of which were not associated with, and therefore not expected from, Negroes. It

has been suggested by many critics that it is this disjunctive feature of Cullen's life that is made manifest again and again in his poetry, though again, a typical feature of American society at this time was the strict enforcement of cultural barriers between blacks and whites. It should be said, moreover, that Cullen did much to cultivate the manner of the sophisticate, and in doing so often alienated his black colleagues while at the same time appearing to affirm black cultural enfranchisement.

Shortly after Cullen's entering New York University in 1922, two significant African American journals heralding the advent of the New Negros—*The Crisis,* the journal of the National Association for the Advancement of Colored People (NAACP) edited at that time by W. E. B. Du Bois, and Charles S. Johnson's *Opportunity,* the magazine of the National Urban League—began to publish some of his poems. Magazines that included a wider and more broadly European American reading public, such as *Harper's, American Mercury,* and *The Bookman,* soon began accepting his work. Harriet Monroe's *Poetry,* one of the famous "little magazines" of this period that had already made its impact on transatlantic literary modernism, also published his poems. Nineteen twenty-five became Cullen's golden year; it was the year of his graduation from New York University and also his election to Phi Beta Kappa, the national honor society. He would go on to earn his Master of Arts in English and French from Harvard in 1926. But in 1925 Cullen would truly begin to make his mark in literary history. He took second place in the Palm Poetry Contest for "Wisdom Cometh with the Years," was the winner of the John Reed Memorial Prize (sponsored by *Poetry* magazine) for "Threnody for a Brown Girl," and won the Amy Spingarn Award for "Two Moods of Love" in a competition in Harlem hosted by *The Crisis.* He also won the Witter Bynner Undergraduate Prize, a national competition for the best undergraduate poetry, for "To a Brown Girl," written in 1923 with its companion work, "To a Brown Boy," which had already been published in *The Bookman* (he had received honorable mention for the Bynner prize in 1924 for "Spirit Birth"). Among the judges was the Chicago poet Carl Sandburg, who would profoundly influence this generation of American writers, both black and white; another judge, the austere George Lyman Kittredge of Harvard, had called "To a Brown Girl" the finest modern rendition of an old ballad that he had ever read.

Color

Cullen also produced his first book of verse in 1925, a slim volume entitled *Color* that brought him wide acclaim among many in the literary community, both black and white. Some of the most often anthologized poems of the Renaissance, "Heritage," "Incident," "To a Brown Girl," "To a Brown Boy," "A Brown Girl Dead," "Saturday's Child," and "Yet Do I Marvel" issue from this first volume. Darwin T. Turner, in his landmark study of Cullen, Zora Neale Hurston, and Jean Toomer, *In a Minor Chord* (1971), calls Cullen's "Heritage" "in imagery and diction . . . the most successful poem he ever wrote." Like Langston Hughes's "The Negro Speaks of Rivers" and "Afro-American Fragment," or Claude McKay's "Enslaved" or "Outcast," "Heritage" is one of the outstanding examples of the "alien-and-exile" theme, a mood of the black lyric made popular during the Harlem Renaissance for its questioning of whether African Americans owe their cultural allegiance to Africa or to the West, knowing as they do that while they are estranged forever from the former, the latter has just as permanently altered them. Cullen's opening strophe reflects this very anguish of Du Boisian double consciousness:

Countee Cullen

What is Africa to me:
Copper sun or scarlet sea,
Jungle star or jungle track,
Strong bronzed men, or regal black
Women from whose loins I sprang
When the birds of Eden sang?
Over three centuries removed
From the scenes his fathers loved
Spicy grove, cinnamon tree,
What is Africa to me?

In one passage the poet seems finally to renounce Africa, bound as he is by the shared rituals and behaviors of the West:

Quaint, outlandish heathen gods
Black men fashion out of rods,
Clay, and brittle bits of stone,
In a likeness like their own,
My conversion came high-priced;
I belong to Jesus Christ,
Preacher of humility;
Heathen gods are naught to me.

Ultimately, however, the indigenous spirit will out, and the poet cries to be mirrored by divinity:

Ever at Thy glowing altar
Must my heart grow sick and falter,
Wishing He I served were black,
Thinking then it would not lack

Precedent of pain to guide it,
Let who would or might deride it;
Surely then this flesh would know
Yours had borne a kindred woe.

If, as Cullen would later write of himself in the preface to *Caroling Dusk,* the chief problem he faced was that of reconciling his Christian background with pagan desires, the union of blackness and divinity—first in "Heritage" and later in "The Black Christ"—would seek to achieve this reconciliation, and it would also attempt valiantly to solve for African America the terrible division of the soul that is the result of disfranchisement. But there is finally no resolution for the poet, overdetermined as his sensibilities are by the West's insistent and thoroughgoing acculturation: *"Not yet has my heart or head / In the least way realized / They and I are civilized."*

Cullen as Critic

Though the critical reception to *Color* was generally favorable, there appeared to be some disagreement as to its focus and impact, falling as it did across the great racial and political divide. Novelist and Secretary of the National Association for the Advancement of Colored People (NAACP) Walter White, while reviewing *Color* in *The Saturday Review of Literature,* said of Cullen that "his race and its sufferings give him depth and an understanding of pain and sorrow." But an anonymous reviewer in the London *Times Literary Supplement* insists that Cullen's African American background and the fact that some of his poems thematize this is irrelevant; the reviewer writes that "it is not only 'the great dark heart' of an insulted people which he lays bare but the dark heart of us all aspiring from primitive passion to spiritual light, in the clear knowledge . . . that the dark passion itself must undergo a vital transmutation." For Clement Wood, writing in the *Yale Review,* "there is no point in measuring [Cullen] merely beside Dunbar, Alberry [*sic*] A. Whitman, and other Negro poets of the past and present: he must stand or fail beside Shake-

speare and Keats and Masefield, Whitman, and Poe and Robinson." In *The New Republic,* however, it is Eric Walrond's "utmost belief" that "dissecting the cosmos of the Negro spirit is Countee Cullen's ultimate concern; certainly the urge in that direction beckons strongest." Despite these discrepant views, however, Cullen would shortly reveal significant aspects of his own aesthetic philosophy.

Another important volume of poetry to have appeared in 1925 was Langston Hughes's *The Weary Blues.* This volume by Hughes, also his first, is very different in tone and style from *Color.* While Cullen employed traditional verse forms and rhythms and was influenced by the poetry of John Keats and Edna St. Vincent Millay, Hughes had practically created a new kind of poetry, based on rhythms to be found in jazz—the then new music of African America—and in the colloquial speech of the urban black masses. That these two works could at the same time elicit such praise from many of the same critical venues was itself a description of the Harlem Renaissance: its aesthetic and thus political branches mark it as a period of great debate as regards African American self-representation. But it was Cullen's conservative perspective toward poetry that helped shape his review of Hughes's volume in the February 1926 issue of *Opportunity.* The review was generally praiseworthy, saying of Hughes that he "represents a transcendently emancipated spirit among a class of young writers whose particular battle-cry is freedom." To those works that observe the standards of structure that Cullen defends, he is generous; but of the jazz poems he is categorically dismissive.

They move along with the frenzy and electric heat of a Methodist or Baptist revival meeting, and affect me in much the same manner. The revival meeting excites me, cooling and flushing me with alternate chills and fevers of emotion; so do these poems. But when the storm is over, I wonder if the quiet way of communing is not more spiritual for the God-seeking heart; and in the light of reflection I wonder if jazz poems really belong to that dignified company, that select and austere circle of high literary expression which we call poetry.

Of Hughes's "The Cat and the Saxophone," Cullen writes: "I cannot say *This will never do,* but I feel that it ought never [to] have been done." The battle lines of the traditional poetic gesture and the bold, new modernist stroke would appear to have been drawn; Cullen's remarks did much to spark a debate that would continue on the pages of Oswald Garrison Villard's *The Nation* during that spring, though Hughes's riposte to Cullen in his famous essay of June 28, "The Negro Artist and the Racial Mountain," would be veiled behind his response to George Schuyler's June 16 article "The Negro-Art Hokum" of the previous week.

After graduating from Harvard and visiting Europe and the Middle East in 1926, Cullen returned in November to become assistant editor of *Opportunity* magazine and editor of its literary criticism section, which he named "The Dark Tower" after one of his poems in his second volume of poetry *Copper Sun* (1927). This poem, "From the Dark Tower," is dedicated to Charles S. Johnson, and strikes a defiant note of race consciousness rhythmically reminiscent of but different in tone from Paul Laurence Dunbar's poem of reticence and restraint, "We Wear the Mask":

We shall not always plant while others reap
The golden increment of bursting fruit,
Not always countenance, abject and mute,
That lesser men should hold their brothers
    cheap;
Not everlastingly while others sleep
Shall we beguile their limbs with mellow
    flute,
Not always bend to some more subtle
    brute;
We were not made eternally to weep.

A'Lelia Walker, the black heiress to the cosmetics fortune of her mother (Madame C. J. Walker) who held parties and teas for Harlemites and those interested in Harlem, had painted on one wall of her salon verses from "The Dark Tower." On the wall opposite was painted a section from Hughes's "The Weary Blues," the title poem of his 1925 book. Despite the very different tones of these poems and their conveyance of different black sensibilities—elements of representation that would be debated throughout the period and well after—their appearance on opposite walls of A'Lelia Walker's salon exemplifies the very kind of gentle disjuncture the Renaissance always appeared to generate. But this artistic and in many ways political contrast was the very description of the New Negro and the conflicting cultural, historical, and political awarenesses that characterized this period.

The poem represents a strain of defiance not often associated with Countee Cullen, one that demands the recognition of black humanity. But both in his poetry and as public intellectual—a responsibility he took seriously as literary critic—Cullen often engaged black defiance, and always with sophistication and nuance. In his inaugural "Dark Tower" column in December 1926 Cullen calls for an even broader recognition of humanity, black and white, who are contributing conspicuously and heroically to the end of racial discrimination, lest the "weary ones" are overtaken by "the conviction that the world is getting worse and race relations more muddled." At a time when white playwrights such as Du Bose and Dorothy Heyward, Ridgely Torrence and Eugene O'Neill were calling for black playwrights to come forward and render through their experiences the sensibilities and aspirations of African Americans to audiences, Cullen's review in the November 1927 issue of *Opportunity* of a production of the Heywards' "Porgy" cautioned against being too hasty in presenting blackness lest such presentations revive and set in relief anti-black stereotypes.

But Cullen would seek also to further his demand for an adherence to artistic standards, and would go beyond this in an effort to deracinate art. At the time that he accepted the post at Johnson's *Opportunity*, he had also been compiling an anthology of African American poetry, *Caroling Dusk*, which appeared with illustrations by Aaron Douglas in 1927 and won the Harmon Foundation Literature Award for that year. In its preface Cullen continued to advance his conservative views on race and poetry, which could not have avoided creating a maelstrom of controversy:

> I have called this collection an anthology of verse by Negro poets rather than an anthology of Negro verse, since this latter designation would be more confusing than accurate. Negro poetry, it seems to me, in the sense that we speak of Russian, French, or Chinese poetry, must emanate from some country other than this in some language other than our own. Moreover, the attempt to corral the outbursts of the ebony muse into some definite mold to which all poetry by Negroes will conform seems altogether futile and aside from the facts. This country's Negro writers may here and there turn some singular facet toward the literary sun, but in the main, since theirs is also the heritage of the English language, their work will not present any serious aberration from the poetic tendencies of their times. The conservatives, the middlers, and their arch heretics will be found among them as among the white poets; and to say that the pulse beat of their verse shows generally such a fever, or the symptoms of such an ague, will prove on closer examination merely the moment's exaggeration of a physician anxious to establish a new literary ailment. As heretical as it may sound, there is the probability that Negro poets, dependent as they are on the English language, may have more to gain from the rich background of English and American poetry than from any nebulous atavistic yearnings toward an African inheritance.

Though Cullen is right to call for an end to the racialization of art, he is here blithely dismissive of the special circumstances of African Americans that make American Negro poetry a truly national poetry. His other literary achievements in 1927 seemed, however, to both compromise and punctuate his theory: *The Ballad of the Brown Girl: An Old Ballad Retold* is a single long poem dealing with miscegenation,

while *Copper Sun* has within its covers only seven poems that discuss the subject of race. But, though Cullen's political views seem unorthodox for an era named that of the New Negro, they are quite in keeping with the tone of that era; understanding and feeling the constraints under which blacks existed, he wrote in a March 1928 "Dark Tower" column that "American life is so constituted, the wealth of power is so unequally distributed, that whether they relish the situation or not, Negroes should be concerned with making good impressions." Though this was perhaps more an appeal for acceptance than, as Jean Wagner remarks was the case with Paul Laurence Dunbar, a "will to whiteness," Cullen nevertheless emerged on the side of wishing away or hiding the behaviors that he and other blacks were convinced whites would prefer not to see. Again, however, it remains not simply the case that a subterranean self-hatred haunts Cullen, but that the period's stifling social inequality fueled that self-hatred and demanded his caution. Additionally, an intellectual rigor with regard to the craft of poetry—a rigor normally not associated by whites with African American art—strongly governed his aesthetic.

Wedlock and Its Aftermath

Perhaps the principal social event of 1928 was Cullen's marriage to Nina Yolande Du Bois, the only child of the putative dean of African American letters, W. E. B. Du Bois. Like her illustrious father, Yolande was a graduate of Fisk University; Cullen met her when he was still a student at New York University. During their courtship Cullen dedicated, either explicitly or implicitly, some of his poems to her. Certainly "Brown Boy to Brown Girl" in *Color*, subtitled "To Yolande," and *Copper Sun*'s "One Day We Played a Game," similarly subtitled, are among the explicit ones. The entirety of *Copper Sun* is dedicated to "The Not Impossible Her," who is likely Yolande. The two were married in April of 1928 by Cullen's adoptive father, the Reverend Frederick Cullen, in his church, and before the notables of African America. The marriage was ill fated, however, and lasted just over a year; toward the end of June, Cullen had received a Guggenheim fellowship and had set sail for France with both the Rev. Cullen and Cullen's close friend, Harold Jackman, leaving Yolande in New York. Though she followed Cullen to Europe in July, the marriage was irrecoverable; upon her return to New York, she divorced Cullen in 1929.

Though he missed Yolande while in Paris and endured an ensuing unhappiness over their breakup, Cullen's homosexual encounters also seemed to be a well-known fact in artistic circles. But, though much of the Harlem community would whisper about the groom's travel abroad not with the bride, but with the best man, no evidence exists of a homosexual relationship between Cullen and Jackman. Newspapers have hinted and teased, but nothing other than a strong friendship and an intellectual affinity between the two men ever surfaced. While those who knew Cullen best speculated, as do contemporary critics, on his apparent lack of fitness for marriage, his marriage in 1940 to Ida Mae Roberson complicates this view of his sexuality; though short-lived because of Cullen's untimely death, this marriage seemed to be one of genuine mutual devotion, and a bond that included Ida Mae's enduring interest in writing and in art, particularly in African art and culture. Ida Mae Roberson-Cullen proved also to be a great aid to Countee's work; as Blanche Ferguson recounts, while Cullen was working on *The Lost Zoo*, he was "pleased to discover that Ida did not think him insane when he declared that the story was being dictated to him by his cat."

The Black Christ and Other Poems

Cullen remained in Paris after the divorce from Yolande, shortly thereafter setting to work on *The Black Christ and Other Poems*, which appeared in 1929. According to Jean Wagner, *The Black Christ* "... is not without grandeur. ... but it also writes a kind of *finis* to his work as a poet." Distressed by the failure of his mar-

riage, but exhilarated by contact with Padraic Colum and other Irish writers and intellectuals in Paris, Cullen did shape a somewhat uneven book that was nevertheless marked in some places by a sublime economy, as in "For the Unknown Soldier (Paris)," the first of "Two Epitaphs":

> Unknown but not unhonored rest,
> Symbol of all Time shall not reap;
> Not one stilled heart in that torn breast,
> But a myriad millions sleep.

And in others, by peregrinations of the spirit to dark venues, as from "Mood":

> I think an impulse stronger than my mind
> May some day grasp a knife, unloose a vial,
> Or with a little leaden ball unbind
> The cords that tie me to the rank and file.
> My hands grow quarrelsome with
>   bitterness,
> And darkly bent upon the final fray;
> Night with its stars upon a grave seems less
> Indecent than the too complacent day.

The companion to this poem, "Counter Mood," seems unconvincing in its effort to render a counter statement, as the resolution is held in abeyance; though the poet's "... nights tend toward the grave, yet I / Shall on some brighter day arise, and live." The love poems in the collection lack the felicity of earlier books, and are filled with a dissonant and regressive, if ironic, music, as in "The Foolish Heart":

> "Be still, heart, cease those measured
>   strokes;
> Lie quiet in your hollow bed;
> This moving frame is but a hoax
> To make you think you are not dead."

Yet Cullen can marshal the ringing human cry against injustice, as he does in "Not Sacco and Vanzetti":

> These men who do not die, but send to
>   death,
> These iron men whom mercy cannot bend

Beyond the lettered law; what when their
  breath
Shall suddenly and naturally end?
What shall their final retribution be,
What bloody silver then shall pay the tolls
Exacted for this legal infamy
When death indicts their stark immortal
  souls?

The Black Christ and Other Poems is illustrated by Charles Cullen (no relation to the poet; he was also the illustrator for *Copper Sun*) with an attention to the form of the human body reminiscent of the engravings of William Blake. As the Blakian influence is most evident in "The Black Christ," the last section of the book, Charles Cullen's detail focuses not only on the perfection of form, but, with this, the power of the body. Unlike Blake's engravings, however, the deeper attention here is to the construction of androgyny in the figures; blended, then, is for Cullen the Manichean duality man-woman, followed by, or blended still, in another, black-white—as well as good-evil, or even Christian-pagan, recalling the irremediable quandary of the speaker in "Heritage." In the title poem of the collection, "The Black Christ," Cullen again enjoins valuations of Christianity that he had long harbored and struggled with.

The religious fundamentalism of Frederick Asbury and Carolyn Mitchell Cullen was in some instances perhaps even embraced by the boy in his early youth, for he was deeply devoted to them. But as he matured, deepened his education, and began to enjoy success and acclaim in the wider world, the tenets of a rigid religious sensibility began to meet in conflict. Ultimately, however, Cullen was accepting of religion, and particularly, the politically aware African American variety. Frederick Cullen's Salem Methodist Episcopal Church was quite politically active, the elder Cullen himself having been a member and president of the Harlem branch of the National Association for the Advancement of Colored People and having co-organized and marched down New York's Fifth Avenue in 1917, with Du Bois and James Weldon Johnson, among others, to protest the riots earlier that summer in East St. Louis, Illinois, in which hundreds of black lives were lost. Christian justice and civil rights, then, were at the center of Frederick Cullen's philosophy, and the younger Cullen could not help but imbibe this spirit.

"The Black Christ" is on its fundamental narrative level the story of Jim, a young black man who rebels against God because of the consistency and the depth with which blacks are offered only second-class citizenship in America. His mother, however, a staunch Christian, retains her faith in spite of the storm. On a beautiful spring day, Jim and a white female companion are seen walking together by a white man, who insults the woman. In the ensuing fight between Jim and the man, the man is killed, and Jim, as he himself understands, must be lynched. Perhaps more so than any of Cullen's other works, "The Black Christ" has had a mixed critical reception. For some, the poem represents a kind of thematic simplicity that might easily insult the sensibilities of the oppressed. J. Saunders Redding, in charting the decline of the poet's power during this period and in determining Cullen to be overall much less the racial poet than his fellows, finds this work "feeble with the childish mysticism of a bad dream." The issue of racial strife is certainly at the poem's center, but, although the poem is "hopefully dedicated to White America," another more transcendent meaning arguably appears evident. Jean Wagner contends that " 'The Black Christ' is a masterly reconstruction of the poet's inner drama," locating in the corpus of American racial drama Cullen's more individual passion of faith and its struggles against adversity. Jim's mother, the symbol of an enduring Christianity in the poem, is at least the temporary balm for her son's bitterness:

Men may not bind the summer sea,
Nor set a limit to the stars;
The sun seeps through all iron bars;
The moon is ever manifest.
These things my heart always possessed.
And more than this (and here's the crown)
No man, my son, can batter down
The star-flung ramparts of the mind.

142

So much for flesh; I am resigned,
Whom God has made shall He not guide?

For Wagner, the mother's faith is not merely that of a single person, but also that of the long-suffering African American masses, whose utter disfranchisement fuels the human cry for God's deliverance. But the atrocity of lynching—which is redoubled in its regularity, its frighteningly swift recurrences—causes Alan Shucard to return to the notion of the poem's simplicity, observing as he does that this Christian acceptance is "extremely facile," and that "Cullen comes to display a degree of faith that would be difficult for all but the most zealous fundamentalist to credit in the shadow of the events of the poem." It is interesting to note that these vastly differing responses are to a poem that presumably represents, for the most part, the ending of Cullen's poetic career, a diminution of the bardic gift. If so, it remains possible that Cullen's last great effort actually defies interpretation by subjoining complexity to simplicity, by refracting the horrifically commonplace into personal and tempestuous spiritual struggle.

Fiction, Drama, and Translation

Cullen returned to the United States in 1930, finding New York and Harlem fast in the grip of the Great Depression. The nation's financial collapse of 1929 that signaled the depression's onset had a crippling effect on the Harlem Renaissance. Though African Americans continued to create art in Harlem and elsewhere through the 1930s—particularly through the programs of FDR's New Deal, manifest for artists in the Federal Writers' and Federal Theater Projects—white interest in Harlem and in the New Negro had begun to disappear. It may have been the case that this event contributed to Cullen's sharp decline in production, for writing would now be less likely to produce steady income. Nevertheless, Cullen's next literary ventures were the adaptation to the stage of Arna Bontemps 1930 novel, *God Sends Sunday,*

and Cullen's only novel, *One Way to Heaven* (1932). Cullen's 1936 stage adaptation of this novel (entitled *Heaven's My Home*) ended in failure.

One Way to Heaven, which satirizes both the religious and intellectual life of Harlem, paints a picture of Harlem familiar to Cullen: the streets, the churches, the salons. Constancia Brandon, the elegant but pretentious hostess of Harlem soirées, provides much of the novel's breeziness and wit as she moves with blithe indifference through the social scene, as do her cohorts: everyone is far more occupied, for example, with the New Negro's raiment than with her constitution. Sam, the one-armed hustler, and his bride Mattie, Constancia's maid, represent the rest of the Harlem community, the masses whose everyday concerns are far from those of the elite and for whom Harlem has a very different landscape. Though their paths cross consistently, Constancia and her crowd never really see Sam and Mattie; the effort toward political connectedness among blacks that Cullen's upbringing and sensibilities would embrace is missed here. For some critics, this is the novel's most unfortunate flaw, for it fails to combine these disparate elements of class into a more cohesive view of Harlem. For others, however, this discrepancy is key to the novel's success: the ultimate class and race fantasies of an urban mulatto elite and the elite's inability to foster alliances with the working masses are the guarantors of separateness, and it is this separateness that is the thematic center of the novel. For his pains, however, Cullen, who had previously enjoyed lavish attention from the black media for being one of the wunderkinder of the Harlem Renaissance, was given only scant mention by *Opportunity* and no review at all from *The Crisis.* Cullen, who at one time upheld poetic standards by citing Langston Hughes's jazz rhythms and diction as insufficient for the construction of verse, had himself transgressed; the arbiters of Renaissance taste would not brook even his negative representations of black America.

God Sends Sunday did not fare well as a drama. At the time of the conception of the project, Bontemps and Cullen understood that the

Depression would make the staging of the play on Broadway difficult. After financial and organizational failures of the Federal Theater Project in both New York and Los Angeles, the drama had difficulty finding support. A new backer, Edward Gross, insisted that the work be redone as a musical, so Cullen and Bontemps worked with the legendary songwriters Harold Arlen and Johnny Mercer to create *St. Louis Woman*. This enjoyed a brief run on the road, staged at the Gilpin House in Cleveland, Ohio, from November 22 to November 26, 1933, and again from June 5 to June 10, 1935, and finally did play, though briefly, on Broadway at the Martin Beck Theatre on March 30, 1946, and again shortly after Cullen's death, appearing in the same venue, later in 1946. The Broadway run starred Rex Ingram and the famous dancers, the Nicholas Brothers; it also debuted singer Pearl Bailey. Before the New York opening, Walter White, who was then the head of the National Association for the Advancement of Colored People and had written glowingly about Cullen's *Color* a generation earlier, criticized the production for displaying blacks as prostitutes and gamblers, thereby perpetuating stereotypes. Though the richly talented Lena Horne had been invited to star in the production, her sensitivity to White's criticism moved her to decline the role. Even after pleas that she reconsider, Horne refused to be associated with the production. It seemed now that even African American interest in Countee Cullen began to dissipate.

While making trenchant claims against so much in the Renaissance that was vacuous and frivolous, however, *One Way to Heaven* seems to lack the mordancy of Wallace Thurman's novel about the period, *Infants of the Spring* (1934), the work to which *Heaven* is often compared. In Thurman's novel, in addition to an oblique yet simple playfulness stretched across the class divide, there is the plight of the artist and a fundamental discussion of what the future of New Negroness will hold as it seeks to create art with so many forces arrayed against it. But despite the equivocations regarding black representation, black artists everywhere were soon faced with the waning days of the Renais-

sance, and Cullen became a junior high school teacher in December of 1934, teaching both French and English at the Frederick Douglass Junior High School in New York. He continued writing, however, and produced *The Medea and Some Poems* (1935). This collection includes Cullen's penetrating poem of protest, "Scottsboro, Too, Is Worth Its Song," a poignant address to American poets who, while the world had waited for its result, had forgotten the unjust trial of nine black boys. Even at this critical moment of change in an illustrious career, Cullen feels and demands from others the social responsibility of the poet and the call of the intellectual to the defense of justice. The collection also includes a translation of Euripides' *Medea* into colloquial English, which made Cullen the first African American writer to translate a major Greek drama into prose. Fellow playwright and poet, Cullen's friend Owen Dodson adapted and successfully staged Cullen's *Medea* on March 15, 1940, at Spelman College in Atlanta, Georgia. In the years after Cullen's death, Dodson produced the play again, changed several of its elements, and renamed it *Medea in Africa* in 1948, placing his own name alongside Cullen's. Dodson also wrote with Cullen *The Third Fourth of July*, Cullen's only published play (appearing posthumously in the magazine *Theatre Arts* in August 1946).

Writing for Children

Writers and artists did what they could to ease the depression-era jitters. Though the worsening economy was on the mind of every American, at least some in the early years sought ways to relax. A'Lelia Walker still threw parties at her Harlem salon, and at one of these Cullen met Ida Mae Roberson, who in 1940 became his second wife. But Cullen produced little after about 1935; perhaps too, the new demands on his time as a teacher made it difficult to concentrate on writing the verse of previous years. Cullen began writing more regularly for children, and in 1940 published *The Lost Zoo (A Rhyme for the Young, But Not Too Young)*, which featured Christopher Cat, the fictional teller of the tale. There is some significance in the fact that Cullen chose a cat to be the narrator. It appears to be connected to an affinity for cats that Cullen developed on one of his sojourns to France during his study of the Symbolist poet Charles Baudelaire. Baudelaire found cats to be inscrutable, and regally so; aloof and utterly independent, cats breathe a rarefied air, and exhibit in their own fashion a commanding manner. While Christopher is not imperious, he nevertheless makes his presence felt, and as Cullen proceeds to undermine Christopher's perspective in places, the cat reasserts authority time and again.

As Gillian Adams has suggested in her article, "Missing the Boat: Countee Cullen's *The Lost Zoo*," the subtitle of *The Lost Zoo* may indicate that the poem is aimed at an adult audience as well as its ostensible children's audience, but the uncertainty of the text—its possible subtlety—has called the conception of an adult audience into question. For this, says Adams, there has been an unfortunate though unsurprising critical neglect. Though many critics have not seen the issue of race as being thematically central to the poem, the structures that Cullen (and Christopher) employ can be seen to reflect modes of discourse normally used between blacks and whites. Cullen's effort to undermine Christopher, for example, can be seen to represent a dismissive, peremptory white authority while Christopher's response reflects, as Adams writes, "to good effect the rhetoric of the social and legally oppressed." Its status as a framed tale, with prose beginning, rhymed verse middle, and prose ending, suggests the possibility that race, or some other distinct representation of difference, was at issue in the poem, especially in the repartée between Christopher and Cullen. In this instance, Cullen would only be following a series of African American writers who have used the frame for teaching an audience about the nuances of difference, a series that includes Charles Chesnutt, Paul Laurence Dunbar, and Zora Neale Hurston. The average junior high school student who might have been introduced to Cullen's text may have found *The Lost Zoo* to be a bit too demanding; this work as

children's literature may therefore have its limitations. But Cullen was an educator beloved by his students, and he sincerely believed that the lessons of life are best taught earliest if taught well. As many critics have suggested, Cullen, who through the 1930s could no longer find an adult audience to listen dutifully to his most urgent messages on race, might now have devoted his messages and his craft largely to children. A second book followed, entitled *My Lives and How I Lost Them* (1942). In this prose work, far from taking up the political stances found in the previous work, Christopher discusses how he used up all but one of his nine lives in a series of adventures.

On January 10, 1946, Cullen died of uremic poisoning at the age of forty-two. The death stunned Harlem and the rest of the literary world, and more than three thousand people attended his funeral. *St. Louis Woman*, his farewell to Harlem and to the still-debated issue of the representation of the black visage and voice, opened that spring. The title of his posthumous collection, *On These I Stand* (1947), seemed a fitting epitaph. At his death, Ida Mae Roberson Cullen had asked Owen Dodson to write an epitaph for notice in the newspaper. Again fittingly, Dodson, the junior poet, composed the farewell in verse:

> Now begins the sleep, my friend:
> You showed us that men could see
> Deep into the cause of Lazarus,
> Believe in resurrection.
> You come back to us
> Now unwinding a shroud and blinking at
>   known light
> But singing like all the famed birds,
> Nightingale, lark and nightjar.

Selected Bibliography

PRIMARY WORKS

POETRY

Color. New York: Harper, 1925. Reprinted, New York: Arno Press, 1969.
The Ballad of the Brown Girl: An Old Ballad Retold. With illustrations by Charles Cullen. New York: Harper, 1927.

Copper Sun. With decorations by Charles Cullen. New York: Harper, 1927.

Caroling Dusk: An Anthology of Verse by Negro Poets. Edited by Countee Cullen. With decorations by Aaron Douglas. New York: Harper & Row, 1927. Reprinted, 1974.

The Black Christ and Other Poems. With decorations by Charles Cullen. New York: Harper & Brothers, 1929. Reprinted, Ann Arbor, Mich.: University Microfilms, 1979.

The Medea and Some Poems. New York: Harper & Brothers, 1935. (Includes Cullen's translation of Euripides' tragedy *Medea.*)

On These I Stand: An Anthology of the Best Poems of Countee Cullen. New York: Harper & Brothers, 1947. (Published posthumously.)

My Soul's High Song: The Collected Writings of Countee Cullen, Voice of the Harlem Renaissance. Edited and with an introduction by Gerald Early. New York: Doubleday, 1991. (This collection includes extensive portions of each of Cullen's volumes of poetry— *Color, Copper Sun, Ballad of the Brown Girl, Black Christ and Other Poems*—his translation of Euripides' *Medea,* his plays, and excerpts from his criticism and his novel, *One Way to Heaven,* as well as an essay commemorating Cullen by the fellow DeWitt Clinton alumnus James Baldwin.)

OTHER WORKS

"Poet on Poet." Review of *The Weary Blues* by Langston Hughes. *Opportunity,* February 1926, Pp. 73–74.

Review of production of "Porgy" by Du Bose and Dorothy Heyward. *Opportunity,* November 1927, p. 336.

One Way to Heaven. New York: Harper, 1932. Reprinted, New York: AMS Press, 1975. (Novel.)

Heaven's My Home. By Countee Cullen and Larry Hamilton. 1935. (Unpublished stage adaptation of Cullen's novel *One Way to Heaven.*)

The Lost Zoo: A Rhyme for the Young, But Not Too Young. By Christopher Cat and Countee Cullen. With illustrations by Charles Sebree. New York: Harper & Brothers, 1940. New edition. With illustrations by Joseph Low. Chicago: Follett, 1969.

My Lives and How I Lost Them. By Christopher Cat in collaboration with Countee Cullen. With drawings by Robert Reid Macguire. New York: Harper & Brothers, 1942. New edition, with illustrations by Rainey Bennett. Chicago: Follett, 1971.(A juvenile autobiography of the fictional character Christopher Cat.)

St. Louis Woman. By Countee Cullen and Arna Bontemps. In *Black Theatre,* edited by Lindsay Patterson. New York: Dodd, 1971. Pp. 1–41. (A musical adaptation of Bontemps's novel *God Sends Sunday* [1930]; first produced at the Martin Beck Theater in New York City on March 30, 1946].

The Third Fourth of July. By Countee Cullen and Owen Dodson. In *Theatre Arts* 30:488–93 (August 1946). (A one-act play.)

Let the Day Perish. By Countee Cullen and Waters Turpin. Unpublished, no date. (Play.)

The Spirit of Peace. Unpublished, no date. (Play.)

Medea in Africa. (Adapted and produced by Owen Dodson in 1948. Based on Cullen's English prose translation of Euripides' *Medea,* which Dodson had first adapted and produced in 1940.)

JOURNALS, CORRESPONDENCE AND MANUSCRIPTS

Cullen's correspondence is fairly widely dispersed; his letters are in folders at the Schomburg Center for Research in Black Culture in New York City, at the main branch of the New York Public Library in New York City, and distributed over several major collections in the Beinecke Rare Book and Manuscript Library at Yale University.

SECONDARY WORKS

CRITICAL AND BIOGRAPHICAL STUDIES

Adams, Gillian. "Missing the Boat: Countee Cullen's *The Lost Zoo.*" *The Lion and the Unicorn* 21, no. 1:40–58 (1997).

Baker, Houston A., Jr. *A Many-Colored Coat of Dreams: The Poetry of Countee Cullen.* Detroit: Broadside Press, 1974.

Bone, Robert. *The Negro Novel in America.* New Haven: Yale Publications in American Studies, 1958. Reprinted, New Haven: Yale University Press, 1965.

Bontemps, Arna, ed. *The Harlem Renaissance Remembered.* With an introduction by Arna Bontemps. New York: Dodd, Mead, 1972.

Bronz, Stephen H. *Roots of Negro Racial Consciousness: The 1920s, Three Harlem Renaissance Authors.* New York: Libra, 1964.

Davis, Arthur P. *From the Dark Tower: Afro-American Writers, 1900–1960.* Washington, D.C.: Howard University Press, 1974.

Dictionary of Literary Biography. Vol. 4, *American Writers in Paris: 1920–1939,* edited by Karen Lane Rood, with a foreword by Malcolm Cowley. Vol. 48, *American Poets: 1880–1945,* edited by Peter Quartermain. Vol. 51, *Afro-American Writers from the Harlem Renaissance to 1940,* edited by Trudier Harris, associate editor, Thadious Davis. Detroit: Gale Research, 1980, 1986, 1987.

Early, Gerald, ed. *My Soul's High Song: The Collected Writings of Countee Cullen, Voice of the Harlem Renaissance.* Edited and with an introduction by Gerald Early. New York: Doubleday, 1991.

Ferguson, Blanche E. *Countee Cullen and the Negro Renaissance.* New York: Dodd, Mead, 1966.

Huggins, Nathan Irvin. *Harlem Renaissance.* New York: Oxford University Press, 1971.

Johnson, James Weldon. *Black Manhattan.* New York: Alfred Knopf, 1930. Reprinted, with a new preface by Allan H Spear. New York: Atheneum, 1972.

———, ed. *The Book of American Negro Poetry.* Chosen and edited and with an essay on the Negro's Creative

Genius by James Weldon Johnson. New York: Harcourt, Brace, 1922. Revised edition. New York: Harcourt, Brace, and Co., 1931. Reprinted, New York: Harcourt, Brace, and World, 1959.

Kramer, Victor A., ed. *The Harlem Renaissance Reexamined.* New York: AMS Press, 1987. Revised and expanded edition. Troy, N.Y.: Whitson Publications, 1997.

Lewis, David Levering. *When Harlem Was in Vogue.* New York: Alfred Knopf, 1981.

Littlejohn, David. *Black on White: A Critical Survey of Writing by American Negroes.* New York: Grossman, 1966.

Locke, Alain. *Four Negro Poets.* New York: Simon & Schuster, 1927.

———, ed. *The New Negro: An Interpretation.* Edited by Alain Locke. With book decoration and portraits by Winold Reiss. New York: Albert & Charles Boni, 1925.

Margolies, Edward. *Native Sons: A Critical Study of Twentieth-Century Negro American Authors.* Philadelphia: Lippincott, 1968.

Rampersand, Arnold. *The Life of Langston Hughes.* Vol. 1. New York: Oxford University Press, 1986.

Redding, J. Saunders. *To Make a Poet Black.* Chapel Hill: University of North Carolina Press, 1939. Reprinted, with an introduction by Henry Louis Gates Jr., Ithaca: Cornell University Press, 1988.

Rosenblatt, Roger. *Black Fiction.* Cambridge, Mass.: Harvard University Press, 1974.

Shucard, Alan. *Countee Cullen.* Boston: Twayne, 1984.

Singh, Amritjit. *The Novels of the Harlem Renaissance: Twelve Black Writers, 1923–1933.* University Park: Pennsylvania State University Press, 1976.

Turner, Darwin T. *In a Minor Chord: Three Afro-American Writers and Their Search for Identity.* With a preface by Harry T. Moore. Carbondale: Southern Illinois University Press, 1971.

Twentieth-Century Literary Criticism. Vol. 4. Detroit: Gale Research, 1981.

Wagner, Jean. *Black Poets of the United States: From Paul Laurence Dunbar to Langston Hughes.* Urbana, Ill.: University of Illinois Press, 1973.

Young, James O. *Black Writers of the Thirties.* Baton Rouge: Louisiana State University Press, 1973.

BIBLIOGRAPHIES

Early, Gerald. "Bibliography." In *My Soul's High Song: The Collected Writings of Countee Cullen, Voice of the Harlem Renaissance.* Edited and with an introduction by Gerald Early. New York: Doubleday, 1991.

Perry, Margaret. *A Bio-Bibliography of Countee P. Cullen, 1903–1946.* Washington, D.C., 1959. Reprinted, Westport, Conn.: Greenwood, 1971.

———. *The Harlem Renaissance: An Annotated Bibliography and Commentary.* New York: Garland Publishers, 1982.

SAMUEL R. DELANY
(1942 –   )

ARTHUR L. LITTLE JR.

IT'S ONLY FITTING that the writer who would more than earn his international reputation as a wunderkind but who would go on to do some of his most significant work after thirty, would today, a few years shy of his sixtieth birthday, walk with a cane and sport a very long and full white beard: without question Samuel R. Delany, known as Chip to his friends, has successfully made the transition from wunderkind to wizard in the world of science fiction and in many worlds outside it. A prolific writer in several genres and sub-genres, including autobiography, Delany is as notable a subject as his many books. To date he has published nearly twenty novels, almost all of which may be classified as science fiction or fantasy fiction: three autobiographical works, four collections of short stories, three pornographic novels, six volumes of critical essays, and two other works of nonfiction.

Ultimately neither Delany's work nor his person can easily be labeled. In many respects a fuller appreciation of Delany often involves first understanding the various ways in which he and his work could be classified, then concluding just how inadequate or unsatisfying such categories become. His marriage to his elementary school classmate and best friend, Marilyn Hacker, provides a rather emphatic and encompassing example of Delany and his

work. We are able to see here Delany's preciousness: even though they were to marry when Delany was only nineteen, by some standards Delany was not so young. After all, by the age of twenty he had already published his first novel. Delany was African American and Protestant (and warned as a child to stay away from the Catholic children on his street); Hacker was white and Jewish. His marriage to Hacker partly demonstrates Delany's refusal to be directed by social, racial, and ethnic strictures placed on himself or on his social relations and choices. (Because of laws against interracial marriage and age-consent laws, the couple had to travel to Detroit in order to get a marriage license.) Also indicative of the kinds of creative and energetic communities with which Delany associated from a very early age onward, Hacker would help pull Delany into the professional world of book publishing through her job as assistant editor at Ace. (It's only fair to point out that Delany submitted his manuscript under a pseudonym, and the editor did not know that Delany was Hacker's husband.) Hacker would later emerge as a poet in her own right, receiving, for example, the National Book Award for her first collection of poetry, *Presentation Piece* (1974). Furthermore, as a sign of the complex milieu and the category-defying place in which Delany immersed himself, he, a self-known gay man before his marriage to Hacker, would find himself with a spouse who would emerge after the end of their nineteen-year marriage as not only a notable American poet but an important lesbian one. Their marriage—its successes and failings—would make its way into various pieces of Delany's writings, including autobiographical work and science fiction. At times he would recall his marriage critically and with a painful honesty; he could also draw on it celebratorily, as he does in *Dhalgren.* His marriage to Hacker gives a rather succinct snapshot of Delany's artistic, social, and personal quests and interrogations.

Notwithstanding, no single piece of Delany's life, however resonant, does finally unleash the complexities of his own story or the depth, richness, or literariness of the stories he writes. His readers remain interested in Delany's life. This interest is not surprising since Delany would successfully bring an African American, urban (inner city), feminist, and gay consciousness to what was still, in the 1960s, a youthful, homogenous, heteronormative, and nearly Aryan identified genre. He would also problematize many of its unexamined structural and social assumptions and would emerge as one of the most important of the "new" science fiction writers coming onto the scene in the 1960s. The "new" writers were more invested in social science than in technology and were not to be confused with the "new wave" writers, a largely British phenomenon associated with Michael Moorcock's takeover and transformation of the journal *New World* and whose stories were set mostly in the near future. The "old" writers were those whose fiction explored technological values. This group includes Isaac Asimov, Arthur C. Clarke, and Robert A. Heinlein. Some of the most notable "new" writers were Harlan Ellison (editor of the groundbreaking volume, *Dangerous Visions*), Ursula K. Leguin, Joanna Russ, and Roger Zelazny.

Early Life

Born April 1, 1942, Delany grew up in Harlem, living above Levy and Delany, a funeral parlor owned by his parents, Samuel R. Delany Sr. and Margaret Carey Boyd Delany. His parents were distinguished members of their Harlem community. His mother was a licensed funeral director and a library clerk. Before Delany was born and before going into the funeral business, Delany Sr. was a jazz musician who sat in a few times with Cab Calloway's band. They were an upper-middle-class family, perhaps even aristocratic by the social and economic standards of African Americans in the 1940s and 1950s. Delany grew up spending part of his summers with his family in, for example, their summer home in Hopewell, New York. In addition to the comforts afforded by his immediate family, his extended family was also a fairly distinguished one, including Delany's paternal grandfather, who was an Episcopal Bishop of North and South Carolina; his maternal uncle and a paternal uncle, who were both judges in New York City; and his aunts, the Delany sisters (the subject of *Having Our Say: The Delany Sisters' First 100 Years,* 1993).

Delany was an only child who nurtured an imaginative universe of his own, sustained by many hours of reading, music, and ballet lessons. He grew up playing both the violin and the guitar, and he even wrote a complete violin concerto at the age of fourteen. As a young adult he would sometimes support himself by playing folk guitar in coffeehouses. Even though Delany as a young adult moved away from relying on publicly performing music for money, music—not only musical characters but also the social and semiotic texture of music—has kept a fairly consistent place in his fiction. As far as the young Delany's reading was concerned, he did, as may be expected, consume science fiction and fantasy stories, but he also avidly read classical mythology and the works of African American writers, especially such Harlem Renaissance writers as Claude McKay, Countee Cullen, James Weldon Johnson, Langston Hughes, and Bruce Nugent. Given when Delany was born, just at a time to reap the hope and the texture of an era, it is possible to read his writing as coming out of a sense not only of new social prospects for Af-

150

SAMUEL R. DELANY

rican Americans but, indeed, of whole new worlds. For a young man energetically crossing the terrain of science fiction with the texts and visions of his own personal experiences of Harlem, the possibilities would seem endless.

At the age of five Delany began attending the private, progressive Dalton School off Park Avenue. With its rather elite and worldly student body, Dalton proved a good fit for Delany. Nonetheless, it would also mark the beginning of his broader social education, since Delany would find himself living in two very different social worlds. In Harlem his friends were the children of working-class parents; at the Dalton School, they were the children of the upper classes, of the social and political elite. He was chauffeured between these worlds in the family's black Cadillac. Like the playing through of a Middle Passage of his own, Delany once described his travels from home to Dalton as a "virtually ballistic trip through a socio-psychological barrier of unrestrained violence." Moving between these worlds comes to signal for Delany the kind of cultural migration, the diasporic machinations, that characterizes much of Delany's fiction. Even though the main character of *Dhalgren*, for example, is Native American (a complex migration story of its own), the African American migratory story ghosts this text as well. When the main character arrives in the supposed utopian world of Bellona, he has lost his name and most of his past, and, notwithstanding his youthful appearance, is then named Kid by someone else, even though he's well into his twenties. To make the diasporic point more emphatic, his name itself allows throughout the novel an easy migration of his name, of his textual presence, from upper to lower case, lower to upper case.

Delany's prestigious education extended beyond the Dalton School. Beginning at the age of six, he spent part of his summers in prestigious upstate New York camps. One such camp, Camp Woodland, is where Delany read some of his first science fiction, and he published a science fiction short story (at the age of eleven) in the camp's magazine. The story

was titled "The End of the World," inspired by his reading Arthur C. Clarke. Not until after the publication of *The Jewels of Aptor*, his first novel, and really not until he began to attend science fiction conventions in the latter half of the 1960s, would Delany consider himself headed toward a career in science fiction. One reason is that for a few years after the publication of *The Jewels*, Delany found playing guitar in coffeehouses a slightly more lucrative enterprise. Still it's fair to say that the precocious Delany began his science fiction writing career by the age of eleven. By the time Delany published *The Jewels* at the age of twenty, this wunderkind had written in part or had completely drafted nine novels: *Lost Stars, Those Spared by Fire, Cycle for Toby, Afterton, The Lovers, The Flames of the Warhog, The Assassination, Voyage, Orestes,* and *Captives of the Flames.*

In 1956 Delany enrolled in the Bronx High School of Science, where he continued to write short stories, publishing them in the school's literary magazine, *Dynamo.* He also began his career of recognitions. In the 1958–1959 school year he received two Scholastic Writing Awards (under the auspices of W. A. Sheaffer Pen Company)—first place for a short story and second place for an essay. The year 1960 marked the real emergence of Delany's writing career. He graduated from Science, received the school's creative writing award, was offered his first professional writing assignment (from the magazine *Seventeen,* even though the article, "The Compleat Folk Singer," was not published until 1962), and received a fellowship to attend the coveted Bread Loaf Writer's Conference in Vermont. (He declined a four-year creative writing scholarship to New York University, an award he was offered on the basis of his short story "Salt.") Among those who mentored him at the conference was Robert Frost. In August 1961, Delany married Marilyn Hacker; in the fall he enrolled in the City College of New York, and in 1962 Ace would publish Delany's first novel. Even Delany's marriage to Hacker seems to have found its own rhythms; for a few months in 1965; Delany and Hacker welcomed a Robert

Folsom, a young man from Florida, into their sexual, emotional, and domestic life. The three became a threesome, or a "triple" as Delany would refer to such relationships in both his fiction and memoirs. In the fall of 1965, Delany and Folsom hitchhiked to Texas in order to work on shrimp boats for about a month. Shortly thereafter, Delany and a new friend, Ron Helstrom, who also had worked on the shrimp boats, left for Europe. Before returning to New York after many weeks of travel, Delany had visited Luxembourg, Paris, Venice, Milos, the isle of Mykonos, Athens, Turkey, and London. Delany saw himself as neither geographically, racially, nor sexually limited.

It seemed as though Delany, in an almost effortless fashion, were headed for personal and professional success. However much Delany may have arrived as a writer and with his personal life seemingly intact, his life had actually come with a series of barriers, ones that may ultimately be said to contribute significantly to the grounding of Delany's novels in social and psychological realism. Even his formal education had its challenges. He had at Dalton been placed in remedial classes until he was diagnosed as dyslexic. Seth McEvoy speculates in his study of Delany's writing that Delany's "structure is a dyslexic view of prose," a commitment to the non-linearity of prose. It's akin perhaps to William S. Burroughs's use of "cut-ups" in a novel such as *The Soft Machine* (1961), where he would cut up a narrative passage and randomly reorganize the parts. One's mental accessibility to texts was not something Delany would ever take for granted and would become one of the leitmotifs of his fiction. Also, however socially popular throughout his first twenty years (he was voted most popular by his Dalton graduating class), he was no stranger to racism and feelings of alienation. And in addition to grappling with his own growing sense of his sexual difference, he underwent what he calls a "rather violent" religious crisis, leading to a short-lived attempt to become a Hindu. Throughout his teens, his relationship with his father became increasingly strained, prob-

ably due in part to his turn away from religion—his father was a very active church member—and Delany's growing sense of his homosexuality. Their relationship was strained to the point where Delany spent his senior year staying away from the house as much as possible and did run away from home several times during his teenage years. In October of 1960, his father died after succumbing to lung cancer. In the spring of 1962, having completed one full term and starting the second, Delany dropped out of City College. He married Hacker but has used words such as "claustrophobic" to describe the first few months of their marriage and "cruel" to describe his behavior in it. Hacker was pregnant when they married; she miscarried after three months. Perhaps as a culminating moment of the first part of Delany's life, in 1964 he suffered a nervous breakdown and was hospitalized at Mount Sinai in New York City. For Delany, this was not the romantic madness of the poet. Delany describes the three-month period leading up to his hospitalization in McEvoy's work: "I seemed to have gotten well on my way to being one of the common, garden-variety madmen you see wandering around New York City: filthy, clothes all unbuttoned, talking to themselves. . . . In my case, I was making daily trips to the subway, where I would sit on the stairs, clutching the banister rails, under the illusion that I was being drawn to the tracks, and something was compelling me to throw myself under a train." And while he and Hacker may have had their marital arrangements, such as with Folsom, the relationship between the two of them was filled with stress. By the time Delany and Helstrom traveled abroad, Delany and Hacker were no longer living together.

Delany's personal life became much more settled after his breakdown and his foreign excursion, especially as he entered the 1970s. He and Hacker finally did have a child, Iva Alyxander Hacker-Delany, born in 1974. Hacker and Delany separated in 1975 and divorced in 1980. The relationship ended amiably and they have remained friends. In the spirit of his coparenting responsibilities, he helped found in the 1980s a group known as Gay Fathers of the Upper West Side.

Beginning in the mid-1970s, Delany has been a prominent academic as well. In 1975 Delany became Butler Professor of English at the State University of New York at Buffalo, and in 1977, senior fellow at the Center for Twentieth Century Studies at the University of Wisconsin at Milwaukee. Since 1988 Delany has been Professor of Comparative Literature at the University of Massachusetts at Amherst. Especially through the 1990s, he has taken on a number of short-term writer-in-residence positions, including at the University of Idaho (1995), the University of Minnesota (1995), Michigan State University (1997), and the Atlantic Center for the Arts (1997).

As iterated, Delany is not a writer whose works may be easily cordoned off in categorical fashion. Notwithstanding, for those readers who wish not only to read Delany but to engage him critically, beginning with an understanding of how Delany and his work reverberate in and draw on the traditions of a number of specific literary and social communities is certainly a very productive way to study or introduce oneself to the density of Delany's fiction and non-fiction. While there are indisputably other Delanys—the feminist, the Marxian, and the public intellectual, for example—the three Delanys that most comprehensively introduce us to his work are Delany as science fiction writer, African American writer, and gay writer. These three are fundamental. As Delany himself says in a 1986 interview, "The constant and insistent experience I have had as a black man, as a gay man, as a science fiction writer in racist, sexist, homophobic America, with its carefully maintained tradition of high art and low, colors contours every sentence I write."

Delany as a Science Fiction Writer

The category that encompasses Delany's work most efficiently is that of science fiction writer,

even though Delany's place within the genre has been frequently challenged by science fiction readers, who have sometimes accused Delany of disrespecting the rules of the genre. While Delany could write *Nova*, which McEvoy argues is a "perfect" science fiction novel—complete with guide, Grail quest, physics, politics, and psychology—Delany is more often seen as violating many of the genre's expectations. To the point, Delany doesn't even allow *Nova* to achieve "perfect" science fiction closure. Hence, the final words of the novel: "The only way to protect myself from the jinx, I guess, would be to abandon it before I finish the last. . . ." In the dense, experimental, and narratively complex *Dhalgren*, for example, Delany's post-war city Bellona becomes itself a metaphor for Delany's text, which may be said to deliver a bold challenge to a genre that Delany found in need of a more epic interrogation of its utopian techno-fantasy at the expense of its yet underappreciated dystopian social possibilities. Investments in such possibilities for the genre of science fiction has sometimes caused readers and critics alike to consider Delany more a social commentator than a science fiction writer, not that Delany himself would ever ascribe to such a culturally telling dichotomy.

However much and in whatever ways Delany may challenge the genre, he remains at heart a science fiction writer. He has received both the prestigious Nebula (granted by the Science Fiction Writers of America) and Hugo (by the science fiction community at large) awards. When asked by an interviewer whether he has ever thought about abandoning the genre, he underscored what particularly attracts him to the field, and it's not just science: it's language. Science fiction, he responded, "uses the scientific discourse to literalize and retrieve for the foreground presentation all sorts of sentences that would be nonsense if they appeared in any other mode of discourse." According to Delany, when he wants to say his "serious thing" he wants to have at his disposal "a full range of [whatever] possible vocabulary." He does not want to work within the restrictions of what he calls "mundane" fiction. And one hears a challenge to mundane fiction even as one gathers a sense of the social possibilities of Delany's science fiction writing: "You can put together more interesting combination of words in science fiction than you can in any other writing . . . [T]he only thing mundane fiction can talk about is either madness or slavery."

His oppositional vision of science fiction here should not be taken too seriously, since so much of Delany's science fiction deals with madness and slavery. The non-pedestrian world of his fiction becomes a rather suggestive site for Delany's exploration of madness, not only on a broader social scale but on a personal level as well—his own bout with madness when he was twenty-two. Slavery and its aftermath haunt Delany's fictional landscapes and, according to much of Delany's fiction, shape our American social consciousness. It is arguable, in fact, that the object of much of his fiction—linked as it is to his interest in archeology—is to excavate, that is, free the individual from the illusions that have covered over that individual's essential and profoundly useful madness. Madness is coterminous with the possibility of freedom in Delany's visionary universe. As just one kind of referent point, it is worth noting that "freedom" functions as much as a dense and centrifugal force in Delany's writing as does "love" in the writing of James Baldwin. In the well-wrought storied, psychological, and linguistic worlds of Delany's fiction, the slavery that prevents one from recognizing oneself as a self is literal, sexual, and semiotic.

Delany's Place in African American Literary Tradition

However much Delany may be read as more a science fiction writer than an African American one, even though of course these categories need not be mutually exclusive, his claims to an African American literary tradition are through more than the incidence of his African American heritage. His fiction gives substantial space to black and other non-white persons. He has given science fiction a list of memorable non-white characters who not only have pivotal roles in their novels but are enlisted patriots, one senses, in Delany's quest to rethink the genre of science fiction: Iimmi, the black sailor, who is a principal character in the rescue effort in *The Jewels of Aptor;* the Asian poet, linguist, and starship commander Rydra Wong and her heroic African friend, the psychotherapist Dr. Markus T'mwarba, in *Babel-17;* the mulatto Lorq Von Ray in *Nova;* the Native American poet and gang leader Kid and the culturally omnipresent and cosmically figured black George in *Dhalgren;* and the black mutant Orpheus, Lo Lobey, in *The Einstein Intersection.* But to reduce Delany's African American vision to a cast of characters would be grossly misleading.

According to Delany, he has "deep within" his work "situated material that encourages the reader's engagement with some of the political questions that the disenfranchised people in this country, victimized by oppression and an oppressive discourse based on the evil and valorized notion of nationhood and its hideous white—no other color—underbelly, imperialism, must face but cannot overcome without internalizing some of the power concepts and relationships inescapably entailed in the notion of 'nation' itself" (Dery, 744). Delany's work also demonstrates that his lack of an explicitly drawn engagement with African American cultural identity stems not from any refusal to engage African American people per se but from the post-structuralist, post-modernist, semiotic-driven and Marxian method Delany calls "strategic efficacy."

Although Delany remains distinct in being the first African American to assume a professional interest in the genre of science fiction, he has since been joined by other African American science fiction writers, namely Octavia E. Butler, whose novels and short stories take up issues of power, environmental exploitation, and parapsychology with multicultural communities; Steven Barnes, whose writing includes several novels tracing the adventures of Aubry Knight, who searches for his humanity in a dystopian world in the near future; and

Charles Saunders, who uses African history and folklore in his African fantasy fiction.

When we consider how these writers have repeatedly shown the metaphorical and literal possibilities the genre offers to African Americans, it's surprising that there aren't more African American science fiction writers. As Mark Dery has put it, "African Americans, in a very real sense, are the descendants of alien abductees; they inhabit a sci-fi nightmare in which unseen but no less impassable force fields of intolerance frustrate their movements; official histories undo what has been done; and technology is too often brought to bear on black bodies (branding, forced sterilization, the Tuskegee experiment, and tasers come readily to mind)." From this perspective, science fiction has within it the material of a diasporic literature.

Delany's place in an African American literary tradition may be undervalued if taken in terms too narrowly conceived. African American science fiction may be considered in terms of African American speculative fiction. In this context Delany continues a tradition in African American literature of using the fantastical in order to present a more liberated view of African American subjecthood. This speculative tradition includes such early texts as Charles Waddell Chesnutt's *The Conjure Woman* (1899) and the 1930s novels of George S. Schulyer, such as his *Black No More* (1931), and more contemporary writers such as Toni Morrison, August Wilson, and Jewelle Gomez. None of this is to say, however, that contemporary critical discussions have failed to appreciate Delany's contributions to African American literature. Robert Elliot Fox, for example, reads Delany's work, along that that of Amiri Baraka and Ishmael Reed, as coming specifically out of a black postmodernist idiom. While Delany does not share Baraka's more visible place in black American sociopolitical and creative struggle, he offers, according to Fox, a vision that is "ultimately more radical." Mark Dery reads Delany's work, within and outside the realm of the strictly literary, as belonging to what he calls "Afrofuturism," that is, creative work—in-cluding comic books and rap, for example—that ponders the concerns of African Americans within the "context of twentieth-century technoculture," appropriating its "images of technology and [those of] a prosthetically enhanced future."

Delany's Sexuality

There may seem to be a natural affinity, a foregone conclusion, between science fiction's investments in alternative worlds and its investments in alternative bodies and sexualities. In the 1960s, when the new science fiction writers began to come onto the scene, science fiction began to deal with explicit sexual matters. Delany, the first openly gay science fiction writer, was one of the first science fiction writers to realize the possibilities science fiction provides for an exploration of marginalized sexualities. He remains one of the three most recognized writers of gay science fiction, or at least of a science fiction that takes seriously its interrogation of a community's sexual constraints and how they affect the psychological and social possibilities of homosexual, bisexual, transgendered, and other sexually marginal characters. The other two writers are Joanna Russ, most famous for her novel *The Female Man* (1975), and Thomas M. Disch, most notable perhaps for his novel *334* (1974). Underscoring Delany's importance not only to a gay science fiction readership but to the gay literary community more generally, in 1993 Delany received the Bill Whitehead Memorial Award for Lifetime Excellence in Gay and Lesbian Literature.

From early on Delany's fiction has attended to the theme of homosexuality and to characters whose sexuality would be seen as marginal by our dominant society. In "Aye, and Gomorrah . . . ," for example, his Nebula-winning short story published in Harlan Ellison's *Dangerous Visions* (1967), the sexual transactions recall those of urban hustlers selling themselves to older men. *Fall of the Towers* includes several references to the homosexual practices among the prisoners who mine the "tetron" ore. *Stars in My Pocket* features Marq, who is gay, as the main character and narrator. The anti-hero Kid in *Dhalgren* is involved in a long, serious, and fully drawn out threesome with the slightly younger, upper-class Lanya and the teenage, streetwise Denny. In *Triton* Bron, in search of love, changes from male to female. And in the Nevèrÿon series, homosexuality has more than a backstage existence. For example, in *Flight from Nevèrÿon*, Delany criticizes New York's gay community's reaction to AIDS by comparing it to his characters' reaction to a sexually transmitted disease in their community.

An in-depth critique of Delany as a gay writer or as a writer of the sexually marginal would also likely attend to his pornographic novels, his autobiographical volumes, and his most recent nonfiction work, *Times Square Red, Times Square Blue.* His work would also benefit from being read within the construct of a black gay male creative tradition, which may be said to move from several Harlem Renaissance writers to the oeuvre of James Baldwin and, more recently, the novels of Larry Duplechan, Melvin Dixon, and James Earl Hardy, the poetry of Essex Hemphill, the dance and choreography of Bill T. Jones, the drama of George C. Wolfe, and the filmmaking of Marlon Riggs. Delany's strategic readings of cultural identity participate in the signifying and re-signifying practices of these African American gay male artists, who are at once within and outside of sexual and racial categories.

To grasp more clearly how Delany incorporates a gay sensibility or a gay consciousness into his work, it is worth noting that when writing in *The Motion of Light* about what "gay culture" means to him, he concludes by saying that "perhaps . . . any 'identity'—semantic, generic, personal, or cultural—is always such an accretive, associative, but finally disjunctive illusion." But, as Delany is not himself hesitant to admit, there does remain that "thing"—that "thang" (to borrow a word he also uses) that makes one feels one's gayness as "essential" (as opposed to "constructed"), that is, as some *thing* very deeply,

perhaps even socio-genetically founded within the self. As in the case of identifying and cataloging Delany as an African American writer, Delany opens himself up to a richer discursive texture than can perhaps be gleamed from thinking about sexual identity too literally, too simply as signifying and identifying a gay body.

Early Writing Career

Delany's first novel, *The Jewels of Aptor*, was published by Ace Books in 1962 as part of an Ace Double Novel. (The other novel was the British science fiction writer James White's *Second Ending.*) *Jewels* would present the first of many dystopian, disaster-torn landscapes found in Delany's fiction. Here, the past continues to make itself felt since The Great Fire, some hundreds of years earlier, has left not only radiation lingering over large areas of land but has rendered significant portions of the population mutants. At the center of the novel is the youthful Geo, one of the many young heroes in Delany's earlier fiction, who is also a poet. He is also one of many artists populating Delany's fiction. Geo's services are enlisted to help release the High Priestess of the white goddess Argo (Greek for "white") and to return three powerful jewels to their rightful place with the Argo Incarnate. Joining Geo's rescue effort is Iimmi, a black sailor and fellow student. The adventure will lead them to the High Priest of the black god Hama (named after the Biblical Ham), who will catch them stealing the final jewel. Already, here in Delany's debut as science fiction novelist, he brings black characters into his fiction and challenges the quest narrative, a staple of the genre. He abandons it for what he calls "ratiocination," a kind of exact thinking. The journey for Geo and Iimmi seems finally more like one of philosophical discovery, more akin to the dialogues of Plato and Socrates than the action-filled quest of science fiction. There were restraints on the young Delany, however: Ace forced him to cut 720 manuscript lines from his original draft. (Ace would restore the lines in the 1968 edition.)

His next major novel was *The Fall of the Towers,* which is actually a trilogy consisting of three published novels: *Captives of the Flame* (1963, originally titled *Out of the Dead City*), *The Towers of Toron* (1964), and *City of a Thousand Suns* (1965). Like *Jewels,* the trilogy presents a devastated landscape, this one as a result of invasions by the Lord of the Flames. At the fore of this novel is Jon Koshar, an outcast criminal who finds himself waging war against evil in order to make possible the birth of a new civilization. The novel has been described as a classic "space opera," a tale of good and evil, alien creatures and space battles. The novel is significant in a few other ways as well. It extends and foreshadows Delany's interest in freedom: freedom moves from the domain of the hero as rescuer or freer, as in *Jewels,* to the hero himself. Furthermore, Jon searches not only for physical but intellectual freedom, particularly in a society under siege, and this embattlement is more than physical. Also, drawing as it does on an allusive interweaving of wars—World War II and Viet Nam—the novel shows Delany thinking through the deep structural material of wars and holocausts as they shape and thwart our very notions of humanity. Here, Delany's social realism is evident. It's even more so when he describes that part of Toromon society known as the Devil's Pot: one is all but forced to compare those socially revealing enclaves: most famously, perhaps, the black Harlem ghetto and the Jewish Warsaw ghetto.

His next novel, *The Ballad of Beta-2,* was published in 1965, shortly after *Thousand Suns;* it is one of his shorter works and also his first novel that takes place in space. It is also the first of his novels to be nominated for a Nebula, whose awarding organization was founded in 1965. Even though *Beta-2* has found a fairly consistent readership since its publication, it remains one of Delany's minor works. Nonetheless, the novel is especially of interest to those excited by the meta-textual Delany, that is, the Delany who is more invested in the textuality of texts than in the affairs of aliens in outer space. *Beta-2* is also a story about intolerance and oppression, of folklore and an-

thropology, conjuring up perhaps the literary domain of Zora Neal Hurston. The novel also speaks to Delany's interest in the cultural texture of music and song. In this novel, Joneny Horatio T'wabaga, a student of galactic anthropology, conducts a historical analysis of the ancient folksong "The Ballad of Beta-2." (Even though Delany will have Joneny's search take Joneny and Delany into outer space, Delany fails to bring any vivid, descriptive detail to this environment.) Joneny's task is to understand the precise meaning of the ballad. The novel becomes a kind of template for reading science fiction, at least for reading Delany's science fiction, for learning to engage the unearthly semiotics of science fiction, the literality of the seemingly metaphorical. Joneny must learn as much before he's able to decipher the ballad and the brutal history it remembers.

Delany's next novel, *Babel-17* (1966), received the Nebula in 1967 and was nominated for the Hugo. The story, a combination of spy fiction and space adventure, revolves around Rydra Wong, interstellar captain, natural linguist, and famous poet throughout many galaxies. She is assisted in her heroic exploits by her former psychotherapist and long-time friend Dr. Markus T'Mwarba (Mocky). The Alliance—a group of planets—request Rydra's help once they realize that a series of attacks on their military installation by a group known simply as the Invaders have been preceded by some kind of radio transmission. The Alliance assumes these transmissions to be some kind of code—they've named it Babel-17. Rydra is called in to decipher the code but discovers that it's not a code but a language; she goes on to theorize about the relationship between language and culture, the way language not only shapes but also determines how and what we think. Culture is, in effect, trapped in its own discourse. After a bit of space adventure, Rydra is able to promise the Alliance an end to war and violence in large part because she will build a new language, Babel-18, which will bring about the desired resolution. In addition to being about the relationship between Babel and language, between alien and human and how language creates knowledge as well as ignorance, the novel covers a fair amount of more familiar cultural space as well. Our heroes are Asian and African; our main hero is a beautiful woman. Rydra is also Delany's attempt to bring a more feminist sensibility to the genre of science fiction, a lack that disturbed his wife and was the subject of numerous conversations between them. In themselves these characters invite Delany's readers into a future in which they may begin to hear and recognize their own linguistic and feminine heritage.

After finishing *Babel* in August, Delany planned and wrote *Empire Star* (1966) within a two-week period in September 1965. This novel came at a rather mobile and exploratory point in Delany's life, perhaps in part as a response to his return from madness and cloistering himself in subways. A few months before writing *Empire* is when Delany worked on shrimp boats; shortly after completing *Empire* is when Delany would make his European excursion. The universe in the novel consists of a three-tier caste system that signifies Delany's own way of signifying on his audience: the simplex are ordinary people, including most readers of Delany's fiction; the complex can perceive both sides of the issue and are more perceptive readers not only of Delany's novel but of the social realities he tries to articulate; and the multiplex comprehend everything, referring less to any particular reader or Delany himself than to Delany's plea for the reader to think of herself or himself most assuredly as more ignorant than knowledgeable about the world. The novel is narrated by the multiplex Jewel, who admits to leaving out some details because his simplex and complex audience would not really be able to grasp them and would only end up confused. The story itself focuses on Comet Jo as she undergoes transformation from a simplex to a complex and finally to a multiplex being. The novel has both a broader philosophical scope and a more particular one. Not only do the Lll allude to the plight of African Americans, but the Lll who pretends to be Oscar Wilde reminds us that within all this social drama there are black gay Americans too, if here it's

only Delany—a persona deeply and ironically marginalized within his own text.

Delany may be said to have a less obscured presence in his next novel, *The Einstein Intersection* (1967), a Nebula winner and a relatively dense and complexly drawn story, especially for its relatively short length and rather accessible prose. Simply told, the story is about the black man-beast Lo Lobey—herder of dragons, musician, and adventurer—who is on a quest to find his girlfriend Friza and bring her back from death. The time of the novel is 40,000 A.D., and even though the story takes place on Earth, at some point in the distant past human beings left Earth and these other beings arrived and attempted to assume the place, the bodies, and the myths of human society. The most encompassing myth of the novel is that of Orpheus, who attempted to bring Eurydice back from Hades. The novel is filled with a multitude of other myths and icons: Greco-Roman, biblical, and American, including a population of allusive others: Billy the Kid, Jean Harlow, and Ringo Starr. The intersection in the title, the novel's primal scene moment when "it" happened, refers to the point of contact between Einstein's idea of the limits of perceivable truths and Gödel's idea of the infinite possibilities of perception within a known system. The unraveling social fabric of the 1960s does haunt this novel in which past, present, and future enfold the one into the others. The temporal, intellectual, and social enfoldings of this novel are not only endlessly suggestive but also promisingly polemical. The novel finally resists a black nationalist sensibility, an adherence to a real black body, as much as it does the phantom whiteness it counters. When thought through Kid Death's words to Lobey, "Like you, lively in your jungle, I was haunted by the memories of those who homed under this sun before our parents' parents come, took on these bodies, loves, and fears," the novel reverses the usual idea of thinking of the African American body as having some white in it. What is at stake, the novel seems to ask, if one perceives instead that what we have here in America are "African Americans" who are black selves inhabiting bodies? Such a primal scene narrative in the 1960s would have been potentially quite politically and socially explosive on either side of the political racial divide. One of the points made by this paradigm shift is not that black Americans are really white people but that here in America there are no white people. One of the things Delany has said is that, at least provisionally, he finds comfort in the fact that Baldwin has advanced such an argument as a rhetorical strategy for talking about race in America.

Delany's next novel, *Nova* (1968), his first hardcover book, would bring to an end the publishing frenzy marking the beginning of Delany's science fiction career. (He published nine novels between 1962 and 1968.) Hailed as a classic "space opera," the novel established Delany's reputation as one of the world's best science fiction writers. Seth McEvoy has described it as a "perfect" science fiction novel, and Douglas Barbour has positively compared it to Greek tragedy. The novel partly earned its reputation because of the way this action-filled quest story seems naturally to unfold, the present dilemma emerging from a web of historical happenings between the principal factions. The novel begins *in media res* with Lorq Von Ray, preparing to set out on a mission to mine the rare element Illyrion from a nova, an exploding star. The element is needed to halt the rival activities of the Red-Shift of Draco Federation. The mad and obsessed Lorq (McEvoy compares him to Captain Ahab in *Moby Dick*) does end up successfully changing the social and economic structure of the galaxy, but he loses his life. Not surprising in Delany's universe, Delany leaves the fuller social realizations of Lorq's more violent accomplishments in the hands of artists—a gypsy musician (Mouse) and a culturally and theoretically astute novelist (Katin).

Later Works

Between the publication of *Nova* in 1968 and *Dhalgren* in 1975, Delany had no major science fiction works. The year 1971 saw the publica-tion of *Driftglass*, a collection of ten previously published Delany short stories, six of which had won or been nominated for a Hugo or Nebula, including "Time Considered as a Helix of Semi-Precious Stones," which won both. Delany's other notable short story collection is *Distant Stars* (1981). In 1973, he published *Tides of Lust* (republished under the title *Equinox*, 1994), the first of his three pornographic novels. *Equinox* would probably have experienced more success had the publisher, Lancer Books, not gone bankrupt just a week after the book was published and after having only just distributed a few thousand copies. *Equinox*, a novel set on the Gulf Coast and about a Black Captain on a Faustian quest and a lady Catherine, explores the relationship between lust and self-awareness, the overlapping of sexual freedom and sexual entrapment. It is also as much about the writing of pornography as it is itself a pornographic novel. *The Mad Man* (1994) tells the story of a philosophy graduate student's obsession with the mysterious death of another philosophy graduate student, murdered years earlier, and the parallels between their rather adventuresome sex lives. *Hogg* (1995), a particularly aggressive blend of sadism, misogyny, and racism (not without their broader strategic purposes), is narrated by a sexually submissive eleven-year-old boy. As a comment, perhaps an ironic one, on the texture of both excessive text and obsessive sex, the narrator says only one word in the novel and that is the novel's final one: "Nothin'." The "other" worlds have become become here horrific sexual landscapes. Ultimately, Delany's pornographic fiction shares a psychological, social, and semiotic pulse with his science fiction.

The period between 1968 and 1975 was not a relaxed professional period for Delany. He wrote and directed two short films, "Tiresias" and "The Orchard"; wrote film reviews for *Fantasy and Science Fiction*; co-edited *Quark* with Hacker (four issues between November 1970 and August 1971); wrote scripts for the *Wonder Woman* comic book; and, of course, wrote *Dhalgren*. He also began his career as teacher and academic critic by teaching at the Clarion

Writers Workshop and writing analyses of the work of other science fiction writers.

When the eight-hundred-page *Dhalgren* appeared in 1975, critics and readers reached their opinions quickly, some claiming the work as a masterpiece of science fiction and others as an indulgent work that stretched too far the boundaries of the genre. The novel went through sixteen printings in eight years, exposed Delany to a broader audience, and finally gave him a readership of over a million. However much *Dhalgren* is a fantasy novel driven by an almost naïve but exacting observant, it is also a novel of social and sexual realism thoroughly permeated with an urban decadence and purposelessness. With a metaphorical literality, the city burns incessantly but is never consumed, never reaches consummation or finality. In this respect, the satire that is *Dhalgren* reads at times like a cross between Lewis Carroll's *Alice's Adventures in Wonderland* (1865) and John Rechy's *City of Night* (1963) or Larry Kramer's *Faggots* (1978). This is not to say that Delany's characters, like Rechy's or Kramer's, are compulsively having homosexual sex or any sex. In fact, late in the novel Lanya observes just how little sex is happening in the scorpion community. It's a poignant absence in the scorpion community, notwithstanding the novel's attention to some particular disturbing sexual moments. Beginning the novel as he does in mid-sentence, Delany also signals his attempt to write a *Finnegan's Wake* (James Joyce, 1939) for his 1960–1970s culture, daring (by the comparison) to present a piece of science fiction as serious fiction.

The story takes place in the present day of the novel itself and is set in Bellona—big beautiful city and/or big war city. The city, somewhere in the United States, acts as far more than a backdrop for the characters and action. Some kind of catastrophe has struck the city and most of its inhabitants, especially its white ones, have left. Outside it, we learn from a few travelers here and there, the rest of the country is going along as usual with little or no news in or out of Bellona. Wherever it's located, Bellona has its own cosmic design. Without explanation a second moon can appear or the sun can rise in the middle of the afternoon with its round shape covering most of the horizon. But Delany's city is still about something more than its mysteries. Without laws and money, Bellona is a land of freedom in which the individual must determine her or his enslavement to materials and ethics: this becomes the novel's real quest. Or is the process of determining itself an illusion? It depends in large part how one thinks through Kid's pivotal question: "Do you think a city can control the way people live inside it? I mean, just the geography, the way the streets are laid out, the way the buildings are placed?" (The question is not unlike Rydra's inquiry into the relationship between language and control in *Babel*.)

The story focuses on the Native American Kid who, having forgotten his name and remembering only bits of his past, enters Bellona, finds a journal, begins to write poetry for the first time, and within hours becomes Bellona's poet laureate. Later he becomes part of a long relationship with Lanya Colson (an upper-class musician and teacher) and Denny (teenage, streetwise kid), and becomes leader of the scorpions, Bellona's main gang. More than a story, however, *Dhalgren* is its characters. Some of these include (many with satiric camp names and descriptions): Tak Loufer, a one-man gay Bellona welcoming committee; idolized "hulking, sadistic, bulk nigger" rapist George Harrison; Ernest Newboy, a poet merely visiting Bellona; Michael Kamp, an astronaut; the Reverend Amy Taylor, a black minister still carrying out her ministry; and the Richards family, adhering still to their "normal" middle-class daily lives and rendered with all the satire of Charles Dickens's Veneerings in Dickens's *Our Mutual Friend* (1864–1865).

Like many of Delany's novels, *Dhalgren* is a study of texts, of reading and writing. It is a virtual explosion of anti-climaxes, authorial contestations, narrative desire, and textual control. In the end Kid leaves, not fulfilled or necessarily wiser (even though he thinks he now knows his name) and not having adopted a more heroic stature.

Triton (1976), subtitled "An Ambiguous Heterotopia," was a relief for some of Delany's science fiction readers: it is a far more conventional science fiction novel than *Dhalgren*, even though they explore similar issues. The novel is about Delany's most explicit and elaborate critique of male chauvenism; it is also Delany's most classic utopian novel. The story takes place in 2112 on Earth and on the Outer Satellites, especially Triton. These Outer Satellites, ruled by a central government, constitute a utopian society: the social, health, educational, art, and daily needs of the citizens are taken care of, and they can, if they so desire and as many times as they like, surgically alter their race, gender, and/or sexuality. (The majority of the people in Triton are bisexual.) The space action focuses on the ongoing cultural strife between the Outer Satellites and the planets, the Satellites being more libertarian-socialist in their beliefs and organization than the planets. A war breaks out between them, leaving the planets near complete destruction. The story is filtered through the narrative of the Mars-born male chauvinistic Bron Helstrom (it's hard not to think "Ron Helstrom," Delany's European co-traveler), who is, despite whatever earnest efforts on his part, a misfit in Triton society. As a solution, but one that does not ultimately give him what he wants or needs, he has his gender changed, deciding to become the kind of passive woman he had hoped to fall in love with; he thinks that he may then find the man who would be like the man he now is and is about to be no longer. This novel too is about freedom and learning to decipher one's own illusions about race, gender, and sexuality. Whereas *Dhalgren* contemplates the way urban geography liberates and restricts one's moral choices; *Triton* examines the way social organizations liberate and restrict one's ability to understand one's very physical presence. Hence, the novel's opening epigraph: "The social body constrains the way the physical body is perceived" (Mary Douglas, *Natural Symbols*).

Stars in My Pocket like Grains of Sand (1984), Delany's first published science fiction novel in eight years, contains many of the con-

cerns found in Delany's earlier fiction. In addition, it also shows Delany's increasing attention to sexual relations as an ingress to his critique of social, psychological, and intellectual spheres. The novel, part of a two-novel story, was supposed to be followed by *The Splendor and Misery of Bodies, of Cities*, which has yet to be published. Set in the distant future, the novel traces the homosexual love and sexual relations between Rat Korga and Marq Dyeth. As a youth, Rat had chosen to undergo a process known as Radical Anxiety Termination (RAT—hence, his name) in order to free himself from violence and antisocial behavior, essentially destroying his capacity for a full emotional range. Rat was enslaved by the RAT Institute (institutional slavery being legal) but was later stolen and sold as a personal slave (illegal) to a sexually abusive woman. Rat's planet, Rhyonon, is then destroyed by some kind of catastrophe that leaves Rat the planet's only survivor. After he's rescued by the Web, an intergalactic organization, he ends up in Velm coupled with Marq Dyeth, who helps undo the RAT surgery. They have a mutually fulfilling relationship until the Web, for reasons not quite clear, takes Rat away from Velm and Marq. There is, indeed, a love story here, but the novel is finally less a fanciful romantic tale than it is Delany's study, on a broader scale, of sex and freedom and, on a more focused scale, of homosexuality and slavery.

His next major group of works were the Nevèrÿon series (1979–1987), which were more clearly fantasy fiction than they were science fiction: *Tales of Nevèrÿon* (1979), *Neveryóna: Or the Tales of Signs and Cities* (1983), *Flight from Nevèrÿon* (1985), and *The Bridge of Lost Desire* (1987, later revised as *Return to Nevèrÿon*, 1989). In 1980, *Tales* was nominated for an American Book Award. While sword-and-sorcery stories are some of the most formulaic of fictional forms, Delany seems to take more delight in breaking the genre's expectations than in telling stories of adventure and rescue, as his hero, Gorik (who is a middle-aged instead of the conventional coming-of-age hero) follows his society's transition from a bartering society to a cash economy. In "The Tale of Gorik," for example, Gorik spends most of his time courting the boy Small Sarg whom he has freed from slavery. As with much of Delany's other fiction, these works become virtual adventure through Delany's theoretical musings on the textuality of texts in a culture of signs, information, reflections, and nostalgia. One of the most notable works in this series is "The Tale of Plagues and Carnivals" in *Flight,* in which Delany explores textuality by including in his fiction entries from his journal observations about the realities of AIDS in New York City. Delany kept journals since his childhood, and he has used entries from his journals in other novels, including, for example, *The Einstein Intersection.*

Delany's next novel, *They Fly at Çiron* (1993), a fantasy one, came six years after the last work in the Nevèryon series, but had actually been first drafted as a much shorter form in 1962. It was reworked with his friend James Sallis and published under both their names in *The Magazine of Fantasy & Science Fiction* in 1971, and reworked again, this time without Sallis's passages, and published as a longer work in 1993. The novel is often cited as a good introduction to Delany's fiction and as a much less complex work than most of his fiction. While the narrative is infused with Delany's social critique, the novel's action is rather continuous and his prose style fairly simple. The novel works as a kind of pastoral tale, showing Delany's commitment throughout his writing career to intertextually engage a number of genres through his science and fantasy fiction. The story focuses on the peaceful Cironian people, whose village is invaded by the malevolent army of Myetra. The army is led by the cruel Nactor, whose name itself seems a crude play on the name Nectar, the drink of the Olympian gods. Nactar and the Myetrans kill many of the villagers and enslave the rest. Rahm, a village boy who has managed to escape, befriends the fearful black Winged Ones, humanoids with bat-like wing, whom the Cironians had previously feared. The Winged Ones defeat the Myetrans. The novel focuses

its story on Rahm, and in keeping with Delany's interest in mythology and sex, Rahm moves through Delany's narrative as a kind of Ganymede, one of Zeus' cup-bearers who is first taken to Olympus by an eagle and made to experience the kind of horrifying ecstasy between Rahm and three Winged Ones that closes the novel.

The three works that make up *Atlantis: Three Tales* (1995) seem to take Delany in a direction away from what his readers have come to expect from his fiction. No intergalactic strife, swords-and-sorcery, or seriously de-familiarized cityscapes here. The book contains one novella, *Atlantis: Model 1924,* and two stories, "*Citre et Trans*" and "Erik, Gwen, and D. H. Lawrence's Esthetic of Unrectified Feeling." These works are at once fictional and semi-autobiographical. *Model 1924* is about Sam, a black 17-year-old naïve high school dropout, who in 1924 takes the train from North Carolina to Harlem in order to live with his older brother Hubert and work. The novella coheres around Sam's exploration of Brooklyn Bridge. Despite the apparent differences between *Model 1924* and Delany's science and fantasy fiction, the novella does explore conventional Delany themes and also uses some of his narrative techniques, such as sometimes splitting the narrative into columns in order to underscore different processes of perception and such. It is a tale of the diaspora, a migration story, a narrative reflection on the artistic heyday of the Harlem Renaissance, evoking such personages as Jean Toomer and Paul Robeson, as well as his own pre-history. The novella seems also to conjure up family members; the reader can now find the Delany sisters' *Having Our Say.* It is also a story about Sam's sexual awakening, about his coming into consciousness. In this novella in which New York City figures as a new Atlantis, a glorious city that would finally be consumed by its own impiety, the tone is at once nostalgic and foreboding. For Delany as black gay artist, witnessing the ravage of AIDS and the cleaning up of his city, perhaps this novel is finally elegiac, the story of a beginning and an end. "Erik, Gwen" is a more straightforward and more autobiographical work than *Model 1924*; it focuses on two figures who influenced the artistic vision and social depth of a young black artist in New York City. And *"Citre et Trans,"* the third and shortest piece, also marked with bits of autobiography, tells the story of a bisexual black artist living in Greece in the 1960s who is forced to deal with his conflicting responses to being raped by two sailors when he encounters one of them again in a train station. Whatever their autobiographical investments, these three pieces do demonstrate Delany's ongoing experimentation with the relationship between myth, narrative, and identity.

While Delany will perhaps remain for most of his readers a writer of science fiction and fantasy, he also has a successful career as a theoretical and critical reader of science fiction. He would receive distinction in this arena as well. In 1985, he received the Pilgrim Award for Excellence in Science Fiction Criticism from the Science Fiction Research Association. To date, he has published six volumes of critical essays, including most notably his first, *The Jewel-Hinged Jaw* (1977); his most critically suggestive, *The American Shore* (1978), a book-length reading of a Thomas M. Disch short story; and his most culturally groundbreaking, *Silent Interviews* (1994). During this same period, he also began publishing autobiographical works: *Heavenly Breakfast* (1978), *The Motion of Light in Water* (1987), and *Bread & Wine* (1999), an illustrated book about the love and sexual relationship between Delany and Dennis, a younger homeless Brooklyn Irishman. Also notable is his critique of the gentrification and "Disnification" of that urban New York that has inspired so many of his science fiction worlds, *Times Square Red, Times Square Blue* (1999). When thinking especially about these last two books, Dennis as the real life incarnation of Delany's earlier fictional Denny and the real city of Delany's fiction being claimed by Disney, one of America's most sterile of fantasies, like so much of Delany's life and like so much of his fiction, it all seems rather just a tad too uncanny.

Selected Bibliography

PRIMARY WORKS

FICTION

The Jewels of Aptor. New York: Bantam Books, 1978. Originally published in 1962.
The Fall of the Towers. New York: Bantam Books, 1986. One-volume edition of the trilogy of novels *Out of the Dead City* (1963), *The Towers of Toron* (1964) and *City of a Thousand Suns* (1965).
The Ballad of Beta-2. New York: Bantam Books, 1982. Originally published in 1965.
The Complete Nebula Award Winning Fiction of Samuel R. Delany. New York: Bantam Books, 1986. Omnibus volume containing *Babel-17*, *A Fabulous, Formless Darkness* (originally published as *The Einstein Intersection*) plus the short stories "Aye, and Gomorrah. . . ." and "Time Considered as a Helix of Semi-Precious Stones."
Babel-17. New York: Bantam, 1984. Originally published in 1966.
Empire Star. New York: Bantam Books, 1983. Originally published in 1966.
The Einstein Intersection. New York: Bantam Books, 1981. Originally published in 1967.
Nova. New York: Bantam Books, 1987. Originally published in 1968.
Driftglass. New York: NAL/Signet, 1971. Short Stories.
Equinox. New York: Richard Kasak/Rhinoceros Books, 1994. Originally published under the title *Tides of Lust.* New York: Lancer Books, 1973.
Dhalgren. Hanover and London: Wesleyan University Press, 1996. Corrected edition of 1975 volume by same title.
Trouble on Triton. Hanover and London: Wesleyan University Press, 1996. Originally published in 1976.
Distant Stars. New York: Bantam Books, 1981. Short Stories.
Stars in My Pocket Like Grains of Sand. New York: Bantam Books, 1984.
Driftglass/Starshards. London: HarperCollins/Grafton Books, 1993. Collected short fiction. Contains "Of Doubts and Dreams, An Introduction," "The Star Pit," "Corona," "Aye, and Gomorrah . . . ," "Driftglass," "We, in Some Strange Power's Employ, Move on a Rigorous Line," "Cage of Brass," "High Weir," "Time Considered as a Helix of Semi-Precious Stones," "Omegahelm . . . Prismatica," "Ruins," "Dog in a Fisherman's Net," "Night and the Loves of Joe Diconstanzo," "Among the Blobs," *"Citre et Trans,"* "Erik, Gwen, and D. H. Lawrence's Esthetic of Unrectified Feeling."
Tales of Nevèrÿon. Corrected edition of the 1979 volume of the same title. Contains "The Tale of Gorgik," "The Tale of Old Venn," "The Tale of Small Sarg," "The Tale of Potters and Dragons," and "The Tale of Dragons and Dreamers."

Neveryóna: Or the Tales of Signs and Cities. Hanover and London: Wesleyan University Press, 1993. Corrected edition of the 1983 volume of the same title.

Flight from Nevèrÿon. Hanover and London: Wesleyan University Press, 1994. Corrected edition of the 1985 volume of the same title. Contains the novels *The Tale of Fog and Granite* and *The Tale of Plagues and Carnivals.*

Return to Nevèrÿon. Hanover and London: Wesleyan University Press, 1994. Corrected edition of the 1986 volume *The Bridge of Lost Desire.* Contains the novel *The Game of Time and Pain* and two stories, "The Tale of Rumor and Desire" and "The Tale of Gorgik."

They Fly at Çiron. Seattle: Incunabula, 1993.

The Mad Man. New York: Richard Kasak Books, 1994.

Hogg. Boulder and Normal: Fiction Collective Two/ Black Ice Books, 1995.

Atlantis: Three Tales. Hanover and London: Wesleyan University Press, 1995. (Also as a first, limited edition from Seattle: Incunabula, 1995.) Contains the novel *Atlantis: Model 1924* and two stories, "*Citre et Trans*," and "Erik, Gwen, and D. H. Lawrence's Esthetic of Unrectified Feeling."

NONFICTION

Heavenly Breakfast: An Essay on the Winter of Love. Flint, Mich.: Bamberger Books, 1995. Memoir of various urban communes and co-ops during 1967. Originally published in 1978.

The Jewel-Hinged Jaw: Notes on the Language of Science Fiction. Elizabethtown, N.Y.: Dragon Press, 1977. Essays. A corrected edition was published by Berkeley-Putnam/Windhover Books, 1978.

The American Shore: Meditations on a Tale of Science Fiction by Thomas M. Disch—"Angouleme." Elizabethtown, N.Y.: Dragon Press, 1978.

Starboard Wine: More Notes on the Language of Science Fiction. Pleasantville, N.Y.: Dragon Press, 1984. Essays.

The Motion of Light in Water: Sex and Science Fiction in the East Village. New York: Richard Kasak/ Masquerade Books, 1993. Originally published in 1987.

Wagner/Artaud: A Play of 19th and 20th Century Critical Fictions. New York: Anzatz Press, 1988.

The Straits of Messina. Seattle: Serconia Press, 1989. Essays.

Silent Interviews: On Language, Race, Sex, Science Fiction, and Some Comics. Hanover and London: Wesleyan University Press, 1994. Selected written interviews.

Longer Views. Hanover and London: Wesleyan University Press, 1995. Contains six essays: "Wagner/ Artaud," "Aversion/Perversion/Diversion," "Reading at Work, and Other Activities Frowned on by Authority: A Reading of Donna Haraway's 'Manifesto for Cyborgs,'" "Shadow and Ash," "Atlantis Revisited," and "Shadows."

Bread & Wine: An Erotic Tale of New York. Illustrated by Mia Wolff; Introduction by Alan Moore. New York: Juno Books, 1999.

Times Square Red, Times Square Blue. New York and London: New York University Press, 1999.

SECONDARY WORKS

Barbour, Douglas. Worlds out of Words: The Science Fiction Novels of Samuel R. Delany. Frome, England: Bran's Head Books, 1979.

Bray, Mary Kay. "Rites of Reversal: Double Consciousness in Delany's *Dhalgren.*" *Black American Literature Forum* 18: 57–61 (Summer 1984).

Dery, Mark. "Black to the Future: Interviews with Samuel R. Delany, Greg Tate, and Tricia Rose." *South Atlantic Quarterly* 92, no. 4: 735–78 (Fall 1993).

Easterbrook, Neil. "State, Heterotopia: The Political Imagination in Heinlein, Le Guin, and Delany." *Political Science Fiction.* Edited by Clyde Wilcox. Columbia: University of South Carolina Press, 1997. Pp. 43–75.

Ebert, Teresa L. "The Convergence of Postmodern Innovative Fiction and Science Fiction: An Encounter with Samuel R. Delany's Technotopia." *Poetic Today: Theory and Analysis of Literature and Communication* 1: 91–104 (1980).

Fox, Robert Elliot. *The Conscientious Sorcerers: The Black Postmodernist Fiction of LeRoi Jones/Amiri Baraka, Ishmael Reed and Samuel R. Delany.* New York: Greenwood Press, 1987.

Golumbia, David. "Black and White World: Race, Ideology, and Utopia in Triton and Star Trek. *Cultural Critique* 32: 75–95 (Winter 1995–96).

Govan, Sandra Y. "The Insistent Presence of Black Folk in the Novels of Samuel R. Delany." *Black American Literature Forum* 18: 43–48 (Summer 1984).

Mathieson, Kenneth. "The Influence of Science Fiction in the Contemporary American Novel." *Science-Fiction Studies* 35: 22–32 (March 1985).

McEvoy, Seth. *Samuel R. Delany.* New York: Frederick Ungar Publishing Co., 1984.

Moore, John. "Singing the Body Unelectric: Mapping and Modelling Sanuel R. Delany's *Dhalgren.*" *American Bodies: Cultural Histories of the Physique.* Edited by Tim Armstrong. New York: New York University Press, 1996. Pp. 186–94.

Moylan, Thomas M. *Demand the Impossible: Science Fiction and the Utopian Imagination.* London: Methuen, Inc., 1986.

Nilon, Charles. "The Science Fiction of Samuel R. Delany and the Limits of Technology." *Black American Literature Forum* 18: 62–68 (Summer 1984).

Peplow, Michael W., and Robert S. Bravard. *Samuel R. Delany: A Primary and Secondary Bibliography, 1962–1979.* Boston: G.K. Hall & Co., 1980. (Also see their supplemental bibliography in *Black American Literature Forum*, vol. 18, no. 2.)

Reid-Pharr, Robert F. "Disseminating Heterotopia." *African American Review* 28: 347–57 (Fall 1994).

Sallis, James. *Ash of Stars: On the Writing of Samuel R. Delany.* Jackson, Miss.: University Press of Mississippi, 1996.

Schweitzer, Darrell. "Algol Interview: Samuel R. Delany." In "Samuel R. Delany." In *The Chelsea House Library of Literary Criticism: Twentieth-Century American Literature.* Edited by Harold Bloom. New York: Chelsea House Publishers, 1986. Pp. 955–68.

Slusser, George E. *The Delany Intersection: Samuel Delany Considered as a Writer of Semi-Precious Words.* San Bernardino, Calif.: Borgo Books, 1977.

Weedman, Jane Branham. *Samuel R. Delany.* Starmont Reader's Guide Series, No. 10. Mercer Island, Wash.: Starmont House, 1982.

W. E. B. Du Bois
(1868–1963)

GEORGE P. CUNNINGHAM

IN A PUBLIC career that stretched from the late 1890s to 1963, William Edward Burghart Du Bois provides the same type of panoramic lens on African Americans in the twentieth century that Frederick Douglass furnishes for the nineteenth century. Successively, as a pioneering architect of the modern African American protest tradition, Pan-Africanism, and cultural nationalism, Du Bois established the basis for an African American alliance with socialists, African nationalists, feminists, and Communists. To a substantial degree Americans both black and white still view and write about the dynamics of race in their country within a spectrum defined by the intellectual, political, and rhetorical frameworks pioneered by Du Bois. He remains *the* central authorizing figure for twentieth-century African American thought.

Above all, Du Bois was a writer. Midway through his career he said of himself in *Dusk of Dawn* (1940): "My leadership was a leadership solely of ideas. I never was, nor ever will be, personally popular. . . . I withdrew sometimes ostentatiously from the personal nexus, but I sought all the more determinedly to force home essential ideas." Beyond the veil of political epitaphs such as "radical democrat," "visionary," "prophet," "race man," "propagandist," and "father of Pan-Africanism" rests a complex, sometimes contradictory, career that was realized primarily through the written word. No other African American of the twentieth century mastered as many political, intellectual, and academic systems of knowledge or essayed in as many intellectual and literary genres.

Although Du Bois wrote poetry, short stories, and five novels, contemporary and later judgments of his work within these purely literary genres have been mixed at best, and only *The Souls of Black Folk* (1903) has an unshakable place in the African American literary canon. Arnold Rampersad's *The Art and Imagination of W. E. B. Du Bois* (1976) is the only book-length study that examines the skills Du Bois brought to his various representations of his ever-shifting intellectual vision. Yet those skills are an integral part of his body of writing. The true drama that is played out in all of Du Bois's work is his struggle to re-create, from the intellectual and literary forms that shape modern consciousness, an African American vision that speaks with urgency to the need to eradicate the racial, sexual, and economic injustices that devalue modern life. Whether he presents his vision through the representational genres of history, the social sciences, and journalism or through the creative genres of literature, each of his works attempts a synthesis of the multiple ways of knowing that he had mastered, a vision of his unchanging sense of ethics, and a call for progressive social change.

David Levering Lewis's *W. E. B. Du Bois* establishes the basic elements of his private as well as public life to 1919, but almost all earlier works are especially dependent on Du Bois's autobiographical writings and the interpretative stamp that he was able to impress on his life through them. Since the age of fifteen, when he became the western Massachusetts correspondent for the *New York Globe,* Du Bois consciously and unconsciously constructed his public persona through the written word. He was aware of the evasions and repressions in all autobiographies, even his own. In *The Autobiography of W. E. B. Du Bois* (1968) he warns his readers of "vast omissions, matters which are forgotten accidentally or by deep design." Lewis's independent documentation of Du Bois's early life greatly enhances our ability to understand the complex process through which he constructed his autobiographical self and is invaluable to an integrated treatment of the private man and his public work.

By accident of birth, Du Bois was culturally, and to a degree psychologically, an outsider in African America. He was born on 23 February 1868 in Great Barrington, Massachusetts. Neither a southerner nor a direct descendant of slaves, he could not, like his principal predecessors, Frederick Douglass and Booker T. Washington, draw a sense of self from the story of a triumph over slavery that provided the basis for the classic nineteenth-century African American public persona. The only child of the short-lived marriage of Alfred Du Bois and Mary Silvina Burghardt, he was descended from generations of free blacks and grew up outside the main cultural, political, and economic currents that shaped the lives of the majority of African Americans in the post-Reconstruction period.

The meaning of his place of birth weighed heavily in Du Bois's autobiographical writings, and his portrait of Great Barrington is as consequential as those of his parents and family. Nestled between the valleys of the Berkshire Hills, "by a golden river and in the shadow of two great hills," as Du Bois often described it, Great Barrington sheltered a culturally homogeneous community in which a small number

of blacks, including the Burghardts, had lived for generations, occupying a secure but not exalted place in the town's social and economic life. He credited the town with a pivotal role in molding his personality and character. "In general thought and conduct" he described himself as "quite thoroughly New England." To his upbringing in Great Barrington he attributed the source of two constants of his personality: his greatest personal failing, a lack of ease with others, and his greatest strength, an intellectual obstinacy. In the *Autobiography* he wrote:

> I am quite sure that in a less restrained and conventional atmosphere I should have easily learned to express my emotions with far greater and more unrestrained intensity; but as it was I had the social heritage not only of a New England clan but Dutch taciturnity. This was later reinforced and strengthened by inner withdrawals in the face of real and imagined discriminations. The result was that I was early thrown in upon myself. I found it difficult and even unnecessary to approach other people and by that same token my own inner life perhaps grew the richer; but the habit of repression often returned to plague me in after years, for so early a habit could not easily be unlearned. (p. 93)

With the exception of a psychobiographical sketch by Allison Davis, most of Du Bois's biographers follow his lead in portraying his childhood as neither unusual nor unhappy, minimizing, as Du Bois did, the pain of some formative incidents that he carried with him throughout his life. His father deserted the family shortly after William's birth. His mother suffered a stroke that left her partially paralyzed and dependent during most of his childhood. In addition, his family history included the awkward fact of his mother's having had an illegitimate child fathered by her first cousin. Du Bois did not seek to integrate these facts in his autobiography and give them weight in the development of his character and personality. Yet his telling different stories about his father's absence, first attributing it to death and then to desertion, suggests that these and simi-

lar events influenced his development more-
deeply than he would admit. In 1890 he wrote
of himself in his diary that "in my early youth
a great bitterness entered my life and kindled a
great ambition." Du Bois the visionary and
Du Bois the scholar, the tireless intellectual
and the "lonely warrior," were as much fathered by that bitterness as by the idyllic life
he portrayed in Great Barrington.

Whatever unhappiness may have been a part
of Du Bois's childhood, Great Barrington and
his family provided compensation in the form
of an education. That opportunity provided
him, as a young man, with a sense of his own
special talents; throughout his life, his assurance of his intellectual abilities provided his
strongest sense of self. He took the college preparatory course at the integrated Great Barrington High School and graduated as valedictorian
in 1884. Although his mother died shortly
thereafter, Du Bois continued an educational
career that would have been unthinkable for
most African Americans at that time.

Du Bois's education both strengthened and
broadened the foundation that was established
in his early life. Through the generosity of several family members and white neighbors, he
entered Fisk University, an all-black institution
in Nashville, Tennessee, as a sophomore. Fisk
was very much at the center of an African
American struggle that Du Bois had seen only
from the margins of Great Barrington. Established at the crossroads of missionary zeal and
Reconstruction politics and staffed by northern
whites steeped in abolitionist traditions, Fisk
was designed to provide a classical education as
a fulcrum for elevating the sons and daughters
of the freed slaves.

Long after Reconstruction ended, black colleges in the South, like Fisk, were the principal
remaining intersection of a disinterested white
philanthropy and the African American project
of "racial uplift." Under the watchful eye of a
mostly white faculty, a small group of blacks
was trained in Greek, Latin, philosophy, math-
ematics, and the natural sciences; were taught
to believe that they had mastered the central
secrets of Western culture; and were sent out
as cultural missionaries, mostly as teachers or

W. E. B. Du Bois

preachers. Coming from Great Barrington, Du
Bois was already the cultural type of African
American Fisk was designed to produce. His experiences at Fisk, however, provided him with
a sense of his importance as an educated African American in the process of racial progress.

Du Bois's experiences at Fisk also unveiled
for him the life and culture of African Americans in the post-Reconstruction South. A central part of the school's history was the story,
already legend by Du Bois's time, of the Jubilee
Singers. In a period of particular financial distress for the school, they were able to raise
money by giving performances of African American spirituals throughout the United States
and before the kings and queens of Europe. The
most imposing building on campus, Jubilee
Hall, was a visible symbol of their work and of
the power of their songs. Equally important, Du
Bois shared with the students of his generation
the experience of teaching in a backwoods

school during the summer. This teaching, as well as his subsequent sociological studies, provided the basis for the poignant portrait of the South that appears in *The Souls of Black Folk*. His time at Fisk afforded him his first glimpse of the terrain of the post-Reconstruction South, which he would spend the next decade scientifically mapping and imaginatively integrating into his vision.

While Fisk provided Du Bois with a sound, nineteenth-century, classical education emphasizing the ethical responsibility of an educated leadership to its race, his further education enabled him to master the emerging disciplines and methodologies that would define the curriculum of higher education in the twentieth century. Graduating with honors from Fisk in 1888, Du Bois entered Harvard University as a junior, where he earned a second bachelor's degree in philosophy, graduating cum laude in 1890. As both an undergraduate and a graduate student, he was exposed to the teaching of Josiah Royce, William James, and George Santayana in philosophy and of Albert Bushnell Hart in history. Through a grant and loan from the Slater Fund, Du Bois was able to attend the University of Berlin, where he studied history and economics. He received his doctorate in history from Harvard in 1895, the first black man to receive a doctorate from Harvard in any discipline. To a degree, at Harvard and the University of Berlin, Du Bois was introduced to, and persuaded of, the social efficacy of empirical methods of studying humankind and society. In the process, he became convinced of the possibilities of finding the truth and advancing the causes of his race through empirical research.

During the period between his receiving the doctorate from Harvard and his full-time appointment as editor of the *Crisis*, the main avenues of Du Bois's multifaceted career began to take shape. He taught at Wilberforce University and Atlanta University; he started two short-lived racial journals, *The Moon* and *The Horizon*; he was secretary of the first Pan-African Conference in London in 1900; he helped found and was president of the American Negro Academy; he directed the Atlanta University conferences, which produced a series of sociological studies; he published two works of history, *The Suppression of the African Slave-Trade to the United States of America, 1638–1870* (1896) and *John Brown* (1909); one sociological study, *The Philadelphia Negro* (1899); a collection of essays, *The Souls of Black Folk*; and a novel, *The Quest of the Silver Fleece* (1911). On 12 May 1896 Du Bois married Nina Gomer; they had two children, Burghardt Gomer and Yolande. His son, however, died before he was two years old.

Du Bois's dissertation, *The Suppression of the African Slave-Trade*, subsequently revised and published as the first volume in the Harvard Historical Series, fixes his work as he was beginning to exploit the new empirical methods. As a monograph, *Suppression* was primarily a study of laws reflecting the then-current idea that the legal evolution of a society represented and embodied the essence of its inevitable developmental history and progress. Although his inquiry was guided by the protocols of this approach, Du Bois refused to fashion through them yet another example of progressive American history. In what would become a standard form of commentary in his scholarly work, he added a coda to *Suppression*, "The Lesson for Americans," that allowed him to reflect on the larger meaning of his study. He concluded that America's involvement in the slave trade evidenced "carelessness and moral cowardice," and he reminded his readers that it "behooves nations as well as men to do things at the very moment when they ought to be done."

In a later phase of his career, Du Bois would suggest that *Suppression* was flawed by his lack of exposure to Freud and Marx. Yet the intellectual vision of these men would not have altered the basic assumption that shaped this study. In this early phase of his career, he insisted that individuals were free agents who bore moral responsibility for their actions. This notion of free agency was essential to Du Bois's understanding of himself and the value of his world. Empirical methods provided not an understanding of fixed laws of society and nature but a scientific basis for establishing a terrain of truth upon which ethically directed men could base their actions.

Du Bois's focus on the moral and ethical responsibility of the individual not only buttressed his own sense of self but also provided the underpinnings of much of his work. Although it was most clearly stated in the 1903 essay "The Talented Tenth," several of his other works evidenced a fascination with the ways in which—for good or ill—individuals embodied for history the distinguishing aspects of their society and culture. His graduation address at Fisk was on Bismarck; that at Harvard was entitled "Jefferson Davis as a Representative of Civilization." His most notable full-length study of the role of an individual was his historical biography of John Brown.

Although Du Bois began his career at Wilberforce in Ohio and worked for a year at the University of Pennsylvania, the main elements of this period belong to the South. In 1897 he was asked to come to Atlanta University to teach economics and history, a job that included directing the newly instituted Atlanta University Conferences on the Negro Problems. In his vision of the Atlanta University studies, Du Bois projected the ideal of enlightened progress. There he could realize his dream of wedding sociology and ethics. He designed an ambitious plan of study, which was to last for a century, in which ten key topics were targeted for study every decade. On the meager resources the university could allocate, Du Bois completed sixteen studies, but during that first decade he was gradually drawn into the political arena.

Suppression and *The Philadelphia Negro*, his second scholarly study, were well received by the academic community. Du Bois was able to publish essays in leading national journals, yet his work had little impact outside the liberal white and African American communities. Unfortunately, he had entered the field of history at precisely the moment it was beginning to be dominated by southern apologists. The two primary fields that touch on African American life, slavery and Reconstruction, were being shaped by Ulrich Bonnell Phillips at Yale and William A. Dunning at Columbia. Both trained generations of graduate students in the new empirical methods of historical research and in a pro-white southern vision. Despite many notable exceptions, the vision of Phillips and Dunning drew the new empirical methods into the service of southern apology throughout most of Du Bois's life. Clearly, Du Bois felt the need to reach beyond his role as a scholar to effect the kinds of changes to which he remained committed.

The turning point in his career came with the publication of *The Souls of Black Folk* in 1903. In *Souls*, Du Bois indisputably achieved two moments of integration. Stitching together his revisions of previously published work with several new essays, Du Bois the sociologist, historian, essayist, polemicist, fiction writer, and poet came together to shape one cohesive intellectual accomplishment. *Souls* also marked the moment that Du Bois's vision became one with the political and intellectual mainstream of African American thought. It is largely through the impact of this work that Du Bois achieved his commanding presence in the African American political and literary imagination.

Souls gives rise to a number of productive tensions. The most visible of them is a duality of styles that, to some degree, informs much of his writing. Arthur P. Davis has suggested that

> the first [is] a style that is smooth flowing, heightened yet controlled, lucid, highly readable, and definitely modern in its rhythms and sentence structure. This is the style he uses when presenting scholarly or social or historical facts. Like all good prose, it is a combination of important content and artistry in the presentation of that content. The second style, however, . . . is inclined to be flowery, emotional, poetic, and essentially Victorian in the unpopular sense of the term. This second style makes too much use of allegorical and mythological terms, has too many apostrophes and invocations, too many "thee's" and "thou's" in it.   (pp. 18–19)

The term "romantic" has most often been evoked to describe Du Bois's second style. Although this "romanticism" characterizes his lapses into an overvalued prose that is indeed difficult for modern readers, it also best describes his stance as visionary.

Through his romantic vision, Du Bois the social scientist found a framework to accommodate, though not always easily, Du Bois the visionary. The stress of romanticism on the transformative power of the individual imagination gave Du Bois a framework for anchoring the passionate and the sentimental in his personality within a larger redemptive vision. The high regard of romanticism for the insights of the primitive or the "folk" allowed Du Bois to draw from the transcendent and mythical elements—the "souls"—of African Americans an external authority for his writing. In addition, in his fiction and some essays, he is drawn to the power of the conventions of the romance—allegory, the power of love, and the importance of character and honor—in order to represent his sense of the drama of the individual and society trapped in great moral and ethical struggles.

Within its historical context, the central essay of *Souls*, "Of Mr. Booker T. Washington and Others," was Du Bois's critique of the then-leading black political leader of the day. President of Tuskegee Institute and a strong advocate of industrial education, Booker T. Washington wielded tremendous powers as the primary black counselor to the Republican party on patronage and to white industrialists on philanthropy. Du Bois had long argued against industrial education; he reiterated his position in "The Talented Tenth," which first appeared in the 1903 volume *The Negro Problem: A Series of Articles by Representative Negroes of Today*:

> If we make money the object of mantraining, we shall develop money-makers not necessarily men; if we make technical skill the object of education, we may possess artisans but not, in nature, men. Men we shall have only as we make manhood the object of the work of the schools—intelligence, broad sympathy, knowledge of the world that was and is, and of the relation of men to it—this is the curriculum of that Higher Education which must underlie true life.
>
> (pp. 33–34)

In the third chapter of *Souls* Du Bois advances a shrewd critique of Washington in the context of Du Bois's own reading of African American history. By comparing him with the leaders of the nineteenth century, Du Bois represents their differences as a struggle of ideals. Claiming the mantle of nineteenth-century abolitionists, he portrays Washington as representing materialism against idealism, accommodation against struggle, and, implicitly, ignorance against true education.

The larger success of Du Bois's critique of Washington and the enduring value of *Souls* lay in Du Bois's ability to infuse each essay in the volume with a sense of a struggle between or toward great ideals. In "Of the Wings of Atalanta," Du Bois draws upon a story from Greek mythology to create an allegory of the struggle between materialism and idealism in the New South. Representing the South is the fleet-footed goddess Atalanta. The fastest of runners, she is bested in a footrace and forced to marry Hippomenes, who drops in her path golden apples that she bends to pick up; Du Bois warns his readers, as he does in the previous chapter, "Of the Meaning of Progress," that the quest for gold or material progress often leads to a loss of the soul.

This pursuit of material possessions, Du Bois implies, ignores the rich spiritual heritage of the African American experience. In the first essay in *Souls*, "Of Our Spiritual Strivings," and two later ones, "Of the Faith of the Fathers" and "Of the Sorrow Songs," Du Bois portrays African Americans as struggling to be true to an identity defined by their unique cultural heritage. He depicts a vision of African American identity based on the folk spirit deriving from Africa. These essays point toward reorienting the ideal for African American identity away from the achievements within an Anglo-American context of the educated and assimilated middle class and toward the lived experience and expressive culture of rural black farmers, the African American "folk." Generations of writers in the United States, the Caribbean, and Africa have followed Du Bois's lead, creating works that draw on and incorporate folklore.

Within the context of this continuous cultural heritage, Du Bois preferred his most frequently quoted statement: "One ever feels his two-ness,—an American, a Negro; two souls, two thoughts, two unreconciled strivings; two warring ideals in one dark body, whose dogged strength alone keeps it from being torn asunder." This sense of a divided African American self—which subsequently sociologists in their notion of marginality and anthropologists in their notion of "liminality" would echo—has struck a responsive chord among students of the African American experience.

Like many who held on to the absolute values of the nineteenth century, Du Bois bitterly rejected the new American ethos of capitalism. He greatly feared that, through education, blacks would adopt the materialistic spirit of the turn of the century. He saw in it the worst kind of social Darwinism; the economically strong were morally free to take advantage of the weak by receiving justification in the form of wealth. The principal obstacle to the complete ascendancy of materialism was the education of men to higher values. Men of culture—"the talented tenth"—who could at least restrain the worst elements of the new system, if not prevent them, would provide wings for the goddess Atalanta and speed her past the temptation of the golden apples.

The possibility that African Americans, especially the "talented tenth," would fail in their mission haunted Du Bois. His sense of possible failures lent a special melancholy and pathos to his portrait of one of his African American intellectual father figures. In "Of Alexander Crummell," a biographical sketch of the preeminent nineteenth-century black intellectual, Du Bois drew a portrait of the ideal racial leader. At each age in Crummell's life he successfully overcame different inner struggles: "the temptation of Hate, that stood out against the red dawn; the temptation Despair, that darkened noonday; and the temptation of Doubt, that ever steals along with twilight." Du Bois portrayed his own struggle to overcome hatred in "Of the Passing of the First-Born," which recounts his bitterness over the death of his son. His ability to focus on inner struggle, to speak,

even in veiled allusion, of inner doubt and alluring temptations, heightened the sense of the larger moral and historical struggles engaged in by the "talented tenth" as a group and as individuals.

His novel, *The Quest of the Silver Fleece*, works out in fiction the themes of *The Souls of Black Folk*, particularly Du Bois's complex vision of African American leadership. Against the social and economic background of the post-Reconstruction South, Du Bois sets in motion the role of vision, doubt, and despair in history. At the center of *Quest* is a heroine, Zora, and her awakening to self-consciousness and search for "the way" in the fragmenting and divided world of the post-Reconstruction South. She possesses "a visionary tenderness; a mighty, self-concealed striving for unknown things," terms that in *Souls* guide African Americans as they seek to enter history. Zora is central among a cast of women—Sarah Smith, the "Yankee schoolmarm"; Mary Taylor Cresswell, a northern schoolteacher who marries into a leading plantation family; and Caroline Wynn, a talented but pragmatically cynical northern black—and dominates the action and the shifting vantage points of the novel.

Through the point of view of women, Du Bois portrays the personal and emotional dimensions of a political and economic world. That world, the emerging "New South," is caught in tensions created by the differing and contending economic and moral orders of northern capitalism and southern post-slavery oligarchy. Blacks and whites, northern and southern, are caught in a common web spun from the "silver fleece," cotton. Du Bois's detailed description of the social, economic, and political empire built on cotton verges on muckraking, but this naturalism avoids economic determinism and serves as the background for a moral allegory of African American redemption. For Zora and the other black characters, the landscape inscribes a separate historical, moral, and social topography; the primary tension comes in the representations of the swamp (personified by Elspeth, Zora's mother), a moral chaos created by slavery but hiding a deeper black spiritual past, and the schoolhouse, personified by Miss Smith, a future projected by the moral faith of northern abolitionists.

The male protagonist, a young student named Blessed (Bles) Alwyn, comes upon the swamp, Elspeth, and Zora. In youthful innocence, "Bles" and Zora fall in love and, with Elspeth's seed "from the old land ten thousand moons ago," try to wrest from the swamp a crop of cotton to pay for their schooling. Ultimately Bles has imbibed too much of the New England moral strictures and cannot reconcile himself to Zora's part in the moral ambiguity of her mother's swamp household, often the site of drinking, gambling, and interracial sexual encounters. His demands for Zora's purity, a concept of little meaning to her, leads her to despair and doubt and cynicism.

Both Bles and Zora leave the South, he for public service in Washington and she for the world of travel and knowledge as a maid to the wealthy and politically influential Mrs. Vanderpool. With the acknowledged assistance of Caroline Wynn and the secret support of Zora and Mrs. Vanderpool, Bles becomes the leading contender for a high appointed office, Register of the Treasury. Yet the moral rectitude that led him to reject Zora gives him the fortitude to resist becoming a servant of Republican commercial interests. He loses Caroline Wynn, who, always pragmatic, forsakes "the one man above men, whom she could respect but would not marry" for the "man like all men, whom she would marry but could not respect." In the meantime, Zora has been assiduously educated by Mrs. Vanderpool and discovers her own sense of purpose, which entails that she sacrifice herself for the greater glory of her people.

In separate decisions, Zora and Bles return to the South, she to build a settlement-style farm cooperative growing out of the school, and he ultimately to help her. In their common struggle against the planter and the commercial interests, they rediscover each other and are married. Significantly, *Quest* belongs between the dominant mode of writing of the nineteenth century and the Harlem Renaissance. The ending is Du Bois's call for a reconciliation between the swamp, the chaos of the African American past in slavery, and the school, the New England moral education. Du Bois also wishes to chart the impediments to that reconciliation, which ultimately must be a triumph of moral will over material circumstances. Bles and Zora return to the South, striving to become men and women who "will not use the world as it is but insist on acting as if it were something else."

Quest glorifies the potential of the folk and the rural southern landscape, yet the novel in many ways marks Du Bois's farewell to the South. After the publication of *Souls*, he became more active in his opposition to Booker T. Washington's leadership. With a group of African American "radicals" he founded the Niagara Movement in 1905. When the all-black Niagara Movement joined forces with radical whites in 1909 to found the National Association for the Advancement of Colored People (NAACP), Du Bois moved to New York, where he became director of publicity and research and the only black on the national board of directors. During this period, his writing was increasingly concerned first with an urban, and then with an international, milieu.

The first issue of the *Crisis* appeared in November 1910, and Du Bois remained its editor in chief until 1934. The period of his editorship marked the portion of his life that is most identified with the mainstream of African American political thought. During this period he was also the guiding force behind the organization of four international Pan-African congresses; he was a strong supporter of rebellions at black colleges; he wrote two further works of history, *The Negro* (1915) and *The Gift of Black Folk* (1924); a second collection of essays, *Darkwater: Voices from Within the Veil* (1920); and a second novel, *Dark Princess* (1928). With the rise of the *Crisis*, Du Bois's voice became synonymous with radicalism and protest in the African American community. As a national journal, the *Crisis* had only one challenger during its first decade, Tuskegee's *Southern Workman*. After the death of Booker T. Washington in 1915, Du Bois and the *Crisis* filled the void in national leadership. In the 1920s the only serious challenge was raised by Marcus Garvey's *Negro World*. As with the two prior journals he had edited, Du Bois insisted on editorial control, a stance that was often a source of concern for the NAACP's board of directors. Indeed, Du Bois did not hesitate to pursue his own ideas rather than the board's policies. The success of the *Crisis,* however, bolstered his ability to be independent. He shepherded the fledgling journal from its initial run of one thousand to a circulation of one hundred thousand in 1918. Although it had a relatively small readership, the *Crisis* became one of the most important national African American periodicals in the country.

Du Bois, who gave great thought to such things, meant the magazine's subtitle, *A Record of the Darker Races,* seriously. His stated purposes were four: (1) to present news from the nation and the world that had an impact on African Americans; (2) to present reviews of scholarly, popular, and creative literature related to racial issues; (3) to present some fiction and poetry by and about African Americans; and (4) to editorialize strongly and independently on racial issues. Underlying these objectives was Du Bois's desire to give a national and cohesive voice to African American political, intellectual, and cultural aspirations. That voice was of course Du Bois's; he hoped to refashion African American consciousness along his lines. He provided a generation of blacks with a radical window on the worlds of America and Africa.

A significant dimension of Du Bois's accomplishment as editor lies in his promoting the creative work of African Americans. From the beginning, the *Crisis* published poetry, fiction, and reviews; and Du Bois always called for the recognition of African Americans as creative artists. That early promotion paid off during the 1920s when the *Crisis,* through literary contests, played a leading role in supporting the artists of the Harlem Renaissance. Many of the writers of this period, including Langston Hughes, Zora Neale Hurston, and Claude McKay, were deeply influenced by *The Souls of Black Folk* and followed Du Bois's warm injunction to find sources for their inspiration in the black folk.

Although he encouraged their work, by the mid 1920s Du Bois had become disturbed at

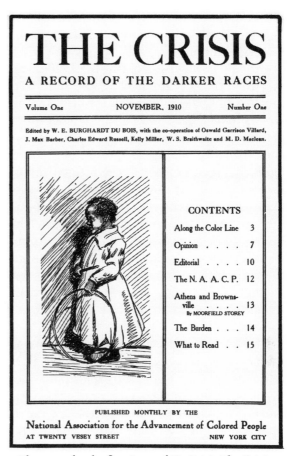

The cover for the first issue of Du Bois's *The Crisis.*

much of what young writers were producing. His vision of the black folk, that outlined in *Souls,* was distinctly rural and romantic, while younger generations explored the urban environment and its sensuality. Du Bois's vision, built on the spirituals, was less than hospitable to those writers who drew on the bawdy secular spirit of the blues. Then, too, Du Bois's vision demanded much of the folk spirit—that it carry a racial zeitgeist and partake in a movement of universal history toward freedom—while the Harlem Renaissance writers were more interested in eliminating the constraints of bourgeois morality. Ultimately, Du Bois was not the urban cosmopolite that many of the younger generation sought to be. His ideal topos was not the multicultural urban city; rather, he most often turned to small town New England and the rural South for visions of ideal communities.

When he did project on the international scene, he envisioned a mythical Pan-African or third world community.

Du Bois's own vision during the 1920s came in two forms—a group of essays that were roughly autobiographical, *Darkwater*, and his second novel, *Dark Princess*. In conception *Darkwater* was much like *Souls*, a mixture of autobiography, fiction, and poetry. In *Princess*, Du Bois remains torn between realism and romance. One of the novel's characters remarks, after having seen a play: "Why can't they try other themes—ours for instance; our search for dinner and our reason for the first balcony. Good dinner and good seats—but the subtle touches, hesitancies, gropings, and refusals that would be interesting," echoing one of the main middle-class criticisms of the new Harlem Renaissance artists.

The realism of *Princess* is Du Bois's answer to that query. Yet another part of the novel (Du Bois subtitled it *A Romance*) explores the need for what its principal character calls "his great dream—his world romance." The male and female protagonists of *Princess* are the questing characters of the romance, while the day-to-day struggles of the black middle class, and to some degree the working class, are sympathetically, sensitively, and realistically portrayed. As always, Du Bois is in search of the power of the individual guided by ideals to transcend the present social and economic orders. In *Princess*, we recognize both a continuity and a shift in the concerns that activated his earlier novel, *The Quest of the Silver Fleece*. The economic determinism that centered the first novel on cotton and the industries and social orders it spawned is absent; in its place is a detailed description of the workings of Chicago's political machine, which seduces characters with the lure of power and wealth, the price of which is moral corruption, cynicism, self-doubt, and passivity.

The male protagonist of *Princess*, Matthew Towns, is a more sophisticated reincarnation of Blessed Alwyn. Although instinctively inclined toward finer things in aesthetics, morals, and politics, his passivity leaves his destiny to be shaped by the world and people around him. In the first section of the novel, "Exile," Matthew is destined for medicine until the medical school refuses to allow him to take a course in obstetrics. He is plunged into despair and takes flight to Europe, where he meets Princess Kautilya, the maharanee of Bwodpur, a large Indian principality that is of extreme geopolitical importance to England's rule of the subcontinent.

Like Zora, Kautilya provides the moral center for the novel and for its protagonist, Matthew, who falls in love with her. She is the acknowledged leader of a highly diversified Pan-Asian movement, the "Great Council of the Darker Peoples," which is forging an alliance with the Pan-African movement. Council members who are with Kautilya doubt the possibility of the African American to participate fully in such a worldwide movement for liberation, and Matthew gives a spirited defense of those possibilities. Kautilya assigns Matthew to return to America and report on the possibility of African Americans' leading a revolt.

In the second section, "Pullman Porter," Matthew returns to America to investigate an organization the Princess believes might show promise of African American potential. Led by Miguel Perigua, the organization represents radical potential. Matthew, employed as a porter, quickly becomes involved in a ride on "the Klan Special," during which one of his colleagues is lynched. He leads a plan for a strike that is aborted because of traitors and strikebreakers. In frustration, he joins Perigua in a plot to blow up the train, only to end up preventing that action after he learns that the princess is a passenger. For refusing to implicate anybody else, he is sent to prison for ten years.

In the third section of the novel, "The Chicago Politician," the plot shifts from romance to realism. In counterpoint to Kautilya is Sara Andrews, the shrewd secretary of a black political boss in Chicago, Sammy Scott. Like Caroline Wynn, she is disillusioned and opportunistic, and through her boss she manipulates the political and economic forces of Chicago, first to secure Matthew's release and pardon, then his election to the state legislature. Matthew assents, passively accepting the political bargains that are made to secure power. In the process, Sara gains independence from her boss and promotes Matthew's nomination to Congress.

In the fourth section, "The Maharajah of Bwodpur," Kautilya's return into Matthew's life leads him to abandon Sara, whom he has married, and live with her. Ultimately they marry, and he becomes the father of her child, the maharajah of Bwodpur and the maharajah-dhirajah of Sindvabad, and the "Messenger and Messiah to all the Darker Worlds."

In the 1920s, the circulation of the *Crisis* declined, and Du Bois's salary was paid by the NAACP. In the 1930s the organization and Walter White, its executive secretary, sought more direct control over the magazine, and Du Bois waged a war for control over the total organization. He lost his bid for independence and advocated a plan of separate black economic development. He finally resigned the editorship in 1934.

Du Bois was, in a fashion, undone by his own success. The NAACP was gradually being transformed from a fringe organization in the shadow of Booker T. Washington, whose principal national leadership was white, to an established African American institution. The goals for African Americans that Du Bois had enunciated with such clarity and force during the first two decades of the organization's existence, and that in some degree he had come to stand for, were, by the 1930s, the public objectives of the educated black middle class. While Du Bois's loyalty to these ideals never wavered, his vision was broad and his mind quickly shifted from one tactic to another. By nature, Du Bois was not comfortable with any constraints on his thoughts and actions.

Forced out of the NAACP, Du Bois was appointed professor and chairman of the sociology department at Atlanta University, a position he held for a decade. Although he never again spoke for the mainstream of African American political thought, he remained the leading African American intellectual. Returning to scholarship, he published two histories, *Black Reconstruction* (1935) and *Black Folk, Then and*

Now (1939), and an autobiographical collection of essays, *Dusk of Dawn;* and founded *Phylon,* a scholarly journal that he edited from 1940 to 1944. In 1944, he returned to the NAACP as director of special research, and remained there until 1948. Against the backdrop of World War II, his primary responsibilities lay in the international arena, and his *Color and Democracy: Colonies and Peace* (1945) and *The World and Africa* (1947) moved to the forefront the globalism that was always a part of his political program. In 1945, he helped to guide the fifth Pan-African Congress, which was attended by most of the figures who would lead African states to independence in the 1950s and 1960s, and was symbolic of a new and international audience for Du Bois's ideas.

Only Du Bois's first two works, *The Suppression of the African Slave-Trade* and *The Philadelphia Negro,* were the products of direct research, and he returned to the life of a scholar as a masterful synthesizer rather than as a researcher. Facing the triumph of southern apologists in American historiography, he turned to the neglected study of Africa and to the study of Reconstruction. In a series of histories beginning with *The Negro* and including *The Gift of Black Folk;* two brief pamphlets, *Africa: Its Geography, People, and Products* (1930) and *Africa, Its Place in History* (1930); *Color and Democracy;* and *The World and Africa,* Du Bois synthesized the scholarship on Africa and linked his study of African Americans to their African past. In the 1940s his approach to the study of Africa was shaped by his increasingly global vision. In *Color and Democracy* and *The World and Africa* he cogently argued the links between European colonial competition and World War I.

Clearly the centerpiece of his writing in this period was *Black Reconstruction,* perhaps his most important work of history, and second in importance only to *The Souls of Black Folk* in his oeuvre. Although it treats only the African American past, it is no less global in its shaping intellectual framework. *Black Reconstruction* joins C. L. R. James's study of the Haitian Revolution, *Black Jacobins* (1963), and Eric William's study of the Atlantic slave trade, *Capitalism and Slavery* (1944), as the triangular base of modern Pan-African thought. It shares with the works of James and Williams a Marxian expositional framework. Although Du Bois cannot truly be considered a Marxist, he found in that framework a mode for portraying the agency of African Americans during Reconstruction as pivotal to the continuing global democratic revolutions. His subtitle, *An Essay Toward the Part Black Folks Played in Reconstructing Democracy*, announces the major theme of his history. As Marx read in the 18 Brumaire of Napoleon the promise of the proletarian revolution in the French Revolution, so Du Bois read the promise of African American freedom in Reconstruction, "an upheaval of humanity like the Reformation and the French Revolution."

Du Bois revised *Black Reconstruction* many times, and his letters to his editor indicate that he placed as much importance on its literary qualities as on its historical accuracy. Writing to persuade and, perhaps, to seduce, he crafted one of his most passionate works. Not satisfied with merely telling the story of Reconstruction from his own viewpoint, he concluded the study with a historiographical essay, "The Propaganda of History," that assailed the "libel, innuendo and silence" of the southern apologist school of historians. A part of Du Bois still looked strongly to empiricism as a guide to ethics, but he stated, "If we are going, in the future, not simply with regard to this one question, but with regard to all social problems, to be able to use human experience for the guidance of mankind, we have got clearly to distinguish between fact and desire."

Throughout the 1950s and until his death in 1963, Du Bois worked against the grain of both American and mainstream African American politics. Against the background of the Cold War and McCarthyism, he became more staunchly committed to the international peace movement and the promise of justice that he found in socialist and Communist revolutions. He was a member of the Council of African Affairs. He chaired the Peace Information Center in 1950, and ran for the U.S. Senate on the American Labor party ticket. For these activities, he was tried (and acquitted) as an unregistered foreign agent and had his passport confiscated. When he was able to travel again, he visited the Soviet Union and China. In 1961 he emigrated to Africa and, at the invitation of Kwame Nkrumah, the president of the newly independent nation of Ghana, became the director of the *Encyclopedia Africana* project. In two symbolic gestures—joining the American Communist party in 1961 and becoming a citizen of Ghana in 1963—Du Bois declared his allegiance to broader socialist, internationalist, and Pan-African audiences.

The 1950s were also marked by a series of personal losses for Du Bois. His wife died in February of 1950, and his daughter died in 1960. He married Shirley Graham on 14 February 1951. The black leadership with whom he had so often disagreed began, largely out of fear over the controversy surrounding his politics, to drift quietly away from him. African American leadership passed to a man more than sixty years his junior, Martin Luther King, Jr. Still, Du Bois, accustomed by temperament to thriving as a singular voice, held and advocated his new commitments with the strength of a man more than half a century his junior. Fittingly, in his last two major works, Du Bois still struggled toward a new synthesis to integrate and reflect the more internationalist and radical, and less racial, vision of his later years. Neither of these works was scholarly. In his last decade Du Bois turned instead toward the freedom offered him by fiction in *The Black Flame: A Trilogy* (1957–1961) and by autobiography in *The Autobiography of W. E. B. Du Bois*.

Published some thirty years after *Dark Princess*, the trilogy has elements of continuity with Du Bois's previous novels as well as telling differences. The tension between the conventions of realism and romance that characterized his earlier works is almost absent. As Du Bois gave up the romance, he also ceded some of the power that he had attached to the individual ability to *transcend* history. The principal characters are less able to transcend the financial and economic structure that shapes day-to-day life. On the whole, from beginning to end it is a more pessimistic story than any of Du Bois's earlier fiction.

The Black Flame consists of three novels whose chronology is controlled by the significant turning points in Du Bois's life and whose scope reflects the ever-expanding canvas upon which Du Bois painted his life. *The Ordeal of Mansart* (1957) covers the period between 1876 and 1916 and takes place mostly in the South; *Mansart Builds a School* (1959) takes place between 1916 and 1936 and, through Mansart's travels, explores the political and economic life of the urban North; *Worlds of Color* (1961) covers the period between 1936 and 1956 and, through the travels of Mansart and other characters, explores Europe and the third world.

The Black Flame is more securely centered on an active male protagonist than are any of his previous works. Through Mansart, Du Bois asks a version of the question that was central to his own life: How does an individual turn history away from the course ordained in his or her past and codified by his or her social and economic structure, and toward a more equitable path? Mansart's struggle, however, is not an interior one, not a struggle for vision, character, or moral strength, as were the struggles of Blessed Alwyn and Matthew Towns. Unlike those predecessors, Mansart does not suffer from or almost succumb to greed, doubt, despair, or hatred. Du Bois's phrasing of the question through a more clearly inwardly directed character perhaps reveals a passing of his own doubts about himself while betraying less faith in his own ability to change the world. Mansart is Du Bois at his most introspective, laying out the life of a visionary.

At the trilogy's end, Du Bois charts out two possibilities for the world. Mansart, who is about to die, calls his family together. Through them the various paths that African Americans have explored in the twentieth century are personified. As a group, his family becomes a medley of African American voices; seeing Mansart as someone who lived "a good life" but one that was "ineffective," these voices attest to the triumph of the world over individuals. Dying, Mansart lays out two visions of the future of the world. The first is pessimistic:

"I have come from Hell—I saw bombs filling the skies—I heard the scream of Death. Moscow was a flame, London was ashes, Paris was a clot of blood, New York sank into the sea. The world was sorrow, hate and fear—no hope, no song, no laughter. Save me, my children. Save the world!"

(*Worlds of Color*, p. 348)

The second is more optimistic:

"I saw China's millions lifting the soil of the nation in their hands to dam the rivers which long had eaten their land. I saw the golden domes of Moscow shining on Russia's millions, yesterday unlettered, now reading the wisdom of the world. I saw birds singing in Korea, Viet-Nam, Indonesia and Malaya. I saw India and Pakistan united, free; in Paris, Ho Chi Minh celebrated peace on earth; while in New York—" (p. 349)

Mansart is unable to complete the second vision. Exhausted, he dies. The task of completion, the choice between the bleak and the noble future, he leaves to his heirs.

In the "Postscript" to *The Ordeal of Mansart*, Du Bois meditates on "the eternal paradox of history" that turned him toward writing historical fiction. In what is almost a coda to his critique of Reconstruction historiography, he places in perspective the discipline of history and, by implication, the faith in empiricism of his early education, saying: "Every historian is painfully aware how little the scientist today can know accurately of the past; how dependence on documents and memory leaves us all with the tale of the past half told or less." The strong imagination of the creative artist fills in the gaps left by the scientist; "lucky or inspired, he may write a story which may set down a fair version of the truth of an era, or a group of facts about human history."

Du Bois's *Autobiography*, completed while he was in Ghana, was published posthumously and appropriately stands as his final word on his life and career. Although he begins the narrative of his life quite self-consciously with the question, "Who and what is this I, which in the last year looked upon a torn world and tried to judge it?" his ensuring "soliloquy" is the most self-assured of his autobiographical writings. Ironically, the man who is such a towering figure of the twentieth century came only slowly to a confident autobiographical voice. Du Bois himself perceived the lineage of his autobiographical self-portraits to begin with *The Souls of Black Folk,* and continue in *Darkwater* and *Dusk of Dawn.* Yet each of these volumes mixed autobiographical writing with historical essays, short stories, and poems. In the *Autobiography,* Du Bois communicates with what he calls a "certain sense of unity," a sense of integration of the various genres he had written in throughout his life in a single vision and a singular sense of himself.

In the *Autobiography,* Du Bois speaks with the same self-possession that he gives to Mansart in the *Black Flame Trilogy.* Not unexpectedly, Du Bois also speaks, as did Mansart, for political radicalism and internationalism. Although a significant portion of the autobiography is devoted to substantially revising *Dusk of Dawn,* Du Bois prefaces his main narrative with five chapters chronicling his trips to Eastern and Western Europe, Russia, and China. That preface is followed by an "Interlude" defending his belief in communism. Concluding this "Interlude," Du Bois speaks directly of his own authority, of the justification of his views by his own life: *Who now am I to have come to these conclusions? And of what if any significance are my deductions? What has been my life and work and of what meaning to mankind? The final answer to these questions, time and posterity must make. But perhaps it is my duty to contribute whatever enlightenment I can. This is the excuse for this writing which I call a Soliloquy."*

W. E. B. Du Bois died in his tenth decade, on 27 August 1963, as a citizen of the youthful independent African nation of Ghana. His death cast little shadow on African America, which preferred to remember him as they imagined he had been during the first three decades of the twentieth century: the author of *The Souls of Black Folk* and the editor of the *Crisis.* Yet if he, the man who spent much of his life in in-ward isolation, could have chosen the time of his death, he would most probably have resolved on the day before the historic civil rights march on Washington in August 1963, as a symbolic reminder of his insistence that his total intellectual and political career was one with modern African American history. Du Bois closes his autobiography by reiterating this characteristic insistence:

> For this is a beautiful world; this is a wonderful America, which the founding fathers dreamed until their sons drowned it in the blood of slavery and devoured it in greed. Our children must rebuild it. Let then the Dreams of the Dead rebuke the Blind who think that what is will be forever and teach them that what was worth living for must live again and that which merited death must stay dead. Teach us, Forever Dead, there is no Dream but Deed, there is no Deed but Memory. (pp. 422–423)

Selected Bibliography

PRIMARY WORKS

NOVELS

The Quest of the Silver Fleece. Chicago: McClurg, 1911.
Dark Princess: A Romance. New York: Harcourt, Brace, 1928.
The Ordeal of Mansart. New York: Mainstream, 1957.
Mansart Builds a School. New York: Mainstream, 1959.
The Worlds of Color. New York: Mainstream, 1961.
Prayers for Dark People. Edited by Herbert Aptheker. Amherst: University of Massachusetts Press, 1980.

POETRY

Selected Poems by W. E. B. Du Bois. Accra: University of Ghana Press, 1964.

AUTOBIOGRAPHY AND ESSAYS

The Souls of Black Folk: Essays and Sketches. Chicago: McClurg, 1903.
"The Talented Tenth." In *The Negro Problem: A Series of Articles by Representative Negroes of To-day.* New York: James Patt, 1903.
Darkwater: Voices from Within the Veil. New York: Harcourt, Brace & Howe, 1920.
Dusk of Dawn: An Essay Toward an Autobiography of a Race Concept. New York: Harcourt, Brace, 1940.
In Battle for Peace: The Story of My 83rd Birthday. New York: Masses & Mainstream, 1952.

The Autobiography of W. E. B. Du Bois: A Soliloquy on Viewing My Life from the Last Decade. Edited by Herbert Aptheker. New York: International Publishers, 1968.

SCHOLARLY WRITINGS

The Suppression of the African Slave-Trade to the United States of America, 1638–1870. New York and London: Longmans, Green, 1896.

The Phildelphia Negro: A Social Study. Phildelphia: University of Pennsylvania Press, 1899.

John Brown. Phildelphia: Jacobs, 1909.

The Negro. New York: Holt, 1915.

The Gift of Black Folk: The Negros in the Making of America. Boston: Stratford, 1924.

Africa: Its Geography, People, and Products. Girard, Kansas: Haldeman-Julius, 1930.

Africa: Its Place in Modern History. Girard, Kansas: Haldeman-Julius, 1930.

Black Reconstruction: An Essay Toward a History of the Part Which Black Folk Played in the Attempt to Reconstruct Democracy in America, 1860–1880. New York: Harcourt, Brace, 1935.

Black Folk, Then and Now: An Essay in the History and Sociology of the Negro Race. New York: Holt, 1939.

Color and Democracy: Colonies and Peace. New York: Harcourt, Brace, 1945.

The World and Africa: An Inquiry into the Part Which Africa Has Played in World History. New York: Viking, 1947.

COLLECTED WORKS

Kraus-Thomson has compiled and reprinted the complete works of W. E. B. Du Bois in 37 volumes published between 1973 and 1986. Several of these volumes, along with the best of the Du Bois collections, are listed below.

An ABC of Color: Selections Chosen by the Author from Over a Half Century of His Writings. Introduced by John Oliver Killens. New York: International Publishers, 1969.

The Black North in 1901: A Social Study. New York: Arno Press, 1969.

W. E. B. Du Bois: A Reader. Edited and introduced by Meyer Weinberg. New York: Harper & Row, 1970.

W. E. B. Du Bois Speaks: Speeches and Addresses. Vols. I–II. Edited by Philip S. Foner. New York: Pathfinder Press, 1970.

The Education of Black People: Ten Critiques, 1906–1960. Edited by Herbert Aptheker. Amherst: University of Massachusetts Press, 1973.

The Correspondence of W. E. B. Du Bois. Vols. I–III. Edited by Herbert Aptheker. Amherst: University of Massachusetts Press, 1973–1978.

Book Reviews. Compiled and edited by Herbert Aptheker. Millwood, N.Y.: Kraus-Thomson, 1977.

W. E. B. Du Bois on Sociology and the Black Community. Edited and introduced by Dan S. Green and Edwin D. Driver. Chicago: University of Chicago Press, 1978.

Contributions by W. E. B. Du Bois in Government Publications and Proceedings. Compiled and edited by Herbert Aptheker. Millwood, N.Y.: Kraus-Thomson, 1980.

Selections from Phylon. Compiled and edited by Herbert Aptheker. Millwood, N.Y.: Kraus-Thomson, 1980.

Selections from the Brownies' Book. Compiled and edited by Herbert Aptheker. Millwood, N.Y.: Kraus-Thomson, 1980.

Writings by W. E. B. Du Bois in Non-Periodical Literature Edited by Others, Vols. I–IV. Compiled and edited by Herbert Aptheker. Millwood, N.Y.: Kraus-Thomson, 1982. Includes "The Talented Tenth."

Selections from the Crisis. Vols. I–II. Compiled and edited by Herbert Aptheker. Millwood, N.Y.: Kraus-Thomson, 1983.

Against Racism: Unpublished Essays, Papers, Addresses, 1887–1961. Edited by Herbert Aptheker. Amherst: University of Massachusetts Press, 1985.

Creative Writings by W. E. B. Du Bois: A Pageant, Poems, Short Stories and Playlets. Compiled and edited by Herbert Aptheker. White Plains N.Y.: Kraus-Thomson, 1985.

Selections from the Horizon. Compiled and edited by Herbert Aptheker. White Plains, N.Y.: Kraus-Thomson, 1985.

Newspaper Columns by W. E. B. Du Bois. Vols. I–II. Compiled and edited by Herbert Aptheker. White Plains, N.Y.: Kraus-Thomson, 1986.

Pamphlets and Leaflets. Compiled and edited by Herbert Aptheker. White Plains, N.Y.: Kraus-Thomson, 1986.

Writings. New York: The Library of America, 1986.

The Oxford W. E. B. Du Bois Reader. Edited by Eric J. Sundquist. New York: Oxford University Press, 1996.

MANUSCRIPTS

The major collection of Du Bois's correspondence and manuscripts is located at the University of Massachusetts at Amherst. His correspondence has been microfilmed (Amherst: University of Massachusetts, 1980).

SECONDARY WORKS

BIOGRAPHICAL AND CRITICAL STUDIES

Andrews, William L., ed. Critical Essays on W. E. B. Du Bois. Boston: G.K. Hall, 1985.

Aptheker, Herbert. The Literary Legacy of W. E. B. Du Bois. White Plains, N.Y.: Kraus International Publications, 1989.

Bell, Bernard W., et al. W. E. B. Du Bois on Race and Culture: Philosophy, Politics, and Poetics. New York: Routledge, 1996.

Broderick, Francis L. W. E. B. Du Bois: Negro Leader in a Time of Crisis. Stanford, Calif.: Stanford University Press, 1959.

Byerman, Keith E. *Seizing the Word: History, Art, and Self in the Work of W. E. B. Du Bois*. Athens: University of Georgia Press, 1994.

Clark, John H., et al. *Black Titan: W. E. B. Du Bois*. Boston: Beacon Press, 1970.

Davis, Allison. *Leadership, Love, and Aggression*. San Diego, Calif.: Harcourt Brace Jovanovich, 1983.

Davis, Arthur P. "W. E. B. Du Bois." In *From the Dark Tower: Afro-American Writers, 1900–1960*. Washington, D.C.: Howard University Press, 1974.

DeMarco, Joseph P. *The Social Thought of W. E. B. Du Bois*. Lanham, Md.: University Press of America, 1983.

Du Bois, Shirley Graham. *His Day Is Marching On: A Memoir of W. E. B. Du Bois*. Phildelphia: Lippincott, 1971.

Horne, Gerald. *Black and Red: W. E. B. Du Bois and the Afro-American Response to the Cold War, 1944–1963*. Albany: State University of New York Press, 1986.

Lewis, David Levering. *W. E. B. Du Bois: A Biography of a Race, 1868–1919*. New York: Henry Holt, 1993.

Logan, Rayford W., ed. *W. E. B. Du Bois: A Profile*. New York: Hill & Wang, 1971.

Marable, Manning. *W. E. B. Du Bois: Black Radical Democrat*. Boston: Twayne, 1986.

Moore, Jack B. *W. E. B. Du Bois*. Boston: Twayne, 1981.

Rampersand, Arnold. *The Art and Imagination of W. E. B. Du Bois*. Cambridge, Mass.: Harvard University Press, 1976.

Reed, Adolph. *W. E. B. Du Bois and American Political Thought: Fabianism and the Color Line*. New York: Oxford University Press, 1997.

Rudwick, Elliott M. *W. E. B. Du Bois: Propagandist of the Negro Protest*. Philedelphia: University of Pennsylvania Press, 1960.

Zamir, Shamoon. *Dark Voices: W. E. B. Du Bois and American Thought, 1888–1903*. Chicago: University of Chicago Press, 1995.

BIBLIOGRAPHIES

Aptheker, Herbert. *Annotated Bibliography of the Published Writings of W. E. B. Du Bois*. Millwood, N.Y.: Kraus-Thomson, 1973.

Partington, Paul G. *W. E. B. Du Bois: A Bibliography of His Published Writings*. Rev. ed. Whittier, Calif.: Partington, 1979. Supplement, Whittier, Calif.: Partington, 1984.

PAUL LAURENCE DUNBAR
(1872 – 1906)

ESTHER NETTLES RAUCH

WITHIN HIS LIFETIME, Paul Laurence Dunbar achieved a superlative reputation. His work was cited as indisputable evidence that literary excellence need not depend on an author's European ancestry. Many published accounts of his life and work emphasize Dunbar's "unmixed" or "pure" African ancestry. This "important" fact was highlighted to counter claims of racist newspaper editors who asserted that no American of African ancestry had ever achieved literary distinction without some mix of European blood. Dunbar's great fame seemed all the more astonishing because of the circumstances of his birth and rearing.

Dunbar's mother and father were both former slaves. His father, Joshua Dunbar, escaped slavery and made his way to Canada through the Underground Railroad. While he was still a slave, Joshua's skills as a plasterer had earned his owner additional income. Virginia Cunningham, one of Dunbar's earliest biographers, and in many respects his most accurate, relates that Joshua had been taught to read and do sums by his owner in order to prevent those who bought his services from cheating him of correct wages. Joshua's reading skills enabled him to follow the course of anti-slavery events in the United States through Canadian newspapers.

When he learned of the impending Civil War, Joshua Dunbar returned to the United States to fight in the Fifty-fifth Massachusetts Infantry, the second black regiment to be organized by the Union Army. After the war, he settled in Dayton, Ohio and in 1871 married Matilda J. Burton Murphy, a widow who was already the mother of two boys. Paul was their only surviving child.

Matilda Murphy had been a house slave for a white Kentucky family. Freed by the Emancipation Proclamation, Matilda moved to Dayton to be near her mother, who had been freed before the war. Joshua and Matilda divorced about five years after their marriage. Joshua, at least thirty years older than Matilda, moved to the local soldiers' home and died there when Paul was about twelve years old.

In a widely reprinted newspaper article (first published in *Argus* on 9 March 1902), Paul Dunbar gives this account of his parents:

> My mother, who had no education except what she picked up herself, and who is generally conceded to be a very unusual woman, taught me to read when I was four years old. Both my father and herself were fond of books and used to read to us when we sat around the fire at night.

Dunbar's parents seem to have been the primary influences in his literary life, a fact he did not acknowledge publicly. He has written about his school days at Central High School in Day-

183

ton, where he was a popular student who wrote poems for special occasions, edited the student newspaper, was elected a member and ultimately president of the exclusive Philomathean Society, and earned excellent grades. Among his classmates was Orville Wright, who printed a newspaper, *The Tattler*, which Dunbar edited and published for the African American community of Dayton. Dunbar's first poems, "Our Martyred Soldiers" and "On the River," were published in the *Dayton Herald* in June and July 1888, when he was sixteen.

In *The Tattler*, Dunbar published his first German dialect poem, "Lager Beer," in imitation of James Whitcomb Riley's Hoosier dialect poems, which he had read and admired. Dunbar wrote most of the articles in *The Tattler* and encouraged the African American community of Dayton to strive for self-reliance and economic independence. He was unable to solicit enough advertisers and subscriptions to continue *The Tattler* beyond eight issues. Nevertheless, the attempt was noble for an eighteen-year-old who had not yet graduated from high school.

What did the world and the community of Dayton, with its fifty-five thousand citizens of European origin and its five thousand citizens of African descent, hold for a talented young man of nineteen upon graduation from high school? Dunbar wished to relate to the great social and political forces of his age. He sought jobs that would permit him to function as a man among men and also provide for the financial needs of his mother, who had supported him by taking in laundry from white people. Fiercely aware of his African and slave heritage, he sought ways to participate in the larger community. The last years of Reconstruction were anything but favorable for a young man with Dunbar's aspirations.

As much as any man of his time, Dunbar fought against the restraints that had been traditionally imposed upon his race. He looked for work as a law clerk—an unlikely prospect for a black man at that time, despite his abilities as a scholar—but was resigned to accept a job as an elevator attendant in Dayton's Callahan Building. During this period he continued to write; he contributed his poems to newspapers (which paid little if anything for them) and studied the styles of published writers. He also gave public readings of his own works to churches and civic groups.

The Western Association of Writers met in Dayton in the summer of 1892. Although most members were unpublished writers, others, like Riley, were well known. Dunbar was invited to compose and deliver a welcome address, and read one of his own poems. He created such a favorable impression that Dr. James Newton Matthews sent a letter about Dunbar's eloquent recital to the newspaper in Matthews's hometown of Mason, Illinois. Dunbar's poem and the letter Matthews had written were picked up by other newspapers, including the *Indianapolis Journal*, where it was seen by Riley. In a letter of encouragement to Dunbar, Riley wrote: "See how your name is traveling, my chirping friend. And it is a good, sound, name, too, that seems to imply the brave, fine spirit of a singer who should command wide and serious attention."

Matthews's epistle describes the audience's reaction to Dunbar's performance, and it explains how Matthews sought out Dunbar in the Callahan Building on the day after the reading. It also provides biographical details about the young poet and reveals Matthews's continuing correspondence with him. Matthews reprints two of Dunbar's poems and ends by challenging: "Show me a white boy of nineteen who can excel, or even equal, lines like these."

Matthews recalls his first view of Dunbar:

. . . a slender Negro lad, as black as the core of Cheops' pyramid. He ascended the rostrum with the coolness and dignity of a cultured entertainer and delivered a poem in a tone "as musical as is Apollo's lute." He was applauded to the echo between the stanzas, and heartily encored at the conclusion. He then disappeared from the hall as suddenly as he had entered it, and many were the whispered conjectures as to the personality of the man, the originality of his verses, none believing it possible that one of his age and color could produce a thing of such evident merit. . . .   (Quoted in Martin, pp. 14–15)

"With it all," wrote Dunbar to Matthews, "I cannot help being overwhelmed by self-doubts. I hope there is something worthy in my writings and not merely the novelty of a black face associated with the power to rhyme that has attracted attention." And yet Jay Martin points out that a Canadian philanthropist named Ross clearly saw in Dunbar a kind of symbolic presence. Ross sent Matthews twenty dollars to buy books for Dunbar, commenting that a "colored poet of sufficient ability" would give to members of his race enlightenment and encouragement. Moreover, his example would evoke respect from European Americans.

Although Matthews had described Dunbar as a black man, Ross's assignment of Dunbar as a "representative" African American was one of the early signs that Dunbar would be the victim of literary segregation by paternalistic but well-meaning white readers. This practice of identifying Dunbar as a spokesman for his race, turning him into a symbol rather than a man or a poet, continues today to circumscribe the analysis and evaluation of his work.

It is astonishing, given the social climate in 1892, that a young black man should have aspired to make his way in life as a writer. Booker T. Washington was preaching the gospel of vocational education and accommodation to counter the resurgence of peonage for the freed slaves and their descendants. Historians describe the 1890s as the nadir in the post-Civil War history of blacks. They recall the overturning of recently won freedoms through the systematic disenfranchising of African Americans. No sphere of life was exempt from this process of reversal. Schools, churches, employment, and all public accommodations—from public conveyances, hotels, and restaurants, to washrooms and water fountains—were separated by race and distinctly unequal. Banks refused business and personal loans to African Americans. In response to this exclusion, separate businesses sprouted up: beauty and barber shops, convenience stores, insurance companies, funeral parlors, real estate agencies, and garbage collection companies all expressed the aspirations and energies of excluded entrepreneurs.

Paul Laurence Dunbar

Dunbar faced a cultural environment that was repressive yet hopeful, segregated but not isolated, hostile but stimulating. Even those excluded from the mainstream businesses were still technically free, in a position to hope and to create their own businesses while working for personal and racial improvement. Similarly, Dunbar's first book of poems, *Oak and Ivy,* was published in 1892 at his own expense. He continued to straddle the two cultures, separate and unequal.

Dunbar was deeply involved in the community life of Dayton but he longed to see the rest of America. In 1893 he visited the World's Columbian Exposition in Chicago (the first World's Fair), where he met many prominent African American writers, artists, and political activists, including, above all, Frederick Douglass. Douglass, leader of the Haitian Pavilion, had already heard about Dunbar and gave him a job as a clerk in the pavilion. In the year following the exposition Dunbar met George Washington Cable, Riley, and Dr. H. A. Tobey, who became a lifelong friend and supporter. The year 1896 saw the publication of Dunbar's second book of poems, *Majors and Minors*, and its review by novelist William Dean Howells. December of that same year brought *Lyrics of Lowly Life* and national celebrity, followed by a tour of readings in Washington, D.C., New York, Boston, and other eastern cities.

During the eastern tour, Dunbar met Alice Ruth Moore. He had admired one of her poems, and he came to admire her as well. Their romance had to wait until Dunbar's tour of England and his collaboration with Samuel Coleridge-Taylor was completed; but their correspondence shows a growing affection. Upon his return to America, Dunbar and Alice Moore were married, on 6 March 1898 in New York. Their marriage was made financially possible by Dunbar's appointment as a reading room assistant in the Library of Congress at a decent salary. Alice, however, learning that the dust in the library and the unhealthy climate of Washington were detrimental to Dunbar's chronically weak lungs, encouraged him to leave the position and to earn his living solely by writing and performing. In search of a healthier climate, they traveled to the New York mountains and then to Colorado.

The peripatetic Dunbar gave a reading in Atlanta, Georgia, at which both Washington and W. E. B. Du Bois presented papers. He traveled to Tuskegee Institute in Alabama, where at Washington's request he wrote the school song. He raised funds for Tuskegee in Boston and continued his program of poetry readings. The constant travel and the gradual decline in his physical strength caused Dunbar to increase his use of alcohol to ease the pain of constant coughing brought on by the early stages of tuberculosis. The alcohol use occasionally interfered with his performances and must also have contributed to a deteriorating marriage. In 1902 the Dunbars separated permanently. Dunbar returned to his mother's home in Dayton.

In 1904 Dunbar's illness became so severe that, except for a trip the following year to participate in Theodore Roosevelt's inaugural parade, he remained at his mother's house in Day-

ton. He died on 9 February 1906, four months before his thirty-fourth birthday.

Dunbar had expressed his views on racial oppression in articles published in newspapers across the country. All of these articles effectively speak from an African American's perspective. In them, there is no suggestion of accommodationism, of racial inferiority, of special pleading. In fact, all of the articles are dignified, reasoned discussions of the overt oppression of African Americans in all aspects of their lives. The articles reveal their writer to be a proud man revolted by the brutality and corruption that was constantly imposed on members of his race, treatment that was regarded as a normal part of their daily lives. For the most part Dunbar approached these themes late in his artistic career, most notably in his last novel; he seems consciously to have relegated these themes to his journalistic efforts.

The political themes of his newspaper articles seldom appear in his poetry, perhaps accounting for Dunbar's dramatic plunge in critical esteem after the Harlem Renaissance. Before that time, Dunbar was without question the central figure in African American literary life. Although he was not the first African American poet, he was the first to secure his living and his reputation solely by the efforts of his pen.

Critical Reception

Dunbar's books were popular and reached a wide audience, most of whom were white; indeed, there would not have been enough African American book-buyers to make Dunbar's work profitable for a major publisher. Yet much of the readers' interest in his poetry may have depended on Dunbar's romanticized version of African American life and language.

The first public critical response to Dunbar's poetry came from Howells, who reviewed *Majors and Minors* in *Harper's Weekly* on 27 June 1896. Howells's response set the pattern for Dunbar criticism to the present day. As the most influential literary critic of his day, Howells determined that Dunbar's poems should be divided, for purposes of analysis, into "literary" and "dialect" English. All subsequent critics have made this division either to agree or to disagree with Howells's appraisal. When *Lyrics of Lowly Life* was published in 1896 with an introduction by Howells (actually the same review of *Majors and Minors* with a few revisions), the opinion of Howells had become gospel. Other reviewers, especially those writing in the *New York Times*, continued to separate the poems into these two categories and to value more highly the dialect poems.

Howells and others had no qualms in their preference for the dialect poems on sociological rather than artistic grounds. They accepted the dialect poems as outward and visible signs of an inward and childlike tenderness, sentimentality, humor, and genial optimism. James Weldon Johnson expresses these common sentiments in the preface to *The Book of American Negro Poetry*:

> The Negro in the United States has achieved or been placed in a certain artistic niche. When he is thought of artistically, it is as a happy-go-lucky, singing, shuffling, banjo-picking being or as a more or less pathetic figure. The picture of him is in a log cabin amid fields of cotton or along the levees. Negro dialect is naturally and by long association the exact instrument for voicing this phase of Negro life.

For an African American to perpetuate in his art a stereotype that blacks themselves were struggling against was viewed by African American scholars as inexcusable. Although their image may not have been entirely false, it was but one of many dimensions of black society; other aspects of life in black America were not presented, or they were overshadowed by that one image.

Johnson praises Dunbar as "the first American Negro poet of real literary distinction," contrasting his work with the poetry of African-born Phillis Wheatley, who successfully imitated English and American poems during an era when there were few, if any, black poets of

great distinction. And although Dunbar did not originate the dialect form, he was the premier writer of dialect poetry. He spawned many imitators, few of whom equalled and none of whom excelled him. Dunbar was the founder of the school of Negro dialect poetry.

Peter Revell argues that among Dunbar's African American contemporaries, Mary Church Terrell comes closest to providing an adequate appraisal of him. Terrell, one of the great African American orators, educators, women's rights activists, and political leaders of her day, wrote an obituary for Dunbar. She chose her words carefully, not resorting to the popular shorthand—"poet laureate of the Negro Race"—in describing Dunbar and his achievements. Terrell asserts that Dunbar must be evaluated on grounds larger than mere poetic achievement; his place is also determined by his historic preeminence and international recognition.

Because many Americans of European descent equated the highest development of human achievement with excellence in the literary arts, Dunbar forced an adjustment in their assessment of the capabilities and humanity of an African American. Dunbar entered the conflict on European terms and was equal to the contest. Other African American writers in this country—Douglass, Washington, and W. E. B. Du Bois—as well as Europeans of African descent—most notably Alexandre Dumas (*père* and *fils*) in France, Aleksandr Pushkin in Russia, and Samuel Taylor Coleridge in England—had obvious interracial origins. But in the case of Dunbar, no miscegenation existed in his family's history. Thus, Dunbar became more than poet; he became a symbol of the essence of the African American. As a symbol, he was placed upon a pedestal and admired, though seldom read or studied seriously. For Americans of European descent he represented a singer of songs in dialect that truthfully mirrored his people's gift for laughter and song. And for African Americans he became a symbol of the heights to which they could aspire.

Most critics in Dunbar's lifetime viewed his poetry through the lens of race and evaluated his achievement as a black man first and as an artist second. After World War I, however, a radical shift occurred in the value placed on Dunbar's work. Instead of praising his achievements, critics complained of Dunbar's affinity for plantation stereotypes and criticized him for writing dialect poetry. He received special vilification for his lyric collaboration in Will Marion Cook's Broadway musicals, which were considered by many to be essentially "coon songs" and minstrel shows. The main criticism leveled against Dunbar is that by writing in the plantation tradition he contributed to the stereotypical view of African Americans as one-dimensional characters.

During the 1920s, Johnson and Alain Locke recognized Dunbar's historical significance while minimizing the importance of his work. Johnson, who had himself written dialect poetry, thought the time for it had passed. Locke praised some new dialect poets of his own day while condemning Dunbar's poetry because it reflected "conscious posing and self-conscious sentimentality." Somehow Locke could excuse dialect poetry if it were addressed only to an African American audience; it would then be similar to the spirituals—but the same poetry addressed to white American audiences became mere minstrelsy.

Locke admired the new dialect poets because, in his view, they avoided the trap in which Dunbar and others of the nineteenth century had been caught. These younger poets had learned, he said, to shun stilted poetic diction, to use fresher and more original language, to omit racial caricature, and to forego pleading on behalf of their race. The new school of dialect poets tried to purge their poetic voices of "false sentimentality and clownishness." Locke believed that these new poets (Langston Hughes, Sterling Brown, and Lucy Ariel Williams [Holloway], among others) surpassed the supposed limits of pathos and humor that Johnson saw in dialect poetry, achieving instead a deep spirituality, quizzical humor, homely secular folksiness, and racial authenticity.

Dunbar was very good at writing dialect, and most critics agree that he elevated the genre. The tradition of dialect poetry was part of a growing interest in the regions that make up America: the Indiana Hoosier, Louisiana Cre-

ole, western cowboy, Boston Brahmin, German immigrant, and so on. So Riley's Hoosier dialect, Irwin Russell and Thomas Nelson Page's poems in Negro dialect (although neither was African American), Joel Chandler Harris's Uncle Remus tales, and a host of other users of dialect were joined by Dunbar.

Twentieth-century evaluation of Dunbar's work has been generally negative. Sterling Brown (1937) and his student Victor Lawson (1941) both follow Locke in their evaluations of Dunbar. Addison Gayle (1971), writing from the perspective of the black aesthetic, pronounces Dunbar an unfortunate victim of his time whose talent suffered from an uncorrected political and social vision. Gayle sees Dunbar as a tragic victim caught between the demands of commercial publishers and his own desire to free himself from racial identity. His reading of Dunbar's poems follows well-established paths and offers few fresh critical insights.

Jean Wagner (1973) chides Dunbar for being too indirect in praise and protest, and casts him in the role of a psychopathological persona who could not ignore his blackness but wished to be white. He characterizes Dunbar as a plantation poet, maladjusted to his race. Wagner's involved psychological exposition of Dunbar's double consciousness has been more completely and correctly described by Du Bois in *The Souls of Black Folk*. Dunbar's poetry need not be read as a "will to whiteness." In fact, if a poet announces plainly, as does Dunbar in "We Wear the Mask," that he is aware of the various roles he must play in order to survive, that poet need not be read as a psychotic, searching through his poetry for ways to reconcile disparate elements within himself.

The negative critical trend was interrupted by Darwin Turner (1967) and reversed by the Centenary Celebration on Paul Laurence Dunbar at the University of California, Irvine, in 1972. The conference made Dunbar one of the first African American writers in history to transcend the critical color boundary of literary academia, and resulted in a revaluation of his work. Again, in 1974 Turner continued the revisionary trend by dispelling the myth that Dunbar was an untutored poet who wrote merely from inspiration by showing the imagistic, metric, rhythmic, and stanzaic diversity in his poems, reasserting Dunbar's primacy as a dialect poet.

Twentieth-century African American poets gained in self-confidence, accepted with better grace their racial identity, felt themselves to be a part of a literary tradition, and identified spiritually with Africa. But the tradition must include and perhaps even begin with Dunbar, who, using Ethiopia as a symbol of Africa, calls her "mother" and celebrates her in an ode. That Dunbar should have heralded Africa is surprising, for high school and college curricula in America in the 1890s ignored African history, except for the chronicling of European "discovery," and colonialization. Africa's people were considered primitive, perhaps even subhuman. His spiritual bifurcation paralleled that of almost every other person of African ancestry in diaspora: European cultural values housed in African facades.

The confidence of men who had either fought alongside other Americans in a global war against a common external foe or who had witnessed those who did, or Rhodes scholars and graduates of Williams and Harvard, like Brown and Locke, with advanced degrees in philosophy or literature, should properly have exhibited more confidence than a nineteen-year-old high school graduate who lived precariously by his pen and presence, as did Dunbar during Reconstruction. That Dunbar's poetry lacks in social protest does not itself justify a negative evaluation of the poet's work, particularly by someone like Locke, who would strip rhetoric and didacticism from poetry. Didactic dialect poetry in the sentimental tradition placed emotion above intellect and emphasized human and family values. Dunbar sought to use the tenets of this tradition in his poetry to effect a change in his audience's attitude toward people of color. He failed, but his failure is more an indictment of his audience's intransigence and hypocrisy than of his own lack of ability.

Revisionist studies of Dunbar's poetry were also undertaken by Houston A. Baker (1974; 1984), Jay Martin (1975), and Peter Revell (1980). These scholars emphasize the impor-

tance of fictive, mythic, psychological, and historical considerations in evaluating Dunbar's works. All demonstrate the ability to sift through the morass of negative historical and sociological analyses, even though they do not include Dunbar among America's most important poets. His is a gift of song rather than symphony. His strength is the lyric rather than the epic. They imply a hierarchy of forms, with epic at the top and lyric at the bottom.

Despite the impressive range of poetic forms, themes, metric patterns, diction, characterization, figures, and tropes employed in their making, Dunbar's poems are not often credited with being finely crafted, highly structured poetic renderings. Dunbar holds firmly in control such features as dialect, which are susceptible to stereotypical treatment. In fact, he uses these attributes often to establish the irrefutable humanity of the characters. Consider, for example, the poem "The Old Cabin" (*Lyrics of Sunshine and Shadow*, 1905), much maligned by critics for its supposed acceptance of servitude. In this poem the speaker, a free man and former slave, reminisces about the days of slavery. He is old now, and says of his youthful days:

'An my min' fu'gits de whuppins,
   Draps de feah o' block an' lash
An' flies straight to somep'n' joyful
   In a secon's lightnin' flash.
         (*Complete Poems*, p. 429)

Surely these recollections of the "deah ol' cabin do' " are sentimental. Nevertheless, the poem also names the horrors of slavery and, at the same time, reveals one of the speaker's techniques of survival: the speaker consciously rejects the visual image and visceral recall of whippings, and concentrates instead on something joyful. Certainly, joyful times came even in slavery. The joy inevitably arises from memories of the family and of laughter shared, which made even the sting of the lash fly away into oblivion. The speaker does not love his slavery nor does he yearn for a return to the plantation; but he does not forget his own humanity even in the face of an indifferent, and even hostile, society. His ability to outlive the

189

institution that sought to destroy him confirms the wisdom of his willful transcendence.

Dunbar's poetry deviates sharply from that of other African Americans writing at the end of the nineteenth century. Richard Wright (1957) notes that after Phillis Wheatley's poems, all literature written by African Americans, unlike the literature by Europeans of African ancestry, can be described as the literature of oppression and lamentation. Wright charges that Dunbar, hiding what he knew to be true, deliberately refrained from the vision of horror that had claimed the exclusive attention of so many African American writers. Wright concedes that Dunbar manages to "wring a little unity" out of the contradiction that was his life.

Many elements struggled for attention and privilege within Dunbar. Schooled in the English Victorian poets and their American imitators or literary successors, influenced by the popular poetry of Riley, Dunbar achieved through the perspective of his African American heritage the integration of these separate— even disparate—elements into a body of work that needs to be examined holistically. Labels that suit the convenience of critics do not necessarily signify any contradiction in the poet's work.

The Poetry

Themes that resonate throughout Dunbar's poems include love, death, social commentary, praise of heroes, human frailty, and music. Dunbar's prose does not reveal a poetic credo. However, in a poem titled "A Choice" (*Lyrics of the Hearthside*, 1899), Dunbar writes:

> They please me not—these solemn songs
> That hint of sermons covered up.
> 'T is true the world should heed its wrongs,
>   But in a poem let me sup,
> Not simples brewed to cure or ease
> Humanity's confessed disease,
> But the spirit-wine on a singing line,
>   Or a dew-drop in a honey cup!
>   (*Complete Poems*, p. 201)

"A Choice" may provide the answer to why Dunbar mutes themes of social protest in his poetry. Aware of the ease with which poetry can be reduced to mere rhetoric, Dunbar sought to achieve delight and instruction in his graceful little verses, a far cry from the direct protest and racial fire of his prose. But even in the poems, some social commentary on racial themes can be detected, although some critics claim that the instruction is sufficiently sugar-coated so as to mask the effect of the message.

Poems of social commentary like "Ode to Ethiopia," "The Haunted Oak," "To The South: On Its New Slavery," and "An Ante-Bellum Sermon," should be included among those that explore the theme of race. The "Ode to Ethiopia" belongs quite clearly in the category of epideictic or ceremonial discourse (which Edward P. J. Corbett calls the most literary discourse); the poet's aim is to inspire. Epideictic's special topics are honor and dishonor, and its means are praise and blame. The "Ode" calls forth generous tribute to a people who are usually despised. The poem's heartfelt sentiments and noble resolutions escape the blight of sentimentality; rather, a contrast is drawn between the lowly status of the people being praised and the emotional exhortations of the poet, whose admiration for his people is evident. In all ceremonial discourse, success depends mainly on the credibility of what is said. Dunbar transcends the denigration of the moment and urges his race to continue its upward climb: "Go on and up!"

The poem "An Ante-Bellum Sermon" (*Lyrics of Lowly Life*, 1896) adds more variety to Dunbar's thematic form of social commentary on race. The poem is written in eleven eight-line stanzas with a complex rhyme scheme whose first stanza creates the pattern *abcbdebe*. In stanzas two and eleven the lines six, seven, and eight rhyme, but all the other stanzas follow the pattern of the first. The poem renders poetically the sermon of a plantation preacher. He has chosen as a text for his sermon the exodus of the Hebrew "chillun" from captivity in Egypt. The speaker carefully cautions his hearers to accept his sermon "in a Bibleistic way."

However, toward the end of his sermon, much stirred by his own eloquence, he forgets his repeated admonitions and looks forward to a modern Moses who will deliver the children of Africa from their captivity.

The preacher makes a sophisticated, imaginative leap of identification with a people of another era who had been enslaved only to be set free by the intervention of God's servant, Moses. The congregation cannot fail to make the connection between the Hebrew "chillun" and themselves, if only because the preacher repeatedly cautions them against making such a connection. The congregation needs the comfort of hope given in this sermon; thus, the preacher risks untrustworthy slaves, menacing masters, and future opportunities to preach. Although its theme is serious, reading this poem without some laughter is nearly impossible. Difficult to scan by eye and pencil, when read aloud the poem's meter is perfect. Readers can hear the longing of the preacher and his congregation for freedom; they can admire the cleverness of the preacher's choice of words.

Dunbar's "choice" is that he shuns using his poem to preach: it is enough for the poet to "brew" here a "simple" through the "spirit-wine" of a "singing line"; for this is a poem that delights as it instructs. It has been read by others as an example of Dunbar's willingness to poke fun at black characters. They have seen this preacher as a cowardly, comic figure who weakens the import of his sermon by limiting its relevance to biblical times. The critic who reads "An Ante-Bellum Sermon" in this fashion ignores the last stanza in which the preacher momentarily loses himself and forgets his caution, shouting,

> But when Moses wif his powah
>   Comes an' sets us chillun free,
> We will praise de gracious Mastah
>   Dat has gin us liberty;
> An' we'll shout ouah halleluyahs,
>   On dat mighty reck'nin' day,
> When we'se reco'nised ez citiz'—
>   Huh uh! Chillun, let us pray!
>   (*Complete Poems*, p. 23)

James A. Emanuel, in his essay "Racial Fire in the Poetry of Paul Laurence Dunbar," names the feature that critics of the 1970s fail to see in Dunbar's poetry. Emanuel insightfully explains various poems—among them "A Banjo Song," "The Old Cabin," "Parted," "When All Is Done," and "We Wear the Masks"—that might be classified under the rubric "racial fire." The widely proclaimed absence of racial pride or criticism of racial and social injustice in Dunbar's poetry cannot be sustained after a careful reading of these poems. With some of Dunbar's poems readers must relinquish their own anachronistic notions about racial relations in his world. In others they must reconsider Dunbar's poetic principles, especially those espoused in a poem like "A Choice."

Dunbar records for posterity the names of battles in which African American troops distinguished themselves in the Civil War, thereby affirming participation in a war that brought about their freedom. History books have neglected the record of these acts, but they live in Dunbar's songs. Therefore his verse serves two functions: it praises those African Americans enlisted in the struggle for human rights, and it shows how African Americans fought for their own freedom alongside other Americans.

In "The Colored Soldiers" (*Lyrics of Lowly Life*) Dunbar shows how the military arts were perceived to be reserved only for white men: " 'These battles are the white man's, / and the whites will fight them out.' " However, as the battles were waged and the casualties mounted, the nation called on the colored soldiers as a last resort. Their eager response to the call, their blazing bravery, earned the respect of their comrades in battle. African Americans suffered and died in the war and Dunbar hopes that "their blood has cleansed completely / Every blot of slavery's shame."

These poems may achieve some of their strength from the fact that Dunbar's father served in the Fifty-fifth Massachusetts Infantry; in celebrating the black soldier and "The Unsung Heroes," Dunbar may have been singing of his father's contribution to their freedom. Certainly the bravery of these men who fought in battle is unquestioned, but African Americans also had to fight for the *right* to fight before they could fight in the war. Southerners were afraid to put weapons in the hands of slaves for fear they might be used against them. Northerners, for all their willingness to fight on behalf of freedom for the slaves, were not certain that the "creatures" possessed the ability or the intelligence to handle weapons in war. Without Dunbar's songs of praise some sense of the slaves' contribution to the war for their own freedom might have been lost.

Death does not evoke despair or pessimism in Dunbar's poems. Instead death summons the voice of stoic resignation or it elicits the hope of peace, as in "A Death Song." A few of the other poems on death may have been written as a result of Dunbar's knowledge of his own approaching death, as in "Worn Out."

Poems on the subject of death, however, do not overshadow poems on the happier themes of music, love, and laughter. Of these themes Dunbar is an acknowledged master. Who has read and not been thrilled by "When Malindy Sings"? The poems "The Corn-Stalk Fiddle," "The Valse," "The Ol' Tunes," and "A Song" ("Thou art the soul of a summer's day") are musical in their structure, metrical pattern, rhyme schemes, sentiments, and stanzas. "The Valse" imitates a waltz rhythm by alternating lines of anapests and dactyls. Ends of lines may occasionally seem to scan improperly; however, when the poems are read aloud, with attention paid to the poetic foot, the waltz-like three-quarter-time rhythm is inescapable.

"The Colored Band" marches down the street to "Sousa played in Ragtime"; "At the Tavern" there is "A lilt and a swing, / And a ditty to sing"; and "The Ol' Tunes" recalls memories of time gone by. "When Malindy Sings," all others who attempt to sing through studying, sing more loudly, or fiddle, must give way before the power, majesty, holiness, and sweetness of Malindy's humble, glorious praises. Malindy's singing is ". . . sweetah dan de music / Of an edicated band." Her songs make children keep still and is as fresh as the "bresh of angels' wings," even though she sings old tunes such as "Rock of Ages" and "Swing Low, Sweet Chariot."

In "The Party" both music and temptation are themes. The speaker regales a friend who missed it with details of a recent party. He recounts an elegant gathering where ordinary souls showed their extraordinary talent for enjoyment. Human foibles abound. The fiddle music—"jigs, cotillions, reels an' breakdowns"—stirs the old, the lame, and the churchgoer. Even the preacher, who has already yielded to the temptation of gluttony because of the variety, kind, and amount of food, must now "tek bofe feet an' hol' dem so's to keep 'em in deir place," as he tries to resist the temptation of the fiddle.

In the Caroline tradition of the English sixteenth century, the beauty who is most fair is also the most beloved. Roses in snow and peaches in cream are the usual descriptions of the beloved's blushing cheeks and complexion. Her hair may be dark but usually it is flaxen or golden. Shakespeare's sonnet to a dark lady of "dun" breasts and "wiry hair" satirizes the tradition of pale beauty rather than celebrating dark—as in African—beauty. In "Dinah Kneading Dough" the speaker knows no lovelier sight than Dinah's "brown arms buried elbow-deep" in dough, keeping "their domestic rhythm." Dinah has "eyes of jet and teeth of pearl, / Hair, some say, too tight a-curl." The speaker prefers her kind of beauty just as he does in several poems in which a woman named Mandy Lou is the object of his love. Then there is "Dely":

Dely brown ez brown kin be,
  She ain' no mullatter;
She pure cullud,—don' you see
  Dat's jes' whut's de mattah?
Dat's de why I love huh so,
  D'ain't no mix about huh,
Soon's you see huh face you know
  D'ain't no chance to doubt huh.
            (*Complete Poems*, p. 238)

These poems of love inspired by an African beauty hard at work contrast vividly with the pale, helpless, indolent ladies who inspire the love poems of white society. Here is beauty and productivity. She was not celebrated before

Dunbar's time, and she will have to wait another quarter of a century for other lyrics that sing of her charms.

The Fiction

Dunbar earned his first income from writing with the sale of two westerns in 1891 to the A. N. Kellogg Newspaper Company. He wrote a hundred short stories in all, eighty-seven of which were published. Despite his large output, some students of the African American short story omit Dunbar from consideration, classifying his short stories as formulaic pulp fiction unworthy of serious study.

Victor Lawson, Robert Bone, Bert Bender, and Peter Revell have commented on Dunbar's short stories. These critics approach the fictions with different assumptions and therefore read the same story in quite different ways. Consider, for example, the following analyses of Dunbar's *The Strength of Gideon and Other Stories.* Lawson (1941) considers the stories as distorted social history that borders on the burlesque because they misrepresent the reality of plantation life by portraying stereotypical families, white and black. Bone (1975) describes the stories as pastorals with an accommodationist worldview that encourages conciliation and discourages dissension. Further, he charges, the stories admonish blacks to forgive and forget the horrors of slavery. Bone's reading implies that Gideon prefers life on the plantation. Bender (1975) believes that the stories, in which a narrator or central character contends with something larger than himself and comes to recognize its futility or inappropriateness, ultimately evolve into veiled social protest against the white supremacist myth of black inferiority. Revell (1980) argues that Gideon is an assertion of the black man's humanity; a bold departure, an extension of the range of the black man's characterization in American fiction.

These comments are typical of the critical commentary on Dunbar's short fiction, and they could be repeated for many of the short stories in each of the four collected editions as well as the other "Ohio Pastorals" (as Dunbar called a group of stories, all set in Dorbury, Ohio, which were published in *Lippincott's Monthly Magazine* between 1901 and 1905). But because the voices of direct and indirect protest do exist in Dunbar's short fiction, universal repudiation such as Lawson's cannot be sustained. Bone separates the stories into distinct categories and identifies one group from the other. Neither Lawson nor Bone seems to recognize, as does Revell, that Gideon's tragic choice lies between his oath of duty to the young master and the vow of duty to his wife.

Bert Bender (1975) believes that Dunbar sought to amuse and to arouse his audience. In all of his stories, argues Bender, "a narrator, or a central character attempts and contends with something larger than himself" and recognizes "the futility or inappropriateness of a reasoned response or of a conventional fictional attempt to understand his situation." Although he writes often about life on the plantation, Dunbar's stories usually present muted, indirect assaults on the myth of black inferiority as held by white supremacists.

Dunbar's poetry aimed at lyrical renderings of the "spirit wine on a singing line." His short fiction essayed the pastoral tradition and voiced indirect protest. His novels share some characteristics of both the emerging naturalistic and protest novels of the period. Critical commentary on his novels centers upon whether *The Uncalled* (1898) is Dunbar's spiritual autobiography and whether it is a protest novel; it condemns *The Love of Landry* (1900) for being a conventional story of the kind found in the popular magazines of the day; and finds *The Fanatics* (1901) structurally unsound. The critics divide on whether *The Sport of the Gods* (1902) continues in the plantation tradition.

When critics discuss the African American novel, Dunbar is usually mentioned as one who failed in his four attempts to achieve any distinction in that form. Recently, however, *The Uncalled* and *The Sport of the Gods* have received critical attention that suggests, at the very least, a new interest, and at best, a total revaluation.

Some critics have observed that the seeds in Dunbar's short stories come to flower in the novels; most critics, however, remain convinced that their uneven quality and high incidence of conceptual and structural defects limit their value. Bone argues persuasively that *The Sport of the Gods* should be included in the company of Charles Waddell Chesnutt's *The House Behind The Cedars* (1900) and *The Marrow of Tradition* (1901) as among the first significant contributions by African Americans to the art of the novel.

Donald Gibson (1969) identifies the city as a mythic place in African American fiction, different in quality from the conception held by white Americans. The North became a place where African Americans could be free. "Going North" came to mean going to Detroit, or Chicago, or New York. Some African Americans moving North stopped in Ohio, others traveled all the way to Canada. According to Gibson, "the journey took on a significance far beyond the fact of itself. It took on a kind of mythical quality, the nature of which related it to universal process. Gibson explains that the trip to the North became a "journey to the city of God." The idea was expressed in the slave spirituals, which were at once a coded language of escape ("Steal Away," "Swing Low, Sweet Chariot"), and a veiled protest against slavery and the expression of a desire for release from it.

The North became identified with the Promised Land of the spirituals. The North symbolizes and becomes the actuality, the reality, the concrete embodiment of the religious ideal. The whole constellation of meanings suggested by Gibson are summed up, he says, in a poem by Lucy Ariel Williams (Holloway) called "Northboun' ":

> O' de wurl ain't flat
> An' de wurl ain't roun',
> Hit's one long strip
> Hangin' up an' down—
> Jes' Souf an' Norf;
> Jes' Norf and Souf.
>
> . . . .
>
> Talkin' 'bout the City whut St. John saw—
> Chile, you oughta go to Saginaw;
> A nigger's chance is "finest Kind,"

> An' pretty gals ain't hard to find.
>
> . . . .
>
> Huh! de wurl ain't flat,
> An' de wurl aint' roun',
> Jes' one long strip
> Hangin' up an' down.
> Since Norf is up
> An' Souf is down,
> An' Hebben is up,
> I'm upward boun'.

That African Americans did not find the Promised Land when they reached the North is abundantly clear. But this reality did not destroy the idea of the city in the mythology of African American artists. Gibson demonstrates conclusively that before and after emancipation, the northern city represented for African Americans the hope for a life better than the one they knew in the South. Gibson believes that the idea of the city illustrated in Langston Hughes's play *Tambourines to Glory*, in Claude McKay's *Home to Harlem* and *Banjo*, and in Richard Wright's *Black Boy* and *Native Son*, was first adumbrated in this way by Dunbar in *The Uncalled*; but *The Sport of the Gods* is the first portrayal in fiction of the African American in Harlem. Gibson does not include novels by African American women; but in their works as well, notably Ann Petry's *The Street* and Dorothy West's *The Living Is Easy*, the tradition continues.

As *The Sport of the Gods* begins, the narrator comments:

> Fiction has said so much in regret of the old days when there were plantations and overseers and masters and slaves, that it was good to come upon such a household as Berry Hamilton's, if for no other reason than that it afforded a relief from the monotony of tiresome iteration.

The Hamiltons have worked for the family of Maurice Oakley for twenty faithful years. Through frugal living, they have been able to save thirteen hundred dollars.

Oakley's profligate brother, Frank, whose dormant career as an artist and active engagement as a gambler leaves him perpetually short of cash, has received money from Maurice to further his art career in Paris. Frank does not want Maurice to find out that he lost the money gambling, so he reports it stolen. Maurice accuses Hamilton of theft. Accusation equals guilt. The southern code of honor reveals itself as a fraudulent facade. A kangaroo court quickly convicts Hamilton and sentences him to ten years of hard labor. The Oakleys then evict the other members of the Hamilton family.

Driven from their homes, bereft of friends, Fannie, Kitty, and Joe Hamilton go North. The narrator explains,

> They had heard of New York as a place vague and far away, a city that, like Heaven, to them had existed by faith alone. All the days of their lives they had heard of it, and it seemed to them the centre of all the glory, all the wealth, all the freedom of the world.
> (p. 98)

They are not prepared for the destructive environment of New York's urban ghetto.

A turn in the novel results when a white reporter, Skaggs, hears about the Oakley-Hamilton affair. He goes south to investigate the matter and learns that Frank had admitted in a letter to Maurice that he squandered the money that Hamilton was accused of stealing. Maurice, led by a fanatical sense of family honor, refuses to besmirch the family's name by acknowledging Frank's guilt. Maurice wears Frank's letter close to his breast in a manner reminiscent of Hester Prynne's scarlet letter. Hester's letter redeemed and released her from punishment; Maurice Oakley's has punished and led him into madness. Skaggs gets his sensational story and Hamilton gets out of prison and immediately heads for New York to reunite with his family.

Berry Hamilton finds his miserable family. Joe is in jail; Kitty is a tramp. Fannie is desolate. Berry and Fannie realize that they are powerless to help Joe and Kitty and cannot survive in the menacing atmosphere of New York. They return to the South, where Oakley's wife entreats them to go back to their former residence. Only in that way can she attempt restitution. On summer evenings, they can hear the howls of Maurice's madness.

Two areas of critical disagreement about *The Sport of the Gods* focus on whether Dunbar recommends that blacks reject the city for a return to the rural South and whether the novel's structural flaws keep it from being considered an artistic success. Few critics doubt its significance to Dunbar studies or to the historical development of the African American novel.

Darwin Turner and Gregory Candela note the presence of irony in *The Sport of the Gods*, but point out that other critics of this novel, like Hugh Gloster and Robert Bone, see in it an attack on northern city life and a recommendation that blacks return to or remain in the South. But Turner and Candela see in Dunbar's conclusion a far more bitter and hopeless resolution. Turner explains that Dunbar's offered alternatives are a restraint of the body in the South and the festering of the soul in the North." Of course, this is no choice at all; or it is like the choice of death by drowning or hanging.

Houston A. Baker observes that most critics have insisted upon interpreting African American literature in a sociohistorical context and thereby miss the benefits of an interpretive strategy grounded in the study of mythic and fictive discourse. In a clarifying exegesis of the sociohistorical interpretations given to *The Sport of the Gods* by Bone, Williams, and Gayle, Baker shows how these critics ignore, minimize, or neglect all aspects of the novel that lie outside of the historical framework.

Baker shows how Bone's sociohistorical interpretation locates the novel in the post-Reconstruction repression. According to this view, Dunbar's main reason for writing is to encourage black people to stay in the South in order to provide disciplined labor for the new plantation economy. Bone thereby presses Dunbar's fiction into the service of his own historical interpretation. Kenny Jackson Williams focuses her interpretation in a critical debate on whether African American writers are, have been, or should be protest writers. She concludes that Dunbar was a protest writer, supplying in this novel a critique of the evil influences the city exerts on black life. Similarly, Addison Gayle situates his argument in an ideological context and argues that Dunbar locates the novel in the context of the old plantation tradition. Gayle's black-aesthetic ideology insists that African American authors should create positive role models, images, and symbols of black life in order to promote the social progress of the race. Gayle holds that Dunbar was unable to contribute to his race because he failed to transcend negative stereotypes.

These critics have certain expectations of the African American novel based on the belief that the African American novel is at least implicitly grounded in historical reality. Baker illustrates the irony in the expectations of these critics: the desire for a historical reading is an a priori justification of their critical explanations. Thus, they achieve what they expect. Baker describes it as "the solacing embrace of a tautological circle."

Baker insists that *The Sport of the Gods* should not be read as a historical document. We do not take up the novel to find out something about the normal, actual everyday context of the lives of the people represented within it. The novel, Baker argues, is "essentially a discourse on the fallibility of human habits of thought." The unfortunate ends to which the characters come result from their inability to rightly understand the world. In the novel's move from "its announced subject of fiction," says Baker, to an implicit reductio ad absurdum of the plantation tradition, the true theft in the novel becomes apparent: it is the theft of Berry Hamilton's "liberty and rightful earnings." Their appropriation "by a bizarre system of social justice is a corollary of the distorted perception that both sanctions and gains support from a plantation tradition."

The novel makes clear that in order to redeem the theft, a new social order and a new theory of fiction must replace the old. The new theory must produce a dramatically new reading of life. Baker concludes that "Skaggs's 'theory,' his fictive, indeed virtually mythic, mode of confronting reality," fulfills the goals implied by the first line of *The Sport of the Gods*:

a plantation tradition's "monotony of tiresome iteration" is transcended by the reporter's "clear, interesting, and strong" story.

New techniques of critical analysis may yield for Dunbar's other fictions the increasing variety of interpretations and critical attention that this novel has begun to attract. His historical significance cannot be denied. His artistic achievement was abundant and fine enough to win a wide and lasting reputation. His literary reputation could take for a metaphor his first job, in which he was an elevator operator. It has gone up and down, according to the literary or critical fashion of the day, and occasionally it has been stalled, but it has always kept moving.

Selected Bibliography

PRIMARY SOURCES

POETRY

Oak and Ivy. Dayton, Ohio: United Brethren Publishing House, 1893 [1892].
Majors and Minors. Toledo, Ohio: Hadley and Hadley, 1895 [1896].
Lyrics of Lowly Life. New York: Dodd, Mead, 1896.
Lyrics of the Hearthside. New York: Dodd, Mead, 1899.
Lyrics of Love and Laughter. New York: Dodd, Mead, 1903.
A Plantation Portrait. New York: Dodd, Mead, 1905.
Chris'mus Is A' Comin' and Other Poems. New York: Dodd, Mead, 1905.
Lyrics of Sunshine and Shadow. New York: Dodd, Mead, 1905.

ILLUSTRATED BOOKS OF POETRY

Poems of Cabin and Field. New York: Dodd, Mead, 1899.
Candle-Lightin' Time. New York: Dodd, Mead, 1901.
When Malindy Sings. New York: Dodd, Mead, 1903.
Li'l' Gal. New York: Dodd, Mead, 1904.
Howdy, Honey, Howdy. New York: Dodd, Mead, 1905.
Joggin' Erlong. New York: Dodd, Mead, 1906.

SHORT STORIES

Folks from Dixie. New York: Dodd, Mead, 1898.
The Strength of Gideon and Other Stories. New York: Dodd, Mead, 1900.
In Old Plantation Days. New York: Dodd, Mead, 1903.
The Heart of Happy Hollow. New York: Dodd, Mead, 1904.

MUSICAL THEATER

Clorindy; or, The Origin of the Cakewal. Music by Will Marion Cook. New York: Witmark Music, 1898.

Dream Lovers: An Operatic Romance. Music By Samuel Coleridge-Taylor. London: Boosey and Co., 1898.

Jes Lak White Fo'ks: A One-Act Negro Operetto. Music by Will and John Cook. New York: Harry Von Tilzer, 1900.

Uncle Eph's Christmas: A One Act Negro Musical Sketch. Music by Will Marion Cook. New York: Will M. Cook, 1900.

In Dahomey: A Negro Musical. Lyrics by Paul Laurence Dunbar and others, music by Will Marion Cook. New York: Harry Von Tilzer; London: Keith Prowse and Co., 1903.

SELECTED ARTICLES

"England as Seen by a Black Man." *New York Independent,* September 16, 1897.

"Our New Madness." *New York Independent,* September 15, 1898.

"The Race Question Discussed." *Toledo Journal,* December 11, 1898.

"The Hapless Southern Negro." *Denver Post,* September 17, 1899.

"Negro Life in Washington." *Harper's Weekly,* January 13, 1900.

"Is Higher Education for the Negro Hopeless?" *Philadelphia Times,* June 10, 1900.

"Negro Society in Washington." *Saturday Evening Post,* December 14, 1901.

"The Fourth of July." *New York Times,* July 10, 1903.

NOVELS

The Uncalled. New York: Dodd, Mead, 1898.

The Love of Landry. New York: Dodd, Mead, 1900.

The Fanatics. New York: Dodd, Mead, 1901.

The Sport of the Gods. New York: Dodd, Mead, 1902.

COLLECTED WORKS

The Life and Works of Paul Laurence Dunbar. Edited by Lida Keck Wiggins. Naperville, Ill.: J. L. Nichols, 1907.

The Complete Poems of Paul Laurence Dunbar, with the Introduction to "Lyrics of Lowly Life" by W. D. Howells. New York: Dodd, Mead, 1913.

Speakin' o' Christmas and Other Christmas and Special Poems. New York: Dodd, Mead, 1914.

The Best Stories of Paul Laurence Dunbar. Edited by Benjamin Brawley. New York: Dodd, Mead, 1938.

Little Brown Baby. Edited by Bertha Rogers. New York: Dodd, Mead, 1940.

The Paul Laurence Dunbar Reader. Edited by Jay Martin and Gossie H. Hudson. New York: Dodd, Mead, 1975.

FACSIMILE EDITION

Numerous facsimile editions have appeared from various presses. *The Life and Works of Paul Laurence Dunbar,* a microfilm version from the Kraus-Thompson Organization (1974), contains nine reels of film facsimile reprints of all volumes of Dunbar's poetry and fiction and a selection of biographical and critical materials.

MANUSCRIPTS

The Ohio State Historical Society's Archives-Library, 1985 Velma Avenue, Columbus, Ohio 43211. Microfilm of major holdings are available. For a catalog of the OHS Dunbar collection, see Sara S. Fuller's *The Paul Laurence Dunbar Collection: An Inventory to the Microfilm Edition* (Columbus, Ohio: Ohio Historical Society Archives-Library, 1972).

The Schomburg Collection of Paul Laurence Dunbar in the Countee Cullen branch of the New York Public Library, West 135th Street, New York. Microfilm of major holdings, including manuscripts, correspondence, and newspaper clippings.

SECONDARY WORKS

BIOGRAPHICAL AND CRITICAL STUDIES

Allen, Caffilene. "The Caged Bird Sings: The Ellison-Dunbar Connection." *CLA Journal* 40:178–90 (December 1996).

Baker, Houston A., Jr. "Paul Laurence Dunbar: An Evaluation." *Black World* 21:30–37 (1971).

———. *Singers of Daybreak: Studies in Black American Literature.* Washington, D.C.: Howard University Press, 1974.

———. *Blues, Ideology, and Afro-American Literature: A Vernacular Theory.* Chicago: University of Chicago Press, 1984.

Bender, Bert. "The Lyrical Short Fiction of Dunbar and Chesnutt." In *A Singer in the Dawn: Reinterpretations of Paul Laurence Dunbar.* Edited by Jay Martin. New York: Dodd, Mead, 1975. Pp. 208–22.

Best, Felton. "Paul Laurence Dunbar's Protest Literature: The Final Years." *Western Journal of Black Studies* 17:54–63 (Spring 1993).

———. *Crossing the Color Line: A Biography of Paul Laurence Dunbar, 1872–1906.* Dubuque, Iowa: Kendall/Hunt, 1996.

Blount, Marcellus. "The Preacherly Text: African American Poetry and Vernacular Performance." *PMLA* 107:582–93 (May 1992).

Bone, Robert. *Down Home: A History of Afro-American Short Fiction from Its Beginning to the End of the Harlem Renaissance.* New York: Putnam, 1975.

Brawley, Benjamin. *Paul Laurence Dunbar: Poet of His People.* Chapel Hill: University of North Carolina Press, 1936.

Brown, Sterling. *The Negro in American Fiction.* Washington, D.C.: Associates in Negro Folk Education, 1937. Reprint, Port Washington, N.Y.: Kennikar Press, 1968.

Candela, Gregory L. "We Wear the Mask: Irony in Dunbar's *The Sport of the Gods.*" *American Literature* 48:60–72 (1976).

Davis, Charles T. "Paul Laurence Dunbar," In *American Writers*. Supp. 2, pt. 1. Edited by A. Walton Litz. New York: Scribners, 1981. Pp. 191–219.

Dunbar, Alice Moore. "The Poet and His Song." *A.M.E. Church Review* 31:121–35 (1914).

Emmanuel, James A. "Racial Fire in the Poetry of Paul Laurence Dunbar." In *A Singer in the Dawn*. Edited by Jay Martin. New York: Dodd, Mead, 1975.

Gayle, Addison, Jr. *Oak and Ivy: A Biography of Paul Laurence Dunbar*. Garden City, N.J.: Doubleday, 1971.

———. *The Way of the World: The Black Novel in America*. Garden City, N.J.: Doubleday, 1975.

Gibson, Donald. "The City and the Black Writer: Mythology and Symbology." *Criterion* (University of Chicago) 7:20–25 (Spring–Summer 1969).

Gloster, Hugh. *Negro Voices in American Fiction*. Chapel Hill: University of North Carolina Press, 1948. Pp. 46–56.

Hudson, Gossie Harold. "A Biography of Paul Laurence Dunbar." Ph.D. diss. Ohio State University (1970).

Inge, Casey. "Family Functions: Disciplinary Discourses and (De)Constructions of the 'Family' in *The Sport of the Gods*." *Callaloo* 20, no. 1:226–42 (Winter 1997).

Johnson, James Weldon, ed. *The Book of American Negro Poetry*. New York: Harcourt, Brace, 1922.

Keeling, John. "Paul Dunbar and the Mask of Dialect." *Southern Literary Journal* 25: 24–38 (Spring 1993).

Kinnamon, Keneth. "Three Black Writers and the Anthologized Canon." In *American Realism and the Canon*. Edited by Tom Quirk and Gary Scharnhorst. Newark: University of Delaware Press, 1994.

Larson, Charles R. "The Novels of Paul Laurence Dunbar." *Phylon* 29:257–71 (Fall 1968).

Lawson, Victor. *Dunbar Critically Examined*. Washington, D.C.: Associated Publishers, 1941.

Locke, Alain. "The New Negro." In *The Negro Caravan*. Edited by Sterling Allen Brown, Arthur Paul Davis, and Ulysses Grant Lee. New York: The Citadel Press (Dryden Press), 1941. Pp. 948–59.

Martin, Jay, ed. *A Singer in the Dawn: Reinterpretations of Paul Laurence Dunbar*. New York: Mead, Dodd, 1975.

Ramsey, William M. "Dunbar's Dixie." *Southern Literary Journal* 32:30 (Fall 1999).

Redding, J. Saunders. *To Make a Poet Black*. Chapel Hill: University of North Carolina Press, 1939. Pp. 56–67.

Revell, Peter. *Paul Laurence Dunbar*. Boston: Twayne, 1980.

Rodgers, Lawrence R. "Paul Laurence Dunbar's *The Sport of the Gods*: The Doubly Conscious World of Plantation Fiction, Migration, and Ascent." *American Literary Realism* 24:42–57 (Spring 1992).

Terrell, Mary Church. "Paul Laurence Dunbar." *Voice of the Negro* 3:271–78 (1906).

Turner, Darwin T. "Paul Laurence Dunbar: The Rejected Symbol." *Journal of Negro History* 52:1–13 (1967).

———. "Paul Laurence Dunbar: The Poet and the Myth." *CLA Journal* 18:155–71 (1974).

Wagner, Jean. *Black Poets of the United States, from Paul Laurence Dunbar to Langston Hughes*. Urbana: University of Illinois Press, 1973.

Williams, Kenny Jackson. "The Making of a Novelist." In *A Singer in the Dawn: Reinterpretations of Paul Laurence Dunbar*. Edited by Jay Martin. New York: Dodd, Mead, 1975. Pp. 152–207.

Wright, Richard. *White Man, Listen!* Garden City, N.Y.: Doubleday, 1957.

BIBLIOGRAPHIES

Blanck, Jacob N. "Paul Laurence Dunbar, 1872–1906." In *Bibliography of American Literature*. Vol. 2. New Haven: Yale University Press, 1957. Pp. 498–505.

Burris, Andrew M. "Bibliography of Works by Paul Laurence Dunbar, Negro Poet and Author, 1872–1906." *American Collector* 5:69–73 (1927).

Cunningham, Virginia. *Paul Laurence Dunbar and His Song*. New York: Dodd, Mead, 1947. Pp. 67–283. New York: Biblo and Tannen, 1969.

Metcalf, E. W., Jr. *Paul Laurence Dunbar: A Bibliography*. Meutchen, N.J.: Scarecrow Press, 1975.

Wagner, Jean. *Black Poets of the United States from Paul Laurence Dunbar to Langston Hughes*. Urbana: University of Illinois Press, 1973. Pp. 529–31.

—The bibliography has been updated for this edition by Keidra Morris.

RALPH ELLISON
(1914–1994)

ROBERT G. O'MEALLY

ONE OF THE "enduring functions of the American novel," Ralph Ellison wrote, "is that of defining the national type as it evolves in the turbulence of change, and of giving the American experience, as it unfolds in its diverse parts and regions, imaginative integration and moral continuity. Thus it is bound up with our problem of nationhood." In *Invisible Man* (1952), probably the most significant American novel since World War II, Ellison gives us a terrifying and yet vibrant national metaphor: we are invisible.

In Ellison's created world, as in American society, the quick pace of change, the caprice, the arrogance alongside the innocence, the newness and the general instability of institutions, and, above all, the impulse to recoil from the awful demands of American democracy—all keep Americans from seeing each other or even themselves. As Ellison noted, the complexity and diversity of American life, along with the development of the novel as a form, have brought forth novels such as *Invisible Man:* "Picaresque, many-leveled . . . swarming with characters and with varied types and levels of experience." More than a "slice of life," Ellison's novel is an attempt at no less than a new definition of the national character, a modern national epic.

Accordingly, the vision in Ellison's *Invisible Man,* and indeed throughout his fiction, is ul-

timately affirmative. Virtually all of his fiction—ten stories published before the novel, eleven after, as well as six additional stories and a second novel published posthumously—features a black youngster stretching toward adulthood. We see in this work the evolution of a central theme: the more conscious one is of individual, cultural, and national history, the freer one becomes. As a young writer, Ellison quickly became dissatisfied with the typical naturalistic scenarios in which characters struggling to survive the merciless American environment are eventually overcome by impersonal forces. To Ellison, this documentary fiction was dull—and failed to capture the richness and variety of American life as he knew it. Influenced by a broad range of writers, including Dostoevsky, André Malraux, and Ernest Hemingway, Ellison began to focus on the person who, by force of character and will, manages to endure.

Ellison's Beginnings

Ralph Waldo Ellison was born in Oklahoma City, Oklahoma, on March 1, 1914. His parents, Lewis Alfred Ellison and Ida Millsap Ellison, left the Deep South for Oklahoma in 1911. At least Oklahoma had no firm tradition of slavery; as it turned out, segregation laws were imported from neighboring Texas and Arkansas. Even so, the blacks who had trekked west in wagon trains to escape southern oppression fought hard for their political rights. The blues lyric (which suggested the title of Ellison's 1986 book, *Going to the Territory*) says, "I'm going to the Territory, baby / I'm going to the nation"; for blacks heading west during this hopeful period it meant "I'm going to be free."

Especially after the death in 1917 of Lewis Ellison (who had worked as a construction foreman and then as an independent businessman, selling ice and coal), the Ellisons were poor— at times extremely poor. Still, Ralph and his brother Herbert were made to feel that the worlds of the rich and the white were approachable. This confidence had been their father's; Lewis Ellison, an avid reader, named his elder son after Emerson. It was reinforced by Ida Ellison, a woman of enormous determination, faith, and purpose. A stewardess at the Avery Chapel African Methodist Episcopal Church who valued forthright action in *this* world, she brought home records, magazines, and books discarded in white homes where she worked as a maid. And she saw to it that her sons had electrical and chemistry sets, a rolltop desk and chair, and a toy typewriter. Her activism extended to politics. "If you young Negroes don't do something about things," she would tell her sons, "I don't know what's going to happen to this race." An ardent supporter of Eugene Debs's Socialist Party, she canvassed for the Party's gubernatorial candidate in 1914. In 1934, after Ralph had gone off to Tuskegee Institute, she was jailed for attempting to rent buildings that Jim Crow laws had declared off limits to blacks. As teenagers, Ellison and his comrades dreamed of being latter-day Renaissance men; they snatched desired symbols along with attitudes and values from blacks, Native Americans, and whites alike. Ellison wanted to read everything he could: fairy tales, James Fenimore Cooper, George Bernard Shaw, and even a translation of Freud's *Interpretation of Dreams*, which he thought to be a fanciful version of the dream books used by certain "scientific" players of the numbers game. He identified with people he met on odd jobs around

town: in private clubs where he waited tables, at buildings where he ran the elevator, on downtown streets where he shined shoes and hawked newspapers. He identified, too, with the tellers as well as the heroes of the tales that he heard in neighbor J. L. Randolph's pharmacy, where he also worked. Not all of Ellison's early job experiences were uplifting. The battle-royal scene in *Invisible Man*, which comprises the first chapter, was suggested not only by similar scenes that he had read about but also by those he had witnessed as a waiter at private clubs.

In the music-centered Oklahoma City of the 1920s, and with musicians as the heroes most revered, it is small wonder that from age eight through his middle twenties, he wanted to be a musician. Ellison himself wanted to be able to read music as well as to improvise. Thanks to Zelia N. Breaux, supervisor of the music program for the black schools in Oklahoma City, he learned music theory at Douglass High School and soon picked up a working knowledge of the soprano saxophone and several brass instruments. As first-chair trumpeter in the Douglass school band, and then as the group's student conductor, he played light classics and marches around town. Meanwhile, the conductor of the Oklahoma City Orchestra taught Ellison privately and invited him to concerts for children. Ellison recalled being "the only brother of colour" permitted to attend these concerts at that time.

Ellison admired the elegance, artistic discipline and seemingly infinite capacity for self-expression that were the hallmarks of the jazz musicians he heard in Oklahoma City. As a high school student, he played occasional dance jobs in pickup groups, sat in on rehearsals, and learned the jazz idiom at jam sessions. In 1933 Ellison left Oklahoma for Tuskegee Institute, where he had been accepted as a scholarship student. He wanted to write a symphony encompassing his varied experiences. Tuskegee was a trade and teachers' school, and its founder, Booker T. Washington, was an apostle of intellectual conservatism; still, Ellison developed there as a musician. The dean of the music school was William L. Dawson, best known as a skillful arranger of spirituals and as the composer of the *Negro Folk Symphony* (ca. 1932). In the face of deeply entrenched segregation laws and customs, Dawson had built Tuskegee into one of the major music centers of the South. As in high school, Ellison played first trumpet in the school orchestra and, on occasion, served as the band's student director.

He also delved into other arts at Tuskegee. He played a leading role in a campus play and in his third year began to test his powers in painting and photography; between school classes he attended an art class to learn watercolor. The instructor, Eva Hamilton, encouraged Ellison to try sculpture. On his own Ellison discovered T. S. Eliot's "The Waste Land," and the poem deeply engaged him: "I was intrigued by its power to move me while eluding my understanding. . . . There was nothing to do but look up the references in the footnotes to the poem." So, said Ellison, began his conscious study of literature. In 1935, as a "reflex" of his reading, Ellison tried his hand at writing poetry. It was at first "an amusing investigation of what seemed at best a secondary talent . . . like dabbling in sculpture."

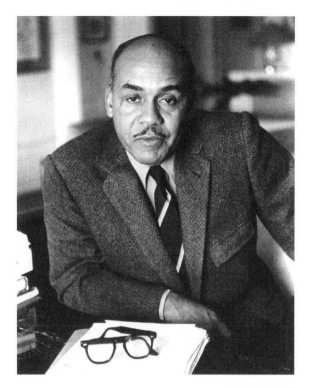

Ralph Ellison

Ellison in New York

Because of a mix-up about his scholarship, at the end of his third year Ellison found that he had neither the forty-dollar tuition fee for the coming term nor any money to live on. He decided to spend the summer of 1936 in New York City, where he thought he could make and save money for the fall more easily than in Alabama. Though she knew that music was his first love—and that his intention was to seek work playing his trumpet—Eva Hamilton was enthusiastic about Ellison's prospects as a sculptor and gave him a letter of introduction to Augusta Savage, the gifted black sculptor in Harlem who had helped to train many artists just coming to town. Fully intending to return to school, Ellison headed north to New York.

Apart from the winter of 1937 spent in Dayton, Ohio, the war years in the merchant marine, and two years (1955–1957) in Rome as a guest of the American Academy of Arts and Letters, Ellison lived in New York City from his arrival there in 1936 until his death in 1994. He was drawn to New York by its glamour and promise of greater freedom. He expected a dazzling fulfillment of "an irrepressible belief in some Mecca of equality." Harlem he supposed to be "a glamorous place, a place where wonderful music existed and where there was a great tradition of Negro American style and elegance."

Harlem was not exactly the promised land heralded by the folklore. Twelve years after coming north, Ellison wrote: "To live in Harlem is to dwell in the very bowels of the city . . . a ruin . . . overcrowded and exploited politically and economically." Black Manhattan he found to be the "scene and symbol of the Negro's perpetual alienation in the land of his birth." Many of the surreal city scenes in Ellison's fiction derive from his attempt to bring into focus the contradictions and confusions actually observed in Harlem.

In the midst of Harlem's fantasticality and turmoil, however, opportunities for personal and artistic growth have abounded. In 1966 Ellison observed that "Harlem was and still *is* a place where a Southern Negro who has a little luck, and who has a little talent, can actually make himself into the man or woman of his dreams."

In 1936, well before World War II (when real estate agents as well as police began to warn whites away from that vast black neighborhood), Harlem was evolving into what James Weldon Johnson called the black American cultural capital, beckoning to artists and intellectuals, black and white. In the 1930s and 1940s Ellison could be found browsing at the Schomburg Library. He would save his nickels and dimes to go to the Savoy Ballroom once or twice a week. Twice a week, often with Langston Hughes, Ellison went to Harlem's Apollo Theater. By 1940 Ellison was going to after-hours hangouts where musicians jammed. "Jazz was part of a total culture, at least among Afro-Americans," said Ellison. And as in Oklahoma City, jazzmen were heroes.

Because he lacked the money for a musicians' union license, and because there was such an abundance of talent in New York, Ellison did not find steady work as a trumpeter. In fact, he performed only once in public: his last engagement as a professional musician was playing the trumpet for a dance recital by Anna Sokolow. But he still wanted to write symphonies and studied for about a year with composer Wallingford Rieger. By the late 1930s, when he became immersed in writing fiction, Ellison laid down his trumpet forever, refusing even to attend concerts for fear of being diverted.

During the Great Depression, finding work of any kind was not easy. At first, still hoping to return to Tuskegee, he worked for almost a year behind the food bar of the Harlem YMCA, where he had a room. Many odd jobs followed, one of the most interesting of which was as substitute receptionist and file clerk for the psychoanalyst Harry Stack Sullivan. That job lasted only a few months, but the experience proved instructive. As he was filing, Ellison would glance through patients' case histories; what he read spurred him to consider again the

importance of dreams, a subject that had interested him as a boy back in Oklahoma, reading Freud. When he began writing fiction and reading authors who employed dreams in their fiction—especially Dostoevsky, who, as Ellison said, "taught the novelist how to use the dream"—the young writer realized how much his stint with Sullivan had shown him.

In 1936 and 1937 Ellison also worked in factories around New York. Later he worked as a freelance photographer and builder of record players and radios. During one series of weeks without work, he slept on the daybed in a friend's living room and on benches in St. Nicholas Park.

In later years Ellison would shrug off his early days of financial instability as the price worth paying to become an artist. For him the point was that not only were the uncertain times part of the writer's fund of usable experience but that despite them his contact with the New York literary world was quickly made. In fact, he had met Langston Hughes quite by chance on his second day in New York. Through Hughes he met Richard Wright, whose poems "I Have Seen Black Hands" and "Between the World and Me" Ellison considered the best ever written by a black writer. Their friendship blossomed. Although Wright was six years older and on the verge of his first major literary success (*Uncle Tom's Children* in 1938), the two were in basically the same predicament: they were radically inclined young black intellectuals with southern backgrounds, trying to survive in New York and struggling to make art in the midst of the Great Depression. They talked endlessly about politics and art, drank, and exchanged jokes and stories.

Wright said candidly that Ellison had started too late to develop into a serious writer, but he was impressed with his friend's ability to discuss literature and urged him to write a short story for *New Challenge*, a leftist literary magazine of which Wright was an editor. Ellison begged off. He was at that time still a musician and lacked writing experience. Wright forced his hand by asking instead for a short review of Waters Edward Turpin's first novel, *These Low*

Grounds. With this review, entitled "Creative and Cultural Lag" (fall 1937), Ellison took the decisive step toward becoming a writer.

When Wright again asked Ellison to write a short story, for the winter 1937 issue of *New Challenge,* Ellison agreed. Drawing on his experience of bumming on trains, he wrote "Hymie's Bull," his first short story. Although heavily derivative of Hemingway, it impressed Wright and got as far as galley proofs. But in the end some new poems by Margaret Walker and others superseded "Hymie's Bull" and the story was dropped. Problems between the other editors led to the magazine's suspension and the winter 1937 issue went unpublished. ("Hymie's Bull" was published posthumously in the 1996 collection, *Flying Home and Other Stories.*)

In February of 1937, Ellison's mother died in Dayton, Ohio. Ida Ellison's death proved a painful initiation into manhood for her son:

I was in my early twenties then, and I had lived through my mother's death in that strange city, had survived three months off the fields and woods by my gun; through ice and snow and homelessness. And now in this windless February instant I had crossed over into a new phase of living. Shall I say it was in those February snows that I first became a man?

Ellison's statement that he survived by his gun through ice, snow, and homelessness is no mere figure of speech. He and his brother both arrived in Dayton almost completely out of money. At night, when the temperature skidded toward zero, they slept in a car parked in a garage open at both ends. They supported themselves by hunting quail, which they either ate or sold to local General Motors executives. Although the Ellison brothers had hunted since childhood, never had it been such a serious enterprise. By reading Hemingway's descriptions of leading a bird in flight, Ellison became an excellent hunter during those lean months. Years later he said of Hemingway, "When he describes something in print, believe him . . . he's been there."

Ellison returned to New York weary and distraught, but one issue was settled: all of his creative energies would be channeled into becoming a good writer.

In Ohio, Ellison had begun writing, as he put it, "in earnest." After hunting all day, he wrote at night and studied James Joyce, Dostoevsky, Gertrude Stein, and Hemingway—"especially Hemingway," he recalled. "I read him to learn his sentence structure and how to organize a story." Ellison began to arrange his life so that writing would be his main focus, "to stake my energy against the possibility of failing." Out of money but determined to continue writing, in 1938 Ellison was hired by the Federal Writers' Project.

Ellison's four-year experience on the project provided $103.50 monthly, enough money to live on and a good deal more. Besides rescuing him from unemployment, the work stocked him with "information and insights about [his] country during a highly formative period of [his] literary life." It also made Ellison aware of being part of a community of writers, black and white, fledgling and established, all trying to perfect their craft.

On the Federal Writers' Project, writers studied folklore and exercised their literary craft transposing the lore into written literature. Ellison collected lore and studied history by day but wrote his own fiction by night. The project inspired some writers' rediscovery of the American vernacular in the 1930s, and in those years Ellison applied his new awareness of language and folklore to the past and to human identity. "The character of a people," he said, "is revealed in their speech." The project's structured examination of language and folklore helped his writing grow beyond the limits of literary realism.

Ellison's Politics

Ellison's increasing maturity as a writer coincided with a gradual shift in his political perspective. During the late 1930s he was an enthusiastic supporter of many Communist Party tenets, but by the mid 1940s he was publicly denouncing the Party. He was first drawn to left-wing politics by his mother's involvement with the Socialist Party in Oklahoma; by his own experience of poverty, segregation, and hard times; and by the impact of such events as the Scottsboro and Herndon cases and the civil war in Spain. André Malraux's political, critical, and fiction writings also affected Ellison profoundly and further stirred in him the prospect of participating in a concerted effort by revolutionary artists, intellectuals, and the people to redeem a world torn by war and depression.

Ellison's friends influenced his leftward progress. Wright was an active member of the Communist Party when they met. Hughes was a charter member of the radical American Writers' Congress and had been writing leftist articles, fiction, and poetry for almost ten years. Though never a member of the Communist Party, Hughes often wrote and spoke on behalf of Party causes.

In the 1930s Ellison joined the chorus of critics calling for realism as the literary mode appropriate for the radical writer. Mirroring the Communist Party position of the day, Ellison's criticism often described black Americans as members of a state or nation (like a Russian soviet) within the United States. The literature of black Americans (the subject of about half of his reviews of the 1930s and 1940s) was, he believed, an emerging national literature that should serve to heighten the revolutionary consciousness of black people. The black writer should instill in his audience not merely "race consciousness" but awareness of class. Ideally, the revolutionary black writer should inspire black working people to unite with workers of other "nationalities" against the bourgeoisie, white and black. From 1937 to 1944 Ellison wrote over twenty book reviews for such radical periodicals as *New Challenge, Direction,* and the *Negro Quarterly;* in 1940 the *New Masses* printed at least one piece by him every month.

While the Great Depression years brought tremendous difficulties, they were also, in Ellison's words, "great times for literature," times for "the conscious writer" to study his society's laws and to examine its citizens' emotions

"stripped naked." Furthermore, the writer could perceive the great American themes of tomorrow shining "beyond the present chaos." The black writer's particular duty was to overcome the handicap of living in racist, capitalist America and to teach his readers to do likewise. His greatest responsibility, said Ellison, echoing Joyce's phrase, was "to create the consciousness of his oppressed nation."

During 1940 and 1941, Ellison published "Stormy Weather" and "Recent Negro Fiction," his longest and most searching critical essays up to that time. They were pioneering works in establishing the creative use of folklore as a touchstone for evaluating black literature.

While reviewing one of Langston Hughes's autobiographies, *The Big Sea,* what Ellison found missing was a certain kind of overtly intellectual presence, a "conscious hero" who could not only report travels and times but who could critically analyze them. This need for a conscious hero was a key theme of Ellison's. In 1942, reviewing William Attaway's *Blood on the Forge* for the *Negro Quarterly,* Ellison again lamented the absence of a conscious heroic presence. While he commended the author's presentation of southern "folk" blacks as harried and even destroyed in the concrete mazes of the urban North, Ellison also pointed out that the artistic vision was incomplete without the inclusion of characters whose consciousness was reborn in the North:

Conceptually, Attaway grasped the destruction of the folk, but missed its rebirth on a higher level. The writer did not see that while the folk individual was being liquidated in the crucible of steel, he was also undergoing fusion with new elements. Nor did Attaway see that the individual which emerged, blended of old and new, was better fitted for the problems of the industrial environment. As a result the author is so struck by the despair in his material that he fails to see any ground for hope in his characters. Yet hope is there.

Later, in "Flying Home" (1944), "King of the Bingo Game" (1944), and *Invisible Man* (1952),

Ellison would present his own black protagonists threatened with liquidation in modern industrial society. His heroes' resiliency, memory, and luck, however, help them to "fuse" with "new elements" in their environment; they are "reborn" better able to deal with the churning world of airplanes and factories. In 1948 Ellison described the bemused protagonist of *Invisible Man*, which he was then writing, as "a character who possesses both the eloquence and the insight into the interconnections between his own personality and the world about him to make a judgment about our culture." Ellison's early desire for conscious heroes in American writing foreshadowed his eventual break with many of his literary and political friends, including Wright.

In his literary essays of the early 1940s, Ellison championed Wright as living testimony to the shining possibilities within the black community. Against all odds, Wright had made himself into a highly conscious activist and writer. But despite Ellison's admiration for his mentor, and despite Wright's encouragement (he inscribed a copy of *Uncle Tom's Children* "To Ralph, who I hope will someday write a better book than this"), by 1940 a degree of "anxiety of influence" afflicted the friendship. Ellison's early fiction style so resembled Wright's that Wright protested. Upon seeing one short-story manuscript, Wright exclaimed, "Hey, that's my stuff!" Ellison deliberately left the piece unpublished, like most of his exercises of the period, and afterward he never showed Wright any work in progress. "You might say," Ellison later commented, that in this awkward scene Wright "influenced me *not* to be influenced by him."

In 1944, when Ellison's disagreement with radical American leftists was already strong, the war policies of the American Communist Party impelled Ellison and many other blacks to leave the organized Left entirely. When the Party lent what Ellison called its "shamefaced support" to segregation in the armed forces, many blacks became bitterly disillusioned with the radicals' vaunted goodwill toward minorities.

The Party blundered in ignoring the fact that "little Hitlers" (white racists and racist policies) plagued blacks at home; for blacks the war against fascism had to continue on the home front as well as overseas. When the Party attacked this position as "narrowly nationalistic," it seemed to Ellison that Soviet foreign policy moved the American Communist Party more than did the plight of its local black members. Party leaders often suffered from what Gunnar Myrdal called "the American dilemma." In Ellison's words:

the Party had inherited the moral problem centering upon the Negro. . . . For in our culture the problem of the irrational, that blind spot in our knowledge of society where Marx cries out for Freud and Freud for Marx, but where approaching, both grow wary and shout insults lest they actually meet, has taken the form of the Negro problem.

In *Invisible Man*, the protagonist's decision to renounce his wholehearted support for the Brotherhood is based on his discovery that the radical group is cynically self-serving and, ultimately, racist. The Brotherhood sacrifices Harlem's interests for the sake of "international" goals and tries to mold the Invisible Man into their conception of the Good Negro: one passively willing to use his energy and his art (which is his oratory) exactly as the party commands. In the novel the Brotherhood stands, to a large extent, for the American Communist Party. But Ellison also wanted the Brotherhood to be seen in a larger context: the Party was not the only group of white American political activists to betray their black countrymen for narrow political ends.

Short Stories

The years 1939 to 1944 were years of apprenticeship for Ellison who, in a *New York Post* feature story of 1943, was identified as "a short story writer." He published eight stories during this period, and his writing grew in eloquence and complexity from one work to the next. He wrote many more stories than he tried to publish, looking upon some as exercises. *Flying Home and Other Stories* brings together six published and six unpublished works from that period (as well as one story from 1956, "A Coupla Scalped Indians") and effectively presents an account of Ellison's early development as a writer.

As we might expect, his first short stories, "Slick Gonna Learn" (1939) and "The Birthmark" (1940), were in the realistic mode and highlighted the jagged edges of the black American environment. These stories offer explicitly political resolutions. But as early as 1940, as Ellison began to draw upon his Oklahoma City background, his vision was not so much that of a political realist as of a regionalist: his first Buster and Riley stories, "Afternoon" (1940), "Mister Toussan" (1941), and "That I Had the Wings" (1943), explored the language, folklore, and unique features of a Southwestern town as seen by two curious and daring black boys. "In a Strange Country" (1944) is a transitional wartime story, important because of its heightened technical complexity. Here, too, an Ellison protagonist first declares his ineradicable Americanness as well as his empowering blackness. Three of the posthumously published stories from this early period—"I Did Not Learn Their Names," "A Hard Time Keeping Up," and "The Black Ball"—significantly foreshadow that declaration.

The final two stories published in the early 1940s, "Flying Home" and "King of the Bingo Game," are more than mere apprentice pieces. In these works the young fiction writer discovers his own surrealistic voice and manages to integrate folklore, ritual, politics, history, and an absurdist vision of American experience in a way that may be termed "Ellisonian." These important early stories center on the individual's struggle to cope with a world that has become machine-mad; in both works a black protagonist struggles to confront the question, who am I?

In 1943 Ellison joined the merchant marine, in part because he had belonged to the National Maritime Union since 1936, when he picketed for the union, but mainly because he "wanted to contribute to the war, but didn't want to be in a Jim Crow army." While still in the service, Ellison was awarded a Rosenwald Fellowship to write a novel. In fact, he already had one outlined: a wartime story in which a black pilot is shot down, captured by the Nazis, and placed in a detention camp. In the camp he is the highest-ranking officer, pitted by his Nazi guards against the white prisoners. Ellison continued working on this novel even after he began *Invisible Man* in 1945. But it never achieved enough unity to satisfy him, and only one section, "Flying Home," was published.

Constructed as a story within a story, "Flying Home" deals with two thwarted flights: that of the black pilot Todd, whose plane collides with a buzzard and crashes in a field in Macon County, and that of Jefferson, who comes to Todd's rescue and who in his "tale told for true" sails from heaven back to the hell of Alabama. Jefferson's uproarious folktale, cataloged by collectors as early as 1919 (listed by the folklorist Richard Dorson as "Colored Man in Heaven"), eases the pain of Todd's injured ankle and his wait for a doctor's help. It also serves an initiatory function for this starry-eyed greenhorn, who, like Jefferson's heavenly flier, must eventually confront the evils of Jim Crow Alabama, however high he has flown. In this brilliantly layered story (which nods to the swing instrumental of the same name and period), various other folk motifs direct the young pilot on his looping homeward flight.

The last story Ellison published before he began to work full time on *Invisible Man* was "King of the Bingo Game." The King is Ellison's first protagonist to witness so directly the frightening surrealism of everyday American life. It is in a wildly imagistic realm, where past and present, dreaming and waking converge, that the King, like the Invisible Man, sees the visions that spell a deepened consciousness, if not salvation. This black southerner sees that life in the urban North is madly unpredictable and that random luck determines much that is known as fate. This being so, the King feels that he must subvert the process that has made losers of him and his generations. His unwillingness to stop turning the bingo wheel suggests this will to subversion. Refusing to play it straight in the game he has been fated to lose, he discovers who he is: "He was reborn. For as long as he pressed the button he was Theman-who-pressed-the-button-who-had-the-prize-who-was-the-King-of-Bingo." Like Invisible Man, King frees himself when he discovers that he has been a sleepwalker, a fool who is naive enough to accept the judgments handed down by an indifferent bingo wheel—of circumstance, of history, of fate. The instant before he is run off the stage, he *is* in control of his fate. Moreover, he is symbolically reborn, as he says, a new person better able to deal with the modern world's absurd turnings. Before the curtain is rung down on him, he hears the taunting laughter in the theater but, foreshadowing *Invisible Man's* Trueblood, King says, "Well, let 'em laugh. I'll do what I gotta do."

Invisible Man

In 1945, exhausted by hard work and by a grueling merchant marine voyage, and hopeless over the unfinished war novel, Ellison went to recuperate at a friend's farm in Wakesfield, Vermont. He had been reading Lord Ragian's *The Hero*, a study of historical and mythic heroes, and had been thinking about leadership in the African American community. Why, he wondered, did black leaders so often seem uncommitted to their black constituents? Why did they so often seem dependent not on the will of blacks but on the largess of white patrons? Along with these questions, Ellison was pondering a number of others—and, overall, the persistent problem of finding a literary form flexible enough to contain his vision of the wild and shifting American hodgepodge of cultures and characters. He determined to write a novel about black identity, heroism, and history, and to write it in a style "unburdened by . . . narrow naturalism."

One morning in 1945, still in Vermont, Ellison scribbled the words, "I am an invisible man"—his novel's first sentence. He recalled that he played with the idea and

> started to reject it, but it intrigued me, and I began to put other things with it. And pretty soon I had a novel going, and I began to work out a conceptual outline on it. And as fast as I could work out the concepts, the incidents started flowing in on me.

Back in New York, Ellison continued work on the novel in his apartment on St. Nicholas Avenue, but he also went downtown every morning to work like any businessman. Using a friend's Fifth Avenue office, he put in at least eight hours a day writing before returning home.

The project was blessed with the support of Ellison's wife, Fanny McConnell, of whom he wrote, "my beloved wife . . . has shown, again and again, through her sacrifices, encouragement and love, more faith in the writer and his talent than the writer has shown in himself." The two met in 1944 and were married in July 1946.

He worked on *Invisible Man* for five years, taking one year off to work on another novel. *Invisible Man* was published in 1952. To many critics the novel seemed like a miraculous first work. But Ellison's first published fiction, "Slick Gonna Learn," and possibly "The Birthmark," had been conceived as part of a novel that he then abandoned. By the 1940s, with "Flying Home" and "King of the Bingo Game," he had discovered a voice and a set of questions and concerns that were timeless but were his own. The sentence "I am an invisible man" started him on a work into which he could pour all he had learned as an apprentice perfecting his craft.

With the publication of *Invisible Man*, Ellison moved suddenly into the front ranks of American writers. His novel evokes visions and tensions peculiar to American life as African Americans know it: Ellison's brown-skinned, nameless seeker suffers and scoots, forth and back, through a thicket of briars well known to American blacks. Yet *Invisible Man* is a modern masterpiece that, as Wright Morris has written, "belongs on the shelf with the classical efforts man has made to chart the river Lethe from its mouth to its sources." Richly expressing the meaning of life in Harlem (and the southern background of that life), Ellison manages to describe what he says he finds in the work of the painter Romare Bearden: "The harlemness of the human condition." *Invisible Man* is a deeply comic novel, with moments of terror and tragedy; it is a bildungsroman in which a young man awakens to consciousness by piecing together fragments and symbols from history, myth, folklore, and literature, as well as his own painful experience.

Set in the approximate period 1930–1950, *Invisible Man* is the story of the development of an ambitious young black man from the provinces of the South, who goes to college and then to New York in search of advancement. This greenhorn at first wants no more than to walk in the footsteps of Booker T. Washington, whose words he quotes at his high school graduation and at a smoker for the town's leading white citizens. At the smoker he is given a new briefcase and a scholarship—emblems of his expected ascent up the social hierarchy. But first he is required to fight blindfolded in a battle royal with other black youths.

This battle-royal scene shows the protagonist to be not just blind but invisible. Obviously, the white town bosses see him not as an individual of promise but as a buffoonish entertainer, a worthless butt of their practical jokes, or, at best, a good colored boy who seems to know his place. The youngster's invisibility also consists of his trust in the myth of advancement, American style. This confidence that he will rise to success (reminiscent of Horatio Alger and Booker T. Washington) renders him willing and eager to suppress his own will and words—his own identity—to be whatever they say he must be to get ahead.

That night he dreams that his grandfather tells him to open the briefcase, which contains a document reading: "To Whom It May Concern, Keep This Nigger-Boy Running." But the youngster remains naive. He goes off to college but is expelled when he makes the fatal mistake of taking a visiting white trustee to a section of the local black community (and, metaphorically, to a level of black reality) never included in the college-town tour. Bledsoe, the college president, sends the hero packing to New York, first giving him a set of private letters of introduction that, he finally discovers, also courteously request that he be kept running—and jobless.

Eventually he does find work in New York, first in a paint factory, where he is discharged after being seriously hurt in an explosion—one that ultimately jars him into a new self-awareness and courage. He gives a moving speech at the eviction of an elderly Harlem couple and is hired by a predominantly white radical political organization called the Brotherhood. The group seems to confirm his childhood wish by telling him he will be made the "new Booker T. Washington . . . even greater than he." But the Brotherhood also sets him running. Despite his success in Harlem, the downtown "brothers" withdraw support for his program.

Why do they sell our hero out? First of all, because he has proven so successful with his uses of such vernacular forms as marching bands and stump speeches that the "scientific" Brotherhood fears that he, and the black community at large, have become dangerously independent in their power. The second, even more cynical, motive here involves Invisible Man's having performed his mission of stirring up Harlem; now, withdrawn from the community, he can perform the Brotherhood's other task of discouraging his followers so that they turn against not only him but also each other. He and the other Harlem leaders are set up to reenact the action of the blindfolded fighters of the novel's first chapter: to self-destruct while the white bosses, this time wearing the colors of the radical Left, protect their power from a safe distance.

A race riot erupts, and, still carrying his briefcase, he falls down a manhole into an abandoned, bricked-up cellar. There he closely examines the mementos in his briefcase and realizes how fully he has been betrayed by those who had professed to help him. And yet he discovers, too, that not only "could you travel upward toward success but you could travel downwards as well." He will remain down there, bathed in stolen light from the power company and in blues-idiom music; he will compose his memoirs in his hole at the edge of Harlem, in hibernation. "Please, a definition: A hibernation is a covert preparation for a more overt action." If others cannot or will not see him, he at least will see himself. His narrative, full of irony, insight, and fury, shows that he has attained full self-awareness—even a certain wisdom—and that he has been able to act, to write this stunning book.

The shape and style of *Invisible Man* bespeak its determination to step toward the universal through "the narrow door of the particular." The novel resounds with black folklore, in which, wrote Ellison,

> we tell what Negro experience really is. We back away from the chaos of experience and from ourselves, and we depict the humor as well as the horror of our living. We project Negro life in a metaphysical perspective, and we have seen it with a complexity of vision that seldom gets into our writing.

Blues, spirituals, sermons, tales, boasts, and other black American folk forms influence the characters, plot, and figurative language in this teeming novel.

The novel is built not only upon the foundation of black lore but also of black literature. It is a benchmark black novel that seems aware of the entire tradition of African American letters. In it one overhears the black and white tricksters (slaves and slaveholders) of slave narrative locked in combat. One senses again the slave's desperate yearning for education, mobility, and individual and communal freedom. There are particularly strong echoes of works by Frederick Douglass, W. E. B. Du Bois, James Weldon Johnson, Zora Neale Hurston, and Richard Wright, all of whom wrote prose portraits of tragicomic characters, "articulate heroes" in search of broader freedom.

But the power of *Invisible Man* is more than that of a repository of black influences. As if in defiance of the single-minded critic, Ellison adapted symbolism and rhetorical strategies from any and every source he felt would enrich the texture and meaning of his work: Sophocles, Homer, Dostoevsky, Malraux, Joyce, and Freud all figure in *Invisible Man.* Some allusions and symbol clusters fade out like wistful jazz riffs; others recur and provide the novel with structure. But no single critical "method" can explain this capacious novel, which owes as much to the symbolist tradition of Herman Melville and Nathaniel Hawthorne as it does to the vernacular tradition of Mark Twain and Hemingway. This is not a "realistic" novel or an understated "hard-boiled" novel, or a symbolist romance (it is not, in any case, to be *only* so categorized); instead, it is an epic novel of many voices, an experimental narrative constructed upon the author's mastery of American language: as he described it, a

> rich babel . . . a language full of imagery and gesture and rhetorical canniness . . . an alive language swirling with over three hundred years of American living, a mixture of the folk, the Biblical, the scientific, and the political. Slangy in one instance, academic in another, loaded poetically with imagery at one moment, mathematically bare of imagery in the next.

The Invisible Man embodies this confluence of traditions. He is a modern Odysseus, a latter-day Candide, a "black boy" comparable to Wright, a black and obscure Jude, a Yankee yokel, a minstrel endman.

Invisible Man is a complex and richly comic novel in which the hero discovers a great deal about American history and culture. In the end he sees that he has been a fool, that he must confront chaos with strength and resiliency—and mother wit—or it will engulf him. When he plunges underground, he vows to stop running the course that Bledsoe and others had set for him.

Ellison's next book after *Invisible Man* was the excellent collection of essays *Shadow and Act* (1964). Its initial appeal seemed to be that in it the "invisible" author would at last emerge from underground: here, as one reviewer proclaimed, was Ralph Ellison's "real autobiography." And *Shadow and Act* does contain autobiographical essays, notably its introduction and "Hidden Name and Complex Fate"; in the book's collected reviews, interviews, and journal pieces the author also draws extensively upon his own experience. Because the essays (none retouched) were written over a twenty-two-year period, they reveal certain aspects of his development from the twenty-eight-year-old, Marxist-oriented Works Progress Administration (WPA) worker of "The Way It Is" (1942) to the seasoned writer of 1964: by the latter date he is not "primarily concerned with injustice, but with art."

Shadow and Act has enduring validity as a unified work of art because of its author's single-minded intention to define the fullness (not just the pain) of African American life. Ellison sometimes gently punctures, sometimes wields an ax against, inadequate definitions of black experience. In place of what he detects as false prophecy, usually uttered by social scientists, he chooses as broad a frame of reference as possible to interpret black experience in richly optimistic terms. "Who wills to be a Negro?" he asks, rhetorically. "I do!"

Juneteenth

Once Ellison had released the galley proofs for *Invisible Man*, he felt emotionally and artistically spent. But he had begun jotting down ideas for a new novel even before *Invisible Man* was published, so that if it failed, he would be too busy to worry. In 1952 he said he had a new novel "on the bench." In 1953, shortly after the National Book Award ceremonies honoring *Invisible Man*, he suggested that his new novel might be an elaboration of the first. "I don't feel that I have exhausted the theme of invisibility," he said. Indeed, he felt that he could salvage some material edited out of the several drafts of the novel. "Out of the Hospital and Under the Bar" (1953), an early version of a chapter in *Invisible Man*, works well as a short story, not as a mere clipping from the larger work; "Did You Ever Dream Lucky?" (1954) concerns Mary Rambo, the novel's Harlem landlady. As early as 1953, however, Ellison had begun laying the structural framework for a totally new novel that he felt sure would be much better and more complex than *Invisible Man*. From then until his death in 1994, Ellison stoked the fires of this new novel—or the second of what he planned to be a trilogy of novels, as it turned out. The work's eight published sections, along with sections read on public television and on

college campuses, made the wait for the finished volumes something of a vigil.

In 1965 Ellison told an interviewer that he wanted to publish a book "in the coming year," adding, "so the pressure's on." Yet the novel never appeared in his lifetime. When he was at all willing to discuss its progress, Ellison recited the history of a wayward work, tedious in the initial construction and reconstruction; destroyed, in part, by fire; bedeviling in the re-reconstruction. After 1977, Ellison refused to publish more selections from the trilogy's then current manuscripts not only because he was "not so strapped for money that I have to publish those pieces" but also because he wanted "the impact of the total book . . . rather than the published pieces." "Can you say when it will be finished?" an interviewer inquired in 1978. "No," responded Ellison. "I've done that too many times and been wrong."

The writing slowed to a baffled halt, for a time, after the hail of assassinations in the 1960s—John F. Kennedy, Martin Luther King, Malcolm X, Robert Kennedy. With the assassination attempt of a major political figure, Senator Adam Sunraider, as the story's central incident, the eruption of real killings "chilled" Ellison, for "suddenly life was stepping in and imposing himself upon my fiction."

That Ellison was far out of step with the most vocal black ideologists of the 1960s also showed in his writing. When Haki Madhubuti (Don L. Lee), Amiri Baraka (LeRoi Jones), and other black writers and social critics were asserting the national identity and the Africanness of black Americans, Ellison stiffly dissented: "I'm not a separatist. The imagination is integrative. That's how you make the new— by putting something else with what you've got. And I'm unashamedly an American integrationist." At Oberlin College in April 1969, Ellison was given a chilly reception by black students, one of whom complained: "His speech was about how American black culture had blended into American white culture."

At Harvard in December 1973, Ellison spoke about the philosopher Alain Locke as a champion of American pluralism. By then the mood on campus had changed. There were awkward silences when Ellison told the gathering that blacks are not an African people but an American one; yet the final applause was enthusiastic. At that point Ellison appeared to have weathered the radical tempest. By 1980 he could look back on these difficult days with irony, defensive pride, and some anger.

As Richard Kostelanetz explained, "One reason Ellison has not been able to complete his second novel is that all these distractions demand so much of his attention, as much to flush the ideological junk out of his own head as to speak about corruption in the social world." Black writers, Kostelanetz comments, seem to have a harder role to play than do white writers because blacks are cornered into commenting on sociopolitical issues that white writers can more easily ignore.

As if these deflections were not enough, in the late 1960s Ellison's summer home in Massachusetts was destroyed by fire, as were 365 pages of the new novel, an entire year's revisions. "I assure you, that's a most traumatic experience," he recalled, "one of the most traumatic of my life." The writer Jervis Anderson has noted: "Perhaps nothing more painful occurred in the working life of a well-known writer since Thomas Carlyle lost the manuscript of the first volume of his history of the French Revolution, a servant in the home of John Stuart Mill having used it to help get a fire going."

While continuing to work on his second novel, Ellison published *Going to the Territory* (1986), a superb gathering of occasional pieces—including personal and cultural essays along with transcribed speeches and an interview—that appeared from 1957 to 1986. As in *Shadow and Act*, blues and jazz provide the book's most vital metaphors. Using language that dances with the inventive energy of a Duke Ellington composition (with both the historical and the created characters taking word solos that at times recall the spirit of Louis Armstrong), Ellison makes his case that it is above all on the level of vernacular culture that the possibility of America being a true "melting pot" was actually fulfilled. And in the irresistible sound of blues and jazz, with their swinging patterns

of give-and-take, one-and-many, call-and-recall, Americans may discover shining examples of what it means to be resilient, daring, free, and yet technically trained enough to face "the territory"—those areas of American life yet to be explored.

Ellison had only recently celebrated his eightieth birthday when he died of pancreatic cancer in New York City on April 16, 1994. Since then, it has been the task of the literary executor of his estate, John F. Callahan, to decide how best to produce the wealth of writings Ellison left behind. Callahan published *The Collected Essays of Ralph Ellison* in 1995, bringing together *Shadow and Act*, *Going to the Territory*, and a number of essays that had previously appeared only in journals, as well as nine works that had never before been published. In 1996, Callahan introduced *Flying Home and Other Stories*, the collection of Ellison's early fiction.

In his 1999 introduction to Ellison's long-awaited second novel, Callahan cautiously asserts, "I think Ellison might have called [this book] *Juneteenth*." Callahan appended a series of the author's notes to *Juneteenth*, the last of which further emphasizes the editor's caution: Ellison wrote, "Incompletion of form allows the reader to impose his own imagination upon the material with too little control from the author. Thus I don't like to show my work until it is near completion." While keeping the reader in mind of his hesitations over publishing Ellison's unfinished work, Callahan attests that *Juneteenth* is indeed "an all but complete novel" with an "organic unity." Most of it, in fact, was finished by the early 1970s; four excerpts were published as separate stories during the 1960s. While the work remains unfinished in that *Juneteenth* is only the second of what Ellison intended to be a trilogy, this second book comprises the "heart" of the trilogy, according to Callahan, in that it tells the story of its two central characters, Hickman and Bliss.

The Reverend Alonzo Hickman—also known as "God's Trombone"—ranks among Ellison's richest creations. An old and revered black preacher in the novel's present (set just prior to the beginning of the Civil Rights movement), the Reverend Hickman was a blues musician before Bliss's arrival turned him into an evangelist. Bliss's mother was a white woman who falsely accused Hickman's brother, Robert, of raping her; in order to conceal the real father's identity, she had Robert lynched. She then gave the baby to Hickman, which the novel recounts in a harrowing flashback. Hickman named him Bliss, *"because they say that's what ignorance is.* Yes, and little did I realize that it was the name of the old heathen life I had already lost."

Bliss constitutes a large part of Hickman's Christian mission: the precocious boy-preacher carries his adoptive father's hopes for breaking down America's racial divide. Yet instead of becoming a powerful political and religious leader who champions racial equality, Bliss abandons his calling, disappears, passes for white, and emerges as the venomously antiblack Senator Adam Sunraider. In a characteristic mixture of allusions, Bliss becomes Sunraider or "Sunrobber," the fatally proud Adam (replete with wounded heel) of the Biblical fall from grace, as well as the heroic Prometheus of Greek myth. Yet this Prometheus, Sunrobber, is more like Icarus and so more like Adam: "Not fire, oh no, that wasn't what Man was yelling about, he wanted the Sun!"

The double-edged emblem of Bliss's extraordinary capacity for rebirth and renewal is the white coffin that terrifies the child and haunts the senator he created. For Hickman, having the boy seem to rise up from the dead like Lazarus out of a coffin to preach at tent revivals is "the art of saving souls" and not "just a bag of tricks." Either way, for Bliss, enduring the coffin is torture. He learns isolation as well as power as a regularly entombed and resurrected child evangelist who can "bring a big man to tears" and whose precocity earns more distance than respect from other boys. At a tent revival celebration of Juneteenth (the commemoration of June 19, 1865, when Union troops brought news of freedom to slaves in Galveston, Texas), Bliss begins to reject his power and especially his isolation as he realizes Hickman's powerlessness in a racist society as well as the possibility that he might not, after all, be an orphan.

Bliss ultimately fails to find his mother and exacts vengeance on his predicament by taking on a more extreme form of power and isolation as Senator Sunraider. For Hickman, identity is composed of a kind of moral commitment, something that connects people to one another, which is why Abraham Lincoln was "one of us." Bliss rather embraces what he knows to be a false but powerful identity at the cost of disconnecting himself from people—emblematized in a recurring dream/nightmare in which he recalls falling in love with and yet deciding to leave Laly, a young black woman he met during a stint as a cross-country filmmaker. He could not fit Laly into his plans to become a white politician, so like Icarus, he gave up everything for the sake of power and freedom.

Where *Invisible Man* is picaresque, *Juneteenth* is more lyrical, its images and narrative strategies echoing Joyce and William Faulkner especially. Structurally, the novel alludes primarily to the prodigal son parable: it opens with the father, Daddy Hickman, searching for his lost son, Bliss; but the son turns back to seek his father only after an assassination attempt threatens his life. Most of the novel takes place as a conversation between the two—often composed of silent recollections or imagined dialogues they never directly communicate to each other—in Senator Sunraider's hospital room. *Juneteenth* draws on a wide range of vernacular traditions, including jazz, blues, film, and sermons, but perhaps above all the antiphonal call-and-response of the black church. Sometimes this call-and-response pattern is so tight that Ellison eschews the quotation marks that would distinguish Bliss's voice from Hickman's, as in a flashback to their early days preaching together when Hickman all but ventriloquizes through the boy. Other times, the separation underlying even their team preaching rises to the fore, and the conversation continues only through each one's unspoken memories; nevertheless the rhythm remains.

Characteristically for Ellison, that rhythm thrives on subtle infusions of wry humor throughout. In Hickman's words, "It was like a riddle or a joke, but if so, it was the Lord's joke and I was playing it straight. And maybe that's what a preacher really is, he's the Lord's own straight man."

The novel begins with Hickman searching for Bliss and ends with Bliss hearing "the sound of Hickman's consoling voice," a voice that seems to symbolize "that vanished tribe" to whom Ellison dedicated *Juneteenth:* "The American Negroes." Yet we have much to learn from both sides of this conversation. Just as we never learn Bliss's racial lineage, we also never learn whether he survives the assassination attempt or whether the prodigal son and Daddy Hickman fully reconcile. Such facile and questionable resolutions are in the end less vital because less instructive than the call-and-response rhythm of the story they tell together, itself a metaphor for what Ellison described as the project of "helping this country discover a fuller sense of itself as it goes about making its founders' dreams a reality": "Keep to the rhythm and you'll keep to life."

While some of Ellison's detractors charge that he doted on the complexity of American experience in order to avoid speaking out against simple injustice, that he hid behind the grand banner of high art rather than "telling it like it is," he, in fact, believed in the reality of the American melting pot and that blacks are as American—in some ways more so—as any Johnny Appleseed. This conviction, some critics say, obscures the fact that African Americans constitute a distinctive group with particular strengths as well as special troubles. As for Ellison's "complexity," it is part and parcel of his discipline as a writer. Ellison told a Harvard gathering in 1973: "All of us are part white, and all of y'all are part colored." The novelist also insisted on the cruel and tragic aspects of American comedy, on the blues side of black religion, on the upper-class elegance of the black poor, on the universality of what Ellison continued throughout his life to call "Negro" experience, and on the "harlemness" of the human condition.

In Ellison's work one finds penetrating and yet lyrical descriptions of black life, an insider's rare perceptions of the contour and meaning of a peculiarly American experience. Very great, nonetheless, was Ellison's sense of America's

confusion and of the bleakly tragic barriers (underrated by most conservatives, liberals, and revolutionaries alike) against which we all struggle. Great, too, was his faith in America's possibility of redemption and his awareness of the difficulty of securing true redemption from that most American sin, vanity. "Remember," he told a graduating class in 1974, "that the antidote to *hubris,* to overweening pride, is irony, that capacity to discover and systematize ideas. Or, as Emerson insisted, "the development of consciousness, consciousness, *Consciousness.* And with consciousness, a more refined conscientiousness, and most of all, that tolerance which takes the form of humor." With his unfailing humor and tragic awareness, Ralph Ellison was an important voice in American fiction, a "man of good hope" whose work embodied his dedication to artistic craft and to the idea that writers are among America's most vital nation-builders.

[The preceding article is a revised and updated version of the author's work that originally appeared in *American Writers Supplement II* (1981).]

Selected Bibliography

PRIMARY WORKS

BOOKS

Invisible Man. New York: Random House, 1952 (30th Anniversary Edition [with a new introduction by the author], 1982).
Shadow and Act. New York: Random House, 1964.
Going to the Territory. New York: Random House, 1986.
The Collected Essays of Ralph Ellison. Edited by John F. Callahan. New York: Random House, 1995.
Flying Home and Other Stories. Edited by John F. Callahan. New York: Random House, 1996.
Juneteenth. Edited by John F. Callahan. New York: Random House, 1999.

UNCOLLECTED SHORT FICTION

"Slick Gonna Learn." *Direction* 2:10–11, 14, 16 (1939).
"The Birthmark." *New Masses* 36:16–17 (1940).
"Did You Ever Dream Lucky?" *New World Writing* 5:134–45 (1954).
"It Always Breaks Out." *Partisan Review* 30:13–28 (Spring 1963).
"Out of the Hospital and Under the Bar." In *Soon, One Morning.* Edited by Herbert Hill. New York: Knopf, 1963. Pp. 242–90.

"A Song of Innocence." *Iowa Review* 1:30–40 (Spring 1970).

"Cadillac Flambé." *American Review* 16:249–69 (1973).

"Backwacking, a Plea to the Senator." *Massachusetts Review* 18:411–16 (Autumn 1977).

SELECTED ESSAYS, REVIEWS, AND INTERVIEWS

"Creative and Cultural Lag." *New Challenge* 2:90–91 (Fall 1937).

"Stormy Weather." *New Masses* 37:20–21 (1940).

"Recent Negro Fiction." *New Masses* 40:22–26 (1941).

"Collaborator with His Own Enemy." *New York Times Book Review*, February 19, 1950, p. 4.

"Harlem's America." *New Leader* 49:22–35 (1966).

Graham, Maryemma, and Amritjit Singh, eds. *Conversations with Ralph Ellison*. Jackson: University Press of Mississippi, 1995.

SECONDARY WORKS

BIOGRAPHICAL AND CRITICAL STUDIES

Adell, Sandra. "The Big E(llison)'s Texts and Intertexts: Eliot, Burke, and the Underground Man." *CLA Journal* 37, no. 4:377–401 (June 1994).

Allen, Caffilene. "The World as Possibility: The Significance of Freud's *Totem and Taboo* in Ellison's *Invisible Man*." *Literature and Psychology* 41, no. 1–2:1–18 (1995).

Benston, Kimberly W. "Ellison, Baraka and the Faces of Tradition." *boundary* 2, no. 6:333–54 (Winter 1978).

———, ed. *Speaking for You: The Vision of Ralph Ellison*. Washington, D.C.: Howard University Press, 1987.

Blake, Susan L. "Ritual and Rationalization: Black Folklore in the Works of Ralph Ellison." *PMLA* 94:121–36 (1979).

Bloom, Harold, ed. *Ralph Ellison: Modern Critical Views*. New York: Chelsea House, 1986.

Busby, Mark. *Ralph Ellison*. Washington, D.C.: Howard University Press, 1991.

Callaloo 18, no. 2:249–320 (Spring 1995). Special section: "Remembering Ralph Ellison."

The Carleton Miscellany 18, no. 3:1–237 (Winter 1980). Special Ellison issue.

CLA Journal 13:217–320 (1970). Special Ellison issue.

Covo, Jacqueline. *The Blinking Eye: Ralph Waldo Emerson and His American, French, German, and Italian Critics, 1952–1971*. Metuchen, N.J.: Scarecrow Press, 1974.

Delta (Paris) 18:1–131 (April 1984). Special Ellison issue.

Eichelberger, Julia. *Prophets of Recognition: Ideology and the Individual in Novels by Ralph Ellison, Toni Morrison, Saul Bellow, and Eudora Welty*. Baton Rouge: Louisiana State University Press, 1999.

Ford, Douglas. "Crossroads and Cross-Currents in *Invisible Man*." *Modern Fiction Studies* 45, no. 4:887–904 (Winter 1999).

Hersey, John, ed. *Ralph Ellison, a Collection of Critical Essays*. Englewood Cliffs, N.J.: Prentice-Hall, 1974.

Hoberek, Andrew. "Race Man, Organization Man, Invisible Man." *Modern Language Quarterly* 59, no. 1:99–119 (March 1998).

Kim, Daniel Y. "Invisible Desires: Homoerotic Racism and Its Homophobic Critique in Ralph Ellison's *Invisible Man*." *Novel* 30, no. 3:309–28 (Spring 1997).

Kostelanetz, Richard. "Ralph Ellison: Novelist as Brown Skinned Aristocrat." *Shenandoah* 20:56–77 (Summer 1969).

List, Robert N. *Dedalus in Harlem: The Joyce-Ellison Connection*. Washington, D.C.: University Press of America, 1982.

Lynch, Michael F. *Creative Revolt: A Study of Wright, Ellison, and Dostoevsky*. New York: Peter Lang, 1990.

Lyons, Eleanor. "Ellison and the Twentieth-Century American Scholar." *Studies in American Fiction* 17, no. 1:93–106 (Spring 1989).

Marvin, Thomas F. "Children of Legba: Musicians at the Crossroads in Ralph Ellison's *Invisible Man*." *American Literature* 68, no. 3:587–608 (September 1996).

McSweeney, Kerry. *"Invisible Man": Race and Identity*. Boston: Twayne, 1988.

Nadel, Alan. *Invisible Criticism: Ralph Ellison and the American Canon*. Iowa City: University of Iowa Press, 1988.

O'Meally, Robert G. *The Craft of Ralph Ellison*. Cambridge, Mass.: Harvard University Press, 1980.

———. "On Burke and the Vernacular: Ralph Ellison's Boomerang of History." In *History and Memory in African-American Culture*. Edited by Genevieve Fabre and Robert O'Meally. New York: Oxford University Press, 1994. Pp. 244–60.

———, ed. *New Essays on "Invisible Man."* New York: Cambridge University Press, 1988.

Parr, Susan Resneck, and Pancho Savery, eds. *Approaches to Teaching Ellison's "Invisible Man."* New York: Modern Language Association, 1989.

Reilly, John M., ed. *Twentieth Century Interpretations of "Invisible Man": A Collection of Essays*. Englewood Cliffs, N.J.: Prentice-Hall, 1970.

Schor, Edith. *Visible Ellison: A Study of Ralph Ellison's Fiction*. Westport, Conn.: Greenwood, 1993.

Schultz, Elizabeth A. "The Illumination of Darkness: Affinities Between *Moby Dick* and *Invisible Man*." *CLA Journal* 32:170–200 (1988).

Stanford, Ann Folwell. "He Speaks for Whom? Inscription and Reinscription of Women in *Invisible Man* and *The Salt Eaters*." *MELUS* 18, no. 2:17–31 (Summer 1993).

Steele, Meili. "Metatheory and the Subject of Democracy in the Work of Ralph Ellison." *New Literary History* 27, no. 3:473–502 (Summer 1996).

Stephens, Gregory. *On Racial Frontiers: The New Culture of Frederick Douglass, Ralph Ellison, and Bob Marley*. New York: Cambridge University Press, 1999.

Stepto, Robert B. *From Behind the Veil: A Study of Afro-American Narrative.* Urbana: University of Illinois Press, 1979.

Sundquist, Eric J., ed. *Cultural Contexts for Ralph Ellison's "Invisible Man."* Boston: Bedford Books of St. Martin's Press, 1995.

Trimmer, Joseph F., ed. *A Casebook on Ralph Ellison's "Invisible Man."* New York: Crowell, 1972.

Watts, Jerry Gafio. *Heroism and the Black Intellectual: Ralph Ellison, Politics, and Afro-American Intellectual Life.* Chapel Hill: University of North Carolina Press, 1994.

—The essay and bibliography have been revised for this edition by Norman W. Jones.

JESSIE REDMON FAUSET
(1882–1961)

LOIS LEVEEN

IF JESSIE FAUSET is today remembered in a single phrase, it is undoubtedly Langston Hughes's designation of her as one of the three individuals "who midwifed the so-called New Negro literature into being." This description has proven to be ironic on a number of levels. The statement pays tribute to the valuable contribution Fauset made as literary editor of the journal *Crisis* from 1919 to 1926, in publishing the work of emerging black writers (particularly Jean Toomer, Countee Cullen, Claude McKay, George Schuyler, and Hughes), but it obscures Fauset's own accomplishments as a prolific writer of poetry, short stories, essays, and four major novels. On another level, metaphorizing Fauset in the female role of the midwife seems to reflect the importance of her position as a woman writer, yet the other two figures Hughes identifies, Charles Johnson and Alain Locke, are men whose prominence was never forgotten in public or scholarly opinion, as Fauset's was for several decades.

Deborah McDowell introduced the 1990 republication of Fauset's second novel, *Plum Bun*, with the rather telling anecdote, "Whenever I cite Jessie Fauset as a writer of the Harlem Renaissance, I get a predictable response: Who is he?" Fauset, well known as a writer and editor from the 1910s through the 1930s, fell into obscurity thereafter, until she became the subject of scholarly attention in the 1980s and

1990s. This resurgence in interest stemmed largely from the increasing number of African American women literary critics, who sought out the work of black women writers, introducing their literary productions to new generations of readers through new editions and inclusion on college and university syllabi. These same critics, however, are often in dispute about the gendered trajectories, as well as the representations of class and skin color prejudices, in Fauset's novels.

Life

On April 27, 1882, Jessie Redmona Fauset was born in Snow Hill Center Township, New Jersey (she would later use the middle name Redmon instead of Redmona). She was the seventh child of Annie Seamon Fauset and Redmon Fauset, an African Methodist Episcopal (A.M.E.) minister. After the death of Annie, Redmon married Bella Huff, a widow with three young children. The couple had three more children. Her father's profession conferred an air of respectability on the family, but it appears that the Fausets were not as well off financially as those critics who label Jessie Fauset the novelist of the black middle class generally assume. Although a number of Annie and Redmon Fauset's children died before Jessie reached the age

217

of twenty, she remained close to her surviving sister, Helen Fauset Lanning, and her stepsiblings and half-siblings, particularly Earl Huff and Arthur Huff Fauset, throughout her life.

In 1900, Fauset graduated with honors from the High School for Girls, a public school in Philadelphia. She had hoped to attend Bryn Mawr College, but the school, unwilling to allow an African American to enroll, instead sponsored a fellowship for her to attend Cornell University. Fauset excelled there, becoming one of the first black women (perhaps the very first, as the historical records are somewhat unclear) to be elected to Phi Beta Kappa. Upon graduating in 1905, however, Fauset could not secure employment within the segregated Philadelphia school system. She moved first to Baltimore to take a teaching position, and then to Washington, D.C., where she taught French for fourteen years at the M Street High School (later renamed Dunbar). In 1918 and 1919 she returned to school as a full-time student, earning a master's degree in French from the University of Pennsylvania.

In 1912, Fauset started publishing poetry, short fiction, and book reviews with *Crisis*, the National Association for the Advancement of Colored People (NAACP) journal edited by W. E. B. Du Bois. At the suggestion of one of her Cornell professors, she had begun to correspond with Du Bois while she was an undergraduate, and he likely had helped her secure a summer teaching position she held at Fisk University in 1904. In 1919, Fauset became literary editor of *Crisis*. In creating this position, Du Bois indicated a desire for the journal to be a venue for creative writing on the theme of black life, and it was Fauset who solicited and edited the literary contributions, often serving as a mentor to the authors whose work was featured. Fauset perceived *Crisis* readers as potential authors as well, including articles on how to write and notices of literary competitions along with the journal's offerings of poetry, fiction, and nonfiction. During Du Bois's frequent absences from New York, Fauset assumed much of the responsibility for running the magazine. In 1920 and 1921, she edited and wrote many of the pieces for *The Brownies' Book*, a short-lived monthly magazine for African American children. It is unclear why she stepped down from her editorship at *Crisis* in 1926, but she did continue to contribute short pieces to the magazine in the years that followed.

Fauset studied French at the Sorbonne and made several trips to Europe and to Africa, often recorded in articles that she published in *Crisis*. Her first novel, *There Is Confusion*, appeared in 1924, and it was followed by three others: *Plum Bun* (1929), *The Chinaberry Tree* (1931), and *Comedy, American Style* (1933). The literary allusions in her novels, as in her shorter pieces, reflect her fluency in several foreign languages (French, German, Greek, and Latin), her familiarity with a vast range of literature, and her assumption that her audience included similarly educated readers. Never fully able to support herself through her writing, Fauset returned to teaching when she left the staff of *Crisis*, working as a French instructor at DeWitt Clinton High School from 1927 through 1944. She married Herbert Harris, an insurance broker, in 1929. Following their marriage, Harris joined Fauset in the Harlem apartment she shared with Helen Fauset Lanning, where the three lived until Lanning passed away in 1936. The couple moved to Montclair, New Jersey, in the early 1940s. Fauset continued teaching in New York and lecturing before a variety of organizations in the area. She served as a Visiting Professor of English at the Hampton Institute in Virginia in the fall of 1949, but after the strain of this physical separation from her husband, Fauset no longer took positions that forced her to live apart from him. Following Harris' death in 1958, Fauset moved to Philadelphia to live with her stepbrother Earl Huff. She suffered from increasing senility and poor physical health in this period, and she died from heart disease on April 30, 1961, at the age of 79, in her stepbrother's home.

Beyond these facts, very little is known about Fauset, particularly in terms of her feelings on such personal matters as the deaths of her parents or her late (for her time) marriage. Carolyn Sylvander's *Jessie Redmon Fauset, Black American Writer* is the sole book-length biography of the author. Sylvander has done an

Jessie Redmon Fauset

some of Arthur's writing in *Crisis*, and she used him as a model for the character of Stephen Denleigh in her novel *The Chinaberry Tree*, so the two certainly enjoyed a close relationship during their adult years. Nevertheless, Arthur was seventeen years younger than Jessie and was well into his seventies at the time Sylvander undertook her research. His recollections therefore provide a more limited perspective on his sister's life than Sylvander acknowledges. The biography focuses on contextualizing Fauset's work in terms of African American women's experience more broadly. When the book was first published in 1981, this context may not have been well understood, but readers today may find this background less necessary, and its inclusion is a bit frustrating given how little information Sylvander is able to provide that is specific to Fauset. Despite these shortcomings, *Jessie Redmon Fauset, Black American Writer* remains a valuable resource for scholars seeking information on Fauset's life.

Readers today most frequently encounter Fauset through her four novels. As the initial novel published during what is now called the Harlem Renaissance, Fauset's *There is Confusion* holds an important place in the African American literary canon. Introducing this novel to a new generation of readers in 1989, Thadious Davis notes its "overextended plot, underdeveloped characters, and unrealistic dialogue," arguing that the novel is "burdened with racial and romantic entanglements for which there is insufficient motivation." Unfortunately, these comments may also be applied, to a greater or lesser extent, to Fauset's later novels. Their imperfections as literary works suggest that Fauset never quite mastered the form of the novel, although the increasing complexity of her two later books indicates that she continually improved as an author. Through the novels, the reader encounters the successes and shortcomings of Fauset's writing, as complicated experiences and conflicting desires are represented through somewhat inadequately developed characters, and then ultimately resolved through simplistic and improbable marriage plot endings. All four novels do succeed at underscoring the concerns facing African

admirable job of locating archival material on Fauset's life (e.g., establishing her true birth year, which is listed incorrectly on her death certificate and which Fauset herself intentionally misrepresented during her lifetime), but unfortunately the written record is relatively scarce and focuses primarily on Fauset's involvement with *Crisis*. While Sylvander argues strongly against the predominant critical assessment of Fauset as the product of a middle-class black background, the sparse information she is able to provide on Fauset's early life comes almost entirely from Fauset's half-brother, Arthur Huff Fauset. Jessie published

219

Americans, especially black women. Fauset's other writings—short stories, poetry, essays, reviews, and translations, most of which appeared in *Crisis*—reveal her importance as an African American intellectual whose prolific production as an author as well as an editor had important influence on black readers and writers of her day.

There Is Confusion

Fauset's first novel, *There Is Confusion*, depicts the lives of middle- and working-class blacks in New York City and Philadelphia during the first two decades of the twentieth century. The main plot centers on Joanna Marshall's relationship with her childhood friend and eventual husband, Peter Bye. The Marshall family represents the financial security that began to be available to blacks in the wake of Emancipation. The family patriarch, Joel, had been born a slave in the South but as an adult established a lucrative catering business in New York City. Although his wealth does not bring the deeper fulfillment he had sought, he supports Joanna's career as a singer and dancer and her brother Philip's political activism—he founds a fictional organization similar to the NAACP—in the hopes that his children can achieve what he could not.

The Bye family of Philadelphia, by contrast, suggests less stability or consistent upward mobility. Peter's great-grandfather works devotedly for the man who had previously owned him. Peter's grandfather refuses such a life, opening a school for black youngsters and steadily building up small holdings in real estate, to demonstrate his independence and respectability. Despite his early ambition to be a doctor, Peter's father squanders his inheritance—thereby negating the achievement of the previous generation—and dies dissolute. Only a young child at the time of this death, Peter is divided between the influence of his father's teachings that the world owes him a living, and his desire to please the only black girl in his class at his new school in New York, the demanding Joanna.

Because the novel depicts not only the childhood, adolescence, and adulthood of Joanna and Peter, but also the lives of Joanna's siblings and their school friends, it enables Fauset to explore a range of themes: both the opportunities open to and the racism faced by African Americans in the wake of black migration; intersections of race and gender and of race and class; and the factors that influence individual development. Fauset's inspiration for writing the novel came from the publication of T. S. Stribling's *Birthright*, in which the biracial characters' most positive traits are characterized as products of their white heritage, in contrast to the degradation of their lives in "Niggertown." Shocked by the white author's depiction of black life, she, Nella Larsen, and Walter White responded, in Fauset's words, "Let us who are better qualified to present that truth than any white writer, try to do so." Readers today can find in *There Is Confusion* diverse documentation of the Northern black experience of the era. Joanna encounters not only the professional limitations of prejudice against black performers, but also the mundane discrimination that confines her to eating in the automat for fear that restaurants in various neighborhoods will refuse to serve her. When Peter joins the army during World War I, he and his fellow African American soldiers find that the equal treatment they receive from the French incites violence on the part of their own white countrymen. Minor characters, such as Joanna's friend Vera, offer other glimpses of African American life. Distraught when her family rejects her dark-complexioned suitor, Vera begins to pass as white, yet she later uses this ability on behalf of the black community, by investigating racial violence in the deep South. Also of interest is the last member of the white branch of the Bye family, who serves with Peter in France. He is as tortured by America's racial history as any black character ever was, and he willingly sacrifices his life to alleviate the burden of that history.

As Thadious Davis argues in her foreword to the 1989 edition of the novel, Joanna's experience depicts inequity in opportunities for black women as opposed to black men—one of the dance troupe directors who reject Joanna comments, "We'll try a colored man in a white company but we won't have any colored women"—and for black women versus white women—when Joanna encounters professionally successful white women, she recognizes that while they have triumphed against gender discrimination, they have had the privilege of not having to fight racism as well. Despite this emphasis on the unique plight of black women, however, *There Is Confusion* reinscribes limitations on them, through the novel's complicated marriage plots, which reflect imbrications of race, gender, class, and ambition.

Maggie Ellersley, who eventually marries Joanna's brother Philip, yearns throughout her childhood and young adulthood for social status and security (Peter is also poor, but he benefits from a family name that confers respectability within the African American community). As Davis notes, although Fauset's choice of the name "Maggie" links this character with the protagonist of Stephen Crane's *Maggie, A Girl of the Streets*, this Maggie is able to overcome poverty and environment, and also the limitations faced by women and African Americans. Nevertheless, the trajectory of Maggie's life is not simply a tale of feminist, racial, or class triumph. When Joanna dismisses the young Maggie's romantic interest in Philip, the poorer girl retreats into a hasty marriage to one of her mother's boarders. After learning that he is a gambler, a source of disgrace, Maggie divorces Henderson Neal and begins to keep company with Peter, who has returned to his native Philadelphia and become estranged from Joanna. In contrast to the latter's professional ambition, Maggie's simple, homey nature appeals to Peter, yet he later realizes that he does not love Maggie, because she cannot compare with Joanna. After he breaks their engagement, Maggie is reunited with Philip, whose service in World War I renders him an invalid. The "happy ending" to their affair is compromised by Philip's early death, which leaves Maggie a young widow who throws herself into managing a chain of hair salons. While Joanna's assumption that Maggie's class position made her an improper partner for Philip is refuted by

Philip's love for Maggie, Joanna's prohibition of marriage between a Marshall and a woman from a lower class who works in a trade has been borne out by Maggie's widowhood. Maggie's repeated romantic failings provide a narrative foil to Joanna's ultimately happy marriage to Peter.

Peter and Joanna's romance follows the often common practice in which each character must change significantly in order for the love match to succeed. Peter must be weaned from the "shiftlessness" of his father, so that he will desire to work hard for his place in the world, thereby representing the ambitions displayed by the era's "Talented Tenth." Conversely, Joanna must cede her ambition for greatness and acknowledge that love is a woman's ultimate goal. Her initial reluctance to sacrifice her career is indicted in an exchange she has with Peter early in the novel:

"Love is a wonderful, rare thing, very beautiful, very sweet, but you can do without it."

"Not much you can't. Better not try it, Joanna. You have to found your life on love, then you can do all these other things."

"Don't talk like a silly, Peter. You know perfectly well that for a woman love usually means a household of children, the getting of a thousand meals, picking up laundry, no time to herself for meditation, or reading or—"

"Dancing! That's through poor management. Marry a man who understands you, Janna [sic], and he'll see that you have time for anything you want."

When Joanna, years later, finally accepts the love Peter identifies as so crucial, he no longer seems willing to give her the time for her own pursuits. As she accepts his marriage proposal, he notes, "I'm afraid you'll have to give up your career, dear Joanna" to tend to the children they will have, a condition to which she immediately accedes. The narrator indicates that this change stems not from Peter's despotism but rather from Joanna's newfound willingness to subsume her desires to his: "Perhaps it is wrong to imply that Joanna had lost her ambition. She was still ambitious, only the field of her ambition lay without herself. It was Peter now whom she wished to see succeed." Juxtaposing the trajectory of Maggie's and Joanna's lives reveals how the novel continues the circumscription of African American women. While Maggie can have a career, and Joanna can have a happy marriage, *There Is Confusion* implies that no woman can have both.

Several aspects of the novel offer more sophisticated and less troubling points of consideration. The Bye orchard serves as a geographic embodiment of America's racial history. Created primarily through the labor of Peter's great-grandfather Joshua, the orchard belongs to the white Bye family, who promote it as a symbol of their success. To overcome the racial bitterness that destroyed his father, Peter must return to the site of the orchard, to bring the last remaining white Bye, the elderly Meriwether, the news of his grandson's death in World War I. Significantly, Fauset locates the orchard at Bryn Mawr, where her own hard work—like that of her creation Joshua Bye—was repudiated by white racism, which impeded her matriculation at Bryn Mawr College, despite her excellence as a student.

Also significant is the novel's commentary on black artistic production. Joanna's great success as a performer comes through her adaptation of a song-and-dance game she sees being played by a group of black children. Although the invocation of African American folk culture in the "high culture" of the Harlem Renaissance is discussed most frequently in relation to the work of Zora Neale Hurston, Fauset has Joanna authenticate her performance for white and black audiences through the use of folk forms. This adaptation signals the value of African American culture, but the role of the black performer still must be asserted judiciously to the white public. When Joanna is given an opportunity to portray "America," she takes to the stage in a mask, to avoid offending the white audience members. Initially reminiscent of Paul Laurence Dunbar's 1895 poem "We Wear the Mask," the scene ultimately suggests that African Americans are now more able to claim their true place in America. Joanna's performance so moves the audience that they shout for her to remove her mask during her encore. When she does, they are momentarily stunned to see that she is black, but she invokes her great-grandfather's service in the Revolutionary War, her uncle's in the Civil War, and her brother's in World War I, as evidence of her Americanness. The audience responds with another round of adoring applause. The narrator carefully notes, "Perhaps it would not have succeeded anywhere else but in New York, and perhaps not even there but in Greenwich Village", yet the episode clearly indicates a belief that the passionate black artist—whether a dancer like Joanna or a writer like Fauset—can help claim African Americans' rightful legacy, by eliciting the respect and recognition of whites.

Plum Bun

Fauset's second novel, *Plum Bun*, focuses more singularly on the development of its protagonist, Angela Murray. Growing up in a lower-middle-class African American neighborhood in Philadelphia, the light-skinned Angela spends her Saturdays passing with her mother, leaving the darker family members—Angela's sister, Jinny, and their father—to entertain themselves. While Mrs. Murray has no desire to pass permanently, she inadvertently teaches Angela to associate whiteness with opportunity. Thus, when her parents die, Angela sells her share of the family home to Jinny and moves to New York City, where she passes as white. Jinny soon moves to New York as well, and her new life in the bustling community of Harlem serves as a contrast to Angela's growing alienation passing as white in Greenwich Village. Angela's isolation is increased by the failure of her affair with a wealthy white man, Roger Fielding, who knows nothing of her family background. Angela eventually chooses to give up passing, in an open embrace of her African American heritage. After doing so, she is united with her true love, Anthony Cross, who has also passed as white but now embraces his blackness.

The sections of the novel are organized around the nursery rhyme, "To Market, to Market / To buy a Plum Bun; / Home again, Home again, / Market is done," and the narrative draws heavily on references to fairy tales in the depictions of Angela's parents' marriage. Ironically, the novel's ending seems as trite and unrealistic as a fairy tale, in which a romantic pairing promises that characters will live "happily ever after." Fauset's attack on the sexual marketplace in which women are reduced to treats for male consumption serves as an important challenge to the eroticizing of women of color, yet the novel ultimately devolves into a sentimental tale in which the heroine once again is happy to sacrifice her potential for professional success in order to assume a constricted role as wife. When Angela reclaims her place in the African American community, she is "rewarded" by ascending to a marriage plot that subsumes the earlier künstleroman plot of her artistic development.

Plum Bun serves as a sometimes troubling meditation on matters of racial representation. Like Joanna in *There Is Confusion* and like Fauset herself, Angela is an artist—a painter. Whereas Joanna fights steadily against discrimination to develop her professional reputation, Angela assumes that if blacks cannot succeed as artists, she must assume a new racial identity. While Angela is living in Philadelphia with her sister, she paints a portrait of Hetty Daniels, a woman who has come to live with the sisters in the wake of their mother's death. Hetty regales Angela with lessons in sexual chastity, yet when Angela regards Hetty as her artistic subject, she sees the embodiment of sexuality: "Her unslaked yearnings gleamed suddenly out of her eyes, transforming her usually rather expressionless face into something wild and avid." Angela believes that if she can capture this sexual wildness in her painting, she will win a prestigious scholarship to study art. Ironically, as she finishes the picture, her art school teacher discovers that Angela is African American (she lives in a black neighborhood with her dark-skinned sister, yet she has been passing whenever she is at the art school), thereby ruining her chances at the scholarship and costing Angela her place at the school. This incident provides the immediate impetus for her to move to Greenwich Village, where she can pass in all aspects of her life.

The episode seems to confirm a belief that black women may be (highly sexualized) subjects represented in art, but that they can never assume the power of being creators of art. Even when the novel later challenges this idea, it invokes a troubling politics concerning skin color. Angela finally does win an art scholarship, to study at the prestigious Fontainebleau in France, and her New York art school classmate, Miss Powell, wins one as well, for her painting "A Street in Harlem." Miss Powell's award is rescinded, however, when a number of white recipients of the award object to traveling to France with a black woman. In response to this news, Angela, already disenchanted with whiteness because of the failure of her relationship with Roger, openly declares that she, too, is African American. The scholarship episode seems drawn from an actual incident involving Augusta Savage, a black sculptor who was denied admission to the summer art program at Fontainebleau in 1923. Blacks and whites joined together to vocalize support for Savage; although the decision to exclude her was never reversed, she was transformed by the event and dedicated herself to challenging racism in the art world. Miss Powell, by contrast, does not even wish to contest the decision, and she asks the group that has organized to support her to leave her name out of their protests. The potential for a radical challenge on the part of Miss Powell is negated, and the novel focuses instead on rewarding Angela for her actions. She is still able to go to France (her trip is financed in part by her sister Jinny, who forgives Angela for snubbing her as soon as she ceases passing), and she, rather than Miss Powell, is lauded for fighting white racism. The episode exemplifies the manner in which the novel at times promotes the seeming privileging of light-skinned African Americans over dark-skinned African Americans.

This privileging also occurs in the novel's complicated romantic pairings. *Plum Bun* continues the plot mechanism of wrong couples needing to be righted, that Fauset incorporated in *There Is Confusion*. Here, Angela discovers that Anthony Cross, an art school classmate with whom she falls in love after the end of her affair with Roger, is engaged to her sister, Jinny. Neither Jinny nor Anthony is aware of this connection. When Angela discovers that Jinny is still in love with Matthew Henson, the object of her childhood crush, she encourages him to contact Jinny. With Matthew and Jinny united at last, Anthony is free to marry Angela. Early in the novel, the dark-complexioned Matthew is often described by the narrator and the African American characters in negative terms (e.g., through references to his "bad hair"), and throughout the narrative his and Jinny's lack of ambition is implicitly linked to their dark skin. Anthony, like Angela, is light-skinned and spends most of the novel passing. By uniting these two couples, the novel again classifies African Americans according to their varying shades of skin.

The Chinaberry Tree

While the narrative trajectories of Fauset's first two novels are fairly similar—a young African American girl comes of age, seeks professional greatness, and discovers her ultimate fulfillment in marriage—the plots of her third and fourth novels are considerably more varied. The subtitle of *Plum Bun*, "A Novel Without a Moral," belies the narrative emphasis on both the value of claiming an African American identity and the troubling sacrifice of female ambition in favor of marriage. By contrast, Fauset prefaced her third novel, *The Chinaberry Tree*, with a somewhat more forthright declaration of her authorial intentions. She begins by proclaiming that she never wrote "to establish a thesis," yet she quickly asserts:

Colored people have been the subjects which I have chosen for my novels partly because they are the ones I know best, partly because of all the other separate groups which constitute the American cosmogony none of them, to me, seems so naturally endowed with the stuff of which chronicles may be made. To be a Negro in America posits a dramatic situation.

Sarcastically describing "the colored American" as "a citizen of the United States whose ancestors came over not along with the emigrants in the Mayflower, it is true, but merely a little earlier in the good year, 1619," Fauset stresses that this novel, which does not deal with immediate experiences of racism, simply evidences the Americanness of African Americans, by making their experiences central to literature.

The Chinaberry Tree focuses on the lives of two cousins, Laurentine Strange and Melissa Paul, in Redbrook, New Jersey. Despite her quiet respectability, Laurentine is rejected by her first suitor, because of her family history: her father, the wealthy, white Colonel Halloway, had taken black Sarah Strange as his lover, securing her in a home and fathering her child. Rather than treating the relationship as a legacy of white male sexual abuse of enslaved women, or even as a source of shame for Sarah and her "illegitimate" daughter, Laurentine, Fauset suggests that Halloway and Sarah were truly in love, as indicated by the former's willingness to risk scandal to continue their relationship throughout his life, and by the latter's continuing devotion to Halloway's memory long after his death. At the time in which the novel was set and written, New Jersey law prohibited interracial marriage, but rather than assuming that nonmarital relationships were necessarily sinful or exploitive, *The Chinaberry Tree* underscores the fact that at least some members of the black community recognize the love and respect Halloway and Sarah shared. Significantly, it is two black males—Laurentine's second suitor, Dr. Stephen Denleigh, a somewhat older man, and Asshur Lane, a teenaged beau of her cousin—who voice most forcefully this understanding of the relationship. Even Laurentine's half-sisters, the product of Halloway's marriage with a white woman, refuse to blame or ostracize Sarah or Laurentine. Instead, they share their inheritance and support Laurentine's training as a seamstress, a process that leads to her financial independence.

Halloway's wife, however, remains bitterly resentful of her husband's commitment to Sarah, and it is her family's political influence that causes the ambitious black man who first courts Laurentine to end their romance. This break coincides with the growing popularity of Melissa, who has recently moved to Redbrook to join her aunt and cousin's household. Melissa assumes a certain superiority over Sarah and Laurentine, yet as the narrative unfolds, she and the reader eventually learn that Melissa, too, was born out of wedlock. Fauset's prefatory assertion of the "dramatic situation" of black life bears out in the way the narrative echoes Greek drama. Melissa is initially popular with the teenagers of Redbrook, but she begins to feel they are shunning her for some unknown reason. The exception is Malory Forten, who, although born in the town, has only recently returned, having been sent away by his mother at a young age. Alienated from his gloomy family, Malory becomes close with Melissa, who feels similarly distanced from her prim cousin. Malory and Melissa plan to elope after graduation, but Malory learns just before this happens that Melissa is his half-sister, the product of his father's extramarital affair with the unwed Judy Strange, Sarah's sister. The Oedipal overtones of this development are underscored by Melissa's recurring dreams, in which Malory wears the mask of tragedy. The threat of the incestuous relationship contrasts with the novel's positive depiction of Sarah and Halloway's interracial romance, and with the marriage plots grafted onto the novel's ending. In the final pages of the narrative both Melissa and Laurentine succeed in finding suitable marriage partners.

These machinations are a bit far-fetched, but Fauset uses them to offer a meditation on propriety, self-righteousness, and judgmental practices within the African American community. *The Chinaberry Tree*, like her earlier novels, depicts the way racism affected even the most minor and mundane aspects of black existence, a painful reality that Fauset could not ignore in her creative writing. One incident, in which Denleigh and Laurentine are subject to the racism of an immigrant restaurant owner and his patrons, was a slightly fictionalized account of an experience Fauset had while dining out with her husband during the writing of the novel. Continuing her focus on how gender and class combine with race in the lives of African American women, Fauset realistically portrays the jealousy and resentment that develop between Laurentine and Melissa, in lieu of any sisterly support and solidarity.

Ironically, although the novel refutes Melissa's belief that the only desirable families are marital, intraracial, and upper middle class, this refutation occurs through the marriages of Laurentine and Melissa. These pairings confirm that neither illegitimacy nor biracial status marks a woman as "undesirable," even as Melissa's acceptance of Asshur, who wants to be a farmer, negates her earlier insistence on marrying only within the professional class. While the emphasis on marriage plot conclusions in *The Chinaberry Tree*, as in the earlier novels, indicates a certain level of literary and moral conventionality, the exploration of the emotional states of the various characters indicates how stultifying not only white racism but the black community's internal snobbery can be. In this sense, the form of Fauset's novel seems to be at odds with the "thesis" she puts forth, a conflict that becomes less pronounced in her final novel.

Comedy: American Style

From its very title, *Comedy: American Style* is more quick to assert its ironic stance. The novel centers on the family of Olivia Blanchard Cary. Like *Plum Bun*'s Angela Murray, Olivia is a light-skinned African American who from childhood on envies the opportunities she associates with whiteness. Openly despising blacks in general and her dark-skinned father in particular, Olivia becomes determined to protect herself and her children from racism by passing. She lacks the professional ambition that marks the female protagonists of Fauset's earlier novels, and at a young age she marries a light-skinned African American doctor. Olivia is as shocked by his willingness to associate with black friends and patients as he is by her obsession with whiteness, an obsession that proves a tragic, not comic, endeavor. Indeed, the dramatic theme of *The Chinaberry Tree* is reinscribed in *Comedy, American Style* through the use of dramatic terms to structure the narrative. The first two sections of the novel, "The Plot" and "The Characters," sketch out the circumstances around Olivia's entrancement with whiteness. Each of the next three sections, labeled "acts," demonstrate how this mania affects her children.

In "Teresa's Act," Olivia's oldest child, a daughter, rebels against her mother's admonition that she pass by becoming secretly engaged to a black man. On the day of their planned elopement, the young couple is intercepted by Olivia, and in trying to assuage her mother, Teresa suggests that her betrothed might pass as Mexican. Indignant at this idea, Henry ends their relationship immediately. When Teresa enrolls in a summer program in France the following year, Olivia orchestrates the girl's marriage to one of her professors. For Olivia, this match seems the pinnacle of achievement, an assurance that her child will be "protected" from being identified as African American and will gain a place in supposedly sophisticated French culture. In fact, Teresa's husband is petty, indifferent, and racist. His interest in the marriage is largely financial, and Teresa is left isolated and miserable in the small French town where she remains. Where Fauset's earlier novels associate happy marriages for the female protagonist with a proclamation of the value of African American identity, "Teresa's Act" uses marriage to contest the privileging of whiteness by revealing how demeaning and discontented the lives of many whites the world over actually are.

The next section of the novel, "Oliver's Act" details an even more sinister effect of Olivia's obsession with whiteness. The youngest of Olivia's three children, Oliver is the only member of his family who is physically recognizable as African American. In his earliest childhood, Olivia sends him off to be raised alternately by his two sets of grandparents. During his teen years, he returns to his parents' home, where his mother has him pose as a Filipino butler whenever she entertains her white friends. Of all Fauset's many depictions of racism, perhaps the most poignant is the emotional effect on Oliver of Olivia's obsession with whiteness. While Teresa, her brother Christopher, and her father are well aware of the reasons for Olivia's mistreatment of Oliver, none of them informs the boy. The teenager discovers a letter from his mother to his father, in which Olivia declares, "Oliver and his unfortunate color has [have] certainly been a mill-stone around our necks all our lives." This revelation, a projection of Olivia's obsession onto the rest of the family, pushes Oliver to commit suicide.

"Phebe's Act," while hardly as tragic as those preceding it, refuses to yield the convenient resolutions common in Fauset's other novels. Focusing on Teresa's childhood friend Phebe, also a light-skinned African American, the section details a series of difficulties the young woman faces. Even as Phebe believes her childhood sweetheart, Nicholas Cambell, is planning to propose, he ends their relationship because of his love for another woman. Rather than admitting this reason, he blames Phebe's coloring, noting that when they are seen in public, strangers assume that she is white and he black, a circumstance that is at best uncomfortable and at worst potentially dangerous. Nicholas' attack on Phebe's very being is quickly followed by the ardent courtship of a wealthy white man, Llewellyn Nash, who believes she is white. When Phebe informs Nash that she is African American, he is at first horrified, but then he offers to take her to Europe as his mistress. Phebe, unlike Angela in *Plum Bun*, does not hesitate to reject such an arrangement, and she soon finds herself pursued by a third suitor, Teresa's surviving brother Christopher.

Even when Phebe and Christopher marry, however, the young woman's troubles continue. The elder Dr. Cary, devastated by his younger son's suicide, has let his practice and his savings dwindle away, so the house Phebe has purchased for her mother, through her labor as a seamstress, now becomes home to herself, her husband, and her in-laws as well. Olivia, hardly affected by her son's death and her daughter's unhappy marriage, continues to pass as white and attempts to manipulate Phebe's mother into posing as her servant, as Oliver had earlier done. In response to the increasing pressure of this situation, Phebe nearly has an affair with Nicholas, who has already grown disenchanted with his wife. At the last moment, she resists and returns home. In her absence, Olivia has departed for Europe, seeking to live out her fantasy of being free from blackness. Phebe and Christopher assert their love, looking toward the promise of the future.

Comedy, American Style does not, however, simply offer a happy ending depicting the bliss of marriage (something Fauset's earlier novels do), as the final section, "The Curtain," indicates. Olivia, living in Paris on her rapidly dwindling savings, barely endures her lonely existence. She finally decides to return home, but she lacks the funds to do so, and when the novel ends it is not clear whether her husband will ever be able to finance her trip back to the United States. Indeed, the final scene of the novel is the most ambiguous conclusion of any of Fauset's works, with the image of the isolated Olivia looking out the window of her Paris pension to see a mother happily joking with her son, a boy who reminds Olivia of Oliver. In *Comedy, American Style*, Fauset best succeeds at using her ensemble of characters, her creative structuring of the narrative, and even the end point of the plot, as tools both to represent the lives of African Americans and to condemn the "American Style" racism they face.

Other Works

Fauset remains most accessible to readers today through her novels, all of which have been reissued, but she was also a prolific writer of poetry, essays, reviews, and short fiction. Readers can gain an understanding of Fauset's larger roles as a writer and thinker through several recent collections that include samples of her work in these other genres: the Northeastern Library of Black Literature edition of *The Chinaberry Tree*, which includes several nonfiction prose pieces originally published in *Cri-*

sis; The Best of "The Brownies' Book", which offers signed and unsigned pieces by Fauset, as well as works by many other writers from the children's magazine Fauset edited; and *The Crisis Reader*, with poetry, essays, and one short story by Fauset. Those readers with access to the many issues of *Crisis* and *The Brownies' Book* to which she contributed as a writer and an editor can enjoy an even fuller appreciation of Fauset's diverse talents and interests.

Fauset's earliest and most frequent contributions to *Crisis* were book and article reviews. She influenced what African Americans of all ages were reading not only through her role as literary editor of *Crisis* and practicing editor of *The Brownies' Book* but also through the numerous reviews she wrote for both journals. In 1912, the first year in which she was a contributor to *Crisis*, she published a poem, a short story, an article, and numerous literary reviews, setting a pattern of eclectic productivity that would continue on and off for seventeen years. During that period she would also translate Francophone Haitian, African, and French poetry and prose for *Crisis* readers to enjoy.

Fauset's first fictional piece for *Crisis*, "Emmy," set the pattern she would later use in her novels, in which love plots are complicated by racial matters. The title character is a black girl growing up in an almost entirely white town in central Pennsylvania. Strikingly, she has no sense of racial inferiority; her boyfriend, Archie, lighter in complexion, moves to Philadelphia after graduating, where he passes so that he may work as an engineer. When Emmy learns that he wishes to postpone their marriage because her coloring will jeopardize his job, she breaks off their engagement. In the wake of this rejection, he tells his boss that he is African American and is immediately fired. He returns to Emmy, and they renew their love, only to learn that the boss has decided he will reinstate Archie. The plot mechanisms at the end of the story, including an abrupt recounting of Emmy's mother's own tragic romance, are rather contrived, yet the character development and the fictional depiction of a polemic about race pride are in some respects smoother and more convincing than Fauset's novels often were.

The masthead of the November 1919 issue of *Crisis* lists Fauset as the literary editor, a position formally announced in the "Men of the Month" column inside. The overall quality of the literary offerings in the journal increased substantially once Fauset assumed this role, and her own work became more varied and sophisticated. In "Mary Elizabeth," a short story in the December issue, a younger African American couple is reconciled in part through their elderly servant's story of her parents' forced separation during slavery. The piece reminds both the main characters and the readers that slavery was not so far removed from the current era, a message reinforced by Fauset's poem "Oriflamme," which was included in the January 1920 issue. Above the poem appears a passage in which Sojourner Truth recalls how her mother would look up at the stars during the nights of her enslavement, thinking of the children whose whereabouts were unknown to her but who at least could look up and see the same stars. Fauset's poem uses this anecdote as a theme to describe how contemporary blacks should relate to slavery:

> I think I see her sitting bowed and black,
> Stricken and seared with slavery's mortal
>   scars,
> Reft of her children, lonely, anguished, yet
> Still looking at the stars.
>
> Symbolic mother, we thy myriad sons,
> Pounding our stubborn hearts on Freedom's
>   bars,
> Clutching our birthright, fight with faces
>   set,
> Still visioning the stars!

The symbolic mother of the race provides the impetus for the fight for freedom and equality in which Fauset clearly saw herself and her contemporaries engaged. Slavery itself becomes the "oriflamme," the heraldic banner, held up to rally support for this fight. While most of Fauset's poetry for *Crisis* consisted of seasonal verse or rarefied meditations on frustrated love, pieces such as "Oriflamme" continue to move readers today.

In addition to her roles as literary arbiter and creative writer, Fauset served as a political and social commentator, promoting ideas in the *Crisis* that were sometimes more radical than those expressed in her novels. Perhaps the most fascinating aspect of Fauset's *Crisis* oeuvre is her international perspective. Her March 1920 article, "Nationalism and Egypt," provides a well-documented history of Britain's involvement in the area, as Fauset argues for the importance of securing Egyptian self-rule. The Diasporic perspective recurs in the September 1920 issue, in which she reviews several books from and about Haiti—and it deviates markedly from the narrow focus on middle-class African Americans found in her novels. Fauset's fluency in French, which she studied at Cornell, the University of Pennsylvania, and the Sorbonne, gave her access not only to the European nation whose racial tolerance was so attractive to African Americans of the era, but also to the writings of Francophone blacks in the Caribbean and in Africa, which she was able to translate for readers who knew no French. Her international emphasis, combined with her quest to provide stories of inspirational blacks, can be seen in pieces such as "The Emancipator of Brazil," a biographical article on Jose De Patrocinio, who fought to abolish slavery, and "Saint-George, Chevalier of France," about the eighteenth-century Guadaloupean who was educated in his white father's native France but refused to renounce his black mother.

Fauset's report, "Impressions of the Second Pan-African Congress," which appeared in *Crisis* in November 1921, further documents her perspective on the African Diaspora. At the convention, Fauset and other African Americans presented their experiences of discrimination to blacks from other nations, and they considered what role they might play in the struggle for self-rule in Africa. The eloquence with which Fauset recorded these events—"Native African and native American stood side by side and said, 'Brother, this is my lot; tell me what is yours!' "—suited the importance of the occasion. Her report enabled readers in the United States to share the emotional triumph she experienced as a delegate, the "feeling that it was good to be alive and most wonderful to be colored." When the Congress moved from London to Belgium, the tone altered, because of the presence of white Belgians whose economic interests in the Belgian Congo made them suspicious of any reforms. In Belgium, Fauset "was able to envisage what Africa means to Europe" and she shared her understanding of how global commerce and colonization continued to affect the lives of Africans with her American readers. She concluded by reminding them that the Pan-African Congress proved the importance and efficacy of organizing blacks throughout the world to work together.

Fauset repeatedly used her trips to Europe and Africa as subject matter for *Crisis* articles. In "Yarrow Revisited," an account of one of her stays in France, she celebrates the opportunity to "have tea ... *at the first tea room which takes my fancy*," in contrast to the constant anticipation of rebuff that blacks had upon entering restaurants in the United States. Yet this praise of the absence of segregated dining is coupled with a strong sense of American identity.

> In Paris I find myself more American than I ever feel in America. I am more conscious of national characteristics than I have ever been in New York. When I say: "We do that differently in America," I do not mean that *we* do it differently in Harlem, or on "You" Street in Washington, or on Christian Street in Philadelphia. I mean that Americans white and black do not act that way.

Distanced from the inevitable "color lines" of American society, Fauset recognizes the commonalities among Americans of all races that ironically are obscured when she is in the segregated United States.

Fauset also reported on crucial aspects of black life within the United States. In "The Thirteenth Biennial of the NACW," she informed readers about the events of the National Association of Colored Women's annual convention. In "The 'Y' Conference at Talladega," she provides a similar summary of a gathering of YWCA leaders. In "Out of the West," she challenges the New Negro focus on Harlem by describing the thriving African American community in Denver, Colorado.

The contributions to *Crisis* offer an important perspective on Fauset as an author. She used her involvement with *Crisis* to hone her craft, for example in the fictional piece "Double Trouble," which is an early version of the story she would develop more fully in *The Chinaberry Tree*. Her impassioned tribute, "The Symbolism of Bert Williams," delineates the limitations placed on the black actor, despite his enormous talent and his notable triumphs. Fauset would later adapt this material for "The Gift of Laughter," her contribution to Alain Locke's collection on the New Negro. The discussion of Williams's artistry and of his struggles perhaps suggests Fauset's thoughts about her own life as a black artist.

Fauset paid great attention to the needs of readers as well as of writers. In January of 1920, she dedicated the premier issue of *The Brownies' Book* with the poem,

> To Children, who with eager look
> Scanned vainly library shelf and nook,
> For History or Song or Story
> That told of Colored Peoples' glory—
> We dedicate The Brownies' Book.

As with *Crisis*, Fauset contributed significantly to this forum as both a writer and an editor. Among her contributions to the new magazine was the regular column "The Judge," which featured dialogues between a fictitious judge and a group of African American children. When one of the children reports that his teacher has asked the class to identify the greatest continent, the judge surprises the children by arguing that the correct answer is Africa. The treatise is clearly intended to educate young black readers about Africa and thus to instill them with pride in their heritage. It also offers a larger lesson, made in reply to one of the character's queries as to why white-authored histories do not include this information: "they tell what they want to think is the truth."

In another column, the Judge delicately explains that although it seems unfair, parents have reasons for forbidding young women from attending public events, such as a neighborhood basketball game, where they might meet with "undesirable people." While the Judge looks to a time free of the injustice of restricting females from doing what their brothers do, the column is designed to encourage girls to accept their parents' prohibitions more willingly. Elsewhere, the Judge explains why boys as well as girls should work to have a neat and clean appearance. These didactic pieces shared spaced with the seasonal poems and amusing short stories Fauset crafted for young readers.

The value of Fauset's canny and kind approach as an editor is evident from the recollections of her that Langston Hughes included in his autobiography, *The Big Sea.* Shortly after graduating from high school, Hughes sent two articles and a short play to *The Brownies' Book.* Fauset responded with letters of praise. Her encouragement paid off when Hughes submitted "The Negro Speaks of Rivers" to her for publication in *Crisis.* Not only was the event a coup for Fauset as literary editor, it was also a significant event in Hughes's career, the first publication of his poetry outside of his high school literary magazine. After Hughes moved to New York, Fauset invited him to lunch with the *Crisis* editors. The young man was initially intimidated, until the "charming" Fauset "thrilled" him with news that readers had written in to laud his poems. As he later recalled, "From that moment on I was deceived in writers, because I thought they would all be good-looking and gracious like Miss Fauset." Although he would come to recognize that the African American critics who decried his poems simultaneously praised Fauset's novels "because they were always about the educated Negro," he did not resent her. Fauset dedicated herself to soliciting literary contributions from a range of authors, whose style and perspective often differed substantially from her own. Her catholic tastes, along with her personal encouragement of emerging writers, greatly enriched the offerings available to readers of *Crisis.*

Hughes responded to Fauset as both a fellow author, identifying her as "the novelist Jessie Fauset," and as a mentor. She provided Hughes and other young writers with opportunities to meet other black artists and intellectuals, hosting gatherings with "quite a different atmosphere from that at most other Harlem good-time gatherings." Even during the "Harlem Renaissance," purely intellectual pursuits were often unavailable to African Americans, and Fauset's cultural salon was greatly enjoyed by those who attended:

> At Miss Fauset's, a good time was shared by talking literature and reading poetry aloud and perhaps enjoying some conversation in French. White people were seldom present there unless they were very distinguished white people, because Jessie Fauset did not feel like opening her home to mere sight-seers, or faddists momentarily in love with Negro life. At her house one would usually meet editors and students, writers and social workers, and serious people who liked books and the British Museum, and had perhaps been to Florence (Italy, not Alabama).

Through these parties, and through her work at *Crisis,* Fauset fostered an atmosphere for black intellectual and artistic achievement.

Her own understanding of the purpose of art was not as strictly defined as that of Du Bois, who in "The Criteria of Negro Art" famously declared "all art is propaganda and ever must be." Nevertheless, Fauset's view did reflect a pragmatism about racial representation. In 1926, Du Bois designed a series of questions concerning artistic depictions of blacks, which Fauset circulated to numerous artists and writers. The results were published in several consecutive issues of *Crisis* under the title, "The Negro in Art: How Shall He Be Portrayed, A Symposium." Fauset's answers were included in the June 1926 issue. In response to the query "What are Negroes to do when they are continually painted at their worst and judged by the public as they are painted?" she responded that, in addition to protesting such representations, African Americans "must learn to write with a humor, a pathos, a sincerity so evident and a delineation so fine and distinctive that their portraits, even of the 'best Negroes,' those presumably most like 'white folks,' will be acceptable to publisher and reader alike." While this portion of her answer indicates Fauset's goals as an author, the rest of the passage underscores an economic imperative that she would not be able to conquer in her own career:

But above all colored people must be the buyers of these books for which they clamor. When they buy 50,000 copies of a good novel about colored people by a colored author, publishers will produce books, even those that depict the Negro as an angel on earth—and the public in general will buy 50,000 copies more to find out what it's all about. Most best sellers are not born—they're made.

Never able to support herself entirely through her writing, Fauset clearly understood the power that consumers had over literary production, even though she could not harness that power for herself. Her answers to the survey emphatically deny that black—or white—artists have any particular obligation to depict blacks positively, yet they also attest to the limited venue for work that portrayed the "best Negroes." Fauset is careful to include the assertion that, in speaking before white groups, she has found ample evidence that whites "are keenly interested in learning about the better class of colored people." Clearly, she found neither the label "the better class," nor the idea that literature could serve as a sort of ethnographic reporting, to be problematic, although both the categorization and the learning process she celebrates seem suspect by today's standards.

The most useful source for understanding Fauset's feelings about her writing is an interview conducted by Marion Starkey and published in May 1932 in *The Southern Workman*, the journal of the Hampton Institute. Fauset, having already published three novels, was working as a French teacher at De Witt Clinton High School, and she expressed the hope that one day her writing might earn her enough money that she could devote herself to it full-time, a dream that never came to pass. Starkey reports that Fauset's next project would be a biography, the subject of which Fauset would not reveal, to be followed by another novel. Although Fauset argued adamantly for the importance of biographies of African Americans, and she included many biographical articles in both *Crisis* and *The Brownies' Book*, the proposed full-length biography was never published, and it is not known who the subject was. She did complete a fourth novel, and later said she was working on a fifth, but that manuscript also appears to have been lost. The interview with Starkey reveals Fauset's struggles as a writer, but it provides no indication of what would cause the long silencing of her pen, from the publication of *Comedy: American Style* through the end of her life.

Fauset's marriage to Herbert Harris was apparently a contented one, but she did not find the facile happy ending through marriage she afforded so many of her fictional heroines. While her professional output was quite substantial, she never fulfilled her own ambitions. The need to support herself financially, the end of the cultural milieu of the Harlem Renaissance, and her own age probably combined to limit her literary production after 1933. Sylvander sums up this unusual career by noting, "Fauset's work was a literature of search more than a literature of protest." In much of her fictional writing, Fauset revealed the host of interrelated challenges her African American characters faced, yet she almost always let her critical fictional representations of social inequity give way to a generic formula of happy endings through marriage. Her novels seem more "old-fashioned" than the work of her Renaissance contemporaries, but her writing continues to speak to readers and interest scholars today.

Selected Bibliography

PRIMARY WORKS

NOVELS

There Is Confusion. New York: Bon and Liveright, 1924. Current edition, Boston: Northeastern University Press, 1995. (Includes a critical introduction by Thadious M. Davis.)

Plum Bun: A Novel Without a Moral. New York: Frederick A Stokes, 1929. Current edition, Boston: Beacon Press, 1990. (Includes a critical introduction by Deborah McDowell.)

The Chinaberry Tree. New York: Frederick A. Stokes, 1931. Current edition, Boston: Northeastern University Press, 1995. (Includes a critical introduction by Marcy C. Knopf and a range of shorter pieces by Fauset that originally appeared in *Crisis.*)

Comedy: American Style. New York: Frederick A. Stokes, 1933. Current edition, Westport, Conn.: Greenwood, 1969.

SELECTED ARTICLES, POEMS, SHORT STORIES

"Emmy (Part One)." *Crisis* 5:79–87 (December 1912).

"Emmy (Part Two)." *Crisis* 5:134–42 (January 1913).

"Mary Elizabeth. A Story." *Crisis* 19:51–56 (December 1919).

"Dedication." *The Brownies' Book* 1:32 (January 1920).

"Oriflamme." *Crisis* 19:128 (January 1920).

"Nationalism and Egypt." *Crisis* 19:310–16 (April 1920).

"The Emancipator of Brazil." *Crisis* 21:208–9 (March 1921).

"Saint-George, Chevalier of France." *Crisis* 22:9–12 (May 1921).

"Impressions of the Second Pan-African Congress." *Crisis* 23:12–18 (November 1921).

"The Symbolism of Bert Williams." *Crisis* 24:12–15 (May 1922).

"The Thirteenth Biennial of the NACW." *Crisis* 24:257–60 (October 1922).

"Double Trouble (Part One)." *Crisis* 26:155–59 (August 1923).

"Double Trouble (Part Two)." *Crisis* 26:205–9 (September 1923).

"The 'Y' Conference at Talladega." *Crisis* 26:213–15 (September 1923).

"Out of the West." *Crisis* 27:11–18 (November 1923).

"Yarrow Revisited." *Crisis* 29:107–09 (January 1925).

"The Negro in Art: How Shall He Be Portrayed: A Symposium." *Crisis* 32:71–72 (June 1926).

"The Gift of Laughter." *The New Negro.* Edited by Alain Locke. New York: Albert and Charles Boni, 1926.

SECONDARY WORKS

BIOGRAPHICAL AND CRITICAL STUDIES

Allen, Carol. *Black Women Intellectuals: Strategies of Nation, Family, and Neighborhood in the Works of Pauline Hopkins, Jessie Fauset, and Marita Bonner.* New York: Garland, 1998.

Hughes, Langston. *The Big Sea.* New York: Knopf, 1940.

Johnson-Feelings, Dianne, ed. *The Best of the Brownies' Book.* New York: Oxford University Press, 1996.

McLendon, Jacquelyn Y. *The Politics of Color in the Fiction of Jessie Fauset and Nella Larsen.* Charlottesville: University of Virginia Press, 1995.

"Men of the Month." *Crisis* 19:341 (November 1919).

Starkey, Marion L. "Jessie Fauset." *The Southern Workman* 61:217–20 (May 1932).

Sylvander, Carolyn. *Jessie Redmon Fauset, Black American Writer.* Troy, N.Y.: Whitston, 1981.

Wall, Cheryl A. *Women of the Harlem Renaissance.* Bloomington: Indiana University Press, 1995.

Wilson, Sondra Kathryn, ed. *The "Crisis" Reader.* New York: Modern Library, 1919.

LEON FORREST
(1937–1997)

JAMES A. MILLER

DURING HIS LIFETIME, Leon Forrest was regarded as a highly original and innovative writer but also as a difficult, sometimes obscure one. Since his death at sixty, in November 1997, his work has steadily achieved more critical acclaim, and the audience for his work continues to grow. This is partly a result of the dedicated efforts of his colleagues at Northwestern University, where he taught from 1973 to 1997, who inaugurated The Leon Forrest Lecture in 2000. But it is also due to the dedicated efforts of a committed group of critics and readers who recognized Forrest's creative genius from the beginning of his career and who have worked constantly to bring his work to a wider audience. More and more, Forrest has become regarded as a major writer whose artistry and complexity of vision rewards the demands he makes on his readers.

Leon Forrest was born at Chicago's Cook County Hospital on January 8, 1937, the only child of two teenage parents. His mother, Adeline Green, came from a New Orleans Creole family that had migrated to Chicago. In his essay "The Light of the Likeness—Transformed," Forrest described his father, Leon Sr., as a "hypersensitive, talented, Mississippi mulatto who did not know his white father, Archie Forrest, so that compensating for his lack of a father and a family unit became everything to him." With his mother, Emma, and his grandmother, Katie,

Leon Sr. left Bolivar, Mississippi, for Chicago in the late 1920s. Leon Sr. had been working since the age of six; in Chicago he rose to the position of a bartender on the Sante Fe railroad, providing his family with a five-room apartment on South Parkway (now Martin Luther King Drive) and a secure position in the lower-middle-class African American community.

Early Influences

Forrest grew up in a traditional African American extended family in which two distinct streams of African American life converged: the Protestantism and values of his father's rural Mississippi upbringing and the Catholic, Creole outlook of his mother's family. His paternal great-grandmother, whose mother had been a slave, lived with the family until Forrest was ten, and Forrest used to read the Bible to her, mainly the Old Testament. Another important member of his household was his "Aunt" Lenora Bell, a seamstress. As he told Kenneth Warren in a 1993 interview, "She wasn't related to us, but had raised my mother and was very instrumental in my raising and rearing. She was a complicated woman, a Republican. . . . She was also quite a good storyteller and would read to me a lot." Forrest often spent weekends with his father's aunt, Maude Richardson, whom he described in his essay "In the Light of Lightness":

> She taught Bible class in the Protestant tradition, which in her ethos was something of a commingling of Baptist and Methodist interpretation, recombined with Negro peasant savvy. She and her husband maintained the ethos of the South and the Negro values of genuine effort, and God-fearing connections. . . . This migrant from Greenville, Mississippi, never let the ethos of Chicago get into the bloodstream of her values. Thus, in the very heart of the slums, where they live, you will find a little Southern patch of vegetables growing in the backyard and Uncle Eddie's flower garden growing in the front—untouched, and even respected, by winos and lost souls of the neighborhood.

On his mother's side of the family, Forrest's Aunt Maude White "ran the cafeteria at St. Elizabeth's Catholic High School. She worked long hours; but she was also rarely without her rosary beads; she took in many orphans from the Catholic Home Bureau. She attended the earliest mass each morning, and took Holy Communion regularly, throughout the week." These three women—Lenora Bell, Maude Richardson, and Maude White—were important influences on Forrest's early development and left their distinct imprints on his fiction.

Forrest also acknowledged other important family influences: "My grand-uncle on my mother's side was a great storyteller and he was a banjo player; he had gone to school with Louis Armstrong in New Orleans. He was also a barber and his story-telling patterns have enriched my memory bank, in the oral tradition." And he described his Uncle George Dewey White as having a "wonderful comic sense, [who] enjoyed imitating the voices of people he spoke of."

At the center of this extended family stood Forrest's parents, both of whom had musical and literary talents and nurtured his imagination. Adeline had a passionate interest in jazz and popular singers, particularly Billie Holiday, and occasionally wrote short stories for maga-

zines—none of which were ever published. A consummate storyteller, Leon Sr. regaled his family with accounts of the celebrities and personalities he met on his railroad runs. He was also a lyricist who had had several of his songs published and enjoyed filming home movies with his eight-millimeter camera. As a child Forrest attended the Pilgrim Baptist Church on Chicago's South Side, where his father had once been a choir member, and his mother's St. Elizabeth's Catholic Church, where, fascinated by its rituals, he received religious instruction and became a communicant.

In the deeply racially segregated world of Chicago in the 1940s, Forrest attended Wendell Phillips School, an all-black neighborhood school. In 1951, he enrolled in Hyde Park High School, a highly regarded, predominantly white school near the University of Chicago. By the early 1950s, the African American student population there had grown to about 25 percent—although there was only one African American teacher. Forrest was an indifferent student, but he sparkled in his creative writing class—encouraged by his teacher Mrs. Edyth Thompson. After graduating from Hyde Park High School in 1955, he enrolled in Wilson Junior College, but he abandoned his studies after a year.

In 1956, Forrest's parents divorced. The following year, Adeline married an accountant, William Harrison Pitts. They opened a liquor store, the 408 Liquors, on Seventy-ninth and South Park, with a package-goods section and a lounge. Forrest worked as a clerk in the store and a relief bartender in the lounge—experiences he would later thoroughly mine in his sprawling epic *Divine Days*. He also took classes at Roosevelt University and was smitten with the music of Charlie Parker, the poetry of Dylan Thomas, and the plays of Eugene O'Neill. At this time, Forrest imagined himself as a potential poet and playwright. In 1960 he enrolled in a playwriting course with Norbert Hruby in the Extension Division of the University of Chicago. Later that year, he dropped out of college and was drafted into the U.S. Army.

After basic training at Fort Leonard Wood, Missouri, and Fort Hood, Texas, Forrest was

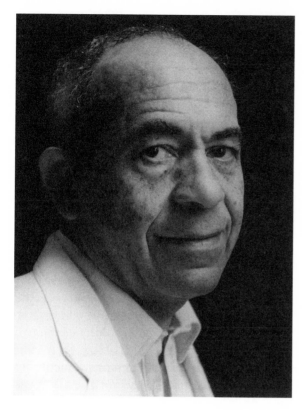

Leon Forrest

shipped to Gelnhausen, Germany, where he spent the remainder of his two-year tour of duty as a Public Information Specialist, writing feature stories for the Third Armored Division newspaper, *Spearhead*. He devoted his free time to playwriting, stage managing the theater group at the military base, and traveling.

The 1960s

In 1962, Forrest returned to Chicago, resuming work at 408 Liquors as manager and bartender. He also returned to the Extension Division of the University of Chicago, where he took a poetry workshop with John Logan and a creative-writing workshop and a course on the modern novel with Perrin Holmes Lowrey, a white Mississippian.

Forrest's encounter with Lowrey marked a turning point in the young man's career. In the writing workshop, Forrest presented a three-act play, *Theatre of the Soul*, that he had begun writing during his military service. In the modern-literature course, Forrest was introduced to the modernist themes and techniques of William Faulkner's *The Sound and the Fury* (1929) and James Joyce's *Portrait of the Artist as a Young Man* (1916). His encounter with these writers inspired him to reread Ralph Ellison's celebrated masterpiece, *Invisible Man* (1952), with renewed enthusiasm. Under Lowrey's tutelage, Forrest began to shift the focus of his literary aspirations from poetry and playwriting to fiction. Through Lowrey, Forrest met another University of Chicago English professor, John Cawelti, who became a lifelong friend and whose efforts as a critic were indispensable in shaping a favorable climate of opinion for Forrest's work.

In August 1964, Forrest's mother died suddenly at the age of 45, after an operation for cancer of the intestine. The following month, Forrest moved into a small room in a building occupied by visual artists, musicians, and writers. There he devoted all of his available time to working on a novel, supporting himself by working as a part-time office boy and as a member of the Catholic Interracial Council's Speaker's Bureau.

In June 1965, Forrest experienced another trauma: Lowrey, his teacher-mentor, was killed in an automobile accident in Sweet Briar, Virginia. Forrest published an eloquent tribute to Lowrey that caught the attention of Ralph Ellison (although it would be seven more years before Forrest would encounter Ellison face-to-face), who had known and liked Lowrey.

In 1966, Forrest published a fictional fragment, "That's Your Little Red Wagon," in a short-lived literary magazine, *Blackbird*; this sketch would later become incorporated into his first novel, *There Is a Tree More Ancient Than Eden* (1973). During the same year Forrest met another University of Chicago professor who would play an important role in his life: the eminent scholar and social anthropologist Allison Davis, whose jointly authored studies *Children of Bondage: The Personality Development of Negro Youth in the Urban South* (1940) and *Deep South: A Social Anthropological Study of Caste and Class* (1941) were

235

highly regarded as classics of social-science investigation and analysis. A professor of educational psychology at the university, Davis was a particularly rich source of insight into the social and cultural life of black Chicago. He and Forrest became fast friends and remained so until Davis' death in 1983.

Forrest had begun writing for and editing weekly South Side newspapers, the *Woodlawn Booster* and the *Englewood Bulletin*, in 1965, continuing to pursue his own writing during his spare time. For a time, he also edited a newspaper of the Woodlawn Organization, a grass-roots community group that gained national attention for its bold organizing strategies.

In 1969, Forrest joined the staff of *Muhammad Speaks*, the national newspaper of the Nation of Islam, under the leadership of the Honorable Elijah Muhammad, as an associate editor. Forrest's managing editor was Richard Durham, whom Forrest described in his essay "Elijah" as "a tremendously interesting and complex man. Sly and subtle, well-educated and very much a race-man in the old-fashioned tradition, Durham was definitely a Marxist in his private faith concerning the ultimate need for a socialistic faith." Durham and Forrest would turn out to be the last non-Muslim editors of *Muhammad Speaks*.

Forrest was deeply influenced by Durham, a man who maintained his commitments to the deepest values of African American life and culture in a theological, political, and working environment that often excoriated and condemned those very values. Forrest was also deeply impressed with the Honorable Elijah Muhammad and attracted to his vision for the black community at the same time that he recognized the dangers of religious charlatanism and racial demagoguery. Forrest expressed his complex and deeply ambivalent responses to the Honorable Elijah Muhammad and the Nation of Islam in his essay "Elijah"; he also revealed them in the novels *The Bloodworth Orphans* (1977) and *Divine Days* (1992) in the form of W. D. Ford, a trickster figure clearly based on the legendary figure W. A. D. Fard, who is said to have delivered the Muslim message to the Honorable Elijah Muhammad before

he mysteriously disappeared. Forrest would continue to work for *Muhammad Speaks* until 1973.

The 1970s

In 1971, Forrest was deeply affected by three major events in his life: his father died of chronic diabetes in April; he married the former Marianne Duncan in September; and he completed a draft of his novel, then called *Wakefulness*, and sent it to a recently promoted senior editor at Random House, Toni Morrison. Forrest met Morrison for the first time in October 1971 and received a contract from Random House the following month. This was the beginning of a long and productive editorial relationship with Morrison that continued through *Two Wings to Veil My Face* (1984), when Morrison left Random House to join the faculty of the State University of New York at Albany as the Schweitzer Professor.

In 1972, Forrest was promoted to managing editor of *Muhammad Speaks*. In November of that year, he met Ralph Ellison, traveling to New York to interview the author in his Riverside Drive apartment for a feature article for *Muhammad Speaks*. Forrest had undertaken an extensive revision and expansion of his manuscript (now known by the title suggested by Morrison: *There Is a Tree More Ancient Than Eden*), and he presented Ellison with a copy of the bound galleys. Ellison subsequently conveyed his enthusiastic endorsement of the novel to Morrison, and his written comments became the foreword to it. *There Is a Tree More Ancient Than Eden* was published in May 1973, boosted by Ellison's foreword and a ringing endorsement by Saul Bellow. On the eve of the novel's publication, Forrest ended his association with *Muhammad Speaks*.

With the publication of *There Is a Tree More Ancient Than Eden*, Forrest's life and work entered a distinct new stage. In June 1973, Jan Carew, chair of African American Studies at Northwestern University, introduced Forrest to the dean of the College of Arts and Sciences, who offered him a faculty appointment in African American Studies. Forrest joined the faculty as an associate professor, without tenure, in September 1973. In 1977, his second novel, *The Bloodworth Orphans*, was published. Although Forrest was now a successfully published novelist and a full-time faculty member, he continued his self-education, pursuing studies in anthropology and immersing himself in western literary traditions. Under the tutelage of Marvin Mirsky, a dedicated literature professor at the University of Chicago's Extension Program for Continuing Education, Forrest pursued in-depth studies of the Bible, William Faulkner, Fyodor Dostoyevsky, James Joyce's *Ulysses* (1932), Marcel Proust's *Remembrance of Things Past* (c.1932–1934), Virginia Woolf, and William Shakespeare.

The 1980s and 1990s

Forrest's third novel, *Two Wings to Veil My Face*, was published in 1984, the same year he was promoted to full professor at Northwestern. That year he also began writing the work that would become his magnum opus, *Divine Days*, a project that commanded his attention for the next seven years. In 1985, Forrest was appointed chair of the African American Studies Department, a position he occupied for the next nine years; he was also given a joint appointment as professor of English.

Although Forrest's first three novels had been critical successes, they had not been profitable. The manuscript of *Divine Days* had swollen to over eighteen hundred pages, and Random House was reluctant to publish it. The efforts of Lee Webster, the founder and publisher of Another Chicago Press, led to the paperback reissue of Forrest's novels and an agreement to publish *Divine Days*. Another Chicago Press brought out fifteen hundred copies to outstanding reviews in July 1992. Regrettably, a fire destroyed some of the remaining stock of the novel in December of that year, and shortly afterward, the distributor for Another Chicago Press went bankrupt. These setbacks did not prevent the *Chicago Sun-Times* from awarding *Divine Days* its Book of the Year Award for 1993.

Other accolades followed. *Callaloo*, one of the premier journals of African American and African literature in the United States, dedicated a special section to Forrest's work in its spring 1993 issue, and there was a five-hour benefit reading of *Divine Days* (modeled on the annual twenty-four-hour readings of James Joyce's *Ulysses* on "Bloomsday," June 16, in Dublin and other cities throughout the world) for Another Chicago Press in May 1993. Shortly after these triumphs, at the end of May, Forrest underwent surgery for colon cancer; the operation was successful, but he was directed by his doctors to undergo chemotherapy for the next six months.

Despite his illness, Forrest maintained an upbeat and optimistic outlook. He delivered the convocation address for Northwestern's College of Arts and Sciences in July 1993. That same month Another Chicago Press and Norton collaborated to bring out a hardback edition of *Divine Days*. In March 1994 Forrest published an important collection of essays, *Relocations of the Spirit* (later reissued in paperback as *The Furious Voice for Freedom*). After Ralph Ellison died in April 1994, Forrest traveled to New York to deliver one of the eulogies at the private funeral. In June, Forrest traveled to Berlin and Hamburg as part of an exchange between Chicago and Berlin writers. Early in 1995, Norton published a paperback edition of *Divine Days*. At the time of his death, Forrest had just completed five novellas, yet unpublished, collectively entitled *Let There Be Light, Let There Be Light!*

There Is a Tree More Ancient Than Eden

The diverse and complex influences that have shaped Leon Forrest's artistic imagination achieve their fullest expression in his verbal exuberance, his sense of sheer exhilaration with the sounds and sweep of African American oral expression: vernacular speech, sermons, blues, spirituals, jazz. This is the most immediately striking aspect of his fiction. As Ralph Ellison explained in the foreword to *There Is a Tree*

More Ancient Than Eden, Forrest is "a word-possessed (and word-possessing) imaginative man from the Negro American briar patch, whose way with words is as outrageously and inventively stunning as this outrageous America which gave him birth!"

Indeed, one way to understand Leon Forrest is as an artist who—like his fictional narrators Nathaniel Witherspoon and Joubert Antoine Jones—avidly listens to, transcribes, edits, and reshapes the voices of the world he inhabits. Forrest defined himself as "a writer who comes out of a culture steeped in the eloquence of the Oral Tradition," and his attempt to capture that eloquence provides an important clue into his aesthetic purposes. Speaking of his literary apprenticeship, Forrest noted, "I was overwhelmed by so many art forms of performance and celebration in the black community and had little confidence in my abilities to make something magical of the overpowering voices I heard all about me." In this sense, his Forest County saga is a record of his struggle to transform these voices into art.

The voices that haunt Leon Forrest, the voices that occupy Forest County—the fictional locale of all of his fiction—are those of Northern-based black characters who have migrated from the South but still carry the weight of their past experiences in their memories and on their tongues. "From the beginning," Forrest pointed out, "my Northern-based black characters emerged from a labyrinth of several worlds. The novels were set in a Northern city (suggestive of 'Chicago'); but the characters and the scenes of my Forest County were fundamentally rooted in a kind of mythical city of body and soul, where the memoirs of the South migrated up to the North." In this respect, Forrest's novels can be read as "migration narratives," as the critic Farah Jasmine Griffin defines the genre, in which the force of southern history and memory continues to shape the outlook, behavior, and destiny of characters in the present.

One of the overarching concerns that therefore connects all of Forrest's fiction is that of memory. For Forrest, the "motherland" of the people who populate Forest County, the source of its "diaspora," is the South, specifically Mississippi and Louisiana: "Undergirding my vision of characterization in the novels is a will to re-create the complex layers of the Afro-American memory, and the impact of history-as-memoir upon the contemporary experience." For Forrest, memory *is* history. It is only through the process of (re)memory, Forrest suggests, through confronting the suffering, pain, and injustice of African American history—embodied in the family and the self—that one can come to terms with the chaos of life and hope to transcend it.

Like his key literary ancestor, Ralph Ellison, Forrest saw African American oral traditions not only as vital expressive forms but as repositories of ritual and value, sources of meaning and hope in the face of suffering and tragedy. The continual desire and capacity for renewal, symbolized by the gift for improvisation that is at the heart of so many African American cultural forms, provides the basis for the redemptive possibilities of black life. As John Cawelti observes in the introduction to *Leon Forrest: Introductions and Interpretations*, African American culture has long "sought 'a way out of no-way' through spirituals, jazz and other musical transformations and through the rich oral poetry, drama, and narration of the streets." But Forrest went much further than Ellison in locating the sources of the redemptive power of African American life in black religion. The world of Forest County is that of the sacred and the profane, the religious and the secular, but in the final analysis, the sources of its deepest values are embodied in the religious faith of wise matriarchs such as Hattie Breedlove Wordlaw and Great-Momma Sweetie Reed Witherspoon.

There Is a Tree More Ancient Than Eden introduces the fictional world of Forest County. Forrest began writing this novel when he was studying Faulkner's *The Sound and the Fury* with Lowrey, and Faulkner's influences are obvious. Forrest shared with Faulkner a concern with geography, with history as it unfolds through family chronicles, and with the burdens of personal and historical consciousness. Forrest's indebtedness to literary modernism is also clear. Highly experimental and symbolically dense, *There Is a Tree More Ancient Than Eden* dispenses with conventional approaches to plot and chronology in its exploration of the multilayered consciousness of his narrator, Nathaniel Turner Witherspoon.

There Is a Tree More Ancient Than Eden begins in the early 1950s with its narrator/hero (born, like his creator, in 1937) riding with his aunt, Hattie Breedlove, in a Cadillac Fleetwood on his way to his mother's funeral. The first section of the novel, "The Lives," sets the stage for the exploration of the many levels of Nathaniel's consciousness by introducing the characters—familial and historical—who impinge on his life, whether he knows it or not. Among them are his parents, his aunt, and his grandfather, Jericho Witherspoon, as well as a gallery of characters including the gay, devout soprano M. C. Browne, the Black Muslim convert Maxwell "Black-Ball" Saltport, and the shape-shifting rebel Jamestown Fishbond. "The Lives" also includes commentary on historical and cultural figures such as Louis Armstrong, Fredrick Douglass, Harriet Tubman, and Abraham Lincoln, suggesting the existence of cultural and historical forces beyond the personal consciousness of Nathaniel Witherspoon.

As the funeral procession wends along, Nathaniel's consciousness is represented in three major sections of the novel: "The Nightmare," "The Dream," and "The Vision." Propelled by grief over the loss of his mother, Nathaniel moves through various stages of consciousness in his struggle toward greater knowledge and self-awareness. His quest is represented in "The Nightmare" by the apple tree, suggestive of the Tree of Knowledge in the Garden of Eden: "My arms aching like apple-tree ladderascending (seeing now through my frozen tears) and aching from my wings to my fingertips, full of the stuffings of patches." The other key image in this section is that of wings—"The wings, lamblike on the outside but yellowed like an ancient scroll, greasy, black and purplish blue, like bruised blood, tough and wolfish underneath"—suggestive of flying and flight and also of freedom and transcendence. The tension between climbing and flying frames the motion of "The Nightmare."

At the center of the novel is the orphan Nathaniel, whose loss of his mother constitutes a break in the ties that link him to his family history and the past. Images of violence and death pervade "The Nightmare" section of the novel. As Nathaniel travels in the automobile, his mind drifts back to experiences he has had in his family, notably the hilarious cantaloupe incident involving Jamestown Fishbond and Nathaniel's light-skinned, middle-class Uncle DuPont; but he also recalls the death of neighborhood children in a fire, the beating death of M. C. Browne, and his mother's death. The family and neighborhood memories are interspersed with other stories: the tragic deaths of the great jazz artists Charlie Parker and Billie Holiday and cascading images of slave ships, runaway slaves and their pursuers, and horrific lynchings. In this section, two powerful, counterposed figures emerge: Jamestown (named after the colony where Africans first arrived on these shores, marking their slow, inexorable process toward becoming African Americans) and Aunt Hattie Breedlove. Jamestown is a gifted artist and rebel whose artistic impulses are thwarted by American racism; he channels his anger into revolutionary politics. Aunt Hattie maintains her devout religious faith, preaching the virtues of patience and trust in God as the path to redemption and salvation. Toward the end of "The Nightmare," Nathaniel appears to be traveling on a train with Jamestown toward the valley of the shadow of death when he thinks he hears Aunt Hattie's preacher quoting the words of Paul: "For we know that if our earthly house of this tabernacle were dissolved, we have a building of God and a house not made of hands; eternal in the heavens."

"The Dream" plunges Nathaniel into another level of consciousness, locating his experience of loss and grief into the wider terrain of African American life. This section is notable for its scrutiny of the various strategies African Americans have pursued to cope with American life. One dialogue between Nathaniel and Aunt Hattie revolves around the aunt's insistence that Nathaniel can transcend his grief through faith in Christ. Another, with Jamestown Fishbond, recounts how Fishbond's father, Moses Booker Fishbond, was raised by his father to accept Booker T. Washington's ideology. Moses rejected this teaching, however, opting for a hustler's life and an early death. The last dialogue revolves around Nathaniel's dream of a confrontation between Jamestown and Nathaniel's grandfather, Jericho Witherspoon, over the political destiny of African Americans. Jericho Witherspoon argues for working within the system of American democracy; Jamestown calls for violent revolution. This unresolved debate leads Nathaniel back to the train and the valley of the shadow of death.

"The Vision," cast within images of the Crucifixion, revolves around the graphic portrayal of a horrific lynching. In the face of this horror, however, Nathaniel's vision of this ritual of dismemberment seems to end on a note of resurrection. After the victim has been lynched, crucified, and brutally torn apart, his eyes remain, confronting the mob. As the crowd moves to destroy these haunting eyes, a band of angels appears, gathers up the pieces of the victim's dismembered body, and restores him to wholeness. The victim then rises and returns to the world, flying. At the end of his multilayered journey through the world of nightmare, dream, and vision, Nathaniel has apparently achieved a vision of how to transform his experience of suffering and grief into a more mature and historically informed understanding. The final section of the novel, "Wakefulness," is a coda on what Nathaniel has undergone, suggesting, however tenuously, that he has achieved a kind of spiritual rebirth that will sustain him in the years to come. At the end of the novel, as John Cawelti has observed, "Nathaniel has arrived at that terribly painful moment between the death of childhood and the birth of maturity."

In the 1988 edition of the novel, Forrest appended a new section, "Transformation." It contains two parts, both dated considerably later than the action of the original novel. The first, "The Epistle of Sweetie Reed," is dated 1967, when Nathaniel is thirty years old. The second is a sermon on the legacy of Martin Luther King Jr. by the Reverend Pompey C.J. Browne in 1980, twelve years after King's assassination. Nathaniel is now forty-three years old. Both of these sections bring the wisdom of historical hindsight to bear on the world of Forest County. "The Epistle of Sweetie Reed," written to President Lyndon B. Johnson, offers her wry and wise reflections on the legislative victories of the Civil Rights movement, the War on Poverty, the rise of student radicals and the Black Power movement, and the Vietnam War. Reverend Browne's sermon occurs at a point in time when the hopes and dreams of the Civil Rights movement seem to have fissured and dissipated. We see that the world Nathaniel inhabited at the age of fifteen has changed considerably, but we also see in retrospect that it continues to teeter between apocalyptic despair and redemptive hope.

The Bloodworth Orphans

Forrest's second novel, *The Bloodworth Orphans*, continues the story of the Witherspoon family, creating a crowded network of characters all linked by their shared sense of orphanhood and their sometimes destructive search for father figures. Like *There Is a Tree More Ancient Than Eden*, *The Bloodworth Orphans* begins with a Faulknerian genealogy. John Cawelti recalls that in response to critics who found the first novel too internalized and impressionistic, Forrest "decided to write enough different characters and actions into his second novel to satisfy everyone." Noting that *The Bloodworth Orphans* was published two years after the phenomenal popular success of Alex Haley's family saga, *Roots*, some critics have suggested that *The Bloodworth Orphans* can be read as *Roots*'s antithesis. Cawelti notes: "Haley's saga portrayed the struggle of an African-American family not only to survive but to retain some memory of lineage and heritage. Forrest, however, feels that there is a more tragic side to the African experience in America which must be acknowledged."

Like Forrest's first novel, the action of *The Bloodworth Orphans* begins with Nathaniel Witherspoon riding in a car, this time a grand Lincoln Continental limousine owned by Regal Pettibone. The novel begins in Forest County on Palm Sunday, 1970. Nathaniel is thirty-three years old. In this novel, he appears as the auditor and witness of the tragedy of the Bloodworth orphans, not as the center of narrative consciousness.

Singer, playboy, and businessman Regal Pettibone is going to pick up his adoptive mother, Rachel Flowers, after the evening service of the River Rock of Eden Baptist Church, in anticipation of his annual Easter Sunday appearance, where he will perform a musical service with his mother. Regal is an orphan who once confided to Nathaniel that he "felt doomed, driven to know his origins, a greater world, to be a king, to know God the true Father, yes . . . Pettibone always felt proud of his unknown, unscaled pedigree in which he envisioned himself an orphan of royalty in search of the true inherited treasures of his lost-found-lost father." Rachel Flowers—"an overwhelming Christian woman, whose love, adoration and service to Almighty God (and her blindness) made her seem more and more 'otherworldly' to the flock at River Rock of Eden Church, where she led the choir and everyone else"—seems, like Hattie Breedlove and Sweetie Reed, to represent the depths of African American religious faith and spirituality. In Rachel's case, however, her religion has become contorted by fanaticism and the will to power—symbolized by her bizarre marriage to Bee-More Flowers, a 350-pound, self-indulgent diabetic.

Rachel is revealed as a key link to the Bloodworth clan—whose curse hovers over the novel—a family of white Mississippi slaveholders founded by Arlington Bloodworth Sr. and whose descendants, black and white, crisscross each other, often without being aware that they are related to each other. Sexually exploited by Arlington Bloodworth III, Rachel has given birth to two of his sons: Industrious and Carl-Rae. Unable to cope with Bloodworth's perverse sexual demands and driven mad by him, Rachel leaves her sons in the care of a black minister and is violently coerced into accepting Christianity by another one. She ultimately settles in Forest County and is reunited with her now grown sons, both of whom are killed in the same year. Rachel tries to atone for her inability to save her sons by adopting Regal Pettibone, but she plunges more deeply into religious fanaticism. Her death from cancer is one of the pivotal events of the novel.

At the same time that Rachel Flowers dies, another major character, Abraham Dolphin, commits suicide. Dolphin, too, is a descendent of the Bloodworths—although he does not know it. The grandson of Arlington Bloodworth II, the son of Bloodworth's mixed-race son, William Body, Dolphin is left to die by his mother in the mud of a river. Discovered by the mentally unbalanced daughter of a plantation owner, Governor Masterson, Dolphin is raised by the Masterson family but remains aware that he is black. He graduates from medical school and establishes a successful practice in the South, but his political activism during the 1952 election makes it necessary for him to flee—north to Forest County. Dolphin successfully reestablishes himself but continues to be plagued by an increasingly frenzied and fruitless search for his family origins. Failing in his quest, Dolphin kills himself.

Nathaniel bears witness to the deaths of Rachel Flowers and Abraham Dolphin and is deeply affected by them. Other tragedies follow. The River Rock of Eden Church is destroyed in a terrible storm. Three more of Nathaniel's acquaintances turn out to be Bloodworth descendants and are revealed as siblings. His beloved friend Regal Pettibone is involved in a passionate affair with La Donna Scales, who turns out to be Regal's own sister. Their brother, Amos-Otis Thigpen, an associate of the late Abraham Dolphin, exposes this incestuous affair, then shoots La Donna and Regal before turning the gun on himself. The frenzied members of the River Rock of Eden Church then unleash their rage on Regal and tear him to pieces. *The Bloodworth Orphans* rises to the crescendo of a bloodbath. In John Cawelti's words, as the action reaches this mythical catastrophe, "we realize that the Bloodworth curse is Forrest's metaphor for the devastating and destructive loss of black identity in American society where the actuality of racial and cultural mixing has been pathologically denied, and the myths of white supremacy and racial purity have exacted a profound and lasting cost on the lives of individuals."

In the aftermath of the tragedy that has befallen the Bloodworth orphans, Nathaniel receives a message from his mother of his childhood friend, Maxwell "Black-Ball" Saltport, that Black-Ball, who had converted to the Black Muslim faith and risen rapidly in its ranks, has fallen into disfavor with its leadership and is hiding out in an abandoned apartment building in the Forest County ghetto. In the middle of a free-wheeling conversation with Black-Ball, Nathaniel is captured in a police raid and incarcerated in Refuge Hospital, a mental-treatment facility. There he encounters the music of Ironwood "Landlord" Rumble, a jazz musician he had heard earlier with Regal Pettibone.

The jazz musician, as represented by Rumble, emerges as a force for transformation and re-creation, a way to transcend the tragic experiences Nathaniel has witnessed. Another strategy for coping with the chaos of life is suggested by Noah Ridgerook Grandberry, an inmate who becomes Nathaniel's spiritual guide. Grandberry is also a Bloodworth descendant and a half-brother to the tragic Bloodworth siblings. Unlike them, however, he has survived because he has learned how to face the forces of chaos with practiced deception. One of the many trickster figures who populate Forrest's fiction, Grandberry shares with Nathaniel the wisdom of his own "tricknology." Despite the increasing chaos of the outside world—a world consumed by violence, gang warfare, arson, and the breakdown of civil order—Nathaniel and Grandberry decide that they must reenter life with all of its chaos, thus symbolizing the renewal of life's possibilities. As they flee the Refuge Hospital, Nathaniel almost stumbles over a box containing a screaming baby. Carrying the baby with them, Nathaniel and Grandberry flee in a stolen police car. The last words of the novel center on the baby: "Then they turned about and looked down upon the back seat in the boot box, at the little black baby's face—perhaps three months old, wailing with fear and life, its trembling little hands reaching upwards towards the two sad-faced sobbing men."

Two Wings to Veil My Face

The third novel in the Forest County saga, *Two Wings to Veil My Face*, is also Forrest's most conventional and accessible one. The action of the novel begins in 1958, and Nathaniel Witherspoon is again the central figure, although—as in *The Bloodworth Orphans*—he functions primarily as an auditor and recorder. His grandmother, Sweetie Reed, now ninety-one years old and ailing, has summoned him to her bedroom to fulfill a promise she made to him fourteen years ago. At the time of the death of Nathaniel's grandfather, Jericho Witherspoon, Sweetie Reed promised Nathaniel that she would explain her bizarre behavior at Jericho's funeral; she also promised to explain why she stopped using her married name, Witherspoon, many years earlier. Nathaniel is now twenty-one, a college dropout, and searching for direction in his life.

From the very beginning of the novel, Nathaniel understands that he is being introduced into the tangled web of relationships that constitutes his family history: "But now the young man Nathaniel Witherspoon . . . wondered if all the storytelling, the loving, the harsh discipline, the praying and the direction had been a preparation for the day, *this* day, when he would have to take over her memories, and business, and even participate in the state of her soul's progress."

To reinforce Nathaniel's active participation in the stories she will tell, Sweetie Reed refuses to allow him to record her, as he has suggested:

No. Just bring along a pen and a pad, not a pencil, either, because too much has been erased in time. Nor an indelible pencil. Write it all down in longhand, with blue-black ink on the pad, in your notebook, and then it will all be recorded on the tablet of your memory and in your heart, as it's transformed from your longhand to your short memory.

Instead of offering an immediate explanation of her behavior, Sweetie Reed launches into a rambling, discursive narrative, spinning stories within stories that begin with an earlier moment in her life: the year 1906, when she returns to the deathbed of her father, I. V. Reed, to listen to *his* rambling vindication of his life.

Roughly half of Sweetie Reed's story concerns I. V. Reed, Nathaniel's great-grandfather, who was born a slave on the Mississippi plantation of Rollins Reed in 1827. Quick, talented, intelligent, and wily, I. V. is a house slave and body servant to Rollins Reed. In a central episode in I. V.'s life, his jealousy of a powerful field slave, Reece Shank Haywood, provokes him to reveal to Haywood that his master, Rollins Reed, has been seen leaving the shack of Haywood's woman, Jubell. I. V. hopes that he can provoke a confrontation between Haywood and Rollins that will lead to Haywood's punishment.

Haywood explodes with rage, however, and almost kills Rollins before being driven away by a rock hurled by I. V's slingshot. I. V. drags Rollins to an ancient African healer, Auntie Foisty, who not only restores Rollins to life but punishes I. V. for what he has done to Haywood. Her curse is that I. V. will forever be the servant and shadow of Rollins Reed; I. V. is literally and symbolically chained to Rollins' bed for the rest of his life.

This episode introduces the theme of betrayal that is played out on a number of different levels throughout the novel. Nathaniel learns of I. V's marriage to Angelina, the daughter of Rollins Reed and possibly Jubell, Haywood's woman; of the birth of Sweetie in 1867 and her early estrangement from I. V.; of the theft of Sweetie and her mother, Angelina, in 1874 and the rape and murder of Angelina (witnessed by Sweetie) before Sweetie is rescued; and of Sweetie's arranged marriage—her sale, in effect—to Jericho Witherspoon, a well-established lawyer, judge, and Forest County resident. Jericho is fifty-five, forty years Sweetie's senior, and sees her only purpose as producing his children.

It is only at the end of this remarkable saga that Sweetie turns her attention to the story she promised to tell. After years of miscarriages and infant deaths, Sweetie fails to produce a child. Jericho Witherspoon betrays her by fathering a child with another woman, Lucasta Jones. He

returns home in 1905 with his son, Arthur, who will become Nathaniel's father, and Sweetie agrees to raise him but separates from Jericho. Nathaniel's father was adopted; the woman he thought was his biological grandmother is not.

Faced with the hard and painful truths that exist beneath the surface of his family history as he thought he knew it, Nathaniel must now grapple with the meanings of his family inheritance. "It is an inheritance fraught with ambiguity," Keith Byerman points out in "The Flesh Made Word." "The polyglossic tale that is black history is not necessarily harmonious, but neither is it easily dichotomous. To insist on either is to descend into sentimentality and self-righteousness." Nathaniel must learn to confront the voices that constitute his family history in all their complexity, for better or worse. There will be no neat or tidy resolution, but without this encounter with the past, with all of its contradictions, *Two Wings to Veil My Face* makes clear, one cannot hope to reinvent oneself in the present.

A major turning point in Forrest's career, *Two Wings to Veil My Face* won the DuSable Museum Certificate of Merit and Achievement in Fiction, the Carl Sandburg Award, the Friends of Literature Prize, and the Society of Midland Authors Award for fiction.

Divine Days

In the last novel published in his lifetime, *Divine Days*—a sprawling comic epic of over eleven hundred pages—Forrest gives full rein to the linguistic virtuosity, the gift for satire, and the wild flights of imagination that have always lurked in his fiction. He also introduces a new protagonist, Joubert Antoine Jones, a first-person narrator who presents the action of the novel in the form of his journal.

Like Leon Forrest, Jones has returned to Forest County after completing a tour of army duty in Germany; like Nathaniel Witherspoon, he is an orphan from a Protestant-Catholic background. But Jones has been raised by his Aunt Eloise, a witty, educated, and cosmopolitan woman from a New Orleans Creole family who

243

is both a talented journalist and a successful businesswoman, part owner of Eloise's Night Light Lounge. And Jones is much more urbane, self-confident, and clear about the direction of his life than Nathaniel Witherspoon. He is determined to become a successful playwright; *Divine Days* recounts a critical week in his pursuit of this goal.

Divine Days begins on Wednesday, February 16, 1966, and concludes exactly one week later. Jones has recently returned to Forest County, where he has resumed his former job as a bartender at Aunt Eloise's lounge—one of the main centers of action in the novel. Shortly before his return to the United States he had received a wire from Aunt Eloise informing him of the death of his childhood idol, Sugar-Groove. This news inspires him to write a play based on his life: "Sugar-Groove, that mythic soul of Forest County, whose early memory was forged mainly in Mississippi. It is his stories, founded upon those memories, that I feel destined to dramatize. During the course of transforming his life, I personally hope to discover a meaning of existence out of this man's divine days upon this planet."

Jones had previously written a play about the notorious hustler, preacher, and cult leader W. A. D. Ford—also a sometime resident of Forest County—which he sent to a producer but which had gotten lost in the mail. From the beginning of *Divine Days*, Sugar-Groove and Ford are inextricably linked in Jones's mind as antithetical forces: he worships Sugar-Groove, but he is fascinated by Ford. A great deal of the novel revolves around Jones's efforts to sort out their relationships—to each other and to him.

A shape-shifting trickster, Ford has flitted in and out of the Forest County saga. He plays a prominent role in *The Bloodworth Orphans* as a mentor to Noah Ridgerook Grandberry, and he continues to function as a shadowy, legendary, mythic figure in *Divine Days*. Ford and his religious sect, it turns out, occupied the property that now houses Eloise's lounge; and Ford's presence haunts the building and Jones's imagination. "Ford clearly represents the dark and manipulative side of human creativity in religion, power, and art," John Cawelti observes

in "Earthly Thoughts on *Divine Days*." "In his shape-shifting demonism Ford also exemplifies the primal energy of chaos, the basic material of creation."

Sugar-Groove—the archetypal hipster and ladies' man—belongs to the tragic, ill-fated Bloodworth family, the unacknowledged son of a prominent southern white man, Wilfred Bloodworth, and his African American mistress, Sarah Belle. Unlike the siblings of *The Bloodworth Orphans*, however, Sugar-Groove has a clear understanding of his family heritage and manages to evade their fate. Jones's first encounter with Sugar-Groove occurs when Jones is a shoe-shine boy in Williemain's barber shop—another prominent locale in *Divine Days*. During a moment when no one else is in the shop, Sugar-Groove regales Jones with riveting stories of his life—stories that Jones devotes a great deal of time recounting in the novel.

One major strand of *Divine Days* revolves around the struggle between Sugar-Groove and W. A. D. Ford, which leads inexorably to the moutaintop struggle between the two antagonists that is one of the highlights of the novel. The other major dimension of the plot recounts the tragic end of Jones's love interest, De Loretto/Imani, who is portrayed as the victim of the ideological excesses of black nationalism. A talented artist and a dedicated social worker, De Loretto/Imani is consumed by her desire to recover a pure African heritage. She lines the walls of her apartment with African art of questionable authenticity, creates works of art that glorify and romanticize the lives of young urban hoodlums, and renames herself and her son with terms derived from the recently created ritual of Kwanza. De Loretto/Imani is finally driven to suicide in the aftermath of a brutal encounter session with other blacks who insist that she rigidly and absolutely define her racial/cultural identity and loyalties. The relationship between De Loretto/Imani's suicide and the epic struggle between Sugar-Groove and Ford clarifies a point of view that has been insistent in Forrest's fiction from the very beginning: any attempt to compromise the dynamism, the complexity, the inventiveness, and the improvisatory will to re-create of African American life and culture is destined to fail, doomed to tragedy.

Like all of Forrest's fiction, *Divine Days* is crowded with colorful characters and scenes from a wide spectrum of African American life. "It's surely no exaggeration," John Cawelti observes, "to say that *Divine Days* is the most encyclopedic account yet created of the whole range of contemporary African-American urban culture." It stands as a fitting culmination to a distinguished literary career.

Selected Bibliography

PRIMARY WORKS

NOVELS

There Is a Tree More Ancient Than Eden. New York: Random House, 1973.
The Bloodworth Orphans. New York: Random House, 1977.
Two Wings to Veil My Face. New York: Random House, 1983.
Divine Days. Chicago: Another Chicago Press, 1992. Paperback edition, New York: W. W. Norton & Company, 1995.

ESSAYS

Relocations of the Spirit: Collected Essays. Mount Kisco, N.Y.: Moyer-Bell, 1993. Reprinted in paperback as *The Furious Voice for Freedom: Essays on Life.* Wakefield, R.I.: Asphodel Press, 1994.

SECONDARY WORKS

CRITICAL AND BIOGRAPHICAL STUDIES

Bethel, Kathleen E. "Leon Forrest: A Bibliography." *Callaloo* 16:448–54 (Spring 1993).
Byerman, Keith. "The Flesh Made Word: Family Narrative in *Two Wings to Veil My Face.*" In *Leon Forrest: Introductions and Interpretations.* Edited by John G. Cawelti. Bowling Green, Ohio: Bowling Green State University Press, 1997, pp. 199–215.
———. "Orphans and Circuses: The Literary Experiments of Leon Forrest and Clarence Major." In *Fingering the Jagged Grain: Tradition and Form in Recent Black Fiction.* Athens: University of Georgia Press, 1985. Pp. 238–74.
Cawelti, John G. "Earthly Thoughts on *Divine Days.*" *Callaloo* 16:431–47 (Spring 1993).
———, ed. *Leon Forrest: Introductions and Interpretations.* Bowling Green, Ohio: Bowling Green State University Popular Press, 1997.
Griffin, Farah Jasmine. *"Who Set You Flowin'?" The African American Migration Narrative.* New York: Oxford University Press, 1995.
Grimes, Johnanna L. "Leon Forrest." In *Dictionary of Literary Biography.* Vol. 33, *Afro-American Fiction Writers after 1955.* Edited by Thadious Davis and Trudier Harris. Detroit, Mich.: Gale Research, 1984. Pp. 77–83.
Miller, James A. "Leon Forrest." In *Oxford Companion to African American Literature.* Edited by William L. Andrews, Frances Smith Foster, and Trudier Harris. New York: Oxford University Press, 1997. Pp. 293–94.
Rosenburg, Bruce A. "Forrest Spirits: Oral Echoes in Leon Forrest's Prose." *Oral Tradition* 9:315–27 (October 1994).
Schultz, Elizabeth A. "The Heirs of Ralph Ellison: Patterns of Individualism in the Contemporary Afro-American Novel." *CLA Journal* 22, no. 2:101–22 (1978).
Taylor-Guthrie, Danille. "Sermons, Testifying, and Prayers: Looking beneath the Wings in Leon Forrest's *Two Wings to Veil My Face.*" *Callaloo* 16:419–30 (Spring 1993).
Thomas, H. Nigel. *From Folklore to Fiction: A Study of Folk Heroes and Rituals in the Black American Novel.* Westport, Conn.: Greenwood Press, 1988.
Warren, Kenneth W. "Thinking beyond Catastrophe: Leon Forrest's *There Is a Tree More Ancient Than Eden.*" *Callaloo* 16:409–18 (Spring 1993).
Werner, Craig. "Leon Forrest, the AACM, and the Legacy of the Chicago Renaissance." *Black Scholar* 23:10–23 (Summer–Fall 1993).
Williams, Dana A. "Leon Forrest." *Contemporary African American Novelists: A Bio-Bibliographical Critical Sourcebook.* Edited by Emmanuel S. Nelson. Westport, Conn.: Greenwood Press, 1999. Pp.158–63.

ERNEST J. GAINES
(1933–)

THADIOUS M. DAVIS

"I THINK ONE of the greatest things that has happened to me, as a writer and as a human being, is that I was born in the South, that I was born in Louisiana," Ernest Gaines reflected in conversation with Ruth Laney in 1974. The centrality of his origins to his work has been a recurrent theme in the many interviews he has granted throughout his career. His remarks to Laney are representative:

> Because I grew up on a plantation in the late thirties and the forties, I'm pretty sure it was not too much different from the way things could have been when my ancestors were in slavery. Oh, we could do a few little things more. But that I went through that kind of experience—there's a direct connection between the past and what is happening today. I'm very fortunate to have had that kind of background.

Few contemporary African American writers have been as candid as Gaines in asserting the formative power of race- and region-specific experiences or as persistent as he in channeling that power into prose fiction.

Early Life

Born on January 15, 1933, at River Lake Plantation in Oscar, Louisiana, Gaines was a child of both the Great Depression and the rural South. His birthplace was in the quarters where African American plantation workers had lived during slavery, and where five generations of his family had made their home while cultivating sugarcane, cotton, and corn. Like his parents, Manuel and Adrienne Gaines, and their ancestors who had known the intensity of labor and poverty under the plantation system, Ernest Gaines went early to work in the fields along False River in Point Coupee Parish. This parish is an area adjacent to the West Baton Rouge and Iberville parishes and one of the thirteen alluvial land parishes where blacks outnumbered whites, on average, ten to one after the Civil War. The oldest of eight brothers and three sisters, Gaines picked cotton at the age of eight, and by the time he was nine years old, he was digging potatoes for wages—fifty cents a day. Gaines has not romanticized growing up on a sugarcane plantation in a time of individual and systemic hardship. In talking to Marcia Gaudet and Carl Wooton for the journal *Callaloo* in 1988, he remembered that his boyhood was enriched by a supportive extended family and community in the River Lake Quarters: "I came from a place where people sat around and chewed sugar cane and roasted sweet potatoes and peanuts in the ashes and sat on ditch banks and told tales and sat on porches and went into the swamps and went into the fields—that's what I came from." Gaines has compressed much of his Louisiana childhood experience into a memory of active people.

The central person in his youth was his great-aunt Augusteen Jefferson, who had lost the use of her legs either at birth or in infancy. Unable to walk, she did not work in the fields; instead she cared for the children too young to accompany their parents in tending crops. She crawled about the cabin, performing household duties, and used benches to elevate herself for cooking and baking in a wood stove or washing clothes in a tin tub. She also made her own garden of beans, cabbages, and tomatoes, and gathered pecans from under the trees in her yard. Not only was Aunt Augusteen the primary caregiver nurturing Gaines in his youth, but she was also his principal moral influence, teaching by the example of her "true dignity." Aunt Augusteen taught him the values of quiet heroism in ordinary life, genuine courage in surviving adversities, and sincere respect for commonplace activities that have characterized his fiction. These values are embedded in all of the older black women who with dignity and strength populate Gaines's fictional world: Aunt Charlotte in *Catherine Carmier* (1964), Miss Julie and Aunt Margaret in *Of Love and Dust* (1967), Aunt Fe in the 1962 short story "Just Like a Tree," Miss Jane in *The Autobiography of Miss Jane Pittman* (1971), and Tante Lou and Miss Emma in *A Lesson before Dying* (1993), among others.

Equally important for the writer Gaines would become, Augusteen Jefferson provided him with access to talk and storytelling. In a family of storytellers, she was a "recorder" who remembered events from the past. However, because she could not easily visit the other residents of the quarters, she received "company," female and male visitors from the community who came alone or in groups to spend time on the outside gallery in summer or around the fireplace in winter: "Sometimes they would sew on quilts and mattresses while they talked; other times they would shell peas and beans while they talked. Sometimes they would just sit smoking pipes, chewing pompee, or drinking coffee while they talked."

Aunt Augusteen required Gaines, the oldest child, to remain within hearing so that he could serve the visitors coffee, water, or homemade brew and retrieve whatever they needed from the cabin. The sound of talk and the practice of listening combined to make him attentive to voice and nuances of speech, particularly the Creole spoken by his aunt and other elders, as well as to oral testimony and folk forms of storytelling.

These formative experiences taught Gaines to avoid folklore in his fiction, as is, for example, the case with Zora Neale Hurston, another southern writer from a self-contained rural black community with a prominent oral culture. Gaines's personal testimony to his aunt and to those who gathered at her house is evident in the preeminence of orality in his written texts, especially in his third novel, *The Autobiography of Miss Jane Pittman*, narrated in the voice of a courageous female witness to more than a century of life in the changing South.

Gaines, however, did not spend all of his youth in Augusteen Jefferson's cabin or in River Lake's fields. Baptized in False River at age twelve, Gaines went to the Baptist church for Sunday school and services. At about the time of his baptism, he wrote and directed a play for his church; his single childhood excursion into creative writing was significant enough to be duplicated in Jimmy Aaron's experience in *The Autobiography of Miss Jane Pittman*. During the week, the church served as the schoolhouse where he received the first six years of his education. From 1945 to 1948, Gaines attended St. Augustine, a small parochial school in New Roads, Louisiana, even though he was not a Catholic. The school required that he attend Mass, but he could not receive Communion. On occasional Friday evenings, he went to see cowboy movies in New Roads, the nearest town with a picture show and the model for Bayonne in his fiction. All of these aspects of his childhood find expression in the short stories written at the beginning of his career, in particular those focusing on the socialization of young black males, such as James in the often-anthologized "The Sky Is Gray."

Gaines left rural Louisiana in 1948, after finishing eighth grade. Because there was no junior or senior high school near Oscar for African Americans, and no relatives with whom he could stay in order to attend a town school, he had to go elsewhere for the educational opportunity that his family believed would break the cycle of peonage in the sharecropping system. He became part of the large post–World War II migration of Louisianans of color to the West Coast. Gaines has recalled packing an old brown leather suitcase with a few clothes, oranges, pecans, and a box of fried chicken, bread, tea cakes, and pralines, sustenance for a black traveler in the age of segregation. He reluctantly took leave of his aunt, the old people, and the children gathered for his departure and set out for Vallejo, California, for the residence of his mother and stepfather, Ralph Norbert Colar Sr., who had planned for the higher education they knew he deserved.

In seeking greater opportunity for themselves and their children, his parents had to leave the South. Adrienne Gaines Colar had first moved from River Lake Plantation to the port city of New Orleans, and from there west to the smaller seaport town of Vallejo with her husband, who was in the merchant marine. Initially the family lived in a government housing project with a large population of Chinese, Japanese, Filipinos, Mexicans, Puerto Ricans, Native Americans, and whites, from among whom Gaines found enough friends to compensate for his longing for Louisiana. After a few months, the family moved to a home in a downtown area where youths were tougher and streetwise.

Although reticent in speaking about his mother and silent about his biological father, Gaines has pointed to his stepfather's influence in shaping his first year in California and, by extension, his existence as a writer. In fact, he has paid tribute to his stepfather: "Very strong. A very handsome man, a big man. Most of my strong characters . . . are built around him." As a seaman, Ralph Colar was frequently away from home, but he was sensitive to the dangers his stepson could face in the neighborhood and strict enough to require him to avoid peer pressure by demanding that he leave the streets.

Ernest Gaines

Gaines quickly discovered the public library and its shelves of novels as a safe haven from the attraction of a rough crowd. His discovery fostered a love of reading, an experience denied him in rural Louisiana, where books had been a scarce commodity. In the beginning, he chose books indiscriminately, on the appeal of a dust jacket or title; however, in a short while he gravitated to books treating the South. In part he wanted to restore his connection to rural life and Louisiana, but he also needed to reaffirm his own experiences and identity. Because the small Vallejo library had a limited number of books by black authors, the southern works he read were written by whites, whose oratorical language, unrealistic dialect, and stereotypical images of blacks did not entirely obscure their ability to evoke and describe the land. As Gaines put it in "Miss Jane and I":

These writers, who so poorly described blacks, did well with the odor of grass and trees after a summer rain; they were especially adept at describing the sweat-odor of the clothes of men coming in from the fields; you could see, better than if you were actually there, the red dust in Georgia or the black mud of Mississippi.

Rapidly, Gaines made his way through all of the southern writers in his local library. His favorites were Mark Twain, whose nineteenth-century images and vernacular remained vivid, and William Faulkner, whose twentieth-century characters and settings evoked his own familiar South. Thereafter, he turned to "any writer who wrote about nature or about people who worked the land." John Steinbeck on the Salinas Valley and Willa Cather on Nebraska stood out among the authors "who would say something about dirt and trees, clear streams, and open sky." Years later, Gaines regretted that in 1948 he had lacked the opportunity to read African American texts on the South, particularly Jean Toomer's *Cane* (1923), which, he subsequently believed, would have exerted the greatest influence on him then. *Cane* has remained his favorite novel by an African American writer. Despite his acknowledgment of Toomer as a black literary forefather, Gaines has demonstrated a greater stylistic and thematic affinity for Faulkner among southern writers and for nineteenth-century Russian authors among the Europeans.

His discovery of European writers was rooted in their portrayal of the soil. From Guy de Maupassant, who was an early favorite because of storytelling marked by simple language and realistic portrayal of the young, Gaines moved on to Anton Chekhov, Leo Tolstoy, Alexander Pushkin, Nikolai Gogol, and Ivan Turgenev, who attracted him because they understood how to write about peasantry without caricature and condescension. As a group they became his favorite authors and have retained his high regard; nevertheless, they did not completely satisfy him. Their icons—cabbage soup, kvass, verst, and steppes—were all foreign to him, and their religious worship, culinary habits, measurement practices, and naming customs were not similar enough to those of his native culture to appease his need for representations of his familiar South. Two experiential

cores, the reading of formal texts and the memory of an oral culture, shaped his turning to writing fiction in which his persistent attempt has been to transmit and transfigure his formative southern experience.

Perhaps predictably, Gaines began writing stories of the Louisiana he remembered, as he relates in "Miss Jane and I":

I wanted to smell that Louisiana earth, feel that Louisiana sun, sit under the shade of one of those Louisiana oaks, search for pecans in that Louisiana grass in one of those Louisiana yards next to one of those Louisiana bayous, not far from a Louisiana river.

This powerful longing for place was not all that attracted him to writing:

I wanted to see on paper those Louisiana black children walking to school on cold days while yellow Louisiana busses passed them by. I wanted to see on paper those black parents going to work before the sun came up and coming back home to look after their children after the sun went down. I wanted to see on paper the true reason those black fathers left home—not because they were trifling or shiftless—but because they were tired of putting up with certain conditions. I wanted to see on paper the small country churches (schools during the week), and I wanted to hear those simple religious songs, those simple prayers—that true devotion. . . . And I wanted to hear that Louisiana dialect—that combination of English, Creole, Cajun, Black. . . . I wanted to read about the true relationship between whites and blacks—about the people I had known.

Consciousness of race, racial identity, and racist practices within his Louisiana also motivated his desire to write and to explain. Memory of the people left behind inspired him in 1949 to begin his first novel as a vehicle for recreating their customs, mores, and language and for commemorating life in the Louisiana that had been his home for his first fifteen years. At the same time, his need for personal identity and subjective affirmation functioned as an added incentive for writing.

Gaines had been in California only a year when he undertook a novel whose working title was "A Little Stream," in which he set out to treat two families divided by a stream of water and by a hierarchy of color. Before the work appeared in 1964 as *Catherine Carmier*, it would receive numerous working titles, all reflecting changes and developments in the plot. In 1949 and 1950, Gaines wrote the novel in longhand, rented a typewriter to complete the manuscript, and mailed it to a New York publisher, who returned it in the original brown paper with a rejection slip. The premature attempt to publish a novel did not weaken his resolve to become a writer of something *he* would want to read about the rural South, though it did destroy his fantasies of immediate publication and instant fortune.

During high school and two years at Vallejo Junior College, Gaines showed less interest in writing. School assignments and summer work left little free time. After being drafted into the army in 1953, he developed interests in pool, pinochle, and softball, so that he wrote only sporadically. While stationed on Guam, he completed a short story and entered it in a writing contest for soldiers on the island. His story won fifteen dollars, a second-place prize in the Guam competition, and was sent on to the competition for soldiers stationed throughout the Far East. Judged at the command headquarters in Japan, the story earned an honorable mention and a ten-dollar prize. Gaines cashed the ten-dollar check immediately but deposited the fifteen-dollar award in a small glass bank, a legacy from his Aunt Augusteen, who had died in 1952.

He enrolled in San Francisco State College in 1955, after being discharged from the army. His intention was to major in writing, but since the college did not offer a writing degree, he chose English on the suggestion of an adviser who pointed out that English was not merely the major closest to writing but also the one that could lead to a teaching job should he fail at writing. During the next two years, he studied for a degree while writing about Louisiana in his free time. Teachers suggested additional readings from among the modernists to advance his writing (James Joyce, Sherwood Anderson, F. Scott Fitzgerald, Ernest Hemingway, William Faulkner), but for the most part they counseled "time and work," especially the latter. In 1956 his first published story appeared in *Transfer*, a San Francisco little magazine, and with its appearance Gaines rededicated himself to a literary career. With his Bachelor of Arts degree in hand in 1957 as well as a Wallace Stegner Creative Writing Award, Gaines allotted the next ten years to becoming a professional writer, after which time, if success eluded him, he would turn to some other livelihood. During 1958–1959 he continued his English studies at Stanford while working on short stories. His story "Comeback" received the Joseph Henry Jackson Literary Award in 1959, but he could not crystallize the novel that he wanted to write about Louisiana.

Return to Point Coupee

In an effort to find himself as a novelist, Gaines planned to join friends in Mexico. The year was 1962, for southern African Americans the beginning of a momentous time following the 1954 Supreme Court desegregation decision, *Brown v. Board of Education of Topeka*, and the 1955 bus boycott in Montgomery. In 1962 James Meredith's successful application of the laws of integration to become the first black student at the University of Mississippi captured Gaines's imagination; the South was being radically transformed and a black male was publicly insisting on recognition of his manhood. Gaines reasoned that "if James Meredith can go through all this—not only for himself, but for his race (and that included me)—then I, too, should go back to the source that I was trying to write about." The decision led to a return to the South in January 1963 and a six-month stay in Baton Rouge with visits back to River Lake Plantation. This period cemented his commitment to narratives of personal transformation, centered in an inescapable past but charged with an inevitable dynamic.

Gaines's return home added the adult's perception of place to the child's vision of it. Point Coupee is an oxbow cutoff of the Mississippi River; the oxbow forms False River and the land forms Point Coupee Parish, which is bounded on three sides by water: on the east, the Mississippi River; on the north, Old River; on the west, the Atchafalaya. To the south, Iberville and West Baton Rouge parishes form the boundary. Within these borders are Lake Moreau, Raccouri Bend, False River, and many bayous, along which are the "fertile lands and extensive plantations" that Samuel Lockett described for an 1869 geographical and topographical survey: "gentle slopes, turfed to the water's edge"; "coast . . . shaded by stately groves of oaks, sycamores, and gums"; dominated by forty-five miles of the Mississippi's "quiet, smooth, transparent expanses." This specific Louisiana has long appealed to the creative writer. In 1884, in *The Creoles of Louisiana*, George Washington Cable, the best-known nineteenth-century Louisiana regionalist writer, observed "a wild and solemn beauty in the shifting scene which appeals to the imagination with special strength," and emphasized the appearance of the land:

the boughs of the dark, broad-spreading live-oak, and the phantom-like arms of lofty cypresses, the long, motionless pendants of pale gray moss; . . . on the banks of the large bayous, broad fields of corn, of cotton, of cane, and of rice. . . . pushing back the dark . . . curtain of moss-draped swamp . . . the neat often imposing residence of the planter, the . . . double row of field-hands' cabins, the tall red chimney and broad gray roof of the sugar-houses, and . . . the huge, square, red brick bagasse-burner, into which, during the grinding season, the residium of crushed sugar-cane passes unceasingly day and night, and is consumed with the smoke and glare of a conflagration.

That Cable's nineteenth-century description reflects a landscape almost identical to the one Gaines experienced in the twentieth century reiterates the time-bound aspect of the plantation area in Point Coupee, the model for Gaines's St.

Raphael, a fictional parish dotted with family plantations all having their literal basis in River Lake Plantation on False River: the Grovers' in *Catherine Carmier*, the Heberts' in *Of Love and Dust*, the Samsons' in *The Autobiography of Miss Jane Pittman*, the Marshalls' in *A Gathering of Old Men*, and the Pichots' in *A Lesson before Dying*. His creation of St. Raphael as a specified, contained fictional landscape is often compared with Faulkner's invention of Yoknapatawpha County, Mississippi, his "cosmos" and "little piece of native soil."

Because the images of the land at Point Coupee are inextricably tied to the plantation and its ordering of life and society, they led Gaines not simply to descriptions of the physical landscape but also to representations of the social and psychological region in which human beings act out tense dramas of individual, class, and caste struggles for survival. From Gaines's adult perspective, one sharpened by the multiculturalism of California and the political activism of the southern Civil Rights movement, the land and its special characteristics shape the distinct groups of people living on it—Creole and Anglo planters, Cajun overseers and tenant farmers, Creoles of color and black sharecroppers, all functioning in dynamic interaction within spatial boundaries, agrarian traditions, temporal suspensions, and racial identities. When he re-visioned his homeplace in 1964, he understood the quarters and the fields not as cultural spaces in which his people gather to talk or to work but as a closed microcosm of the larger economic society.

Carved out of the historical reality of the plantation system and inseparable from the fields enclosing them, the quarters where Gaines had grown up existed both because of and in spite of that history. The home of slaves in the nineteenth century and of sharecroppers in the twentieth, the quarters are isolated from the larger world. Still dependent upon agriculture for a livelihood, the residents in the modern period find themselves even more victimized by race than they had been in the early decades of the twentieth century, when it was still possible to making a living cropping the land with Creole cotton mules or Missouri sugar mules.

Though the owners have not removed the residents of the quarters from their homes, they have displaced them in the fields by renting the land to the Cajuns, who use technology and tractors for efficient, modern farming. Upon his return in the 1960s, Gaines observed the paralyzing effect of these changes on the quarters.

The result was that during his six-month visit he adopted the view of Louisiana that has remained consistent, but not static, in his fiction. "Louisiana's probably the most romantic and interesting of all southern states," he told Ruth Laney, identifying "the land, the language, the colors, the bayous, the fields" as the dramatic pulls on his imagination. His imaginative impulse, dependent upon the land and its actual and perceived meanings, and his writing, grounded in an initial consideration of place rather than character or incident, ranges beyond the romance of locality to the historical caste and class relationships to the land, to the stultifying effects of mandated social decorum, and to the contemporary upheaval of codified behavior, to the disruption of traditional institutions.

Gaines worked on his novel five or six hours a day, and during the remainder of the day he absorbed life and talk in the community. Though the South was on the verge of enormous change, the plantation folk were almost untouched by the fifteen years that had passed since Gaines's departure. Some of the elders had died, but it appeared to him that "the ones living could talk about them and did talk about them as though they had simply walked into another room only a few minutes before." Struck by the continuity with the past and by the impinging of a different present, he returned to San Francisco and in six months finished the seven-hundred-page novel. He had arrived at the ideological position which remained constant in his career—that of a cultural artist basing his creative expression upon racial awareness and historical consciousness.

Catherine Carmier

"A Little Stream" became "Catherine," Gaines's Louisiana novel incorporating everything he remembered and knew about his homeplace: "There were house fairs, with gumbos and fried fish, soft drinks and beer; there was much lovemaking, and, of course, there had to be illegitimate children; there were deaths, wakes, funerals, baptisms, even threats of race violence." But the novel published as *Catherine Carmier* in 1964 contained only half of the material Gaines had poured into the manuscript. Not without some initial resistance, he followed the advice of an editor and reduced the main plot to a love story between a Creole woman of color and an African American man, two people from the same yet different Louisiana culture; nevertheless, he did not completely erase the social, economic, and racial tensions existing in the intertwined lives of three groups—blacks, Creoles of color, and Cajuns—who also operate in the foreground but who are dominated by the presence of the planter class of landowning whites in the background.

Patterned after Turgenev's *Fathers and Sons*, the novel tells the story of Jackson Bradley, a dark-skinned son of the quarters who returns with a college degree and an outsider's perspective, and of Catherine Carmier, a daughter of the quarters who remains within her environmental and familial heritage. Jackson's more expansive cultural conditioning has modified his ability to participate in the ceremonies of the quarters and has made him appear to reject the community's values. His travels "up North," representing Gaines's ten years in California, have violated the community's assumed homogeneity. He considers his return temporary, although his Aunt Charlotte expects that he has come home to teach in the plantation school.

In contrast to Jackson's travels, Catherine Carmier's physical movement has been limited. She "was a Negro, but with extremely light skin. With her thin lips and aquiline nose, with her high cheekbones, dark eyes, and dark hair, Catherine Carmier could have easily passed as an Indian." Imprisoned by her Creole heritage and its restrictive notions of skin color, she has spent her life isolated in the quarters and devoted to her father, Raoul. He epitomizes a jealous, possessive paternalism but also a standard of manhood—an insistence on recognition as a man—and he emerges as tragically heroic in support of this standard.

Catherine and Jackson renew their childhood attraction, and this brings upon them a confrontation with what it means to be black in a modern world, colliding with history and roots, with place and tradition. Their reunion in a combined search for racial identity is overshadowed by historical caste and class relationships and by the social decorum appropriate to those hierarchical relationships. In representing their struggle, Gaines addresses the complexity of impending modernity on a time-bound society partly as a conflict between the past and the changing present. However, he also provides as the psychological backdrop for the action the psychological position of the reflective individual experiencing the effect of not merely coming into an education, as Jackson literally does, but also coming into a meaningful awareness of the dominant white world—through immersion in that world—as it responds to the otherness of blacks. Jackson's reflections mirror the questions about existence that the ordinary blacks, Creoles, or Cajuns in this multilayered, multicolored environment perceive intuitively but cannot pose: how does the individual live and where does he or she focus loyalties and find values as the old world passes and is destroyed.

Gaines's demystification of Catherine and Creoles of color is illuminating, especially for the ghosts exorcised from his own experience as a brown-skinned youth in a community privileging fair skin; nonetheless, the most consequential aspect of Louisiana life in *Catherine Carmier* is his treatment of the Cajun population. In Gaines's rendering, the Cajuns, the white sharecroppers and tenant farmers, have capitalized upon their color, their primary bond with the white plantation owners, in order to gain the best lands and to remove the blacks from the lands and from the quarters as well, by the quantity of their production and the speed of their new technology.

Descended from hundreds of Acadians who settled in Louisiana between 1764 and 1767 after the British drove them out of Acadia in 1755, the Louisiana Cajuns settled primarily in what has come to be called Acadiana, the southwest parishes of Lafayette, Vermilion, St. Martin, St. Mary, and Iberia, though they are found in clusters in other parishes throughout Louisiana. Like their French peasant forebears who settled old Acadie between 1603 and 1605, the Cajuns are primarily farmers and fishermen. In the early nineteenth century, they were the major group of independent farmers *(petits habitants* or *paysans)*; in the twentieth, they are more frequently tenant farmers on large acreages. Despite their being hardworking and closely knit, Cajuns have been viewed as tolerating an element of violence, which Gaines depicts in the murder of Robert Carmier and the conspiracy to ruin Raoul Carmier.

As late as the 1950s and early 1960s, the Cajun small farmer, like the black sharecropper, was still working the land with mules and walking plows. But the plantation owners had favored Cajun sharecroppers by giving them the better lands, which also brought increased opportunity for higher yields and greater profits. While Cajuns purchased the new farm equipment that ensured their superior position in agriculture, blacks found themselves less and less able to support themselves on the land. The landowners had thus ensured that a new group of whites would dominate the plantation. In *A Gathering of Old Men*, one character summarizes the problem:

> We had got the worst land from the start, and no matter how hard we worked it, the people with the best land was go'n always be in front. All you old people know this already. After the plantation was dying out, the Marshalls dosed out the land for sharecropping, giving the best land to the Cajuns, and giving us the worst—that bottomland near the swamps. Here, our own black people had been working this land a hundred years for the Marshall plantation, but when it come to sharecropping, now they give the best land to the Cajuns, who had never set foot on the land before.

From *Catherine Carmier* through *A Gathering of Old Men*, Gaines has portrayed the Cajuns in the process of destroying the quarters and its black residents by moving their fields into the quarters, plowing between the cabins and up to the doors of the blacks, and tearing down the structures as soon as a black family gives in and moves out. The Cajuns are Gaines's version of Faulkner's Snopeses, modern and acquisitive, scheming and aggressive. At the same time and equally important, they are his transformational men who shake off the restrictions of their own past deprivations and are hardworking and productive. They regenerate themselves at the expense of others, primarily the blacks and Creoles of color. Gaines shows that essentially the Cajuns, like both the blacks and the Creoles, are victims of the economic system and ethnic structure of rural Louisiana.

The operation of the Cajuns in destroying the old culture forces a reconsideration of that culture and necessitates a questioning of technology and change, technique and ideology, as well as of the past and value, of the past and meaning. Not only do the Cajuns and their machines make the work of the black sharecroppers obsolete, but their technological progress promotes a retrieval of what is valuable in a cultural past and a movement into modernity and away from the legacy of slavery. The innovations of the Cajuns clearly erode the old ways and values of the blacks, but those values have not been altogether laudatory or worth preserving, because the blacks have been too complacent and accepting of their lot in the quarters and in servitude on the plantation. Gaines's conception of Cajuns is the keystone to his philosophical concerns, and is as crucial to his fiction as is his view of blacks, because it involves social dynamics affecting the lives, traditions, and aspirations of his black characters. In portraying the Cajuns, Gaines dramatizes the conflict between the past and the present fundamental to all of his writing.

Despite containing a storehouse of creative materials, *Catherine Carmier* was not a financial success, and it attracted little critical notice. Only in the 1980s did it begin to receive retrospective analysis from writers such as John A. Williams. While Gaines seemingly remained confident about the importance of writing about

Louisiana, he switched directions in the year-and-a-half following the publication of his first novel. Turning his attention to the other half of his lived experiences—to California—he wrote three novels set in San Francisco. They have not appeared in print; he claims they were "three of the worst novels ever written by a published writer." The experience of attempting fiction in an environment different from Louisiana was cathartic, because it renewed his vision of the potential of other fictions drawing upon the known and remembered Louisiana and encouraged his patience in seeking an appropriate creative vehicle.

Gaines returned to Louisiana in 1965. During that visit he learned that a childhood friend had been killed by a black man in Baton Rouge and that, true to the patterns of justice involving black-on-black crimes in the South, the murderer had been released from prison after only a brief time. The incident combined imaginatively with lyrics from a Lightnin' Hopkins blues, "Mr. Tim Moore's Farm," recounting a black man's move with his family to a farm whose white owner promised to keep him out of jail if he could keep himself out of the grave. Gaines immediately began work on a story about a black murdering another black. The result was "Three Men," published in *Bloodline* (1968).

His inspiration from a blues song was not accidental. "I have learned as much about writing about my people by listening to blues and jazz and spirituals as I have by reading novels," he said. In the late 1970s, Gaines had collected more than five hundred recordings of African American, European, African, and Native American works. He readily admits his inspiration from jazz, which he says has " 'fired his imagination as much as anything in literature." However, he maintains a preference for blues: "The rural blues, maybe because of my background, is my choice in music."

Of Love and Dust

During the summer of 1966, the incident of the black-on-black murder and the blues song by

Lightnin' Hopkins recombined, and with financial assistance from a National Endowment for the Arts grant, Gaines began writing his second novel, *Of Love and Dust*, set not in Baton Rouge but on a False River plantation. He recalled that he wanted "to say something about my past, something of what I had left out of *Catherine Carmier*. I wanted to talk about the fields a little bit more, about the plantation story, the river, the church, the house fairs." In *Of Love and Dust*, he narrates from the first-person point of view (an approach with which he had already experimented, in writing nearly a dozen short stories during the 1960s). The novel assumes the immediacy of an oral tale performed for a gathering of intimates. The voice of the narrator reverberates with the sounds of his community's storytelling traditions; indeed, the critic John Callahan has said that Gaines creates "a world of kinship ties based as much on reciprocal speaking and listening as on blood."

Jim Kelly, the narrator of *Of Love and Dust*, is a plantation worker who by middle age has gained trust and respect in his years of mediating between the black workers and the white managers (the Cajun overseer Sidney Bonbon and the landowner Marshall Hebert). In the process, Kelly has been cautious to maintain his small stake in the economic hierarchy, and thus has accepted his victimization and that of the other blacks. Analytical and detached, he achieves a greater wisdom about social order and deeper self-knowledge when he promises the elderly Miss Julie Rand to look after her godson, Marcus Payne, who has been released from prison to work on the plantation. Miss Julie has been a cook on the Hebert plantation for forty years and knows how to extract a promise from Jim Kelly:

> Miss Julie looked at me so long, I turned my head . . . I just didn't feel comfortable with her looking at me like that. Old people look at you like that for two reasons. One, when you've done something wrong. The other is when they want you to do something for them. The thing they want you to do usually turns out to be a burden. The heavier the burden, the longer they look at you. And Miss Julie looked at me a long, long time.

Jim discovers that though he is a country blues–man who plays guitar and sings songs of his missed opportunities and lost loves, Marcus is a blues subject, the urban "badman" in open defiance of and in conflict with conventional authority. Gaines's portrayal of Marcus as societal rebel challenging complacency in conduct and belief suggests that *Of Love and Dust* is a play upon Faulkner's *Intruder in the Dust*. In an inversion of the relationship between Faulkner's youthful narrator, Chick Mallison, and his elderly antagonist, Lucas Beauchamp, in Gaines's work a mature narrative consciousness, Jim Kelly, learns from a young antagonist, Marcus, that the prevailing racial codes must be violated.

Though Marcus' godmother makes a case for the young man's goodness, he is guilty of stabbing a man. Unrepentant and hostile, Marcus is dangerous not because of this one deed but because, in attitude and manner, he is a rebel, unwilling and unable to accept the narrow social space designated for black men. Sidney Bonbon attempts to break his spirit by brutalizing him in the fields; as overseer, Bonbon assumes that his straw boss, Jim Kelly, will cooperate in forcing Marcus to work under the worst conditions. Kelly finds himself mystified by Marcus' refusal to realize his place, but he is committed to protecting Marcus because of the promise to Miss Julie.

Marcus attempts to get even with the whites, particularly the overseer, by openly courting the black woman Pauline, who is Bonbon's mistress and the mother of his two children. He discovers what the rest of the quarters has always known and ignored about the interracial affair: that Bonbon loves Pauline more than he loves his white wife, Louise, and that she loves him. That discovery and Pauline's rejection flame Marcus' desire for revenge and for Louise, who has lived with the knowledge of her husband's infidelity. Marcus cares little about the certainty of violent retaliation against himself and the entire black community should his violation of the strict sexual code prohibiting relationships between black males and white females become known. Selfishly and recklessly, he begins a relationship with Louise, a relationship that develops into mutual love.

Jim Kelly functions conservatively in listening to Aunt Margaret express the community's fears and in warning Marcus about his behavior. He resents Marcus' disrespect in labeling him a traitor to his race, but precisely because he has cooperated with the whites and accepted their treatment of blacks, Jim is helpless to dissuade the troublemaker or prevent the tragedy. His own years of accommodation and submission become unnecessary and meaningless, except as a contribution to his own emasculation. His failure becomes clear when Hebert, under the pretense of arranging an escape, deceives the lovers by betraying them to Bonbon, who kills Marcus in a bloody fight. The events precipitate Jim's transformation and his recognition of Marcus's insistence on pride and dignity in black manhood, and his recognition as well of the landowner's underhanded manipulation of the Cajun and the black to solve his own difficulties. Jim reflects:

> Bonbon had said, "We is nothing but little people. They make us do what they want us to do and they don't tell us nothing." So why blame Marcus?" . . . No, I didn't blame Marcus any more. I admired Marcus. I admired his great courage. . . . He was the bravest man I knew, the bravest man I had ever met.

Jim Kelly leaves the plantation with the hope of reshaping his life and redeeming his manhood. In leaving, and refusing to accept a recommendation from Marshall Hebert, he assumes the risks concomitant to any life worth living and accepts the message, if not the model, of Marcus' resistance.

Gaines received a measure of critical acclaim for his second novel, though it did not generate great public interest or sales. Nonetheless, the work revealed his mastery over the folk materials and idioms of the oral storyteller, and it manifested his talent for capturing the ambivalences of the social fabric in Louisiana and for

unpacking the conventions of its social and economic system.

Short Stories

In the year after *Of Love and Dust,* Gaines's only collection of short stories appeared. *Bloodline* (1968) contains five stories. "A Long Day in November" (1958), "Just Like a Tree" (1962), and "The Sky Is Gray" (1963), the three written and published before his first novel, can be counted among his major achievements; the other two, "Three Men" and "Bloodline," are strongest in their linking of heritage and lineage as determinants of the black male's maturation.

Ordered so as to emphasize the successive development of African American male narrators, the first four stories exhibit what Gaines in conversation with John O'Brien termed "a constant growth." Sonny, the narrator of "A Long Day in November," is six years old and hard-pressed to understand the marital conflict between his parents. James, the eight-year-old narrator of "The Sky Is Gray," travels with his mother into the town of Bayonne and, in the process, learns the meaning of a dignified manhood even in a segregated society. Gaines has linked his moving account of a boy's developmental journey and a mother's tough love to Eudora Welty's short story "A Worn Path." In "Three Men," Proctor Lewis, a nineteen-year-old jailed for stabbing a black man, narrates a dilemma of self-definition given his limited options: either accepting responsibility for his crime by remaining imprisoned, or becoming dependent upon whites and the system designed to emasculate him by choosing work release into field labor. In "Bloodline" narrated by seventy-year-old Felix, Copper Laurent, a black veteran, tries to claim his birthright and achieve recognition as the only son of a white landowner. The story line is similar to the one concerning Lucas Beauchamp in Faulkner's *Go Down, Moses.*

Narrated by a chorus of voices, the final story, "Just Like a Tree," recounts the last days of Aunt Fe, an elderly black woman being removed from her rural home because of her grandnephew's activities in the Civil Rights movement. Friends and family members visit her on the night before her departure; ten of their voices present Aunt Fe's life and that of the entire community of blacks and whites, young and old, males and females. Neither Emmanuel, the activist grand-nephew, nor Aunt Fe functions as narrator, but each represents the meanings, past and present, of intergenerational living on the land. Aunt Fe, who wills her death to avoid leaving, is like the tree of the spiritual from which the title is taken. She "will not be moved" because, for her, to be uprooted from her place is to lose her spiritual sustenance and face a meaningless existence. "Just Like a Tree" culminates the cycle of precarious existence and corrective transformation in black southern life.

The Autobiography of Miss Jane Pittman

After completing his first two novels and his collection of stories, Gaines realized that the movement in his fiction had been farther back each time into his individual and racial past. Inspired by the form and idea of "Just Like a Tree," he began to construct what he termed a "folk autobiography." In *The Autobiography of Miss Jane Pittman* (1971), according to "Miss Jane and I," he found a creative vehicle for giving value to the common people missing from historical narrative and erased from discourses on history:

> I knew at least two years before I started writing on the novel that eventually I would write *The Autobiography of Miss Jane Pittman*. Maybe I had known it all my life, because it seems that I started writing it many, many years before when I used to sit on the porch or the steps and write letters for the old people. But it took me at least two years after I first conceived the idea to start working on the book. I held back as long as I could because I did not know enough.

With this work and the film version aired on television in 1974, Gaines achieved his first major popular and critical success.

Partly a personal reminiscence and partly racial history, the text depends upon the credibility of one individual's observation of and participation in African American life from slavery to the second emancipation of the modern Civil Rights movement. Miss Jane talks her own life into focus and foregrounds the personal and racial pasts often submerged in history attuned to great men and events. Divided into four books—"The War Years," "Reconstruction," "The Plantation," and "The Quarters"—the novel frames Miss Jane's narrative with an introductory account of the text. Written by a young African American history teacher responsible for tape-recording Miss Jane's life story, the introduction explains the process of gathering the oral materials and shaping a written version: "Miss Jane would talk about one thing one day and the next day she would talk about something totally different." Out of his experience of learning to listen, the editor comes to understand the oblique interconnections dramatized in Miss Jane's personal life and racial history.

Masterful in its evocation of a life defined by restrictive social realities, *The Autobiography of Miss Jane Pittman* constitutes a text about an indefatigable female spirit who survives because of unlimited internal resources. A subtext is the question of how to tap Miss Jane's gendered racial strength for future generations, specifically for a generation of young African American males. Gaines's achievement lies not only in his meticulous attention to the racial content of Miss Jane's historical existence but also in his considerable sensitivity to the nature of her femaleness. He has attributed his ability to create a realistic bond of identification with his heroine to being raised by his Aunt Augusteen, yet aside from this familial prototype, he must also have continued close and sympathetic observation of black women who were engaged in sustaining meaningful lives.

In My Father's House

The success of *Miss Jane* led to a Guggenheim Fellowship in creative writing for 1973–1974. Gaines's project "The House and the Field," which later became *A Gathering of Old Men* (1983), was interrupted by the persistent call for attention emanating from ideas that took shape as *In My Father's House* (1978). This fourth novel, he told Jeanie Blake, was the most difficult to write. Although he attributed his difficulty to problems with handling the omniscient point of view, it seems also that *In My Father's House*, like *Catherine Carmier*, explores the psychological recesses of a personal past that Gaines has been unable to discuss openly. Throughout the text he scatters references to his own mother, Adrienne Gaines Colar: the town is St. Adrienne, a character's surname is Colar. Gaines explores the destructive impact of illegitimacy upon a firstborn son and the male child's desire for recognition from his long-absent father. Set in the civil rights era of the 1960s, the novel is a discourse on paternal responsibility and on filial need. Rather than foregrounding the son's obsessive search for an errant father, the text uncovers the psychological states of a black man forced to confront his failure to acknowledge and nurture his offspring.

Phillip J. Martin is a minister at Solid Rock Baptist Church who has transformed his behavior from youthful dissipation in the rural South to dedicated activism in the urban Civil Rights movement. Religion saved him from drinking and gambling, but his past returns, in the form of the illegitimate son he had abandoned, to challenge his self-righteous satisfaction with his achievements. Robert X, formerly named Etienne, is the rootless son who searches for his father, ostensibly to confront him for ruining his life and that of his mother, Johanna, and his siblings, Antoine and Justine, but also to find meaning for his own existence. In appearance he is haggard and ghostlike. His alienation and suffering are refracted in the weariness and futility that overshadow any possibility that protest marches and simple idealism could be effective in the late 1960s. Robert X adopts his new name and sheds the old, Etienne, partly to accept a new identity but mainly to cast off the stigma of his illegitimacy. He refuses to accept Martin's attempt to lay the blame for his actions on the legacy of slavery and holds him personally responsible for his weakness.

Turning from his plans for new economic demonstrations and thus from his social responsibility as a community leader, and returning to the plantation of his youth to confront his private responsibility as a father, Martin eventually comes to understand that he cannot absolve himself from the sins of his past. His explanation of his youth cannot repair the damage he has done:

> I was paralyzed. Paralyzed. Yes, I had a mouth, but I didn't have a voice. I had legs, but I couldn't move. . . . It took a man to do these things, and I wasn't a man. I was just some other brutish animal who could cheat, steal, rob, kill—but not stand. Not be responsible. Not protect you or your mother. They had branded that in us from the time of slavery.

Neither can Martin effect a reconciliation with his children. Justine and Antoine are gone, and Robert X, already psychologically dead, commits suicide, an act that completes the punishment of the father. Martin's words in the conclusion, "I'm lost, Alma, I'm lost," position his grief and despair against the comforting notion of his wife, Alma, that they will begin anew.

Although a powerful psychological drive is embedded in the narrative, *In My Father's House* suffers from inadequate development of characters, motive, and incident, as well as from a truncated time frame. Too much is told obliquely in monologue and not enough is rendered in action. Despite underdevelopment, the novel hauntingly evokes the meaning of manhood and the presence of the past, both of which are recurrent themes in Gaines's fiction, especially in the novel interrupted by the writing of *In My Father's House*.

A Gathering of Old Men

A Gathering of Old Men, conceived in 1973 but published ten years later, returns to the first-person narrative technique that has distinguished Gaines's most effective writing. Told from multiple perspectives, the story reveals the motivations of eighteen elderly black men who make their first overt stand against the racism in their rural Louisiana community. The murder of a son of a prominent Cajun in the black quarters precipitates their stand. Encouraged by the young white owner of the plantation, Candy Marshall, who has concocted a scheme to save Mathu, the eighty-year-old black man who had helped raise her, the old men all confess to murdering Beau Boutan though they know that his father, Felix "Fix" Boutan, has been the Cajun most committed to violence, retaliation, and revenge. Each not only claims responsibility for the killing but articulates his motive for the act. In no case is the murder unjustified, though in several the grievances are generations old.

Uncle Billy tells of his son being beaten by Fix's crowd after he returned from World War II: " 'They beat him till they beat him crazy, and we had to send him to Jackson. He don't even know me and his mama no more.' " Jacob's sister Tessie, "one of them great big pretty mulatto gals" who had chosen to live in the quarters with blacks, had been killed by white men on Mardi Gras Day in 1947; Jacob joins the old men not only because of what whites had done to his sister but also because he had adhered to his color-conscious mulatto family's refusal to accept Tessie's body back from the people of the quarters. The grievances suffered in the past unite the group to show that they can be men, that they can overcome their own internal caste and color divisions, that they can stand together against the whites.

Unlike these downbeaten elders, Mathu has been strong, even rebellious, in his years as a plantation worker, but he does not tell of his own past or of his version of the present. He becomes the powerful silence at the center of the drama and of the history of oppression voiced by a generation of submissive black males. His representation foregrounds the viability of a courageous African American manhood and emergent identity in spite of brutalizing slavery and systematic suppression.

The novel not only concerns the transformation possible among black men; it also portrays the changes taking place among the whites, perhaps most dramatically among the Cajuns.

The brutality Sheriff Mapes has shown in dealing with all blacks ceases as he develops respect for the elders who would stand up to him and for themselves. Fix Boutan, aging no less than the black men, no longer demands vigilante action from his family and other Cajuns; he accepts that the law and courts can be responsible for justice. His son Gil, a student at Louisiana State University, is part of a new code of race relations; education has changed his inherited attitudes toward blacks, in part because of a general exposure to a wider world than the self-contained Cajun one, and in part because of specific association with a black teammate, who with Gil makes up the high-scoring football duo "Salt and Pepper." Candy Marshall, the plantation owner, also learns that change is necessary. She discovers that although she conceived the plot to confuse the authorities, the old men do not need or want the paternalism and patronage of a white landowner. While her age, gender, and sympathies make her a nontraditional landowner, they do not compensate for her place in the conventional order of systematic oppression. In the face of the old men's determined self-actualization, she must relinquish her notions of leadership, protection, and control.

Like *The Autobiography of Miss Jane Pittman*, *A Gathering of Old Men* was made into a film for television. The 1987 movie revived interest in Gaines's career and fostered a critical retrospective of his work. Not only literary critics but also creative writers began to reassess Gaines's fiction. The novelists Barry Beckam, John Wideman, and John A. Williams and poets Alvin Aubert and Michael Harper are only a few of the prominent African American artists who have called attention to his focused yet expansive canon and to his imaginative and eloquent evocation of time and place.

In the 1980s, Gaines began dividing his time between teaching at the University of Southwestern Louisiana in Lafayette and writing in San Francisco. The first allowed him to keep his sense of place, people, and subject accessible, and the second provided the perspective of distance. His permanent position as writer-in-residence at Southwestern has afforded him both an especially supportive community of students and colleagues and a rejuvenated connection to Louisiana. Since his 1993 marriage to Dianne Saulney, an assistant district attorney in Miami and a native of New Orleans, he has also spent a part of the year in Miami. But he has maintained his fascination with his native state and its rural people, as the documentary, *Ernest J. Gaines: Louisiana Stories* produced by Louisiana Public Television, made apparent in focusing on his social history and cultural background and their relationship to his writing.

A Lesson before Dying

Gaines's sixth novel, *A Lesson before Dying*, appeared in 1993 to critical acclaim. Awarded the National Book Critics Circle Award for fiction and nominated for a Pulitzer Prize, the novel concerns Grant Wiggins, a conflicted and disillusioned teacher at a plantation school, whose aunt, Tante Lou, enlists him to help Jefferson, a black youth slated for electrocution for a murder he did not commit. The twist is that the despairing Grant, who believes that nothing has ever changed or will ever change in their separate but unequal rural community, is to assist Jefferson not in obtaining a reprieve for killing a white man, but in facing his inevitable death in an electric chair with dignity and humanity.

The narrative is set in the 1940s because, as Gaines told Jeanie Blake in 1983, "I don't know if I could write about contemporary Louisiana." The setting recaptures a time when the criminal justice system in the South was still all-white, as well as all-male, and the plantation communities were still intact social entities. Within that temporal and spatial frame, a discourse on manhood, commitment, responsibility, and ultimately faith and belief unfolds. Its dramatic logic and its compelling argument for change resonate with much of Gaines's earlier fiction, in particular with the outsider figures Jackson Bradley in *Catherine Carmier* and Marcus Payne in *Of Love and Dust*.

Beautifully written in the evocative language, dialect, and idiom of rural Louisiana in the late 1940s, *A Lesson before Dying* presents both the first-person vision of the college-educated Grant and the colloquial communal perspective of members of the plantation community and small town community, alongside the emotion-charged diary entries written by Jefferson prior to his execution.

Miss Emma, Jefferson's *nannan* (godmother), believes that Grant can teach Jefferson how to be a man and how to die with dignity. Her fear is that Jefferson will go to his death reduced to the animal level and without fully recognizing his own humanity. The defense attorney's summation has raised the specter of Jefferson as a cornered animal lacking in intelligence and a thing acting out of instinct:

> Gentlemen of the jury, look at him—look at him—look at this. Do you see a man sitting here? I ask you, I implore, look carefully—do you see a man sitting here? Look at the shape of this skull, this face as flat as the palm of my hand—look deeply into those eyes. Do you see a modicum of intelligence? Do you see anyone here who could plan a murder, a robbery, can plan—can plan—can plan anything? A cornered animal to strike quickly out of fear, a trait inherited from his ancestors in the deepest jungle of blackest Africa—yes, yes, that he can do—but to plan? . . . No gentlemen, this skull here holds no plans. What you see here is a thing that acts on command. A thing to hold the handle of a plow, a thing to load your bales of cotton, a thing to dig your ditches, to chop your wood, to pull your corn.

In pleading for mercy for Jefferson, the defense concludes: "What justice would there be to take this life? Justice, gentlemen? Why, I would just as soon put a hog in the electric chair as this."

Miss Emma has been rightly offended by the language chosen by Jefferson's defense attorney in pleading for his life: "Called him a hog. . . . I know he was just trying to get him off. But they didn't pay that no mind. Still give him death." Her request is simple: " 'I don't want them to kill no hog,' she said. 'I want a man to go to that chair, on his own two feet.' " Miss Emma and her friend, Grant's aunt, become determined to disprove the derogatory and negative construction of Jefferson life, even if he has only a brief time to live.

Reluctant to become involved, Grant cannot deny the request of the two elderly black women, despite his protests that he hates the quarter and wishes only to get away from all it represents. The problem for Grant is that though he lives in the quarter and teaches the children of the quarter, he is spiritually alienated from the place, from its practices and beliefs. He is especially at odds with the black church and the pie-in-the sky theology it teaches through ministers like the Reverend Mose Ambrose, the preacher at the plantation church, who acquiesces to the unfair treatment of blacks in the community while espousing faith in God's justice and mercy.

Although he is not physically imprisoned, Grant feels trapped. He wants to leave Louisiana, but cannot. He confesses to Vivian Baptiste, the Creole woman whom he loves, " 'I need to go someplace where I can feel I'm living. . . . I want to be with you, someplace where we have a choice of things to do. I don't feel alive here.' " Grant's own condition causes him to question whether he can help Jefferson: "What do I say to him? Do I know what a man is? Do I know how a man is supposed to die? I'm still trying to find out how a man should live." Grant's questions give way to halting efforts to communicate with Jefferson who has accepted both the death sentence and the subhuman categorization imposed by whites. With patience and talk, as well as food provided by Miss Emma and Tante Lou, Grant demonstrates that he is capable of teaching and of caring.

Do you know what a myth is, Jefferson? . . . A myth is an old lie that people believe in. White people believe that they're better than anyone else on earth—and that's a myth. The last thing they ever want to see is a black man stand, and think, and show that common humanity that is in us all. It would destroy their myth. They would no longer have justification for having made us slaves and keeping us in the condition we are in. As long as none of us stand, they're safe. They're safe with me. They're safe with Reverend Ambrose. I don't want them to feel safe with you anymore.

Grant Wiggins reduces Jefferson to tears when he says: "I want you to chip away at that myth by standing. I want you . . . to call them liars. I want you to show them that you as much a man—more a man than they can ever be." The tears signify that the lessons are ultimately not lost on Jefferson, who moves from anger and silence to verbal and written expression of his feelings and thoughts, those aspects of his being which reveal his humanity:

i kno i care for nanan but i don't kno if love is care cause cuttin wood and haulin water and things like that i don't know if thats love or just work to do an you say thats love but you say you kno i got mo an jus that to say an when i lay ther at nite and cant sleep i try an think wha you mean i got mo cause i aint done this much thinkin and this much writin in all my life befor

The pencil and notebook he has received from Grant become a means to self-actuation, self-knowledge, and self-assertion.

Jefferson's resultant move from object to subject produces a concomitant move on Grant's part from despair to belief and to Grant's acknowledgment to Jefferson:

I need you. . . . I need you more than you could ever need me. I need to know what to do with my life. I want to run away, but go where and do what? I'm needed here and I know it, but I feel that all I'm doing here is choking myself. I need someone to tell me what to do. I need you to tell me, to show me. I'm no hero; I can just give something small. That's all I have to offer. It's the only way we can chip away at that myth.

Grant's faith in Jefferson is well placed, though Grant himself cannot find the strength to witness the execution. Jefferson's last words, conveyed to Grant by the sympathetic white deputy Paul, are " 'Tell Nannan I walked.' And straight he walked, Grant Wiggins. Straight he walked. I'm a witness. Straight he walked." This message, which encodes Grant's own words, produces a reciprocal reduction to tears. Like Jefferson's, Grant's tears signal a change of heart and action: "I turned from him [Paul] and went into the church. Irene Cole told the class to rise, with their shoulders back. I went up to the desk and turned to face them. I was crying." Grant's words, the revelation of his tears, conclude the novel.

In examining a life struggling for meaning within the debilitating contexts of a racial and cultural past, *A Lesson before Dying* signals that Ernest Gaines is at the height of his creative powers. Long considered one of the premier and distinctive writers of modern fiction, he was awarded a MacArthur Foundation fellowship in 1993 after the publication of the novel. Often referred to as the "genius" awards, the MacArthur is one of the most prestigious and coveted American awards because it is given in recognition of the special creativity of the recipients and offers a generous five-year stipend to free them to pursue their own interests. In Gaines's case, the award came in his extraordinary sixtieth year—a year in which he received major prizes for his writing, and a year in which he ended his lifelong bachelorhood and married a soul mate who seemed to step out of his fiction: "We have a very close relationship . . . I keep telling Dianne we've been married for thirty-three years, because this relationship is the one I dreamed of when I was writing *Catherine Carmier*" he told Ruth Laney. The award-winning *A Lesson before Dying*, which was also adapted for film (in 1999), is dedicated to his wife.

In other interviews, Ernest Gaines has revealed that his work in progress includes three novellas, one of which has the working title, "The Man Who Whipped Children" and concerns a black man on a Louisiana plantation who helped parents discipline their children. The other two novellas will explore the relationship between light- and dark-skinned African Americans, a subject Gaines has returned

to throughout his career. These new projects suggest that Ernest Gaines will continue to call upon his Louisiana heritage and its dynamic polarities for some time to come.

Selected Bibliography

PRIMARY WORKS

NOVELS

Catherine Carmier. New York: Atheneum, 1964.
Of Love and Dust. New York: Dial, 1967.
The Autobiography of Miss Jane Pittman. New York: Dial, 1971.
In My Father's House. New York: Knopf, 1978.
A Gathering of Old Men. New York: Knopf, 1983.
A Lesson before Dying. New York: Knopf, 1993.

SHORT STORIES

Bloodline. New York: Dial, 1968.
A Long Day in November. New York: Dial, 1971.

SHORT WORKS

"Home: A Photo-Essay." *Callaloo* 1, no. 3:52–67 (May 1978).
"Miss Jane and I." *Callaloo* 1, no. 3:23–38 (May 1978).
"The Turtles." In *Something in Common: Contemporary Louisiana Stories*. Edited by Ann Brewster. Baton Rouge: Louisiana State University Press, 1991. Pp. 89–97.
"A Very Big Order: Reconstructing Identity." *Southern Review* 26:245–53 (1990); also published as "The Autobiography of Mr. Ernest Gaines." *Cultural Vistas* 1, no. 1:4–6, 15–16 (Spring 1990).

SECONDARY WORKS

INTERVIEWS

Gaudet, Marcia, and Carl Wooton. "Talking with Ernest J. Gaines." *Callaloo* 11, no. 3:229–43 (Spring 1988).
———. *Porch Talk with Ernest Gaines: Conversations on the Writer's Craft*. Baton Rouge: Louisiana State University Press, 1990.
Ingram, Forrest, and Barbara Steinberg. "On the Verge: An Interview with Ernest J. Gaines." *New Orleans Review* 3:339–44 (1972).
"An Interview: Ernest Gaines." *New Orleans Review* 1:331–35 (1969).
"Interview with Ernest Gaines." *Xavier Review* 3:1–13 (1983).
Laney, Ruth. "A Conversation with Ernest Gaines." *Southern Review*, n.s., 10:1–14 (Winter 1974).
Lavasseur, Jennifer, and Kevin Rabalais. "An Interview with Ernest Gaines." *Missouri Review* 22, no. 1:95ff. (1999).
Lepschy, Wolfgang. "A *MELUS* Interview: Ernest J. Gaines." *MELUS* 24, no. 1:197–208 (Spring 1999).
Lowe, John, ed. *Conversations with Ernest Gaines*. Jackson: University Press of Mississippi, 1995.

O'Brien, John. "Ernest J. Gaines." In *Interviews with Black Writers.* Edited by John O'Brien. New York: Liveright, 1973. Pp. 79–93.

Rickels, Patricia. "An Interview with Ernest J. Gaines." *Southwestern Review* 4:33–50 (1979).

Rowell, Charles H. " 'This Louisiana Thing That Drives Me': An Interview with Ernest J. Gaines." *Callaloo* 1, no. 3:39–51 (May 1978).

BIOGRAPHICAL AND CRITICAL STUDIES

Andrews, William L. " 'We Ain't Going Back There': The Idea of Progress in *The Autobiography of Miss Jane Pittman.*" *Black American Literature Forum* 11:146–49 (Winter 1977).

Babb, Valerie Melissa. *Ernest Gaines.* Boston: Twayne, 1991.

Beavers, Herman. *Wrestling Angels into Song: The Fictions of Ernest J. Gaines and James Alan McPherson.* Philadelphia: University of Pennsylvania Press, 1995.

Bryant, Jerry H. "From Death to Life: The Fiction of Ernest J. Gaines." *Iowa Review* 3:106–20 (Winter 1972).

———. "Ernest J. Gaines: Change, Growth, and History." *Southern Review,* n.s., 10:851–64 (Autumn 1974).

Burke, William. "*Bloodline:* A Black Man's South." *CLA Journal* 19:545–58 (June 1976).

Byerman, Keith E. "Ernest Gaines." *Dictionary of Literary Biography.* Vol. 33, *Afro-American Fiction Writers after 1955.* Edited by Thadious M. Davis and Trudier Harris. Detroit: Gale Research, 1984. Pp. 84–96.

———. *Fingering the Jagged Grain: Tradition and Form in Recent Black Fiction.* Athens, Ga.: University of Georgia Press, 1985.

Cable, George Washington. *The Creoles of Louisiana.* New York: Scribners, 1884.

Callahan, John. "Image-Making: Tradition and the Two Versions of *The Autobiography of Miss Jane Pittmann.*" *Chicago Review* 29:45–62 (Autumn 1977).

———. "Hearing Is Believing: The Landscape of Voice in Ernest Gaines's *Bloodline.*" *Callaloo* 7, no. 4: 86–112 (Winter 1984).

———. *In the African-American Grain: The Pursuit of Voice in Twentieth-Century Black Fiction.* Urbana: University of Illinois Press, 1988. Pp. 189–216.

Callaloo 1, no. 3 (May 1978). Special issue devoted to Gaines. (Contains essays and poetic tributes by Alvin Aubert, Barry Beckam, Todd Duncan, Michel Fabre, Michael S. Harper, and John Wideman.)

Davis, Thadious M. "Headlands and Quarters: Louisiana in *Catherine Carmier.*" *Callaloo* 7:1–13 (Spring–Summer 1984).

Estes, David C., ed. *Critical Reflections on the Fiction of Ernest J. Gaines.* Athens, Ga.: University of Georgia Press, 1994.

Gaudet, Marcia. "The Failure of Traditional Religion in Ernest Gaines' Short Stories." *Journal of the Short Story in English* 18:81–89 (Spring 1992).

———. "Miss Jane and Personal Experience Narrative: Ernest Gaines' *The Autobiography of Miss Jane Pittman.*" *Western Folklore* 51, no. 1:23–32 (1992).

Griffin, Joseph. "Calling, Naming, and Coming of Age in *A Gathering of Old Men.*" *Names* 40, no. 2:84–97 (June 1992).

Hicks, Jack. "To Make These Bones Live: History and Community in Ernest Gaines's Fiction." *Black American Literature Forum* 11:9–19 (Spring 1977).

———. *In the Singer's Temple: Prose Fictions of Barthelme, Gaines, Brautigan, Piercy, Kesey, and Kosinski.* Chapel Hill: University of North Carolina Press, 1981.

Laney, Ruth. "Bard from the Bayou." In *Conversations with Ernest Gaines.* Edited by John Lowe. Jackson: University Press of Mississippi, 1995. Pp. 276–81.

McDonald, Walter R. " 'You Not a Bum, You a Man': Ernest Gaines's *Bloodline.*" *Negro American Literature Forum* 9:47–49 (Summer 1975).

Potter, Vilma Raskin. "*The Autobiography of Miss Jane Pittman:* How to Make a White Film from a Black Novel." *Literature/Film Quarterly* 3:371–75 (Fall 1975).

Puschmann-Nalenz, Barbara. "Ernest J. Gaines: 'A Long Day in November.' " In *The Black American Short Story in the Twentieth Century: A Collection of Critical Essays.* Edited by Peter Bruck. Amsterdam: Grüner, 1977. Pp. 157–67.

Roberts, John W. "The Individual and the Community in Two Short Stories by Ernest J. Gaines." *Black American Literature Forum* 18, no. 3:110–13 (Fall 1984).

Rowell, Charles H. "The Quarters: Ernest Gaines and the Sense of Place." In *Afro-American Writing Today: An Anniversary Issue of the "Southern Review."* Edited by James Olney. Baton Rouge: Louisiana State University Press, 1989. Pp. 146–63.

Shelton, Frank W. "Ambiguous Manhood in Ernest J. Gaines's *Bloodline.*" *CLA Journal* 19:200–09 (December 1975).

———. "*In My Father's House:* Ernest Gaines after Jane Pittman." *Southern Review* 17, no. 2:340–45 (Spring 1981).

———. "Ernest J. Gaines." In *Fifty Southern Writers after 1900: A Bio-Bibliographical Sourcebook.* Edited by Joseph M. Flora and Robert Bain. Westport, Conn.: Greenwood Press, 1987. Pp. 196–205.

Simpson, Anne K. "The Early Life of Ernest Gaines." *Louisiana Literature* 7:71–87 (1990).

———. *A Gathering of Gaines: The Man and the Writer.* Lafayette: Center for Louisiana Studies, 1991.

Stoelting, Winnifred L. "Human Dignity and Pride in the Novels of Ernest Gaines." *CLA Journal* 14:340–58 (March 1971).

Werner, Craig Hansen. *Paradoxical Resolutions: American Fiction since James Joyce.* Urbana: University of Illinois Press, 1982.

Wertheim, Albert. "Journey to Freedom: Ernest Gaines's *The Autobiography of Miss Jane Pittman.*" In *The Afro-American Novel since 1960.* Edited by Peter Bruck and Wolfgang Karrer. Amsterdam: Grüner, 1982. Pp. 219–35.

Williams, John A. Review of *Catherine Carmier,*

American Book Review 4, no. 5:13 (July–August 1982).

Williams, Sherley Anne. *Give Birth to Brightness: A Thematic Study in Neo-Black Literature.* New York: Dial, 1972.

BIBLIOGRAPHIES

Doyle, Mary Ellen. "Ernest J. Gaines: An Annotated Bibliography, 1956–1988." *Black American Literature Forum* 24, no. 1:125–50 (1990).

Rowell, Charles H. "Ernest J. Gaines: A Checklist, 1964–1968." *Callaloo* 1, no. 3:125–31 (May 1978).

FILM ADAPTATIONS

The Autobiography of Miss Jane Pittman. Teleplay by Tracy Keenan Wynn. Directed by John Korty. CBS, 1974.

The Sky Is Gray. Teleplay by Charles Fuller. Directed by Stan Lathan. Learning in Focus, 1980.

A Gathering of Old Men. Teleplay by Charles Fuller. Directed by Volker Schlöndorf. Zenith, 1987.

A Lesson before Dying. Teleplay by Ann Peacock. Directed by Joseph Sargent. Home Box Office (HBO), 1999.

LORRAINE HANSBERRY
(1930–1965)

MARGARET B. WILKERSON

IN 1959 WHEN Lorraine Hansberry's first produced play, *A Raisin in the Sun,* won the New York Drama Critics Circle Award, few people would have predicted that the play would become an American classic. At the time, plays by black writers were considered too parochial to last beyond a short run in the professional theater. Yet *A Raisin in the Sun* has enjoyed numerous productions in the years since its original presentation, and in 1989 a made-for-television version of the play, which restored cuts in the original script, broke television viewing records across the country.

Lorraine Hansberry's work is frequently mentioned along with that of such major American playwrights as Arthur Miller, Eugene O'Neill, and Tennessee Williams, despite the fact that she died in 1965 at the age of thirty-four after a scant six years in the professional theater. The popularity of *A Raisin in the Sun,* during some of the most intense years of the civil rights movement, catapulted her to fame at the age of twenty-nine. She quickly became an articulate spokesperson for black Americans in the struggle for civil rights, and she was a vocal critic of racial, sexual, and class discrimination, themes that were reflected in her plays. Although only two of her plays were professionally produced in her lifetime, two subsequent works were produced and published posthumously, and her artistic reputation has continued to grow.

Born on 19 May 1930 in Chicago, Illinois, Lorraine Vivian Hansberry was the youngest of four children; seven or more years separated her from Mamie, her sister and closest sibling, and two older brothers, Carl, Jr., and Perry. She was born into a family of means. Her father, Carl Augustus Hansberry, was a successful real-estate broker who had moved to Chicago from Mississippi after completing a technical course at Alcorn College; like thousands of southern rural blacks, he had migrated north in the early years of the twentieth century seeking better economic opportunities. Despite the economic stringencies of the Great Depression, he built a real-estate company that he ran as a family business, hiring other relatives who wanted to leave the South or who needed employment. A prominent businessman, he made an unsuccessful bid for Congress in 1940 on the Republican ticket and contributed large sums of money to causes supported by the NAACP and the Urban League. Hansberry's mother, Nannie Perry, was a schoolteacher and later a ward committeewoman who had come north from Tennessee after completing teacher training at Tennessee Agricultural and Industrial University. The Hansberrys were at the center of black social life in Chicago and often entertained important political and cultural figures who were visiting the city. Thus young Lorraine was exposed to such personages as Paul Robeson,

Duke Ellington, Joe Louis, and Jesse Owens. Another frequent and influential visitor was her father's brother, William Leo Hansberry, who was a professor at Howard University and a pioneer in the study of African history. Because her uncle coordinated the visits of college students from Ethiopia and from other African countries, Hansberry made early acquaintance with young people from the African continent.

Despite the Hansberrys' comfortable middle-class economic status, they were subject to the racial segregation and discrimination characteristic of the period, and they were active in opposing it. Restrictive covenants in which white home-owners agreed not to sell their property to blacks created a ghetto that was known as the "Black Metropolis" in the midst of Chicago's Southside. Although large numbers of blacks continued to migrate to the city, restrictive covenants kept the boundaries static, creating serious housing problems. Carl Hansberry knew well the severe overcrowding in Black Metropolis. He had, in fact, made much of his money by purchasing large, older houses vacated by the retreating white population, dividing them into small apartments, each one with its own kitchenette; he thus became known as "the kitchenette king." Lorraine Hansberry used this type of apartment as the setting for her play *A Raisin in the Sun*, and the history of struggle for better housing as the driving action of the plot.

Carl Hansberry challenged this housing pattern in 1938 by purchasing a home in a white area. A court order forced the family to leave, but not before they were threatened by a white mob, which threw a brick through the window, narrowly missing Lorraine. Nannie Hansberry strongly supported her husband's action, at one point standing armed and prepared to fend off the intruders. Hansberry fought the case (*Hansberry* v. *Lee*) to the Supreme Court and won a favorable judgment. Nevertheless, the legal victory did not immediately open up housing opportunities for blacks in Chicago. Disillusioned and bitter, Lorraine Hansberry's father moved to Mexico in 1946 and was making preparations to move his family when he suddenly died. Lorraine was sixteen years old. Years later, in a

1964 letter to the *New York Times*, she would defend civil disobedience with a reference to her father's method of fighting white supremacy:

> The fact that my father and the NAACP "won" a Supreme Court decision, in a now famous case which bears his name in the lawbooks, is—ironically—the sort of "progress" our satisfied friends allude to when they presume to deride the more radical means of struggle. The cost, in emotional turmoil, time and money, which led to my father's early death as a permanently embittered exile in a foreign country when he saw that after such sacrificial efforts the Negroes of Chicago were as ghetto-locked as ever, does not seem to figure in their calculations.

Hansberry's education was not traditional for one with her family's means. Although her parents could afford private education, she attended public elementary and high schools, graduating from Englewood High School in 1947. In a 1964 speech for a *Monthly Review* benefit for black college libraries, Hansberry described herself as "the product of [a] Jim Crow grade school system," attributing her difficulty with computation to a substandard education. Although she could read at the university level in the sixth and seventh grades, she had learned so little elementary arithmetic she could not make "even simple change in a grocery store." Patently uninspired by most of her teachers, she earned average grades throughout her primary and secondary years. Hansberry, however, shaped her own education, reading avidly and widely from her earliest years. Her schoolmates remember her as politically astute for her age.

This pattern of self-education continued throughout her life, rendering formal education virtually irrelevant to her intellectual development. Breaking with the family tradition of attending southern black colleges, Hansberry chose to attend the University of Wisconsin at Madison, moving from the ghetto schools of Chicago to a predominantly white and somewhat elite university. She integrated her dormitory, becoming the first black student to live at Langdon Manor. Although the campus was known for its politically liberal scholars, Hansberry found most of her courses and professors lacking in creativity.

Hansberry's years at Madison, however, gave sharper focus to her political views, as she worked in the Henry Wallace presidential campaign and in the activities of the Young Progressives of America, becoming campus president of the organization in 1949, during her last semester at the university. Her artistic sensibilities were heightened by a university production of Sean O'Casey's *Juno and the Paycock*. Deeply moved by O'Casey's ability to universalize the suffering of the Irish without sacrificing specificity, she wrote: "The melody was one that I had known for a very long while. I was seventeen and I did not think then of *writing* the melody as *I* knew it—in a different key; but I believe it entered my consciousness and stayed there." A few years later, *A Raisin in the Sun* captured that suffering in the idiom of the Negro people. In 1950, she dropped out of university and moved to New York City for "an education of another kind," one which would rival any formal curriculum.

In Harlem she worked for *Freedom,* a progressive newspaper founded by Paul Robeson. In 1952, she became associate editor of the newspaper, writing and editing a variety of news stories that expanded her understanding of domestic and world problems: the overcrowded, understaffed schools of Harlem; legal battles and demonstrations over civil rights; the revoking of Paul Robeson's passport and the ensuing controversy; protests against false imprisonment of black Americans; special reports on the growing revolution in colonial Africa; and many others. She also wrote reviews of local theater productions and various new books on literature, art, and politics. Her job at the newspaper brought her into contact with Robeson and other people who became her literary and political mentors: the political activist and thinker W. E. B. Du Bois, from whom she took a seminar on Africa; Louis Burnham, the charismatic editor of *Freedom*; and the poet Langston Hughes. In 1952 she attended the Intercontinental Peace Congress in Montevideo,

Lorraine Hansberry

Uruguay, taking the place of Paul Robeson, whose passport had been revoked by the U.S. State Department. Living and working in the midst of the rich social, political, cultural, and progressive activities of Harlem stimulated Hansberry to begin writing short stories, poetry, and plays. She wrote a pageant that was performed to commemorate *Freedom's* first anniversary; she also experimented with transforming various public incidents into dramatic literature, such as the trial of a young black man on draft-dodging charges. But it was several years before she found her definitive theatrical voice.

In 1952, while covering a picket line protesting discrimination in sports at New York University, Hansberry met Robert Barron Nemiroff, a white student of Jewish heritage who was attending the university. They dated for several months, participating in political and cultural activities together. In a letter dated 26 December 1952, Hansberry told Nemiroff of her love for him and then went on to talk about her work, declaring: "I am a writer. I am going to write. . . ." They married on 20 June 1953, at the Hansberry family home in Chicago. Hansberry and Nemiroff took various jobs during the early years of their marriage. Nemiroff was a part-time typist, waiter, multi-lith operator, reader, and copywriter. Hansberry left the *Freedom* staff in 1953 in order to concentrate on her writing. For the next three years, she worked at writing plays while holding a series of jobs: tagger in the garment-fur industry, typist, program director at Camp Unity (a progressive, interracial summer program), teacher at the Marxist-oriented Jefferson School of Social Science, and recreation leader for the handicapped.

A sudden change of fortune freed Hansberry from these odd jobs. Nemiroff and a friend, Burt D'Lugoff, wrote a folk ballad, "Cindy Oh Cindy," which became a hit. Money Nemiroff earned from the popular song allowed Hansberry to quit her jobs and devote all her time to her writing. It was then that she began to write "The Crystal Stair," a play about a struggling black family in Chicago, which would eventually become *A Raisin in the Sun*.

Drawing on her knowledge of the lives of working-class black people who had rented from her father and with whom she had attended school on Chicago's Southside, Hansberry wrote a realistic play with a theme inspired by Langston Hughes' poem "Harlem": "What happens to a dream deferred . . . Does it dry up like a raisin in the sun . . . Or does it explode?" In Hansberry's play, three generations of Youngers have struggled to survive financially and spiritually for too many years in a cramped, roach-infested kitchenette apartment with shared bathroom. When $10,000 insurance money is paid to Lena (Mama), elder of the household, on the death of her husband, she and her thirty-five-year-old son, Walter, differ sharply on the disposition of the windfall. Walter, frustrated by his dead-end job as a chauffeur, wants to invest in a liquor store as a means of freeing the family from its economic and psychological trap. But Mama, seeking more physical space for the family and the psychological freedom a real home would bring, puts a down payment on a house that happens to be in a white neighborhood. Her decision devastates

Walter, who views the money as his last chance to gain some economic control over his life. When Mama realizes how deeply her decision has hurt her son, she entrusts him with the remaining money—a portion is to be placed in a savings account for his sister Beneatha's college education, but the rest goes to Walter to do with as he wishes. Walter's good fortune is short-lived, however, because he loses the money in a dubious business deal. A disillusioned man, he faces his mother and family in a highly emotional scene. When presented with the opportunity to recover his losses by selling the house to the Clybourne Park Association (which is determined to keep the neighborhood white), he decides to take the offer despite its demeaning implications. Walter eventually comes to realize that he cannot live with this denigration of his family's pride, and in a very dramatic, climactic scene he rejects the offer. The play ends as the family begins to move to the new house.

Hansberry read a draft of the play to several colleagues. On one such occasion Phil Rose, a friend who had employed Nemiroff in his music-publishing firm, optioned the play for a Broadway production. Although he had never produced a Broadway play before, Rose and co-producer David J. Cogan set forth enthusiastically on this new venture. They approached major Broadway producers, but a "Negro play" was considered too risky a venture for Broadway. The only interested producer insisted on changes in director and cast that were unacceptable to Hansberry. So Rose, Cogan, and others raised the cash independently and took the show on tour without guarantee of a Broadway house. Audiences in the tour cities—New Haven, Philadelphia, and Chicago—reacted ecstatically. A last-minute rush for tickets in Philadelphia finally made the case for acquiring a Broadway theater.

A Raisin in the Sun opened at the Ethel Barrymore Theatre on 11 March 1959. The show was an instant success with both critics and audiences. New York critic Walter Kerr praised Hansberry for reading "the precise temperature of a race at that time in its history when it cannot retreat and cannot quite find the way to move forward. The mood is forty-nine parts anger and forty-nine parts control, with a very narrow escape hatch for the steam these abrasive contraries build up. Three generations stand poised, and crowed, on a detonating-cap."

The original cast and director were outstanding—and would later prove to be legendary, as they went on from this production to make significant contributions to American theater as actors, directors, and playwrights: those involved included Sidney Poitier, Claudia McNeil, Ruby Dee, Glynn Turman, Lou Gossett, and Diana Sands. Ossie Davis later replaced Poitier in the cast. The director, Lloyd Richards, was a newcomer to the professional scene; he became the first black director of a Broadway show since the 1920s, and many years later he assumed the directorship of the Yale Repertory Theatre.

Critics praised the play for its "honesty" and for creating a family of blacks with whom whites could identify. The extraordinary timeliness of the play contributed to its popularity. The spirit and struggles of the Younger family symbolized the social progress and setbacks characteristic of the 1950s. Desegregation of the nation's schools had been ordered by the Supreme Court only five years before. Boycotts and sit-ins had intensified as federal troops were used to enforce the court order and as black and white freedom riders demanded an end to segregation in transportation and other public accommodations. The newly militant mood of black Americans, born of anger, frustration, and deferred dreams, had been captured in the explosive and desperate Walter Lee. The sudden decision of Rosa Parks, whose refusal to move to the back of a bus precipitated the historic Montgomery bus boycott, was mirrored in Lena Younger's apolitical decision to live in Clybourne Park and her consequent challenge to the restrictive covenants of the day. The rise of independent African nations was reflected in the presence of the African student Asagai, who brought to the play the reality of his people's struggle for liberation; Beneatha's adulation of things Africaine anticipated a new wave of hair and dress styles that black Americans would soon adopt. Hansberry's prescience even extended into the next decade, to the struggle for

women's rights; assertive Beneatha aspires to be a doctor, and loyal, loving Ruth seriously contemplates an abortion in order to save her marriage. The play touched the vibrating nerve of a country on the verge of change and a people on the move.

Hansberry became a celebrity overnight, and she enjoyed her success immensely. "It's wonderful and I'm enjoying it," she said. "I've tried to go to everything I've been invited to and . . . so far I've tried to answer every piece of correspondence I get," which she estimated was twenty or thirty pieces a day.

The play was awarded the New York Drama Critics Circle Award in 1959, making Lorraine Hansberry the first black writer, the youngest person, and the fifth woman ever to win that award. Letters and telegrams poured in from around the world; invitations for interviews, speaking engagements, and many other opportunities took up much of her time for the next two years. Although she complained that she did not get much writing done during this period, she completed a television play within the year and made significant progress on several other projects.

In 1960, NBC producer Dore Schary commissioned Hansberry to write the opening segment for a television series commemorating the Civil War. Her subject was to be slavery. Recognizing that no serious treatment of slavery had been attempted on television before, Hansberry thoroughly researched the topic, reading the major studies of the Civil War and the slavery period and seeking out primary documents from libraries in New York and Washington, D.C. The result was *The Drinking Gourd*, a television play that neither sentimentalized nor apologized for slavery, but focused on the effects the slave system had on the families of the plantation master and on the poor white as well as the slave.

Hansberry portrayed slavery as an uncontrollable and totally victimizing institution designed to exploit cheap labor. Even Hiram, the slavemaster and a central figure in the play, who tries to run a humane plantation, finds that he cannot prevent the mutilation of the son of his favorite slave. Zeb, a poor white, is sucked into service of the slave system as over-seer because he cannot compete with the grow-ing power of plantations that are buying up the land. In viewing the white, both rich and poor, as victims, Hansberry stepped-outside the ra-cial categories so rigidly defended by society. Hiram's favorite slave, Rissa, whose son has been blinded for learning to read, turns her back on Hiram in his dying moments, thus shatter-ing the stereotype of the black mammy servant who puts her master's welfare above everything else.

NBC television executives deemed the play too controversial, and despite Schary's objec-tions it was shelved, along with the entire pro-ject. The network apparently was fearful that the project would offend some regions of the United States, particularly the South, although a studio vice-president had labeled it superb. Hansberry was paid well for *The Drinking Gourd*, but it was never produced by network television.

Hansberry was successful, however, in bring-ing her prize-winning play *A Raisin in the Sun* to the screen a short time later. In 1959, a few months after the play opened, she sold the movie rights to Columbia Pictures and began work on drafts of the screenplay, incorporating several new scenes. These additions, which were rejected for the final version, sharpened the play's attack on the effects of segregation and revealed with surer hand the growing mil-itant mood of blacks. Among them was a pow-erful scene in which a street orator articulates the economic exploitation of blacks and calls for militant action. Another shows Walter en-during the patronizing attitude of a white shop-keeper whom he asks for business advice. After many revisions and rewrites, the film was pro-duced with all but one of the play's original cast and released in 1961. The major textual loss in the film is the deletion of Asagai's third-act analysis of African liberation movements and their relationship to the struggles of the African American. In the film Asagai is reduced to a handsome, albeit quite intelligent, love interest for Beneatha. Nevertheless, the film was widely acclaimed and was invited for screening at the Cannes Film Festival in 1961.

Hansberry's celebrity as a playwright gave her a public platform from which to voice her advocacy for the black struggle and the need for social change. Among her most notable speeches was one delivered to a black writers conference sponsored by the American Society of African Culture in New York. Written during the pro-duction of *A Raisin in the Sun* and delivered on 1 March 1959—two weeks before the Broadway opening—"The Negro Writer and His Roots" is in effect Hansberry's credo. In this speech Hansberry declares that "all art is ultimately social." She called on black writers to be involved in "the intellectual affairs of all men, everywhere," and to address the major illusions of their time and culture. One of the most persistent and dangerous illusions, she argued, was the idea that people exist indepen-dent of the world around them, an attitude that she believed led to adolescent plays and the portrayal of man as helpless "in the face of a fate he cannot call by name." She went on to deny the notion that middle-class problems and values represent the problems of the na-tion and the world, noting that many peoples of the world remain alienated from the United States' abstract notions of destiny and the American dream. Finally, she declared the ur-gency of bringing about equality in the United States, warning that time was running out. Black writers, she felt, were in an enviable po-sition, poised to reclaim the past, to expose the dangers of materialism, and to affirm the he-roic potential of humankind. These ideas formed the framework for her later plays as well as *A Raisin in the Sun* and dictated her involvement in the world as both activist and artist.

As the civil rights movement intensified, Hansberry helped plan fund-raising events to support organizations such as the Student Non-violent Coordinating Committee (SNCC) and publicly agreed that Negroes should defend themselves against terrorist attacks when nec-essary. She expressed her disgust with the red-baiting of the McCarthy era and called for the abolition of the House Un-American Activities Committee. She criticized President John F. Kennedy's handling of the Cuban missile crisis,

Claudia McNeil and Sidney Poitier from the 1959 debut of *A Raisin in the Sun.*

arguing that his actions endangered the cause of world peace.

In 1961 Hansberry began work on several new plays: *The Sign in Sidney Brustein's Window, Les Blancs,* and an untitled work about Mary Wollstonecraft. Even though *The Sign in Sidney Brustein's Window* (1964) would be her next play produced, she first finished a favorite project, a screen adaptation of the Haitian novel *Masters of the Dew* by Jacques Roumain. A film company had requested the screenplay, but contractual problems prevented the production from proceeding.

Despite progress on her work, Hansberry struggled with self-discipline. Still heavily in demand for public appearances, she also faced the distractions of letter-writing and her own activism.

In an effort to minimize the interruptions brought on by fame, in 1962 she moved to Croton, a semirural suburb about forty-five minutes north of Manhattan. The peace and quiet of her new home, with its acreage of wooded

land, offered the solitude necessary to continue and to complete what was then her most pressing project, *The Sign in Sidney Brustein's Window.* Auditions for the play were to open in September 1963, with Hal Prince directing and coproducing; she had much to do. Early in April 1963, however, she had "a weird attack" and fainted. Hospitalized at University Hospital in New York City for nearly two weeks, she underwent extensive tests. The results suggested cancer of the pancreas, but she was not told of her specific condition.

Despite the progressive failure of her health during the next two years, she continued her writing projects and political activities. In May 1963 she was invited to join a multiracial assembly that included James Baldwin, Harry Belafonte, and Lena Horne at a meeting in New York City with Attorney General Robert Kennedy to discuss the escalating protests and violence in the South. After a passionate query by Jerome Smith, a young black freedom rider, as to the lack of positive leadership on the part of the United States government in the South, Hansberry admonished Kennedy that he must listen to the voices of men like Smith if he were to understand the needs of black Americans. Although she worked intensively on *The Sign in Sidney Brustein's Window*, she took time to organize a meeting in Croton to raise funds for the SNCC and a rally to support the Southern Freedom Movement. In an effort to treat her health problems she went to the Lahey Clinic in Boston, where a draining tube was inserted and removed a month later. Meanwhile disagreements with Hal Prince erupted, and he soon withdrew from the production of *The Sign in Sidney Brustein's Window*.

Although her health was in rapid decline, Hansberry greeted 1964 as a year of glorious work. Despite frequent hospitalization and bouts with pain and attendant medication, she completed a photo essay for a book on the civil rights struggle, *The Movement: Documentary of a Struggle for Equality* (1964), and continued with the many other projects on her writing schedule.

In March 1964 she quietly divorced Robert Nemiroff, formalizing a separation that had occurred several years earlier, although they continued to collaborate as colleagues and friends. Those outside their close circle of friends and family learned about the divorce only when Hansberry's will was read in 1965.

Hansberry spent the rest of 1964 in and out of hospitals, as the cancer spread to her bones and neck. She struggled with final revisions on *The Sign in Sidney Brustein's Window* and attempted to remain involved in civil rights activities. In May she was released from the hospital to deliver a speech to the winners of the United Negro College Fund's writing contest, where she coined the now-famous phrase "Young, gifted and black." A month later she left her sickbed to participate in the Town Hall debate "The Black Revolution and the White Backlash," at which she and fellow black artists challenged the criticism by white liberals of the growing militance of the civil rights movement.

From October 1964 to January 1965 she moved back and forth between the hospital and the Hotel Victoria in New York, where she stayed to be near the rehearsals of *The Sign in Sidney Brustein's Window*. A few days after the play's opening, the cancer entered Hansberry's brain. She lapsed into a coma for two weeks, but later recovered long enough to attend some performances of her play.

The Sign in Sidney Brustein's Window opened on 15 October 1964 at the Longacre Theatre to mixed reviews. Critics were somewhat surprised by this second play from a woman who had come to be identified with the black liberation movement. Writing about people she had known in Greenwich Village, Hansberry had created a play with a cast that was primarily white and with a theme that called for intellectuals to get involved in the social problems and issues of the world.

Her target was her own generation, which had been marked by the postwar existentialist debate surrounding Jean-Paul Sartre and Albert Camus. A play of ideas, *The Sign in Sidney Brustein's Window* drew upon the wit, philosophical sophistication, and ennui of the Greenwich Village intellectual and artistic community. Sidney Brustein, a bohemian of Jewish background who owns a small, alternative newspaper, gets involved in a local political campaign only to discover that his candidate is linked to the criminal elements that exploit the community. A series of revelations, especially about his wife and her sisters, set Sidney on a personal odyssey toward self-discovery. Symbolizing her generation as the "Western intellectual poised in hesitation before the flames of involvement," Hansberry wrote a play designed to jolt that generation out of its passivity.

Some critics considered the play too diffuse, too depressing, and marred by too much talk, charging that it lacked the warmth of *A Raisin in the Sun*. A review in *Newsweek* by Richard Gilman even called it "borrowed bitchery" and "a vicious sitting in judgment on others." Other critics raved that it was a courageous and compassionate play that revealed the confusion of contemporary life. Playwright William Gibson noted that the reaction to the play was as much a comment on the state of Broadway theater and audiences as on the work itself: "How

274

can it be that, of the hundreds of thousands who roared with pleasure and wept tears at her *Raisin in the Sun,* so few have the intellectual appetency to hear what her mind has been at work on since?" The cautious and negative responses would have been enough to close the show, except for a network of friends and pre-eminent theater artists (including playwright Sidney Kingsley and actresses Shelley Winters, Viveca Lindfors, and Diana Sands) who quickly mounted a tireless campaign to keep the production open.

Finally on 12 January 1965, Lorraine Hansberry's battle with cancer ended. She died at University Hospital in New York City at the age of thirty-four. The list of telegrams and cards sent to her family read like a *Who's Who* of the civil rights movement and the American theater. *The Sign in Sidney Brustein's Window* closed on the night of her death.

Lorraine Hansberry left a number of finished and unfinished projects in her papers. Among them were the book for a musical adapted from Oliver La Farge's novel *Laughing Boy;* an adaptation of *The Marrow of Tradition,* by Charles Chesnutt; a film version of *Masters of the Dew,* adapted from Jacques Roumain's impressive novel about Haiti; a play about the Egyptian pharaoh Akhnaton; sections of a semi-autobiographical novel, "All the Dark and Beautiful Warriors"; a number of essays, including a critical commentary written in 1957 on Simone de Beauvoir's *The Second Sex,* a book that Hansberry said had changed her life, and many other works. In her will she designated her former husband, Robert Nemiroff, as executor of her literary estate.

Despite the brevity of her theatrical life and the fact that only two of her plays were produced during her lifetime, Hansberry's contribution to American theater was more than a simple "first," to be commemorated in history books and then forgotten. *A Raisin in the Sun* was the turning point for black artists in the professional theater. Numerous black writers and actors were inspired by or directly helped by its production and success. *The Black Theatre Movement from "A Raisin in the Sun" to the Present* (1979), a documentary film pro-

duced and directed by Woodie King, Jr., has recorded the immense impact of this play on a generation of black artists. Of more than sixty people who were interviewed for this project, at least two-thirds said they were influenced or aided, or both, by Lorraine Hansberry and her work. Among these were Woodie King, Jr., Lloyd Richards, Ivan Dixon, Rosalind Cash, Douglas Turner Ward, Lonne Elder, Robert Hooks, Ossie Davis, Ruby Dee, Ron Milner, Glynn Turman, and many others who were either in the original cast or subsequent casts of *A Raisin in the Sun,* or who simply saw the play and were inspired to seek a career in theater.

In the introduction to Hansberry's *To Be Young, Gifted, and Black,* James Baldwin wrote of the play, "Never before, in the entire history of the American theater, had so much of the truth of black people's lives been seen on stage." Those qualities of authenticity and candor combined with the timeliness of the work to make it one of the most popular plays ever produced on the U.S. stage. The original production ran for 538 performances on Broadway, attracting large audiences of whites and blacks alike.

The artistry of the play in presenting fully realized black characters made it an excellent vehicle for overcoming racial attitudes in the theater and exposing white audiences to truths of black life at a time when the nation's attitudes were polarized. Walter Lee exemplified frustrated young black men struggling to define their manhood in a materialistic society, much like the angry young men who strode the boards of the black arts theater in the 1960s and 1970s. Beneatha's intelligence, assertiveness, and high aspirations became characteristic of the works of women writers in the 1970s, as the women's movement found its particular voice. Asagai, the African intellectual, superior in intelligence and sensibility to the American men around him, was the first such character seen on the U.S. stage. A Pan-Africanist like her mentor W. E. B. Du Bois, Hansberry was the first to emphasize the positive connections between black Americans and emerging African nations in a major American play. Anticipating the Black Arts movement of the 1960s and 1970s, Hansberry addressed issues unfamiliar at the time but soon to be inescapable: concepts of black beauty, male-female relationships, generational conflict, class differences, value systems of black families, questions of identity, and black Americans' relationship to their African past.

One of the most important and elusive contributions of Hansberry's plays is her assertion of the heroic dimensions of modern man's struggles. At a time when impotence and despair dictated the fate of figures in American drama, Hansberry created characters who affirmed life in the face of brutality and defeat. She credited her roots in black American culture for her positive spirit. In the *Village Voice* essay "Willy Loman, Walter Younger, and He Who Must Live," she argued that Walter survives and grows because he is supported by a culture of hope and affirmation, unlike Arthur Miller's protagonist in *Death of a Salesman*. Accordingly, in *The Sign in Sidney Brustein's Window*, the rootless Sidney, lacking cultural support, must resist the temptation to despair by sheer act of will and reaffirmation of his linkage to the human family. Through her plays and essays, Hansberry offered a strong, opposing voice to the drama of despair.

Hansberry succeeded in creating believable, rounded black characters who were both authentic racially and accessible to nonblacks. An early interview in the *New York Times* misquoted her as saying that *A Raisin in the Sun* is "not a Negro play," and that she was a writer who "happened to be Negro." This quote, interpreted in light of the extraordinary success of the play, led some critics to label her "integrationist" and to claim that her characters were not authentically black. Some contemporary critics have built their assessment of Hansberry on this idea. In fact, however, Hansberry argued that her characters were distinctly Negro and even more specifically from Chicago's Southside, asserting that art must be very specific in order to achieve the universal. *A Raisin in the Sun* indeed achieved the universal and has endured as an American classic. It is produced by high schools, colleges, and

community theaters regularly each year. During its twenty-fifth anniversary season in 1983–1984 it was revived to critical acclaim by the Goodman Theater in Chicago, the St. Louis Repertory, and the Yale Repertory, as well as theaters in San Francisco and Off-Broadway in New York. Reviews during this season revealed that the intervening years had dulled the novelty of black figures on the stage and therefore allowed critics and audiences to recognize Hansberry's perceptive portrayal of a family struggling to maintain human values of pride and dignity in the face of materialistic temptations as well as to appreciate the particular difficulties of a black family.

Robert Nemiroff, who was literary executor and owner of Hansberry's papers until his death in 1991, edited, published, and produced much of Hansberry's work after her death. In 1969 he adapted some of her unpublished writings for the stage under the title *To be Young, Gifted, and Black*. The longest-running drama of the 1968–1969 Off-Broadway season, it toured colleges and communities in the United States during 1970 and 1971; a ninety-minute film based on the stage play was first shown in January 1972.

In 1970, Nemiroff produced Hansberry's *Les Blancs*, a full-length play set in the midst of a violent revolution in an African country, a project which Hansberry had worked on with excitement during the last year of her life, even during the run of *The Sign in Sidney Brustein's Window*. *Les Blancs* is unusual for its forthright discussion of the inevitability of revolution when concrete gains toward freedom are not made. Its major character is an articulate, European-educated black African, who eloquently sets forth the reasons why his people cannot wait for freedom but who at the same time hesitates to join the revolution. Critical response was mixed on the play's premiere production at the Longacre Theatre in New York City; several critics accused Hansberry of fomenting revolution, while others, particularly black reviewers, welcomed her exposition of the communication gap between whites and blacks. Nemiroff edited *Les Blancs: The Collected Last Plays of Lorraine Hansberry* (1972), which made available *Les Blancs* and *The Drinking Gourd* as well as *What Use Are Flowers?*, a short play about the consequences to civilization of nuclear holocaust. In 1973 *A Raisin in the Sun* returned as a musical, *Raisin*, produced by Nemiroff and for which he won a Tony Award.

In 1989 Robert Nemiroff produced on educational television the most complete version of *A Raisin in the Sun*, including scenes never before seen on stage or television. Nielsen ratings indicated that the broadcast, produced by the American Playhouse and featuring Danny Glover and Esther Rolle, had the highest black viewership in the history of public television. The response indicated that thirty years after its premiere, the play endured as a work that articulates in ethnically specific terms the universal struggle between materialistic and spiritual values.

With the growth of women's theater and feminist criticism in the 1970s and 1980s, Hansberry was rediscovered by a new generation of women in theater. Indeed a revisionist reading of her major plays reveals that she was feminist long before the rise of the women's movement. The female characters in her plays are pivotal to the major themes. They may share the protagonist role, as in *A Raisin in the Sun*, where Mama is co-protagonist with Walter. Or a woman character may take the definitive action, as in *The Drinking Gourd*, in which Rissa, the house slave, defies the slave system (and stereotype) by turning her back on her dying master and arming her son so that he can escape to the North. In *The Sign in Sidney Brustein's Window*, Sidney is brought to a new level of self-awareness through the actions of a "chorus" of women—the Parodus Sisters. Likewise, the African woman dancer is ever-present in Tshembe Matoseh's mind in *Les Blancs*, silently and steadily moving him to a revolutionary commitment to his people. Hansberry's portrayal of the character Beneatha, a young black woman with aspirations to be a doctor, and her introduction of abortion as an issue for poor women in *A Raisin in the Sun* signaled her feminist attitudes early on. These and other portrayals challenged prevailing stage stereotypes

of both black and white women and introduced feminist issues to the stage in compelling terms. In the 1980s, Hansberry's "anonymous" letters to *The Ladder* came to light, revealing not only her sensitivity to homophobic attitudes, but her own homosexuality. These letters have further stimulated feminist interest in her work. As more of her papers are released for publication by the current literary executor and owner of her papers, Dr. Jewell Gresham Nemiroff, and as more scholars examine her role in twentieth-century theater and literature, the full scope of Lorraine Hansberry's work will emerge.

Selected Bibliography

PRIMARY WORKS

DRAMA

A Raisin in the Sun: A Drama in Three Acts. New York: Random House, 1959.

The Sign in Sidney Brustein's Window: A Drama in Three Acts. New York: Samuel French, 1965.

Lorraine Hansberry's "A Raisin in the Sun" and "The Sign in Sidney Brustein's Window." With a foreword by John Braine. New York: New American Library, 1966. Includes Robert Nemiroff's "The One Hundred and One 'Final' Performances of *Sidney Brustein: Portrait of a Play and Its Author*." Nemiroff's essay describes critical response to *The Sign in Sidney Brustein's Window*, discusses Hansberry's characterization of the Western intellectual, and relates the story of the struggle to keep the Broadway production of *Sidney Brustein* alive. Expanded twenty-fifth anniversary edition, 1987. Reprint. New York: Vintage Books, 1995.

To be Young, Gifted, and Black. New York: Samuel French, 1971. Stage play. Also published as *To Be Young, Gifted and Black: Lorraine Hansberry in Her Own Words*. New York: Vintage Books, 1995.

Les Blancs: The Collected Last Plays of Lorraine Hansberry. Edited By Robert Nemiroff. New York: Random House, 1972. Includes *Les Blancs, The Drinking Gourd*, and *What Use Are Flowers?* Reprinted as *The Collected Last Plays*. New York: Vintage Books, 1994.

Raisin. New York: Samuel French, 1978. Musical.

"Toussaint: Excerpt from a Work in Progress." In *Nine Plays by Black Women*. Edited by Margaret B. Wilkerson. New York: New American Library, 1986.

SCREENPLAY

A Raisin in the Sun: The Unfilmed Original Screenplay. Edited by Robert Nemiroff. New York: Penguin Books, 1992.

NONFICTION

The Movement: Documentary of A Struggle for Equality. New York: Simon & Schuster, 1964. Reprinted as *A Matter of Colour: Documentary of the Struggle for Racial Equality in the USA.* London: Penguin, 1965.

To Be Young, Gifted, and Black: Lorraine Hansberry in Her Own Words. Edited by Robert Nemiroff. With an introduction by James Baldwin. Englewood Cliffs, N.J.: Prentice-Hall, 1969. Biography drawn from letters, journals, essays, memoirs, poetry, and dramatic scenes.

FICTION

"All the Dark and Beautiful Warriors." *Village Voice,* August 16, 1983. Pp. 1, 11–16, 18–19.
"The Buck Williams Tennessee Memorial Association." *Southern Exposure,* September–October 1984. Pp. 28–30.

ESSAYS AND ARTICLES

"Willy Loman, Walter Lee Younger, and He Who Must Live." *Village Voice,* August 12, 1959. Pp. 7–8.
"On Summer." *Playbill,* June 27, 1960. Pp. 3, 25–27.
"This Complex of Womanhood." *Ebony* 15:40 (August 1960).
"Images and Essences: 1961 Dialogue with an Uncolored Egghead Containing Wholesome Intentions and Some Sass." *Urbanite* 1:10–11, 36 (May 1961).
"Thoughts on Genet, Mailer and the New Paternalism." *Village Voice,* June 1, 1961. Pp. 10, 15.
"A Challenge to Artists." *Freedomways* 3:33–35 (Winter 1963).
"The Black Revolution and the White Backlash." *National Guardian,* July 4, 1964. Pp. 5–9. Transcript of Town Hall forum.
"The Nation Needs Your Gifts." *Negro Digest* 13:26–29 (August 1964).
"The Legacy of W. E. B. Du Bois." *Freedomways* 5:19–20 (Winter 1965).
"The Scars of the Ghetto." *Monthly Review* 16, no. 10:588–91 (February 1965).
"Original Prospectus for the John Brown Memorial Theatre of Harlem." *Black Scholar* 10:14–15 (July–August 1979).
"The Negro Writer and His Roots: Toward a New Romanticism." *Black Scholar* 12:2–12 (March–April 1981).
"Simone de Beauvoir and *The Second Sex:* An American Commentary (An Unfinished Essay-in-Progress)." Edited with an introduction by Margaret B. Wilkerson. In *Words of Fire.* Edited by Beverly Guy-Sheftall. New York: The New Press, 1995. Pp. 125–42.

SECONDARY WORKS

BIOGRAPHICAL AND CRITICAL STUDIES

Baldwin, James. "Sweet Lorraine." *Esquire,* November 1969. Pp. 139–140. (The introduction to *To Be Young, Gifted and Black.*)

Baraka, Amiri (Leroi Jones). "*Raisin in the Sun's* Enduring Passion." *Washington Post,* November 16, 1986. Section F. Pp. 1–3.
Bigsby, C. W. E. *Modern American Drama, 1945–1990.* New York: Cambridge University Press, 1992. Pp. 269–76.
Bond, Jean Carey, ed. *Lorraine Hansberry: Art of Thunder, Vision of Light, Freedomways* 19 (1979). (Special issue on Lorraine Hansberry, with extensive bibliography.)
Brown, Lloyd W. "Lorraine Hansberry as Ironist: A Reappraisal of *A Raisin in the Sun.*" *Journal of Black Studies* 4, no. 3:237–47 (March 1974).
Carter, Steven R. "Lorraine Hansberry." In *Dictionary of Literary Biography.* Vol. 38, *Afro-American Writers After 1955: Dramatists and Prose Writers.* Edited by Thadious M. Davis and Trudier Harris. Detroit: Gale Research, 1985.
———. *Hansberry's Drama: Commitment amid Complexity.* Urbana: University of Illinois Press, 1991.
Cheney, Anne. *Lorraine Hansberry.* Boston: Twayne, 1984.
Cruse, Harold. "Lorraine Hansberry." In *The Crisis of the Negro Intellectual.* New York: William Morrow, 1967. Pp. 267–84.
Domina, Lynn. *Understanding "A Raisin in the Sun": A Student Casebook to Issues, Sources, and Historical Documents.* Westport, Conn.: Greenwood Press, 1998.
Friedman, Sharon. "Feminist Concerns in the Works of Four Twentieth-Century American Women Dramatists." Ph.D. diss. New York University (1977).
Grant, Robert Henry. "Lorraine Hansberry: The Playwright as Warrior-Intellectual." Ph.D. diss. Harvard (1982).
Keppel, Ben. *The Work of Democracy: Ralph Bunche, Kenneth B. Clark, Lorraine Hansberry, and the Cultural Politics of Race.* Cambridge, Mass.: Harvard University Press, 1995.
McKissack, Patricia C., and Fredrick L. McKissack. *Young, Black, and Determined: A Biography of Lorraine Hansberry.* New York: Holiday House, 1998.
Nemiroff, Robert. "From These Roots: Lorraine Hansberry and the South." *Southern Exposure,* September–October 1984. Pp. 32–36.
Phillips, Elizabeth C. *The Works of Lorraine Hansberry: A Critical Commentary.* New York: Monarch Press, 1973.
Scheader, Catherine. *They Found a Way: Lorraine Hansberry.* Chicago: Children's Press, 1978. (A biography for young readers, with many photos.)
Schiff, Ellen. *From Stereotype to Metaphor: The Jew in Contemporary Drama.* Albany: State University of New York Press, 1982. Pp. 155–60 and passim.
Wilkerson, Margaret B. "*A Raisin in the Sun:* Anniversary of an American Classic." *Theatre Journal* 38:441–52 (December 1986).
———. "The Dark Vision of Lorraine Hansberry: Excerpts from a Literary Biography." *Massachusetts Review* 28:642–50 (Winter 1987).
———. "Lorraine Vivian Hansberry (1930–1965)." In *Black Women in America.* Edited by Darlene Clark

Hine. Brooklyn, N.Y.: Carlson Publishing Inc., 1993. Pp. 524–29.
———. "From Harlem to Broadway: African American Women Playrights at Mid-Century." In *The Cambridge Companion to American Women Playwrights*. Edited by Brenda Murphy. Cambridge: Cambridge University Press, 1999. Pp. 134–52.

AUDIO RECORDINGS AND FILMS

Lorraine Hansberry Speaks Out: Art and the Black Revolution. Caedmon Records TC 1352 (1972). Record album.
Lorraine Hansberry: The Black Experience in the Creation of Drama. Princeton, N.J.: Films for the Humanities, 1976.

A Raisin in the Sun. Columbia Pictures (1961). Film.
To Be Young, Gifted, and Black. WNET, Educational Broadcasting Corp. (1972). Film.
A Raisin in the Sun. American Playhouse Production (1989). Videotape.

BIBLIOGRAPHIES

Kaiser, Ernest, and Robert Nemiroff. "A Lorraine Hansberry Bibliography." In *Lorraine Hansberry: Art of Thunder, Vision of Light*. *Freedomways* 19 (1979).
Leeson, Richard M. *Lorraine Hansberry: A Research and Production Sourcebook*. Westport, Conn.: Greenwood Press, 1997.

FRANCES ELLEN WATKINS HARPER
(1825–1911)

FRANCES SMITH FOSTER

AUTHOR OF ALMOST a dozen books, several short stories, and numerous separately published poems, essays, and letters, Frances Ellen Watkins Harper was impressively productive, even by current standards. Her pioneering efforts in journalism made her, in I. Garland Penn's words, "the journalistic mother, so to speak, of many brilliant young women who have entered upon her line of work so recently" *The Afro-American Press and Its Editors* (repr. New York: Arno, 1969). Harper's literary versatility and political influence made her the preeminent African American writer prior to the twentieth century.

Harper belongs to the cadre of writers that included John Greenleaf Whittier, Harriet Beecher Stowe, Harriet Jacobs, Maria W. Stewart, Frederick Douglass, and William Wells Brown, writers who did not divide their words from their works; consequently, her achievements with the written word, remarkable as they are, are not the sole basis for her prominence. She was one of the first American women to become a professional lecturer. In her work for various abolitionist, temperance, civil rights, and peace organizations, she shared the platform with such notables as Susan B. Anthony, Elizabeth Cady Stanton, and Sojourner Truth. Frances Harper also served on the national boards of or as officer of numerous organizations, including the Women's Christian Temperance Union (WCTU), the American Association of Educators of Colored Youth, the National Women's Suffrage Association, the National Council of Negro Women, and the National John Brown Memorial Association of Women.

Harper's contemporaries recognized and praised her contributions in various ways. Local and national newspapers routinely noted her activities, advertised her lecture tours, and generally promoted her career. Histories such as William C. Nell's *Colored Patriots of the American Revolution* (1855), William W. Brown's *The Rising Son; or, The Antecedents and Advances of the Colored Race* (1873), Phebe A. Hanaford's *Daughters of America; or, Women of the Century* (1883), and N. F. Mossell's *The Work of the Afro-American Woman* (1894) regularly refer to her achievements. She was included in such compendium articles, published in *A.M.E. Church Review*, as "Some Negro Poets" (4, 1888), Fannie Bentley's "The Women of Our Race Worthy of Imitation" (6, 1890), and S. Elizabeth Frazier's "Some Afro-American Women of Mark" (8, 1892). Many African American women's service clubs named themselves in her honor, and across the nation, in cities such as St. Louis, Pittsburgh, and St. Paul, F. E. W. Harper Leagues and Frances E. Harper Women's Christian Temperance Unions continued to thrive long after her death. The national WCTU recognized Harper's contributions posthumously in 1922 by making her the only African American on its Red Letter calendar.

By any standard, Frances E. W. Harper was an extraordinary woman, but as of 2000 there is only one full-length biography and no full-length critical analysis of her work. While every major discussion of nineteenth-century women's or African American literature mentions Harper's writings, the scholarship has, until the 1980s, been strikingly narrow and repetitive, the breadth and scope of her canon largely undiscovered. Biographical entries appear in virtually all the standard reference books, but relatively little is known about her life. Since 1871 most accounts have relied heavily upon the anecdotes, letters, and interpretations that her longtime friend and colleague, William Still, published that year in *The Underground Rail Road*.

The self-educated son of slaves, William Still had worked his way from janitor and clerk in the Philadelphia antislavery office to head of the local Underground Railroad station, correspondent for several national antislavery periodicals, prominent businessman, and community leader. Most likely Still was referring to his own home when he noted that upon her arrival in Philadelphia, Frances Harper made "her home at the station of the Underground Rail Road, where she frequently saw passengers and heard their melting tales of suffering and wrong, which intensely increased her sympathy in their behalf."

Since their correspondence shows that William Still, his wife, Letitia, and their daughters, Caroline and Mary, all considered Harper (who lived with them off and on for twenty years) part of the family, Still's knowledge of Harper was probably as extensive as any, and the heavy reliance of later biographers upon his account is not inappropriate. However, the facts and correspondence that Still made public, while informative and reasonably accurate, emphasize her abolitionist activities and omit the last forty years of her life.

From Still, we know that Harper was born Frances Ellen Watkins to free parents in Baltimore, Maryland, on 24 September 1825. By the

age of three, she was orphaned and living with relatives. William Still does not specifically identify the relatives who took her in, but most likely the young child lived in the household of her uncle, William Watkins. A deeply religious and politically active man, he was a former shoemaker who had decided that "his true vocation [was] that of training the mind and saving the soul," according to Rev. William H. Morris, writing in the *A.M.E. Church Review* in 1886. He spent his life as a writer, educator, minister, and social activist of singular and intense effect. For many years in Baltimore he operated the William Watkins Academy, a school devoted to the education of free colored youth that was renowned for its academic rigor and strict discipline.

Biographical sources generally follow Still's lead and suggest that Harper's childhood was unusually serious, even melancholy. They frequently reprint the words (from a letter Harper wrote to Still) that suggest she was a lonely child: "Have I yearned for a mother's love? The grave was my robber. Before three years had scattered their blight around my path, death had won my mother from me. Would a strong arm of a brother have been welcome? I was my mother's only child." Still provides this remark, however, from an unknown context, and it may not adequately express Harper's general attitude toward her childhood. The Watkins family was large, close-knit, and respected among middle-class black Baltimoreans. Frances Watkins, though "noted for her industry, rarely trifling away time as most girls are wont to do in similar circumstances," was no Cinderella. She had an uncommonly thorough education, and early on she earned many accolades for her academic and literary accomplishments at the Watkins Academy, which was known for producing committed black professionals and leaders, not the least of whom were Watkins's five sons, Richard, William, George, Henry, and John, and his niece Frances Ellen. From her uncle's precept and practice, she early developed skills in writing and elocution, a strong interest in radical politics and religion, and a special sense of responsibility and dedication to the noble and lofty ideals of the world.

Some of Harper's autobiographical poems and stories encourage a more balanced view. For example, an untitled poem published in *The Anti-Slavery Bugle* in 1860 declares that she had no desire to return to the days of her youth, not because they were unhappy but because they were so carefree:

> Oh! childhood had laughter, song and
>   mirth,
> The freshness of life, the sunshine of earth;
> But instead of its gilded dreams and toys,
> I have loftier hopes and calmer joys.

Though her early years were certainly not without their problems and griefs, it seems more likely that Harper had as normal a childhood as that of any middle-class free African American child of a politically active family in a slave state.

Frances Harper was one of the very few women of her generation to have the luxury of attending school for a sustained period but, as was customary for all but the most privileged students, the classroom had to give way to the workroom at an early age. When she was about thirteen, Harper began working for the Armstrong family. Her duties were to learn sewing, to watch over the children, and to care for the house. Still says that young Frances had "an ardent thirst for knowledge and a remarkable talent for composition" and that her employers allowed her free access to their bookstore.

Sometime around 1845, Harper reportedly published a small collection of her writings called *Forest Leaves*. Unfortunately, no copy is known to have survived. About five years later, she was hired as the first female teacher at the newly established Union Seminary near Columbus, Ohio. For a year she taught sewing at the struggling young institution, established by the African Methodist Episcopal Church as a training school for African American youth. According to the annual report, she was quite successful. J. M. Brown, the principal, wrote: "Miss Watkins has taught a class in embroidery, which numbers 12; also a class in plain Sewing. . . . [She] has been faithful to her trust, and has manifested in every effort a commend-

Frances Ellen Watkins Harper

able zeal for the cause of Education; and sacrificing spirit, so that it may be promoted."

Despite this favorable evaluation, the next year Harper took another teaching position in Little York, Pennsylvania. She was not happy with her new position. Although she found the education of African American youth philosophically compatible work, the physical and emotional realities of trying to control "fifty-three untrained little urchins" were not. In a letter published by Still she expressed her dilemma thus:

What would you do if you were in my place? Would you give up and go back and work at your trade (dress-making)? There are no people that need all the benefits resulting from a well-directed education more than we do. . . . It is a work of time, a labor of patience, to become an effective school teacher; and it should be a work of love in which they who engage should not abate heart nor hope until it is done.   (Still, p. 785)

In Little York, Harper frequently encountered fugitive slaves, and these experiences, coupled with her own refugee status (the result of a Maryland law that made it a crime, punishable by enslavement, for a free black person to enter the state), moved her toward more direct political involvement. It angered her that African Americans were "treated worse than aliens among a people whose language we speak, whose religion we profess, and whose blood flows and mingles in our veins," and she found it intolerable that they were "homeless in the land of our birth and worse off than strangers in the home of our nativity."

Then, an event occurred that caused the young woman to make a drastic and dangerous decision. The case of one particular hapless soul victimized by the new Maryland law attracted considerable attention: the man had been arrested and sold into slavery, escaped, only to be recaptured, beaten, and sent farther south. Shortly afterward he died as a result of his beating and the harsh conditions of his enslavement. "Upon that grave, I pledged myself to the Anti-Slavery cause," Harper later wrote in a letter.

Quitting her job, she moved to Philadelphia, where she associated with the local antislavery network by attending lectures, reading and writing abolitionist material, and working in whatever capacity she could. She learned a great deal of the theory and practice of abolitionism, but the newcomer was not allowed to be as active and responsible as she had hoped. According to Still, "her modesty prevented her from pressing her claims; consequently as she was but little known, being a young and homeless maiden (an exile by law), no especial encouragement was tendered her by Anti-slavery friends in Philadelphia."

There was a substantial African American middle class in Philadelphia, and the city was a center for African American literature, supporting several literary societies and nurturing a relatively large number of publishing writers. Undoubtedly these were the models for the "conversaziones" that frequently appear in Harper's later fiction. Frances Harper was soon recognized as one of the city's most talented young artists, but she was unable to gather the support necessary to publish her book-length manuscript. Undaunted, she continued to submit individual pieces for publication and to build a national reputation.

The appearance of Harriet Beecher Stowe's novel *Uncle Tom's Cabin* in 1852 sparked an unprecedented literary and social response, and Frances Watkins was one of many writers inspired by the images and purpose of that work. In her poem "Eliza Harris" Harper re-imagines Stowe's famous scene of Eliza's desperate flight across the ice-blocked Ohio River, retelling the familiar incident with a focus subtly but profoundly different from the original. Both writers relate the scene from a third-person perspective, but Stowe describes the sight and sounds of Eliza's flight, includes Eliza as one of several characters, and privileges the thoughts and actions of her white characters. Haley, the slave-master, pursues Eliza "like a hound after a deer." And Stowe's Eliza desperately reacts with an instinctive ability more like that of a pursued animal than that of a determined individual. Stowe's narrator tells the reader that Eliza leaped with "wild cries and desperate energy," that she "saw nothing, felt nothing, till dimly, as in a dream, she saw the Ohio side, and a man helping her up the bank." Stowe provides a Mr. Symmes, the white southern neighbor who just happens by in time to rescue the dazed woman, to assure her, "You've arnt your liberty, and you shall have it, for all me," and to point the way to the house of white Quakers who will take care of her.

Harper, on the other hand, forcefully manipulates Stowe's simile of the pursued and pursuing: "Like a fawn from the arrow, startled and wild, / A woman swept by us, bearing a child." The metaphor emphasizes the swiftness and desperation of the flight, but Harper's version makes it clear that it is a "woman" with a "child" being chased. The next lines emphasize Eliza's humanity, carefully describing her physical features that convey her purposeful decision. Harper provides phrase after phrase that define the resolve and determination that compelled Eliza's extraordinary physical feat. Her narrator interrupts the action, not to discuss the creaking of the ice and the loss of Eliza's clothing as she stumbles across the raging river, but to reflect upon the nature of a society within which such a scene would occur. Harper's Eliza is aided not by a friendly white man but by "Heaven" and "the friends of humanity" who open their doors. And, most significantly, the lines "For she is a mother—her child is a slave—/ And she'll give him his freedom, or find him a grave!" balance any sentimentalized notion elicited by the image of Eliza as a doe.

"Eliza Harris" is an important work from this early period not only because it demonstrates a technique that Harper was to use throughout her career but also because the controversy surrounding its publication helped make Frances Ellen Watkins a nationally known name. Apparently the aspiring poet had submitted "Eliza Harris" to several papers. William Lloyd Garrison published it in the *Liberator* on 16 December 1853, and it appeared in *Frederick Douglass' Paper* on 23 December 1853. However, Douglass published the poem with the caption "For Frederick Douglass' Paper," thus prompting an irate note from W. H. H. Day, the editor of *The Alienated American*, informing Douglass that he had printed that same poem a week earlier, and since the poem was sent on a "printed slip," his paper had not claimed that it was written exclusively for it. "Since then," Day continued, "we have received a fine piece written "for the *Alienated American*" which piece was published last week." Such territorial squabbling had more to do with competition between the editors than with any impropriety of the author, but it certainly drew attention to the budding writer.

Despite, or in defiance of, the controversy with the *Alienated American*, Douglass continued to publish Harper's works, including the other two poems of her *Uncle Tom's Cabin* trilogy, "To Mrs. Harriet Beecher Stowe" (February 1854) and "Eva's Farewell" (March 1854). Douglass often prefaced Harper's poems with flattering remarks about her lectures, predictions of her continued success as a leader of the movement, and recommendations of her books. William Lloyd Garrison also regularly allocated

space in the *Liberator* for Harper's writings. Thus it comes as no surprise that the resistance of the abolitionist leadership in Philadelphia and the encouragement of prominent abolitionists in Massachusetts would result in the young activist's moving farther north.

Shortly after her relocation, Harper was hired as an agent by the Maine Anti-Slavery Society, apparently making her the first African American woman to become a professional lecturer. Her services were in great demand. Between 5 September and 20 October 1854, she gave at least thirty-one lectures in about twenty cities. Despite such a grueling schedule, she found time to write and to publish poems, essays, and letters and to arrange the fall 1854 publication of *Poems on Miscellaneous Subjects*, a collection of poems and essays for which William Lloyd Garrison wrote the preface. *Poems on Miscellaneous Subjects* was an immediate success. Within four months an enlarged edition was published in Philadelphia. In 1855 both the Boston and the Philadelphia editions were reprinted. By 1857, over ten thousand copies had been printed. During Harper's lifetime the collection was reprinted at least twenty times.

Included in *Poems on Miscellaneous Subjects* are several of the poems for which Harper is best known today, poems that, as most scholars acknowledge, ushered in the tradition of African American protest poetry. Clearly redirecting the African American poetic tradition, such works as "The Slave Mother," "The Slave Auction," and "The Fugitive's Wife" are classic antislavery poems that focus upon the separation of families and the devastating pain that women, in particular, suffer in bondage. However, the majority of the poems and the three essays in *Poems on Miscellaneous Subjects* do not focus directly upon abolitionist themes. Some, like "The Syrophenican Woman" and "Ruth and Naomi," are retellings of Bible stories. Some, such as "The Drunkard's Child" and "The Revel," are temperance poems. And some, such as "Report" and "Advice to Girls," are strong feminist statements.

Harper maintained the dominant themes in her early lectures and writings for the rest of her career: Christian living, civil rights, and racial pride. Among her important poems published during the antebellum period but not included in *Poems on Miscellaneous Subjects* are "Be Active" (*Frederick Douglass' Paper,* 1 November 1856), a testimony to individual responsibility in rectifying social wrongs; "The Burial of Moses" (*Provincial Freeman,* 24 May 1856), which invents a conclusion to the biblical account of that great leader's death; and "Lessons of the Street" (*Liberator,* 14 May 1858), a catalog of the people and lives that one encounters "through life's dusty highways."

Harper was consistently described as "a noble Christian woman," "one of the most scholarly and well-read women of her day," and a woman with a "nature most femininely sensitive." Her writings do display strong evidence of classical training and contemporary awareness, and a very fundamental Christianity pervades all of her writings. However, this "bronze muse," as she was dubbed by Grace Greenwood of the *Independent,* was anything but removed from earthly activity. She characteristically told a friend, "If there is common, rough work to be done, call on me." Harper's tenure with the Maine Anti-Slavery Society took her to much of New England and parts of Canada, working on a grueling schedule, speaking daily in different towns, sometimes lecturing two or three times a day. After a tiring, cold journey, she often found the audience diminished by inclement weather or the meetinghouse locked, the advertising inadequate or the arrangements for bed and board incomplete. The routine hardships of nineteenth-century travel were complicated by the danger to abolitionists from mobs of rowdies and pro-slavery advocates. As a young African American woman Frances Harper faced particular difficulties, for nineteenth-century public sentiment did not generally favor women or African Americans who spoke publicly to integrated audiences. Nevertheless, she followed her tenure with the Maine Anti-Slavery Society by signing as an agent and lecturer for the Pennsylvania Society for Promoting the Abolition of Slavery. And after that, she began a series of tours that took her to Ohio, Indiana, Michigan, and Ontario, Canada.

During the antebellum period, letters signed by "Frances Ellen Watkins" appeared frequently in such papers as the *Anti-Slavery Bugle* (Salem, Ohio), the *National Anti-Slavery Standard* (New York City), *Frederick Douglass' Paper* (Rochester, New York), the *Provincial Freeman* (Ontario, Canada), and the *Liberator* (Boston). A letter published in the 23 April 1858 issue of the *Liberator* regarding a recent experience on the Philadelphia streetcars illustrates Harper's use of this genre to garner support for social issues, but it also shows that the young poet did not write pleas that she herself was not prepared to heed. According to her own description, Harper willfully violated the custom of restricting blacks to the outside platform of the public streetcars by holding the nineteenth-century version of a sit-in. Not only did she refuse to leave the car until she reached her destination, but when she was about to disembark and the conductor would not accept her proffered fare, she threw it at his feet. In this act, Harper was certainly a foremother of Rosa Parks. Her action did not directly mobilize a transportation boycott, but it was one of a series of defiances that helped desegregation of public transportation to become a major issue in Philadelphia during the 1860s; in 1867 a law was passed desegregating public transportation in the state of Pennsylvania.

As the repressive measures against blacks, especially those in slavery, increased, Harper's writings became increasingly militant. In a discussion of the U.S. Constitution on 9 April 1859, Harper chastises a nation "so fresh from the baptism of the Revolution" for making "such concessions to the full spirit of Despotism," and she warns that such concessions remind her "of the fabulous teeth sown by Cadmus—they rise, armed men, to smite." Later that year, when the group of armed men led by John Brown stormed the arsenal at Harper's Ferry and colleagues such as Frederick Douglass found it expedient to flee the country while others maintained a discrete silence, Harper took a leading role in providing moral and physical support for the captured men and their families. She wrote letters of support and joined efforts to raise money for the families of the jailed men. Several of her letters to John Brown, Mary Brown, and others involved in that action were published in the press, and William Still tells us that during the two weeks in which Mary Brown awaited the execution of her husband, Harper was her companion.

By 1860, Harper was publicly supporting direct physical confrontation. When several men who had defied the fugitive slave law and tried to rescue a captured runaway were jailed in Philadelphia, Harper wrote in *The Weekly Anglo-African* of 23 June 1860:

> It is not enough to express our sympathy by words; we should be ready to crystalize it into actions. . . . Do not stop to cavil and find fault by saying they were rash and imprudent, and engaged in a hopeless contest. Their ears were quicker than ours; they heard the death-knell of freedom sound in the ears of a doomed and fated brother, and to them they were clarion sounds, rousing their souls to deeds of noble daring.

Harper's stance was a complex mixture of pragmatism and idealism, and it is quite probable that she directly violated the fugitive slave laws by accompanying runaway slaves along the Underground Railroad. Nonetheless, her writing was, in fact, her most consistent and obvious contribution to the struggles for freedom and civil rights.

In 1859 the prospectus for a new publication for and about African Americans advised that it would be "devoted to Literature, Science, Statistics, and the advancement of the cause of human freedom." Among its contributing editors were such prominent figures as Mary A. S. Cary, Frederick Douglass, Henry Highland Garnet, J. Mercer Langston, Grace Mapps, Bishop Daniel Payne, Dr. J. W. C. Pennington, Charles Lenox Remond, and Dr. James McCune Smith. Within a few months, the masthead of *The Anglo-African Magazine* added Harper to that stellar group. She contributed poems, essays, and a story, "The Two Offers," generally considered the first published short story by an African American.

"The Two Offers," published in the September–October 1859 issue of the magazine, is a provocative work that argues against social complacency and asserts that marriage is but one of several options for a woman of intelligence and social conscience. As was typical in fiction by women of that time, "The Two Offers" has two leading characters, one of whom serves as a foil for the other. The protagonist, Janette Alston, orphaned at an early age, has managed to acquire a sound education and to develop a strongly independent and self-confident spirit. The talented and beautiful Janette has an accomplished and beautiful cousin, Laura Lagrange, "the only daughter of rich and indulgent parents, who had spared no pains to make her an accomplished lady," but Laura had not developed a strength of character equal to her cousin. Although she knows that she is intellectually superior and emotionally uncommitted to both her suitors, Laura believes that the only choice her life offers her is which man to marry. Ignoring Janette's counsel that a marriage based upon such assumptions is "a mere matter of bargain and sale, or an affair of convenience and selfish interest," that there are worse fates than becoming "an old maid," Laura chooses a dashing husband of fine appearance but with lax character and "no appreciation of life's highest realities." He becomes a gambler, a reveler, and a drunkard. Laura, virtuous and refined but naively dependent, dies of a broken heart, while Janette, having followed her own clear and courageous vision, finds satisfaction and fulfillment as a successful writer and an "earnest advocate" for righteous causes.

The themes, situations, and images that appear in "The Two Offers" are consistent with those in Harper's poetry and lectures. In poems such as "Saved by Faith," "The Contrast," and "The Drunkard's Child" (all in her 1854 volume), Harper emphasizes the importance of personal faith and self-discipline, warning against the tragic results of neglecting these virtues. In "Advice to the Girls" (also in the 1854 volume), she specifically cautions against choosing a husband by his appearance, and recommending instead:

... marry one who's good and kind,
  And free from all pretence;
Who, if without a gifted mind,
  At least has common sense.

Eventually the young activist's heavy schedule began to take a physical, and perhaps psychological, toll. Still reports that she began to suffer health problems and to yearn to return to her "own kindred and people," but that the slave laws of Maryland made this impossible. He states that she wrote several poems expressing these sentiments, one of which was the popular "Bury Me in a Free Land," first published in the *Anti-Slavery Bugle* (20 November 1858). A letter dated 9 December 1859 and published in the *National Anti-Slavery Standard* fits this analysis. After stating that she was lecturing in Ohio about the fugitive slave bill and commenting on a recent case there, Harper adds, "The doctor thinks my lungs are weak, and that I need rest more than medicine. That rest may soon be the unbroken slumber of the grave."

In November 1860, however, Frances Watkins married Fenton Harper, a widower with three children, purchased a farm near Columbus, Ohio, and went into semiretirement from political life. The Harpers had one child, Mary. In a letter dated 5 July 1871, Frances Harper remarked that if someone had entered her "humble log house," they would have discovered her "kneading bread and making butter." The requirements of rearing four children in rural Ohio certainly would have made such scenes routine and activities such as writing and lecturing less possible, but newspapers in neighboring states and cities continued to report her occasional lectures and to publish such new poems as "To the Cleveland Union Savers" (*Anti-Slavery Bugle*, 23 February 1861), "God's Judgment" (*Weekly Anglo African*, 8 February 1862), and "To My Daughter" (*Weekly Anglo African*, 15 February 1862).

In 1864, Fenton Harper died. Debtors claimed the property, its livestock, and all the furniture, including the widowed mother's milk crocks, washtubs, and featherbed. Frances Harper returned to the lecture circuit to support herself

and her children. Within months, she was speaking to large and attentive audiences on such topics as "The Lessons of War," "The Claims of the Negro," and "The Mission of War and the Demands of the Colored Race in Reconstruction."

Although she was a veteran fighter in the political arena, Harper, as an African American woman, had never been able to vote. Naturally she was willing to join Frederick Douglass, Robert and Harriet Purvis, Sojourner Truth, Susan B. Anthony, Lucretia Mott, Elizabeth Cady Stanton, and others in the fledgling American Equal Rights Association. However, the blatantly racist arguments of Stanton, Anthony, and some other whites against the proposed Fifteenth Amendment's extension of the vote to black men but not to women created crisis in that organization. When it split into the National Woman's Suffrage Association (which excluded men) and the more liberal American Woman's Suffrage Association, Harper affiliated with the latter but remained cooperative with both. One of the few African Americans to gain national recognition as a feminist, Harper consistently challenged her white sisters to confront their racism and to acknowledge that they bore some responsibility for the sufferings of others:

> Talk of giving women the ballot-box? Go on. It is a normal school, and the white women of this country need it. While there exists this brutal element in society which tramples upon the feeble and treads down the weak, I tell you that if there is any class of people who need to be lifted out of their airy nothings and selfishness, it is the white women of America.
>
> (*Proceeding of the Eleventh Annual Woman's Rights Convention* [n.p., 1866], p. 48)

Harper's equal rights advocacy was complicated by the racism of her feminist colleagues and the sexism of some of her black brothers. She often assumed the role of mediator between sometimes naive, often competitive, and frequently hostile sectors. "We are all bound up together in one great bundle of humanity," she repeatedly admonished.

After the Civil War, many educated northern women, both black and white, traveled into the South to teach and to provide other social services for the newly freed slaves. Most of these women were hired or supported by organizations such as the American Missionary Society or the Freedman's Bureau, and they traveled in groups to preselected sites where they set up schools, hospitals, and homes for children and dependent adults. Frances Harper, however, operated independently, generally traveling alone and without financial support.

From 1866 to 1871 she crossed and recrossed the South, visiting every state but Arkansas and Texas, teaching and lecturing to southern audiences and recording her impressions for northern readers. It was a time of physical danger, intellectual challenge, and intense self-discovery. Southern poverty was beyond anything she had previously experienced, but the hospitality, optimism, and hard work of most blacks and many whites surpassed her expectations. Finding "ignorance to be instructed; [and] a race who needs to be helped up to higher planes of thought and action," Harper wrote in a letter dated 1 February 1870, "whether we are hindered or helped, we should try to be true to the commission God has written upon our souls."

Some of her lectures were summarized by journalists and a few were excerpted in periodicals, but the texts of most of Harper's Reconstruction lectures are not available. Titles such as "The Mission of War," "The Work Before Us," and "The Colored Man as Social and Political Force" suggest that in general her message to Southerners was the same as her message to Northern audiences before, during, and after the Civil War. "Our greatest want," she repeatedly stated, is "men and women whose hearts are the homes of a high and lofty enthusiasm, ... who are ready and willing to lay time, talent, and money on the alter of universal freedom."

Harper argued that the future of the nation depended upon the ability of its citizens to unite behind a common goal. "Between the white people and the colored there is a community of interests," she asserted, "and the sooner they find it out, the better it will be for both parties, but that community of interests does not consist in increasing the privileges of one class and curtailing the rights of the other, but in getting every citizen interested in the welfare, progress and durability of the state." Her other theme, and the one that increasingly dominated her published writings, was that the Emancipation had opened a new era, a time for blacks, particularly black women, to "consecrate their lives to the work of upbuilding the race."

This era-of-opportunity theme characterizes Harper's many poems, essays, letters, and fiction of that period. Most often she illustrates this idea by portraying individuals who make courageous and self-sacrificing choices. For example, in "Minnie's Sacrifice," a serialized novel that ran from March to September 1869 in *The Christian Recorder*, both Minnie and her future husband, Louis, are rescued temporarily from the bondage of racism by well-intentioned whites who defy social custom and rear the two children as if they were white. These were two separate situations, but both foster parents chose to keep secret from others and from the children themselves their African ancestry. Their decisions, while well intended, ultimately create significant personal and psychological complications that contribute to the suspense of the narrative and at the same time suggest that the solution to racism is not one of individual privilege but one of collective action. When Minnie and Louis discover that they are African American, each chooses to identify with and work for the liberation of their oppressed race. As she does in her later novel, *Iola Leroy* (1892), Harper concludes "Minnie's Sacrifice" with a note to the reader that the story's characters are "ideal beings, touched here and there with a coloring from real life" and that the "lesson of Minnie shall have its place among the educational ideas for the advancement of our race."

Harper believed that literature has a vital social role, and in "Minnie's Sacrifice" she wrote not only to inspire more noble actions among her readers, but to provide models for other writers. Wrote Harper in "Minnie's Sacrifice":

> While some of the authors of the present day have been weaving their stories about white men marrying beautiful quadroon girls, who in so doing were lost to us socially, I conceived of one of that same class to whom I gave a higher, holier destiny; a life of lofty self-sacrifice and beautiful self-consecration, finished at the post of duty, and rounded off with the fiery crown of martyrdom.

The first chapter of "Minnie's Sacrifice" explicitly compares Louis's situation to that of the Hebrew leader Moses. After reading a Bible story wherein the king's daughter rescues a baby from slavery, Camille, the slavemaster's daughter, says, "Now I mean to do something like that good princess." The allusion is neither coincidental nor casual. About the same time she was writing "Minnie's Sacrifice," Harper published *Moses: A Story of the Nile. Moses* (2nd ed., 1869) is approximately seven hundred lines of free verse that re-create the life and times of the Hebrew leader who led his people from slavery. It is a startling departure from Harper's typical four-line, heavily rhymed stanzas but an excellent example of her use of African American tropes. Just as Phillis Wheatley had done with her poem "David of Goliath" nearly a hundred years earlier, Harper chose an Old Testament subject and emphasized details that invited comparisons between biblical situations and current conditions.

The enslavement of the Hebrews in Egypt was an especially common African American trope for the American slave experience. In both oral and written literature, the South was Egypt, the slavemaster was the Pharaoh, the Ohio River was the Jordan River, and the North was the Promised Land. The African American leaders, such as Harriet Tubman and the other conductors who led fugitives to freedom, were called Moses. In *Moses* Harper conflates African American literary conventions and the present moment, joining her personal symbol with the public one. Moses had long been one of her favorite literary subjects. One of her ear-

liest poems was titled "The Burial of Moses" (1856), and in 1859 Harper described the focus of *Moses*. In "Our Greatest Want" she wrote:

> I like the character of Moses. He is the first dis-unionist we read of in the Jewish Scriptures. The magnificence of Pharaoh's throne loomed up before his vision, its oriental splendors glittered before his eyes; but he turned from them all and chose rather to suffer with the enslaved, than to rejoice with the free. He would have no union with the slave power of Egypt. When we have a race of men whom this blood stained government cannot tempt or flatter, who would sternly refuse every office in the nation's gift, from a president down to a tidewaiter, until she [the government] shook her hands from complicity in the guilt of cradle plundering and man stealing then for us the foundations of an historical character will have been laid.
>
> ("Our Greatest Want," *Anglo-African Magazine* 2:160 [1859])

Whereas Harper usually wrote short, heavily rhymed narrative poems, in *Moses* she employs blank verse to create a poetic drama in nine chapters. The poem begins as a dialogue between Moses and Charmian. This conversation summarizes his earlier life, emphasizing the brave love that Charmian had manifested in adopting the Hebrew infant and rearing him as a member of the royal family. Charmian's brave love also allows her to accept Moses' decision to sacrifice the privileges of his adoption and to identify himself with his oppressed people. Harper's heroic depiction of the Egyptian princess is consistent with her earlier revisions of well-known stories to reflect more complex and assertive female roles. Harper retells the Moses story as an example of high ideals and personal sacrifice. Her implicit comparison of the two heroic acts invites comparison between the biblical and the antebellum enslavements while it also critiques the possibilities of women and African Americans in resisting oppression.

In 1871, two years after the second edition of *Moses* appeared, Harper published her second Reconstruction volume, *Poems. Poems* does not obviously continue the technical experimentation that marks *Moses,* but its subjects and themes of piety, politics, and promise generally echo Harper's antebellum best-seller, *Poems on Miscellaneous Subjects.* However, close reading of the individual poems frequently reveals modifications of theme or tone that identify *Poems* as a Reconstruction work.

The poems in this volume generally treat one of three themes: motherhood, separation and death, and public experience. Such poems as "Thank God for Little Children" and "To a Babe Smiling in Her Sleep" celebrate motherhood and family. Although Harper's mothers and children generally evoke only pain and pathos in *Poems on Miscellaneous Subjects,* they are sources of love and fulfillment. Harper still idealizes motherhood, but to the fugitive mother running with infant in arms and to the sorrowful slave mother being auctioned away from her child she adds the mother of "The Mother's Blessing," who serenely says, "Hope and joy, peace and blessing, / Met me in my first born child." The poems of separation and death in this volume continue to focus on the division of the family, especially on death's sundering mother from child, child from mother. But such postbellum works as "The Bride of Death," "The Dying Child to Her Blind Father," and "The Dying Fugitive" offer more complex or less tragic divisions. While earlier poems—such as "The Slave Mother," in which a woman grieves over her imminent parting from her child, or "The Slave Mother, a Tale of Ohio," in which a woman chooses to kill her infant rather than see it return to slavery—suggest final, irrevocable partings, the poems in this volume offer hope of reunion. In "The Dying Mother" a woman blesses her children with her last words, comforted by the knowledge that her husband and family will remain together, that God will watch over them, and that they will be united in "the brighter world above." From the horrific and unnatural experiences that slavery created, her poems now turn to the redemptive suffering of divinely ordained separations.

Together, the new images of motherhood, the death poems, and the third category, the ce-lebratory poems of public experiences, including "Fifteenth Amendment," "Lines to Miles O'Reiley," and "President Lincoln's Proclamation of Freedom," establish a Reconstruction ideal of heroic effort, sacrifice, and courage rewarded. Overall, *Poems* strikes a more mature, contemplative, and hopeful tone than does the earlier collection. This shift reflects both Harper's personal experiences and the social spirit of Reconstruction with which she aligned herself.

A year after *Poems,* Harper published her third Reconstruction volume, *Sketches of Southern Life.* The first edition of *Sketches* is really a pamphlet—only nine poems—but its small size belies its great significance. *Sketches* begins with a poem of appreciation to "Our English Friends" for their support of the American antislavery struggle. Its final two poems are "I Thirst," a dramatic dialogue about death, responsibility, and perhaps suicide, and "The Dying Queen," the final recitation of a woman who chooses to die as she has lived, with her eyes wide open. In all the poems, the details of southern geography and culture reveal the affect of Harper's southern sojourns.

The heart of this volume is a series of six poems, narrated by Aunt Chloe, that form at once the autobiography of a former slave woman and an oral history of slavery and Reconstruction. Aunt Chloe may well prove to be Harper's most important contribution to American letters. As Emily Stipes Watts has pointed out, postbellum women writers represented a more diverse spectrum of society, including more women from the western frontier, the recently formed middle class, and the various and growing ethnic groups of the United States. These women tended to write about women of "independent and aggressive spirits," and their poetry, especially, reflected the current debate over "woman's place." Like other women writers, Harper created what Sandra Gilbert and Susan Gubar call "Byronic heroine[s]," that is, women who reject "cultural commandments that failed to meet the needs" of their souls. Harper's Aunt Chloe and her equally strong-minded women friends survived slavery because of their courage and faith. Aunt Chloe is sixty years old, but she ignores her detractors who say she is too old, and learns to read. Although she can't vote, she takes an active interest in politics and does what she can to ensure that the men "voted clean." She helps build schools and churches for the community, and she works to buy herself a cabin, which she enlarges to accommodate all her children after they are reunited.

Sketches of Southern Life is a true benchmark in Harper's poetic career and a touchstone for African American literature. Unlike the slave narratives, Harper's polemical essays, and much of her antebellum poetry, *Sketches* does not have to emphasize its authenticity as a depiction of what is and what should be. As an epic poem about slavery, the Civil War, and Reconstruction, it is one of the first examples of the use of slavery as a literary construct. To be sure, Harper certainly intended her work to instruct and to inspire, but with slavery a thing of the past and Reconstruction still appearing to promise an improved future, there was more room for play, for humor, and for the exploration of racial diversity.

The characters and episodes in the poems closely resemble those which Harper discussed in her letters and lectures. For example, in an address delivered before the Women's Congress in 1877 and reprinted in 1878 in the *Englishwoman's Journal* as "The Coloured Women of America," Harper cites numerous examples to prove that African American women in the South "as a class are quite equal to the men in energy and executive ability." In fact, Harper continues, "I find by close observation, that the mothers are the levers which move in education. The men talk about it, . . . but the women work most for it."

Each of Harper's Reconstruction volumes may be read as a political work, and politics continued to command her interest and intervention after she settled in Philadelphia sometime around 1871. The passage of the Fifteenth Amendment and the deconstruction of Reconstruction were making it abundantly clear that women's suffrage and racial integration were long-term goals. Harper's attitude during these times is well represented by one of her most frequently printed speeches, the address at the centennial anniversary of the Pennsylvania Society for Promoting the Abolition of Slavery in 1875. "The white race has yet work to do in making practical the political axiom of equal rights, and the Christian idea of human brotherhood," Harper declared, but she continued, "The most important question before us colored people is not simply what the Democratic party may do against us or the Republican party do for us; but what are we going to do for ourselves?" Harper operated under the conviction that people of all races had a long way to go toward ameliorating American civilization's two great wants, "a keener and deeper, broader and tenderer sense of justice" and "a deeper and broader humanity."

Harper's poems were increasingly concerned with individual commitment despite what might appear to be formidable odds. Such poems as "Vashti," "Something to Do," "Go, Work," and "Peace" (all reprinted in *A Brighter, Coming Day*), stress the necessity for self-sacrifice, moral integrity, and Christian service. The last stanza of "Peace" is typical:

Bury deep your proud ambitions.
  Cease your struggles, fierce and wild;
Oh, 'tis higher bliss to rescue,
  Than to trample down God's child.
Better far to aid the feeble,
  Raise the groveler from the clod;
Lives are only great and noble,
  When they clasp both man and God.

Between 1873 and 1874, Harper contributed a series to the *Christian Recorder* called first "Fancy Etchings," and later "Fancy Sketches." Both were dramatized essays, similar to those that Langston Hughes made popular with Jesse B. Semple in the twentieth century. In brief conversations between Jenny, a young poet, and her mentor, Aunt Jane, Harper depicts various social, economic, and political situations that African Americans, especially young women, were confronting and suggests the best ways to resolve them.

Among those issues was temperance, a cause that Harper had previously supported and that now became her first priority. The Women's

Christian Temperance Union was segregated, but Harper refused to let human imperfection interfere with what she felt to be a divine movement. She wrote and spoke to any and all who would listen, but she concentrated upon organizing temperance associations within the African American communities. From 1875 until 1882, she was superintendent of the Colored Section of the Philadelphia and Pennsylvania WCTU, and in 1883 she became head of the Colored Section of the national WCTU.

Harper regularly published such essays as "The Women's Christian Temperance Union and the Colored Woman" (*A.M.E. Church Review* 4 [1888]) and "Temperance—a Symposium" (*A.M.E. Church Review* 7 [1891]). She wrote numerous poems on the subject, and rarely did her fiction of the period not mention temperance issues. In some works it was the central theme, as in her 1876 serialized novel, "Sowing and Reaping: A Temperance Story," which not only put forth her fundamental arguments that alcoholism was socially and morally debilitating and the sale of alcohol immoral, but also explored such subtleties as the correct stance toward social drinking and toward suitors who occasionally imbibed. In other works, such as "Trial and Triumph," temperance was one of several issues addressed.

Published serially in the *Christian Recorder* between October 1888 and February 1889, "Trial and Triumph" is one of Harper's most obvious attempts to combat the inroads that the plantation school literature was making in creating a mythology of the chivalrous South, the happy slave, and the treacherous free black. "Trial and Triumph," in the tradition of the novel of manners, revolves around the adventures of Annette Harcourt and Clarence Luserne, Laura Lusette and Charley Cooper, and their families and friends, who comprise the black middle class in the city of A.P. As its title implies, the story presents episodes that try the faith and futures of these representatives of African America. For some such as Mrs. Lasette, it is having her children barred from attending the neighborhood school because of racial prejudice. For Charley Cooper it is losing his job as a cashier when it is discovered that he is of Af-

rican ancestry. For Annette it is having her desire to graduate from school and to become a published poet ridiculed because she is an African American woman. Through the experiences of both the major and the minor characters, Harper demonstrates the obstacles to and the responses of African Americans who attempt to realize the American Dream. Those who choose the less virtuous strategies are thwarted, but those who struggle to improve themselves while exercising their Christian faith learn that while they may "be disciplined by trial and endeavor," eventually their lives will be "be rounded by success and triumph."

"Trial and Triumph" was widely publicized in the national African American press. It was so popular that when a chapter was not published as scheduled, the editor found it necessary to apologize to readers and reassure them that the next issue would include the missing installment. However, to combat the assault of the plantation school, African American writers had to publish where they could expect large, integrated audiences. Consequently, Harper resorted to the strategy that had made *Poems on Miscellaneous Subjects* a best-seller. She used commercial printers for *Iola Leroy* and arranged for publication in both Philadelphia and Boston.

The strategy worked. When *Iola Leroy* appeared in 1892, it was greeted with positive reviews in white periodicals such as the *Nation* and the *New York Independent*, the latter paper praising Harper as "one of the most accomplished literary women the colored race has numbered among its members" and rating her book as "unrivaled in extent and character." The Philadelphia *Public Ledger* praised *Iola Leroy* for its "natural" plot, realistic characters, and, most especially, for its language, calling the dialogue "exceeding clever, full of pathos, human, and authentic." And, according to the *African Methodist Episcopal Review*, *Iola Leroy* was "the crowning effort of [Harper's] life."

In *Iola Leroy*, her most important and best-known work, Harper adapted the techniques of the historical romance to increase her readers' "sense of justice and . . . Christlike humanity." In many ways the story is an extension of the narrative poems she had written since her earliest days under the influences of Elizabeth Barrett Browning, Charles Dickens, Henry Wadsworth Longfellow, and John Greenleaf Whittier. But more significant are the ways in which Harper consciously adopted and modified the characters, plots, and methods of the earlier African American novels.

Iola Leroy is similar to William Wells Brown's *Clotel* (1853) and Frank Webb's *The Garies and Their Friends* (1856), in that its title character is a beautiful, educated, and refined paragon of womanhood whose appearance and background do not reveal her African heritage. Iola is one of three children from the marriage of Marie and Eugene Leroy. Her Northern education and European ancestry have erased the external signs of Marie's African heritage, and the children grow up not knowing that their elegant and beautiful mother was born a slave. Iola lives the life of a beloved and economically privileged young student until her father dies suddenly. Then her father's cousin is able to have Marie's emancipation invalidated and trick Iola back to the South, where he claims the entire family as his property. Iola is sold away from her mother. When the Union army arrives and rescues her from slavery, Iola remains with the troops and works as a nurse.

Although she is similar in superficial ways to the figure of the tragic mulatta, Iola differs markedly from the suffering victims of the earlier works. Her life as a slave is only vaguely mentioned, and she is rescued before she loses her beauty, self-esteem, and chastity. After her initial shock at learning that she is black and a slave, she does not experience any sense of tragedy or racial confusion. As a Civil War nurse, she wins the respect and admiration of her patients and the love of the white doctor with whom she works. Although she is fond of Dr. Gresham, Iola barely hesitates before rejecting his marriage proposal, explaining that while she has not chosen her lot in life, she is determined to accept it. "I must serve the race which needs me most," she says. And Gresham, with "sympathy, love and admiration" knows it is "useless to attempt to divert her." Iola devotes her life and her energies to reuniting broken families, fighting for equal employment opportunities, teaching, and working for the progress of her race. Unlike Janette Alston in "The Two Offers," Iola finds both love and important work. She marries Dr. Latimer, a man who has also dedicated his life to Christian reform, and with him she returns to the Reconstruction South.

Harper's primary intention in *Iola Leroy* was to present a story of slavery and Reconstruction that offered a panoramic view of the lives of slaves and former slaves. The novel's opening conversations among field and house slaves refute both the notions of "class" divisions and of political ignorance or apathy among slaves and assert the slaves' strong desire for freedom, general adherence to Christian ethics, and great respect for education. Despite its title, *Iola Leroy* does not focus solely on the perils and problems of the title character, nor does it concentrate upon the black middle class. Iola Leroy is not even mentioned until chapter 5, and it is not until chapter 9 that the Leroys are introduced. Harper pairs her mulatto characters with "pure African" counterparts who are generally superior to their noble and accomplished lighter-skinned friends. Extending her story beyond the earlier African American novels, Harper includes several folk characters whose intelligence, dedication, and resourcefulness become models for the emerging middle class.

After *Iola Leroy*, Harper published at least five collections of poetry: *The Sparrow's Fall and Other Poems* (ca. 1894), *Atlanta Offering: Poems* (1895), *The Martyr of Alabama and Other Poems* (ca. 1895), *Poems* (1900), and *Light Beyond the Darkness* (n.d.). Most of the poems in these collections had already been published. Although there is a marked increase in her emphasis on Christian faith and heavenly reward, Harper did not abandon political and social issues. The title poem of *The Martyr of Alabama* was written in response to the lynching of a young boy in December 1894. And her frequent contributions to the official journals of schools, churches, and other organizations included titles such as "The Lake City Tragedy" (*The Peacemaker and Court of Arbitration* 18 [1899]), "Woman's Work" (*Chris-*

tian Recorder, 7 February 1889), and "The Vision of the Czar in Russia" (*A.M.E. Church Review*, July 1898).

As Harper entered her seventies, age forced her to slow down, but she refused to stop. She had told her audience at the World's Congress of Representative Women held at the Columbian Exposition in 1893 that they stood "in the threshold of woman's era." Clearly intending to cross that threshold before she died, Harper continued to work with the National Council of Women, the Universal Peace Union, the Women's Christian Temperance Union, and other predominantly white organizations. She was featured speaker at their annual meetings, her poems and essays appeared in their journals, and, according to Alfred H. Love, president of the Universal Peace Union, she "acquired the title of 'Empress of Peace and Poet Laureate.' "

Harper genuinely believed, as she wrote in "The Burdens of All" (*Poems* [1900]), that

We may sigh o're the heavy burdens
  Of the black, the brown and white;
But if we all clasped hands together
  The burdens would be more light.

She also knew, however, that even after a lifetime of working for equal rights, she and the two other African American women who participated in the World's Congress of Representative Women were invited to do so only after a strong and concerted campaign to include black women in that conference took place.

During the last years of her life, it appeared that the struggle against racism was in many ways just beginning. Like her friend and colleague, Anna Julia Cooper, Harper believed, as Cooper put it, that "there is a call for workers, for missionaries, for men and women with the double consecration of a fundamental love of humanity and a desire for its melioration through the Gospel. But superadded to this we demand an intelligent and sympathetic comprehension of the interests and special needs of the Negro." Despite her declining health, she continued to participate in the national meetings of organizations such as the American As-

sociation of Educators of Colored Youth and the National Colored Woman's Congress. In 1896, along with such other elders as Harriet Tubman, Charlotte Forten Grimke, and Fanny Jackson Coppin, Harper joined several younger activists, including Mary Church Terrell, Ida B. Wells-Barnett, and Alice Dunbar Nelson, in founding the National Association of Colored Women, of which she served as vice president and as consultant for several years.

In his memorial tribute to Harper in 1911, Alfred H. Love describes her last years this way:

When taken sick and seemingly unable, because of age, to earn money, she was offered homes in different quarters, some she helped to establish, but replied: "I have always been independent; I love liberty; I supported myself without charity, and I shall stand by my record."

And so we found her up to the 87th year of her age. She had lost her valuable and devoted daughter, Mary, a short time before, but friends were not wanting to see that she was in a family where all was welcome and affection.

Harper died on 20 February 1911. Her funeral was held in Philadelphia at the Unitarian Church on Chestnut Street, and she was buried in Eden Cemetery. For over sixty years she had worked and written to inspire and instruct "in the full development and right culture of our whole natures." She did not do so for personal glory, but believed, as did Iola Leroy, "what matters it if they do forget the singer, so they don't forget the song?"

"Let me make the songs for the people," Frances Harper wrote, "Songs for the old and young; / Songs to stir like a battle-cry / Wherever they are sung." During her career, Harper worked in virtually every literary genre available to her, changing themes and techniques in accordance with the trends and expectations of the changing times. Although she appreciated beauty and enjoyed the accolades she received, Harper believed that literature which could not be used to represent, to reprimand, and to revise was frivolous and useless. Born during slavery,

Harper was buried during the period that historians now refer to as the nadir of American race relations. Through it all she combined pragmatic idealism, courageous action, and lyrical words to dispel the shadows and usher in what she knew would be brighter coming days.

Selected Bibliography

PRIMARY WORKS

POETRY

Forest Leaves. N.p., n.d. [ca. 1845].

Poems on Miscellaneous Subjects. Boston: J. B. Yerrinton & Sons, 1854. Reprinted Philadelphia: Merrihew & Thompson, 1857.

Moses: A Story of the Nile. 2d ed. Philadelphia: Merrihew & Son, 1869.

Poems. Philadelphia: Merrihew & Son, 1871.

Sketches of Southern Life. Philadelphia: Merrihew & Son, 1872.

"Fancy Etchings." *Christian Recorder*, April 24, 1873, p. 1; May 1, 1873, p. 1; May 22, 1873, p. 1; July 3, 1873, p. 1.

"Fancy Sketches." *Christian Recorder*, January 15, 1874, p. 1.

The Sparrow's Fall and Other Poems. N.p., n.d. [ca. 1894].

Atlanta Offering: Poems. Philadelphia: privately printed by George S. Ferguson, 1895.

The Martyr of Alabama and Other Poems. N.p., n.d. [ca. 1895].

Light Beyond the Darkness. Chicago: Donohue & Henneberry, n.d.

Poems. Philadelphia: n.p., 1900.

FICTION

"The Two Offers." *Anglo-African Magazine* 1:288–92, 311–13 (1859).

"Minnie's Sacrifice." *Christian Recorder*, March 20–September 25, 1869.

"Sowing and Reaping: A Temperance Story." *Christian Recorder*, August 10, 1876–February 8, 1877.

"Trial and Triumph." *Christian Recorder*, October 4, 1888–February 14, 1889.

Iola Leroy; or, Shadows Uplifted. Philadelphia: Garrigues Brothers, 1892. Reprinted with an introduction by Frances Smith Foster. New York: Oxford University Press, 1988.

ADDRESSES AND ESSAYS

"Address to the Fourth Anniversary of the New York City Anti-Slavery Society; Delivered May 13, 1857." *National Anti-Slavery Standard*, May 23, 1857.

"The Great Problem to Be Solved." *Programme of the Centennial Anniversary of the Pennsylvania Society for Promoting the Abolition of Slavery.* Philadelphia, 1875.

"The Coloured Women of America." *Englishwoman's Review*, January 15, 1878.

"Duty to Dependent Races." *National Council of Women of the United States: Transactions.* Philadelphia: Lippincott, 1891.

Enlightened Motherhood: An Address by Mrs. Frances E. W. Harper Before the Brooklyn Literary Society, November 15, 1892. N.p., n.d.

"Woman's Political Future." In *World's Congress of Representative Women.* Chicago: Rand McNally, 1894. Pp. 433–37.

COLLECTED WORKS

The Complete Poems of Frances E. W. Harper. Edited by Maryemma Graham. New York: Oxford University Press, 1988.

A Brighter Coming Day: A Frances E. W. Harper Reader. Edited by Frances Smith Foster. New York: Feminist Press, 1990.

Minnie's Sacrifice, Sowing and Reaping, Trials and Triumphs: Three Rediscovered Novels. Boston: Beacon Press, 1994.

SECONDARY WORKS

BIOGRAPHICAL AND CRITICAL STUDIES

Ammons, Elizabeth. *Conflicting Stories: American Women Writers at the Turn of the Twentieth Century.* New York: Oxford University Press, 1991.

Bacon, Margaret Hope. " 'One Great Bundle of Humanity': Frances Ellen Watkins Harper (1825–1922)." *The Pennsylvania Magazine of History & Biography* 113:21–43 (1989).

Boyd, Melba Joyce. *Discarded Legacy: Politics and Poetics in the Life of Frances E. W. Harper, 1825–1911.* Detroit: Wayne State University Press, 1994.

Carby, Hazel V. *Reconstructing Womanhood: The Emergence of the Afro-American Woman Novelist.* New York: Oxford University Press, 1987.

Christian, Barbara. *Black Women Novelists: The Development of a Tradition, 1892–1976.* Westport, Conn.: Greenwood Press, 1980.

Daniel, Theodora Williams. "*The Poems of Frances E. W. Harper*, Edited with a Biographical and Critical Introduction and Bibliography." Master's thesis, Howard University, 1937.

Ernest, John. *Resistance and Reformation in Nineteenth-Century African-American Literature.* Jackson: University Press of Mississippi, 1995.

Filler, Louis. "Frances Ellen Watkins Harper." *Notable American Women, 1607–1950: A Biographical Dictionary.* Vol. 2. Cambridge, Mass.: Harvard University Press, 1971.

Foster, Frances Smith. "Gender, Genre, and Vulgar Secularism: The Case of Frances Ellen Watkins Harper and the AME Press." In *Recovered Writers/Recovered Texts: Race, Class and Gender in Black Women's Literature.* Edited by Dolan Hubbard. Knoxville: University of Tennessee Press, 1997. Pp. 46–59.

Graham, Maryemma. "Frances Ellen Watkins Harper." In *Dictionary of Literary Biography.* Vol. 50, *Afro-American Writers Before the Harlem Renaissance.* Edited by Trudier Harris and Thadious M. Davis. Detroit: Gale Research, 1986.

Hill, Patricia Liggins. " 'Let Me Make the Songs for the People': A Study of Frances Watkins Harper's Poetry." *Black American Literature Forum* 15:60–65 (Summer 1981).

Lauter, Paul. "Is Frances Ellen Watkins Harper Good Enough to Teach?" *Legacy* 5:27–32 (Spring 1988).

Love, Alfred H. "Memorial Tribute to Mrs. Frances E. W. Harper." *The Peacemaker and Court of Arbitration* 30:118–19 (1911).

Leeman, Richard W., ed. *African-American Orators: A Bio-Critical Sourcebook.* Westport, Ct.: Greenwood Press, 1996.

McDowell, Deborah E. " 'The Changing Same': Generational Connections and Black Women Novelists." *New Literary History* 18:281–302 (Winter 1987).

Peterson, Carla L. *Doers of the Word: African American Women Speakers and Writers in the North (1830–1880).* New York: Oxford University Press, 1995.

Redding, J. Saunders. *To Make a Poet Black.* Chapel Hill: University of North Carolina Press, 1939.

Sterling, Dorothy. *We Are Your Sisters: Black Women in the Nineteenth Century.* New York: Norton, 1984.

Still, William. *The Underground Rail Road.* Philadelphia, 1871. Reprint, Chicago: Johnson, 1970.

Walden, Daniel. "Frances Ellen Watkins Harper." In *Dictionary of American Negro Biography.* Edited by Rayford Whittingham Logan. New York: Norton, 1982.

Washington, Mary Helen. *Invented Lives: Narratives of Black Women 1860–1960.* New York: Doubleday/Anchor, 1988.

Watts, Emily Stipes. *The Poetry of American Women from 1632–1945.* Austin: University of Texas Press, 1977.

Williams, Kenny J. *They Also Spoke: An Essay on Negro Literature in America.* Nashville, Tenn.: Townsend, 1970.

Yacovone, Donald. "Sacred Land Regained: Frances Ellen Watkins Harper and 'The Massachusetts Fifty-Fourth,' A Lost Poem." *Pennsylvania History* 62: 90–110 (1995).

MICHAEL S. HARPER
(1938–)

SCOTT SAUL

POET MICHAEL HARPER is a riddler with purpose, an artist who does not flinch from the painful enigmas he sees at the heart of American life. In his first collection *Dear John, Dear Coltrane* (1970), Harper offered the following puzzle under the title "American History":

> Those four black girls blown up
> in that Alabama church
> remind me of five hundred
> middle passage blacks,
> in a net, under water
> in Charleston harbor
> so *redcoats* wouldn't find them.
> Can't find what you can't see
> can you?

"American History" is a typical Harper "cryptogram," a poem that provokes through its no-frills clarity. It recalls the persistence of racial terror in American history—connecting the Birmingham church bombing of 1963 to the violence of the middle passage from Africa into slavery—but more searchingly, it seeks to understand the meaning of this terror. Why have the traditional places of sanctuary—the church, the net, the harbor—become mere death traps for American blacks?

Harper's answer has much to do with the invisibility of black suffering, the assumption (here made by Charleston's revolutionary patriots) that blacks are not human beings but mere instruments of a larger national will. They can be drowned and no one will mourn, because the "redcoats," the nation's greater enemy, have been defeated by the ruse. Harper's last two lines, however, underscore the feebleness of this alibi. Addressing the reader directly, Harper suggests that the deception has been worked upon us as well as the "redcoats": the taunt, seemingly borrowed from the schoolyard where the four girls might have played, asks what we have hidden from our own sight, what we have repressed for fear of what it might reveal.

Throughout his career, Harper has sought to fight this prevailing amnesia and recover the repressed history of blacks within America, a history writ large and small. The title of Harper's second collection, *History Is Your Own Heartbeat* (1971), might serve as the motto of his poetry as a whole: he has grounded his civic poetry in the world of personal experience, exploring ceaselessly the relation between individual lives and the broader expanse of American history.

Both emphatically black and keenly American, Harper has acted as a key tradition maker in the wake of the Black Arts Movement. A master of the art of homage and elegy, he has created a rich legacy of poems attesting to the treasures, and trials, of the black artistic tradition—from jazz figures like John Coltrane and Bessie Smith to literary ancestors like Richard Wright, Zora Neale Hurston, and Sterling Brown. And he has probed the story of his own life and family—his own heartbeat—in poetry that is sometimes stark, sometimes warmly intimate, and often both at once. Harper's poetry is full of heroic action, but his underlying theme is that heroism never comes on the cheap: it is earned through struggles won and lost, courage tempered by grief.

Harper was born on March 18, 1938, in his parents' Brooklyn home. Characteristically, Harper has described the birth as a moment of ancestral sustenance and familial extension: he was delivered by his grandfather Roland R. Johnson, a physician, and his birth was celebrated partly because he was the first male child on either side of his family. Harper's family background was solidly professional, though his parents' means were modest. His father, Walter Warren Harper, worked for the U.S. Post Office as a supervisor; his mother, Katherine Johnson Harper, worked in medical stenography. His parents had a large record collection and, although they expressly forbade him from listening to the music, Harper began a furtive acquaintance with jazz that blossomed into a lifelong love affair.

Churchgoing and jazz were intertwined at an early age—a premonition of Harper's fascination with music as a sacred art. Before he was ten, Harper would regularly attend a Sunday Baptist service, where he would participate in the rituals of the choir, the collection box, and the baptismal font; then he would head on the subway to 52nd Street, where he would search for bebop legend Charlie Parker. In a perhaps apocryphal tale, Harper claims to have held Parker's saxophone case as the two of them walked back to the subway station, at which point Parker gave him his fare home.

At age thirteen, Harper moved with his family—which then included his younger brother, Jonathan Paul, and his sister, Katherine Winifred—to a largely white neighborhood in West Los Angeles. Harper has reflected that he "wouldn't have become a poet had I not moved from Brooklyn to Los Angeles; at thirteen the world was both collapsing and full of possibilities." A persistent theme in Harper's recollections is the struggle to have his potential recognized, and to recognize it himself. He entered Susan Miller Dorsey High School, a putatively integrated school, and was initially tracked into an industrial arts rather than an academic program. He wrote "secretly, in high school, buried in the back of some English class for fear that I'd be asked to stand and recite a memorized poem of Donne, Shakespeare, or John Keats." Harper, who suffered from an extreme case of asthma, failed gym class because he would not "strip down"—and as a result he did not make his high school's honor roll, despite his high grades in other subjects.

Meanwhile his neighborhood and school bore witness to the larger struggles in the 1950s over integration. Black-occupied homes nearby were bombed, and Harper has recalled that his school had little "sharing across the board, except on the playing fields." He was not encouraged to use his high school's facilities and, despite his passion for reading, never once entered its library.

After graduating from high school in 1955, Harper enrolled in Los Angeles State College (now California State, Los Angeles) and worked nights at the post office. Both environments gave Harper a schooling in the literary arts. "I learned about narrative at the post office," Harper has said, adding that the long hours forced his fellow black employees to sharpen their wits through "woofing on a large scale": "I was surrounded by Ph.D.'s who couldn't get employment in the private sector. . . . [T]hey were formidable people, witty, zany, and with spunk. You looked forward to their verbal assaults on the facing table, and in airmail."

Harper's teachers at LA State College invited him to mine his talents and explore the literary tradition. British dramatist Christopher Isherwood prodded him to send out his work—plays and stories, not poetry— to magazines; Isherwood also helped shape Harper's suspicion of politicized writing, cautioning him that extremist politics on the left or right could impinge on a writer's creative freedom. Two other young teachers, the poet Henri Coulette and the novelist Wirt Williams, deepened Harper's appreciation of the literary moderns—Faulkner, Fitzgerald, Yeats, Eliot, Pound—and also encouraged Harper to attend the Iowa Writers Workshop, their alma mater and one of the premier breeding grounds of American fiction writers and poets.

In 1961 Harper entered the Iowa master's program, where he was struck by his cultural and artistic singularity. The "only blood in either fiction or poetry," Harper enrolled in both workshops and soon contended with the expectations foisted upon him. "Several teachers asked me was I going to be another [James] Baldwin," Harper has reminisced. "All the writers in the workshop at the time were victims of the New Criticism, the poets writing in rhyme and meter, the fiction writers reading [Henry] James and [E. M.] Forster." Harper's experiences outside the workshops may have left the strongest imprint. Among his friends were the writer Ralph Dickey, whose writings he collected and edited under the title *Leaving Eden,* and the painter Oliver Lee Jackson, later a key figure in the black avant-garde.

The advanced degree from Iowa did have its uses, however, and Harper embarked on a career as a poet-teacher. Throughout the sixties, he moved up and down the Pacific coast, teaching at Contra Costa College in San Pablo (1964–1968), Reed College and Lewis and Clark College in Oregon (1968–1969), and California State College (now University), Hayward (1969–1970)—all the while publishing his verse in small magazines like *Carolina Quarterly, Negro Digest, Poetry, Poetry Northwest,* and *Southern Review.*

Harper's career took off in 1970, when the University of Pittsburgh Press published *Dear John, Dear Coltrane* at the behest of fellow poet Gwendolyn Brooks, who called Harper's poetry "vigorous as well as brilliant," poetry that was "obvious blood-stuffed life." Nominated for the National Book Award, the collection stands as one of the signal postwar collections of African American poetry, an ambitiously harrowing and sensitive response to the cultural turbu-

Michael Harper

lence of the 1960s. The book established Harper's reputation and laid out the themes that would animate much of his later writing. Love and loss, heroism in the face of extreme emotional pain, the redemptive power of music—these were Harper's main subjects, and they were explored in a striking number of different settings, both topical and personal.

Although Harper kept his distance from the Black Arts Movement—he has said that he did not "have the disposition" to be "a joiner"—he did welcome the "excitement in the air," the intense energies unleashed as black artists organized, socialized, and agitated together. His poetry shared the movement's broad concerns, if not its specific political agenda, dwelling on issues of black pride, black creativity, and black manhood in a possibly revolutionary age.

Many of Harper's poems took on a public mantle and interpreted main political episodes of the black freedom struggle: the life and death of Malcolm X ("Malcolm's Blues," "Dead-Day: Malcolm, February 21"), the urban riots of the late sixties ("On Civil Disorders," "Aftermath"), the African liberation movements ("Biafra Blues"), and the protest of Black Power athletes at the 1968 Mexico City Olympics ("Ode to Tenochtitlan"). Also, like forthright radicals such as Amiri Baraka and Sonia Sanchez, Harper used the renaissance in black music—the experimental jazz and soul music of the postwar period—to explore the culture of black heroism.

Harper's enthusiasm was often laced with skepticism, and *Dear John, Dear Coltrane*'s first poem, "Brother John," asserted black pride even as the poem questioned it through ambiguous formal play:

Black man:
I'm a black man;
I'm black; I am—
A black man; black—
I'm a black man;
I'm a black man;
I'm a man; black—
I am—

Bird, buttermilk bird—
smack, booze and bitches
I am Bird
baddest nightdreamer
on sax in the ornithology-world
I can fly—higher, high, higher—
I'm a black man;
I am; I'm a black man— . . .

Already in his first book, Harper was taking great risks: "Brother John" relies on the provocative power of syntax and repetition, while pointedly refusing elaborate metaphor, rhyme, or other traditional poetic resources. Jazz was both the poem's subject and its method: Harper sets in motion one foundational phrase, "I am a black man," manipulating it like a jazz improviser alive to the different conjugations of a single melody. Perhaps no phrase had more political charge during the Black Power Movement, and Harper worries the line, breaking down the different aspects of identity—"black," "man," "I am"—into their constituent parts. The odd phrasing and punctuation create an ef-

fect that blends incantation and hesitation, public assertion and private doubt. The stanza builds to full attainment, the completion and repetition of the phrase "I am a black man," then spills again into fragments.

The effect of hesitation dissolves in the second stanza, which translates into poetry the African American oral form of the boast. Like later stanzas touching on trumpeter Miles Davis and saxophonist John Coltrane, it amplifies the meaning of black manhood through its incarnation in a musician—here saxophonist Charlie Parker, or "Bird." Bird is a Staggerlee figure, a black folk hero whose "badness" is a matter of "smack, booze and bitches"; he is black manhood on extended wings, flying "higher, high, higher."

Written as a kind of chant, the poem allows its reader/speaker to pass through four different incarnations of black manhood: Bird, Miles, Coltrane, and finally Brother John, who "plays no instrument" but shares a solidarity with the musicians because he, like them, sings the phrase "I am a black man." The poem is a ritual invocation of ancestors, one that circles and gives strength back to the present.

Harper did not limit himself, however, to the solidarity of black men. In *Dear John, Dear Coltrane*, his vision radiated outward to a larger American community, at a moment when liberation movements like Black Power, the American Indian Movement, feminism, and gay rights were each reclaiming the value of "pride." Harper offered his own version of the American anthem in the poem "Strange Song," and it sounded like the blues:

in America you have
three sons and a woman
and the metaphors
of all this
colliding and colliding
in dissonant music
someone's said
is a symphony:
reds, browns, blacks
all humming
the same old tune:
love me,

love me painlessly—
but you can't.

"Strange Song" showcases the unique sup-
pleness of Harper's poetic voice: his quick,
short lines, which often reverse themselves
with stunning clarity (as in the last couplet);
the mix of incantation and precision, conver-
sational fluency and jibe; a skepticism that
strips away superfluous words as it inquires
into superfluous desires; and a lucidity that has
emotional warmth, since it is driven by the
search for love's meaning.

Here Harper reaffirms the American dream
of democracy—the "symphony" of reds, browns,
and blacks singing about the pursuit of happiness—but does so with a sense of tragic reen-
actment and limitation. We repeat the "same
old tune," not understanding that our pursuit
of happiness, our search for painless love, is destined to fail. And this failure comes not because
we will never find love, but because love must
be painful if it is to be comprehensive, embracing our terrors as well as our hopes. The dissonance of our shared history—the "colliding and
colliding" of our lives—ensures this fate.

Love and its difficulties preoccupy the more
personal poems in *Dear John* also. Two of
Harper's sons, Reuben and Michael, died from
complications in childbirth, and Harper wrote
movingly about his own and his wife's sense of
loss. In these elegies, Harper achieves a stoic
consolation by seeing his loss within a larger
national drama: "American History," with its
recognition of the four girls "blown up" in the
Alabama bombing, immediately precedes these
poems, and the poem "Deathwatch" ends with
another devastating Harper couplet, one that
enlarges our field of vision:

America needs a killing.
Survivors will be human.

The nation at present is murderous, even
hungry for death, but the future is compelled to
be different, in part because the survivors have
been schooled, terribly, in their humanity. The
elegy "We Assume: on the Death of Our Son,
Reuben Masai Harper" similarly finds consolation in the midst of unnerving heartbreak:

We assume
that in 28 hours,
lived in a collapsible isolette,
you learned to accept pure oxygen
as the natural sky;
the scant shallow breaths
that filled those hours
cannot, did not make you fly—
but dreams were there
like crooked palmprints on
the twin-thick windows of the nursery—
in the glands of your mother
. . . .
We assume
you did not know we loved you.

Harper tries to reclaim his son's brief life by
imagining it from the inside out: what did the
infant Reuben learn, know, dream? The key
word "assume" echoes the opening of Walt
Whitman's "Song of Myself"—"And what I assume you shall assume"—with its promise of
mutuality in mind and body. But Harper also
stresses the unknowability of his son's mind:
what could be less knowable than the mind of
an infant, since no one remembers what they
thought as a baby? Harper offers his son the qualified transcendence of an angel with clipped
wings: he has the ability to "accept pure oxygen" but not to fly, the power of dreams aslant
like "crooked palmprints."

The poem builds from this chastened poignancy to a heartbreaking conclusion: the last
couplet, with its quick and stark second line,
has a revelatory finality. If his son dies innocent, then he also dies unaware of his parents'
love. Harper reverses the sentimental hope—
that his son should, somehow, have divined his
parents' love—and comes face-to-face with his
grief, the certainty of both his love and his loss.

The presiding force in *Dear John, Dear Coltrane*—announced by the title, and present
directly or by implication in seven of the collection's poems—is the saxophonist John Coltrane, whose quartet pioneered a particularly
spiritual and searching form of jazz in the 1960s.
Throughout Michael Harper's career, Coltrane
has served as the poet's self-proclaimed Orpheus, his spiritual kin and artistic double:

Harper's second book, *History Is Your Own Heartbeat*, features the powerful "Here Where Coltrane Is"; his later collection *Healing Song for Inner Ear* (1985) includes the remarkable sequences "My Book on Trane" and "Peace on Earth"; and his recent *Honorable Amendments* (1995) recalls the anniversary of Coltrane's death in "Late September Refrain." Harper even wrote extensive liner notes, combining prose and poetry, for a Coltrane re-release on Prestige Records.

For Harper, Coltrane is both inspiration and model, an ancestor who teaches how to shatter older aesthetic and social restrictions. Harper has remarked on "the energy and passion with which [Coltrane] approached his instrument and music. Such energy was perhaps akin to the nature of oppression generally and the kind of energy it takes to break oppressive conditions, oppressive musical structures, and oppressive societal structures." In Coltrane's most celebrated work, *A Love Supreme* (1964), he departed from older jazz song-form, which was based in Tin Pan Alley structures and relied on constantly shifting harmonic patterns, and in its place launched a "modal," more open-ended form. In so doing, Coltrane tilted jazz away from light entertainment—he was not interested in catchy melodies—and toward intense spirituality: his art aimed to suffuse a single musical force-field, or modality, with the workings of the spirit, as a way of bringing his bandmates and audience to a state of communion.

In brief, Coltrane transformed the blues from "good-time" or "devil's" music into an oracular, inclusive, and devotional rite. Harper in turn seized on Coltrane's technique as a model for his own: "My poems are modal," he said. "By modality I mean the creation of an environment so intense by its life and force as to revivify and regenerate, spiritually, man and community.... The blues singer says 'I' but the audience assumes 'We'; out of such energy comes community and freedom. A Love Supreme!"

"Dear John, Dear Coltrane" is one of Harper's earliest Coltrane poems, and in fact its composition eerily predated Coltrane's death. It describes Coltrane's visionary quest to find and channel "a love supreme," but this heroic quest-romance has a contradictory, ascetic aspect: Coltrane discovers his individual power by purifying himself, by converting the traumas and annihilations of the past into the communal exaltation of the present. Coltrane himself spoke of his need to always "clean[] the mirror," by which he meant the need to look at and erase oneself at the same time. To clean the mirror is to assert oneself through an act of submission—a paradoxical process that is alive in Coltrane's art, where personal anguish is twinned to a fundamental act of empowerment.

Harper's poem begins with the terrors at the root of Coltrane's music, and then it mimes this cleansing ritual of spiritual uplift:

a love supreme, a love supreme—
a love supreme, a love supreme—

Sex fingers toes
in the marketplace
near your father's church
in Hamlet, North Carolina—
witness to this love
in this calm fallow
of these minds,
there is no substitute for pain:
genitals gone or going,
seed burned out,
you tuck the roots in the earth,
turn back, and move
by river through the swamps,
singing: a love supreme, a love supreme;
what does it all mean?
. . . .
Dawn comes and you cook
up the thick sin 'tween
impotence and death, fuel
the tenor sax cannibal
heart, genitals and sweat
that makes you clean—
a love supreme, a love supreme—

Why you so black?
cause I am
why you so funky?
cause I am

why you so black?
cause I am
why you so sweet?
cause I am
why you so black?
cause I am
a love supreme, a love supreme:

So sick
you couldn't play *Naima,*
so flat we ached
for song you'd concealed
with your own blood,
your diseased liver gave
out its purity,
the inflated heart
pumps out, the tenor kiss,
tenor love:
a love supreme, a love supreme—
a love supreme, a love supreme—

In the opening stanza of the poem, Harper gives us not the spirit of Coltrane but a dismembered body: "sex fingers toes/in the marketplace." Harper here invokes the maimed bodies of lynching victims, which were indeed traded "in the marketplace" as baubles of white supremacy. More specifically, Harper has said that he was recalling a harrowing scene from the life of W. E. B. Du Bois, who—while walking to a newspaper office to protest the lynching of farmer Sam Hose—discovered that Hose's knuckles were displayed in an Atlanta storewindow. Du Bois became a more forthright activist; Coltrane, meanwhile, created a testamental art out of such common terrible beginnings.

Harper has commented elsewhere on the centrality of terror for black artists: "black people in this country have been under a continuous assault, and the response to that assault has a lot to do with the vibrancy, not to mention the rigor, of the artistic expression." In "Dear John, Dear Coltrane," Harper describes both the terror and the response—both the fugitive slave "mov[ing]/by river through the swamps" and his conjure roots buried in the earth, both the "genitals gone or going" and the song "a love supreme."

In the second stanza, Harper focuses on how Coltrane's suffering is, ironically, a source of exaltation. Confining himself to an elemental vocabulary of the body (heart, genitals, sweat) and metaphysics (sin, impotence, death), Harper then connects the two with simple verbs of transformation (cooking, fueling, making). This elemental vocabulary allows Harper to describe several scenes at once: we witness Coltrane's drug addiction (heroin was "cooked up" to be ingested) and his grueling musical performances (a "cooking" session was also a musical jam), and, more abstractly, we see his alchemical process of self-transformation, where he consumes his own body, like a "cannibal," in order to cleanse himself. Thus does Harper convey, in the multiple ambiguities of his own poem, how Coltrane could destroy and purify himself at the very same time.

For Coltrane to succeed, however, he must not only lift himself up but also speak to his community. In the next stanza, Harper employs the fundamental technique of black church ritual—call-and-response—to affirm and broaden Coltrane's message of spiritual uplift. Again, Coltrane reverses the logic of shame—"why you so black?" "why you so funky?"—by refusing to be thrown on the defensive. Instead he responds, again and again, with a godlike affirmation of himself: "cause I am" is a loose vernacular translation of the biblical Yahweh, commonly rendered as "I am."

Coltrane wrests praise out of the degraded language of insult—and, even more strikingly, empowers the members of his audience, who are meant to join in the repeated choruses, "cause I am" and "a love supreme." This sense of empowerment is confirmed in the final stanza, which again moves from the sufferings of the past (the "diseased liver" which "gave/out its purity") to the beloved community of the present. The "inflated heart"—a heart grander than any single individual—"pumps out" its offering, the "tenor kiss" and "tenor love."

Harper's second collection, *History Is Your Own Heartbeat,* found the poet extending his reach, linking shorter poems into conceptual sequences. Winner of the Poetry Award of the

Black Academy of Arts and Letters, the book was divided in three parts: "Ruth's Blues," a series that examines his mother-in-law's illness in order to explore issues of interracial dependence and mutuality; "History as Personality," twenty-eight poems on music, color, and culture; and "High Modes," a brilliant series dedicated to the avant-garde painter Oliver Lee Jackson and an attempt to model, at length, the ritual of exaltation so central to "Dear John, Dear Coltrane."

The book jacket of *History Is Your Own Heartbeat* was telling: the title and author's name appeared as if written on a shattered mirror, the words coming apart yet held together in a fragile assemblage. Within the collection itself, Harper continued to investigate both the dark and the redemptive aspects of American history. The poems were suffused with violence, illness and death, even as they aimed to find reconciliation within the experience of pain.

In the sequence "Ruth's Blues," Harper considered how the fate of his mother-in-law, Ruth McLaughlin Buffington, was entwined with his own—and how, on a broader scale, history depended on such intimate yet strained relationships between men and women of all colors. In an interview he has remarked that "everyone has a kind of kinship tie with everyone else, if only can find the keys, *and there are keys.*" Understanding someone else is a necessary vehicle for understanding oneself. In the last stanza of "Love Medley: Patrice Cuchulain," Harper ruminated on the interdependence of his mother-in-law's illness and his son Patrice's birth:

> As you breathe easily, your mother's
> mother is tubed and strapped,
> hemorrhaging slowly from her varices;
> your two dead brothers who could
> not breathe are berries
> gone to rot at our table:
> what is birth but death
> with complexity: blood, veins,
> machinery and love: our names.

In contrast to the baby Patrice, whose umbilical cord has been cut, his grandmother is "tubed" and "strapped": she has become like a newborn with his or her lifeline still attached. This sense of reversal—the baby is independent and at ease; the adult is dependent and troubled—is compounded by a series of striking enjambments (the "brothers who could/not breathe", the "berries/gone to rot") and sets up the philosophical conundrum of the final three lines. "Complexity" is a much honored term in Harper's lexicon, and here it serves to yoke together terms that seem unshakably opposed: birth and death, machinery and love.

Such "complex" dichotomies are resolved in a final term, "our names"—names that testify to both our kinship and our singularity, defining us as individuals while renewing our ties to the past. As in "Brother John" and "Dear John, Dear Coltrane," the act of naming—carried elsewhere by the simple declarative "I am"—is central to Harper's project of communal affirmation.

The sequence "High Modes" may represent Harper's most extended meditation on the "modal" form he wished to create, a form open-ended enough to allow for both combat and exaltation, antagonism and uplift. Dedicated to his friend Oliver Jackson, the sequence wrestled centrally with the recent suicide of Jackson's wife, Gail, who had swallowed rat poison in an act of despair. The purpose of the sequence, then, was to answer this despair: what kind of ritual might redeem this suffering? And how would this redemption destroy and remake the world as it had been?

The sequence's first epigraph—"Supernigger's dead; long live the mf!"—gives a devious cue to its subsequent direction. Recasting the slogan "The king is dead; long live the king!," Harper telegraphs that this story of resurrection will be salted with vulgarity, devoted to the triumph of the lowly. This parodic epigraph is twinned, however, with a second epigraph that is poker-faced and metaphysical (and comes, notably, from the late John Coltrane): "Music, being an expression of the human heart, expresses what is happening." Toggling between parody and the earnest expression of "what is happening," Harper engages in a double maneuver typical of early-seventies black literature:

he both subverts a dominant tradition (here identified with the forces that led Gail to suicide) and reaches toward a new way of happening, a new form.

At this point in his career, Harper began speaking at greater length of the power of his modal forms, which he hoped would lead him away from "the Western orientation of division between denotative/connotative, body/mind, life/spirit, soul/body, mind/heart." Modality, in his view, offered an alternative to Western reason, substituting an inclusive logic (what he called "both/and") for an exclusive one ("either/or"). Fittingly, Harper's idea of a spiritually rejuvenating "modality" drew together an astonishing array of developments, in fields as diverse as popular music, academic anthropology, and the visual avant-garde. First and most transparently, Harper was indebted to the modal jazz spearheaded in the 1960s by John Coltrane and Miles Davis. Linked to religious musics like the ragas of India, modal jazz highlighted the qualities of "energy" and "action"—qualities that signified a gathering spiritual intensity.

Second, Harper took note of the philosophical anthropology of Africanists like Marcel Griaule, Janheinz Jahn, and William Abrahams, all of whom described how the peoples of sub-Saharan Africa had developed sophisticated and all-embracing cosmologies, enacted through aesthetic ritual. In fact, Harper first encountered the concept of modality in Abraham's *The Mind of Africa* and Jahn's *Muntu: An Outline of the New African Culture*, the latter of which emphasized the roles of repetition, rhythm and process in African poetry.

Last, Harper drew upon the "Neo-African" painting of Oliver Jackson himself, who helped lead St. Louis's "Black Artists Group" along with the jazz saxophonists Oliver Lake and Julius Hemphill, the poet Quincy Troupe, and the painter Emilio Cruz. Like much earlier Abstract Expressionist painting, Jackson's Neo-African art emphasized the flatness of the canvas and the action of the artist, but it also infused these ideas with the ethos of Jahn's African culture. "Neo-African" meant that improvisation and process were valued above de-

liberation and finality; the viewer was invited to participate in a field of energy, not to scrutinize a well-wrought object.

All three of these influences—music, Africanist anthropology, and abstract art—are evident in the sequence's culminating poem, "High Modes: Vision as Ritual: Confirmation." The poem's refrain—repeated four times at the beginning and end of the poem, and interspersed throughout—is *Black Man Go Back To The Old Country*. The command might first be read as an insult, since it seems to expel black men from America in a sort of segregationist's dream. Once again, however, Harper reverses the common language of insult. The phrase becomes an originary myth, a way of describing how artists create their world:

And you went back home for the images,
the brushwork packing the mud
into the human form; and the ritual:
Black Man Go Back To The Old Country

Harper sees the painter Oliver Jackson in an elemental, godlike act of creation, his "brushwork" molding man out of clay. The "Old Country" is a symbolic space of recovery and attainment, not the Africa of a journalist.

As the poem builds, it becomes clear that Harper is not only describing this ritual of recovery: he is *enacting* it, through a language that is simultaneously abstract and actively concrete. Chanting in simple declarative and imperative sentences, Harper relishes the power of repetition, since repetition allows him to describe the continuity of tradition:

Bird was a mode from the old country;
Bud Powell bowed in modality, blow Bud;
Louis Armstrong touched the old country,
and brought it back, around corners;
Miles is a mode; Coltrane is, power,
Black Man Go Back To The Old Country
Black Man Go Back To The Old Country
Black Man Go Back To The Old Country

Harper conjugates the concept of the mode through every register: it is archetypal ("Bird was a mode"); it is an atmosphere ("Bud Powell bowed in modality"); and finally it is the element of human possibility, or "power." Percussive and forthright, the stanza tries to move the reader into the realm of intuition and experience. We are meant to become more bare and powerful, like the heroes who "go back to the old country."

The success of *Dear John, Dear Coltrane* and *History Is Your Own Heartbeat* brought Harper greater security as a poet, and the next five years witnessed the blossoming of his career: four new books of poetry, a new and selected poems, and a shower of professional honors. In 1970, Brown University appointed Harper as an associate professor, partly in response to student activists who demanded greater diversity in the curriculum and on the faculty. While he took various leaves from Brown—serving as a fellow at the Center for Advanced Studies at the University of Illinois from 1970 to 1971, teaching part-time at Harvard from 1974 to 1977, and holding visiting appointments at Yale (1976), Carleton (1979) and the University of Cincinnati (1979)—Harper became a cornerstone of Brown's English faculty. He was named a full professor in 1974, and he served as the director of the Graduate Creative Writing Program until 1983, when he was awarded an endowed chair, the Israel J. Kapstein Professorship. (As he adopted Rhode Island as his community, so Rhode Island adopted him: he was named the state's Poet Laureate and published *Rhode Island: Eight Poems* in 1981.)

The title of Harper's next full-length collection, *Song: I Want a Witness* (1972), attested that he was still interested in rituals of call-and-response and collective redemption. The title poem frames the collection, appearing at both beginning and end, and aims to convert the experience of terror—here set on the riot-torn streets of urban America—into a healing ritual of rescue. It opens with an almost surreal, gold-tinted account of urban disorder:

Blacks in frame houses
call to the helicopters,
their antlered arms
spinning; jeeps pad

these glass-studded streets;
on this hill are tanks painted gold.

The blacks here seem to be appealing to the authorities, "call[ing] to the helicopters"; and these authorities seem harmless, their jeeps "pad[ding]" around like so many city dogs, their tanks "painted gold" in a glistening vista that includes "glass-studded streets."

Soon, however, Harper twists the mood around, revealing that "This scene is about power,/terror, producing/love and pain and pathology." Harper places himself as a sympathetic observer, but not one interested in revenge: while his urban blacks are full of "love and pain and pathology," they are not driven to fantasies of destruction. His last image is double-edged, fitting for this moment of crisis. He sees

blacks here to *testify*
and testify, and testify,
and redeem, and redeem,
in black smoke coming,
as they wave their arms,
as they wave their tongues.

A plume of "black smoke coming," Harper's blacks are ready to detonate. Yet even more striking than this hint of militance is Harper's last figure, the symmetry of the arms and tongues waving: he memorably ties together the need for rescue and the need for poetry— for redemption *and* for testifying.

Ironically, given this framing poem, *Song: I Want a Witness* has few chant-poems like "Brother John" or "High Modes," few poems of ritual performance. In these earlier poems, Harper had aimed to become his material: he had modeled his voice on the articulate "blowing" of Coltrane and Parker, illuminating their lives by adopting their phrasing. In *Song: I Want a Witness* and later collections, Harper remained attached to jazz as an art of spiritual heroism, but he stopped identifying with musicians on such intimate, even otherworldly terms. As a rule, his poems became more retrospective, full of immediacy yet not written to be chanted; they did not import Harper's artistic forbears *into* a continuous present, but instead focused on the layered impact of historical events and decisions *upon* the present.

As Harper explained in an epigraph that would become the title of his sixth book, "Nightmare begins responsibility." This responsibility is a matter of historical debt: if we wish to wake from our nightmares, we must found better myths, recover a fuller story. Harper has repeatedly distinguished between open and closed myths, the latter of which he sees as the driving force behind American violence. "[T]he fantasy of a white supremist [sic] America with its closed myths has always been a fantasy of a white country," he has said. "Out of that kind of fantasy came genocide, Indian massacres, fugitive slave laws, manifest destiny, open-door policies, Vietnam, Detroit, East St. Louis, Watts, the Mexican American War, Chicago and the Democratic Convention of 1968."

Harper contrasts these closed myths with the "open-ended" stories that admit the power of individuals to change the world, stories that expose how history is made, diverted, repressed, and retold. "I try to speak with eloquence for losers," Harper has said. "I'm concerned with those particular people who have no voice."

In the three main sections of *Song: I Want a Witness*, Harper aimed to speak for these "losers," both by acknowledging their bitter experience and by finding new ways to tell the American story of "discovery." The series "Homage to the New World" was largely a paean to the virtues of simplicity and tranquility, a hymn to his wife who was "the hearth of this house," but it ended with an ominous flashback to the muted violence of the past:

these fatherless whites
come to consciousness
with a history of the gun—
the New World, if misery had
a voice, would be a rifle cocking.

Likewise, the sequence "Love Letters: The Caribou Hills, The Moose Range" comments on the murderousness at the root of the American settling. Written as a response to William Faulkner's "The Bear," the poem narrates a moose hunt in Alaska, but it refuses to glorify its violence, ending with the image of bloody hands. The legacy of conquest is the impoverishment of everyone, hunter and hunted alike. "One does not sell the earth upon which the people walk," Harper says in an epigraph.

In the sequence "Photographs: Negatives," Harper tried to write an open-ended myth of the American past. "The Indian is the root of an apple tree; history, symbol, presence," he suggests. "[T]hese voices are not lost on us, or them." Not being lost on *us*, they summon us to action; not being lost *on them*, they resonate as living presences. In the poem "History as Apple Tree," Harper claims a solidarity with disparate voices in the American past— with native Americans, with the black men who escaped into the tribes near Providence, with the Puritan John Winthrop, and with the heretic Roger Williams. This motley company brings him to a new myth of origins, a story where the apple tree brings an enabling knowledge:

As black man I steal away
in the night to the apple tree,
place my arms in the rich grave,
black sachem on a family plot,
take up a chunk of apple root,
let it become my skeleton,
become my own myth:
my arm the historical branch,
my name the bruised fruit,
black human photograph: apple tree.

Here Harper reinvents the scene of dying (the "rich grave") as a place of rebirth: he finds his skeleton in the native American burial ground, but it is an empowering kind of self-recognition. "Stealing away" like a slave bound for freedom, he remakes history in his own image, becomes his "own myth." Harper deploys three different metaphors: the apple tree as the root of knowledge, the family tree as the account of origins, and the photograph as a record of history. All three converge as collective history becomes one with personal knowledge.

In his next book, *Debridement* (1973), Harper experimented with new technical resources as he investigated, more pointedly, the meaning of heroism in a world where social justice seems indelibly linked to the threat of violence. If power concedes nothing without an astringent demand, how far should a hero go?

The first sequence of twenty poems, "History as Cap'n Brown," retells the story of abolitionist John Brown—how he massacred proslavery settlers, gathered troops, and raided Harper's Ferry to spur a slave rebellion—through a "found poetry" that relies much on W. E. B. Du Bois's biography *John Brown*. Taking as his epigraph Du Bois's formula that "The price of repression is greater than the cost of liberty," Harper does not sit in judgment of Brown. Rather, he allows Brown to tell his own story, in a matter-of-fact tone that attests to Brown's steely determination and stoic approach to pain. "I will give my life for a slave," Brown says—"with a gun my secret passage." Although Brown's raid was a failure, he did succeed as a prophet of emancipation, and Harper captures keenly how his prophecy took the form of a blood sacrifice: "We wrote our names on the hideout walls/hung by the heavens in blood."

The second sequence of ten poems, "Heartblow," ruminates on the achievement and limitations of black intellectual Richard Wright. "Heartblow" was Harper's first extended meditation on his literary influences, and it forecast much of the work in his next book, *Nightmare Becomes Responsibility*, where Harper claimed a catholic tradition of African American writers as his ancestors. Wright's achievement, for Harper, was to illuminate the "parable of black man, white woman/ the man's penis slung to his shin"—the myth of black supervirility and violence that Harper has elsewhere called "the national sickness." But Wright, a "double-conscious brother in the veil," also had trouble extricating himself from his own mythologies: "souls said you dealt your own heartblow," Harper concludes his series.

The third and most powerful sequence, "Debridement," tells the story of John Henry Louis, a military hero troubled by his brutal experience in Vietnam. Harper recounts his alienation from both the military and his Detroit neighborhood, in a sequence that juxtaposes two different voices together: an "official" rolling psychological report on Louis's mind, and the voice of Louis himself, as he struggles to remember Vietnam and integrate himself back into his community. Ultimately, Louis is gunned down by a white storeowner, and Harper wants to understand the meaning of this sacrifice. Like John Brown, Louis dies from the "schizophrenia" of our national ideals, the gap between our supposed commitment to freedom and our reliance on terror and violence. This gap is reflected pointedly in the distance between the official reports on Louis and his own self-consciousness. The clinical reports are, in Harper's words, "body poetry torn asunder," a form of spiritual mutilation.

The term "debridement" acts as a complex metaphor for the workings of the poem. It refers to a medical procedure—the cutting away of dead tissue in order to stave off a larger infection—but its meaning shifts depending on the answer to the question: who is being saved by the sacrifice? On the one hand, the term bitterly describes the operation behind Louis' death: Louis is one of many black men infected by American myths, then sacrificed so that America can restore itself to a clean bill of health. According to Harper, Louis's roles in Vietnam and Detroit reflect how he had "no options at all: to be an executioner . . . or be a victim." After he becomes both in turn, the nation closes up its wounds: Louis is buried in Arlington National Cemetery, with an "army honor guard/in dress blues," surrounded by the Kennedy Memorial and the Pentagon. It is the funeral of a well-behaved patriot.

On the other hand, Harper also suggests that Louis' "debridement," however painful, may heal the community of his friends and kin. The poem "A White Friend Flies in from the Coast" is both brutal and delicate as it describes Louis' narrow world of choices through the eyes of his white platoon mate:

> *Burned*—black by birth,
> *burned*—armed with .45,

burned—submachine gun,
burned—STAC hunted VC,
. . . .
burned—killed faceless VC,
burned—over and over,
burned—STAC subdued by three men,
burned—three shots: morphine,
burned—tried killing prisoners,
burned—taken to Pleiku,
burned—held down, straightjacket,
burned—whites owe him, hear?
burned—I owe him, here.

Harper plays with the different meanings of "burned" as he hammers on the word: it refers to Louis's race ("black by birth"); it conjures up images of black victimization, the lynched body, and of black rioting (the slogan "burn baby burn"); it refers to the unremitting violence in Vietnam; and it captures the sense of being cheated. In the final two lines, though, Harper suggests that there may be relief from this great American fraud, the sacrifice of black men in the name of ideals that the country systematically betrays. The "friend" moves to a realization of racial exploitation ("whites owe him, hear"), then echoes this with a sense of personal indebtedness ("I owe him, here"). As Harper has said about "open-ended myths," they do allow for unexpected solidarities.

In *Nightmare Begins Responsibility* (1975), Harper became a virtuoso in the art of homage, concentrating for the first time on his literary forbears and his own extended family. The poems are awash in gratitude, studded with telling dedications—to his wife; parents; the sports heroes Jackie Robinson and Willie Mays; the singer Mahalia Jackson; the poets Sterling Brown, Ralph Dickey, and Robert Hayden; and the writers Leon Forrest, Ernest Gaines, Jean Toomer, and Alice Walker.

The section "Sterling Letters" announced Harper's devotion to Sterling Brown, a poet, folklorist, and professor who became a literary institution at Howard University. Harper was inspired early on by Brown's recordings in a San Francisco library; later he repaid his debt by editing and ushering into publication *The Collected Poems of Sterling Brown* (1980). With his appreciation for folklore, his razor-edged wit, and his novel grasp of blues intonations and rhythm, Brown was a natural mentor for Harper, who also grounded his poetry in musical and vernacular forms. Harper's homage to Brown, "Br'er Sterling and the Rocker," calls out Brown as a spiritual brother ("Br'er") and trickster (the hint of "Br'er Rabbit"), and aims to be poetry of the rocking chair itself—wisdom dispensed by a savvy tongue:

Any fool knows a Br'er in a rocker
is a boomerang incarnate; look at the blade
of the rocker, that wonderous crescent
rockin' in harness is a poem.
To speak of poetry is the curled line
  straightened;
to speak of doubletalk, the tongue
gone pure, the stoic line a trestle
whistlin', a man a train comin' on:

Many of the strongest poems in *Nightmare Begins Responsibility* memorialize Harper's extended family. "Grandfather," like many Harper poems, tells of that brand of heroism that sinks under its own weight. Harper recalls how his grandfather, while young, fended off a lynch mob inspired by the movie *Birth of a Nation*. Now he sits on a porch, pondering "the great white nation immovable," "his weight wilt[ing]." In "Alice Braxton Johnson," Harper wrestles with the infirmity of his grandmother, who herself grapples with the unexpected death of her son. They are enmeshed, and numbed, in their grief.

In "Alice," the concluding poem of *Nightmare Begins Responsibility*, Harper entwines literary and family homage, paying respects to fellow writer Alice Walker and to his grandmother. Walker had tracked down writer Zora Neale Hurston's unmarked grave, and Harper responds by honoring the power of folklore—the conjure traditions that Hurston had explored in her fieldwork—as well as the kinship circles that sustained them:

And for this I say your name: Alice,
my grandmother's name, your name,
conjured in snake-infested field
where Zora Neale welcomed you home,

and where I speak from now
on higher ground of her risen
black marker where you have written
your name in hers, and in mine.

In 1977 Harper brought out *Images of Kin*, largely a selection of his earlier poems. The book spooled backward from Harper's most recent work to *Dear John, Dear Coltrane*, as if to illustrate Harper's proposition that the present is a needful gateway to the past.

Among the new poems were "Tongue-Tied in Black and White," a powerful tribute to the poet John Berryman that probes their friendship in light of Berryman's reliance on minstrel dialect; "Healing Song," a tribute to Robert Hayden that emulates Hayden's own efflorescent rhetoric; and the series "Uplift from a Dark Tower," which considers different historical approaches to "uplift the race," from the ethos of Booker T. Washington to the missionary activity of Harper's own great-grandfather in the African Methodist church. A summation of the most prolific phase of Harper's career, the book won the Melville-Cane Award and was nominated in 1978 for the National Book Award.

After producing six collections of poetry in as many years, Harper spent nearly a decade preparing his next, *Healing Song for Inner Ear* (1985). *Healing Song* was predominantly a collection of elegies, and its tone was unmistakably retrospective, wistful, and chastened. In "The Drowning of the Facts of a Life," about the death of his brother, Jonathan, Harper began by questioning the motives behind the elegy itself:

Who knows why we talk of death
this evening, warm beyond the measure
of breath . . .

Tonight we talk of losses in the word
and go on drowning in acts of faith
knowing so little of humility,
less of the body,
which will die in the mouth of reality.

The poem, like so many in *Healing Song*, reveals the influence of poet W. H. Auden in both its speaker's voice and cadence. There is an elegance to Harper's metaphysics, in the way "death" echoes through the passage ("breath," "faith," "mouth") or in the light rhymes of "humility," "body," and reality." Moreover, Harper writes with fluent formality, staging his private grief as a greater parable of loss, humility, and unfulfilled promise. Jonathan, breathing through a respirator, is beyond the consolation of poetry: there is "no chant sound enough/to lift him from the rest/ of contraption/to the syncopated dance of his name."

Healing Song was also Harper's most global work, reflecting his travels in Egypt, England, Sweden, and particulary South Africa, where he returned to the township that his great-grandfather had served as a missionary. In "Stutterer," published first in the *New York Times*, Harper anatomizes the surveillance operations of a Soweto police station where the poet was detained for a few hours. Likewise, in "The Militance of a Photograph in the Passbook of a Bantu under Detention," Harper weaves the history of his own great-grandfather with the history of a man tortured by the apartheid regime. "This is no simple mug shot," he says, adducing that its "militance" is a matter of living history, a passbook passed on.

The title of Harper's next book of poems, *Honorable Amendments* (1995), signaled that Harper was both amending his usual style and extending it in an "honorable" direction—that is to say, in the service of a democratic cultural tradition. Harper took one of his epigraphs from John Kouewenhoven's *The Beer Can by the Highway*, a book which Ralph Ellison had also appraised highly:

By a "commitment to democracy" I mean a commitment to the idea that there are no fixed or determinable limits to the capacities of any individual being, and that all are entitled, by inalienable right, to equal opportunities to develop their potentialities. Democracy in this sense is an ideal, not a political system, and certainly not an actual state of affairs.

Honorable Amendments is a testament to this conception of cultural democracy, one that understands individual achievement as the means of community empowerment. It hails a wide spectrum of individuals who share the drive to realize their genius—the musicians Lester Young, Sarah Vaughn, and Dexter Gordon; the athletes Ernie Banks and Joe Louis; the writer Sterling Brown; and the painter Romare Bearden. In "Study Windows," Harper underscores that "you code your life/ with the ability to work," and *Honorable Amendments* showcases both his love of artistic discipline and his own openness to work in new ways, his adventurous approach to his material.

Perhaps the most ambitious sequence is "Songlines from a Tessera(e) Journal: Romare Bearden, 1912–1988," a praisesong for the painter who created indelible collages, bright in color and jagged in composition, of black life. A "Tessera(e) Journal," the sequence aims to be a sort of collage itself: its five parts form a mosaic, with each piece giving a different vantage point on Bearden's art and life. The first poem, "Quilting Bee (Mecklenburg County)," takes inspiration from Bearden's canvas "Quilting Time" and from the act of quilting itself, a folk form of collage involving creative overlay and juxtaposition. It employs a much longer poetic line—up to sixteen syllables—as it imitates how Bearden's canvas captures the work of a quilting bee in progress: "the diamonds and gold of musicians humming without voice."

The rest of the Bearden sequence is similarly inventive, as Harper strives to capture other facets of Bearden's aesthetic. In "Homage to the Brown Bomber," he dances around the subject of boxer Joe Louis, improvising around his moves ("Speed of the punch/its dancing, rhythmic fluency/in short space, short duration"). In "Journey Through the Interior," he creates an interior monologue to suggest how Bearden may have explained his collages to himself: "It was strenuous repetition/tempering of volumes," "the music of optics." Then in "Odd Facts About the Painter (On Causality)," he muses on why Bearden became a compelling artist. His reasons swing from being absurdly focused ("because Savoy had good stride-piano") to being mind-boggling and abstract ("because vari-

ous problems of relationship/condense negative space of temperament").

After such formal play, the last poem "Dear Romie: Rock Formation Epistles" is shockingly straighforward: a forty-five-line litany of "thanks" that crisscrosses the whole of Bearden's life. It begins with "Thanks for the drawing of Judith Jamison," becomes increasingly complicated as Harper extemporizes on different Bearden compositions, then culminates with simple grace: "Thanks for your pace at the fair." We are back in the world of the quilting bee, the stately world of black ritual and rhythm that Bearden honored—but we have gotten there through the disjunctive juxtapositions, the cut-and-paste of collage, that Bearden used to fabricate his art.

Harper's desire to honor his "kin," to realize networks of influence and inspiration, has also propelled him into the role of mentor and editor. From the late seventies into the new century, he has been a key shaper of the African American literary tradition. As a teacher at Brown, his students have included the novelist Gayl Jones and the poets Sherley Anne Williams, Melvin Dixon, George Barlow, and Anthony Walton, many of whom have dedicated portions of their work to Harper.

As an editor, Harper consolidated an African American canon just as it began to crystallize in university curricula. In 1977 he edited, with Robert Stepto, two special issues of *Massachusetts Review* that grew into *Chant of Saints* (1979), a seminal collection of African American literature, art, and criticism. *Chant*'s impact can be measured by the way that the wider literary culture has adopted as its own the book's contributors: Sterling Brown, Robert Hayden, Leon Forrest, Ralph Ellison, Derek Walcott, Toni Morrison, Chinua Achebe, Ernest Gaines, and Jay Wright, among others. Two of *Chant*'s contributors subsequently won the Nobel Prize in Literature.

The historian John Hope Franklin compared the book with *The New Negro*, the keynote text of the Harlem Renaissance, and praised its "air of security, if not solidarity and self-esteem," which he traced to the professionalism of its contributors, the fact that they made their living from their art. Such canon-making did have its critics, however. Amiri Baraka, after calling Harper "rhythmless," denounced him as one of the "Ivy structuralists" who "want to distort Afro-American literary history and Mandrake up a tradition of elegant (?) copout as the heavy mainstream." The bite in Baraka's criticism came from his sense that Harper hesitated to marshall art in the service of black liberation and deferred to a middle-class sense of literary propriety.

Harper has repeatedly called himself a "both/ and" poet, and his recent editorial work reflects his spirit of inclusiveness. *Every Shut Eye Ain't Asleep* (1994), an anthology of post–World War II African American poetry that Harper co-edited, is notable for its catholic tastes. While it is grounded in long selections from Gwendolyn Brooks and Robert Hayden, it also features experimental poets like Clarence Major and Nathaniel Mackey, less well known poets like Marilyn Nelson Waniek and Cornelius Eady, and (Baraka's broadside notwithstanding) openly political voices like Sonia Sanchez, Haki Madhubuti, and Baraka himself.

Harper's express aim—and one he honors as editor and poet—is to "focus attention on the entire spectrum of African-American poetic practice." While his own career emerged with the starburst of the "New Black Poetry" of the 1970s, Harper has carried on a longer tradition personified by his mentor Sterling Brown, where the poet is at once a historian, teacher, and moralist. He has advanced the art of black America while striving always for a visionary poetry that—through some magic fusion of improvisation and discipline, imagination and hard moral truth—could go beyond the veil of race.

Selected Bibliography

PRIMARY WORKS

POETRY

Dear John, Dear Coltrane. Pittsburgh: University of Pittsburgh Press, 1970.
History Is Your Own Heartbeat: Poems. Urbana: University of Illinois Press, 1971.
Photographs: Negatives: History as Apple Tree. San Francisco: Scarab Press, 1972.
Song: I Want a Witness. Pittsburgh: University of Pittsburgh Press, 1972.
Debridement. Garden City: Doubleday, 1973.
Nightmare Begins Responsibility. Urbana: University of Illinois Press, 1975.
Images of Kin: New and Selected Poems. Urbana: University of Illinois Press, 1977.
Rhode Island: Eight Poems. Roslindale, Mass.: Pym-Randall Press, 1981.
Healing Song for Inner Ear: Poems. Urbana: University of Illinois Press, 1985.
Honorable Amendments: Poems. Urbana: University of Illinois Press, 1995.

AUTOBIOGRAPHY

"Robert Hayden and Michael S. Harper: A Literary Friendship." Edited by Xavier Nicholas. *Callaloo* 17, no. 4:975–1016 (Fall 1994).

SELECTED ARTICLES

"My Poetic Technique and the Humanization of the American Audience." In *Black American Literature and Humanism.* Edited by R. Baxter Miller. Lexington: University Press of Kentucky, 1981. Pp. 27–32.
"Magic: Power: Activation: Transformation." In *Acts of Mind: Conversations with Contemporary Poets.* Edited by Richard Jackson. Birmingham: University of Alabama Press, 1983.
"It Is the Man/Woman Outside Who Judges: The Minority Writer's Perspective on Literature." *TriQuarterly* 65:57–65, 80–83 (Winter 1986).

EDITORIAL WORK

Ralph Dickey. *Leaving Eden: Poems.* Providence: Bonewhistle Press, 1974.
Chant of Saints: A Gathering of Afro-American Literature, Art, and Scholarship. Edited by Harper and Robert B. Stepto. Urbana: University of Illinois Press, 1979.
Brown, Sterling Allen. *The Collected Poems of Sterling A. Brown, 1st ed.* Edited by Harper. New York: Harper & Row, 1980.
The Carleton Miscellany: A Ralph Ellison Festival 28:3 (Winter 1980). Edited by Harper and John Wright.
Every Shut Eye Ain't Asleep: An Anthology of Poetry by African Americans Since 1945, 1st ed. Edited by Harper and Anthony Walton. Boston: Little, Brown, 1994.

SECONDARY WORKS

BIOGRAPHICAL AND CRITICAL STUDIES

Brown, Joseph A. "Their Long Scars Touch Ours: A Reflection on the Poetry of Michael Harper." *Callaloo* 9, no. 1:209–20 (Winter 1986).
Callahan, John F. "The Poetry of Michael Harper." *New Republic*, May 17, 1975, pp. 25–26.
———. "The Testifying Voice in Michael Harper's *Images of Kin.*" *Black American Literature Forum* 13:89–92 (Fall 1979).

Dodd, Elizabeth. "Another Version: Michael S. Harper, William Clark, and the Problem of Historical Blindness." *Western American Literature* 33, no. 1:61–72 (Spring 1998).

Forbes, Calvin. Review of *Honorable Amendments. African American Review* 32:508–10 (Fall 1998).

Fussell, Edwin. "Double-Conscious Poet in the Veil." *Parnassus Poetry in Review* 4, no. 1:5–28 (Fall/Winter 1975).

Grimes, Kyle. "The Entropics of Discourse: Michael Harper's Debridement and the Myth of the Hero." *Black American Literature Forum* 24:417–40 (Autumn 1990).

Lenz, Gunter H. "Black Poetry and Black Music: History and Tradition: Michael Harper and John Coltrane." In *History and Tradition in Afro-American Culture.* Edited by Gunter H. Lenz. Frankfurt: Campus, 1984. Pp. 277–319.

Lieberman, Laurence. "Derek Walcott and Michael S. Harper: The Muse of History." *Yale Review* 62:284–96 (October 1973).

"Michael S. Harper: American Poet." *Callaloo* 13, no. 4:749–829 (Fall 1990).

Rampersad, Arnold. "The Poetics of Michael S. Harper." *Poetry Miscellany* 6:43–50 (1976).

Stepto, Robert B. "After Modernism, After Hibernation: Michael Harper, Robert Hayden, and Jay Wright." In *Chant of Saints: A Gathering of Afro-American Literature, Art, and Scholarship.* Edited by Harper and Stepto. Urbana: University of Illinois Press, 1979. Pp. 470–86.

———. "Michael S. Harper: Poet as Kinsman: The Family Sequences," *Massachusetts Review* 17:477–502 (Autumn 1976).

———. "Michael Harper's Extended Tree: John Coltrane and Sterling Brown." *Hollins Critic* 13, no. 3:2–16 (June 1976).

INTERVIEWS

Chapman, Abraham. "An Interview with Michael S. Harper." *Arts in Society* 2:463–71 (Fall/Winter 1974).

Lloyd, David. "Interview with Michael Harper." *TriQuarterly* 65:119–28 (Winter 1986).

Martin, Reginald. "An Interview with Michael Harper." *Black American Literature Forum* 13:441–51 (Autumn 1990).

O'Brien, John. "Michael Harper." *Interviews with Black Writers,* 95–107. New York: Liveright, 1973.

Randall, James. "An Interview with Michael Harper." *Ploughshares* 7, no. 1:11–27 (1981).

Rowell, Charles. " 'Down Don't Worry Me': An Interview with Michael S. Harper" *Callaloo* 13, no. 4:780–800 (Fall 1990).

Young, Al, Larry Kart, and Michael Harper. "Jazz and Letters: A Colloquy." *TriQuarterly* 68:118–58 (Winter 1987).

315

ROBERT HAYDEN
(1913–1980)

ROBERT M. GREENBERG

FROM 1940 UNTIL shortly before his death on 25 February 1980, Robert Hayden published poems of unusual diversity and breadth of experience. A range of modern poetry from the dialect verse of Langston Hughes to the Byzantium poems of William Butler Yeats figured in his development. In broadest terms his work deals with the tensions between the conditional realities of men's lives and their human aspirations, between a tragic and irredeemable world and the possibilities for transcendence that exist in sensory delight, art, and religion.

As a black American, Hayden is concerned with history. The relationship between harsh empirical facts—especially the realities of American slavery—and the moral and imaginative use of these facts is an important element of his verse. Although at times his poems rise above the evil of the world, most often history and a hostile universe limit the possibilities of the present. In "Locus" (*Words in the Mourning Time,* 1970), a poem about the undying presences and deadly nature of the southern landscape, Hayden writes:

> Here violent metamorphosis,
>   with every blossom turning
> deadly. . . . Here wound-red earth
>   and blinding cottonfields,
> rock hills where sachems counseled,

where scouts gazed stealthily
    upon the glittering death march
of De Soto through Indian wilderness.
    Here mockingbird and
cottonmouth, fury of rivers.
. . . .

> Here spareness, rankness, harsh
> brilliances; beauty of what's hardbitten,
> knotted, stinted, flourishing
>   in despite, on thorny meagerness
> thriving, twisting into grace.

In "Locus" past and present, shade and brightness, beauty and violent undergrowth twist into qualified "grace." Embodiment of the violent history of the South, the landscape thwarts the ample blossoming of beauty or the poet's transcendent contemplation. By contrast, in the same volume the poet is able, briefly, in "Monet's 'Waterlilies' " to escape history through the contemplation of art:

> Today as the news from Selma and Saigon
> poisons the air like fallout,
>   I come again to see
> the serene great picture that I love. . . .
> . . . .
> Here space and time exist in light
> the eye like the eye of faith believes.
>   The seen, the known
> dissolve in iridescence, become

317

illusive flesh of light
    that was not, was, forever is.

In these poems we see a manifestation of what Wilburn Williams, Jr., calls Hayden's "bipolar" imagination. Both poems emerge out of the conflict between man's imaginative-spiritual nature and the immitigable aspects of existence. In "Locus" the evil in man and nature condemns the transcendental impulse to unending terrestrial struggle. In "Monet's 'Waterlilies' " the poet is able for a short while to rise beyond "the seen, the known" to a sphere of iridescent serenity. Williams says of Hayden's verse: "The realities of imagination and the actualities of history are bound together in an intimate symbiotic alliance that makes neither thinkable without the other." Michael S. Harper observes similarly that "Hayden has always been a symbolist poet struggling with historical fact, his rigorous portraits of people and places providing the synaptic leap into the interior landscape of the soul."

Hayden himself suggested to John O'Brien, only partly in jest, that perhaps he was a "romantic realist." Acknowledging elements of romanticism, symbolism, and realism in his poetry, Hayden often underscored in interviews his mistrust of the commonplace sense of "reality" and his belief in the reality of the subjective. (The word he preferred is "fantasy.") He said to Dennis Joseph Gendron, ". . . we live so much of our lives in our own minds. What we consider fantasy and unreality—these things are so much a part of us and determine so much of us. I have always been fascinated by this. The line between the real and the fanciful is a very thin line."

Unquestionably the reality of "fantasy" or what we shall call "subjectivity" exerted a persistent influence on Hayden's verse. Yet if this attitude placed him squarely in the mainstream of modern poetry, it did not always win him approval or even attention. "There is a chronic American belief," Lionel Trilling observes in "Reality in America" (1940), "that there exists an opposition between reality and mind and that one must enlist oneself in the party of reality." This tendency to view reality as "ma-terial reality," "wholly external" and "always easily to be known," emerges particularly in economically depressed times and amid economically oppressed groups. Sometimes it leads to a complete subordination of art and intellectual life to economic and political "realities." At other times, as was common during the 1960s and 1970s among radical blacks, mind—but only "black" mind—is admitted as part of reality. Stephen Henderson, for example, in *Understanding the New Black Poetry* (1973), defines contemporary black verse exclusively in terms of black themes, black feeling for life (Henderson's term is "saturation"), and structural effects arising from black speech and music as "poetic references." Other themes, feelings, or references are not important in understanding black poetry.

Although it made Hayden the subject of occasional attack, he always opposed such ethnocentric attitudes. Their fault lay for him in their defining of the boundaries of reality for the artist and establishing ethnic or political criteria upon which to judge a writer's selection and treatment of material. In Hayden's view, craft and universality are the criteria upon which a work ought to be judged. Blackness to Hayden, as Blyden Jackson says, "was . . . a point of departure into that magic realm where all artists of unmistakably superlative merit . . . become ecumenical and universal."

Responding to real or anticipated pressure from black quarters, Hayden described himself in his own anthology of black poetry as "opposed to the chauvinistic and the doctrinaire." Significantly, he went on to say that he "sees no reason why a Negro poet should be limited to 'racial utterance' or to having his writing judged by standards different from those applied to the work of other poets."

Robert Earl Hayden was born in Detroit, Michigan, on 4 August 1913. He grew up in a poor neighborhood, later affectionately, though not without irony, named Paradise Valley by its inhabitants. In the 1920s, blacks, Jews, Germans, Italians, and some southern whites lived there; by the 1930s, with the black migration to the North, the neighborhood was inhabited solely by blacks.

The quality of life in Paradise Valley is best evoked in " 'Summertime and the Living . . .' " (*Selected Poems,* 1966). In contrast with the languid environs of George and Ira Gershwin's *Porgy and Bess,* the living, according to the poem, was anything but easy. The adult speaker recalls how "sunflowers gangled there sometimes / tough-stalked and bold / and like the vivid children there unplanned." He also remembers how, as a child, there were never any roses

Robert Hayden

. . . except when people died—
and no vacations for his elders,
so harshened after each unrelenting day
that they were shouting-angry.
But summer was, they said, the poor
   folks' time
of year. And he remembers
how they would sit on broken steps amid
The fevered tossings of the dusk, the
   dark,
wafting hearsay with funeral-parlor fans
or making evening solemn by
their quietness. . . .

Hayden's family life was riddled with emotional complication and trauma more than with poverty. His parents' marriage ended when he was still young. His mother placed him in the care of a childless neighborhood couple, then went to Buffalo, New York, in search of work. Robert remained with William and Sue Ellen Hayden permanently. He assumed their name, and they reared him with the love of actual parents. "All through my childhood my mother was a kind of vision, a kind of imaginary person, Hayden said, trying to describe the impression the visits of his real mother left on him. When he was a teenager, she returned, not merely to Detroit but to live with the Haydens; and then, when jealous conflict with Sue Ellen Hayden made that impossible, to the house next door.

Until Hayden was forty, he thought that he had been legally adopted by the Haydens, and that his original name was Robert Sheffey. He learned when applying for a passport that there never had been a legal adoption, although the

"old ones" had told him so; his legal name was Asa Bundy Sheffey. "You know, I am in many respects a divided person," Hayden told Gendron. Hayden's tendency to think of both sets of adults as parents and his prolonged living with divided loyalties and ambivalent feelings help one to understand the man. It also offers valuable insight into the sources of the dogged courage he displayed during his long career as a poet.

Learning to live amid violently contending demands as a youth may ultimately have helped Hayden to resist the pressures he faced as an adult from black nationalists to be a "black poet" and from white liberals to be a "spokesman for his race." Also, Gendron suggests that, from the circumstances of his youth, certain themes manifested themselves in his work: "The search for and definition of what constitutes identity, the significance of names, and the dilemma of a man caught between two worlds." Furthermore, rather than immobilizing his sense of self (though for periods this evidently occurred), his struggle with identity seems finally to have given him a penetrating and coherent sense of character. One wonders, after reading his poems about Malcolm X and Nat Turner, what sort of novelist he might have made.

Hayden was always extremely nearsighted. Limited to indoor play because of this and turned inward by the tensions at home, he spent most of his early years in solitary activity. Recalling the summer in late adolescence when he discovered modern poetry, he told Paul McCluskey: "Instead of playing baseball . . . or taking part in the other so-called 'normal' activities of the boys in my neighborhood, I would spend hours reading poetry and struggling to get my words down on paper. From that summer on, I continued working at poetry, hoping someday to be known as a poet." By the age of eighteen, he had taken the first step. A poem imitating Countee Cullen's "Heritage" appeared in *Abbott's Monthly*, a Chicago magazine.

Hayden attended Detroit City College (now Wayne State University) from 1932 to 1936 and majored in foreign languages. After college he joined the Federal Writers' Project of the Works Progress Administration (WPA) and until 1938 did research on the Underground Railroad in Michigan and the antislavery movement. He probably acquired his appetite for historical research from this stint with the WPA. In the 1940s, Hayden continued to read about the slave trade, plantation life, slave revolts, and the Underground Railroad; and this material, both as general background and as documentary detail, made the composition of his historical poems possible.

During his college years and afterward, Hayden also acted in Detroit and wrote for the stage. A play of his about Harriet Tubman, *Go Down, Moses*, was produced several times. He served as an arts critic for a black weekly, the *Michigan Chronicle*; and he was also tangentially involved in left-wing labor organizing in Detroit. At one mass meeting, he told Gendron, he was voted "the people's poet." "These Are My People" (*Heart-Shape in the Dust*, 1940), a long protest poem describing the poverty and idleness of blacks in America during the Great Depression, was "a great thing . . . in Chicago and Detroit" and was performed by groups.

From 1941 to 1946 Hayden did graduate work in English at the University of Michigan, where he studied with and was befriended by W. H. Auden. He received an M.A. in 1944. He had married Erma Morris, a musician and teacher, in 1940; and they had a child, Maia, two years later. In 1946 Hayden moved his family to Nashville, Tennessee, to teach at Fisk University. He spent twenty-two years at Fisk. Although the faculty was racially mixed, socialized together, and lived in an integrated enclave, he described (in his interview with Richard Layman) feeling limited in "the kind of experience we could have . . . the kind of things we could do." His daughter had to attend a segregated school. Also, there was a "provincialism in the South," frustrating to his and Erma's interest in avant-garde painting and dance.

Thus, although Fisk was a "pretty sophisticated place" and he felt he "could be of some service to the young people there," Hayden would have liked to return to the North. But it was impossible to find a position. In the years when he might have been at the height of his productive powers, he found his stamina drained away in "earning a living."

Although Hayden worked in relative obscurity, without significant popular or critical recognition, he did have his share of awards and honors, some of major importance. He won the Avery Hopwood Award for poetry at the University of Michigan in 1938 and 1942, and received a Rosenwald Fellowship in 1947 and a Ford Foundation grant to write and travel in Mexico in 1954. In 1966—the same year that Julius Lester recalls his being attacked as an Uncle Tom by students and writers at a writers' conference at Fisk—Hayden received a major international honor, the Grand Prize for Poetry in English at the First World Festival of Negro Arts; he was personally awarded the prize, for *A Ballad of Remembrance* (1962), by Leopold Senghor, the president of Senegal. In 1975 he was elected a fellow of the American Academy of Poets, and in 1976 he became the first African American to be appointed poetry consultant to the Library of Congress. From 1968 until his death in 1980 Hayden was a professor of

English at the University of Michigan at Ann Arbor.

Kaleidoscope, the word used by Hayden as the title of his anthology of black poetry, can be used in its adjectival form to describe Hayden's body of work. In terms of subjects and styles, his poetry is kaleidoscopic. While there are, of course, representative traits in his various styles and representative patterns of thought, the impression his work gives is of relative freedom from thematic or stylistic obsession. His poetic treatments convey a sensibility able to interact with new material in a fresh and inquisitive manner. In his poems Hayden moved through subjectivity and private anguish to a plane where the possibilities for objectivity, clarity, imaginative freedom, and artistic realization lay. Art for him involved language and design cleansed of the egocentric.

Hayden's philosophy of poetry was that it must not be limited by the personal or ethnic identity of the poet. Though inescapably rooted in these elements, poetry must rise to an order of creation that is broadly human and universally communicative. Yeats is the figure Hayden admired and pointed to in his effort to articulate his own goals. This is because Yeats was able to reconcile his private self with both his common humanity and the folk culture and myths of his ethnic group. "I think I always wanted to be a Negro poet . . . the same way Yeats is an Irish poet," Hayden said to Gendron. He then went on to speak of his intense response to Yeats's "Easter 1916" (in which Yeats speaks of "All changed, changed utterly") in the aftermath of the Detroit riots: ". . . that is the kind of poetry I want to write. Yes, it may reflect a certain kind of experience, a certain kind of awareness, but it's human rather than racial. It speaks to other human beings and it's not limited by time and place and not limited by the ethnic."

The manner in which these goals manifest themselves most prominently in Hayden's verse is the movement of his imagination away from the autobiographical and toward the impersonal. In "Summertime and the Living . . . ," for instance, Hayden referred to himself in the third person in order to obtain perspective and objectivity about his childhood. In "The Burly Fading One" (*Selected Poems*) he took the early work history of his foster father, William Hayden, and the experience of seeing an early photograph of him, and then enlarged the characterization to mythic outlines about a hard-living, hard-dying "bullyboy" American, Uncle Jed.

Hayden's poems are not necessarily factual. There is no reason, for example, to assume from "Free Fantasia: Tiger Flowers" (*Angle of Ascent,* 1975) that Hayden ran errands for St. Antoine Street prostitutes. Given the spirit of the poem, it is more reasonable to assume that it expresses an unchecked wish, an old man's fantasy drawn from the materials of childhood. Similarly, in " 'Mystery Boy' Looks for Kin in Nashville" (*Words in the Mourning Time*) it would be unfortunate for a reader to stop at the identification of Hayden's own conundrum about parentage. Far better if the projected emotions that visit and torment the boy from within trees and behind walls are perceived as universal to a parentless condition. And better still to view the boy as the man-child in any individual, so that the real subject of the poem can be seen as the psychic grotesquerie beneath the cliché search for identity." Hayden said in an address at the Library of Congress in 1977 that he thought of his poetry "as a way of coming to grips with reality, as a way of discovery and definition. It is a way of solving for the unknowns."

Hayden's commitment, then, was to a truth deeper than realism can provide; it was to a dimension of mind and cultural truth beyond naturalistic fact. And because, for him, that realistic surface was the means to a deeper end, he was a symbolist. Heavy reliance on autobiographical material will not carry a reader to the essence of his poems.

On the other hand, Pontheolla T. Williams's 1987 book on Hayden has brought to the surface a facet of his rejection of overtly personal poetry that may necessitate a reevaluation of his approach. From conversations with the poet and from notebooks he gave her, Williams has concluded that Hayden had troubling "homoerotic tendencies" and that his "preoccupation with his sexuality" is the veiled subject of several poems, such as "The Diver" (*Selected Poems*), "Sphinx," " 'Mystery Boy,' " and "The Mirages" (*Words in the Mourning Time*). If her conclusion is correct and Hayden's gnomic statements of psychic torment are "cleansed" treatments of his struggle with bisexuality, then the question reemerges as to whether the desire to avoid shameful feelings about sexuality or race is at the back of Hayden's aesthetic philosophy. The reader ought to remember, however, that the limitations of a poetic approach do not necessarily invalidate the approach; they may simply indicate limits. In Hayden's defense, it needs to be pointed out, moreover, that the very subject of shameful feelings about the body and their relation to the genesis of art is explored in "For a Young Artist" (*Angle of Ascent*) and "The Tattooed Man" (*American Journal*, 1982). Furthermore, even if he did not always choose to say what he was desperate about, Hayden persistently treated the fact of psychic desperation. "I am desperate still" he says in one of his last poems ("Letter," *American Journal*, 1982).

Swinging from a hazy romantic and proletarian vantage point in *Heart-Shape in the Dust* (1940) to an aesthetic allied with dense linguistic and formal effects in *The Lion and the Archer* (1948), Hayden's mature work did not appear in significant quantity until *A Ballad of Remembrance* in 1962. *A Ballad*, retaining and revising some of the poems from *The Lion and the Archer* and *Figures of Time* (1955), and abandoning all the apprentice work of *Heart-Shape*, presents the first consolidated view of Hayden's protean subjects and styles, as well as his rare devotion to craft. *Selected Poems* (1966) extends this impression with some new poems as well as a thoughtful grouping of his previous work.

After *Selected Poems*, Hayden continued to evolve, responding both to the times and to his internal rhythms, the former tendency somewhat more prominent in his volume of writings from the 1960s, *Words in the Mourning Time* (1970), which contains a poem about Malcolm X and the long title poem responding to the war, riot, assassination, and racial militance of that decade. Hayden's volumes since then— *The Night-Blooming Cereus* (1972), the eight new poems in *Angle of Ascent* (1975), and *American Journal* (1978 and 1982)—reflect a poet entering his seventh decade and coming to terms with his deeply aesthetic nature and his love of art and beauty for their own sake. They are roughly comparable with Yeats's devotion to "monuments of unaging intellect" in his Byzantium poems in *The Tower* (1928).

Chronological development is not the soundest basis on which to discuss Hayden's work. There is neither the set of philosophical preoccupations nor the persistent subject matter to warrant serial study. Because he was ever responsive to new subjects and to the truths intrinsic to these subjects, it is in terms of style and technique—and then only in terms of limited clusters of subjects and themes—that the kaleidoscopic Hayden yields to broad generalization. In "Kodachromes of the Island" (*Words in the Mourning Time*), Hayden concludes a descriptive poem about a Mexican island with the following lines:

> Alien, at home—as always
> everywhere—I roamed
> the cobbled island,
>
> and thought of Yeats,
> his passionate search for
> a theme. Sought mine.

The roving quality, "alien, at home . . . / everywhere," reveals a basic quality of Hayden's nature: he was a peripatetic modern with a lingering sense of the past, but ever open to the new, to the flow of the contemporary.

Hayden wrote in a spectrum of styles that range from the severely economical to the highly decorative. Toward one end of the spectrum his work is typified by the qualities of concreteness, conciseness, and clarity of effect. Hayden wrote in the concrete and was not usually in agreement with Wallace Stevens that "Life consists of propositions about life." Hayden's lines may rise to the reflective and the abstract, but abstractive lyricism is not the plane on which he usually created. At times, in fact, Hayden gravitated toward the poetics of imagism: "dry," "hard" lines without sentiment or generalization; total dependence on image for emotional and intellectual content; *haiku*-like concentration. "The Moose Wallow," "Smelt Fishing," "Kodachromes of the Island," and "Gulls" fall into this category. More commonly, though, Hayden's brief lines and clear effects have a sensuous and rhythmic litheness, such as is found in "The Night-Blooming Cereus."

Another of his styles relied on a heavier application of language in order to achieve the effect of dense, sensuous imagery. This is Hayden's tropical side, reflecting acute sensory equipment and a love of rare, colorful language. "I must confess that I like the exotic, and I go in for exoticism," he told Gendron. Always he had to "tone it down" because he loved to "deal in exotic textures" and "atmospheric words." Yet in "The Diver" (*Selected Poems*) and "Market" (*A Ballad of Remembrance*) he does not tone it down; he lavishes it on like a painter going from paintbrush to palette knife; and the result, especially in the latter, Mexican poem, is a virtuoso performance. The poet becomes utterer, namer, creator of reality:

> Ragged boys
> lift sweets, haggle
> for venomgreen
> and scarlet gelatins.
> A broken smile
> dandies its weedy
> cigarette
> over papayas too ripe
> and pyramids
> of rotting oranges.
> Turkeys like feather-
> duster flowers
> lie trussed in bunchy smother.

Occasionally Hayden wrote in a style that was still more elaborately ornamented, which he liked to describe as "baroque." This decorative, denser style was used when he treated disturbing material; it served both to reflect and to explore the tension between an ornamental surface and a dark problem, between an embel-

lished defense and a private or social pathology. It appears in "Witch Doctor" (*A Ballad of Remembrance*). It is present also in "A Ballad of Remembrance," in which Hayden describes the Zulu parade of blacks that was a feature of the Mardi Gras and tries to convey the tension of their lives, balanced between gaudy spectacle and underlying racial nightmare.

In the 1960s and 1970s Hayden's poems showed less attraction to ornate diction and elaborate effects. The spirit of imagism prevailed over the rococo temptation. His verse became sinuous, colloquial. Colorful subjects—objects of art or beautiful flowers—satisfied the need for "exoticism" that was formerly satisfied by densely wrought presentations.

Hayden often wrote poems about people—ballads or character poems such "Unidentified Flying Object," "Aunt Jemima of the Ocean Waves," and "The Dream" (all in *Words in the Mourning Time*). The need in these poems to render the speech or thoughts of his characters led him to refine a technique that is of special interest. Widespread throughout Hayden's verse, this technique is the careful blending of a narrator's voice with a folk character. The narrator's voice in these instances carefully avoids learned diction, so as to blend imperceptibly with the speech or consciousness of the character. The poet is able to enlarge his control over mood, setting, or narrative point of view without overshadowing the protagonist. James Weldon Johnson in the preface to *The Book of American Negro Poetry* (1922) says that a Negro poet needs "a form that is freer and larger than dialect, but which will still hold the racial flavor. . . ." If we add "regional" to "racial," we can understand how Hayden, by means of this technique, enlarged the field of his materials and was able to write about folk culture and local color anywhere.

An unusual philosophical influence on Hayden should be examined before discussing his themes and subjects. This is Hayden's Baha'i faith and his allusions to the prophet Bahaullah in some of his poems. Hayden and his wife became Baha'is in the early 1940s, when Hayden was attending the University of Michigan. He was the poetry editor for the Baha'i magazine,

World Order. Some of his poems—for example, "Full Moon" and " 'From the Corpse Wood-piles, from the Ashes' "—contain references to Bahaullah as "Him" or "The Glorious One" or the "exiled One." "Words in the Mourning Time," part III, in *Angle of Ascent,* contains the most explicit treatment of Bahaullah as a rec-onciling and redeeming figure for our age:

> I bear Him witness now—
> mystery Whose major clues are the heart of
>   man,
>   the mystery of God:
>
>   Bahá'u'lláh:
> Logos, poet, cosmic hero, surgeon, architect
>   of our hope of peace,
>
>   wronged, exiled One,
> chosen to endure what agonies of
>   knowledge, what
>   auroral dark
>   bestowals of truth
> vision power anguish for our future's sake.

As a Baha'i, Hayden explained to Layman, he obtained important—perhaps crucial—spiritual resources: for one, a belief in "the essential one-ness of all people" and the "basic unity of all religions," and, for another, a belief that "the work of the artist is . . . a form of service to mankind" and "a kind of worship." John Hatcher argues in his critical study *From the Auroral Darkness* (1984) that Hayden's Baha'i faith "confirmed and advanced" the poet's most powerful themes and gave Hayden's oeuvre "its overall significance." On the other hand, other critics have argued that Hayden's immersion in the universalist content of Bahaullah's message may sometimes have obscured from Hayden the fact that to Western readers his faith seems not so much humane and unifying as strange and sectarian. This has involved Hayden, they feel, in at least the appearance of a contradic-tory stance, since he conceived and described his poetry as "opposed to the chauvinistic and the doctrinaire."

Although his Baha'i faith provided Hayden stable ideals to live by, his poetry itself deals with fluctuations of viewpoint, ambivalences explored, uncertainties succumbed to, despair lived to the bottom. In his poetry the self lives in conflict or in dialectical relation with higher truths. Finite identity and material reality strain against imagination and transcendental longing. Resolution is never more than partial, respite never more than temporary, equilibrium attainable only by maintaining the terms of the struggle. When pursued directly, the dream of unity brings dissolution of the self. At the same time, resignation to the prison of the self and the material realm is a denial of one's spiritual imaginative nature. One's ultimate responsibil-ity is to keep one's powers alive through the struggle with self and God.

In "Veracruz" (*A Ballad of Remembrance*) the terms of the struggle are "reality" and "dream." Under the term *reality* are allusions to the finiteness of the self and to poverty, his-tory, power; under the term *dream* are the plea-sures of the senses and the flesh, the impulse to merge with the boundless natural world, and the problem of romantic illusion.

In "The Diver" (*Selected Poems*) the impulse to yield to death, to slough off the will, is at first irresistible. Through the diver's descent, merging with nature is simulated. Echoing John Keats's "Ode to a Nightingale," the diver-poet finds release for his imagination as he sinks "through easeful / azure." At once chill and floridly delicious, his descent—his death wish—opens a private psychological realm that is dis-orienting but has its own subaqueous logic. Reminiscent of " 'Mystery Boy' Looks for Kin in Nashville," the diver imagines a "hide and / seek of laughing I faces." He then declares:

>   I yearned to
> find those hidden
> ones, to fling aside
> the mask and call to them,
> yield to rapturous
> whisperings? . . .

The "hidden ones" (dead family members? forbidden lovers?) draw him into their circle. He yearns to "have / done with self and / every dinning / vain complexity." Yet regression is not in the service of the ego if the "hidden ones" prevail and he succumbs. He flees "the numbing / kisses" that he craves. "Reflex of life-wish" reasserts itself. A "measured rise" begins.

The subject of "A Ballad of Remembrance" is not the desire for unity either with nature or with the past. Rather, it is a descent into the nightmare of southern racism and the perversion of imagination that such a milieu exacts. Social institutions, reaching back into the "shadow" and "blood" of the past, shape the highly charged, subjective setting, a Walpurgis Night of hysteria, menace, confusion, and hallucination. The poet is overwhelmed by a Mardi Gras spectacle. The parade floats, costumes, and tawdry shops possess him as though the boundaries of his ego were shattered, and events move through rather than past him. Unable to separate subject from object, he is victimized by monstrous choices, threatened with monstrous metamorphoses. Finally the poet is "released from the hoodoo"—the black magic—"of that dance" by the arrival of a friend who is "meditative, ironic, / richly human," (The friend is identified as Mark Van Doren.) The terrifying metamorphoses cease; integrated selfhood returns.

The transience of subjective "dreams"—indeed, the transient and dreamlike nature of life—begins to emerge with more prominence in the poems Hayden published in the 1970s. Many of these poems respond to the passage of time and may be usefully thought of as the art of old age. The title poem in *The Night-Blooming Cereus*, by describing the ephemeral beauty of the nocturnal cactus flower, evokes the terrible poignancy and "plangency" of life itself. "The Point" (*American Journal*) speaks of "land's end," where "sound and river come / together, flowing to the sea." In golden elegiac light the poet contemplates "all for a moment . . . inscribed / on brightness" "like memories in the mind of God." Hayden's principal means of dealing with the flow of time and the ebbing away of life is art, even if, as with Yeats, it is art "of what is past, or passing, or to come."

The high point of Hayden's verse about art as a means of redemption from time is "The Peacock Room" (*The Night-Blooming Cereus*). An old man visits a historical room exhibited in a museum. The room, with extravagant peacocks painted on the paneled walls, was commissioned by a wealthy English shipowner to set off a James Whistler painting. The old man is familiar with the room because it was moved to Detroit from England in 1919 and a friend of his in the 1960s told him about attending a party there when she was twelve. Because the friend is dead, personal and historical associations flood his mind. He is filled with a sense of loss and a heightened awareness of time; but there is also stirred within him an uncanny appreciation of the survival of the room. The room becomes a symbol of art. It generates meditations about time, history, art, imagination, and the nature of reality. Yeats's "Among School Children" is an influence, especially in the stanzas in which a woman's anecdote about her youth is recalled. Yet this in no way diminishes the level of achievement of the poem, nor the sense that Hayden is able, with some frequency, to compose poems of major or near-major rank.

The poem begins with a statement that art is long and life is short, and follows with the question "Which is crueller / life or art?" The cruelty of life is obvious, but the cruelty of art is that it mocks man's impermanence. This is one of the major themes of the poem. Another theme is the aggressiveness that always underlies artistic activity. And a third is that "reality" and "art," even when they move in opposite directions, are never entirely disparate. Even an effete, ornamental art, which the room represents, has some of the savagery of the real.

Hayden is best known for his historical poems. In 1941, while reading Stephen Vincent Benét's *John Brown's Body* (1928), he was strongly affected by a passage in which Benét confesses his limitations:

Oh, black-skinned epic, epic with the black
    spear,
I cannot sing you, having too white a
    heart,
And yet, some day, a poet will rise to sing
    you

325

And sing you with such truth and
    mellowness. . . .

At this time Hayden, nearly thirty, conceived
the ambition to be the poet to sing the history
of black Americans—to end the neglect of their
past, correct the stereotypes, and bring the in-
extinguishable urge of black men and women
for freedom into current consciousness. He
planned to write poems about slavery and the
Civil War and a sonnet series about outstanding
antislavery figures. Regrettably, only part of
this plan was carried out. By 1942 enough poems were finished for him to submit them under the title *The Black Spear* and to win the
Hopwood competition at the University of
Michigan for the second time. As Reginald Gibbons has been able to illustrate by publishing
some of these poems in *TriQuarterly,* they both
"compel attention as finished work" and "point
to an early impulse that Hayden later refined
. . . toward framing the injustice of racial discrimination explicitly in his poems." One can
see as well early experiments with the character poem technique and the early stages of
"Runagate Runagate" (*Selected Poems*).

The finest of these poems is "Middle Passage," published in various periodicals in the
mid 1940s and appearing in final form in *A Ballad of Remembrance.* The primary historical
sources for the poem are Brantz Mayer's *Adventures of an African Slaver* (1928) and the
second chapter of Muriel Rukeyser's biography
Willard Gibbs (1942), in which the story of the
Amistad mutiny and the legal battle that followed it are narrated. The literary influence is
Benét's *John Brown's Body.*

The marvel of "Middle Passage" is its ability
to evoke the entire period of the Atlantic slave
trade, yet achieve a highly unified effect. From
research in actual documents, Hayden creates
log entries, court depositions, and trial testimony, all of which give the work its air of historical truth. Careful coordination of this "documentary" material to sustain the themes of
inhumanity, greed, moral disease, and blindness is one of the sources of the unity of the
poem; the other is the consistent manner in
which this material is handled. The moral

bankruptcy of the white "Christians" is allowed to reveal itself. Although the poet selects
what they say, he does not comment actively.
Documentary objectivity with a reliance on
dramatic irony is his major strategy.

The first part comprises a mosaic of the
physical and spiritual torments endemic to the
slave trade. The conditions described support
the opening assertion that the middle passage
is a "voyage through death" or, in spiritual and
literary terms, a descent into hell. Illness, con-
finement, squalor, and suicidal despair afflict
the Africans; fear of disease and rebellion, guilt,
desperate prayer, and sexual degeneracy beset
the whites. The names of ships that the poet
intersperses between sections of the poem suggest the pervasiveness of these conditions.

Multiple voices are employed to yield both
scope and immediacy. First there is the narrator's omniscient voice, which frames the narrative and offers a moral vision of the action;
then the alarmed journal notations—concrete,
concise, yet rich in psychological atmosphere—
of an officer or crew member; the narrator's adaptation of a disembodied voice of conscience
follows next (other italicized passages differ
from this one); then the hymns, double-spaced,
so that they seem to drift mournfully over the
scene as they drift across the page; and last the
deluded prayers of crew members asking "safe
passage to our vessels bringing / heathen souls
unto Thy chastening." The first part concludes
with a court deposition revealing the disintegration of authority and the brutal lusts aboard
the *Bella J.* The fire that envelops the ship symbolizes the fires of sinfulness much as the oph-
thalmia on another ship has overtones of the
traders' moral blindness.

The second part, using the reminiscences of
a retired slaver, enlarges the canvas to include
the complicity of African kings. The simplicity
of the second part provides respite from the
complex structure of part I. Part II also conveys
the moral imperturbability of the whites, even
when privileged with hindsight about their "adventures in the slave trade."

Having begun by describing the middle passage as a "voyage through death / to life upon
these shores," the poem in part III reaches for

some sustaining actuality, some affirmative human basis, upon which life on these shores will be possible—not only for the survivors of the crossing but also for succeeding generations. Here the moral imagination of the poet exerts a more pronounced influence. Although the use of testimony from the trial of the *Amistad* mutineers returns to the documentary method, the narrator's shaping moral vision obtrudes more strongly both in the opening section, which speaks of the "dark ships" as "shuttles in the rocking loom of history," and in the portrayal of the leader of the *Amistad* mutiny as a symbol or icon for the "immortal human wish, / the timeless will" of men to be free.

Charles T. Davis writes about the "mystical emergence of freedom from circumstances that appall and degrade" in Hayden's history poems; and it is this very mystical sense of the inevitable assertion of manhood that Hayden tries to compress into his few words about the leader of the rebellion. In the poem Cinquez is not developed as an individual. He is a "life that transfigures many lives"; and with his efforts to gain freedom, life on the "actual shore" can begin.

In "Runagate Runagate" (*Selected Poems*) Harriet Tubman rises like Cinquez from the "anguish" and "power" of her people. "Runagate" is conceived also as a historical panorama, in this case of the Underground Railroad. As a collage of slave voices and verse, snippets of song, ads for runaways, and wanted posters for Tubman, it is somewhat reminiscent of John Dos Passos's sketches of prominent Americans in *U.S.A.* (1937). The title "Runagate" derives from an archaic form of the word "runaway." The first part is self-consciously literary, unable to escape the rhythms of an "inspired" tone. Richest and most memorable are the instances of folk idiom and imagination in part II, in which the "freedom train" of the spirituals becomes fused with the idea of crossing over to the North:

> *Midnight Special on a sabre track*
> *movering*
> *movering,*
> *first stop Mercy and the last Hallelujah.*

We see this also in the final lines:

> Come ride-a my train
> Mean mean mean to be free.

One passage captures beautifully the whispered tensions of nocturnal flight:

> And this was the way of it, brethren
>   brethren,
> way we journeyed from Can't to Can.
> Moon so bright and no place to hide,
> the cry up and the patterollers riding,
> hound dogs belling in bladed air.
> And fear starts a-murbling, Never make it,
> we'll never make it. *Hush that now,*
> and she's turned upon us, levelled pistol
> glinting in the moonlight:
> Dead folks can't jaybird talk, she says;
> you keep on going now or die, she says.

Because it is about the leader of the 1831 slave revolt in Virginia, "The Ballad of Nat Turner" (*A Ballad of Remembrance*) was grouped by Hayden with his other historical poems; yet it might just as appropriately be grouped with poems about religious experience, such as "Bahá'u'lláh in the Garden of Ridwan." Narrated in the first person, it is a historical character poem in which Turner describes his quest in the Dismal Swamp of Virginia for a vision of divine approval. At first, visions of death visit the tormented wanderer:

> And came at length to livid trees
>   where Ibo warriors
> hung shadowless, turning in wind
>   that moaned like Africa,
> their belltongue bodies dead, their eyes
>   alive with the anger deep
> in my own heart.

As he wanders further,

> . . . wild things gasped and scuffled in
>   the seething night; shapes
> of evil writhed upon the air.

Finally Turner experiences an Old Testament vision of a war of angels, patterned on Ezekiel. With Miltonic detail he sees "angels at war / with one another, angels in dazzling /

battle." He describes "the shock of wing on wing and sword / on sword," and how he saw

> . . . many of
> those mighty beings waver,
> waver and fall, go streaking down
>   into swamp water, and the water
> hissed and steamed and bubbled.

In the end "the conqueror faces . . . were like mine." Free of his burden of doubt, reassured of his divine mission, he returns to the "blazing fields, to the humbleness," and bides his time.

Williams observes that "although . . . Hayden's mind ventures backward over time" in his history poems, they "invariably close with a statement or action that points forward." Cinquez makes life upon these shores possible. Harriet Tubman's poem reverberates with the unceasing sounds of the freedom train: "Mean mean mean to be free." Nat Turner has his revolt still before him. And in the one as-yet-unmentioned poem of this group, the sonnet commemorating Frederick Douglass, the great fighter is envisioned as a living influence that flows into the present. Williams puts it well: "The poet emphasizes that the dead hero is still a vital force, and the reality his poem ostensibly commemorates has its full realization in the future. . . . In the final analysis the poem celebrates not a man who has been but a man still coming into being."

Besides poems about nineteenth-century antislavery figures, Hayden wrote other character poems. About known figures of the modern world (Bessie Smith, Malcolm X) and unknown figures from strange corners of black life (a religious charlatan, a circus Aunt Jemima), these poems exemplify the fertile conceptions and high degree of realization of Hayden's work. Tone is the quintessential ingredient, the crowning grace, of some; in others a bold use of syntax or unusual verbal texture is the facilitating technique.

Dramatic or narrative elements also figure in some poems. A dialogue in "Aunt Jemima of the Ocean Waves" (*Words in the Mourning Time*) between the low-key speaker and "Aunt Jemima" brings out the pathos in the downhill life of the "Sepia High Stepper" of the 1920s. In "El-Hajj Malik El-Shabazz" (*Words in the Mourning Time*), the phases or "masks" of Malcolm's development from "Home Boy" and "Dee-troit Red" to his "final metamorphosis" in Mecca are narrated with a brevity that captures his abbreviated lifespan.

"Homage to the Empress of the Blues" (*A Ballad of Remembrance*) employs a particular syntactic structure to describe the origin of Bessie Smith's blues and the ironic splendor of her stage presentation. Each sentence begins with a "because" clause that is long and highly descriptive of the background of black life or the blues tradition that has risen from it; and each sentence ends with an independent clause that gives the result, the triumphant éclat with which Bessie comes out on stage:

> Because there was a man somewhere in a
>   candystripe silk shirt
> gracile and dangerous as a jaguar and
>   because
> a woman moaned
> for him in sixty-watt gloom and mourned
>   him
>   faithless love
> twotiming love oh love oh careless
>   aggravating love,
>
> she came out on the stage in yards of
>   pearls,
>   emerging like
> a favorite scenic view, flashed her golden
>   smile
>   and sang.

In the first sentence old blues, such as W. C. Handy's "Careless Love Blues," and in the second sentence poverty, persecution, and fantasy are defined as the formative elements of her art. This art, the poem goes on to say, involves a shared sense of experience with her audience and a communal celebration of the triumph of the self over circumstance.

The promiscuous woman who is, at the same time, an inspired singer in the church choir is the subject of "Mourning Poem for the Queen on Sunday" (*A Ballad of Remembrance*). Spoken in the idiom of the black church, as if by a chorus of mourners, the poem approaches the circumstances of the singer's death (she was murdered, presumably for two-timing) with a high ironic tone, half mock-lament, half genuine dismay. Infinitely wry, the poem pivots teasingly on the refrain, "Who would have thought / she'd end that way?" Yet the void in spiritual terms is real, even if the adulation of church members has always contained lurking suspicions about her. The righteous and the sinner alike are losers:

> Oh who and oh who will sing Jesus down
> to help with struggling and doing without
>   and
>   being colored
> all through blue Monday?
> Till way next Sunday?

Bewitching artifice is the theme of "Witch Doctor" (*A Ballad of Remembrance*), a poem that describes a day in the life of a religious charlatan. Included is all the drapery of his mystique—the chic surfaces of his style of life, the tailored movements and calculated effects on his congregation. Not only does his mystique answer the hunger of his followers for some fantasied being who is opulent, erotic, and unreal, but it also feeds the preacher's own "outrageous" narcissism. Mutual fantasy, Hayden seems to say, is the basis for the rapport; manipulation, the unspoken formula that yields "euphoria" for the members and "mystery and lucre" for their leader. A poetry that moves toward the conjurer's art captures this obscure pact. Present-tense verbs and participles usher the "prophet" through the decadent textures of his day. Exotic belongings fill his artificial world—mirrors everywhere, a cinquecento stair, a lilac limousine with black leopard-skin interior, the smoke of Egyptian cigarettes. Though it is repellent and luridly funny, the spell on the reader (like the spell on the congregation) is seductive. It taps some deep vein of delusional need and is as suggestive about the poet's temptation by the magical powers of language as it is about the magnetism of the prophet of Israel Temple. "Witch Doctor," like "Mourning Poem

for the Queen of Sunday," is among Hayden's perfect poems.

As Hayden's interest was aroused by a variety of people, so, too, did diverse places engage him as poetic subjects. Earlier a set of lines from "Kodachromes of the Island" ("Alien, at home—as always / everywhere—") was introduced to suggest the breadth of his subject matter. In discussing a final group of poems about places, a perspective intrinsic to these lines can now be brought into greater definition. Sometimes alienation defines the quality of an experience for Hayden; more often estrangement and "at homeness" coexist.

On the one hand Hayden confronted a changing and frightening world as a lonely modern; on the other hand he was able to perceive emotional and intellectual connections with a new environment. This ability to discern meaningful relations in ostensibly alien places derived from his sense of continuity between past and present.

In "Zeus over Redeye" (*Words in the Mourning Time*), a poem about a visit to the Redstone Arsenal in Alabama, a sense of alienation and dread predominates; yet even here the past offers a reference point for his fears. Myths of the Greek gods (for whom the rockets are named) are the only analogue for the "new mythologies," the new powers and gods breeding in the desert. The rockets are "totems of our fire-breathing age" and the grounds of the arsenal are "terra guarded like / a sacred phallic grove."

In another poem in the same volume, "On Lookout Mountain," the poet visits a Civil War battleground in Tennessee. He thinks of "Union soldiers struggling up / the crackling mountainside," where now "Sunday alpinists / pick views and souvenirs." "A world away," he remarks, scions of that earlier climb are falling—in Vietnam. And because of Vietnam and the racial warfare at home, he refers to the Civil War battle as "dubious victory."

In the best of these poems in which the past contributes to the imaginative rendering of the present, it is the poet's psychic refraction of the past that colors the present, not formal history or intellectual tradition.

329

In "Locus" and "Tour 5" (*A Ballad of Remembrance*), this Hawthornean aspect of Hayden's imagination achieves its highest expression. The southern landscape, with its psychic subsoil of Indians, slaves, bloody war, and aristocratic dreams, becomes a "soulscape . . . of warring shades" that lacerates the bright present.

Having begun with "Locus," let us conclude with "Tour 5," a poem emblematic of the nature of the poetic intelligence that has been suggested: roving yet not deracinated; alive to the luminous present yet inescapably haunted by, caught up with the harsh chromatics and shadowy phantoms of the past. The title derives from a guidebook description of a contemporary route to Jackson, Mississippi. The poem itself includes references to the "old Natchez Trace," which Hayden described (in the McCluskey interview) as "originally an Indian trail going from Nashville . . . down through Mississippi and beyond," "a dangerous and sinister road, used by escaped criminals, highwaymen, murderers." More than simply informational, this background emerges in the poem as a group of associations that is symbolic of a dangerously angry state.

The speaker and his party are on an auto trip through the autumn "blazonry of farewell scarlet / and recessional gold." Past the car window scenes move—"cedar groves," "static villages" with Indian names. But with an inevitability linked with the tragic history of the South, the holiday mood is dampened. As they "buy gas and ask directions of a rawboned man," his eyes "revile" them "as the enemy." Suddenly there is internal difference. Physical journey becomes mental journey; the festive enjoyment ends:

> . . . Shrill gorgon
> silence breathes behind his taut civility
>
> and in the ever-tautening
> air that's dark for us despite the Indian
> summer glow. We drive on, following
> the route of phantoms, highwaymen, of
>   slaves
> and armies.

Children, wordless and remote,
wave at us from kindling porches.

Ancestral wounds have begun to bleed. An everyday event has punctured the most human of pleasures. The cruel southern past seeps into a final vision of the present:

> . . . And now
> the land is flat for miles, the landscape
>   lush,
> metallic, flayed; its brightness harsh as
> bloodstained swords.

Descriptive, symbolic, human—this is vintage Hayden. A surface is beautifully rendered; an internal anguish is subtly conveyed; a vision of the inner nature of things emerges with detached and passionate intensity. Hayden has brought us more fully and humanly into the world. That was his purpose, his calling.

Selected Bibliography

PRIMARY WORKS

POETRY

Heart-Shape in the Dust. Detroit: Falcon Press, 1940.
The Lion and the Archer. With Myron O'Higgins. Counterpoise series, no. 1. Nashville, Tenn: Hemphill Press, 1948.
Figure of Time. Counterpoise series, no. 3. Nashville, Tenn.: Hemphill Press, 1955.
A Ballad of Remembrance. London: Paul Breman, 1962.
Selected Poems. New York: October House, 1966.
Words in the Mourning Time. New York: October House, 1970.
The Night-Blooming Cereus. Heritage series, no. 20. London: Paul Breman, 1972.
Angle of Ascent: New and Selected Poems. New York: Liveright, 1975. (Contains poems Hayden wished to collect from previous volumes.)
American Journal. Taunton, Mass.: Effendi Press, 1978; New York: Liveright, 1982. (The 1982 edition contains ten poems not included in the earlier edition.)

COLLECTED WORKS

Collected Prose. Edited by Frederick Glaysher. Ann Arbor: University of Michigan Press, 1984. (Contains Layman, McCluskey, and O'Brien interviews listed below.)
Collected Poems. Edited by Frederick Glaysher. New York: Liveright, 1985.

ROBERT HAYDEN

LETTERS

Nicholas, Xavier, ed. "Robert Hayden and Michael Harper: A Literary Friendship." *Callaloo* 17: 980–1016 (Autumn 1994).

OTHER WORKS

Kaleidoscope: Poems by American Negro Poets. Edited by Hayden. New York: Harcourt, Brace, and World, 1967.

Afro-American Literature: An Introduction. With David J. Burrows and Frederick R. Lapides. New York: Harcourt Brace Jovanovich, 1971.

SECONDARY WORKS

BIOGRAPHICAL AND CRITICAL STUDIES

Chrisman, Robert. "Go Down, Moses: An Introduction." *Michigan Quarterly Review* 37: 782–802 (Fall 1998).

Davis, Charles T. "Robert Hayden's Use of History." In *Modern Black Poets: A Collection of Critical Essays.* Edited by Donald B. Gibson. Englewood Cliffs, N.J.: Prentice-Hall, 1973. Pp. 96–111.

Faulkner, Howard. " 'Transformed by Steeps of Flight': The Poetry of Robert Hayden." *CLA Journal* 21:282–91 (1977).

Fetrow, Fred M. "Robert Hayden's 'Frederick Douglass': Form and Meaning in a Modern Sonnet." *CLA Journal* 17:79–84 (1973).

———. " 'Middle Passage': Robert Hayden's Anti-Epic." *CLA Journal* 22:304–18 (1979).

———. "Portraits and Personae: Characterization in the Poetry of Robert Hayden." In *Black American Poets Between Worlds, 1940–1960.* Edited by R. Baxter Miller. Knoxville: University of Tennessee Press, 1986.

———. *Robert Hayden.* Boston: Twayne, 1984.

Galler, David. "Three Recent Volumes." *Poetry* 110:267–269 (1967). (Contains a review of *Selected Poems.*)

Gendron, Dennis Joseph. "Robert Hayden: A View of His Life and Development as a Poet." Ph.D. diss., University of North Carolina at Chapel Hill, 1975. (A pioneering dissertation on Hayden's life and development; includes the transcript of a four-day interview with the poet in March 1974.)

Gibbons, Reginald. "Robert Hayden in the 1940's." *TriQuarterly* 62:177–86 (Winter 1985).

Glaysher, Frederick, "Re-Centering: The Turning of the Tide and Robert Hayden." *World Order* 17:9–17 (Summer 1983).

Greenberg, Robert M. "Robert Hayden." In *American Writers.* Supp. 2, pt. 1. Edited by A. Walton Litz. New York: Scribners, 1981. Pp. 361–83. (Includes detailed analyses of several poems, in particular "Veracruz," "A Ballad of Remembrance," and "The Peacock Room.")

Harper, Michael S. "Angle of Ascent." *New York Times Book Review,* February 22, 1976. Pp. 34–35.

———. "Remembering Robert Hayden." *Michigan Quarterly Review* 21:182–88 (Winter 1982).

Hatcher, John. *From the Auroral Darkness: The Life and Poetry of Robert Hayden.* Oxford: George Ronald, 1984.

Jackson, Blyden. Foreword to *Robert Hayden: A Critical Analysis of His Poetry,* by Pontheolla T. Williams. Urbana and Chicago: University of Illinois Press, 1987.

Lester, Julius. "Words in the Mourning Time." *New York Times Book Review,* January 24, 1971, pp. 4–5, 22.

Lewis, Richard O. "A Literary-Psychoanalytic Interpretation of Robert Hayden's 'Market.' " *Negro American Literature Forum* 9:21–24 (Spring 1975).

Mullen, Harryette, and Stephen Yense. "Theme & Variations on Robert Hayden's Poetry." *The Antioch Revue* 55:160–74 (Spring 1977).

Novak, Michael Paul. "Meditative, Ironic, Richly Human: The Poetry of Robert Hayden." *Midwest Quarterly* 15:276–85 (Spring 1974).

O'Sullivan, Maurice J., Jr. "The Mask of Allusion in Robert Hayden's 'The Diver.' " *CLA Journal* 17:85–92 (1973).

Pool, Rosey. "Robert Hayden: Poet Laureate." *Negro Digest* 15:39–43 (1966).

Post, Constance J. "Image and Idea in the Poetry of Robert Hayden." *CLA Journal* 20:146–75 (1976).

Rice, William. "The Example of Robert Hayden." *The New Criterion* 8, no. 3: 42–45 (November 1989).

Rodman, Selden. "Negro Poets." *New York Times Book Review,* October 10, 1948, p. 27. (Includes a review of *The Lion and the Archer.*)

Turco, Lewis. "*Angle of Ascent:* The Poetry of Robert Hayden." *Michigan Quarterly Review* 16:199–219 (Spring 1977).

Williams, Pontheolla T. *Robert Hayden: A Critical Analysis of His Poetry.* Urbana and Chicago: University of Illinois Press, 1987.

Williams, Wilburn, Jr. "Covenant of Timelessness & Time: Symbolism & History in Robert Hayden's *Angle of Ascent.*" *Massachusetts Review* 18:731–49 (Winter 1977).

Wright, John S. "Homage to a Mystery Boy." *The Georgia Review* 36:904–11 (Winter 1982).

BIBLIOGRAPHY

Xavier, Nicholas. "Robert Hayden." *Bulletin of Bibliography* 42:140–53 (1985).

INTERVIEWS

Gendron, Dennis Joseph. "Robert Hayden: A View of His Life and Development as a Poet." Ph.D. diss., University of North Carolina at Chapel Hill, 1975. Pp. 150–234.

Layman, Richard. "Robert Hayden." In *Conversations with Writers.* Vol. 1. Edited by Matthew Bruccoli, C. E. Frazer Clark Jr., et al. Detroit: Gale Research, 1977. Pp. 156–79.

McCluskey, Paul. "Robert Hayden, the Poet and His

Art: A Conversation." In *How I Write/1.* Edited by Judson Philips and Lawson Carter. New York: Harcourt Brace Jovanovich, 1972. Pp. 133–13.

O'Brien, John. "Robert Hayden." In *Interviews with Black Writers.* Edited by John O'Brien. New York: Liveright, 1973. Pp. 106–23.

CHESTER HIMES
(1909–1984)

ALAN M. WALD

WHEN CHESTER BOMAR Himes launched his career as a novelist by publishing *If He Hollers Let Him Go* in 1945, he was quickly typecast by reviewers as an exponent of protest literature in the Richard Wright school of hard-boiled naturalism. The label stuck and occurs in most of the first scholarly books and essays that treat post-World War II African American fiction. Yet Himes lived another four decades to witness the rebirth of his reputation as an author through assorted incarnations.

The most noteworthy came in the late 1950s, when Himes achieved acclaim in his newly adopted country of France as the skillful craftsman of violently surreal detective thrillers set in Harlem, such as *For Love of Imabelle* (1957). In the 1960s, these popularly oriented works won a fresh audience in the United States, assisted by the notoriety of *Pinktoes* (1961), a ribald satire about interracial sex. In the 1970s, with the appearance of his two-volume autobiography, Himes was aggressively championed by a new generation of African American writers such as John A. Williams and Ishmael Reed. They embraced the full sweep of his writings, charging that Himes had been the victim of neglect by the literary establishment due to his articulation of disquieting truths about the psychological effects of racism.

The Crucible of Biography

Conventional mappings of Himes's literary life have also tended to characterize his first five novels as autobiographically based "serious" fiction, followed by a spate of nine or so commercially motivated mass-market novels completed under financial duress. Himes himself bolstered this view by volunteering remarks in interviews emphasizing the formulaic aspect of his Harlem detective fiction. Yet recent scholarship points to cogent elements of continuity throughout his fifty-year career.

Many of Himes's short stories from the early 1930s are in the same hard-boiled mystery-thriller genre as his works in midcareer; for example, "He Knew," a story in the December 1932 issue of *Abbott's Monthly and Illustrated News*, features a team of rugged African American policemen who augur the two detectives in his Harlem series, Coffin Ed Johnson and Grave Digger Jones. Biographers Edward Margolies and Michel Fabre have noticed that Himes's first novel, *If He Hollers Let Him Go*, was incipiently visualized as a mystery and that its "terse, deadpan prose" attests to the sway over Himes of the hard-boiled private-eye fiction he read in the journal *Black Mask.*

On the other hand, autobiographical background, while most explicit in his first five novels, also appears in the Harlem thrillers, some of which draw on Himes's experiences in Cleveland, Ohio, in the 1920s and 1930s. Personal acquaintances and autobiographical incidents additionally play a part in the New York and Paris settings of *Pinktoes* and *A Case of Rape* (1980). Moreover, his final nonfiction works, *The Quality of Hurt* (1972) and *My Life of Absurdity* (1976), readily employ techniques of fiction (and perhaps some fictional embellishments) to propel forward the autobiographical anecdotes.

Further muddling any tidy classificatory system is the scrambled chronological sequence of the first five novels, which are customarily viewed as fictionalized autobiography. *If He Hollers Let Him Go* and *Lonely Crusade* (1947) derive from Himes's left-wing and working-class periods in Cleveland during the late 1930s and in Los Angeles in the World War II era. *Cast the First Stone* (1952) revisits his earlier seven years in prison for robbery, and *The Third Generation* (1954) goes back further to the painful turmoil of his childhood and adolescence. *The Primitive* (1956) shoots forward to New York City in the 1950s to dramatize an intense and mutually ruinous interracial love affair.

In Himes's rendition of his family drama, his parents were engaged in a domestic war over color and class that left him snared in the center. Himes recollected his father as dusky, proficient in mechanical skills, and compliant to whites; he remembered his mother as fair enough to pass for white, repelled by most other African Americans, yet militant in the face of personally experienced racism. Himes's most astute biographers, Margolies and Fabre, have unearthed material suggesting some degree of overstatement in these recollections, but Himes was assiduous in making this remembrance the groundwork of both the fictional and nonfictional interpretations of his early life.

Most conspicuous in Himes's first decades is the extravagant disparity between the middle-class propriety in which he was raised and the amoral personal rebellion of his young adulthood. At the time of his birth on July 29, 1909, in Jefferson City, Missouri, his father, Joseph Sandy Himes, was employed by the Lincoln In-

stitute, a land grant college, as a teacher. The young Himes spent much of his first decade in genteel surroundings, and the family was able to purchase a car at the time of World War I. Through the early 1920s, Himes and his two older brothers, Edward and Joseph, were extensively taught at home by their mother, Estelle Bomar Himes. She was an educated musician who introduced Chester to Greek mythology, classical music, and the literature of Charles Dickens, Edgar Allan Poe, and William Makepeace Thackeray.

Yet marital strife and puzzling employment problems tormented Himes's parents. Following a 1923 accident in which the middle brother, Joseph, was mostly blinded, the family moved to Saint Louis, Missouri, and then to Cleveland seeking improved medical treatment. As the parents persevered in their course of disaffection, a second accident occurred. Chester, working as a hotel busboy following graduation from East High School, fell down an elevator shaft, resulting in major back injuries and a long hospitalization.

Himes subsequently spent part of a year at Ohio State University (1926–1927). He had grown up in somewhat protected African American communities in the South and shared friendships with students of all colors in Cleveland. Even while in college Himes did not seem particularly absorbed by the sundry forms of discrimination and segregation and was mainly captivated by the black underworld of prostitution and gambling. When asked to leave school due to his poor scholastic record, Himes succumbed utterly to his fascination with the criminal underworld, where he was known as "Little Katzi." After several arrests he was convicted of armed robbery in 1928 and sentenced to a minimum of twenty years at the Ohio State penitentiary. During his incarceration (1928–1936) Himes began writing fiction about prison experiences and criminal activities, publishing them in African American periodicals such as *Abbott's Monthly Magazine* (Chicago) the *Pittsburgh Courier*, and the *Atlanta Daily World*, as well as in the more prestigious *Esquire* magazine. Paroled in 1936, he married Jean Lucinda Johnson a year later and then drafted an early

Chester Himes

Fellowship to finish a novel. *If He Hollers Let Him Go* appeared to laudatory reviews in 1945, succeeded by *Lonely Crusade* in 1947. The response to the latter was more disapproving, and the book reaped fewer sales, demoralizing Himes and adding to the disorder of his domestic life.

During these years he shifted back and between New York City and the West Coast, ultimately remaining in the former after he separated from his wife in 1950 and published *Cast the First Stone* in 1952. In 1953 he departed for Paris, where he connected with the expatriate milieu that included left-wing cultural figures such as Richard Wright, Ollie Harrington, and William Gardner Smith. *The Third Generation* appeared in 1954, attaining complimentary but uneven reviews, and *The Primitive* came out in 1956, achieving little notice.

Suffering financially and with his personal life in upheaval, Himes accepted an offer to start writing detective fiction for a French publisher, Marcel Duhamel, in 1956. His first volume, *For Love of Imabelle*, won the Grand Prix de la Littérature Policière award for the year's outstanding detective novel in 1958; this propelled Himes to new financial security and recognition. The following year he began a romantic relationship with Lesley Packard, an English journalist whom he would later marry, and published *The Crazy Kill* and *The Real Cool Killers*. The next year he issued *All Shot Up* and *The Big Gold Dream*.

In 1961 Himes shifted course with *Pinktoes*, which is rooted in his experiences in New York in the late 1940s, and he traveled to the United States the next year to participate in a French documentary film about Harlem. While taking a side trip to Mexico, Himes suffered a stroke and returned to France in 1963, the same year that his roman à clef about French racism, *"Une Affaire de viol"(A Case of Rape)*, was published in France. In the next seven years he issued *Cotton Comes to Harlem* (1965), *Run Man Run* (1966), *The Heat's On* (1966), and *Blind Man with a Pistol* (1969).

In 1970 a film version of *Cotton Comes to Harlem*, the most triumphant movie based on his fiction, was released. Next he published his

version of the prison novel that would be published in 1952 as *Cast the First Stone* and posthumously in a longer version as *Yesterday Will Make You Cry* (1998).

In Cleveland in the late 1930s Himes was employed as a laborer and then library research assistant by the federal government's Works Progress Administration (WPA). He was ultimately transferred to the Ohio branch of the Federal Writers' Project (FWP) and contributed to a history of Cleveland. During his last year in Ohio he retained a post doing domestic service for Pulitzer Prize-winning novelist Louis Bromfield, who motivated Himes to move to Los Angeles where he might discover an opportunity as a writer in the motion picture industry.

The Himeses spent four arduous years in Los Angeles and San Francisco. Failing to discover work in Hollywood, Himes was chiefly hired in war industries and participated in his own fashion in activities of the Communist movement. He continued to publish fiction in magazines— now including *Crisis, Every Opportunity*, and *Negro Story*—and in 1944 secured a Rosenwald two-part autobiography, *The Quality of Hurt* and *My Life of Absurdity*, as well as a collection of short fiction and prose, *Black on Black* (1973), and an unfinished French version of *Plan B*, which concluded his Harlem "domestic" series. After his death there were English-language versions of *A Case of Rape* (1980) and *Plan B* (1993), a nearly comprehensive volume of *The Collected Stories of Chester Himes* (1990), and earlier and unexpurgated versions of his early novels *Cast the First Stone* and *The Primitive*, retitled *Yesterday Will Make You Cry* (1998) and *The End of a Primitive* (1997), respectively. Among the most notable new scholarly resources to have appeared are Fabre, Robert F. Skinner, and Lester Sullivan's *Chester Himes: An Annotated Primary and Secondary Bibliography* (1992) Fabre and Skinner's *Conversations with Chester Himes* (1995); and Margolies and Fabre's *The Several Lives of Chester Himes* (1997).

From the Great Depression to World War II

Autobiographical sources provide the major flow of continuity in Himes's fiction, but another can be found in his standpoint on the socioeconomic system of his native land. Most important, there is a cohesion in political thought (Himes's belief in the necessity of organized violent revolution), social philosophy (his view of the absurdity of racism), and psychological portraiture (his relentless depictions of sexual relations warped by white supremacism). Himes's judgment to designate his detective series as the "Harlem Domestic" novels indicates that he saw their makeup as conveying a cultural critique of the effects of racism in a black enclave of his native land, even if some formal features of the writing were derived from the genre of detective fiction pioneered by Dashiell Hammett.

Himes's sociopolitical perspective was initially forged during the Great Depression and early 1940s, undergoing a sequence of transformations and modifications throughout the Cold War, his European exile, the new radicalization

of the 1960s, and his more comfortable and balanced final years. Himes evidently enacted so many of his deeds in these early narratives that when it came to writing his memoirs, he only briefly referred to his youthful Marxist-oriented radicalism, his Los Angeles and prison experiences, and other episodes that he had previously fictionalized. As a result, various critics noticed that the autobiography is too silent on crucial issues while inordinately concerned with secondary matters such as Himes's pets and automobiles. However, neither the fictional nor the nonfictional renditions of his political ideas and activities from the last years of the Great Depression in Cleveland through his wartime experiences in Los Angeles and San Francisco contain data that indicates what attachments pulled him so forcefully to the Marxist Left for at least five or six years. One can only speculate on the character and depth of his early radicalization based on deductions from his first two novels, his short stories of the era, clues that appear in his interviews, and other scant primary sources.

Himes asserted in his memoirs that the issue of racism did not impress him overtly or disturb him during his youth, college, or prison years; he contended that the "shock" of white supremacism only struck full force when he arrived in Los Angeles at the onset of World War II. While this may be an overstatement, it is notable that both of the published versions of his novel about his prison experiences employ a white convict as Himes's autobiographical persona; compared with fictionalized treatments of other periods in his life, race in these works is relegated to the background. Race figures even less pivotally in his first class-conscious political stories published in the late 1930s.

These latter works appeared in *Crossroad*, a magazine out of Cleveland with left-wing connections. On the editorial board was Himes's friend Dan Levin, a future novelist and at that time a Communist sympathizer who would be the model for "Rosie," the Jewish Marxist exemplar of *Lonely Crusade*. Among the contributors was the radical Jewish lesbian and fellow WPA employee Ruth Seid (later known as novelist Jo Sinclair), who had made her literary debut by contributing an antilynching story to the Communist Party's *New Masses*, a weekly magazine, in 1936 and who contributed plays to Cleveland's left-wing theater movement. Seid and other *Crossroad* collaborators addressed racism in their stories and poems, but Himes's three pieces of fiction in 1939–1940 ("With Malice toward None," "A Modern Fable," and "Looking down the Street: a Story of Import and Bitterness") were above all class based and Marxian. This was also the case with an unpublished story ("The Shipyards Get a Welder") that Himes donated to. a projected WPA collection that never appeared.

From the late 1930s until the postwar era, Himes more or less partook of the dominant Left view of his time: the Soviet Union had achieved the closest approximation of an egalitarian society; the working class of the United States, organized by the CIO (Congress of Industrial Organizations), was the primary vehicle for progressive change; and the Communist Party was in the vanguard of the struggle. This outlook was still in place at the date of the publication of *If He Hollers Let Him Go*. In the May 1944 issue of the *Crisis*, Himes confirmed that "the communist-dominated socialist state of the USSR" was closest to an existence "wherein every one is free"; in contrast, the United States capitalist system had advanced only to a situation "wherein a ruling class or race is free." When interviewed by the *Chicago Defender* on December 22, 1945, Himes observed of communism: "Today you have a nation that represents a new ideology in which the masses of people have more freedom. It is a new way of life which would be better for the people, and, in Russia, has passed from theory to practicality."

There are other indications that Himes's outlook was attuned with pro-Soviet Marxism in those years. Himes's opinions on World War II roughly paralleled those of the Communist movement, although he treated domestic race issues far more centrally. Nine months into the Hitler-Stalin Pact, a time when the Communist movement was isolated from most of the Left, Himes was featured in the May 21, 1940, *New Masses* symposium of views about Wright's

Native Son; and as late as 1946 Himes drafted a review for *New Masses* of Ann Petry's novel *The Street*. His first book was applauded enthusiastically and with considerable insight by a leading African American Communist in the December 30, 1945, issue of the Party's *Daily Worker*.

Nonetheless, by the time of the publication of *Lonely Crusade*, Himes's estimation of the Party had shifted spectacularly. This evolution paralleled that of two other black pro-Communist writers with whom Himes was personally acquainted, Richard Wright and Ralph Ellison. Wright, a public member, had quietly distanced himself from the Party in 1942, officially resigning in 1944. Wright then published his embittered memoir, "I Tried to Be a Communist," in the August and September issues of the *Atlantic*, just preceding Himes's first novel. Ellison, who had contributed significantly to Party publications and was diligent in the leading councils of the Party-led League of American Writers, also drifted away during his wartime service in the merchant marine from 1943 to 1945.

Thus, the *Lonely Crusade* is in certain particulars the ancestor of both Ellison's *Invisible Man* (1952) and Wright's *The Outsider* (1953). The three novels are cognate in placing the accent more on what repelled them than on what attracted them to communism, dramatizing the Machiavellian and manipulative aspects of the Party. Yet Himes's work is politically singular in that its concluding sections reaffirm his non-Party yet communist ideology, faith in the working class, and commitment to the union movement. In *Lonely Crusade* the expelled Communist, but still Marxist, Abe "Rosie" Rosenberg, becomes the avatar of this utopian hope, and the African American protagonist, Lee Gordon, martyrs himself to the "cause" of the proletariat at the novel's climax.

Two Radical Novels

Generally speaking, both *If He Hollers Let Him Go* and *Lonely Crusade* are affiliated with the tradition of the proletarian or radical novel, notwithstanding peculiar twists and revisions. One such innovation is Himes's prioritization of interracial sexual tensions as the site of a primordial power struggle as well as the source of philosophical and psychological insight. Another is his view of Communism, which is never simplistically "pro" or "anti." In the first novel his appraisal of the Party appears on balance to be neutral. In the *Lonely Crusade,* however, Himes anticipates the bitter rage of *Invisible Man* and *The Outsider* toward the Party but aggressively affirms a left-wing working-class orientation. Thus, he seeks to extract the essence of communist ideals from what he now sees as the sordid reality of the Communist political movement. Still radical and anticapitalist, *Lonely Crusade* is such a furious assault on the Party and its members (one of whom is depicted as an outright killer) that Himes could only have calculated to elicit the outraged condemnation from the Party about which he later complained.

Set in the summer of 1944, *If He Hollers Let Him Go* has some aspects of a "regional" novel of Los Angeles, although it may agglomerate some of Himes's former life in San Francisco and Cleveland. The protagonist, Bob Jones, a middle-class college-educated shipyard worker from Ohio, lives with a working-class black family but is wooing Alice Harrison, the light-skinned daughter of a successful black physician. Organized around a work week in which the narrative of each day originates with a recital of a symbolically revealing nightmare, Himes's novel depicts race and class war on the home front.

Although President Roosevelt's wartime directives commanded U.S. industry to cease discrimination, Bob and the other black workers remain segregated with the lowest jobs, obliged to battle for the simple rights that whites take for granted, such as access to blueprints. When Bob, recently advanced to the rank of the company's first black leadman, tries to enlist a southern white woman, Madge Perkins, to his work crew, the two end up reciprocating hate epithets. Bob is then downgraded to mechanic and classified as suitable for the military draft by an unfriendly white supervisor. Next, when

Bob triumphs in a dice game, a white worker named Johnny Stoddart accuses him of cheating and knocks him out. As critic Gilbert Muller notes, the attack turns Bob into a loser even when winning, in this study of an all-pervasive racialized power system.

Bob is both an engaged actor in events and a spectator in a warlike world as he journeys through the sundry levels of society in Los Angeles. From his working-class domicile he visits the Harrisons, who live in the moneyed black district. Alice, a social worker, proclaims that she will love Bob only if he goes back to school to become a professional. As Muller explains, Bob's "powerful, assertive blackness" is an embarrassment to her.

The novel diverges from the mainstream of earlier protest literature with its many absurd elements that render people and situations nearly freakish. Himes's approach here has as many bonds with the semisurrealist radical novels of Nathanael West as it does with the work of Great Depression social realists such as Richard Wright, James T. Farrell, and John Steinbeck. Often it seems as if Bob's nightmares occur when he is awake as well as asleep. Unlike in much naturalism, characters and events are not impersonally presented but refracted through Bob's consciousness, fashioning a surfeit of comically violent happenings.

Nonetheless, in some ways Bob's entrapment is depicted as inversely analogous to that of Wright's Bigger Thomas in *Native Son.* Himes's protagonist, Bob Jones, is an educated man; his lover, Alice, is well-to-do; and Jones's white female nemesis, Madge, is working class. All of this contrasts with Wright's unemployed Bigger Thomas; his girlfriend, Bessie, who works as a domestic; and the upper-class Mary Dalton, whose insensitive behavior leads to her own murder and Bigger's demise. Despite the different class configurations of the two narratives, Bob and Bigger experience corresponding pressures stemming from the long-term legacy of racism. This is eminently indicated in the incendiary sexual situation that occurs whenever Madge and Bob are alone. As in the case of Bigger and Mary, "normal" interaction between black men and white women is precluded, and the threat of some violent consequence hovers over any attempt at intimacy.

The psychological direction of Himes's analysis of racism's effects blends well with his organizational strategy in the novel. As James Lundquist detects, the narrative moves forward by its succession of dreams—of tethered dogs, crippled men—that add structural and thematic unity. One dream is of a beating by two white southerners supervised by the president of the shipyard who is outfitted in the garb of a military officer. The prose style, however, is dedicated to dramatization; an auctorial voice infrequently butts in, pontificates, or explicates.

Himes's handling of sex and race benefits from his interweaving of class angles, due to the faithful backdrop of what Gilbert Muller calls "the social landscape." Through Bob's association with Alice Harrison, Himes reveals the habit of mind of the African American aristocracy. Mrs. Harrison adulates Booker T. Washington; Dr. Harrison is a sexual predator; and their daughter's recoil from the black working class is displayed in a veiled lesbianism and abashment at Bob's color, occupation, and bluntness of speech.

Madge Perkins, conversely, a working-class, blond Texan, exhibits a grotesque syndrome as she counterfeits a loathing of black men while covertly lusting after them. Bob, too, alternates between aversion and desire for Madge—somewhat inexplicably, since her physical charms are rather modest. When he visits her apartment at night, her ultimatum that he rape her depletes him of ardor. The implication of Bob's fascination with Madge seems to be that the allure is less physical than based on Madge's latent power as the mechanism of his ruination. As the novel advances, Madge is unveiled to be somewhat dull witted, fatuous, and wearisome. This magnifies the import of *If He Hollers Let Him Go* for its unforgettable enactment of an abiding proposition in Himes's oeuvre: that the destructive "power" of interracial sex is largely a cultural construct in which the distraught imaginations of the participant-victims—primarily black men and white women—perform a crucial role.

In *If He Hollers Let Him Go* the wartime setting functions ironically. The war itself is presumably being fought against Hitler's white supremacy. Yet people of color in the United States, from first to last, are under racist attack within the boundaries of their own homeland. Early in the novel Bob witnesses the forced relocation of Japanese Americans. On the last page, he is marched with two Chicanos to an induction center, where he will be given the opportunity to sacrifice himself for the system that almost sent him to jail on a sham rape charge. While not disputing the official war aims, the novel is a bitter commentary on the hypocrisies of racial capitalism.

As Edward Margolies notes, Bob Jones is a forcefully memorable character because of the way he combines a cognizance of what is happening to him with an inability to save himself. Nevertheless, the novel is the work of a revolutionary who is averse to the social system. In a political altercation with Alice's white liberal friends about Lillian Smith's *Strange Fruit* and Wright's *Native Son*, Bob articulates a pose that remained Himes's for the rest of his life: "The only solution to the Negro problem is a revolution. We've got to make white people respect us and the only thing white people have ever respected is force." Twenty-five years later, in the April 3, 1972, issue of *Publishers Weekly*, Himes would remind the interviewer, "I have always believed in a black revolution by violent force."

Himes's follow-up novel, *Lonely Crusade*, is in many respects an even more excruciating character study of another educated black worker who also has certain features in common with Himes. The same technique of shocking and explosive language and situations is used. This style not only asserts the state of mind of the characters but also enables Himes to proffer his case with bold urgency. Steven J. Rosen has noted that most critics regard this novel as Himes's most poignant effort to articulate a vision and philosophy.

Lee Gordon, born in 1912 to parents who work as house servants and educated at UCLA with a sociology major, is thirty-one years old. To some he seems green and boyish, but not to his wife, who discerns him as precipitately aged. Lee has been fiercely molded by certain formative episodes of his youth. Bedeviled by the mystery of white females, as a schoolboy Lee had spied on the women's locker room, and when he was apprehended, his family was hounded out of the city. Subsequently, his father, while returning from his janitorial job, is wrongly shot down by a police officer who imagines that he is a burglar.

As a consequence, Lee is timorous of whites and discharges his animosity by beating and raping his wife. He seems to be very aware of race yet poorly educated about the lives of most African Americans. Lee also upholds a resentment against the Communist Party, to which he was once sympathetic; after Pearl Harbor he lost his post-office job due to his antiracism, but the Party was no longer around to defend him due to its prowar orientation. Now Roosevelt's executive order has brought him a job as a labor organizer at Comstock Aircraft Company, and the Party is anxious to make use of him. Through most of the narrative Lee oscillates back and forth between hunting for a kind of ethical immaculateness and embracing debasement forced on him by a racist order. Yet he finally develops from scapegoat to a resolute martyr; he elects his ultimate action willfully, thereby achieving distinction.

Lee is surrounded by a band of fantastic characters. One African American factory worker from Georgia is called Lester McKinley, although there is some mystery about his real name, which was changed after he witnessed a lynching at age twelve. In response to the violence that he saw, Lester feels a compulsion to kill whites. Although he had been an outstanding student of Latin in Atlanta, he is obligated by his homicidal urges to move out of the South, and he chooses Albany, New York. When his obsession remains unabated, Lester is counseled by a psychologist to marry a white woman. Lester and his new family move to California, but he is disconsolate in his work. He entertains a scheme to assassinate Lewis Foster, the capitalist scoundrel of the novel. Yet the naive Lee comes to venerate Lester, imagining that through his marriage and children,

Lester has mastered the racism of society. Lester, however, disappears precipitously before any genuine action comes to pass.

Luther McGregor may be the only bona fide person of deeds in the body of story, although Lee himself will at last move conclusively at the very end. A union organizer for the Communist Party, Luther is from Mississippi, was on a chain gang, worked for the WPA, and has been taken up by several affluent white women. Unlike Lee, who falls in love with and idealizes a white female Communist, Jackie Forks, Luther has no illusions about his relation to white women; Luther knows that to them he is just an device of sexual gratification.

A number of happenings imply some sort of intimate link between Lee and Luther. Luther presents himself as if he had formerly met Lee and later avows that he was the behind-the-scenes figure who obtained for Lee his current union job. Visiting Lee's apartment for the first time, Luther appears to be so much at home that the atmosphere becomes eerie. Later, when Lee wants to kill a policeman after he and Luther are beaten, it is Luther who actually carries out the murder.

Luther has an imposing political record as an organizer of agricultural workers; this experience confers on him a distinguished status in the union. Yet he has no sincere political convictions—he will take money from the capitalists as well as the Communist Party. He is faithful only to himself and other blacks, including Lee. He has a breed of cold mental clarity, hinting that he is a man who lives his life independent of illusions, an attribute suggesting an existentialist antihero. At one point Luther recites the African American folk song "Signifying Monkey" to end discord among a group of black workers, but the song is really about the dissembling side of Luther to which Lee is blind. There is yet another perplexing feature of this haunting character: Lee perceives Luther in stereotypically racist images, as a dangerous jungle beast, yet in his own house Luther relaxes to Sibelius' First Symphony, and he had previously been a short story writer.

Another bizarre character, Lewis Foster, is the major shareholder and manager of Comstock

Company, the large plant that Lee and Luther seek to organize. Comstock has a thirty-thousand-person workforce on three shifts that includes three thousand black men and women (exactly the required number of 10 percent). Foster himself abhors blacks unless they have a deferential attitude, but he also doesn't want them to hate him. He offers a $5,000 salary to buy off Lee with a job in the personnel department. Foster, a stock villain, is a longtime adversary of unions and is resourceful about exploiting patriotic sentiments.

Several militants in the union are consequential in the narrative. Marvin Todd is the racist chairman of the union local; at first his appearance seems to insert a question mark about the nature of unions, yet in the climactic episodes of the novel Todd harbors Lee from the police. Smitty, a white union organizer, is down to earth and pragmatic, and he proves to be a dependable friend to Lee. Joe Ptak is an experienced union leader from the east, professional and tough, whose aim is to organize the plant and then move on to next job. Joe, however, reveals his core of masculine courage through his actions in the closing pages and points the way forward for Lee.

The moral center of the book is Abe "Rosie" Rosenberg, a Jewish Marxist mentor to the persecuted black worker, a figure somewhat analogous to Wright's Mr. Max in *Native Son*. Rosie is the oldest member of the local Communist Party, an intellectual who espouses a humanistic Marxism combined with earthy humor. Lee first perceives him as a semitic stereotype, but this changes after Rosie tells Lee that black antisemitism is the most harmful result of racial prejudice. Eventually Rosie becomes a kind of spiritual guide for Lee and tries to educate him in the habits of survival that link all oppressed people in every sector of society.

Lee's dialogues with Rosie help to structure the novel. They lead Lee from a stance of passivity and wavering convictions finally to authentic commitment. In his last six days Lee recreates himself. Rosie's philosophy, that people are indivisible, prepares Lee for his death. Yet Lee is not merely a creation of Rosie; his own thinking, the support afforded by Smitty, and

the final example of Joe forge conditions for Lee's acceptance of Rosie's guidance.

Among the female characters, the most fully drawn are Ruth and Jackie. Ruth is Lee's wife of eight years. Their relationship is a sadomasochistic one, in which Lee needs to demonstrate a power over her that he is denied in the "real" world. There is a sharp discrepancy between Lee's idealism and his behavior in his marriage. While Ruth often demonstrates a forceful character, she is beaten down by disillusionment with Lee. In retaliation Ruth torments Lee with nasty remarks because she makes more money and jeers at the idea that he could be loved by a white woman. She can't forgive Lee for the woe he has caused her, but she can't relinquish him either. Moreover, she sees herself as a professional and superior to the working class—she rejects the Communist Party due to her certitude in the American dream. Only after Lee discards her for Jackie does Ruth turn to the looking glass and for the first time feel inferior as an African American.

Jackie Forks, whose name, it has been pointed out, insinuates both a fork in road and a devil's pitch fork (connoting a diabolical temptation), enacts the myth of white female sexual power. She herself is perplexed by her own responses. She feels a sexual fascination for Lee but is afraid of being snared in a messy situation in which she is the "other woman" in a contest with a black wife. Moreover, as a Communist, she believes she must use Lee for political ends dictated by the Party. The reader senses some sort of deep connection between Lee's sexual crisis with Jackie and the social crisis of racist society. Their distorted sexual feelings are a product of the delusions distorting the body politic.

In the final confrontation of the novel, Himes presents a bottom-line Marxist view of a class society: working people aligned against the police who are preserving the interests of the ruling elite. Lee, who has been hunted by police, takes the erect union flag from fallen Joe Ptak and walks deliberately toward the guns that are beaded on him in preparation to fire. His last thoughts are an enigmatic statement about marching toward this "knowledge of truth." He has embraced the possibility that the road of rebellion leads to death because Rosie, the model of the integrated man, has told him that one will not be afraid if one resolves one's indecision. Yet even as Lee appears to abandon personal concerns for a symbolic act of defiance, he is also striving to regain his own masculinity and contribute to Rosie's dream of human solidarity.

Stephen Milliken observes that the point of view in *Lonely Crusade* is that of a disembodied, omniscient third-person narrator. This strategy is sustained throughout but always influenced by a strong subjective bias. That is, the narrator tends to identify with whatever character happens to be on center stage at the moment, both registering and analyzing his or her secret thoughts. Such a technique enables Himes to develop rather fully a large cast of characters in addition to Lee, probing the issues in the novel from many distinct angles. Yet the work that results is sprawling and bulging.

The plot itself ranges over about fifty days. Six of these are consecrated to the stormy romance with Jackie, and another six cover the marathon to get out the union vote. All the copious secondary plots connect to the primary thread—Lee's crusade for a vision. But there are some independent interconnections between these rather sketchy subplots, ones that narrate the private ordeals of six or more major characters beyond Lee. The structure of the novel invokes the image of a character trapped between forces in the class struggle—Lewis Foster on behalf of capitalism and the Communist Party on behalf of the working class. Critics have regarded Lee as an Odysseus navigating between the straits between Scylla and Charydbis.

The portrait of the Communist Party in this novel is of an organization committed to the exploitation of individuals for its rather murky objectives dictated by a hunger for power. Two Communists attempt to become Lee's friends—the black worker Luther and the white woman Jackie—but it is only to use him. The union, too, is shown to be vulnerable to opportunism. As Milliken notes, Smitty and Joe easily accept the Party's decision to frame Jackie as a suspected spy, simply in order to quell discontent.

They also want to protect Luther, a union stalwart, when he falls under suspicion for duplicitous behavior. Only the heretical Communist Rosie is willing to go after Luther, demanding his expulsion from the Party. Instead, Rosie's own purge results, placing Marxist integrity clearly outside the organization.

Himes's novel has an important relation to the tradition of radical strike novels. As James Lundquist observes, it focuses on problems of union organization in relation to bosses, police violence, sellouts, the divisiveness of racism, and the backwardness of southern white workers. Instead of building to an actual strike, however—a thematic motif that scholar Walter Rideout uses to theorize the arc of narrative action in such books—Himes's novel culminates in a police confrontation on the day of a vote for or against unionization. Yet the situation Himes depicts of a workers' rally threatened by police violence performs the same dramatic function as a strike. What is distinct about Himes's contribution to the genre is his paramount focus on racial strife and the attempt to establish a revolutionary pole to the Left of the Communist movement.

Moreover, the crux of the novel dramatizes a variant of the emblematic theme of Himes's writing: the use of interracial sex as a kind of litmus test of the warping power of white chauvinism. The pain caused by white supremacism has forced Lee to view sexual intercourse as necessary to reaffirm his manhood, but sex with a black woman fails to perform that function. Still, after intercourse with Jackie he feels impotent because the fantasy that he will regain his masculinity from the sexual act is deflated. Jackie, on the other hand, seems to get a strong sense of empowerment from her control over a black man.

The Absurdity of Racism

Himes's political themes received less attention in his three subsequent novels, published in the early 1950s, but they returned in full force in his Harlem Domestic series. These popular works, while devoid of sympathy for Marxism, socialism, and the union movement, are nevertheless politically anticapitalist. As in his first two novels, Himes continued to see the violent exploitation of blacks as a necessary part of the system, rather than an aberration. Himes's black detective-protagonists, Coffin Ed Johnson and Grave Digger Jones, must walk a difficult path if they are to remain true to their community. The established themes of Himes remain omnipresent: the inherent violence of racial capitalism, the absurdity of racism, and interracial sexuality as a flash point of power relations.

John Reilly has emphasized the extent to which the series recalls classic tough-guy fiction in its attitude. Although they are police officers, not private eyes, Himes's detectives are nevertheless outsiders, loners who are as cynical and pragmatic as the protagonists of Dashiell Hammett and Raymond Chandler. For them, the pursuit of thieves and killers comes before family, comfort, or monetary gain. In *Cotton Comes to Harlem* Ed even refuses the proposition to have sex with an alluring but corrupt woman, recalling similar episodes involving the classic detectives Philip Marlowe and the Continental Op.

The very setting of the novels reflects conditions produced by class and caste system of racial capitalism, and Himes can be very graphic in showing character as determined by social conditions. At least one individual, Sheik, in *The Real Cool Killers*, recalls Himes's own disposition at the time he emerged from his troubled family background to participate in self-destructive conduct in the 1920s. In a memorable episode in *The Crazy Kill*, the Black Harlem residents observe black Sonny Pickens pursue white Ulysses Galen through the streets with a drawn gun as if it were a free spectacle; the explanation for this attitude is that the chase was a pleasant relief from the more archetypal Harlem scene of beholding a white man after a black. Himes's characters often must lead double lives to get through the ghetto hell, as with the lesbian Billie Belle in *Cotton Comes to Harlem*: she despises men but dedicates herself to summoning their lust through her famous nude dances.

Fred Pfeil has observed the importance of the themes surrounding illegal, as opposed to official, violence in the books. And as Michael Denning has noted, the new forms and ideology of Himes's brutality require special literary conventions, including fast-moving, terse sentences, short paragraphs, a large amount of dialogue, tough-guy wisecracking, and sometimes caricatured characters. Denning also maintains that Himes's books should not be regarded fundamentally as detective stories because the police are not invariably so central as in the other works that define the genre.

As a group, Himes's detective novels include some formulaic features in their plots. Usually, for example, there is a quest for a mysterious object, and Digger and Ed are brought into the chase narrative as the result of a crime or because of some other connection with the events. Violence is omnipresent, growing out of the oppressed environment of Harlem.

The first book in the series, *For Love of Imabelle*, which features various scams and a search for a gold-filled trunk, introduces the detective team quite late in the narrative. Other books in the series show various influences. For example, *The Crazy Kill*, which begins with a Harlem preacher tumbling out a window into a loaf of bread, is one of the novels most effectively influenced by Faulkner (especially *Sanctuary*). *Blind Man with a Pistol*, introduced by three forewords and a poem, employs experimental techniques to depict the effort to solve the murder of a white homosexual and others. Himes's last contribution to the series, *Plan B*, is the draft of a blueprint for an African American Revolution in which a secret black network arises to wage armed struggle against white power.

Run Man Run is the one work connected with the series that does not feature Coffin Ed Johnson and Grave Digger Jones. Instead, Jimmy Johnson, a law student working as a night porter, becomes the casualty of a psychotic vice-squad detective who needs to frame Jimmy to cover up one of his own murders. Margolies and Fabre suggest that the fast-moving plot has elements of an allegory of Himes's flight "from his own inner demons, which from time to time he projected as white males—despite the fact that many of his dearest friends . . . were white men."

The literary technique employed in *Cotton Comes to Harlem*, with its velocity and crowding of freakish incidents, is representative of the Harlem thriller series. There is little adherence to conventional chronology. Himes dashes from what one set of characters is doing at one moment to what another is doing hours before or later, without shifting tense. The incidents depicted in *Cotton Comes to Harlem* are a product of Himes's creed that blacks must make their way in the culture in which they find themselves. They can acquire consolation neither in Africa nor in a glorified past but must speak to the present-day United States.

In this series Himes goes to enormous lengths to re-create Harlem as a black colony within a larger, oppressive social order. The white Lieutenant Anderson is as much an outsider in Harlem as Ed and Digger are at home there. Yet the detectives make an odd team; at first one is struck by their ordinariness as well as their similarity. As the series progresses, however, Ed (possibly unhinged by the facial disfiguration that resulted from acid once thrown at him) reveals himself to be more rash and impetuous, while Digger tends to be more pensive and crafty. From this angle they express two well-known aspects of Himes's own personality; they could even be considered a surrogate for the artist, aspiring to carry out on the mean streets of the ghetto an intervention into life that is in some sense analogous to the cultural work of Himes's imagination.

Robert Skinner has noted that the biographies of Coffin Ed and Grave Digger can be progressively assembled from assorted pieces of background information that pop up at different moments. The detectives, in their mid-thirties, share a past: both are World War II veterans and both were raised in Harlem. They even attended public school together during the Great Depression. Both are jazz enthusiasts, they own matching guns, and their wives (Molly Johnson and Stella Jones) go shopping together. The men rarely disagree, and they have at their disposal a massive network of stool pigeons.

At times Digger has to restrain Ed during interrogations. In fact, the wanton brutality employed by both men when in pursuit of "justice" raises the question of whether Himes wished to impart near-fascist traits on them. They sometimes seem to justify their violence according to autocratic logic; their moral judgments can seem simplistic and unsubtle even if one finds them to be ultimately complicated as men. On occasion the two seem to be simply cops on the take; at other times they appear to be basically honest and loyal to the community. Moreover, Digger and Ed manage to combine some characteristics of familiar detective heroes with the "bad niggers" of black folklore. Figures of defiance, with considerable masculine strength, they exude a raw personal power and seem indifferent to physical danger.

It is noteworthy that even though Himes depicts Harlem as seen through the lens of "crime," the characters paraded in the numerous novels are quite varied. He seemed to thrive in creating personalities who shed light on the anatomy and codes of the ghetto at same time as they come alive to the reader. Raymond Nelson has studied the variety of character types to be found in the series, which he regards as a grotesque comedy of violence narrated in a spare, descriptive style. Himes openly embraced the popular crime-novel formulas, yet he also incorporated rich traditions of the folk. Nelson sees the detectives as proverbial symbols of defiance, recalling the rebel slave Nat Turner and the Stackalee of myth and song, modernized and urbanized. If there is a thematic progression in the series, it may be a change from pessimism to optimism about the possibilities that an eventual uprising might reorganize the social system.

Nelson also argues for an assessment of Himes's Harlem series as a retrospective embrace of Harlem Renaissance cultural pride in African American folklore and the unique mores of the traditional black community. Himes himself had not investigated the Harlem Renaissance tradition in the Great Depression, although he had personally known some of its leading cultural figures, such as Langston Hughes. But his impulse in writing fiction at that time drew him toward the hard-boiled writers, as well as Ernest Hemingway and William Faulkner. Thus, his Harlem Domestic series enabled him to retrieve some of the Harlem Renaissance essence without surrendering to the naïveté for which it has sometimes been reproved. Nelson concludes that Himes fashioned the spirit of two literary eras into a single balanced response to African American life.

The Achievement of Himes

Chester Himes's achievement is increasingly considered to be a central contribution to mid-20th-century culture, particularly due to its psychosexual focus and imaginative power. These two traits lend themselves to renewed appraisals and rereadings by fresh generations of students and scholars. Himes's early novels *Cast the First Stone, The Third Generation,* and *The Primitive,* however, still await the extensive and contemporary reconsiderations accorded to his other novels. All three are rooted explicitly in Himes's life before his European exile, and none are "political" novels in the manner of his first two radical books or the later Harlem Domestic thrillers. Yet they relentlessly examine questions of race and gender from stimulating and complex angles animated by a compelling social vision.

Cast the First Stone, which Himes drafted before his first two published works, depicts a white southerner from Mississippi, Jim Monroe, who has been convicted of armed robbery after an earlier forgery conviction. He is incarcerated in a state prison in the post-World War II era, a shift in time to some twenty years after Himes's own sentence. The book covers the five years following his admission and leading up to Monroe's transfer to a prison farm. Brutalization is a constant theme of the novel, with one dramatic episode involving a prison fire. The most startling feature, especially in the unabridged version published in 1998, is Monroe's strong same-sex love relationship with a character named Dido. This aspect of the novel was considerably cut in the 1952 version, but its restoration in the version entitled *Yesterday Will*

Make You Cry caused Bruce Franklin to declare it "a profoundly affirmative homosexual love story" for which "America in 1952 was not ready."

The Third Generation fictionalizes the Himes family as the Taylors. The incompatible couple, of different colors and social backgrounds, has three sons. The youngest, Charles, becomes the object of the mother's devotion; she is fixated on straightening his hair and perpetuating his "white" features. Gradually, Charles responds by transferring his affection to his mother, with whose grooming he has also reciprocally been involved. When Charles assaults his father to defend his mother in one episode, an oedipal relationship is strongly suggested. Milliken regards the book as part of the bildungsroman tradition, along with James Joyce's *Portrait of the Artist as a Young Man,* for its "detailed account of the genesis of an artist's special sensitivity."

The Primitive focuses on a weeklong sexual encounter between an aspiring black author, Jesse Robinson, and a middle-class white woman, Kriss Cummings. Each exploits the other—the black man idealizing Kriss as the ideal of beauty, the white woman viewing Jesse as a sex machine. The deeply pessimistic theme is the anatomy of lost souls caught up in social myths. Gilbert Muller concludes that "the obsessive, almost hysterical sexuality that links Kriss and Jesse in a prolonged and destructive embrace demands consideration of cultural symptoms and the racist pathologies that cause it."

Once transplanted to Europe, Himes avowed that he experienced new freedoms. He also augmented his literary repertoire there. Among the first of his new books written abroad was *Pinktoes,* published several years later. The book took Himes's career in a novel direction as a light satire narrating the adventures of an upper-middle-class Harlem hostess, Mamie Mayson, who specializes in arranging interracial sexual encounters through her parties. These social affairs are ostensibly held to address race issues, but the attraction is the sex. The plot centers on Mamie Mayson's machinations to lure the wife of an eminent light-skinned black leader into her activities.

A *Case of Rape* is a rare example of Himes's employing European materials, although he also provides his customary focus on racist stereotypes centering around black male sexuality. The four black defendants charged with rape are all attracted to white women. One of the men, Scott Hamilton, has brought an old lover to his room, where three of his friends are present. A figure suggesting Richard Wright undertakes an investigation of the events that subsequently led to the woman's death and the accusation of rape against the African American men. The findings demonstrate that all are ensnared within their racial and sexual destinies.

Himes died on November 12, 1984. He was seventy-five and had suffered strokes, partial paralysis, and many bed-ridden months in Spain, where he resided for his last fifteen years. Since then he and his work have remained the object of a steady stream of academic books, essays, and conference papers. Fascination with his life and writings has been fueled by the republication of unedited and unexpurgated versions of early works, the English-language editions of previously untranslated writings, and important biographical research. Himes is one of the mid-20th-century African American writers to benefit most from the evolving concerns of the post-1960s generation of scholars, which includes a long overdue frankness about the interrelationship of racial and sexual oppression. When such perspectives are brought to bear on the new primary materials, the result has been the production of numerous innovative considerations of his oeuvre, most recently including those that address topics such as national identity, diasporic culture, gender, masculinity, social history, and narrative theory.

Selected Bibliography

PRIMARY WORKS

NOVELS

If He Hollers Let Him Go. New York: Doubleday, Doran and Company, 1945.
Lonely Crusade. New York: Knopf, 1947.
Cast the First Stone. New York: Coward-McCann, 1952. Reprinted in unabridged version as *Yesterday Will Make You Cry.* New York: Norton, 1998.

The Third Generation. Cleveland. Ohio: World Publishing, 1954.
The Primitive. New York: New American Library, 1956. Reprinted in unabridged version as *The End of a Primitive.* New York: Norton, 1997.
For Love of Imabelle. Greenwich, Conn.: Fawcett World Library, 1957. Reprinted as *A Rage in Harlem.* New York: Avon, 1965.
The Crazy Kill. New York: Avon, 1959.
The Real Cool Killers. New York: Avon, 1959.
All Shot Up. New York: Avon, 1960.
The Big Gold Dream. New York: Avon, 1960.
Cotton Comes to Harlem. New York: Putnam, 1965.
Pinktoes. Paris: Olympia Press, 1961; New York: Putnam, 1965.
The Heat's On. New York: G.P. Putnam and Sons, 1966. Reprinted as *Come Back, Charleston Blue.* New York: Berkeley, 1972.
Run Man Run. New York: Putnam, Stein & Day, 1966.
Blind Man with a Pistol. New York: Morrow, 1969. Reprinted as *Hot Day, Hot Night.* New York: Dell, 1970.
A Case of Rape. New York: Targ, 1980.
Plan B. Jackson: University Press of Mississippi, 1993.

SHORT STORIES AND NONFICTION COLLECTIONS

Black on Black: "Baby Sister" and Selected Writings. New York: Doubleday, 1973.
The Collected Stories of Chester Himes. London: Allison & Busby, 1990. Reprint, New York: Thunder's Mouth Press, 1991.

AUTOBIOGRAPHIES

The Quality of Hurt. New York: Doubleday, 1972.
My Life of Absurdity. New York: Doubleday, 1976.

PAPERS

Amistad Research Center. Tulane University.
Beinecke Rare Book and Manuscript Library. Yale University.
Julius Rosenwald Fund Archives. Fisk University.

SECONDARY WORKS

BIOGRAPHICAL AND CRITICAL STUDIES

Bell, Bernard W. *The Afro-American Novel and Its Tradition.* Amherst: University of Massachusetts Press, 1987.
Bone, Robert A. *The Negro Novel in America.* New Haven, Conn.: Yale University Press, 1965.
Braham, Persephone. "La Novela Negra from Chester Himes to Paco Ignacio Taibo II." *Journal of American Culture* 20:159–69 (Summer 1997).
Crooks, Robert. "From the Far Side of the Urban Frontier: The Detective Fiction of Chester Himes and Walter Mosley." *College Literature* 22, no. 3:68–90.

Davis, Arthur P. *From the Dark Tower: Afro-American Writers 1900–1960.* Washington, D.C.: Howard University Press, 1974.

Denning, Michael. "Topographies of Violence: Chester Himes' Harlem Domestic Novels." *Critical Texts* 5, no. 1:10–18.

Hughes, John Milton Charles. *The Negro Novelist.* New York: Citadel, 1953.

Lundquist, James. *Chester Himes.* New York: Frederick Ungar, 1976.

Margolies, Edward. *Native Sons: A Critical Study of Twentieth Century Negro American Authors.* New York: Lippincott, 1968.

Margolies, Edward, and Michel Fabre. *The Several Lives of Chester Himes.* Jackson: University Press of Mississippi, 1997.

Milliken, Stephen F. *Chester Himes: A Critical Appraisal.* Columbia: University of Missouri Press, 1976.

Muller, Gilbert H. *Chester Himes.* Boston: Twayne, 1989.

Murray, Stephen O. "An African-American's Representation of Internalized Homophobia during the Early 1930s: Chester Himes's *Cast the First Stone.*" *Journal of Homosexuality* 34, no. 1:31–46.

Nelson, Raymond. "Domestic Harlem: The Detective Fiction of Chester Himes." *Virginia Quarterly Review* 48:260–76 (Spring 1972).

Pfeil, Fred. "Policiers noirs." *Nation,* November 15, 1986, pp. 523–25.

Reckley, Ralph. "Chester Himes." In *Dictionary of Literary Biography.* Vol. 76, *Afro-American Writers, 1940–1955.* Edited by Trudier Harris. Detroit, Mich.: Gale Research, 1966. Pp. 89–103.

———. "The Use of the *Doppelgänger* or Double in Himes' Lonely Crusade." *College Language Association Journal* 20:448–58 (June 1977).

Reed, Ishmael. "Chester Himes: Writer." *Black World* (March 1972): 23–38, 83–86.

———. "Chester Himes' Last Visit Home." *Black Scholar* 28:5–7 (Spring 1998).

Reilly, John M. "Chester Himes' Harlem Tough Guys." *Journal of Popular Culture* 9:935–47 (Spring 1976).

Rideout, Walter B. *The Radical Novel in the United States, 1900–1954: Some Interrelations of Literature and Society.* Cambridge, Mass.: Harvard University Press, 1956.

Rosen, Stephen J. "African American Anti-Semitism and Himes's *Lonely Crusade.*" *MELUS* 20:46–68 (Summer 1995).

Skinner, Robert E. *Two Guns from Harlem: The Detective Fiction of Chester Himes.* Bowling Green, Ohio: Bowling Green State University Popular Press, 1989.

Yarborough, Richard. "The Quest for the American Dream in Three Afro-American Novels." *MELUS* 8, no. 4:33–59 (Winter 1981).

INTERVIEW

Fabre, Michael, and Robert E. Skinner. *Conversations with Chester Himes.* Jackson: University Press of Mississippi, 1995.

FILMS BASED ON THE WORKS OF HIMES

Cotton Comes to Harlem. Screenplay by Ossie Davis; directed by Ossie Davis, United Artists, 1970.

Come Back Charleston Blue. Screenplay by Bontche Schweig and Peggy Elliot; Samuel Goldwyn Jr., 1972.

A Rage in Harlem. Screenplay by John Toles-Bey and Bobby Crawford; directed by Bill Duke, Miramax, 1991.

BIBLIOGRAPHY

Fabre, Michel, Robert F. Skinner, and Lester Sullivan. *Chester Himes: An Annotated Primary and Secondary Bibliography.* Westport, Conn.: Greenwood Press, 1992.

PAULINE HOPKINS
(1859–1930)

DAPHNE A. BROOKS

A PERFORMER OF some notoriety in the 1870s and 1880s before taking up journalism and fiction writing, Pauline E. Hopkins would endorse the powers of theater and performance as key political tools necessary for the empowerment of African Americans throughout her career as an author. By the time Hopkins published her last and perhaps most ambitious serialized novel, *Of One Blood*, in 1902–1903, it was evident that one character's exclamation at a key point in that sprawling epic—"Pleasure! . . . Oh Lord! You've come to the wrong place. This is business, solid business"—could easily apply to Hopkins' views on the urgency of black cultural production and its critical significance as a weapon in the battle for social and political enfranchisement. Hopkins' work aggressively seeks to mix the "business" of African American uplift with the "pleasure" of popular aesthetic production and consumption.

A novelist, journalist, essayist, short-story writer, dramatist, actress, and singer, Hopkins employed multiple generic forms and themes, blending journalism with the sentimental novel, history with Westerns, theater and performance with sensation fiction, and Pan-Africanist ideology with the culture of spiritualism. Elizabeth Ammons points to the very hybridity of Hopkins' work as evidence of the writer's imaginative "disruliness" as an artist and her distinct "rebellion" against the narrow restrictions of aesthetic genres in the articulation of African American history and culture. Like her more famous contemporaries, W. E. B. Du Bois and Paul Laurence Dunbar among them, Hopkins invoked multiple expressive strategies to contribute to contemporaneous black liberation movements as well as the burgeoning concepts of a "New Negro" identity, and a postslavery, post-Reconstruction, "modern" African American literature and culture. Hopkins not only participated in this movement in politics and letters, she crafted fiction, prose, journalism, and theater that collapsed and transgressed generic boundaries, creating a uniquely popular *and* political form of African American cultural production at the turn of the twentieth century. Hopkins produced one published dramatic musical, one novel in book from, three serialized magazine novels, a full-length historical survey, and over thirty periodical articles, and she also delivered numerous public lectures in her career.

Despite her prolific work as a writer (Richard Yarborough has referred to her as "the single most productive black woman writer at the turn of the century") and her high-profile position as literary editor and contributor at *Colored American Magazine*, Hopkins, until the late twentieth century, was largely overlooked in literary and historical studies of African

American letters and culture. Nellie McKay credits Pulitzer-Prize–winning poet Gwendolyn Brooks with having been among the first contemporary writers to attempt to reclaim Hopkins, and reposition her within the African American canon. Brooks wrote the afterword to the first modern reprint of Hopkins' first novel, *Contending Forces*, in 1978. Subsequently, in the 1980s and 1990s, and particularly in the wake of Hopkins' inclusion in the landmark Schomburg Library of Nineteenth-Century Black Women Writers series, feminist and cultural critics from a wide variety of disciplines have produced critical studies of the author's work. Critics have cited Hopkins and her ambitious political and historical fiction and journalism as crucial precursors to both the African American cultural nationalist movement of the 1960s and 1970s and the black feminist narrative epics of Toni Morrison and Sherley Anne Williams. Hopkins' work is still only beginning to be perceived for its worth as early evidence of the effort to conceive, enact, and manifest a culture of "black modernity."

Hopkins' fiction evolves out of three distinct nineteenth-century cultural fields: theater, journalism, and spiritualism. All were forms of cultural production that influenced and first shaped Hopkins' drama and later her novels and short stories published in *Colored American Magazine* between 1900 and 1904. She cultivated a distinct kind of literary style, grafting scenes of performance, journalistic documents, spectacles of mesmerism, and "new psychology" into the sentimental, domestic, sensation, and detective novel forms. Hopkins' prose makes broad and sweeping allusions to European and American canonical lyric and prose in epigraph form, citing Ralph Waldo Emerson, and Alfred, Lord Tennyson, for instance. Yet it is also apparent from her fiction that Hopkins was as much a fan of popular, trans-Atlantic literature as she was to become a producer and innovator of the hybrid form. The late eighteenth- and early nineteenth-century sentimental novels of Susanna Rowson and Hannah Foster, the serialized narrative stylings of Charles Dickens, the detective novels of Wilkie Collins, the sensation fiction of Elizabeth Brad-

don, and the Gothic suspense of Ann Radcliffe all come to surface in Hopkins' fiction. Her prose is also clearly informed by the black feminist journalistic endeavors of Mary Ann Shadd Cary, the rigorous and forthright antilynching editorials of Ida B. Wells, as well as the the spiritualist and occult explorations of her contemporaries: Du Bois, William James, and Charles Chesnutt, and the Pan-Africanist musical productions of Bert Williams and George and Aida Overton-Walker. Hopkins made use of as many creative and expressive forms as possible to develop a renegade style of black feminist narrative authority and to represent and articulate, as Claudia Tate describes, the "political desires" of African Americans as they made the transition from the nineteenth to the twentieth century, from southern agrarian life to northern intellectual culture, from slavery to full social political enfranchisement in the American landscape. As Hopkins herself emphasized in 1900 in the preface to *Contending Forces*, "No one will do this for us; we must ourselves develop the men and women who will faithfully portray the inmost thoughts and feelings of the Negro with all the fire and romance which lie dormant in our history."

Life and Early Career

Born in Portland, Maine, in 1859, the only child of migrant Virginian Northrup Hopkins and New Hampshire native Sarah Allen, Hopkins grew up and lived her entire professional life in Boston, Massachusetts, a city that would serve as the setting for many of her fictional narratives. She attended the public Girls High School in Boston and in her student years demonstrated an early interest in literary endeavors. In 1874, at the age of fifteen, Hopkins entered an essay contest organized by the Congregational Publishing Society of Boston, a group financially supported by the former black abolitionist activist, author, and entrepreneur William Wells Brown. Her essay, entitled "Evils of Intemperance and Their Remedy," won first prize and anticipated Hopkins' role as a social activist engaged in literary production. Probably Hopkins' most significant and influential activity prior to her prolific *Colored American Magazine* period began in 1879 at the age of twenty when she completed her first play, entitled *Slave's Escape; or, The Underground Railroad* and later changed to the title *Peculiar Sam; or, The Underground Railroad*. The play was brought to the stage and performed by her family's theatrical troupe, the Hopkins Colored Troubadours, a company that included Hopkins, her mother, her father, and at least one other male performer. *Peculiar Sam* debuted in1879 at the Boston YMCA and culminated in an 1880 run at the city's Oakland Gardens, on one warm summer night playing before a large amusement park audience. The Hopkins Colored Troubadours were accompanied by the well-known Hyers Sisters performance troupe and a chorus of more than sixty people.

The Hopkins Colored Troubadours toured and performed throughout the Boston area and parts of the northeast for twelve years, and Hopkins played a central role in the group's success, becoming known as "Boston's Favorite Soprano." Indeed, Hopkins gave occasional recitals and concerts during her stage career; she also lectured on black history and is believed to have written at least one other drama during this period, but it is not known whether the play was ever produced. In addition to the troupe's performances of *Peculiar Sam*, the family's repertoire consisted of ambitious musicals that celebrated and provided narrative scope to the recent black historical past, tackling weighty concerns such as social reform, emancipation, and Reconstruction's ill-fated promise of economic and social opportunities for African Americans. This fusion of historical events and theatricality would clearly leave its mark on Hopkins' writing style as she made the successful transition from playwright to popular magazine novelist at the turn of the century.

In the 1890s, as Hopkins entered her thirties, she sought additional means of financial support and began training in stenography, a trade on which she would depend at several points in her career, particularly, it seems, in the years following her departure from *Colored American Magazine*. On occasion Hopkins even in-

corporated the image of that corporate trade in her prose, representing her first major heroine, Sappho Clark in *Contending Forces*, as a southern migrant to the north who supports herself through stenography. Beyond the financial practicality of the field, one might assume that Hopkins capitalized, as she did in her journalism, on the concept of documentation and the need for African Americans to diligently record their own histories.

From theater and stenography work, Hopkins leapt, like so many of her adventurous dramatic and fictional characters, into the worlds of journalism and fiction writing on a full-time basis, beginning in 1900 when a new journal, the *Colored American Magazine*, was born.

Colored American Magazine and the Era of the "New Negro"

Conceived and created by a group of Boston African Americans, *Colored American Magazine* preceded both Du Bois's *Crisis* and A. Phillip Randolph's *The Messenger* as a critical periodical intended specifically to "uplift the race." Unlike *The Crisis*, *Colored American Magazine* was owned and published by blacks, becoming one of the first major twentieth-century instruments of the media controlled by blacks. *Colored American Magazine* also set a historical precedence by maintaining its finances through the organization of a cooperative comprised of readers and contributing writers who supported the journal's monthly budget. It was in this thriving cultural and political context that Hopkins produced her most noteworthy and most influential works as a novelist and journalist.

Beginning in May 1900, Hopkins began her productive career as a contributor to the journal, publishing her short story "The Mystery Within Us," an exploration of new psychology and mesmerism's focus on the "transmigration" of the soul, mapping what many critics believe to be a direct precursor to her final serial novel, *Of One Blood*. The same year in which

Colored American Magazine was created and Hopkins joined its staff, Booker T. Washington and Fannie Barrier Williams published the anthology *A New Negro for a New Century*, a project comprised of essays and portraits that according to Henry Louis Gates Jr., marked an early point in the "New Negro" movement and a new juncture in the historical period of Reconstruction. The era of the "New Negro," spanning the years of the 1890s to the 1920s, is defined as "the crux of the period of black intellectual Reconstruction." The context for Hopkins' work was thus a period of great productivity and self-conscious projects that attempted to revise popular images of African Americans in the social and cultural mass conscious.

Black political and aesthetic leaders made claims that "a New Negro" had been born, a figure that contested and ultimately sought to displace the stereotypical hegemonic images of African Americans as "sambos" and "mammies." As a critical resistance to the remnants of the still-popular minstrel tradition born out of theater culture, black leaders thereby endeavored to erase narrow, caricatured figures by engaging in the rhetoric of rebirth and "newness." Washington's and other turn-of-the-century social leaders' conception of "newness" was grounded in the ability to transcend and ultimately "look past the past" of black history toward an idealized tomorrow. As the century progressed, influential black radicals such as A. Phillip Randolph also made widespread use of the term for "militant" purposes so as to arouse African Americans into a strong, defensive self-consciousness.

The best-known figure of this period was W. E. B. Du Bois, who, like Hopkins, straddled the fields of fiction, journalism, historical and cultural research, and numerous other disciplines. The first African American to receive a doctorate from Harvard and an icon of African American letters, Du Bois's life literally spanned the Reconstruction era to the early stages of the contemporary Civil Rights movement. He is a particularly important figure to juxtapose with Hopkins. As scholars such as Eric Sundquist and Cynthia Schrager have dem-

onstrated, both Du Bois and Hopkins explored the intersections of spiritualism and the African diasporic liberation movements.

According to Schrager, each used the "transpersonal" themes associated with mesmerism to great effect. Both Hopkins and Du Bois' works made reference to concepts and images rooted in nineteenth century spiritualism, the trans-Atlantic movement dedicated to the study of the human soul and traversing the boundaries between life and death. Each author applied the existential and philosophical questions embedded in spiritualist culture to questions of racial identity and the politics of the colorline. Moreover, spiritualism offered a convenient site for "cultural nationalists" such as Hopkins and Du Bois to imagine a fluid frontier between North America and West Africa for black Americans to travel spiritually in their pursuit of racial ideological revelations. This similarity in philosophical, spiritual and political concerns is particularly evident in Hopkins' *Of One Blood* and in Du Bois' treatise on twentieth century race relations, *The Souls of Black Folk* (1901).

Unlike Du Bois, however, Hopkins employed spiritualism in her work both as a tool for Pan-Africanist sociopolitical movements and as a specific representational strategy designed to articulate a black feminist agenda and African American women's quests for narrative agency in the postbellum era.

To this end, Hopkins operated in concert with the critically influential and tirelessly active black women's club movement of the turn of the century by engaging the movement's most pressing issues in her prose. She, for example, explored mob rule and the lynching epidemic in North America, disenfranchisement, and the problem of the color line and institutionalized Jim Crow. Hopkins also addressed the obstacles specifically facing African American women in their quest to reappropriate the discourses of morality, social propriety, and their own bodies from slavery's legacies of the systemic rape and concubinage of black women. Hazel Carby points out that by delineating the ways in which the lynching of black men in the South and the rape of African American women in slavery worked in tandem to repress the social and political empowerment of the black community, Hopkins' work reflects the sophisticated, militant journalism of her contemporary Ida B. Wells. It was Wells who, following the lead of Mary Ann Shadd Cary in the decades before her, set a new standard of innovation and bold, unapologetic political activism in her antilynching editorials and investigative reports for the *Free Speech* newspaper in Memphis, Tennessee, and for the *New York Age* periodical in the 1890s. Wells's method of attempting to condemn the architects of lynch mob murders "by their own hands," through the incorporation of transcribed confessions and reprints of prosegregation articles, signaled a new level of structural fluidity in African American cultural production—even within the context of nonfictional prose. Hopkins would expand on this sort of fluidity of form by not only writing fiction, journalism, and historical surveys, such as the twin series *Famous Women of the Negro Race* and *Famous Men of the Negro Race*, but also by imaginatively combining these forms within the context of the sentimental novel genre. Although she is often overshadowed in literary criticism by her legendary contemporary Du Bois, it is evident that, from the advent of Hopkins' ambitious and relatively short-lived forays into literary production, she deftly rewrote the script, as it were. of African American letters at the turn of the century.

Peculiar Sam

Written in 1879, roughly two decades before the major box-office successes of black musical companies such as Williams and Walker and Black Patti's Colored Troubadours, *Peculiar Sam* is, according to Leo Hamalian and James V. Hatch, one of the earliest musical dramas in the history of black theater. Although it clearly builds on the basic plot of William Wells Brown's abolitionist play *The Escape, or the Leap for Freedom* (1858) in its emphasis on tracing the trajectory from slavery to freedom among its African American characters in the

antebellum south, *Peculiar Sam* is early evidence of Hopkins' ongoing investment in engaging antebellum issues in the postbellum era. It thereby recalls the abolitionist ideological activism of that era as well. Hopkins' text differs from Brown's in its almost ritualistic invocation of music—slave spirituals in chorus, extravagant solos, lively duets—in the structure of the drama. Rather than subsuming music within its plot, *Peculiar Sam* employs singing and dancing in the forward movement of the play so that performance operates as an allegorical means to liberation and as a kind of "escape art" in and of itself within the text. The three-act play is structurally built around the escape plot of the enslaved Sam, who is described in the stage directions as "a peculiar fellow." The conflict between Sam and the black overseer, Jim, who remains psychologically as well as physically shackled in the regime of slavery until his "conversion" late in the play, functions as the major action of the musical. Sam's relationship with the stationmaster, Caesar, on the underground railroad, his camaraderie with friends Pete and Pomp, and his blooming romantic relationship with Virginia, "the plantation nightingale," all operate as significant subplots in Sam's escape plan and his elaborate method of foiling the jealous and conspiratorial Jim. Sam's sister, Juno, and his ever-devoted mother, Mammy, serve as the supportive, female-centered core of his domestic life on the plantation.

Peculiar Sam opens with a foregrounding of plantation performance; the stage directions call for the "unseen chorus" to sing as the curtain rises and Sam and Pete trade dance steps in the stolen time away from work. Within moments of the opening lines of the play, Sam expresses his desire to be free, a desire that marks his critical "difference," his "peculiarity," throughout the drama. He proclaims to Pete that "de spirits a movin' in me," and in his first solo of the play, he prophetically confesses to having powerful dreams of an inverted world of possibility where "the sun was shinin' bright in the middle of the night." Several choruses later, as the cast of characters enters, Sam is the first to broach the subject of escape. Resoundingly, he concludes that he will, through plot machinations, carry his entire family and community of comrades to Canada because "dars been suthin a growin' an' a growin' inter me, an' it keep sayin' 'Run'way, run away, Sam. Be a man, be a free man." It is in this scene that Sam is marked by his mother in terms of difference, as being "pecoolar." Thus, Hopkins uses the figure of Sam to embrace and distinguish heroic characters and to appropriate social "deviance" as a space of resistant social and political innovation.

Jim, Sam's foil, vows to thwart the escape plan and to keep Sam in his "proper" place as a subservient plantation field hand. Although Jim, too, reads Sam as a "culiar coon," he, unlike Mammy, finds Sam's difference threatening and problematic. From act 1 forward, however, Sam consistently rejects Jim's tyrannical execution of slave system ideology. He seizes the whip away from Jim in their initial confrontation, symbolically marking the ways in which southern slaves attempted to literally remove the weapons of power from their former oppressors during Reconstruction. Jim, "Marser's pet," as Sam refers to him, is an object of scorn throughout acts 1 and 2. His character prefigures other equivocal black figures that receive scorn and critique in Hopkins' later fiction, such as John Langley in *Contending Forces*, one of the earliest black villains in African American fiction. Through such characters, Hopkins expressed a political interest in addressing internal schisms within postbellum black communities and examining the nature of the social, moral, and political character of African Americans as they made the trek out of slavery and into the twentieth century.

With the exception of Jinny (Virginia), Sam's love interest and the "young mulatto girl" of the plantation, all of *Peculiar Sam*'s characters speak in shifting layers of black vernacular. The exclusion of Jinny from this kind of characterization reflects a pattern not only in Hopkins' later fiction but in popular literary production of the nineteenth century as well. For instance, in Harriet Beecher Stowe's enormously successful 1851 novel *Uncle Tom's Cabin*, the mulatto characters such as Casey and George and Eliza Harris each speak in standard English and

execute what would become some of the iconographic forms of "heroic escape" in American letters. In contrast, "dark-skinned" characters run the gamut from minstrel-show buffoonery—for example, Topsy, whose malapropisms and slapstick humor evoked the major tropes of the theatrical blackface stage genre—to Uncle Tom's passive yet divinely heroic black Christ figure who speaks in a kind of "noble" dialect to express his willingness not to flee slavery but to redeem and convert the enslaved to a life of religious faith and spiritual liberty. Unlike *Uncle Tom's Cabin* or the minstrel show, *Peculiar Sam* distinguishes itself from either of those generic constructions of black characters in dialect. While Hopkins would fall prey to the literary convention of putting particular emphasis on the virtues of mulatto characters throughout her career as a writer, *Peculiar Sam* represents a crucial departure from the aforementioned stereotypes of dark-skinned black characters in nineteenth-century literature.

Rather than employing dialect in the play to mark the characters as clownish, Hopkins used the vernacular to manipulate language and mount a clever critique of dominant culture. Through her use of the vernacular, she worked from the inside out, as it were, to revise black caricature by manifesting signs of rebellion in the very language that her characters speak. Mammy's early concern over Sam's escape plot, that it might bring "disrace onter" her, exemplifies how Hopkins used the veil of black dialect to address critical concerns regarding the political nature of African American identity and which kinds of social acts constituted the formation of that identity. In addition, through their escape to Canada, Sam and Juno execute a successful conversion from speaking dialect to speaking standard English. Through the use of the vernacular, Hopkins emphasized the social forces influencing the formation of black identity and likewise, the critical transformations open to African Americans as they crossed the divide from bondage to freedom.

Indeed, transformation is a recurring theme in the play, particularly in act 2, the pivotal act between plantation life and liberation in the musical. In the closing scene of act 1, Sam appears in disguise as the overseer Lucas and puts into play his plot to deceive Jim and throw the latter off of the trail of tracking his comrades' escape route. Act 2 focuses in detail on the confrontation between Sam and Jim, who recognizes the former in his disguise as Lucas but whose own plot to trick Sam back into the bounds of slavery is foiled by Sam's superior ability to read through Jim's machinations. Sam is presented as the more skillful trickster of the two, and Juno assumes the militant role of guarding and suppressing Jim from ultimately ruining the escape plan of the others. Indeed, Juno functions as one of the most militant black female characters in nineteenth-century letters, brandishing a pistol, "playing" at "shooting" Jim, and psychologically terrorizing the overseer into a long-standing state of submission.

The transitional act 3 underscores Hopkins' view of performance as a means to liberation in and of itself in *Peculiar Sam.* This short act takes place on the "banks of a river," and is comprised almost completely of songs sung by the chorus as the cast crosses over the river, "shaking hands" and expressing joy in their newfound liberation.

Act 4, set in the post–Civil War period, repositions the characters, (many of whom have lost their dialect) within the context of new professional and political roles within the black community and the nation at large. Sam has become a congressman and Jinny a singer. Hopkins again juxtaposes politics and performance, and demonstrates, as the famous cakewalk dancer Aida Overton-Walker would also suggest two decades later in print, the viability of performance as a form of both financial support and leadership for black Americans in the postbellum era. Jim again encounters Sam's cadre of friends and family and reveals himself to have conclusively rejected the plantocracy ethos of slavery. The final recuperation of Jim affirms Hopkins' ultimate and long-standing agenda to illustrate the power of both socioeconomic and ideological convertibility among African Americans entering into the "New Negro" era in her work.

Peculiar Sam was Hopkins' greatest success as a playwright. Yet it is rarely discussed in relation to the rest of the writer's corpus. In addition to this musical, she is believed to have at least written several other dramatic works, including a musical drama, *Aristocracy* (1877), and a five-act play entitled *Winona* (1878), which may in fact have been a precursor to her serialized novel of the same name that appeared years later in *Colored American Magazine.* After *Peculiar Sam,* Hopkins also completed the unproduced "One Scene from the Drama of Early Days," based on the biblical story of Daniel in the lion's den. At the age of forty-one, now with an extensive dramatic and oratorical background, she joined the staff of *Colored American Magazine* and assumed a high-profile role as writer and public voice in the northeastern black community. In 1900 she also published an epic and ambitious first novel that both invoked the historical and political content of her past theater work and marked a new engagement with multiple and intersecting literary forms of the period.

Contending Forces

Contending Forces was published by the same production company that sponsored *Colored American Magazine.* Its subtitle, "A Romance Illustrative of Negro Life North and South," suggests the narrative's attempts both to engage in realist "illustrations" of black life in a new era of transition between "north and south" and to apply the genres of sentimentality and domestic fiction to representations of the African American experience in the post-Reconstruction era. Although she addressed many of the issues also of great concern to Ida B. Wells, Hopkins employed fiction to expand the ways in which to articulate the political economy of desire, social discontent, and hopes for reform from within the black community. Indeed, fiction may have operated for Hopkins as an alternative format to journalism in the quest for literary avenues to examine the controversial topics of lynching, rape, and concubinage. The fiction of Hopkins and other black female intellectuals from the turn of the century, such as Frances Harper, offered a way to enact an imaginative form of narrative agency over their own texts, as well as a way to represent and recuperate their own bodies in narrative form.

Postbellum black female novelists and fiction writers such as Hopkins explored a complex expression of "social and political desire" through the genre of the sentimental novel and the romance narrative. Originating in eighteenth-century Great Britain, the sentimental and domestic fiction genres were of great use to burgeoning black women authors, as Claudia Tate and Valerie Smith have each demonstrated. Many of these writers, including Hopkins, sought to invoke sentimentality and domestic themes of family, marriage, and matrilineal relations in order to work in concert with the adventure and political themes of many texts by black male writers such as Frederick Douglass and Sutton Griggs. By engaging in the sentimental novel and exploring the realm of familial and communal space, as opposed to exclusively tracing interracial conflict, the fiction of black feminist postbellum authors situated itself centrally within post-Reconstruction black communities. Moreover, for African American women, the "cult of domesticity" previously championed by Anglo women such as Catherine Beecher and her sister Harriet Beecher Stowe took on greater significance beyond the original claims of providing a "moral" influence on American culture. Rather, black women's sentimental fiction was yet another platform to directly engage with the period's political concerns. Domestic themes could address the dual concerns of political and social activism and affirm black women's place within the context of "true womanhood," a sphere previously denied them precisely because of their history as victims of sexual abuse in slavery. Hence, nineteenth-century black women's narrative, as Gabrielle Foreman, Barbara Christian, and other critics have revealed, encompassed communal as well as specifically feminist agendas.

Hopkins' first novel strategically mediates the genres of romance and realism. Her work self-consciously combines the genre of journalistic documentation with that of domesticity and sentimentality. Although various critics have argued that these sorts of discourses are commensurate with Booker T. Washington's accommodationist rhetoric of the period, feminist scholars have convincingly shown how sentimentality provided an alternate means of politicized resistance to the social and political repression characteristic of the turn of the century. Through sentimentality, as well as a multiplicity of popular modes of expression, Hopkins aligned herself with radical protest sentiments of the period, efforts to ban lynching, and club movements that actively produced literature to promote the high morals of black womanhood. She espoused these sentiments with increasing complexity throughout her literary career.

As evidenced by her journalism published at the time *Contending Forces* appeared, Hopkins believed firmly in the value and political significance of cultivating a people's arts and literature as a sign of social progress and spiritual redemption. She proclaimed in the preface to *Contending Forces* that "fiction is of great value to any people as a preserver of manners and customs-religious, political and social. It is a record of growth and development from generation to generation." Years before Du Bois expressed a similar sentiment in his role as editor of *The Crisis,* the "record of the darker races" in the 1910s, Hopkins strongly encouraged the documentation of the African American experience. To her, writing and aesthetic representation symbolized the ways in which black communities could actively insert themselves into the national imaginary. Ultimately, as a fiction writer and editor of *Colored American Magazine,* she popularized the concept of using cultural arts as an avenue to revise dominant culture and to assert race pride on a popular level. Hopkins' views placed her in direct opposition to Washington's philosophies, which appealed to the interests of southern whites by stressing, among other things, suffrage restrictions, socially unequal segregationist standards, and an underlying support of southern, white patriarchal and juridical standards. It was with deep irony that in 1904 Hopkins would be ousted from her prolific and influential role at *Colored American Magazine* by none other than representatives of Washington's "Tuskegee machine."

At the beginning of Hopkins' tenure at the periodical, however, her work affirmed and embodied the ambitiousness and hopefulness considered characteristic of the "New Negro" era. *Contending Forces* stands as a representative landmark of the powerful convergences between political realism, domestic fiction, and aggressively anti-accommodationist rhetoric. The plot of the narrative foregrounds the struggles of the mixed-race Smith family—Ma Smith, her daughter, Dora, and son, Will—and their experiences in turn-of-the-century, post-Reconstruction Boston running a boarding-house in the middle-class black community. The opening chapters begin earlier in the century, tracing the experiences of the Smith's ancestors, the Montforts, and their odyssey from running a plantation of slaves in Bermuda to their decision to resettle in antebellum Virginia. In their move from the Carribean to the American South, the Montforts experience a "fall" from being slave owners to being American slaves themselves. The two sons in the family ultimately escape slavery as one marries into a free black northern family and the other into an aristocratic, white philanthropist English family. Here, the narrative splits. One part traces the reunification of the lost British side with the American side. The other portion focuses on the postbellum experiences and courtships of two African American heroines: Dora Smith and Sappho Clark. Dora negotiates a stormy relationship initially with the villainous John Langley, himself a product of illicit, miscegenational relations in slavery. She later marries the noble Dr. Arthur Lewis. The alluring and enigmatic Sappho Clark embarks on a complex and heady relationship with the political and intellectual activist and leader Will Smith, whom she ultimately marries. Although the novel ends by affirming the classic "marriage plot" of turn-of-the-century black novels, the heroines must first confront their equally turbulent and intricate respective histories of rape, lynching, and incest that inform their mixed-race heritage. Sappho in particular must confront her repressed past and status as an "immoral," unwed mother coerced into concubinage by a white uncle. Hence, the fulcrum of the novel's plot emphasizes the redressing of history and the reappropriation of black, and particularly black women's, autonomy in the wake of slavery and at the dawn of a new social, cultural, and political era.

To this end, Hopkins' characters operate as mouthpieces of the contemporaneous debates between Washington and his political foil, Du Bois. Arthur Lewis, a black southern businessman, functions as the Washington character while the Harvard-educated Will Smith, the romantic hero of the text, articulates a consistently vociferous belief in African American franchisement and education. The second half of the narrative focuses at length on Smith's arguments during a meeting of the Colored American League, an organization that anticipates by nearly a decade the actual historical creation of the National Advancement for the Association of Colored People. These debates, which outline the black struggle to obtain federal condemnation of the southern lynching problem, are prefigured by the political dialogue between the dual black female heroines, Dora, Will's sister, and the mysterious mulatta figure and southern migrant Sappho Clark. Indeed, Dora and Sappho's lengthy discussions about "race troubles," as well as the pros and cons of marriage, family, and the "woman question," establish the primacy of black women's voices, social, and political concerns within the narrative. Rather than dividing the space between public and political space and private and domestic space along gender lines, Hopkins demonstrates the exigencies of mixing the personal and political, the domestic and the legislative in her vision of New Negro America.

The narrative brings to life Du Bois's vision of a "talented tenth" by centralizing black intellectual, artistic, and cultural activities within the confines of Ma Smith's thriving lodging house. It is here that Hopkins' characters indulge in literature and music as a communal activity. Each person is given the chance to perform unique talents and aesthetic talents. The gatherings serve as an outlet for self-expression and spiritual renewal, as an alternative cultural space to the potential trade work of many communal participants, thus anticipating the representation of "porch-life" in Zora Neale Hurston's *Their Eyes Were Watching God*. Through the representation of songs, poetry, and musical recitals in Ma Smith's lodging house, the narrative affirms the critical importance of African American cultural production and artistic and intellectual activity within the context of the larger political struggles of the period.

Alongside the emphasis on domesticity and the arts, *Contending Forces* engages in the genres of realism and journalistic documentation to further politicize and lend credence to the narrative agency of its author. Like the work of Ida B. Wells, the novel expresses an awareness of and an engagement with fact-finding and fact-revealing. Hopkins proclaimed in her preface that she "tried to tell an impartial story, leaving it to the reader to draw conclusions. I have presented both sides of the dark picture—lynching and concubinage—truthfully and without vituperation, pleading for that justice of heart and mind for my people." She also explained that the goal of her narrative is directly linked to the response of her audience. Her preface echoes Wells's influential antilynching propaganda pamphlets in that Hopkins on the one hand characterizes her discourse as "impartial" and objective and yet simultaneously argues that she is writing specifically and unabashedly for a particular cause, in support of black liberation ideology. Her work thus straddles the borders of documentation and fictional persuasion. Both Hopkins and Wells appeal to the sentiment of their readers, but they also underscore the centrality of revealing the "truth" of turn-of-the-century racial inequalities. Hopkins thus closely associated her fiction with "fact," acknowledging that "incidents portrayed in the early chapters of the book actually occurred." She indicated in her preface, for instance, that she culled many of the oratorical passages presented during the political debates at the Colored American League meeting from actual historical sources.

A narrative of the intricacies of mixed blood lines, rape, and miscegenation, *Contending Forces* influenced the direction of Hopkins' work for the remainder of her literary career. The early, near "primal scene" of rape sets the main action of the narrative into play and ultimately affects and haunts each of the characters in the text. The novel deploys the murder of reconciliatory slave owner Charles Montfort and the graphic allegorical "whipping" of his racially ambiguous wife, Grace Montfort, as a way of conjoining the themes of lynching and rape in the narrative. Both Charles and Grace are coded as being of potential "mixed blood"; thus, their demise at the hands of working-class, proslavery Virginians operates as a symbolic act of white supremacy and racial tyranny that would repeat itself in the postbellum era. Rape and lynching in this scene operate as twin tools of hegemony; Hopkins used this kind of symbolism to engage her readers with the urgency of outlawing both mob rule and the sexual exploitation of black women.

This point is brought home even more fully in the narrative's portrayal of Sappho. Threatened by the advances of John Langley, Sappho must confront the horrific trials of her past. Although she has changed her name to the classical Sappho in an effort to reinvent herself, Sappho must battle with Langley's unwanted advances, which potentially resituate her in a personal history of violent sexual abuse. Through Langley's character, Hopkins inverts and undermines the prosouthern ideological undergirdings of mob rule by attacking the propaganda of miscegenation. In response to the white supremacist agenda that attacked African Americans for potentially "mongrelizing" the race, Langley's mistreatment of both Sappho and Dora suggests that white—not black—blood has the potential to disrupt racial and therefore moral codes of purity. The text presents Langley as a clichéd example of racial amalgamation "gone bad," but it suggests that he inherits this passion from his white grandfather, Anson Pollock, the seditious overseer who rapes Grace and enslaves her servant, Lucy. *Contending Forces* suggests a legacy of white male sexual violence that has literally permeated the African American community through race mixing. The narrative posits a way of reading against popular notions of black moral "impurity" by calling into question Anglo moral politics as well. Indeed, through the figure of Langley, Hopkins also emphasizes the importance of black men supporting and coming to the aid of those women who survive sexual abuse (just as African American women have aided in the struggle to fight lynching). In this sense, the novel presents Will Smith as an alternative paradigm of black manhood, who ultimately re-values Sappho as a partner in the black liberation struggle.

In addition to the domestic, the antilynching, and the antirape agendas of *Contending Forces*, the text underscores the critical value of relationships between African American women as central to the major action of the novel. Stressing female solidarity, the novel suggests the various ways that relationships between women are perhaps more fulfilling than marriage. Although the potential for competition between Sappho and Dora exists, the two nevertheless enter into a passionate and long-lasting relationship with one another. Hopkins presents these two women as reciprocal characters. Neither figure dies off, as do many classic sentimental heroines who experience some sort of social "fall." Rather, it is the villainous John Langley who seeks to disrupt Dora and Sappho's friendship and who ends up suffering the traditional fate of the tragic sentimental heroine. In opposition, Sappho successfully resists patriarchal narrative possession. She assumes authority over her own life and narrates her story to an all-female audience, the women of the holy convent to whom she flees in the final stages of the narrative before her reunion with Will. Sappho reappropriates the role of mother of her own child and thus claims authorship of her own "text." She embraces and revalues her "duty" as a mother, a domestic heroine, and in turn siezes narrative control over her traumatic past. This powerful statement would be the first of many for Hopkins in her transformation into an early twentieth-century novelist and fiction writer.

Hagar's Daughter and *Winona*

Two lesser-known serialized novels came on the heels of *Contending Forces* in the years 1901 and 1902. *Hagar's Daughter* originally appeared in *Colored American Magazine* in March and April 1901. This text is most often discussed in terms of its careful focus on and critique of the law in the wake of Plessy v. Ferguson, the Supreme Court decision that federally sanctioned segregation until the mid-twentieth century.

Like *Peculiar Sam* and *Contending Forces*, *Hagar's Daughter* splits the narrative timeframe, in this case, between plot development in 1860s Maryland and an 1880s courtroom. In the antebellum plantation section of the novel, two prominent families are united in a marriage that ultimately inflicts far-reaching political, legal, and domestic disorder on future generations. The heroine Hagar Sargeant, a mixed-race and orphaned woman, weds Ellis Enson, the dashing heir to a prosperous plantation family. In spite of this union, Hagar preserves ties with her maternal figure, Aunt Henny, and Henny's daughter, Marthy. In the wake of the birth of Hagar and Ellis's first child, the domestic tranquility of Hagar's extended family life dissolves. The narrative introduces the villainous slave trader Walker as an agent symbolic of slavery's relentless policing of black bodies. Walker reveals Hagar to be a "slave child" raised by the Sargeant family. Claiming Hagar as his property now, Walker—in a well-crafted conspiracy with Ellis's profligate brother, St. Clair Enson—makes plans to "repossess" Hagar for his own profit. The "unveiling" of Hagar's racial heritage challenges Ellis's own racial politics, but he eventually renews his committment to his wife and pledges to flee to Europe with his family. Death, however, presumably destroys this plot and Hagar, in 1862, is in danger of being sold back into slavery. She manages to escape and, building on famous scenes from *Uncle Tom's Cabin* and William Wells Brown's novel *Clotel* (1853), Hagar leaps with her child into the Potomac river as an alternative to enslavement.

The remainder of the narrative takes place in the post-Reconstruction era, shifting from the "private" world of the plantation to national and judicial politics. Although names have been altered, the original characters are still in place; thus the text concerns itself with revealing identities through courtroom dramas revolving around property, inheritance and racial lineage. Politicians and government officials central role in the latter half of *Hagar's Daughter*.

A wealthy senator, Zenas Bowen, surfaces with his wife Estelle and his daughter Jewel. This political family is linked to even greater prominence with the impending marriage of Jewel to Cuthbert Sumner, the private secretary to General Charles Benson, a representative of the treasury department. Senator Bowen is Jewel's adopted father, who rescued her from drowning in the Potomac river. He operates as the link between the younger girl and his newly betrothed wife, Estelle. In turn, Estelle is revealed, in fact, to be both Jewel's biological mother and Hagar in disguise. In actuality, the murderous General Benson, intent on marrying Jewel himself and squandering her inheritance, is St. Clair Enson. Walker has transformed into Major Madison, a villain intent on employing his own dauthter Aurelia as a pawn to we Cuthbert Sumner for his fortune. At the crux of all these shifting personas is the patriarch Ellis Enson, who resurfaces at as the detective and chief of the Secret Service, Henson. As Henson, Ellis Enson restores social order by resolving the hidden familial and racial identities of Hagar, Jewel, and Aurelia—all women of African descent. In an added emphasis on the power and legacy of masquerades, Venus, a product of Marthy and Henny's matrilineal line, assists Henson in solving the mysteries of geneaology by cross-dressing as a character named "Billy," and serving as a spy for the detective's case. Kristina Brooks has observed that *Hagar's Daughter* is a text which encourages the exploration of racial amalgamation politics and the tenuousness of racial identity boundaries. This is a theme that Hopkins would repeatedly return to in her fiction.

The second serialized novel, *Winona: A Tale of Negro Life in the South and Southwest*, from 1902, is perhaps even more unwieldly in plot structure than *Hagar's Daughter*. Parts western, romance, fugitive slave narrative, and political novel, the narrative revolves around the dissolution and reconstruction of a mixed-race North American family. It begins in the Edenically rendered "wilderness" of the Niagra River, between the free-territory of Canada and the volatile U.S. western region of the mid-ninteenth century. The narrative traces the vicissitudes of a family headed by a white fatehr living life as an Indian by the name of "White Eagle."

As a widower whose wife, an African-American ex-slave, has already passed away when the narrative begins, White Eagle is in the position of raising a multicultural family alone on the western range. Settling in the woods surrounding the river, he cares for his adopted African-American son Judah, and he and his wife's only natural-born child, Winona. Hopkins weaves the historical figure of militant abolitionist John Brown, his band of radicals, and the pre-Civil War Free Soil conflict of the midwest into the obstacles and events which Winona, Judah, and White Eagle must surmount. The fragility of their uniquely interracial family unit is placed in jeopardy, as in both *Contending Forces* and *Hagar's Daughter*, by the tyrannical, far-reaching effects of slavery. Almost immediately, the family is forced into a quest for re-stability following the two children's tumultuous catapult into bondage. Elizabeth Ammons points out that the struggle over "familial legitimacy," the "fall" into bondage, and the restoration of the matrilineal and patrilineal lines all rearticulate the dominant themes of Hopkins' prose.

Of One Blood

All of Hopkins' works lead to *Of One Blood*, the author's final serialized novel and according to many critics, her most boldly executed and challenging literary work. First published in 1902–1903 in *Colored American Magazine*, *Of One Blood* spans three continents while tracing African American protagonist Reuel Briggs's search for cultural, historical, and individual meaning through a series of scientific experiments and expeditions. A Harvard-educated doctor, Reuel passes for white in the narrative; as the plot rapidly unfolds, readers come to discover that he is in actuality a lost African prince. The narrative underscores Reuel's deep interest in spiritualist research, supernatural phenomena, and especially mesmerism. The fascination with mysticism provides a potential opiate for his inner turmoil and his proclaimed sense of dislocation in the universe caused by his disguising his racial identity. Much of the circuitous plot centers on Reuel's doctor-patient relationship with Dianthe Lusk, the fictional star performer of the Fisk Jubilee Singers whom Reuel initially encounters at a choir concert. As fate would have it, Dianthe (also a "white-looking" black character) has a mysterious and mystical past of her own that promises to collide with Reuel's professional goals and personal history.

In one of the more significant plot twists (and there are many), following the concert Dianthe is rushed to a local hospital, the victim of a train wreck and suffering from presumably fatal injuries. Reuel, called in to administer to the singer, miraculously revives her out of a state of only "seeming rigor mortis." The doctor's chivalric energies draw him into a romantic relationship with Dianthe, which leads to marriage. Unbeknownst to Reuel, however, his friend and confidant, the transplanted southern plantation heir Aubrey Livingston, also desires Dianthe and engineers a scheme to send Reuel away on an archaeological expedition to Ethiopia.

This plot development shifts the remainder of the text into a journey narrative built around Reuel's movement toward Africa and toward the discovery of multiple "hidden selves" in the narrative. In Africa Reuel uncovers the hidden city of Telassar, an area steeped in ancient Ethiopian culture. Here, he is reunited with what turns out to be his lost tribal community, his "hidden self"; through clairvoyant methods, he not only learns of Aubrey's duplicity and his plan to both murder Reuel and force Dianthe into concubinage but he also confronts the horror that he, Dianthe, and Aubrey are all "of one blood" and that the three characters have thus been embroiled in an incestuous triangle. The narrative ends with Aubrey's hasty poisoning of Dianthe, Reuel's vengeful return to the States to hypnotize Aubrey to die by his own hand, and Reuel's final return to Telassar to ascend the throne and unite in leadership with a bronze Dianthe look-alike, Candace.

Of One Blood's skillful use of African American historical, cultural, and performative discourses reflects the diversity of nineteenth-century theatrical space as a site of racial, gender, and communal reconstruction. The novel begins by offering the theater as an answer to Reuel's emotional and intellectual desolation. Inspired by his spiritualist readings (which are in actuality passages from William James's 1890 essay "The Hidden Self"), Reuel asserts that he is indeed in search of what James calls in his essay that "undiscovered country" waiting to be mined internally. Reuel prompts Aubrey to join him in carrying forward his search for the secrets of the soul. Aubrey responds to Reuel's proposition with an invitation to the theater; his proposed "amusement" is none other than an African American student choir, the Fisk Jubilee Singers. Describing the concert to Reuel, Aubrey notes that the event is "a new departure in the musical world." The text's positioning of Aubrey's comment regarding the "newness" and mystery of black musical performance suggests that the concert might serve the double purpose of "amusing" Reuel and inspiring him to recast his analytical energies in a new direction, away from the "mysteries" of the universe and toward the titillating spectacle of African American performance. Thus, the narrative abruptly shifts in focus from Reuel's vast and largely solitary philosophical debate regarding the self and existential positionality toward (black) performative relief in a public setting.

Music and performance are heavily contextualized and politicized as sites of social resistance and development in the Reconstruction era as depicted in *Of One Blood*. Hopkins extends this point by weaving the landmark concerts of the enormously popular Fisk Jubilee

Singers into the plot, setting the stage for the pivotal role that performance will play in the novel. The event highlights theatricality as a site of both audience and performer pleasure, as an African American political device, and as a forum for solving the broad theoretical questions of self that threaten to consume Reuel Briggs. The text specifically articulates the symbolic social and political significance of the concert, pointing out that "these were representatives of the people for whom God had sent the terrible scourge of blood upon the land to free from bondage." As figures on stage before an all-white audience, the singers serve as a vehicle for relating the history of a people to an audience enticed by the deeply affective quality of such a representation. Through their renditions of Negro spirituals, the choir taps into the audience's emotional core and its relationship with a turbulent history of slavery and abolition still fresh in its memory.

This performance scene introduces the notion of musical performance as a visceral as well as ideological theme that binds the African American characters together in the narrative. Dianthe Lusk's soprano solo, for instance, demonstrates the ability to carry Reuel "out of himself" during the course of the concert. So wrought with "divine fire" and historical weight is Dianthe's performance that "all the horror, the degradation from which a race had been delivered were in the pleading strains of the singer's voice." The link between the communal expressiveness found in Dianthe's singing and Reuel's initial ability to be carried "outside" of what one might read as his "passing" self anticipates the role of the performative in the lives of *Of One Blood*'s characters. Beyond the visceral catharsis that music seems to offer black individuals in crisis, such as Reuel, the novel affirms the function of performance as a means of reawakening and reformulating African American identity in the post-Reconstruction era.

Dianthe's relationship to her performative past vividly articulates the union between constructions of blackness and performance culture; she is the exemplary figure of racial identity remade through performance. Following

her near-death experience and subsequent resuscitation, Dianthe is left with little memory of her successful past as a Jubilee Singer. Under the care of Reuel, Aubrey, and the latter's fiancée, Molly Vance, the singer flourishes in New England, upper-class culture, where "she accepted the luxury of her new surroundings as one to the manner born." Unrecognized and unable to recollect her past as the graceful, "fair-skinned" black choir soprano, Dianthe is fully accepted into an elite Anglo community populated by doctors and socialites. Reminders of her former self, however, hint at a unique complexity in the representation of Dianthe's African American lineage. At an afternoon function featuring an Anglo women's singing group, for instance, "the grand, majestic voice that had charmed the hearts from thousands of bosoms, was pinioned in the girl's throat like an imprisoned song-bird. Dianthe's voice was completely gone along with her memory. But music affected her strangely." Voice and former (black) self have been symbolically lost, suggesting a powerful link between performative expression and African American identity.

This connection is driven home later in the plot when music serves as the catalyst for the return of Dianthe's memory. Following a waltz at the Vances, Dianthe is drawn, as if in a trance, toward the parlor piano, where she assumes "a strange rigid appearance." Falling into a familiar rendition of "Go Down, Moses," she holds yet another group of white spectators in awe, while disrupting their notion of her "true" self. On the heels of this startling, impromptu performance, "memory . . . return[s] in full save as to her name," and Aubrey proceeds to relate the past to Dianthe, having, along with Reuel, concealed this information from her, ostensibly to protect her psychological health. Music even permeates the way in which Dianthe experiences this narration of her black past; as she listens to Aubrey tell her tale, "the pulsing music of the viols beating and throbbing in her ears like muffled drums" provides a dramatic, if contrived backdrop while again yoking the rediscovery of black identity and musical culture together. The black female figure becomes representative of the "New Negro" self here, a self reconnected to a communal as well as an individual past. Dianthe's reunion with a distinctly intermingled African American and performative cultural history reveals how *Of One Blood* aggressively characterizes performance as a way to access a cultural past and the "reconstruction" of black identity.

Reuel's relationship with Dianthe reinforces this union of performance and black culture, extending the bond so as to allegorically represent the ritualized resuscitation of African American communal identity as well. Given Reuel's professional interest in mesmerism and "the reanimation of the body after seeming death," he is particularly fascinated with Dianthe's near-fatal condition after the train accident. His ability to revive Dianthe gets quickly labeled a miracle and a product of the supernatural. This performance, much like Dianthe's own singing, which revives a history of a people, restores life into a physical black body believed to be deceased. Dianthe's literal "rebirth," which prefigures her cultural reawakening, spurs Reuel forward in his quest to answer the questions "why are we created? [and] for whose benefit?"

Critics such as Jennie Kassanoff read this plot development as the key point that reveals Dianthe's ultimate lack of agency in the greater narrative, which ends with her death and Reuel's climactic ascent to African royalty. Critics cite the "reanimation" scene, which serves as such a remarkable symbol of nation building, as nevertheless vexing in its (dis)placement of Dianthe's figure. Reuel's studied role as mesmerist and his successful manipulation of Dianthe's body before an eager white audience of doctors operates as an allegory for the "reanimation" of the African diaspora, dispelling the dominant culture's doubts regarding black self-renewal. His "miracle" seemingly works at the expense of Dianthe's autonomy and performative agency. Indeed, upon reviving the performer, he poses to "marry her before she awakens to consciousness of her identity. . . . I will give her life and love and wifehood and maternity and perfect health." Reuel's Frankenstein-like obsessiveness with Dianthe illustrates the way in which

he envisions her body as a conduit through which he will attempt to symbolically unmake and remake black culture.

This sort of a reading of Dianthe's role in the narrative fails to take into consideration Hopkins' personal engagement with performance as a representational strategy of empowerment for black women. Indeed, given Hopkins' investment in theater culture, one could read Dianthe's reanimation as a different kind of performance, one that recuperates and transforms the politics of the narrative authority she initially deploys in her gospel solos. As spiritualist medium, she engages in a legacy of black women's mystical performances that provide the crucial link between the American and African landscape in the narrative.

Dianthe's role as Reuel's medium certainly depends on a complex formulation of her figure, which makes it at times difficult to mark her agency in the novel's many spiritualist exchanges. Her body suffers different levels of affliction as a result of her mesmerism-induced "trance-states," which presumably render her abject, a "slave" to her body. We are told that during her initial trip to the hospital, Dianthe is already the subject of mysterious (and never fully explained), pre-Reuel mesmeric influences.

Although Reuel confesses an early desire to capitalize on Dianthe's vulnerability and to potentially convert Dianthe's identity through spiritualism, his own narrative authority in such exchanges is repeatedly called into question and complicated. For instance, he assures his medical colleagues after his startling treatment of Dianthe that he is but "an instrument" in the larger spiritualist and scientific projects to which he has dedicated himself. And perhaps more important, Reuel's own trance-states, in which he initially envisions an ephemeral Dianthe, find him struggling to maintain his own agency. We are told that at the sight of Dianthe's silhouetted, floating figure, it is Reuel who is seemingly abject as he unsuccessfully "tries to move" but is in fact powerless at the sight of the (preaccident) vision. Reuel and Dianthe's shifting mesmeric positions thus prevent an oversimplistic reading of gender dynamics and spiritualist culture in *Of One Blood*. Rather, spiritualism sustains the theme of cross-gender partnership, which Hazel Carby reads as being central to Hopkins' plot. Carby argues that Dianthe becomes "the mediating figure" for Reuel's first coalition building with the black community and that he engages Dianthe as a partner in his philosophical, spiritual, and racial odyssey. Spiritualism and mesmerism allow for a terrain on which to develop an open field of cross-association and identification between African Americans in the quest for social and cultural empowerment through a method that ultimately transcended the parameters of the body itself.

Dianthe, in particular, critically transforms the role of medium; her character confronts and manipulates the threat of bodily and psychological subjugation in mesmerism, which comes precisely as a result of her serving as the mesmerist's patient. As the medium, she is forever perceived as "enshrouded" and in the words of one nineteenth-century preacher who campaigned obsessively against women's engagement in spirit rapping (supposed communication from the spirits of the dead through a series of raps), duplicitous and "veiled." Dianthe is consistently linked in the narrative to veil imagery, but in an interesting twist, the text takes this symbol of the veil, associated with both Du Boisian "double consciousness" and hidden female sexuality, and reinvents its symbolism. While in a trance-state Dianthe proclaims to Reuel that she is at times especially attuned to reading the enigmatic trope, arguing that, "I see much clearly, much dimly, of the powers and influences behind the Veil . . . Some time the full power shall be mine; and mine shall be thine." Here she assumes the role of the Du Boisian seer-figure, who sagely decodes the complexity of the color line. Moreover, the novel showcases her gospel performances as "veiled" spectacles, rising and falling upon every wave of the great soprano, and reaching the ear as from some strange distance." This latter imagery conversely acknowledges a kind of Pan-African desire that Du Bois articulated in his configuration of the veil in *The Souls of Black Folk*, where the veil represents the double consciousness of African Americans and a mystic vision that connects lost souls to a distant land. By positing Dianthe as capable of traversing the veil through clairvoyance and engaging in a kind of performance that allows her voice to reach "a strange distance," *Of One Blood* successfully mediates and revises Pan-Africanist ideology that often displaced or elided the significant role of black women in global uplift movements.

In 1904, following the publication of *Of One Blood*, Hopkins was ousted from her position as literary editor for *Colored American Magazine*. Although she would occasionally publish historical surveys and would contribute in 1916 to *New Era* magazine, a short-lived periodical, Hopkins' literary career came to halt by 1920. Little is known about her life in the fourteen years following her publications in *New Era*, but records show that she continued her stenographer work at the Massachusetts Institute of Technology before dying in 1930 at the age of 71, the victim of a fire in her home in Cambridge, Massachusetts. For a woman whose literary work remains so richly textured and imaginatively complex, the silences surrounding her later years and the tragic circumstances of her death leave a difficult and challenging void that students and fans of Hopkins' groundbreaking contributions to the African American canon have yet to fill.

Selected Bibliography

PRIMARY WORKS

NOVELS

Contending Forces: A Romance Illustrative of Negro Life North and South. Boston: Colored Co-operative, 1900. Reprint. Miami, Fla.: Mnemosyne, 1969. Reprint, with an afterword by Gwendolyn Brooks. Carbondale: Southern Illinois University Press, 1978. Reprint, with an introduction by Richard Yarborough. New York: Oxford University Press, 1988.

Hagar's Daughter: A Story of Southern Caste Prejudice. Colored American Magazine, March 1901–March 1902. Published under the pseudonym Sarah A. Allen. Reprinted in *The Magazine Novels of Pauline*

Hopkins. New York: Oxford University Press, 1988. Pp. 1–284.

Winona: A Tale of Negro Life in the South and Southwest. Colored American Magazine, May 1902–October 1902.

Of One Blood; or, The Hidden Self. Colored American Magazine, November 1902–November 1903. Reprinted in *The Magazine Novels of Pauline Hopkins.* New York. Oxford University Press, 1988. Pp. 439–621.

The Magazine Novels of Pauline Hopkins: 1901–3. New York: Oxford University Press, 1988. With an introduction by Hazel Carby. Includes *Hagar's Daughter, Winona,* and *Of One Blood; or, The Hidden Self.*

DRAMA

Peculiar Sam; or, The Underground Railroad. 1879. Reprinted in *The Roots of African-American Drama.* Edited by Leo Hamalian and James V. Hatch. Detroit, Mich.: Wayne State University Press, 1991. Pp. 100–123. Words and music also in *African American Theater: Out of Bondage* (1876) and *Peculiar Sam; or, The Underground Railroad* (1879). Edited by Eileen Southern. New York: Garland, 1994. Pp. 117–205.

SELECTED ESSAYS

Famous Men of the Negro Race. A series published in *Colored American Magazine.* ("Toussaint L'Overture," November 1900, pp. 9–24; "Hon. Frederick Douglass," December 1900, pp. 121–32; "William Wells Brown," January 1901, pp. 232–36; "Robert Browne Elliot," February 1901, pp. 294–301; "Edwin Garrison Walker," March 1901, pp. 358–66; "Lewis Hayden," April 1901, pp. 473–77; "Charles Lenox Remond," May 1901, pp. 34–39; "Sargent Wm. H. Carney," June 1901, pp. 84–89; "Hon. John Mercer Langston," July 1901, pp. 177–84; "Senator Blanche K. Bruce," August 1901, pp. 257–61; "Robert Morris," September 1901, pp. 337–42; "Booker T. Washington," October 1901, pp. 436–41.)

"A Dash for Liberty." *Colored American Magazine,* August 1901, pp. 243–47. Reprinted in *Short Fiction by Black Women, 1900–1920.* Edited by Elizabeth Ammons. New York: Oxford University Press, 1991. Pp. 89–98.

Famous Women of the Negro Race. A series published in *Colored American Magazine.* ("Phenomenal Vocalists," November 1901, pp. 45–53; "Sojourner Truth," December 1901, pp. 124–32; "Harriet Tubman," January–February 1902, pp. 210–23; "Some Literary Workers," March 1902, pp. 41–46; "Educators (Continued)," June 1902, pp. 125–30; "Educators (Concluded)," July 1902, pp. 206–13; "Club Life among Colored Women," August 1902, pp. 273–77; "Artists," September 1902, pp. 362–67; "Higher Education of Colored Women in White Schools and Colleges," October 1902, pp. 445–50.)

"Talma Gordon." *Colored American Magazine,* December 1902, pp. 113–19. Published under the pseudonym Sarah A. Allen. Reprinted in *Short Fiction by Black Women, 1900–1920.* Edited by Elizabeth Ammons. New York: Oxford University Press, 1991. Pp. 205–17.

"Heroes and Heroines in Black: I. Neil Johnson, American Woodfolk, et al." *Colored American Magazine,* January 1903, pp. 206–11.

"The Dark Races of the Twentieth Century." *Voice of the Negro,* February 1905, pp. 108–15; March 1905, pp. 187–91; May 1905, pp. 330–34; June 1905, pp. 415–18; July 1905, pp. 459–63.

"Topsy Templeton." *New Era Magazine,* February 1916, pp. 11–20, 48; March 1916, pp. 75–84.

SECONDARY WORKS

BIOGRAPHICAL AND CRITICAL WORKS

Ammons, Elizabeth. *Conflicting Stories: American Women Writers at the Turn into the Twentieth Century.* New York: Oxford University Press, 1991.

Brooks, Kristina. "Mammies, Bucks, and Wenches: Minstrelsy, Racial Pornography, and Racial Politics in Pauline Hopkins's *Hagar's Daughter.*" In *The Unruly Voice: Rediscovering Pauline Elizabeth Hopkins.* Edited by John Cullen Gruesser. Urbana: University of Illinois Press, 1996. Pp. 119–57.

Bruce, Dickson D., Jr. *Black American Writing from the Nadir: The Evolution of a Literary Tradition, 1877–1951.* Baton Rouge: Louisiana State University Press, 1989.

Campbell, Jane. *Mythic Black Fiction: The Transformation of History.* Knoxville: University of Tennessee Press, 1986.

Carby, Hazel. *Reconstructing Womanhood: The Emergence of the Afro-American Woman Novelist.* New York: Oxford University Press, 1987.

Christian, Barbara T. *Black Women Novelists: The Development of a Tradition, 1892–1976.* Westport, Conn.: Greenwood Press, 1980.

DuCille, Ann. *The Coupling Convention: Sex, Text, and Tradition in Black Women's Fiction.* New York: Oxford University Press, 1993.

Foreman, P. Gabrielle. "'Reading Aright': White Slavery, Black Referents, and the Strategy of Histotextuality in *Iola Leroy.*" *The Yale Journal of Criticism* 10, no. 2:327–54 (1997).

Gaines, Kevin Kelly. "Black American Racial Uplift Ideology as 'Civilizing Mission': Pauline E. Hopkins on Race and Imperialism." In *Cultures of United States Imperialism.* Edited by Amy Kaplan and Donald E. Pease. Durham, N.C.: Duke University Press, 1993. Pp. 433–55.

Gillman, Susan. "The Mulatto, Tragic or Triumphant? The Nineteenth-Century American Race Melodrama." In *The Culture of Sentiment: Race, Gender, and Sentimentality in Nineteenth-Century America.* Edited by Shirley Samuels. New York: Oxford University Press, 1992. Pp. 221–43.

Gruesser, John Cullen, ed. *The Unruly Voice: Rediscov-*

ering *Pauline Elizabeth Hopkins.* Urbana: University of Illinois Press, 1996.

Hamalian, Leo, and James V. Hatch. "Pauline Elizabeth Hopkins (1859–1930)." In *The Roots of African-American Drama: An Anthology of Early Plays, 1858–1938.* Detroit, Mich.: Wayne State University Press, 1991. Pp. 96–99.

Kassanoff, Jennie. "'Fate Has Linked Us Together': Blood, Gender, and the Politics of Representation in Pauline Hopkins's *Of One Blood.*" In *The Unruly Voice: Rediscovering Pauline Elizabeth Hopkins.* Edited by John Cullen Gruesser. Urbana: University of Illinois Press, 1996. Pp. 158–81.

McKay, Nellie. Introduction to *The Unruly Voice: Rediscovering Pauline Elizabeth Hopkins.* Edited by John Cullen Gruesser. Urbana: University of Illinois Press, 1996. Pp. 1–20.

Schrager, Cynthia D. "Pauline Hopkins and William James: The New Psychology and the Politics of Race." In *The Unruly Voice: Rediscovering Pauline Elizabeth Hopkins.* Edited by John Cullen Gruesser. Urbana: University of Illinois Press, 1996. Pp. 182–209.

Shockley, Ann Allen. "Pauline Elizabeth Hopkins." In her *Afro-American Women Writers, 1746–1933.* Boston: G. K. Hall, 1988. Pp. 289–95.

Smith, Valerie. "'Loopholes of Retreat': Architecture and Ideology in Harriet Jacobs's *Incidents in the Life of a Slave Girl.*" In *Reading Black, Reading Feminist: A Critical Anthology.* Edited by Henry Louis Gates Jr. New York: Meridian, 1990. Pp. 212–26.

Somerville, Siobhan. "Domestic Renovations: The Marriage Plot, the Lodging House, and Lesbian Desire in Pauline Hopkins's *Contending Forces.*" In *Burning Down the House: Recycling Domesticity.* Edited by Rosemary Marangoly George. Boulder, Colo.: Westview Press, 1998. Pp. 232–56.

Sundquist, Eric J. *To Wake the Nations: Race in the Making of American Literature.* Cambridge, Mass.: Harvard University Press, 1993.

Tate, Claudia. *Domestic Allegories of Political Desire: The Black Heroine's Text at the Turn of the Century.* New York: Oxford University Press, 1992.

Walker, Aida-Overton. "Colored Men and Women on the Stage." *The Colored American Magazine* IX, no. 4:571–75 (October 1905).

Washington, Mary Helen. *Invented Lives: Narratives of Black Women, 1860–1960.* Garden City, N.Y.: Anchor, 1987.

Yarborough, Richard. Introduction to *Contending Forces: A Romance Illustrative of Negro Life North and South,* by Pauline Hopkins. New York: Oxford University Press, 1988. Pp. xxvii–xlviii.

BIBLIOGRAPHY

Walther, Malin LaVon. "Works by and about Pauline Hopkins." In *The Unruly Voice: Rediscovering Pauline Elizabeth Hopkins.* Edited by John Cullen Gruesser. Urbana: University of Illinois Press, 1996. Pp. 221–30.

LANGSTON HUGHES
(1902 – 1967)

ARNOLD RAMPERSAD

IN MARCH 1966, about a year before his death, Langston Hughes flew from his home in New York City to Africa, to the city of Dakar in Senegal, to attend the widely heralded First World Festival of Negro Arts. As a leader of the large United States delegation, but more so as an individual in his own right, Hughes stood out among the more than two thousand visitors who had come from all over the world to celebrate the international appeal and influence of black culture. Known at home as the "poet laureate of the Negro race" and as the dean of African American writers, in this international setting he was honored for the worldwide impact of his lifetime of writing about the lives and cultures of his fellow blacks. Langston Hughes was both respected and immensely popular. While the poet-president of Senegal, Léopold Sédar Senghor, who had organized the festival, singled him out for his historic contribution to the development of black poetry and the concept of negritude, the *New York Times* also reported of Hughes that "young writers from all over Africa followed him about the city and haunted his hotel the way American youngsters dog favorite baseball players."

This honoring on an international scale in Africa followed on the heels of national honors at home that testified to the stature Hughes had achieved by the end of his life. In 1961 the National Institute of Arts and Letters had elected

him a member, and in 1960 the National Association for the Advancement of Colored People (NAACP), then probably at the height of its prestige because of the civil rights movement, had awarded him its annual Spingarn Medal for his contribution to the lives of black Americans. These honors were the result not only of diligent efforts but also of a striking identification on his part. From virtually the start of his career Hughes had forged a special bond with black readers in the United States and abroad through his conspicuous love of his people, which he demonstrated not simply by creating attractive portraits but also by saturating his art in the most significant popular expressive forms within the community, as well as in the struggles, sorrows, victories, and joys in the day-to-day lives of ordinary black people.

James Langston Hughes was born on 1 February 1902, in Joplin, Missouri, but grew up mainly in Lawrence, Kansas, in the home of his maternal grandmother, Mary Langston. Hughes and his mother, Carrie Langston Hughes, moved to Lawrence after his ambitious father, James Nathaniel Hughes, frustrated by racism in his determination to be a lawyer in Oklahoma, left his family behind and emigrated to Mexico. From his grandmother Hughes learned constantly about the need to struggle on behalf of the ideals of social justice and African American progress. A radical abolitionist in her youth, she had lost her first husband, Lewis Sheridan Leary, when he was shot and killed as a member of John Brown's band in its doomed assault at Harper's Ferry. Her second husband, Charles Langston (Hughes's grandfather), had himself taken part in a celebrated abolitionist action, the Oberlin-Wellington rescue, on behalf of a fugitive slave; and Charles's brother, John Mercer Langston, also an ardent abolitionist, had become one of the most famous black Americans of the nineteenth century as a lawyer, an educator, a diplomat, and a United States congressman from Virginia in the 1890s.

In spite of this colorful and prestigious background, Hughes passed his boyhood in poverty, as his mother searched for jobs to support her son and her mother. The frequent absences of his mother and the increasing withdrawal of his aging grandmother combined to make him a troubled child, according to his own account, "unhappy for a long time, and very lonesome." He was rescued from sadness by his discovery of books: "Then it was that books began to happen to me, and I began to believe in nothing but books and the wonderful world in books— where if people suffered, they suffered in beautiful language. His love of reading, then of writing, was first fostered by both his grandmother and his mother, who herself wrote verse and acted, and even hoped for a career on the stage.

As he later recalled, Hughes wrote his first poem after he left Lawrence for Lincoln, Illinois, where he spent a year with his mother between 1915 and 1916. But his main apprenticeship as a writer came in high school in Cleveland, Ohio, where he lived from 1916 to 1920. In the monthly school magazine he published short stories that showed an early concern with questions of social justice, though not with racism. His poetry in the magazine, at first undistinguished, revealed at one crucial point the decisive influence of Walt Whitman and then of Carl Sandburg, the Illinois poet of radical democracy—and free verse—whom Hughes remembered as my "guiding star." Under this influence, as well as that of Paul Laurence Dunbar and W. E. B. Du Bois from earlier in his life, he matured quickly. Within a year of graduating from high school, Hughes had

composed memorable poems in what would later be regarded as his authentic voice: "The Negro Speaks of Rivers," in which he quietly extolled the historic beauty and dignity of the African peoples; "Mother to Son," composed entirely in dialect but free of the stereotypes of low comedy or extreme pathos that had come to mar most black dialect verse; and "When Sue Wears Red," which ecstatically praises the beauty of a black woman and links her honorably and dramatically to Africa.

These poems were Hughes's first major literary response to the racism and segregation he had personally encountered, but more so to the plight of blacks in less fortunate circumstances than he had experienced as a young black in the Midwest. In addition to the tales of slavery and freedom told to him by his grandmother, he also knew from her and other blacks about the complex network of segregation, whether de jure or de facto, that marred the lives of blacks particularly in the South but also virtually across the country, and about the reign of terror through lynchings to which southern blacks were subjected. He himself had first experienced segregation and racist insult as a small child in Lawrence. However, Cleveland had proved a relatively benign place for his adolescent years, and he had actually flourished at Central High under conscientious teachers and with students, many of them the children of European immigrants, who in his senior year elected him class poet and editor of the annual.

Between his departure from high school in 1920 and the appearance of his first book in 1926, Hughes led an almost compulsively varied life. A disastrous year with his father in Mexico, when he finally faced the fact that "I hated my father" for his harshness and materialism, was followed by a disappointing year (1921–1922) at Columbia University, which Hughes found cold and hostile. He then descended into a succession of humble jobs, including delivery boy for a florist in Manhattan and worker on a vegetable farm on Staten Island (also in New York City). A desire to go to sea led to several months as a messman on ships anchored in the Hudson River, then to steamer voyages to Africa that allowed him to visit ports on the west coast of Africa from Senegal in the north to Angola in the south. Next came a similar job on a ship in Europe, where, after jumping ship, he passed several months in Paris as a dishwasher in a nightclub that featured black American entertainers.

Hughes returned to the United States near the end of 1924, then passed the following year in Washington, D.C., where his mother was living. Again he worked at lowly jobs—in a laundry and in restaurant kitchens, for example. During all this time of travel and work in the early 1920s, however, he had been diligently publishing poems—at first mainly in the *Crisis*, edited for the NAACP by W. E. B. Du Bois; then in Charles Johnson's *Opportunity*, sponsored by the Urban League; and in a widening circle of journals. Thus he had returned from Paris relatively well known to black lovers of poetry. In 1925 he finally made the decisive contacts that led to the publication by Alfred A. Knopf, in January 1926, of his first volume of verse, *The Weak Blues*.

From his first publication of verse in the *Crisis*, Hughes had reflected his admiration for Sandburg and Whitman by experimenting with free verse as opposed to committing himself conservatively to rhyme. Even when he employed rhyme in his verse, as he often did, Hughes composed with relative casualness—unlike other major black poets of the age, such as Countee Cullen and Claude McKay, with their highly wrought stanzas. He seemed to prefer, as Whitman and Sandburg had preferred, to write lines that captured the cadences of common American speech, with his ear always especially attuned to the variety of black American language. This last aspect was only a token of his emotional and aesthetic involvement in black American culture, which he increasingly saw as his prime source of inspiration, even as he regarded black Americans ("Loud laughers in the hands of Fate— / My People") as his only indispensable audience.

Early poems captured some of the sights and sounds of ecstatic black church worship ("Glory! Hallelujah!"), but Hughes's greatest technical accomplishment as a poet was in his fusing of the rhythms of blues and jazz with traditional

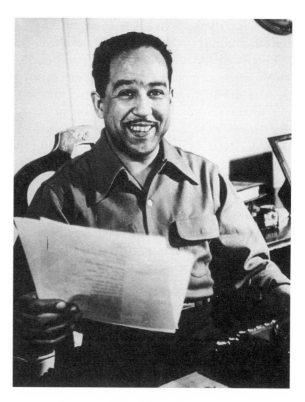

Langston Hughes

poetry. This technique, which he employed his entire life, surfaced in his art around 1923 with the landmark poem "The Weary Blues," in which the persona recalls hearing a blues singer and piano player ("Sweet Blues! / Coming from a black man's soul") performing in what most likely is a speakeasy in Harlem. The persona recalls the plaintive verse intoned by the singer ("Ain't got nobody in all this world, / Ain't got nobody but ma self") but finally surrenders to the mystery and magic of the blues singer's art. In the process, Hughes had taken an indigenous African American art form, perhaps the most vivid and commanding of all, and preserved its authenticity even as he formally enshrined it in the midst of a poem in traditional European form.

"The Weary Blues," a work virtually unprecedented in American poetry in its blending of black and white rhythms and forms, won Hughes the first prize for poetry in May 1925 in the epochal literary contest sponsored by *Opportunity* magazine, which marked the first

369

high point of the Harlem Renaissance. The work also confirmed his leadership, along with Countee Cullen, of all the younger poets of the burgeoning movement. For Hughes, it was only the first step in his poetical tribute to blues and jazz. By the time of his second volume of verse, *Fine Clothes to the Jew* (1927), he was writing blues poems without either apology or framing devices taken from the traditional world of poetry. He was also delving into the basic subject matters of the blues—love and raw sexuality, deep sorrow and sudden violence, poverty and heartbreak. These subjects, treated with sympathy for the poor and dispossessed, and without false piety, made him easily the most controversial black poet of his time.

The previous year (1926), with his essay "The Negro Artist and the Racial Mountain" in the *Nation*, he had composed the manifesto of the younger artists who were determined to assert racial pride and racial truth in the face of either black or white censure or criticism:

> We younger Negro artists . . . intend to express our individual dark-skinned selves without fear or shame. If white people are pleased we are glad. If they are not, it doesn't matter. We know we are beautiful. And ugly too. The tom-tom cries and the tom-tom laughs. If colored people are pleased we are glad. If they are not, their displeasure doesn't matter either. We build our temples for tomorrow, strong as we know how, and we stand on top of the mountain, free within ourselves.
>
> (*The Nation* 122:694 [June 1926])

Now, with *Fine Clothes to the Jew*, he faced a volcano of criticism from black reviewers. Never before had a black poet so clearly exposed these aspects of black culture to the white world, and the middle-class black critics responded to the volume with outrage. Langston Hughes was a "SEWER DWELLER," blared one headline; to another journal, he was the "poet 'low-rate' of Harlem"; yet another called the book "about 100 pages of trash" that reeked of "the gutter and the sewer." But Hughes refused to retract a line. Most blacks were of the lower class, he asserted; "even I my-self, belong to that class." In any event, "I have a right to portray any side of Negro life I wish to."

In 1926, seeking a greater degree of stability in his life, Hughes joined the almost all-black student body at Lincoln University in Pennsylvania, from which he graduated in 1929. About this time another, more private involvement proved to be at least as important. In 1927 he began to benefit from the patronage of the remarkable Mrs. Charlotte Mason, or "Godmother," an older white woman whose generosity to black writers and artists included support for Zora Neale Hurston and Alain Locke, among others. A firm believer in parapsychology and in the spiritual power of the darker races contrasted to the materialism of Europe, Mrs. Mason applied her powerful, highly volatile temperament to the task of guiding Hughes in his career. Alternately pampered and stimulated by her, and driven by her relentless editing, he somewhat unwillingly wrote his first novel, *Not Without Laughter* (1930). This often lyrical, charming, and moving story of a black Midwestern boyhood reflects only slightly the actual details of Hughes's past. However, this story of an old black mother, her three grown daughters, her son-in-law, and her grandson Sandy as they struggle for survival and even respectability against racism, poverty, and natural disaster is both a graphic portrait of a broad aspect of the black American world and a projection of Hughes's own desire as a child for a loving family, especially a father and a mother to shower him with the love he had craved and missed.

Hughes's sudden and highly dramatic expulsion by Mrs. Mason—for reasons still altogether unclear—virtually upended his life early in 1930. Deeply hurt but chronically unable to vent anger, he fell ill. His sickness was compounded when Zora Neale Hurston—with whom he had written *Mule Bone*, a folk comedy set in the deep South, while both were under Mrs. Mason's patronage—claimed the play as her sole property and denounced him as a liar. With four hundred dollars from the Harmon Prize for literature in 1930, he fled to Cuba and Haiti. He did not return until he had passed several weeks living almost aimlessly on the north coast of Haiti, near the famed citadel begun by Jean-Jacques Dessalines and completed by Henri Christophe, the most imposing symbol of black ambition and determination in the Western Hemisphere. During this time, however, Hughes clearly brooded on the major choices he had made in his life, and came to decisions about changes for the future.

Returning to the United States, which had started its downward slide into the Great Depression, Hughes moved swiftly toward the far Left. He published anti-imperialist essays and poems in *New Masses* and elsewhere, and made ready to work closely with the Communist John Reed Club of New York. Then, aided by a Rosenwald Fund grant, he headed south to begin a yearlong tour bringing his poetry to the people. Reading mainly in black churches and school halls for modest fees, and selling books, pamphlets, and posters from the back of a Ford driven by a friend, he moved steadily through the South before heading west. He stirred vicious controversy and risked his life at least twice: by making a rare appearance at the all-white University of North Carolina in Chapel Hill and by involving himself in the Scottsboro Boys controversy, first by visiting the town where the condemned black youths had been captured and accused of the rape of two white women, then by visiting some of the accused on death row in an Alabama prison.

By this point Hughes had given up blues and lyric poetry for militantly radical socialist utterance, such as *Scottsboro Limited* (1931), a verse play about the Scottsboro case. His radicalism reached its zenith following his reading tour, which took him as far as Oregon and Washington, when he joined a band of twenty-two young blacks recruited in the United States for a film on American race relations to be made in the Soviet Union. In June 1932, Hughes arrived in Moscow, but the poorly planned film project soon collapsed in a mire of controversy. Warmly received as a writer, he decided to spend a year in the Soviet Union. He traveled in the Central Asian republics with fellow writers, including the young journalist Arthur Koestler. In a small book published in Moscow,

A Negro Looks at Soviet Central Asia (1934), he contrasted the humane Soviet treatment of its ethnic minorities with the horrors of American segregation.

While in the Soviet Union, Hughes wrote and published the most radical verse of his life, including "Good Morning Revolution," "Columbia" (a sensational attack on American imperialism), and his single most controversial work, "Goodbye Christ," in which the speaker caps his or her rough dismissal of various well-known evangelists of dubious integrity with the dismissal of Christ in favor of "Marx Communist Lenin Peasant Stalin Worker ME—." This poem was published in the German-based radical magazine *Negro Worker*, apparently without Hughes's knowledge or permission. However, he did not repudiate it on its appearance, as he would later do.

In August 1933, Hughes returned to the United States via China and Japan. Noël Sullivan, a liberal patron of the arts whom he had met in San Francisco during his tour the previous year, then arranged to support Hughes's writing of a series of short stories for a year at Sullivan's cottage in the wealthy resort village of Carmel, on the Monterey Peninsula. Neither patronage nor friendship prevented Hughes from showing his new cynicism about race relations in America in the stories penned in Carmel, which formed the heart of his important collection *The Ways of White Folks* (1934). In stories such as "These Blues I'm Playing" and "Slave on the Block," he attacked the insincerity and confusion of many whites in their dealings with blacks. Other stories pilloried racism in various forms, at times with such harsh psychological realism that the collection in some ways sounded a note of unprecedented bitterness in African American fiction. It also established Hughes with the leading magazines as a writer of fiction, a major consideration given his determination to live solely by his writing.

At the end of his Carmel year, late in 1934, the death of his father, whom he had not seen since 1921, took Hughes to Mexico. His hopes for a legacy were soon dashed, but he remained in Mexico for several months. His major work there was an act of typical generosity and cosmopolitanism—the translation of several short stories written by progressive young Mexicans, for possible publication in the United States. Unfortunately, nothing came of this project; American editors were uninterested in such material. Almost penniless, Hughes returned in 1935 to the United States to join his mother, who was then living in Oberlin, Ohio, where her parents had passed some of their youthful abolitionist days before the Civil War.

Almost at once his career took a sudden turn with the news that his *Mulatto: A Play of the Deep South*, about miscegenation and written in 1930, was about to open on Broadway. In *Mulatto*, Hughes drew to some extent on his family history, in that his grandfather Charles Langston had been the somewhat rebellious son of a white Virginia planter and a slave, Lucy Langston, with whom the planter had lived as if in marriage, even bequeathing most of his property to his children upon his death. In the play, a mulatto son of a similar "marriage" demands recognition by his father. When Colonel Norwood refuses, he inaugurates an action that ends with his death at the hands of his son, who is soon on the brink of being lynched even as his grieving mother goes mad. Thus Hughes dramatized the tragedy of American race relations as epitomized in the segregated South, with its denial of the humanity of blacks and their essential part in the nation, and the disaster awaiting the republic as a result of that denial.

With certain sensational changes in Hughes's text and with a series of ingenious publicity ploys, the white producer of *Mulatto* kept the play alive in spite of harsh reviews that questioned Hughes's skill as a playwright. *Mulatto* remained on Broadway longer than any other play by a black playwright until Lorraine Hansberry's *A Raisin in the Sun* (with its title from a Hughes poem) more than a generation later. In the next few years, working closely with the Karamu Theater in Cleveland, Hughes tried to repeat the success of *Mulatto*. First came the farce *Little Ham* (1936), set mainly in a shoeshine parlor, with its diminutive bootblack hero, Hamlet Hitchcock Jones, and his many women friends and admirers and his passion for

playing the "numbers." In 1936, Karamu staged the premiere of *Troubled Island* (later retitled *Emperor of Haiti*), Hughes's drama of the Haitian revolution, with its emphasis on the failure of Jean-Jacques Dessalines to sustain the national spirit that had won independence from France. Not long afterward, the Cleveland group staged Hughes's *Joy to My Soul*, a broad comedy about a rich but dim young man come from Texas to Harlem in search of a bride. Still later in the 1930s Karamu staged the melodrama *Front Porch*, about a striving black family living uneasily in a mainly white neighborhood, and a daughter who is forced into an abortion that kills her.

None of these Karamu plays resulted in a commercial or a major critical success. Among Hughes's other plays in the 1930s, the brief *Soul Gone Home* is a provokingly macabre comedy about a dead young man who "comes alive" to scold his heartless mother as she prepares to go out on the town. *Don't You Want to Be Free?* was written by Hughes for his radical Harlem Suitcase Theater, which he founded in 1938 after returning from several months in besieged Madrid as a war correspondent for a black newspaper. This radical play, which combines several of Hughes's poems with the music of the blues and a loose story line that ends in a rousing call for class unity and for revolution, ran for over one hundred performances in Harlem. The year 1938 also marked the appearance of Hughes's only collection of radical socialist poetry, *A New Song*, with an introduction by the radical writer Mike Gold. It was published by the leftist International Workers Order, which was also behind the Harlem Suitcase Theater.

None of these plays made Hughes much money. In fact, most made him virtually nothing, so that throughout the 1930s he lived close to poverty. In 1939 he accepted with alacrity the chance to work as a writer in Hollywood with the black actor and singer Clarence Muse on *Way Down South*, a movie intended as a vehicle for the popular boy singer Bobby Breen. To Hughes's chagrin, the movie, set on a plantation in the days of slavery, was denounced in progressive circles when it opened later that year. He soon had another setback of at least equal consequence. A major book luncheon at a hotel in Pasadena, California, at which his freshly published autobiography, *The Big Sea* (1940), was to be featured, was canceled following picketing by an evangelical group who accused Hughes of atheism and communism. At the heart of their objections was his 1932 poem "Goodbye Christ." Hughes then repudiated the poem as an aberration of his youth, and ended his decade-long identification as a radical socialist.

The Big Sea, written before this repudiation, shows clearly that Hughes was already well prepared to make the shift; the volume makes virtually no mention of socialism. Penned in the clear, simple, unpretentious prose characteristic of Hughes, the book unfolds in a succession of brief, episodic chapters narrated in an often droll manner. However, this approach does not entirely conceal some of his more serious purposes and concerns, notably his anger at his parents and his unhappy childhood. In a disarming manner, Hughes portrayed his father as a Satan-like figure who tries to tempt the young black poet with an offer of untold riches in Mexico if only Hughes will surrender his soul—that is, give up blacks and poetry for profit. Hughes also tells frankly of his disaster with his patron, "Godmother," his inability to vent his anger, and his resulting serious illness. At the center of the text is a smiling, even-tempered young black hero who gracefully endures the vicissitudes of life, including those heaped specially on blacks, without ever falling into bitterness or despair. *The Big Sea* is also invaluable in that it provides a firsthand account, never surpassed, of the main personalities and events of the Harlem Renaissance.

With the entry of the United States into World War II, Hughes completed his withdrawal from the Left. His next volume of verse, *Shakespeare in Harlem* (1942), took him back, as he put it, to "Nature, Negroes, and love." The volume is dominated by the blues, which he had neglected as a writer throughout the preceding decade. Near the end of 1942, he started another line of work that would sustain him for the rest of his life. He accepted an invitation to write a column, "Here to Yonder," for the black weekly *Chicago Defender*. The column was conventional until early 1943, when Hughes related a conversation he had had in a bar with a man he called only "My Simple Minded Friend." This friend, barely literate but highly opinionated and possessed of a powerful, sometimes even bizarre, racial pride, eventually was identified as Jesse B. Semple, or "Simple"; the rather stuffy narrator was identified early on as Langston Hughes but was later called "Boyd." First intended as a ploy by Hughes to bolster support for the war effort among blacks, many of whom felt a sense of kinship with the non-white Japanese in the war, Simple quickly grew into by far the most popular aspect of the column and one of the more original comic creations in American journalism. The column lasted for more than twenty years, and was edited and adapted by Hughes into five books of Simple sketches, including *Simple Speaks His Mind* (1951), *Simple Takes a Wife* (1953), and *The Best of Simple* (1961). A musical play, *Simply Heavenly*, opened successfully off Broadway in 1957.

In retreating from the far Left around 1940, Hughes shifted his considerable energy back in the direction of matters pertaining to segregation and civil rights for blacks—the direction, in a sense, from which he had started. His decision to write for the *Chicago Defender* was of a piece with this shift, as was his collection of propagandistic verse, *Jim Crow's Last Stand* (1943). On the other hand, he saw this new emphasis in his work as consistent with a broad view of American and world culture. The centrist magazine *Common Ground*, edited by M. Margaret Anderson for the Common Council for American Unity, published more of his poems in this decade than did any other journal.

These gestures toward a more centrist position coalesced at some point with Hughes's desire, as he grew older, to enjoy at last a measure of financial security. Thus in the early 1940s he wrote dozens of songs both in support of the war effort and in vain hope of a commercial hit. His songwriting at last paid off in 1947, with the Broadway premiere of the musical play *Street Scene*, a fusion of opera and Broadway on which Hughes had worked as lyricist with the composer Kurt Weill and the dramatist Elmer Rice. Weill and Rice had turned to Hughes, they explained, because of the simple lyricism, as opposed to slickness, of his verse. *Street Scene* closed after only five months on Broadway, but it had been hailed as a milestone in American musical theater and opera. It also netted Hughes enough money to buy a house of his own at last, in the heart of Harlem at 20 East 127th Street, where he lived for the rest of his life.

The year 1947 also saw the appearance of Hughes's only volume of poetry entirely without racial reference, *Fields of Wonder*. Some critics emphasized the beauty of his verse, others its apparent lack of purpose and originality. Two years later, Hughes's next volume of verse, *One-Way Ticket* (1949), returned him squarely to the black urban world and its rich cast of characters; the work included a suite devoted to one of Hughes's most brilliant creations, Alberta K. Johnson—"Madam to You." In between these two volumes, he had begun work on yet another volume of verse. The richly symbolic and emotional event of finally having his own home appeared to inspire, just after he moved in, his finest volume in many years, *Montage of a Dream Deferred* (1951). This collection of poems, which Hughes offered as really one long poem about Harlem, reflected his keen sense not only of the tremendous pressures of northern urban life on black migrants from the South but also of the spectacular way in which the jazz musicians maturing around the end of World War II responded to those pressures in the new "bebop" jazz. His book-length poem, Hughes wrote, "is marked by conflicting changes, sudden nuances, sharp and impudent interjections, broken rhythms, and passages . . . punctuated by the riffs, runs, breaks, and disc-tortions of the music of a community in transition." At least one of the poems, "Harlem" ("What happens to a dream deferred?"), joined the long list of his poems known widely and cherished among blacks for their special insight into the African American condition.

As the decade of the 1940s closed and the cold war intensified, Hughes found himself increasingly under fire from organized right-wing forces for poems and essays written years before, and in particular for "Goodbye Christ." In vain he protested that he had never been a member of the Communist party and was no longer sympathetic to the far Left. The effort to censure him reached its climax in March 1953, when a subpoena brought him before Senator Joseph McCarthy's investigating committee concerned with Communist subversion in the United States. In contrast to other writers called, Hughes generally cooperated with McCarthy although he had little respect for him and his aims. He agreed that the presence of some of his books in official American libraries overseas was odd, given his politics at the time they were written (he did not identify any particular book), and he again repudiated "Goodbye Christ." Although Hughes was criticized by elements on the Left for appeasing McCarthy, he spared himself the fate of black leaders such as Paul Robeson and W. E. B. Du Bois, and preserved his special relationship with black institutions and his special place in the black community.

Although attacks from the right wing never ceased completely, Hughes was now free to exploit his considerable talents and his distinguished record as a writer. His output, always steady, became voluminous as he accepted contract after contract for a variety of books, plays, and musical projects. In addition to his five Simple collections, he published two new collections of short stories, *Laughing to Keep from Crying* (1952) and *Something in Common* (1963), as well as an amusing little novel of somewhat dubious origin, *Tambourines to Glory* (1958), which had started as a gospel musical play before Hughes converted it into fiction. *The Sweet Flypaper of Life* (1955), a small volume comprising a brief but spiced urban narrative inspired by Roy DeCarava's accompanying photographs of Harlem, was hailed as an extraordinarily fine marriage of image and text.

Hughes's main work in poetry after *Montage of a Dream Deferred* came almost a decade later with the publication of *Ask Your Mama* (1961). The genesis of this poem in twelve parts was his agitated response to a riot by young whites in 1960 in Newport, Rhode Island, after they were shut out of a session of the Newport Jazz Festival, of which Hughes had for some years been an officer. Based on the "dozens," the game of ritual insult played in black American culture especially by young men, *Ask Your Mama* is freighted with musical references and annotations; indeed, the main text demands accompaniment by jazz and blues music, which offsets the fragmented and at times almost incoherent modernist language of Hughes's poetic lines. Like the riot over black jazz that inspired it, the poem ominously anticipated the explosive pressures on American society that would surface soon in the 1960s. Nevertheless, the volume was generally either ignored or ridiculed by literary critics, who evinced no interest in responding to the challenges posed by its allusions and innovations.

Another important aspect of Hughes's career was his writing for children. In 1932, he and Arna Bontemps had published their affecting children's tale *Popo and Fifina,* set in Haiti and drawing on Hughes's visit to the country in 1931. Well received by the critics, the book also sold well over several years. His *The First Book of Negroes* (1952), which offered information about blacks to young children, began a constant effort on Hughes's part to write for this market. In part, this was a commercial decision; in larger part, however, the effort reflected his sincere love of young people and his concern for their education. Other "First" books (in a series from the publisher Franklin Watts) included *The First Book of Rhythms* (1954) and *The First Book of Jazz* (1957), as well as others on the West Indies (1956) and on Africa (1960). The book on jazz drew particular praise from reviewers in the field. For a somewhat older youth audience, he emphasized history in volumes that included *Famous American Negroes* (1954) and *Famous Negro Music Makers* (1955).

Sometimes with historic results, Hughes also kept busy as editor and anthologist. His 1949 anthology with Arna Bontemps, *The Poetry of the Negro 1746–1949,* included work by Caribbean writers as well as "tributary" verse on blacks by white writers. As the first such book since James Weldon Johnson's revised edi-

tion of *The Book of American Negro Poetry* in 1931, the anthology brought an entire generation of poets before the general public for the first time. Hughes's alertness to the new forces in black literature, and his unstinting desire to assist younger writers, resulted in other anthologies such as *New Negro Poets USA* (1964), with a foreword by Gwendolyn Brooks, and *The Best Short Stories by Negro Writers* (1967), which included the first story published by Alice Walker.

A major effort in collaboration with Milton Meltzer, who provided most of the pictures, resulted in *A Pictorial History of the Negro in America* (1956), the first volume of its kind to be published in the United States. The two men collaborated again on *Black Magic: A Pictorial History of the Negro in American Entertainment* (1967). Hughes edited a sampling of his own work in *The Langston Hughes Reader* (1958) and again in *Selected Poems* (1959). The latter volume is notable not least of all for its strenuous exclusion of the poet's socialist verse.

From early in his life, Hughes had a powerful sense of internationalism, which his traveling reinforced. Reasonably fluent in French and Spanish, he translated or helped to translate four books. The first was Federico García Lorca's *Gypsy Ballads* (1951), most of which Hughes translated while living in Madrid in 1937. Poems by Nicolas Guillén, *Cuba libre* (1948), capped his long friendship with Cuba's national poet. On Hughes's visit to Havana in 1930, Guillén had been decisively influenced by the American's work on the blues. His first book of poems, *Motivos de son,* was a landmark in Cuban writing because of its radical employment of African-based popular music and dance. *Selected Poems of Gabriela Mistral* (1957) was the first American book-length translation of the Chilean-born Nobel Prize winner. The novel *Masters of the Dew,* by Jacques Roumain, perhaps Haiti's finest writer of this century, was translated by Hughes and the scholar Mercer Cook of Howard University. Hughes had first met Roumain in Haiti in 1931, and had shared many of his radical socialist sympathies for the poor of that country.

With the exception of the poems by Gabriela Mistral, where critics questioned Hughes's appropriateness as a translator of a woman s poetry and his decision not to translate certain poems he found too complex, his translations were well received. Two anthologies of African writing, *An African Treasury: Articles, Essays, Stories, Poems by Black Africans* (1960) and *Poems from Black Africa, Ethiopia, and Other Countries* (1963), introduced the writings of a wide range of Africans to readers in North America. Many of the writers who later achieved major international success, including Wole Soyinka, Amos Tutuola, and Chinua Achebe, were represented in these anthologies, which benefited from Hughes's various visits to Africa in the 1950s and 1960s. At least two other anthologies are worth noting: *The Book of Negro Folklore* (1958), compiled with Arna Bontemps and the first comprehensive collection ever published on the subject; and *Book of Negro Humor* (1966), also largely unprecedented.

Fight for Freedom (1962), commissioned by the NAACP, was a lively and well-researched history of the organization. (As a radical, Hughes had opposed the NAACP, especially in its struggles with Communists over the Scottsboro case, but he supported it staunchly in the later stages of his life.) His major prose effort of the 1950s and 1960s, however, was unquestionably his second volume of autobiography, *I Wonder as I Wander* (1956). Here Hughes traced his life from 1931, where *The Big Sea* ended, to 1938, as he prepared to leave Europe, over which war clouds were gathering, after his grim experience of the Spanish Civil War. The volume reflects a coming to terms with the Left, in that much of the book is devoted to a detailed account of Hughes's year in the Soviet Union. Although many of the inconveniences and weaknesses of the Soviet system are pointed out, the book is entirely free of the anti-Soviet hysteria of the cold war. *I Wonder as I Wander* retains the genial tone and episodic structure of *The Big Sea* but is even less revealing of Hughes's inner life. On the other hand, it is a larger, denser narrative, highly satisfying as an account of one segment of an American life of almost unique variety.

In all this prodigious output, perhaps the most significant aspect of Hughes's career in his last twenty years was his work for the stage, starting with *Street Scene* in 1947 and his opera with the black composer William Grant Still, *Troubled Island*, in 1949. For the classical composer Jan Meyerowitz, a refugee from Germany who had immigrated to the United States at the end of the war, he wrote several librettos and related texts. Probably their most successful collaboration was the opera *The Barrier*, based on Hughes's 1935 Broadway play *Mulatto*. To excellent critical reviews, *The Barrier* had its premiere at Columbia University in 1950. Later, however, it failed miserably on Broadway. But Hughes's main interest was in the commercial theater. His first fruitful attempt in this area after *Street Scene* led him to collaborate with the Harlem composer David Martin in their production *Simply Heavenly*, which opened to steady interest and applause off-Broadway in 1957. This jaunty Harlem comedy, susceptible to being played as farce and even burlesque in spite of its author's intentions, drew heavily on the Simple newspaper columns.

In this collaboration, as with Meyerowitz, Hughes deferred in musical matters to the composer. Even before the premiere of *Simply Heavenly*, however, he was at work on another play that would find him making more inventive use of black music. Fascinated by the rise of black gospel music, itself a fusion of the hymn and the blues, he decided to address it in the theater as he had addressed the blues and jazz in his verse. The first result was *Tambourines to Glory*, set in the colorful world of the black storefront evangelical church. With much of its music written by Harlem composer Jobe Huntley, *Tambourines to Glory* marked the first use of gospel music on the theatrical stage. Unfortunately, the broadly comic aspects of the show, with its burlesque of religion, offended many critics, included blacks, and it fared poorly when it reached Broadway late in 1963.

From this point, Hughes ceased collaborating with composers but delved more experimentally into the fusion of gospel and the stage. The resulting productions often featured spare but stunning narrative lines married to effulgent music drawn from the burgeoning gospel tradition. Among these were *Black Nativity* (1961; a black gospel counterpart, perhaps, to Gian Carlo Menotti's internationally popular opera *Amahl and the Night Visitors*), which seldom failed to arouse audiences; *Jericho-Jim Crow* (1964), on the civil rights movement, which earned Hughes the most celebratory reviews of any of his stage ventures in his life; and *The Prodigal Son* (1965), which also garnered fine reviews.

Hughes was hard at work on various literary projects—including the posthumously published collection of verse *The Panther and the Lash* (1967), which focuses on the civil rights movement and the nascent black power movement—virtually until his death in a New York hospital on 22 May 1967.

The sheer quantity and the variety of his written work inevitably have led some critics to question whether Hughes sacrificed his integrity and his talent as an artist for a more functional vision of himself as a man of letters. Hughes himself seemed to have few such misgivings, although he often joked about the multiplicity of his commitments and jobs, and ruefully called himself, more than once, a "literary sharecropper." In the end and to the end, nevertheless, he was proud to have been the first black American, as far as he knew, to live solely by his writings. He had established and maintained his career at great personal sacrifice. He was proud that his career had been tied closely to the African American community, and he was even proud that the height of his fame found him living securely in the middle of a typical black neighborhood in Harlem—and not in a suburb or, above all, in exile.

From the start, Hughes's art was responsive to the needs and emotions of the black world even as he held to an inclusive view of America and the whole world. In his artistic experimentations, he increasingly looked to blacks, especially black musicians, for direction and inspiration. Much of his work, even his broad comedies, celebrates the dignity and humanity of black culture. In turn, while many other major black writers looked elsewhere for approval

and endorsement, Hughes basked in the high regard of his primary audience, which was black.

His poetry, with its original jazz and blues influence and its prominent demotic element, almost certainly is the most influential written by any black in this century. Certain of his pieces, such as "The Negro Speaks of Rivers," "Mother to Son," and "Harlem," are virtual anthems of black America. He strove hard in the theater, and while his success was mixed, his record of productivity and innovation establishes him as one of the main voices of the black American stage. His "Simple" is probably the most memorable figure to emerge from black journalism. "The Negro Artist and the Racial Mountain" is timeless as a statement of the young black artist's constant dilemma, caught between the contending forces of black and white culture, and caught between class divisions within his or her own racial group. Arguably, Langston Hughes was black America's most original poet. Certainly he was black America's most representative writer and a significant figure in world literature in the twentieth century.

Selected Bibliography

PRIMARY WORKS

POETRY

The Weary Blues. New York: Knopf, 1926.
Fine Clothes to the Jew. New York: Knopf, 1927.
Montage of a Dream Deferred. New York: Henry Holt, 1951.
Selected Poems. New York: Knopf, 1959.
Ask Your Mama: Twelve Moods for Jazz. New York: Knopf, 1961.
Collected Poems. Edited by Arnold Rampersad and David Roessel. New York: Vintage Books, 1995.

FICTION

Not Without Laughter. New York: Knopf, 1930.
The Ways of White Folks. New York: Knopf, 1934.
The Best of Simple. New York: Hill and Wang, 1961.
The Return of Simple. Edited by Donna Akiba Sullivan Harper. New York: Hill and Wang, 1994.

AUTOBIOGRAPHY

The Big Sea: An Autobiography. New York: Knopf, 1940.

I Wonder as I Wander: An Autobiographical Journey. New York: Rinehart, 1956.

JOURNALISM

Langston Hughes and the Chicago Defender: Essays on Race, Politics, and Culture, 1942–1962. Edited by Christopher C. DeSantis. Urbana: University of Illinois Press, 1995.

DRAMA

Five Plays of Langston Hughes. Edited by Webster Smalley. Bloomington: Indiana University Press, 1963.

ANTHOLOGIES

The Langston Hughes Reader. New York: George Braziller, 1958.

Good Morning Revolution: Uncollected Social Protest Writings by Langston Hughes. Edited by Faith Berry. Westport, Conn.: Lawrence Hill, 1973.

SECONDARY WORKS

BIOGRAPHICAL AND CRITICAL STUDIES

Barksdale, Richard. *Langston Hughes: The Poet and His Critics.* Chicago: American Library Association, 1977.

Berry, Faith. *Langston Hughes: Before and Beyond Harlem.* Westport, Conn.: Lawrence Hill, 1983.

Bloom, Harold, ed. *Langston Hughes.* New York: Chelsea House, 1989.

———. *Langston Hughes: Comprehensive Research and Study Guide.* New York: Chelsea House, 1998.

Dace, Tish, ed. *Langston Hughes: The Contemporary Reviews.* New York: Cambridge University Press, 1997.

Emanuel, James A. *Langston Hughes.* New York: Twayne, 1967.

Gates, Henry Louis, Jr., and K. A. Appiah, eds. *Langston Hughes: Critical Perspectives Past and Present.* New York: Amistad, 1993.

Harper, Donna Akiba Sullivan. *Not So Simple: The "Simple" Stories.* Columbia: University of Missouri Press, 1995.

Jemie, Onwuchekwa. *Langston Hughes: An Introduction to the Poetry.* New York: Columbia University Press, 1976.

McLaren, Joseph. *Langston Hughes: Folk Dramatist in the Protest Tradition, 1921–1943.* Westport, Conn.: Greenwood, 1997.

Miller, R. Baxter. *The Art and Imagination of Langston Hughes.* Lexington: University Press of Kentucky, 1989.

Mullen, Edward J. *Langston Hughes in the Hispanic World and Haiti.* Hamden, Conn.: Archon Books, 1977.

O'Daniel, Therman., ed. *Langston Hughes, Black Genius: A Critical Evaluation.* New York: William Morrow, 1971.

Ostrom, Hans. *Langston Hughes: A Study of the Short Fiction.* New York: Twayne, 1993.

Rampersad, Arnold. *The Life of Langston Hughes.* Vol. 1, *1902–1941: I, Too, Sing America.* Vol. 2, *1941–1967: I Dream a World.* New York: Oxford University Press, 1986–1988.

Tracy, Steven C. *Langston Hughes & the Blues.* Urbana: University of Illinois Press, 1988.

Trotman, C. James. *Langston Hughes: The Man, His Art, and His Continuing Influence.* New York: Garland, 1995.

BIBLIOGRAPHIES

Dickinson, Donald C. *A Bio-Bibliography of Langston Hughes: 1902–1967.* 2nd ed., rev. Hamden, Conn.: Archon Books, 1972.

Miller, R. Baxter. *Langston Hughes and Gwendolyn Brooks: A Reference Guide.* Boston: G. K. Hall, 1978.

ZORA NEALE HURSTON
(1891–1960)

CHERYL A. WALL

IN 1973 ALICE Walker traveled to Florida to piece together as much as she could of the puzzle that was Zora Neale Hurston's life. As a writer, Walker had found in Hurston's fiction and folklore an empowering legacy. Walker set out on her journey in search of the woman herself. She met people who had known Hurston, but their recollections were contradictory and dim. No one even knew for certain where Hurston was buried. But when Walker stood in the waist-deep weeds of the "colored" cemetery in Fort Pierce, Florida, and called out "Zora," she found herself standing on what she took to be Hurston's grave. Her parting tribute was to mark the site with a stone that reads:

Zora Neale Hurston
"A Genius of the South"
1901–1960
Novelist, Folklorist, Anthropologist

The essay that records Walker's pilgrimage is entitled "Looking for Zora." Its title and its structure, which italicizes conflicting quotations from critics and contemporaries, demonstrate the difficulty of finding out the truth about Hurston, a woman who regularly misrepresented the facts about her life. The unmarked, untended grave symbolizes the terrible neglect that Hurston and her work suffered. Most profoundly, the essay conveys the power

of the legacy that speaks from the grave, as it were, to respond to Walker's call.

That legacy has been reclaimed not only by Alice Walker, who edited the first anthology of Hurston's writing, but also by a generation of African Americanist and feminist critics and scholars who have begun to restore Hurston's work to its rightful place among the literary traditions of the United States. As the author of seven books, Hurston was more prolific than any black woman writer before her. She published four novels, two volumes of folklore, and an autobiography, as well as more than fifty short stories, essays, and plays. Her work was reviewed favorably in leading journals, yet none of her books was in print when she died.

Three decades after her death her novel *Their Eyes Were Watching God* (1937) became an acknowledged classic in the canon of modern American fiction, and the volume of folklore *Mules and Men* (1935) is a key text in African American literary and cultural studies. All of her books have been reprinted, and her short stories and essays have been collected for the first time. Robert Hemenway has reconstructed the fascinating story of her life in a meticulously researched biography, and numerous monographs, critical essays, articles, and bibliographies have been published about Hurston and her work. Most significantly, Hurston's influence on African American literary tradition continues to grow. Novelists, poets, and playwrights—including Michael Harper, Toni Morrison, Gloria Naylor, Ishmael Reed, Ntozake Shange, George Wolfe, and Alice Walker—allude to, interpret, and revise Hurston's work. It seems inconceivable that her writing will be lost to readers again.

Hurston's art is rooted in the cultural traditions of rural black southerners. More than half a century ago, Hurston boarded a train in New York to return to her native Florida and begin a pilgrimage of her own. She went not in search of an individual—Hurston knew of no literary foremother to seek—but in search of a cultural legacy that she had known "from the earliest rocking of [her] cradle."

At a time when some black intellectuals adopted a rhetoric of uplift that would educate their people out of their culture, Hurston told the reporter Frank L. Hayes, "It would be a tremendous loss to the Negro race and to America, if we should lose the folklore and folk music, for the unlettered Negro has given the Negro's best contribution to America's culture." She was, as the first line of *Mules and Men* proclaims, "glad when somebody told me, 'you may go and collect Negro folk-lore.' " She traveled the South collecting folktales, recording sermons, spirituals, and blues, and apprenticing herself to hoodoo doctors to learn their curses and cures.

The years she spent in the field not only yielded *Mules and Men* but also shaped Hurston's entire oeuvre: "I picked up glints and gleams out of what I had and stored it away to turn to my own use." Hurston's writing is suffused with the similes, the metaphors, and the rhythms that are the poetry of black vernacular expression. Her desire, in Karla Holloway's phrase, "to render the oral culture literate" led to the technical innovations of her prose. Her effort was not merely to interpolate folk sayings in her fiction; it was to create a literary language informed by the poetry as well as the perspective of the "folk."

The first stop on Hurston's journey back was her hometown of Eatonville, Florida, the "first Negro community in America to be incorporated." It was not, she emphasized in her au-

tobiography *Dust Tracks on a Road* (1942), "the black back-side of an average town," but "a pure Negro town—charter, mayor, council, town marshal and all." Her parents, John and Lucy (Potts) Hurston, had been tenant farmers in their native Alabama, but in Eatonville, John Hurston was thrice elected mayor and wrote the village laws. Her father's experience exemplifies the political and psychological significance of Eatonville; it allowed black people to assume roles in keeping with their image of themselves, rather than internalizing the subservient images a dominant white society prescribed. Finally, Eatonville's significance was cultural. Joe Clarke's store was "the heart and spring of the town," the site of the "lying sessions" that defined the town's cultural identity. In these folktales or "lies," "God, Devil, Brer Rabbit, Brer Fox, Sis Cat, Brer Lion, Tiger, Buzzard, and all the wood folk walked and talked like natural men." For the child Zora, the store porch was the most interesting place in town. Hurston the writer retained the fascination even as she remarked the exclusion of women from the store porch ritual.

John Hurston was a carpenter by trade but a minister by calling; as a preacher-poet, he played a major role in Eatonville's cultural life. From her father's example, Zora Hurston perceived how verbal agility conferred status within the community. His sermons demonstrated as well the capacity of his language to convey the complexity of his parishioners' lives. In her fiction she homed in on the connection between voice and selfhood, between the power of speech and personal status. Revelatory moments in her novels occur when a character claims his or her own voice.

Lucy Hurston was a smart, feisty woman who had no public forum but encouraged her children to "jump at de sun." Her relation to her culture's rituals was problematic, at least at the time of her death. In *Dust Tracks*, Hurston describes the pivotal event of her childhood. Her mother, having instructed Zora to protest the ceremonial acts the village performed for the dying, lay silent upon her bed: "But she looked at me, or so I felt, to speak for her. She depended on me for a voice."

The passage might be accorded wider significance. Although one could argue that Zora Hurston set out to honor her father's art and that of the Eatonville storytellers, the history of her writing career is, to some extent, the history of her efforts to recover her mother's voice. Reflecting these dual motives, her evocation of African American vernacular culture is always part celebration and part critique.

Although in *Dust Tracks* Hurston identifies the precise date on which Eatonville was incorporated, the closest she comes to dating her birth is January, during "hog-killing time." In practice, Hurston celebrated her birthday on 7 January and most frequently gave 1901 or 1903 as the year of her birth. She lied. According to the 1900 census, Zora L. Hurston was born in January 1891. She was her parents' fifth child and second daughter. Her birthplace is listed as Alabama. Throughout her career Hurston persuaded everyone she met that she was at least ten years younger than she was in fact—no mean accomplishment. The discrepancy concerning her birthplace is altogether less important. Whether she was born there or not, Eatonville was assuredly Zora Hurston's home.

After her mother's death in 1904, however, she was never again a permanent resident. She attended school in Jacksonville for a time. She was hired and fired from a series of menial jobs. Perhaps she married, though no record of a marriage exists. In 1917 she made her way from rural Florida to Baltimore. Through the force of her intellect and her tenacious will, she completed a course at Morgan Academy in Baltimore and enrolled first in the secondary department, then in the undergraduate college, at Howard University in 1918.

In *Dust Tracks*, Zora Neale Hurston remembers that, "feeling the urge to write," she moved to New York City in January 1925, with "$1.50, no job, no friends, and a lot of hope." She had arrived friendless and penniless in Baltimore and Washington, too, yet she had achieved academic success. Literary success in New York seemed within her grasp.

The timing was fortuitous. Hurston's arrival in New York coincided with the advent of the New Negro or Harlem Renaissance, the great

Zora Neale Hurston

cultural awakening that riveted the attention of countless white Americans on black music, dance, and theater and created a smaller but substantial audience for black literature and the visual arts. Alain Locke, the philosopher of the Renaissance and Hurston's mentor at Howard, wrote in "Negro Youth Speaks" that "Negro genius today relies upon the race-gift as a vast spiritual endowment from which our best developments have come and must come." The finest expression of the race gift was folk art, and those vernacular forms of spirituals, sermons, and folktales were the raw material out of which New Negro art would be refined. One of the few writers of the period to have grown up in the rural South, Hurston claimed this rich cultural legacy by birthright. A talented young writer whose contributions to her college literary magazine had been reprinted in national publications, she was committed to exploring this legacy in her fiction. Zora Hurston seemed destined to play a leading role in the Harlem Renaissance.

Good notices came quickly. In May 1925, her short story "Spunk" took second prize at the Opportunity Awards; a dinner marking the first annual competition sponsored by the magazine *Opportunity* was attended by an array of well-known black and white literary figures. "Spunk" was subsequently published in *The New Negro*, the landmark anthology Locke edited. The following year Hurston was one of several associate editors of *Fire!!*, an avant-garde journal whose single issue won it a place in African American literary history. The young artists who produced *Fire!!* included Langston Hughes, poet Gwendolyn Bennett, painter Aaron Douglas, bohemian writer Richard Bruce Nugent, and the venture's guiding spirit, novelist Wallace Thurman. Hurston's contributions were the play *Color Struck* and "Sweat," a remarkable short story. Not only was Hurston's work being published and garnering modest attention, but she seemed to have found an artistic community whose members shared similar goals and sensibilities. Neither the incipient fame nor the sense of community would endure.

Years later Langston Hughes referred to the Harlem Renaissance mordantly as the period when the Negro was in vogue. Alain Locke and other intellectual leaders of the New Negro movement—including Jessie Fauset, Charles S. Johnson, and James Weldon Johnson—hoped, vainly as it turned out, that the cultural recognition the artists achieved would be translated into social and political progress for the race. As Hurston made clear in the essay "How It Feels to Be Colored Me," written at the height of the Renaissance, she was not sympathetic to the political project:

> But I am not tragically colored. There is no great sorrow dammed up in my soul, nor lurking behind my eyes. I do not mind at all. I do not belong to the sobbing school of Negrohood who hold that nature somehow has given them a lowdown dirty deal. . . . No, I do not weep at the world—I am too busy sharpening my oyster knife.
>
> (*I Love Myself When I Am Laughing*, p. 153)

Hurston's verve does not mask the defensive anger that simmers beneath the surface of this article. She contrasts her happiness in Eatonville, where she was "everybody's Zora," insulated from racism and oblivious to racial distinctions, with the alienation she experienced once she left her hometown and was defined solely in terms of race. Recognizing that this definition renders her a victim and nothing more, she rejects it. But she found it difficult as an adult to express her identification with her race in positive terms. When she writes about her reaction to a Harlem jazz band, she can only parody the exotic primitive myth. When she claims that discrimination "astonishes" rather than angers her, she seems hopelessly naive.

Hurston's situation was inherently problematic. She had a sincere commitment to express the moral and aesthetic value of the culture that had nurtured her. Superficially, the zeitgeist of the 1920s welcomed her subject; however, the prevailing myth of the exotic primitivism of African Americans distorted what she had to say. In this atmosphere it was not easy to explain "how it feels to be colored me."

Anthropology seemed to offer a key. Hurston studied anthropology at Barnard under the tutelage of Franz Boas and Gladys Reichard and alongside Margaret Mead, all of whom are major figures in American anthropology. The cultural relativity of anthropology freed Hurston from the need to defend her subjects' alleged inferiority. Her homefolk were neither exotic nor primitive; they had simply selected different characteristics from what Ruth Benedict, another pioneering anthropologist trained by Boas, called the "great arc of human potentialities." Such truths could pay literary dividends, but by the time she graduated from Barnard in 1927, Zora Hurston was convinced her future lay elsewhere.

Mules and Men (1935), the first book of folklore by a black American, is a widely recognized if underdiscussed classic in African American literature and American anthropology. It records seventy folktales, including the well-known Brer Rabbit tales and the less familiar stories of the heroic slave John. It is, however, more than a compilation of tales. Hurston devises a unifying narrative that provides a context for the tales and allows her to present a range of black southern verbal art. Moreover, through the narrative Hurston subtly reveals both the ways in which women are relegated to subordinate roles in the culture she otherwise celebrates and the means by which these women gain access to creative expression and power. In effect, the subtext of *Mules and Men* is the narrative of a successful quest for female empowerment.

The opening scenes represent the ways in which Eatonville women resist but more often accept their gendered roles. For example, the first event the narrator, Zora, attends is a toe-party, at which women stand behind a curtain, revealing only their feet, as men bid for their company. Not surprisingly, the totally passive Zora, who defers to someone else for every decision made in the first chapter, is selected five times. This Zora soon recedes from the narrative, and a more assertive figure begins to choreograph the action. The group she invites to gather on the store porch is made up of women and men. Interspersed among the tales they tell are highly charged exchanges between couples, exchanges that constitute what Hurston once described in a letter to Boas as "the between story and business."

Implicitly acknowledging that the most highly regarded types of performance in African American culture, such as storytelling and sermonizing, are in the main the province of men, Hurston uses "between-story conversation and business" to give voice to women in *Mules and Men*. Through smart talk, or "sass," women on the store porch counter the crude sexism of the male storytellers and attempt to negotiate respect for themselves. These exchanges are both extremely funny and painful, for "sass" is ultimately resistance of a very passive kind.

As the narrator continues her quest, she travels farther South to Polk County, Florida, which represents the matrix of African American expressive culture. In a lumber camp, the increasingly outspoken Zora meets Big Sweet, who becomes her guardian and guide. This woman's name—with its suggestions of physical power and sexual attractiveness, of strength and tenderness—aptly defines her persona. Unlike the women in Eatonville, Big Sweet's actions match her words.

Well-tutored and emboldened by her encounter with Big Sweet, Zora is prepared to navigate the spiritual mysteries of hoodoo; these in turn unlock the key to her personal power, the power of the word. In 1931 Hurston had published the first scholarly article on hoodoo, the pre-Christian, Afrocentric system of belief to which many black southerners secretly adhered. In *Mules* hoodoo becomes an intrinsic part of that "which the soul lives by"; it is a means by which African Americans exert control of their interior lives. Metaphysically decentered and clerically nonhierarchical, hoodoo offered some women a more expansive vision of themselves than Christianity. Within hoodoo, women were the spiritual equals of men; they had similar authority to speak and act. Under the providential guidance of the spirit of the legendary New Orleans priestess Marie Leveau, "Zora" is completely transformed.

Hurston spent five years in the field collecting the material that appeared in *Mules and Men*. However gratifying and exciting fieldwork may have appeared from the distance of New York's Morningside Heights, up close it was physically grueling and psychologically demanding. Among the personal consequences of her professional commitment were two failed marriages. In May 1927 Hurston married Herbert Sheen, whom she had met at Howard. Although their romance had outlasted Hurston's New York sojourn, their marriage lasted only four months. Unable to reconcile the competing demands of marriage and career, Hurston resumed her collecting while Sheen returned to medical school. A second marriage, in 1939, to Albert Price, ended quickly as well.

Fieldwork was also expensive. In order to raise the money to conduct her research, Hurston entered into one of the most intense, problematic, and controversial relationships of her life. She acquired a patron, Mrs. Rufus Osgood Mason, who underwrote her expenses from December 1927 to September 1932. It is perhaps more accurate to say that Hurston was acquired by Charlotte Mason, a woman of great wealth and distinguished lineage. Mason lent support to numerous Harlem Renaissance artists, including Langston Hughes, Claude McKay, sculptor Richmond Barth" painter Aaron Douglas, and choirmaster Hall Johnson. Only Hurston broke the vows of silence Mason imposed, never to reveal publicly her name as a patron. In committing some details of their relationship to print, Hurston exposed herself to contemptuous criticism.

She wrote in *Dust Tracks* of the "psychic bond" between her and the beloved Godmother (as Mason was known to both Hughes and Hurston) who "was just as pagan as I." Mason could read her mind, Hurston averred, even when she was thousands of miles away. Accusatory letters would find Hurston in Alabama or Florida: "You have broken the law. You are dissipating your powers in things that have no real meaning. . . . Keep silent. Does a child in the womb speak?" Talk of pagan godmothers and psychic bonds seemed spurious to many of Hurston's peers, though a few testified privately to psychic experiences with their benefactor. In truth, although Charlotte Mason believed devoutly in her telepathic power, her power to write checks was paramount.

The terms of her agreement with Hurston were anything but ethereal. In a contract—signed, witnessed, and notarized—Mason spelled out exactly what she was offering and what she expected to receive. She employed Hurston to "collect all information possible, both written and oral, concerning the music, poetry, folklore, literature, hoodoo, conjure, manifestations of art and kindred subjects relating to and existing among the North American Negroes" (quoted in Hemenway, p. 109). The material collected would *belong* to Mason; Hurston was forbidden to share it with anyone without Mason's permission. As compensation, Hurston was to receive a stipend of $200 per month for a year. The period of the original contract was one year, starting in December 1927, but its terms were subsequently extended.

Given the terms of this Faustian compact, it is remarkable that Hurston was ever able to claim any voice of her own. She devised what loopholes she could. She corresponded with Boas, seeking his counsel about her work, and later aided, clandestinely, one of his protégés investigating music in New Orleans. Secretly she shared her findings with Langston Hughes, who realized as well as she that a people's folklore could not be owned. She and Hughes eventually collaborated on the ill-fated comedy "Mule Bone," which drew extensively on the material Hurston had collected. The project ended disastrously, with the play unfinished and the friendship with Hughes destroyed. Mason's influence was largely to blame.

Despite its high personal toll, Mason's support allowed Hurston to conduct research she otherwise would have had to forgo. Nevertheless, not until she was forced off the payroll in 1932 could Hurston declare her artistic independence. Significantly, the platform she chose was the theater. In a series of concerts variously entitled *The Great Day* (1932), *From Sun to Sun* (1933), and *Singing Steel* (1934), she presented her material to audiences in New York, Chicago, and Florida. Hurston not only conceived these productions, she performed in them; through her performances she was able to lay claim to her material in a far more intimate way than academic publication allowed. The concerts demonstrated an important lesson she had learned in the field: "Every phase of Negro life is highly dramatised. . . . Everything is acted out."

Hurston outlined this and other concepts in "Characteristics of Negro Expression," an article that she contributed to Nancy Cunard's anthology, *Negro*, in 1934. The article described the way in which language was used to heighten the drama that permeated black life. "The will to adorn" that characterized black speech was expressed through the use of metaphor and simile, the double descriptive, and verbal nouns. Taking up a long-standing argument that African American art was not original, that the spirituals, dance, and folklore were merely imitations of white models, Hurston argued that all art is modification or revision. African Americans, who lived in the midst of a white civilization, reinterpreted everything for their own use; in so doing they created an art of their own.

Hurston's novel *Jonah's Gourd Vine* (1934) was actually written after *Mules and Men* but was published first. In both books, Hurston shares at length the discoveries of her field-work, but in the novel this became a liability. A contemporary reviewer objected that her novel's characters were mere "pegs" on which she hung their dialect and folkways. Hemenway refers to the novel more sympathetically as a "series of linguistic moments." Hurston's determination to demonstrate the African-American's "will to adorn" is everywhere evident.

Loosely based on the lives of Hurston's parents, *Jonah's Gourd Vine* tells the story of Lucy and John Pearson's courtship and marriage, John's swift rise to prominence as a Baptist preacher, his equally swift fall resulting from his marital infidelities, Lucy's strength and perseverance, and the family's ultimate dissolution. All this takes place against a background of social and technological change occurring in the South at the turn of the century. These changes are subordinate to the cultural traditions that remain intact: the sermons and sayings, children's games and rhymes, hoodoo beliefs and practices. In the foreground are the experiences of John and Lucy.

John's story takes precedence. Hurston wrote in a letter to James Weldon Johnson that she intended her protagonist to stand for "the common run of us who love magnificence, beauty, poetry and color so much that there can never be too much of it." But he was to represent more: "He becomes the voice of the spirit when he ascends the rostrum." Yet the novel never adequately explores the reasons why this gifted preacher-poet repeatedly contravenes the dictates of the spirit and misreads his own metaphors.

Lucy is also unable to achieve an identity between word and deed, even though she possesses the insight that her husband lacks. In a passage echoed in the maternal deathbed scene in *Dust Tracks*, Lucy Pearson warns her daughter, "Don't you love nobody better'n you do yo'self. Do you'll be dying befo' yo' time is out." Loving John too much, Lucy has acquiesced in her own suppression. At her death, she remains on the threshold of self-discovery.

Unlike Lucy, Janie, the heroine of *Their Eyes Were Watching God* (1937), is a fully realized

character. During the twenty-odd years spanned by the plot, she grows from a diffident teenager to a woman in complete possession of herself. Analogously, Zora Neale Hurston the artist is in total command of her talent here, the folk material complementing rather than overwhelming the narrative. The sustained beauty of Hurston's prose owes much to the body of folk expression she had recorded and studied, but Hurston here transmutes that expression into a literary language that is distinctively her own. The result is what Henry Louis Gates designates "a speakerly text."

The action of the novel proper begins when Janie is sixteen, beautiful, and eager to struggle with life, but unable to communicate her wishes and dreams. Her consciousness awakens as she watches bees fertilizing the blossoms of a pear tree. Although critics have debated whether the novel is aesthetically flawed because the narrative voice is not Janie's, many agree that the following scene and most of the novel are told from her perspective:

She was stretched on her back beneath the pear tree soaking in the alto chant of the visiting bees, the gold of the sun and the panting breath of the breeze when the inaudible voice of it all came to her. She saw a dust-bearing bee sink into the sanctum of a bloom; the thousand sister-calyxes arch to meet the love embrace and the ecstatic shiver of the tree from root to tiniest branch creaming in every blossom and frothing with delight. So this was a marriage! She had felt a pain remorseless sweet that left her limp and languid. (1990 ed., pp. 10–11)

The lyricism of the passage mutes somewhat its intensely sexual imagery: "Oh to be a pear tree—*any* tree in bloom!" Janie is prepared to accept sexuality as a natural part of life, a major part of her identity, but before she has a chance to act on this belief, her grandmother interposes a radically different viewpoint.

To Nanny, her granddaughter's nascent sexuality is alarming. Having been unable to protect herself and her daughter from sexual exploitation, Nanny determines to safeguard Janie.

The only haven is marriage, which had not been an option for the grandmother, who as a slave was impregnated by her master, nor for her daughter, who was raped by a black school-teacher. Helpless to fulfill her dreams of what a woman should be for herself and her daughter, "Ah wanted to preach a great sermon about col-ored women sittin' on high, but they wasn't no pulpit for me," Nanny has saved the text for Janie.

Even without a pulpit, Nanny is a powerful preacher. Her half-sung, half-sobbed "chant prayer" runs on for several pages. In it she en-visions Janie on the pedestal reserved for south-ern white women, far above the drudgery that has characterized Nanny's own life—the drudg-ery that has made the black woman "de mule uh de world." When she explains her plan for Janie to marry Logan Killicks, an old man whose sixty acres and a mule constitute his el-igibility, the impact of Nanny's words is over-whelming: "The vision of Logan Killicks was desecrating the pear tree, but Janie didn't know how to tell Nanny that."

Joe Starks offers Janie an escape from her loveless marriage. Stylishly dressed and citi-fied, he is a man of great initiative and drive. He is like no *black* man Janie has ever seen. He reminds her vaguely of successful white men, but she cannot grasp the implications of the re-semblance, though she can appreciate his big plans and the élan with which he courts her. Tempering her reservations that "he did not represent sun-up and pollen and blooming trees," Janie determines that "he spoke for far horizon. He spoke for change and chance."

It quickly becomes apparent that, like Nanny, Joe has borrowed his criteria for success from the white world. He takes Janie to Eatonville because there he can be a "big voice" and a "ruler of things." His ambition is soon realized. He buys property and opens a store that be-comes the town's meeting place. He decrees that roads be dug, a post office established, a street lamp installed, and town incorporation papers drawn. Already landlord, storekeeper, and postmaster, Joe runs for mayor to consoli-date his power. His brashness elicits equal measures of respect and admiration from the townspeople. As much as they admire his ac-complishments, they take exception to his manner. One citizen's observation is widely shared: "He loves obedience out of everybody under de sound of his voice."

"Everybody" naturally includes Janie. Joe as-signs her the role of "Mrs. Mayor Starks." She must set herself apart from the townspeople, conduct herself according to the requirements of his position. Most significantly, she must not speak in public. Starks first imposes this rule during a ceremony marking the opening of the store. The ceremony has occasioned much speechmaking, and toward the end Janie is in-vited to say a few words. Before she can re-spond, her husband takes the floor to announce: "Thank yuh fuh yo' compliments, but mah wife don't know nothin' 'bout no speech-makin'. Ah never married her for nothin' lak dat. She's uh woman and her place is in de home." Joe's announcement catches Janie off guard. Although she is not sure she even wants to speak, she resents being denied the right to decide for herself.

Joe's prohibitions increase. He forbids Janie to participate in the lying sessions held on the store porch; she is hustled inside when they be-gin. Janie loves these conversations and notes that Joe, while not deigning to join in, stays around to listen and laugh. Being forbidden to speak is a severe penalty in an oral culture. It short-circuits Janie's attempt to claim an iden-tity of her own; it robs her of the opportunity to negotiate respect from her peers. Barred from speaking to anyone but Joe, she loses the desire to say anything at all: "So gradually, she pressed her teeth together and learned to hush."

Although in the seven years of marriage Janie yields to Joe's requirement of total submission, she retains a clear perception of herself and her situation, a perception that becomes her sal-vation. On one occasion after Joe has slapped her—her submission has not slowed his verbal or physical abuse—she experiences the follow-ing revelation:

She stood there until something fell off the shelf inside her. Then she went inside there to see what it was. It was her image of Jody tumbled down and shattered. . . . She found that she had a host of thoughts she had never expressed to him, and numerous emotions she had never let Jody know about. . . . She was saving up feelings for some man she had never seen. She had an inside and an outside now and suddenly she knew how not to mix them.   (1990 ed., pp. 67–68)

Facing the truth about Joe allows Janie to divorce him emotionally. She accepts her share of responsibility for the failure of the marriage, knowing that if Jody has used her for his purposes, she has used him for hers. Although she cannot claim her autonomy because she is not yet capable of imagining herself except in a relationship with a man, she is no longer willing to jeopardize her selfhood for the sake of any such relationship.

This determination motivates Janie's act of "specifying" or "signifying" against Joe. Critics disagree whether it is her self-division or the integration of her divided selves that empowers her speech. But in an often-quoted scene, Janie, sensing that her womanhood as well as her intelligence is under attack, responds to Joe's persistent taunts: "Humph! Talkin' 'bout *me* lookin' old! When you pull down yo' britches, you look lak de change uh life." The public humiliation hastens Joe's death. As he lies dying, Janie confronts him with more painful truths, revealing how well she comprehends the effect of his domination: "Mah own mind had tuh be squeezed and crowded out tuh make room for yours in me."

This episode signals Janie's break with the past, and her emergence as a different woman is metaphorically rendered: Just after Joe dies, Janie stands before a mirror and recalls that years before "she had told her girl self to wait for her in the looking glass. . . . The young girl was gone, but a handsome woman had taken her place." Janie integrates her inside and outside selves—seeing herself whole, she reflects on her past and realizes that her grandmother, though acting out of love, has wronged her deeply. At the base, Nanny's sermon had been about *things*, when Janie wanted to journey to the horizon in search of *people*. Janie is able at

last to reject her grandmother's way and to resume her original quest, one that culminates in her marriage to Tea Cake, with whom she builds a radically different relationship. Having discarded Nanny's text, she is free to improvise one of her own.

Tea Cake is a troubadour, a traveling bluesman whose life is dedicated to joyful pursuits. With this character, Hurston explores an alternative definition of manhood, one that does not rely on external manifestations of power, money, and position. Tea Cake has none of these. He is so thoroughly immune to the influences of white American society that he does not even desire them. Tea Cake is at ease being who and what he is. Consequently he fosters the growth of Janie's self-acceptance. Unlike Joe, he has no desire to be a "big voice"; he wants a woman to talk to, not at. They engage in small talk and invent variations of traditional courtship rituals. They play checkers, fish by moonlight, and display their affection freely. Janie soon concludes that Tea Cake "could be a bee to a blossom—a pear tree blossom in the spring." Over the protests of her neighbors, she marries Tea Cake, who is several years younger than she, and whose only worldly possession is a guitar.

Though their courtship is certainly idyllic, Tea Cake is not a completely idealized character. As a son of the folk culture Tea Cake is heir to its prejudices as well as its wisdom. Moreover, female autonomy cannot be granted by men, it must be demanded by women. Janie gains her autonomy only when she insists upon it. An important turning point occurs shortly after their marriage. "So you aims tuh partake wid everything," he asks, and she responds affirmatively.

They embark on a nomadic existence that takes them to the rich farmland of the Florida Everglades. On the "muck," Janie joins Tea Cake in the fields—work freely chosen and inspired by love. The work also strengthens the bond not only between herself and her husband, but also between her and the group. Like the Eatonville store, Janie and Tea Cake's cabin becomes the focal point of the community, a place where Janie "could listen and laugh and . . . tell big stories herself from listening to the rest."

Immersed in the cultural traditions of her people, Janie grows into the woman she has always had the potential to be. She and Tea Cake achieve a remarkably egalitarian marriage; they both work in the fields and they both do household chores. For a sweet season, they sustain the intensity of their love.

Although the marriage ends in the wake of a fierce hurricane, vividly evoked in the novel, culminating in Tea Cake's violent death, the conclusion of *Their Eyes Were Watching God* is not tragic. With Tea Cake as her guide, Janie has explored the soul of her culture and learned how to value herself.

Hurston never duplicated the triumph of *Their Eyes Were Watching God*. In her subsequent novels she changed the direction of her work dramatically. *Moses, Man of the Mountain* (1939) is a seriocomic novel that attempts to fuse biblical narrative and folk myth. *Seraph on the Suwanee* (1948) is a psychological novel whose principal characters are upwardly mobile white Floridians. Neither of her new settings is as compelling as the Eatonville milieu, and although the impact of black vernacular expression is always discernible, it is diminished, as is the power of Hurston's own voice. In these novels the question of female autonomy recedes in importance, and when it is posed in *Seraph*, the answer is decidedly reactionary. What interests the reader is Hurston's reworking of themes identified in her earlier work.

Hurston's protagonist in *Moses* is a combination of biblical lawgiver and African American hoodoo man. Officially a highborn Egyptian but according to legend a Hebrew, he neither wholly rejects nor accepts the legend, and uncertainties about his identity complicate his quest for fulfillment. That quest conforms, in part, to patterns outlined in Hurston's earlier work, for Moses becomes a great manipulator of language, and much of his authority derives from the power of his words. As an educated man, he has learned the formal language of the Egyptian elite, but with the Midianites he adapts the rhythms of a rural culture and learns to speak the black vernacular English of the Hebrews; and when he becomes their leader, Moses masters their tongue. A man of action, as befits a leader, he fights most often for the rights of those under his stewardship. Though he knows he would be more beloved as a king and more popular as a politician, Moses rejects the accoutrements of power. He has as little use for class distinctions as have Janie and Tea Cake. In Moses, Hurston has developed a character who was already a certified hero not only in the biblical tradition but also in African American culture. She draws on the longstanding identification of blacks with the enslaved Hebrews, an identification that inspired the majestic spiritual "Go Down, Moses," among many sacred and secular expressions.

What she adds are new points of emphasis, although these had precedents in her earlier work and her research into the African-derived spiritual traditions of vodun in Haiti, a subject explored in *Tell My Horse*, published the year before *Moses*. In both *Tell My Horse* and the earlier *Mules and Men*, Hurston notes the coexistence of seemingly antithetical religious beliefs in the lives of her informants. Implicit is her attempt to reconcile the biblical Moses and her conception of Moses as conjurer, though one looks in vain for a synthesis of the two belief systems to which the hero is heir. In a novel whose protagonist seeks and achieves cosmic fulfillment, the failure to explicate the spiritual sources of that fulfillment is serious indeed.

Throughout the 1940s and 1950s Hurston's political instincts grew markedly conservative. At her publisher's request, she excised the more militant political views from the manuscript of *Dust Tracks on a Road*, and in its sanitized form the autobiography seemed a celebration of American individualism. The book elicited sharp criticism from black reviewers who, following the lead of Sterling Brown and Richard Wright in their critiques of her earlier books, deplored the absence of political protest.

Her last novel, *Seraph on the Suwanee*, further alienated Hurston from the black literary community. In a somewhat misguided attempt to universalize the major themes of *Their Eyes Were Watching God*, the novel traces the development of its protagonist, Arvay Henson Meserve, who, like Janie, searches for selfhood.

She is hindered in the quest by the deep-rooted inferiority she feels about her family's poverty, but for the wrong reason comes to the right conclusion. As Hurston depicts her, she is inferior to her husband, Jim, and is able to achieve an identity only by accepting a subordinate role as his wife. Hurston endows Jim Meserve with a mixture of the attractive qualities found in Joe Starks and Tea Cake—though his more crudely chauvinistic character is treated with amazing tolerance. Equally problematic, Arvay lacks the inner resources that would permit her to claim autonomy: though she "mounts the pulpit" at the end of the novel, she has no words of her own to speak.

Ultimately, Arvay's weakness may be less personal than cultural. Unlike Hurston's earlier protagonists, Arvay cannot achieve selfhood through a profound engagement with an expressive culture, because she has no culture to engage. To a substantial degree, the culture of African Americans, whom Arvay despises, has supplanted her own. For example, the speech of white characters in the novel reflects the influence of black vernacular expression, and Arvay's musician son learns his art from the family's loyal black employee. To the extent that it analyzes the cost whites pay for their denial of the diverse roots of American culture, *Seraph on the Suwanee* is less reactionary than its depiction of gender roles and race relations makes it appear.

Although *Seraph on the Suwanee* did not enhance Hurston's literary reputation, its publication fueled journalistic interest in a scandal in which Hurston was unjustly, but contemporaneously, implicated. In September 1948 Hurston was arrested in New York on a charge of committing an immoral act with a ten-year-old boy. The charge was groundless. Eventually Hurston proved she was out of the city when the crime was alleged to have occurred. But she was devastated by the charge and the sensational way black newspapers reported it. By the time the indictment was dismissed in March 1949, Hurston had begun to withdraw from public life.

She did not stop writing. In the early 1950s, her byline appeared in the *Saturday Evening Post, American Legion Magazine,* and *Negro Digest.* Many of the articles reflected her political conservatism. She supported Republican candidates and defended the South as being no less racist than the North. Hurston's politics had long been unpopular among blacks; but when she condemned the Supreme Court's 1954 school integration decision, some leaders accused her of betraying the race.

In a letter to a Florida newspaper denouncing the decision, Hurston took issue with the Court's implication that black children could learn only when they went to school with whites. Although she did not elaborate, Hurston rejected the decision, perhaps because it seemed to deny the worth of her childhood in all-black Eatonville and the value of African American culture in general. Regrettably, she did not contemplate the ways in which the cultural traditions she cherished might survive the dismantling of the oppressive social and political system in which they were spawned.

Zora Neale Hurston died, penniless and forgotten, on 28 January 1960. Those who reclaim her legacy see her not as a political reactionary but as one who recognized that African Americans, despite their oppression by whites, had created alternative spaces, at least in language, where they asserted their selfhood. Black women, despite their suppression by men, negotiated spaces where they could do the same. Hurston's art recuperates the cultural riches these diverse negotiations have both reflected and produced.

Selected Bibliography

PRIMARY WORKS

NOVELS

Jonah's Gourd Vine. Philadelphia: J. B. Lippincott, 1934. Reprinted with introduction by Larry P. Neal, 1971. Reprinted with foreword by Rita Dove. New York: Harper & Row, 1990.

Their Eyes Were Watching God. Philadelphia: J. B. Lippincott, 1937. Reprinted with introduction by Sherley A. Williams. Urbana: University of Illinois Press, 1978. Reprinted with foreword by Mary Helen Washington. New York: Harper & Row, 1990.

Moses, Man of the Mountain. Philadelphia: J. B. Lippincott, 1939. Reprinted with introduction by Blyden Jackson. Urbana: University of Illinois Press, 1984.

Reprinted with foreword by Deborah McDowell. New York: HarperPerennial, 1991.

Seraph on the Suwanee. New York: Scribners, 1948. Reprinted with foreword by Hazel Carby. New York: HarperPerennial, 1991.

FOLKLORE

Mules and Men. Philadelphia: J. B. Lippincott, 1935. Reprinted with introduction by Darwin Turner. New York: Harper & Row, 1970. Reprinted with introduction by Robert Hemenway. Bloomington: Indiana University Press, 1978. Reprinted with foreword by Arnold Rampersad. New York: Harper & Row, 1990.

Tell My Horse. Philadelphia: J. B. Lippincott, 1938. Reprinted Berkeley, Calif.: Turtle Island, 1981. Reprinted with foreword by Ishmael Reed. New York: Harper & Row, 1990.

AUTOBIOGRAPHY

Dust Tracks on a Road. Philadelphia: J. B. Lippincott, 1942. Reprinted with introduction by Larry P. Neal, 1971. 2nd ed., edited and with introduction by Robert Hemenway. Urbana: University of Illinois Press, 1984. Reprinted with foreword by Maya Angelou. New York: HarperPerennial, 1991.

DRAMA

Mule Bone: A Comedy of Negro Life. With Langston Hughes. New York: HarperPerennial, 1991.

ANTHOLOGIES

I Love Myself When I Am Laughing . . . And Then Again When I Am Looking Mean and Impressive: A Zora Neale Hurston Reader. Edited by Alice Walker. With an introduction by Mary Helen Washington. Old Westbury, N.Y.: Feminist Press, 1979.

The Sanctified Church. Edited by Toni Cade Bambara. Berkeley, Calif.: Turtle Island, 1981.

Go Gator and Muddy the Water: Writings by Zora Neale Hurston from the Federal Writers Project. Edited by Pamela Bordelon. New York: Norton, 1999.

Spunk: The Selected Short Stories of Zora Neale Hurston. Berkeley, Calif.: Turtle Island, 1985.

The Complete Stories. Edited by Henry Louis Gates Jr. and Sieglinde Lemke. New York: HarperCollins, 1995.

Zora Neale Hurston: Folklore, Memoirs, and Other Writings. Edited by Cheryl A. Wall. New York: Library of America, 1995.

Zora Neale Hurston: Novels and Short Stories. Edited by Cheryl A. Wall. New York: Library of America, 1995.

SECONDARY WORKS

BIOGRAPHICAL AND CRITICAL STUDIES

Awkward, Michael. *Inspiriting Influences: Tradition, Revision, and Afro-American Women's Novels.* New York: Columbia University Press, 1989.

————, ed. *New Essays on "Their Eyes Were Watching God."* New York: Cambridge University Press, 1990.

Baker, Houston. *Workings of the Spirit: The Poetics of Afro-American Women's Writing.* Chicago: University of Chicago Press, 1991.

Carby, Hazel. *Reconstructing Womanhood: The Emergence of the Afro-American Woman Novelist.* New York: Oxford University Press, 1987.

Christian, Barbara. *Black Women Novelists: The Development of Tradition, 1892–1976.* Westport, Conn.: Greenwood Press, 1980.

Cronin, Gloria, ed. *Critical Essays on Zora Neale Hurston.* New York: G. K. Hall, 1998.

DuCille, Ann. *The Coupling Convention: Sex, Text, and Tradition in Black Women's Fiction.* New York: Oxford University Press, 1993.

DuPlessis, Rachel. *Writing Beyond the Ending: Narrative Strategies of Twentieth-Century Women Writers.* Bloomington: Indiana University Press, 1985.

Gates, Henry Louis, Jr. *The Signifying Monkey: A Theory of Afro-American Literary Criticism.* New York: Oxford University Press, 1988.

Gates, Henry Louis, Jr., and K. A. Appiah, eds. *Zora Neale Hurston: Critical Perspectives Past and Present.* New York: Amistad Press, 1993.

Harris, Trudier. *The Power of the Porch: The Storyteller's Craft in Zora Neale Hurston, Gloria Naylor, and Randall Kenan.* Athens: University of Georgia Press, 1996.

Hemenway, Robert. *Zora Neale Hurston: A Literary Biography.* Urbana: University of Illinois Press, 1977.

Hill, Lynda. *Social Rituals and the Verbal Art of Zora Neale Hurston.* Washington, D.C.: Howard University Press, 1996.

Holloway, Karla F. C. *The Character of the Word: The Texts of Zora Neale Hurston.* New York: Greenwood Press, 1987.

Howard, Lillie P. *Zora Neale Hurston.* Boston: Twayne, 1980.

Johnson, Barbara. *A World of Difference.* Baltimore: Johns Hopkins Press, 1987.

Jones, Gayl. *Liberating Voices: Oral Tradition in African American Literature.* Cambridge, Mass.: Harvard University Press, 1991.

Kaplan, Carla. *The Erotics of Talk: Women's Writing and Feminist Paradigms.* New York: Oxford University Press, 1996.

Kubitschek, Missy Dehn. *Claiming the Heritage: African-American Novelists and History.* Jackson: University Press of Mississippi, 1991.

Lowe, John. *'Jump at the Sun': Zora Neale Hurston's Cosmic Comedy.* Urbana: University of Illinois Press, 1994.

Meisenhelder, Susan. *Hitting a Straight Lick with a Crooked Stick: Race and Gender in the Work of Zora Neale Hurston.* Tuscaloosa: University of Alabama Press, 1999.

Nathiri, N. Y., ed. *Zora! Zora Neale Hurston: A Woman and Her Community.* Orlando: Sentinel Communications, 1991.

Plant, Deborah. *Every Tub Must Sit on its Own Bottom: The Philosophy and Politics of Zora Neale Hurston.* Urbana: University of Illinois Press, 1995.

Sundquist, Eric J. *The Hammers of Creation: Folk Culture in Modern African-American Fiction.* Athens: University of Georgia Press, 1992.

Turner, Darwin. *In a Minor Chord.* Carbondale: Southern Illinois University Press, 1971.

Walker, Alice. *In Search of Our Mothers' Gardens: Womanist Prose.* New York: Harcourt Brace Jovanovich, 1983.

——. *Anything We Love Can Be Saved: A Writer's Activism.* New York: Random House, 1997

Wall, Cheryl A. *Women of the Harlem Renaissance.* Bloomington: Indiana University Press, 1995.

——, ed. *"Sweat," by Zora Neale Hurston.* New Brunswick, N.J.: Rutgers University Press, 1997.

——, ed. *Zora Neale Hurston's "Their Eyes Were Watching God": A Casebook.* New York: Oxford University Press, 2000.

Wallace, Michelle. *Invisibility Blues: From Pop to Theory.* London: Verso, 1990.

Washington, Mary Helen. *Invented Lives: Narratives of Black Women, 1860–1960.* Garden City, N.Y.: Anchor Press, 1987.

Willis, Susan. *Specifying: Black Women Writing the American Experience.* Madison: University of Wisconsin Press, 1987.

BIBLIOGRAPHIES

Davis, Rose P. *Zora Neale Hurston: An Annotated Bibliography and Reference Guide.* Westport, Conn.: Greenwood Press, 1997.

Newson, Adele S. *Zora Neale Hurston: A Reference Guide.* Boston: G. K. Hall, 1987.

CHARLES JOHNSON
(1948–)

SONNET RETMAN

ANY APPRAISAL OF Charles Richard Johnson's rich and varied career as an artist must begin with the caveat that such an assessment will inevitably compress the complexity and power of his vision. Known chiefly as a novelist, he has also worked prodigiously as a cartoonist, a critic, a philosopher, a screenwriter, a playwright, a martial-arts expert, and a teacher. Though they are disparate in form, all his works engage fundamental ethical, ontological, and epistemological questions about the nature and possibility of liberation. Through his deft experimentation with concepts of chronology and fact, identity and language, Johnson joins writers such as Ishmael Reed and Toni Morrison in advancing an affirmative postmodernist recovery of history. As we review the twentieth century from the vantage of the twenty-first, it is clear that Johnson is one of the most important contemporary American writers. Yet only in the past decade has his work received the critical attention it deserves.

In both Johnson's philosophical fictions and his philosophy of fiction, he interrogates questions of subjectivity in relation to language and literary form. In his phenomenological treatise on African American fiction, *Being and Race* (1988), he calls for art that is "dangerous and wickedly diverse, enslaved to no single idea of Being, capable if necessary of unraveling, like Penelope, all that was spun the night before and creating from entirely new social and scientific premises . . . or adjusting the seminal work of the past to address issues relevant to this age." His fiction follows this dictate: it limns our literary inheritance for old forms to be used in the service of new investigations of meaning. In keeping with this ethos, Johnson has also been active in the recovery of overlooked written and oral texts, such as folklore and slave testimonials. Through these efforts, he challenges the orthodoxy that impels black writers to adhere to realism as a primary literary mode. Rejecting what he deems "calcified vision," Johnson cautions the writer against adopting "preestablished models . . . for our experience, or for any experience."

Instead, Johnson calls for the (black) writer to grapple "again with the perceptual flux of experience that characterizes the black world— and all worlds—to originate new meaning." In his view, good fiction should not only transgress generic boundaries, it should strategically stage these traversals in the service of liberty for the benefit of the reader and the writer. By attempting to dismantle hierarchies of race and gender, self and other, as well as traditional literary forms and their typical modes of reception, Johnson refigures subjectivity from a radically layered perspective. He collapses these conventional oppositions and perspectives, in part, by introducing Eastern modes of thought into his writing. Here, he draws upon extensive academic training in philosophy; his scholarly interests in Buddhism, Taoism, and Hinduism; and his long-standing commitment to Kung Fu and meditation. In works such as *Faith and the Good Thing, Oxherding Tale, Middle Passage,* and *Dreamer,* Johnson addresses human bondage, in all of its psychic, physical, and metaphysical formations by way of a cross-generic, intergenerational approach.

Johnson was born in Evanston, Illinois, in 1948. His father and mother raised him in the Ebenezer Baptist Church, where he was baptized and later married to his wife, Joan, and where his son, Malik, would later be baptized as well. His father had moved from rural South Carolina to Evanston to work for his uncle, an entrepreneur who first owned a milk business and then began a construction company. A firm believer in the Protestant work ethic, Johnson's father held two jobs, as a construction worker and a night watchman, in addition to doing odd jobs on the weekends. We might conjecture that Johnson's prolific output reflects his father's values. In interviews, Johnson also cites the significance for him of growing up attending integrated schools: his high school, ranked third in the nation at the time, was comprised of 15 percent African American students. Johnson's mother was an avid reader, and she shared this interest with him as well as encouraging his childhood passion for drawing, a passion that would determine his artistic direction in his late teens and early twenties.

In 1966, he entered Southern Illinois University at Carbondale, where he became a philosophy and journalism major. By the time he had completed his undergraduate degree, he had published two collections of political cartoons, influenced by black nationalism—*Black Humor* (1970) and *Half-Past Nation Time* (1972)—and he hosted, wrote, and produced his own drawing program on PBS, *Charlie's Pad,* in 1971. In 1970, he turned to fiction, as he states in *Oxherding,* "with no intention of becoming a novelist," in order to wrestle with questions about the nature of the self and experience in both the

Western and Eastern philosophical traditions. Despite his reservations, the novel has proved to be Johnson's most long-standing mode of expression, perhaps because it is an artistic form overtly devoted to constructing and exploring a discourse of the self. Influenced by the Black Aesthetic and the social protest genre, in particular the writing of Richard Wright, James Baldwin, and John A. Williams, Johnson penned what he deems, according to his comments in *Being,* "six bad, apprentice novels." In the fall of 1972, when Johnson was pursuing a master's degree in philosophy at Southern Illinois University, he fortuitously initiated a tutorial with the acclaimed novelist and writing teacher John Gardner, beginning his work on a seventh novel, *Faith and the Good Thing.*

In broad terms, this first novel (really the seventh) defines the intertwined philosophical and aesthetic project that occupies Johnson in all of his subsequent works: the fusion of diverse literary forms, philosophies, and religious systems to investigate the nature of the self within the context of history. In *Faith,* Johnson traverses an array of genres—"folklore, myth, philosophy, naturalism and fantasy"—in order to tell the story of a young woman named Faith Cross who searches for self-identity and the illusive "good thing," at her mother's death bed behest. The novel begins with the injunction:

> It is time to tell you of Faith and the Good Thing. People tell her tale in many ways—conjure men and old gimped grandmothers whisper it to make you smile—but always Faith Cross is a beauty, a brown-sugared soul sister seeking the Good Thing in the dark days when the Good Thing was lost or, if the bog-dwelling Swamp Woman did not lie, was hidden by the gods to torment mankind for sins long forgotten. Listen.

Grounded in communal storytelling conventions, the novel adopts the immediacy of an oral tale performed for a gathering of acquaintances. It situates the narrative voice as that of the conjurer, and it foregrounds the imperative of both telling and listening in the process of narrative invention.

Through the character of Faith, Johnson ruminates on the specificity of the black female experience within a U.S. context. More broadly, he pursues questions about subjectivity in relation to different forms of human bondage. Faith's encounter with the metaphysical—the loss of her mother and her visit to the ultimate conjurer, the Swamp Woman—occasions her physical journey from her folk origins in Hatten County, Georgia, to Chicago. Once in the city, Faith undergoes a series of experiences ranging from horrific to blissful: she is raped, consigned to whoredom; she is haunted by the ghost of a philosopher; she marries the wrong man, becomes pregnant by the right man; she loses her newborn baby in a terrible fire that nearly kills her as well; finally, she shape-shifts, trading places with the Swamp Woman. With her rape, Faith loses all sense of herself. After this trauma, she believes she has found the answer in materialism, but to obtain these goods, she, in turn, must transform herself into an object, a thing for sale. When Faith trades prostitution for a loveless bourgeois marriage, she substitutes one form of bondage for another, becoming part of "the dead living," an "IT," whose body moves but whose soul is dead. She is awakened by the reappearance of her adolescent flame, Alpha Omega Holmes, an economically impoverished but spiritually rich ex-convict painter. After they make love for the first time, Faith asks him about the Good Thing and he replies, "You were good. . . . That story was good. The dinner was good." Faith begins to understand that one experiences the Good Thing in "its small reflections." As she works her way along the "path of the pristine young innocent," she achieves a greater understanding of human existence—she leaves behind a static view of identity and begins to conceive of life as a series of paths.

The primary manifestation of the Good Thing in the novel is storytelling. Narrative is the vehicle for reinvention, the means to an infinite variety of paths, for, according to the conjure woman, there are "a thousand 'n one ways to look for what's good in life." As Faith reflects on her journey, she sees how "she'd suffered several roles: the innocent, the whore, the

Charles Johnson

housewife. . . . And now the werewitch herself. . . . There would be others. . . . There had to be. . . . She was more than one path, or the total of them all. . . . She would glean from each its store of the Good Thing, would conjure it up." By the novel's end, Faith, like her father, becomes another godlike spinner of metaphysical yarns. Johnson offers us, by way of his own metaphysical yarn, a Buddhist notion of self-authorship, a mode of conjuration beholden to the past, present, and future. He departs from realism, viewing genre as something akin to the paths available to Faith. Much like Alpha Omega Holmes, the painter in the novel who grasps the reflections of the Good Thing, Johnson's vision is "incredibly precise" and at the same time, refreshingly "unreal." As the Swamp Woman cautions Faith at the beginning of the tale, "Before you ask if anythin's true, first ask y'self if it's good, and if it's beautiful!" *Faith and the Good Thing* transforms "the infinity of worldly sensations" into a momentary order, a narrative, that is both "good" and "beautiful."

After publishing *Faith* in 1974, Johnson entered the Ph.D. program in philosophy at SUNY

Stony Brook. (His dissertation proposal would later become *Being and Race.*) In 1976, just as he completed his exams, he accepted an offer from the University of Washington to teach creative writing. He and his wife, Joan, moved to Seattle, where they would raise their children, Malik and Elizabeth. In the midst of this transition, Johnson was working on his masterpiece, *Oxherding Tale,* a second novel that would take seven years to complete, with little encouragement from his mentor Gardner or his agent and friends. In Johnson's own words, "I often [refer] to it as my 'platform' book . . . meaning that everything else I attempted to do would in one way or another be based upon and refer to it." Above all, the novel exemplifies Johnson's own protean dictate: it is a postmodern subversion of the classical American slave narrative with resonances of an Eastern parable. It "performs" myriad versions of genre and identity in order to attain ontological and narrative freedom. Through his reclamation of the nineteenth-century slave narrative, he examines in his own words "a black man's desperate bid for liberation from numerous kinds of 'bondage' (physical, psychological, sexual, metaphysical)."

His enslaved, biracial protagonist, Andrew Hawkins, can only achieve emancipation by comprehending his own subjectivity as process, as heterogeneously constructed out of the interstices between "house" and "field" and "white" and "black." Andrew in his role as narrator must also transcend first-person perspective and the confines of traditional autobiography in order to enact a "first-person universal." By extension, according to Johnson in *Being,* he forces his readers to confront the limitations of a conventional, realist reading method (as he calls it, "a heavily conditioned seeing"), proposing as an alternative, a more liberated mode of readership. In keeping with its Buddhist underpinnings, the novel insists that only by *defeating* a desire for the pleasure of constructing a seamless, rational "reality" can we truly inhabit the story. As the text foregrounds the ways that the reader acts upon the text and the text acts upon the reader, it engages with the emancipating effects of this dynamic relationship.

Johnson's metafictional strategy is borrowed, in part, from the rhetorical posture of self-consciousness in the nineteenth-century slave narratives. His textual manipulations insert his readers directly in the midst of conflicting narrations of slavery, thereby thwarting our traditional interpretations of his novel and forcing us to participate in a more intricate reading of the subject of slavery and its attendant debates. *Oxherding Tale* avoids the trap of either a postmodernist "radical indeterminacy" or an essentialist rhetoric of fixedness. Instead, it effectively employs various strategies of fiction to enact previously overlooked truths.

In Johnson's revisitation of the nineteenth-century slave narrative, he also explores many of its limitations and consequent omissions, specifically in its bid for realism (instead of complex character development) as a means of moral persuasion. To be convincing in their argument against slavery, slave narratives presented a carefully constructed public self to a predominantly white, female audience—this representation reflected the values abolitionist Americans would find most compelling and, accordingly, was shaped out of the most popular literary genres of the day, the picaresque and the sentimental novel. While maintaining the picaresque and sentimental aspects of the genre, Johnson sheds the encumbrance of realist representation and its repressive ontological implications. As the novel charts its protagonist's journey from enslavement, in all of its manifestations, to freedom, it is strategically unpredictable in its comical language, its plot frame, and its narrative techniques. In this way, much like its protagonist, it functions as a kind of trickster text.

Oxherding Tale is nothing if not funny. While slave narratives are rarely humorous, certain comic modes serve as an effective if limited means of empowerment in the face of oppression. Following the mode of the carnivalesque, if the slave can outwit or ridicule the slave driver, the hierarchy is momentarily reversed. Thus, escapist devices—fabrication, masquerade, paradox, and word play—become a part of the slave's bid for linguistic and literal freedom. Johnson borrows this ironic humor and uses it as a filter for rereading the narratives and inventing his own. This is no more apparent than in the first chapter "Part One: House and Field." The narrator (and narrative's) origins are ludicrous. Andrew is the product of a bed-switch ruse concocted by his master and his father, a house slave, one ill-fated, whiskey-laden evening. This scenario signals a literal reversal (the husbands swap nuptial beds for the night) as well as a reversal of history and generic convention. Put simply, Andrew's origins are linked to a black paternal presence rather than the black maternal presence found in most narratives. (Andrew was the product of Master Polkinghorne's ill-advised proposal to exchange wives; thus, Polkinghorne "fathered" the plan that begets Andrew.) This scene is all the more ridiculous for its flowery asides and melodramatic imagery.

If humor and comic reversal present one aspect of the text's tricksterism, then the protagonist's unlikely training in Continental and Eastern philosophy represents another. Overturning convention once again, Andrew is educated at his white master's behest: Andrew is destined to be either a philosopher or an improved piece of property or some ambiguous combination of the two. We are to understand that Andrew has received the "perfect moral education": he has been trained in European philosophy, Eastern mysticism, and American transcendentalism, an archive of knowledge to which he refers throughout the novel. These allusions have a notably alienating effect on the reader—for how much do we know off-hand about the errors in Hegel's *Lectures on the Philosophy of History*? Unless the reader is fairly well versed in philosophy, these references carry limited associations; in other words, through Andrew, Johnson handily signifies on us as well.

Even equipped with this vast knowledge of Western intellectual history, Andrew must work his way toward a more complex Eastern understanding of selfhood to achieve enlightenment. As several critics have noted, Andrew's trajectory dramatizes a specific Buddhist parable allegorized in Kuo-an Shih-yuan's *Ten Oxherding Pictures*, a twelfth-century zen series that de-

picts an oxherder's path to enlightenment as he loses and then gains his true self. Much like Faith, Andrew must learn the difference between subjection and subjectivity. The chapters "Homeleaving" and "Living in the Service of the Senses" detail Andrew's induction into the sexual world as well as his preliminary move toward freedom. When Andrew informs Master Polkinghorne of his desire for a deed of manumission for himself and Minty, the young slave woman he wishes to marry, Polkinghorne agrees to sign the papers on the condition that Andrew first work for a year at Flo Hatfield's plantation, aptly named Leviathan. His initiation neatly divides into two sections: his first sexual experience with Minty and his sexual apprenticeship with Flo. Together, they comprise an ontological continuum, representing two related but crucially different ways of being, one according to a mode of desire and one according to a mode of hedonism. By learning the difference between the two, Andrew is able to locate a subjectivity apart from subjection.

Andrew's union with Minty is the impetus for his discovery that he desires liberty. It leads him to ask his first existential questions: "Was beauty truly *in* things? Was touch in me or in the things I touched?" As Andrew experiences the exhilaration of merging with the other, he loses himself and gains his first taste of freedom. His very perception shifts: "physical shortcomings . . . seemed (to me) that afternoon to be purified features of a Whole, where no particular facet was striking because all fused together to offer a flawed, haunting beauty the likes of which you have never seen." This more complex view is the product of a series of contradictions: not only are Minty's deficits her assets, but the conventional grounds for such an assessment are inverted; boundaries between the internal and external are confused; one facet simultaneously constitutes another. Andrew's query reveals the self to be a figure of relation and possibility, an ongoing process. Underscoring the interdetermination of subjectivity and social context, these transformations comprise the "Whole" to which Andrew alludes. Thus, Andrew's desire to "own" Minty forcefully brings him to the realization that all enslavement is intolerable, that no one should be owned by anyone.

Andrew's new desire for freedom ironically propels him to Flo Hatfield's plantation, the place of his further subjugation and, ultimately, the site from which he escapes. In a general sense, this plot progression mimics the pattern of the traveling rogue in the picaresque novel, but with a twist. Andrew is at the mercy of a hedonist and so he must become one, too, in accordance with her desires. Shackled to his own sexual coming of age, he performs masculine roles found in both the picaresque and the classic slave narrative. As Flo's personal male servant, her concubine, Andrew must be the polymorphous "lover of [her] fantasy . . . husband, ravager, teacher, Galahad, eunuch, swashbuckler, student, priest, and, above all else, *always there.*" When he begins to see beyond the hazy pleasures of sex and opiates, and prepares for his escape, he realizes that the "dead-end, wheel-spinning life of desire" he shares with Flo is nothing but "a male fantasy" to which they are both enslaved. Reb the Coffinmaker, an African from the vaguely Taoist Allmuseri tribe, tells Andrew, "Without you, she don't know who she *is.* Without her . . . you ain't nothin' without somethin'—or somebody—to serve, Freshmeat." Flo defines herself through and against him, desiring to empower herself through "serving" a man. And since Andrew's very life depends on the services he renders her, he is nothing without her. Andrew's blackness makes him an ideal candidate for her victimized projections twice over—because he is a man, she directs them toward him, and because he is her black slave, he has no power to stop her from doing so. While Flo's hedonistic bondage is pathetic and her treatment of Andrew is deplorable, Johnson makes us understand that both Flo and Andrew are manipulated by a larger system of white patriarchy. In this way, Johnson points to a broader definition of slavery that includes complex, oppressive power relations in their overt and subtle expressions.

If Andrew survives his tenure with Flo Hatfield through a protean performance of masculine roles, this mode also serves him in his es-

cape. Moreover, through Johnson's cunning play with narration itself, he effectively extends this trick/trickster motif to include the very writing of the text. To escape, Andrew adopts a "white" persona, claiming that Reb is his slave. Simultaneously, Johnson begins to liberate the narrator's perspective from the limits of first person and his readers from a realist practice of interpretation.

Andrew's escape begins with his request for monetary compensation for his services from Flo. Insulted, she banishes him to the mines along with Reb. Just as they arrive at the mines, Andrew concludes a story about his boyhood tutor Ezekiel, detailing his feelings when he died bereft and alone: "he sobbed . . . a bony ruin . . . his heart overheating—searing pain in his chest, and then even the work of this bloody, tired motor went whispering to rest, his spirit changed houses." At this point in the story, we are drawn in by this sad remembrance, unaware of the text's subtle shift into omniscience. The transition that follows, then, is utterly unanticipated:

> You will object, and rightly, that I cannot know what Ezekiel Sykes-Withers felt when he died, for this work is first-person, the most limited form. But even this philosophical problem of view-point—the autobiographical I—will be answered, I assure you, and I confess, for now, that this account is a tale woven partly from fact, partly from fancy.

Here, Johnson echoes the highly self-conscious escape scene found in many nineteenth-century narratives in which details are omitted so as not to reveal routes and methods potentially still in use by other fugitive slaves. He adapts the mode of direct address from the classic narratives—its tone of confessional familiarity—to comment instead upon autobiographical narration itself. This aside jolts us out of a passive acceptance of the text, making us aware of our own reading as well as of Johnson's writing of the text. We become uncomfortably aware of our own press for familiar narrative codes and chronological coherence. While Andrew's sudden omniscience is implausible, the true trick here is that this implausibility does not surface until our narrator directly suggests that we might object to his duplicity. In other words, the narration is not only unreliable, it is one step ahead of us. As we consider our textual bearings, the boundaries between "fact" and "fancy" become further blurred or, in Johnson's terms, "woven" together. The text walks us into an interpretive quandary, daring us to conflate the narrator with the author. Who is the implied "I" in this passage? Is it Andrew or Johnson?

This unstable textual moment foreshadows the book's two "essayist interludes" entitled "On the Nature of Slave Narratives" and "The Manumission of First-Person Viewpoint." Each interlude provides the reader with a self-conscious disposition on the nature of writing and point of view. The escape scene and these two interludes cunningly push the limits of first-person perspective and challenge our own stance as readers. Significantly, once Andrew achieves an expanded authorial control, he is able to contemplate taking control of his own life: "I still had no plan for escape, only a feeling that . . . I could wing a way to liberation." As our guide, he first gains mastery over the way he tells the story and then over the events within his account: significantly, the narrator's bid for omniscience precedes the planning or execution of his actual escape. In this way, *Oxherding Tale* proposes a subject that is constructed through an ongoing process of narration. With his protagonist's bid for freedom, Johnson begins the process of freeing his novel from the limitations of the "autobiographical I." He slowly casts away the slave narrative's first-person point of view, which, for polemical reasons, often emphasized the system of slavery at the expense of individual character development. Andrew's escape plan requires him to pass for white, an act that allows him to explore his mulatto identity, both black and white. Thus, Johnson suggests that the act of writing from multiple points of view (omniscient and autobiographical, for example) is akin to the act of passing.

Johnson further dismantles the classic slave narrative's reliance on fixed categories of "au-

thentic" identity in the final section of the novel when Andrew must undergo his last trial of escape before he reaches freedom. In "The White World," Johnson invokes another trickster figure, the slave catcher of all slave catchers, Horace Bannon, better known as the Soulcatcher. As the runaway attempts to escape, the Soulcatcher psychically apprehends his victim by reading his or her desires. He explains to Andrew:

It ain't so much in overpowerin' him physically, when you huntin' a Negro, as it is mentally. . . . The Negro-hunt depends on how you use destiny. You let destiny outrace and nail down the Negro you after. From the get-go, hours afore Ah spot him, there's this thing Ah do, like throwin' mah voice. Ah calls his name. The name his master used. Mah feelin's and my voice, fly out and fasten onto that Negro. . . . You *become* a Negro by lettin' yoself see what he sees, feel what he feels, want what he wants. . . . You look for the man who's policin' hisself. . . . That's yo Negro. When you really onto him, the only person who knows he's a runaway—almost somebody he kin trust—you tap him gently on the shoulder, and he knows; its the Call he's waited for his whole life.

Like Flo Hatfield who attempts to stay one step ahead of her men and Andrew who stays one step ahead of her, the Soulcatcher mentally switches positions with his victim in order to anticipate the next move. This reversal is predicated upon his ability to imitate the hunted slave and gain a kind of insider knowledge. When the Soulcatcher speaks about bounty hunting, he reveals its theatrical tenets: he "becomes" the runaway slave by throwing his voice, by ventriloquizing his victim. In this role-playing, he unseats the essentialist, racist demarcations that gird chattel slavery. Once the slave quavers on the run, believing he or she is really a slave, the Soulcatcher fulfills this prophecy: he acts as "destiny."

In this exchange, the course of Andrew's life lies in the balance, dependent on the quality of his acting and the lens through which the spectator (namely the Soulcatcher and the reader) perceives him. Andrew eludes the Soulcatcher, explaining to Reb, " 'Maybe rabbits enjoy the hunt, too'. . . . because I knew his techniques, the strategies that poisoned my father, I could stare them down, second-guess Bannon and escape destruction." To survive in the face of the Soulcatcher, Andrew must ultimately reject his father's view of race: he refuses to emulate his father's internalized racism and self-hate, his insistence on a notion of "authentic" black identity in strict opposition to whiteness. By not allowing himself to invest in a fixed notion of authentic blackness or whiteness, by feeling himself, almost from birth, to be located somewhere between "the house and the field," between "the white world" and "the black world," Andrew is able to pass successfully for white. In a sense, he defines himself through all of these roles and none in particular. Johnson points to the ways that race is first and foremost a narrative construct, yet, nonetheless, a construct with profoundly real, material effects. Instead of seeing the world through his father's "spell of hatred," Andrew sees the world through all of its "rich senses," a spell of hatred and love, both. With Andrew's marriage to Peggy, a white woman, in spite of his father's probable disgust, the novel resuscitates love, so often hidden in the interstices of the traditional slave narrative, as a means of achieving a liberating subjectivity.

Yet when Andrew falls in love with Peggy, this development recalls the disappearance of Minty, his first love. Once his catalyst for running away and winning freedom, Minty has since been ravaged by bondage and condemned to the "auction circuit." When Andrew first falls for Minty, she has an earthy sensuality reminiscent, in Andrew's mind, of an African landscape. With her death, she melts back into this landscape "form into formlessness." Just before Minty dies, Peggy tells Andrew that she is pregnant. Minty's dying state and Peggy's fertile condition emphasize the gendered, cyclical nature of life and death. Some critics have found this portrayal of Minty troubling: the most significant black woman in the text virtually disintegrates by the end of the novel. Her death appears to engender the white woman's progeny and she becomes a kind of all-giving mother Africa. Given the novel's claims to a polymorphy of being and identity, this retreat into essentialism is inconsistent at best.

By the novel's conclusion, Andrew has learned that " the heart could survive anything by becoming everything." This lesson not only describes the mutability of Andrew's approach to identity but Johnson's protean approach to genre. In the final scene, after discovering that Reb has defeated the Soulcatcher and thereby won freedom for himself as well, Andrew asks about his dead father (previously captured by the Soulcatcher): "Did he speak of me? What I must know is if he died feeling I despised him, or if he died hating me." In a last gesture of redemption, the Soulcatcher undoes his shirt, commanding Andrew to look closer. The Soulcatcher's tattooed chest becomes a theater of moving figures, all his earlier kills:

I lost his figure in this field of energy, where the profound mystery of the One and the Many gave me back my father again and again, his love, in every being from grubworms to giant sumacs, for these too were my father and, in the final face I saw in the Soulcatcher, which shook tears from me— my own face, for he had duplicated portions of me during the early days of the hunt—I was my father's father, and he my child.

Slavery is written quite literally on the bodies of its chattel, in particular, on Minty's disintegrating body. In the end, it is permanently inscribed on the body of the abuser, the Soulcatcher. The life cycle doubles on itself, forming a nonlinear, simultaneously historical and ahistorical pattern of life; fathers become sons and sons become fathers. Hence, Andrew and Peggy's daughter, Anna, becomes a revision of her grandmother, Anna Polkinghorne.

The metaphysical performance on the Soulcatcher's chest exemplifies the narration's final shift to "first-person universal," enacting "the manumission of first-person viewpoint," the crucial escape foreshadowed in the second narrative interjection of the novel. Andrew reconnects with past and present experiences—this "cosmic costume ball"—as the narration extends beyond his telling. *Oxherding Tale* recounts the lives represented on the Soulcatcher's chest, which is itself one fluid oxherding tale. As the narrator suggests, "No form . . . *loses* its ancestry; rather, these meanings accumulate in layers of tissue as the form evolves. . . . and [that] all a modern writer need do is dig, dig, dig . . . until the form surrenders its diverse secrets." Johnson plays with the slave narrative and its evolved meanings to create a variegated "palimpsest" out of its own "diverse secrets." Like the Soulcatcher, Johnson's fiction becomes the old genre it traces and finally catches. Johnson liberates both the first person and Andrew Hawkins and ambitiously attempts to emancipate the reader as well from the traps of realism.

In the seven years during which Johnson labored over *Oxherding Tale,* he also began the first of many screenplay assignments for PBS, including the story of a black cowboy, the oldest living American, *Charlie Smith and the Fritter Tree* (1978). (In subsequent years, he wrote a program on Booker T. Washington, *Booker* [1984] and a host of other historical projects.) He also published several short stories—"The Education of Mingo" (1977), "Alethia" (1979), "Exchange Value" (1981), and "China" (1983)—which resonate with the central philosophical questions posed in *Oxherding Tale.* These stories provided the basis for a short story collection, *The Sorcerer's Apprentice: Tales and Conjurations,* published in 1986. These diverse stories deploy the parable, the tale, the animal fable, science fiction, and memoir as specific modes of narration; some are set during slavery while others take place in the contemporary moment. In spite of their diversity, the stories unify some of Johnson's most pressing concerns: the difference between having and being; the relationship between consciousness, perception, and experience; the dissolution of racial, moral, and ontological dualisms within Buddhist thought; and the aim of enlightenment as one of process rather than stasis.

The first story, "The Education of Mingo," is an antebellum parable, a creation tale like Mary Shelley's *Frankenstein,* about the vanity of playing God with another person's life. In the story, an aging Illinois farmer, Moses Green, purchases a bondsman named Mingo, the youngest son of the Allmuseri tribe (the fictitious phenomenological African tribe Johnson also invokes in *Oxherding Tale, Middle Passage,* and *Dreamer*). Moses teaches Mingo everything he knows: he thinks of Mingo "now like a father, now like an artist fingering something fine and noble from a rude chump of foreign clay." In purchasing Mingo, Moses provides himself with a surrogate son, an other to be formed in "his own spitting image," like God "remaking the world so it looked more familiar." Mingo becomes Moses' alter ego: "The boy was all Moses wanted to be, his own emanation, but still . . . himself." In this way, Moses' ownership enacts the central paradigm of the story, "how being and having were sorta the same thing," for Moses lives through his property, Moses.

Mingo learns by imitation but seemingly misunderstands some of the crucial tenets of Moses' thinking: at the turning point of the story, Mingo reverses Moses' dictum, that one should "kill chicken hawks and be courteous to strangers," killing Moses' troublesome neighbor, Isaiah. It occurs to Moses that Mingo acted on behalf of his innermost desires. As Moses explains the consequences of the murder, Mingo slyly responds: "What Mingo know, Massa Green know. Bees like *what* Mingo sees or don't see is only what Massa Green taught him to see or don't see. Like Mingo lives through Massa Green, right? . . . Bees Massa Green workin', thinkin', doin' *through* Mingo." In exploring the master slave dialectic, the story not only reveals the vanity of Moses' position but also the potential for education to become another form of mastery like slavery. By the parable's conclusion, "owner and owned magically dissolved into each other like two crossing shafts of light." After Mingo makes another "mistake," killing Moses' potential love interest, the two men escape to Missouri, symbolically running deeper into the heart of slavery. The themes in this story resonate with others in the collection, especially "Exchange Value," a tale about material possession as a means of enslavement rather than emancipation, and "The Sorcerer's Apprentice," a folktale about knowledge as process rather than product.

Several stories in the collection, "Alethia," "Popper's Disease," and "China," narrate the stories of childless black men who ponder and transform their middle-aged, middle-class existences. In particular, "China" tells the contemporary story of Rudolph, a hypochondriac postman in his fifties, who reconstitutes his masculinity through Buddhist practice and Kung Fu. In so doing, he disrupts his marriage with his pious wife, Evelyn, the narrative filter for the story. (This story is loosely based on Johnson's long-standing practice of Kung Fu since 1967. Since 1987, he has codirected one of grandmaster Doc Fai Wong's Kung Fu schools in Seattle.) Throughout the story, we are told the depressing details of their lives. For example, Evelyn's nightstand is cluttered with a "water glass from McDonald's, Preparation H suppositories and Harlequin romances." Imprisoned in a world of mass-produced goods and fantasies, Evelyn finds solace at her church; Rudolph, in his ill-health. Together, they share "the comfort every Negro couple felt when, aging, they knew enough to let things wind down." That is, until they happen to go to the movies for their staid Saturday-night outing and witness a coming attraction for a Kung Fu film, which features a man leaping "twenty feet in the air in perfect defiance of gravity." This image shocks Rudolph into consciousness, both literally and figuratively, as he asks "Can people really do that? Leap that high?" After his first Kung Fu lesson, Rudolph comes to the realization that "I've never been able to give *everything* to *anything*. . . . The world never let me." Kung Fu requires him to "give *every*thing, body and soul, spirit and flesh."

As Rudolph begins his physical and metaphysical journey into the martial arts culture of Seattle, Evelyn is left behind to experience a kind of death-in-life, reminiscent of Faith's spiritual enslavement as a bourgeois housewife. Paradoxically, the mass-packaged masculine fantasy represented in the Kung Fu film clip allows Rudolph to transcend the world of materialism, a transcendence seemingly unavailable to Evelyn in her consumption of popular narratives of femininity in the form of Harlequin romances. In contrast to Evelyn's increasing alienation and her failing vision, Rudolph gains a multiracial group of male friends (from Vietnam, Puerto Rico, and elsewhere) and more significantly, the ability to perceive the universe as "infinite . . . any point where he stood would be at its center—it would shift and move with him." The story concludes with Evelyn attending Rudolph's tournament at the Kingdome, Seattle's old sports coliseum. After a flash of retinal blindness, she sees "a frame of her husband, the postman, twenty feet off the ground in a perfect flying kick that floored his opponent . . . and the fighting in the farthest ring, in herself, perhaps in all the world, was over." As Rudolph becomes the cinematic image that initiates his quest, Evelyn's battle with him is over, leaving the reader to ponder the ambiguity of this ending. We are unsure if Rudolph's triumph signals a new beginning for their relationship or Evelyn's final defeat. As with many of the stories in the collection, "China's" very ambiguity, its suggestion of an ongoing story that exceeds the narrative's conclusion, underscores Johnson's deft use of the disciplined form of the short story to grapple with larger existential questions.

Being and Race (1988), Johnson's book-length treatise on black fiction since 1970, consolidates many of the thematic issues raised in *The Sorcerer's Apprentice* as well as Johnson's other fiction. It takes a phenomenological approach toward the craft of writing. The first half of the book investigates notions of "being" in relation to race, fiction, and form. The second half of the book evaluates a range of contemporary black writers. In his argument, Johnson traces the tradition of black letters to its most prevalent nineteenth-century forms, black social criticism and the novel, as well as the violent context of their production, slavery. This trajectory suggests to Johnson that "the black American writer begins his or her career with—and continues to exhibit—a crisis of identity. . . . If anything, black fiction is about the troubled quest for identity and liberty, the agony of social alienation, the longing for a real and at times a mythical home."

Reviewing the history of black literary movements, from the Post-Reconstruction writings of Charles Chesnutt to the black cultural nationalist writings of Amiri Baraka, Johnson sites "image control" as the primary aim of most writers. In other words, through "this control and reconstitution of images," African American writers mean to "counteracting cultural lies" about blackness. Johnson links together the Negritude movement of the 1930s and 1940s with the Black Arts movement of the 1960s as moments that mark the crystallization of this effort. He sees their doctrinaire approach to being and experience as the primary source of their failure. In his view, these movements lapse into the stasis of kitsch by insisting on the utility of art to fix the image—they retreat from "ambiguity, the complexity of Being occasioned by the conflict of interpretations." This evaluation leads Johnson to make his controversial assertion that "black fiction philosophically still remains a form of genre writing." To break free of these limitations, Johnson advocates an approach toward writing that spurns ideology. This is a position with which many critics have disagreed, on the grounds that Johnson's claims to political neutrality are untenable, that his own stance has political and ideological ramifications equal to, albeit different from, those writers whom he comments upon.

Johnson's call for an artistic practice that moves beyond didacticism supports his theory of "whole sight," a concept first elaborated upon in his 1984 essay "Whole Sight: Notes on New Black fiction," which he wrote as the guest editor of *Callaloo.* In Johnson's definition in *Being,* "whole sight" indicates a way of seeing that advances our search for "innumerable perspectives on *one* world." Johnson claims that "language is transcendence. . . . And so is fiction. . . . They comport us 'other there' behind the eyes of others . . . suddenly our subjectivity is merged with that of a stranger." In other words, good fiction bridges the gap between self and other. By implication, good fiction also bridges the gap between black and white, male and female, and any number of other dualities which support the status quo. He concedes that this analysis may be overly optimistic, yet he suggests that the attempt to collapse the most fundamental of oppositions—self and other—is an emancipating process in and of itself: "perhaps we can never know others. . . . Phenomenology aside, perhaps all we shall ever know are the workings of our own nervous system. . . . But real fiction tries. Its faith is that of transcendence." At the same time, he views language as "the experience, the sight (broad or blind) of others formed into word"—when reviewing the cannon of American literature, these others have most often been "white" and "male," writers "*not* sympathetic with their [contemporary black and feminist writers'] sense of things." Marginalized writers navigate this "communal aspect" of language with the understanding that "language is not fixed but evolving."

With this caveat, Johnson proposes a "cross-cultural" approach to writing that spans a vast range of contemporary and ancient genres. In his view, the "fictional forms we inherit remain fertile fields for new explorations of meaning." Thus, the accomplished writer will manifest a "formal virtuosity," wrought from relentless practice and forged out of a keen respect for "the brilliance of our predecessors" and an understanding of "their inevitable oversights." This approach will usher in "a fiction by Americans who happen to be black, feel at ease both in their ethnicity and in their Yankeeness, and who find it the most natural thing . . . to go about 'singing the world.'" While critics have disagreed over Johnson's take on African American fiction and his vision of the black writer's responsibilities, at the very least, *Being and Race* offers us a compelling description of Johnson's own fictional approach. Furthermore, it contributes to the ongoing dialogue about race and narrative from the unique vantage of a philosopher-practitioner.

In 1990, Johnson finally gained the recognition he long deserved with the publication of *Middle Passage.* For this novel, Johnson was awarded the National Book Award, the first black man to win it since Ralph Ellison won for

Invisible Man in 1952. *Middle Passage* is a Melvillian sea tale, a perverse adventure novel about the nineteenth-century slave trade, based loosely on the story of Odysseus, the Amistad mutiny, and Olaudah Equiano's slave narrative. Written as a ship's log, the tale is narrated by Rutherford Calhoun, a newly freed slave who, leaving his life of petty crime in New Orleans, stows away on a slaver, the *Republic*. He takes this action to avoid being blackmailed into marriage with Isadora Bailey, a prim yet compassionate schoolteacher from Boston. In choosing the *Republic*, Rutherford unwittingly undertakes the journey of the Middle Passage backward: as a free black man, he travels to the origin of enslavement and back again. Moreover, the ship's human cargo is comprised of the Allmuseri, Johnson's ancient (and fictitious) African tribe who exemplify his theory of intersubjectivity. The book's title refers to the nightmarish middle leg of the slave trade between Africa and America where an estimated 1.2 to 2 million Africans died. Johnson takes this traumatic historical moment as the setting for his novel.

As many critics have noted, Johnson not only represents the Middle Passage with historical accuracy, he also limns that history for its metaphorical significance as well. When Rutherford boards the *Republic*, he experiences it as a sentient being, "a wooden sepulcher whose timbers moaned with the memory of too many runs of black gold between the New World and the Old . . . the ship . . . felt conscious and disapprovingly aware of my presence." Later, he discovers that the ship "was, from stem to stern, a process." This designation symbolizes the cross-cultural fertilization that occurs on the boat, between Rutherford, the rest of the ship's crew, and the enslaved Allmuseri, under the oppressive conditions of colonialism in its most extreme form. Rutherford is in the middle, in temporal, spatial, and relational terms: he is in a state of becoming, and part of this process depends on his mediary position in relation to the rest of the characters in the story. As tensions mount on the ship, Rutherford experiences himself as a go-between by virtue of his outsider status. The ship's captain,

an unscrupulous American soldier of fortune, Ebenezer Falcon, asks Rutherford to spy on his crew, while his crew, led by the noble if misguided First Mate, Peter Cringle, calls upon Rutherford to assist them in their plan for mutiny. At the same time, the enslaved Ngonyama, the leader of the last surviving Allmuseri, befriends Rutherford.

A thief through and through, "it's [Rutherford's] nature to be in places he ain't supposed to be." As a result, his allegiances are confused at best. Every faction who calls upon him understands this fact. For example, during their plans for an uprising, one of the mutinous crew suggests:

> Suppose we tell'em the stowaway done in the skipper? . . . Once we reach New Orleans, the rest of us kin sign on to other ships and Calhoun'll go his own way, like he always done, believin' in nothin', belongin' to nobody, driftin' here and there and dyin', probably in a ditch without so much as leavin' a mark on the world—or as much of a mark as you get from writin' on water.

While this estimation sums up Rutherford's central problem, his total alienation, its prophecy is ultimately incorrect, for the text we read is the mark Rutherford leaves on the world. In fact, this "mark" seems to become Rutherford's raison d'être, the answer to his self-loathing query, "But what were my interests?" Though one might expect Rutherford to feel a bond with the enslaved Africans on the ship, even that tie is circumscribed: after the slave mutiny, Ngonyama comforts him with the assertion that "no one will hurt you here. . . . These men are your brothers," to which Rutherford thinks, "How I wish I could believe him." For Rutherford, there can be no easy alliance based on skin color and the experience of bondage; he views himself as different from the Allmuseri on cultural and national grounds. It is no accident that at this point in the narrative, when Rutherford is more desirous for home than ever, Johnson disallows him the reductive answer of Africa, his ancestral homeland. As several critics have suggested, Johnson demonstrates the tendency of colonization to render its victims homeless. In Rutherford's words, "Some part of me was a fatherless child. . . . Alone in an alien world. . . . Wanting to belong somewhere and to someone. . . . But no answers came." By the novel's conclusion, his only viable "home" is the text he writes, which documents the violent displacements of the colonial system.

Rutherford's inability to align himself with one faction or another indicates his in-between status and also underscores his ultimate resistance to the Western dualisms of capital and empire so clearly epitomized in the philosophical views of Falcon, the ship's captain. As a soldier of fortune, Falcon believes that "social conflict and war were, in the Kantian sense, a *structure* of the human mind." In accordance with this position, he asserts that "conflict . . . *is* what it means to be conscious. . . . Dualism is a bloody structure of the mind. . . . Subject and object, perceiver and perceived, self and other—these ancient twins are built into the mind like the stem-piece of a merchantman. . . . We cannot *think* without them." This philosophy stands in sharp contrast to the phenomenological intersubjectivity of the Allmuseri who were a "process . . . not fixed but evolving," a "four-dimensional culture"; they seemed "less a biological tribe than a clan held together by values." The Allmuseri are grounded first and foremost in a moral understanding of the world that resists individualistic categories such as "clan." As Rutherford maneuvers between the ships' factions, his in-between status situates him in the interstices of the self/other opposition that Falcon sees as integral to existence.

In this tenuous position, Rutherford experiences a crisis of self-definition. As he pleads for "mercy" in this moment of turmoil, his cries issue from "an inner wasteland into the larger emptiness . . . the voiceless shadows out there." Through all of his mediations, he finds himself, "[a] man remade by virtue of his contact with the crew." Much like Andrew's final reckoning with his father on the chest of the Soulcatcher, Rutherford comes out of this crisis through a reconciliation with his long-dead father in his meeting with the African god in the hold of the ship. As the god shape-shifts into the form of

his father who abandoned him when he was a child, the grounds of Rutherford's perception change as well. He merges with them both in a fluid "we," beyond self/other, now/then distinctions: "I had to listen harder to isolate him from the We that swelled each particle and pore of him, as if the (black) self was the greatest of all fictions. . . . He seemed everywhere, his presence, and that of countless others, as well as the chamber. . . . Suddenly I knew the god's name: Rutherford."

Adopting the Allmuseri's emphasis on process, Rutherford learns to understand his personhood as a multiple layering of fluid selves. From this point of view, his perceptions reveal "a uniqueness so radical I felt I could assume nothing about anyone or anything." Rejecting the "invisible economic realm"—capitalist notions of property as constitutive of being—he no longer comprehends life experience as "a commodity, a *thing* we could cram into ourselves." Rather, "the voyage had . . . made of me a cultural mongrel, and transformed the world into a fleeting shadow play I felt no need to possess or dominate, only appreciate in the ever extended present." Rutherford attributes this new way of seeing to the asceticism of the Middle Passage, specifically, to the slaves who survived the journey, and in this way, he connects with the cosmology of his ancestors.

The Allmuseri are no less affected by the violence of their encounter with the Western slave trade. As they murder the crew to gain control of the ship, they injure themselves by extension, for they believe that "what came *out* of us, not what went in, made us clean or unclean." Their responsibility for the murders on the ship causes a "vast rupture" within themselves: having entered the breach of "us" versus "them," they are "[n]o longer Africans, yet not Americans either." Fittingly, after the ship goes down, the only Allmuseri survivors are three children, one of whom Rutherford has adopted as his own charge. The Allmuseri's transformation is symbolized in the form of this new generation of interlopers who will grow up in America.

Rutherford's New World legacy, his mark, is the book we read. As he reluctantly takes Falcon's "logbook from the ruins" at the captain's behest, he promises himself that the story "would be, first and foremost, as I saw it since my escape from New Orleans." With this declaration, Rutherford writes from his unique status, as one of the formerly colonized who mediates between the colonizers and those about to be colonized into slavery. His role as the narrator enacts his new conception of selfhood: as he explains, "I was but a conduit or window through which my pillage and booty of 'experience' passed." No longer owning experience, Rutherford makes restitution for his feelings of indebtedness to all the people who have touched him by allowing us to undergo his experiences by proxy, in the form of the novel. At the tale's conclusion, once Rutherford has been rescued by a floating gin palace and reunited with Isadora, he feels "a need to transcribe and thereby transfigure all we had experienced and somehow through all this I found a way to make my peace with the recent past by turning it into Word." The metafictional implications of Rutherford's desire are clear: through the transformative process of writing, Johnson and his protagonist act upon the past, revising history from the perspective of the recently colonized.

In 1998, the same year that Johnson was awarded the prestigious MacArthur award, he published *Dreamer. Dreamer* continues his exploration of "a philosophy of Being" through its skillful layering of fact, fiction, and history in the narration of the last years of Martin Luther King Jr.'s life. Set against the escalating violence of the Civil Rights movement in the late 1960s, the novel traces King's internal struggle over the efficacy of his nonviolent tactics in fighting the entrenched institutional racism of Chicago and the North while his more militant detractors call for an explicitly black nationalist approach. In the novel's prologue, narrated through a limited third-person perspective, we are privy to King's despair, his weariness and his certainty of his own imminent death:

[m]ore tired, acclaimed, hated, gaoled, and hunted than any other Negro in history. . . . No matter how he looked at it, his calling

meant that from the moment he donned his robe the laws governing his life were different from those of the vast majority of men; indeed, it was no longer his life to do with as he pleased. The world owned him long before he could own himself. As it is with candles, so it was with him: the more light he gave, the less there was of him.

In addition to his self-sacrifice, King comprehends the difficult nature of his doctrine, the possibility that "his deeper, esoteric message of freedom had barely been heard." The novel provides us with an intimate portrait of King, representing his spiritual philosophy as a "truth-seeking process," at once suspended between doubt and supreme faith and complicated by its profound costs to his personal life. Johnson grapples with King's legacy in a deeply lyrical manner, enabling us to better comprehend both the conceptual elegance and compassion of King's moral leadership as well as the moral ambiguities of personal sacrifice.

Johnson's work adds to the ongoing reassessment and reclamation of King's achievement by Clayborne Carson, Michael Dyson, and other scholars. Yet Johnson departs from a factual account of King's life, gaining entry into this recent history by deploying a doppelganger, one Chaym Smith, a broken man whose startling resemblance to the great leader inevitably brings their lives together. The men's shared appearance and intellectual proclivities ironically underscore their vastly divergent philosophical perspectives: throughout the novel, Johnson plays Chaym's informed cynicism against King's ecumenical faith, further limning the underpinnings of King's spirituality. The novel also centers on King's young aide, Matthew Bishop, an insecure, shy, bookish twenty-four-year-old who records the inner workings of the movement for posterity. Accordingly, the narration is told primarily from Matthew's first-person perspective, interspersed with periodic chapters of King's internal monologues told from a limited third-person perspective. Though Matthew downplays his own role in the movement, describing himself as a "callow prop in the background of someone else's story," his role as narrator proves to be far more significant than he knows.

After the novel opens with King's despair over his Northern campaign, Chaym appears, a degenerate junkie painter, offering himself as a double, a decoy who can confuse potential assailants. King agrees to Chaym's proposal, but not without intense soul-searching. Chaym's appearance occasions King's meditation on the fundamental inequities of life, for if King was raised in a "commodious, two-story Queen Anne-style home in Atlanta," Chaym grew up (figuratively, at least) in one of the shacks across the street "crammed with the black poor." The men's similar appearance only heightens the profound differences in their life circumstances. King's contemplation of the moral ambiguity and bad luck that characterize Chaym's life foregrounds several of the novel's most important themes: the relation of self and other; the meaning of collective struggle; the particularities that make one human being distinct from another. In a broad sense, Johnson's recourse to the doppelganger plot not only permits him an ingenious method of recuperating King's life through fiction, it also speaks directly to the foundation of King's theology. For, from Johnson's perspective, King's teachings, writings, and activism all speak to the fundamental schism between self and other that lies at the center of human experience: "Every social evil he could think of, and every 'ontological fear,' as he was fond of saying lately, arose from that mysterious dichotomy inscribed at the very heart of things: self and other, I and thou, inner and outer, perceiver and perceived." In providing us with this pair, one chosen and one fallen, Johnson casts the problem of self and other in concrete terms, literalizing this schism in the plot of his novel.

If Johnson's previous fiction has examined this opposition primarily along a racial axis of black and white, in *Dreamer* the figuration of self and other is displaced upon two black men who could be twins. This enables Johnson to focus on the particularity of material conditions such as class, as well as more abstract factors, such as talent, which differentiate one hu-

man being from another. And, of course, the story of two brothers, one good and one bad, is one of the oldest stories of Western civilization. As the narrator informs us, the name "Chaym" is an etymological variant of "Cain." In Johnson's inimical fashion, he uses the story of Cain and Abel to interpret King's and Chaym's relationship, and in turn, those two fraternal relationships reflect the ontological problem of self and other in King's theology.

Chaym's link to Cain is most clearly explicit in the chapters that document his transformation into King's perfect double. He is given over to the guidance of Matthew and the beautiful, smart Amy, another Southern Christian Leadership Conference (SCLC) volunteer with whom Matthew is secretly in love: the three leave Chicago for Amy's ancestral farm house in southern Illinois in order to train Chaym in the teachings and physical gestures of King, so that he can pass for the leader. In the process, each undergoes a spiritual awakening (though we are privy mostly to Matthew's and Chaym's growth): "we three were subtly transformed, Amy no less than I as we looked to impress the matrix of the minister onto our charge." In particular, as Chaym learns how to perform King, he simultaneously instructs Matthew about their shared status as outcasts, as Cainites as opposed to Abelites: "Outcasts know each other. . . . Until the day we die, we're drifters. . . . And that's okay. I accept that. Hell, I embrace it. . . . The only thing is, I don't want to be forgotten. . . . I want to *do* something to make [God] remember this nigger—*me*—for eternity." In this way, Chaym positions himself and Matthew as outsiders and, implicitly as artists, who will never find a home in this life but, nonetheless, may ultimately establish a place for themselves in the immortality of their work.

Throughout the novel, Chaym's character not only symbolizes Cain but also echoes the trickster figure of the Soulcatcher in *Oxherding Tale* and the Allmuseri god in *Middle Passage*, manifesting one of Johnson's central formulations about identity as a kind of ongoing performance rather than a fixed or static self. As Matthew watches Chaym speak, he sees him "fluidly shifting from one mask to another as the occasion demanded, as if maybe the self was a fiction—or, if not that, a multiplicity of often conflicting profiles." As we see throughout the novel, Chaym is a loose configuration of many selves, an identity formation as instrumental to Matthew's own development as King's model of moral largesse. Moreover, King himself seems to possess something of Chaym's ability. In one of the most important episodes of the novel, Chaym is called upon to accept an award for King at a black middle-class AME church in Evanston, "his first real performance as double." As Chaym begins to understand the magnitude of his task, he begins to unravel. Amy takes Chaym back to the kitchen to help him compose himself and Matthew joins the congregation. Moments later, "Amy walked in behind King—it was most certainly King, not Chaym Smith" and King begins his acceptance speech, the only complete oration of King's in the entire novel. As King speaks, Matthew contemplates his grace, which comes from his selflessness: "Something in him was dead, extinguished so long ago." The church's pastor asks King if he feels disillusioned and King's response to this question comprises his oration:

> The answer to the question is that no man can bring me so low to make me hate him. . . . after being in the storm so long I've learned to accept only one problem: What is God? Every night when I get down on my knees to pray or close my eyes in quiet meditation I'm holding a funeral for the self. I'm digging a little grave for the ego. . . . After a time, I tell you, a man comes to see only a We, this precious moment as a tissue in time holding past, future, present, with all of us in the red, everlasting debtors—ontological thieves—in a universe of interrelatedness. . . . Every man and woman is a speculum, our mirror. Our twin . . . Brothers and sisters, Reverend Coleman, no one can make me hate. I have no choice but to love others because I *am* the others.

In this passage, the very heart of the novel, King's sermon offers a perfect synthesis of the meaning of Cain and Abel in the narrative. As we read, we are unsure if the speaker is King or Chaym. We have only Matthew's perception with which to judge this performance, and half way through the preaching, it occurs to him, "The more I listened and looked, the more I suspected that it was Smith, not King at the microphone." Thus, we are suspended between the two men, trying to locate the actual speaker with every new word. Ultimately, the beauty of the speech obviates this search.

Through this narrative confusion, Johnson enacts the meaning of King's philosophy, for the speech is a melding of Chaym and King, self and other. After the speech, Chaym despairs, "How *does* he *do* that? Some of the things he said . . . That was *my* stuff. Not things I've ever said, but stuff I've felt. Like my spirit is trapped in his, which is so much clearer and bigger and cleaner. His voice . . . It feels when he's preaching like his words come from inside me, not outside—like he gives my soul a voice." King's extinguishing of the ego and desire allows him to become the ultimate "ontological thief," to become the other. In this way, King achieves the selflessness central to a Christian theology defined in broad terms: he achieves agape (divine love) in Christianity or Vedantic thought. As the sermon so aptly demonstrates, King collapses boundaries of self and other and accesses the redemptive collective spirit of his theology.

This scene signals several other mergings as well. When Johnson provides us with King's oration, he enacts a metatextual doubling, showing his hand as a writer. As the writer, he stands in for King, inventing a speech worthy of the great leader's oeuvre. And this suggests yet another doubling in the text, as Matthew embodies the figure of the writer, standing in for Johnson. As a recorder of the revolution, Matthew's job is to preserve "its secrets for posterity . . . particularly what took place in the interstices. Naturally, this is where the stories of all doubles occur." While Matthew refers literally to his recording of Chaym's progress in learning King's ways, in a larger sense, his summation refers to the way the writer functions as a double (even a decoy) for his subject.

Throughout the novel, we witness Matthew come into his own as a man and a writer, a Cainite genius "in the shadows."

If King's Way is agapic love, "a daily praxis," Matthew's Way is writing, and it requires a similar skill, the ability to collapse distinctions of self and other, to be both at once. Matthew's struggle with the efficacy of narrative—the accusation made by Chaym that "all narratives are lies"—parallels King's turmoil over the efficacy of his teachings. Matthew discovers his answer to this accusation in his definition of the self:

> The self we constructed was anything more than a fragile composite of other selves we'd encountered . . . indebted to all spoken languages, all evolutionary forms, all lives that preceded our own . . . when we spoke, it could be said, in the final analysis, subjectivity vanished and the world sang in every sentence we uttered. (And thus narrative was not a lie.)

In this way, narrative and language are a palimpsest of past, future, and present usages. They are lies in the same sense that "selves" are lies: they are borrowings, ontological units at once individual and vastly interrelated.

Herein lies the novel's ultimate achievement. While some critics have objected that the novel sheds no new factual light on the conspiracy behind King's assassination, this complaint misses the point and, in fact, runs counter to Johnson's entire artistic project. His historical fiction pointedly breaks with the tenets of realism, in order to argue for a more fluid and layered vision of history, one that strives for contingent and interrelated truths located in the interstices of past, present, and future. In this way, perhaps *Dreamer* is Johnson's most risky novel, because it addresses recent history, a period about which many contemporary readers feel proprietary. But as Johnson asserts in *Being*, "writing doesn't so much record an experience—or even imitate or represent it—as it *creates* that experience." In engaging this history through fiction, in suggest-

ing that facts are not the whole key to the truth, Johnson unites the writer and the reader as participants who act upon history through interpretation, who produce the living truths of King's life.

As Johnson so aptly demonstrates, perhaps the most important aspect of King's legacy is his radical agapic teaching, his understanding of good and evil in complex interfaith terms (an understanding that sheds light on his assassination in fundamentally moral and philosophical terms). We learn about King through the story of his double—"from an oblique angle of alienation"—for in the end, both men are emblematic of King's prophetic vision. In deploying the trope of the doppelganger, Johnson locates the magnitude of King's message in his ability to transcend the duality of self and other through a vision "lapped and folded in as few as three words: Others first. Always." This message is refracted through the dizzying proliferation of doubles in the novel: as Chaym doubles for King, in turn, they double as a pair for Cain and Abel and any number of legendary brothers; Johnson stands in for King in the writing of the sermon (and the larger narrative); Matthew, the movement's scribe (propitiously named after the writer of the first gospel) stands in for Johnson the writer; in a sense, too, Matthew and Johnson function as our double as we strive to know King's story. And with King's assassination, he becomes Christ, having died for our sins. Each of these displacements performs the most fundamental doctrine of King's philosophy: "white and black, male and female, Jew and Gentile, rich and poor—these were ephemeral garments. . . . To gain the dizzying heights of the mountaintop the self's baggage had to be abandoned in the valley." Finally, by the novel's conclusion, we are all Cainites, restless seekers in our quest for knowledge in the story of King. In undertaking this spiritual journey, in grasping even partial truths about King's legacy, Johnson suggests, "even . . . the fatherless exiles . . . might sometimes—and occasionally—doeth well."

In the 1990s, Johnson rose to prominence as a writer. At the same time that he won the National Book Award, he was named the first Pollock Professor of English at the University of Washington. In 1994, Southern Illinois University inaugurated the Charles Johnson Award for Fiction and Poetry, a competition for college students. Along with a Writers Guild Award, a Guggenheim Fellowship, and a MacArthur Fellowship, Johnson was one of twelve African American authors honored in an international stamp series celebrating great writers of the twentieth century, an honor that marks his long-deserved ascendancy in the pantheon of the nation's best writers, past and present. In 1997, he published an anthology devoted to an exploration of black masculinity in America, *Black Men Speaking*, which he edited with John McCluskey and John McCluskey Jr., alongside a compilation of his own essays, poetry, cartoons, novel excerpts, interviews, and critiques entitled *I Call Myself an Artist: Writings By and About Charles Johnson* (1999). He also completed a companion work to the PBS documentary, *Africans in America: America's Journey Through Slavery* (1999), in which his short fictional narratives about slavery dovetail with Patricia Smith's historical anecdotes and commentary. In addition, since the publication of *Middle Passage*, Johnson adapted the book into a screenplay. In Johnson's evolution as a creative artist, from his first published novel to his later endeavors, we see him grappling with a set of fundamental epistemological questions about the relationship between being and identity, language and history. Echoing the work of John A. Williams and Ralph Ellison, Johnson's fiction embraces a postmodernist experimentation with chronology, fact, and narration. Moreover, in its revision of significant historical events and its telling of stories previously untold, Johnson's projects intersect with the literary endeavors of writers such as Ishmael Reed and Toni Morrison, helping to reshape the contours of American literature. Johnson's literary corpus surely deserves our greatest esteem, for he exceeds his own standards, exemplifying "the protean writer, the performer . . . who slides from genre to genre, style to style, leaving his . . . distinctive signature on each form

lovingly transfigured and pushed toward new possibilities."

Selected Bibliography

PRIMARY WORKS

NOVELS AND SHORT STORIES

Faith and the Good Thing. New York: Viking, 1974.
Oxherding Tale. Bloomington: Indiana University Press, 1982.
The Sorcerer's Apprentice: Tales and Conjurations. New York: Atheneum, 1986.
Being and Race: Black Writing Since 1970. Bloomington: Indiana University Press, 1988.
Middle Passage. New York: Athenuem, 1990.
Dreamer: A Novel. New York: Scribner, 1998.

OTHER WORKS

Fiction: A Special Issue. *Callaloo* 7, no. 3 (1984).
Black Men Speaking. Edited by Charles Johnson, John McCluskey, and John McCluskey Jr. Bloomington: Indiana University Press, 1997.
Africans in America: America's Journey through Slavery. Charles Johnson, Patricia Smith, and the WGBH Series Research Team. New York: Harcourt Brace and Co., 1998.
I Call Myself an Artist: Writings By and About Charles Johnson. Edited by Charles Johnson and Rudolph P. Byrd. Bloomington: Indiana University Press, 1999.

ARTICLES

"The Primeval Mitosis: A Phenomenology of the Black Body." *Juju: Research Papers in Afro-American Studies,* Winter 1976, pp. 48–59.
"Essays on Fiction." *Intro* 10:xi–xiii (1979).
"Philosophy and Black Fiction." *Obsidian* 6:55–61 (1980).
"Whole Sight: Notes on New Black Fiction." *Callaloo* 7, no. 3:1–6 (1984).
"A Phenomenology of 'On Moral Fiction.'" *Thor's Hammer: Essays on John Gardner.* Edited by Leonard Butts, Jeff Henderson, and Kathryn Van Spanckeren. Conway: University of Central Arkansas Press, 1985. Pp. 147–56.
"John Gardner as Mentor." *African American Review* 30, no. 4:619–24 (1996).

CARTOONS

Black Humor. Chicago: Johnson Publishing, 1970.
Half-Past Nation-Time. California: Aware Press, 1972.

TELEVISION

Charlie's Pad, PBS, 1971.
Charlie Smith and the Fritter-Tree, PBS, 1978.
For Me Myself, PBS, 1982.

A Place for Myself, 1981.
Booker, coauthored with John Allmann, PBS, 1984.

SECONDARY WORKS

CRITICAL AND BIOGRAPHICAL STUDIES

Benesch, Klaus. "The Education of Mingo." *The African American Short Story*. Edited by Wolfgang Karrer and Barbara Puschmann-Nalenz. Trier, Germany: Wissenschaftlicher, 1993. Pp. 169–79.

Boccia, Michael, and Herman Beavers, eds. "Charles Johnson." *African American Review* 30:517–675 (1996).

Brown, Bill. "Global Bodies/ Postnationalities: Charles Johnson's Consumer Culture." *Representations* 58: 24–48 (1997).

Byrd, Rudolph P. "*Oxherding Tale* and *Siddhartha*: Philosophy, Fiction, and the Emergence of a Hidden Tradition." *African American Review* 30:549–58 (1996).

Coleman, James. "Charles Johnson's Quest for Black Freedom in *Oxherding Tale*." *African American Review* 29, no. 4:631–44 (1995).

Fagel, Brian. "Passages from the Middle: Coloniality and Postcoloniality in Charles Johnson's *Middle Passage*" *African American Review* 30, no. 4:625–33 (1996).

Gleason, William. "The Liberation of Perception: Charles Johnson's *Oxherding Tale*." *Black American Literature Forum* 25:706–28 (1991).

Goudie, S. X. " 'Leavin' a Mark on the Wor(l)d': Marksmen and Marked Men in *Middle Passage*." *African American Review* 29:109–22 (1995).

Griffiths, Frederick T. " 'Sorcery is Dialectical': Plato and Jean Toomer in Charles Johnson's *The Sorcerer's Apprentice*." *African American Review* 30, no. 4:527–38 (1996).

Hayward, Jennifer. "Something to Serve: Constructs of the Feminine in Charles Johnson's *Oxherding Tale*." *Black American Literature Forum* 25:689–703 (1991).

Little, Jonathan. "Charles Johnson's Revolutionary *Oxherding Tale*." *Studies in American Fiction* 19, no. 2:141–51 (1991).

———. "From the Comic Book to the Comic: Charles Johnson's Variations on Creative Expression." *African American Review* 30, no. 4:579–601 (1996).

———. *Charles Johnson's Spiritual Imagination*. Columbia: University of Missouri Press, 1997.

Muther, Elizabeth. "Isadora at Sea: Misogyny as Comic Capital in Charles Johnson's *Middle Passage*." *African American Review* 30, no. 4:649–58 (1996).

O'Keefe, Vincent A. "Reading Rigor Mortis: Offstage Violence and Excluded Middles 'in' Johnson's *Middle Passage* and Morrison's *Beloved*." *African American Review* 30, no. 4:635–47 (1996).

Parrish, Timothy L. "Imagining Slavery: Toni Morrison and Charles Johnson." *Studies in American Fiction* 25, no. 1:81–100 (1997).

Retman, Sonnet. " 'Nothing was Lost in the Masquerade': The Protean Performance of Genre and Identity in Charles Johnson's *Oxherding Tale*." *African American Review* 33:417–37 (1999).

Rushdy, Ashraf H. A. "The Properties of Desire: Forms of Slave Identity in Charles Johnson's *Middle Passage*." *Arizona Quarterly* 50, no. 2:73–108 (1994).

———. "The Phenomenology of the Allmuseri: Charles Johnson and the Subject of the Narrative of Slavery." *African American Review* 26, no. 3:373-94 1992.

Scott, Daniel M. "Interrogating Identity: Appropriation and Transformation in *Middle Passage*." *African American Review* 29, no. 4:645–55 (1995).

Storhoff, Gary. "The Artist as Universal Mind: Berkeley's Influence on Charles Johnson." *African American Review* 30, no. 4:539–48 (1996).

Walby, Celestin. "The African Sacrificial Kingship Ritual and Johnson's *Middle Passage*." *African American Review* 29, no. 4:657–69 (1995).

Whatley Smith, Virginia. "Sorcery, Double-Consciousness, and Warring Souls: An Intertextual Reading of *Middle Passage* and *Captain Blackman*." *African American Review* 30, no. 4:659–74 (1996).

INTERVIEWS

Boccia, Michael. "An Interview with Charles Johnson." *African American Review* 30, no. 4:611–8 (1996).

Little, Jonathan. "An Interview with Charles Johnson." *Contemporary Literature* 34, no. 2:159–81 (1993).

McCullough, Ken. "Reflections on Film, Philosophy, and Fiction: An Interview with Charles Johnson." *Callaloo* 1, no. 4:118–28 (1978).

Myers, George. "Being and Race: An Interview with Charles Johnson." *Gargoyle* 35:30–35 (1988).

Rowell, Charles H. "An Interview with Charles Johnson." *Callaloo* 20:531–47 (1997).

JAMES WELDON JOHNSON
(1871–1938)

J. T. SKERRETT JR.

ANY RECITAL OF the richly varied life of James Weldon Johnson is likely to inspire critical interest even as it defies any ambition to encompass his many activities in a single study. During his working life, Johnson was a principal of an elementary school, the publisher and editor of a daily newspaper, a practicing attorney, the lyricist of a songwriting team, a diplomat for the consular service of the U.S. State Department, a journalist, a field officer and then executive secretary of the National Association for the Advancement of Colored People, and, finally, a professor of literature at Fisk University.

Despite the fact that he excelled at each of these careers and enterprises, Johnson has earned his place in American cultural history as a writer. Like the Victorian gentleman that in many ways he was, Johnson viewed his work as poet, novelist, essayist, and editor as an avocation. Although Johnson sought satisfaction in positions of political and social leadership, he also found satisfaction in the cultural leadership that his literary work represented, struggling to strike a balance between his sense of responsibility for the advancement of black Americans and the pleasure of art.

Johnson's background was atypical of the generation of blacks born just after the Civil War. Neither of his parents had been slaves before the war. His father, James Johnson, was a freeborn person of color born in Virginia in 1830, who by 1860 was established in New York City. His mother, Helen Dillet, born in 1842 in the Bahamas, was part French, part Haitian, and a member of the Bahamian black middle class. The Johnsons married in the Bahamas in 1864. When economic depression struck Nassau a few years later, James moved his family to Jacksonville, Florida, taking a position as head-waiter at a luxury hotel. The Johnsons' eldest son, James William (he became "James Weldon" in 1913) was born in Jacksonville on 17 June 1871.

James's artistic gifts seem to have come to him through his mother, who taught elementary school in Jacksonville. She played the piano, sketched, wrote poetry, and interested her children in varied forms of genteel self-expression. From his father, James inherited both a strong will to succeed and a confidence equal to any challenge. James Johnson, Sr., provided his family with a middle-class life accessible to only a small minority of blacks in the South of the late 1800s. Family contacts in Nassau and New York, friendships with political activists, and the presence in the Johnson home for nearly ten years of a Cuban boy James's age all served to add to Johnson's store of useful and unusual experiences. He learned something of party politics and of black relations with and expectations of the political system. As a teenager

Johnson visited New York and was fascinated by city life. He learned to speak fluent Spanish at a relatively young age. At seventeen, trapped in Jacksonville by a yellow fever epidemic that made it impossible for him to return to high school in Atlanta, James worked as secretary to a sophisticated white physician. Dr. Thomas Osmond Summers greatly influenced Johnson with his model of the modern gentleman: a public person and a research scientist and physician who worked for the common good, Summers was also a man who retained a nonconforming private self; he was an atheist and a poet and a man who rejected racism. Summers treated young Johnson as a social and intellectual equal, giving him books to read and discussing them with him; he also encouraged Johnson to write poetry and analyzed his work. He took Johnson to New York and Washington, D.C., and let him experience life as a first-class citizen—sitting at the captain's table while shipboard, sharing rooms in hotels, and sightseeing. The exposure to the cultured and cosmopolitan Dr. Summers had a lasting influence on Johnson. In *Along This Way* (1933), Johnson's autobiography, he boldly states that he "made him [Dr. Summers] my model of all that a man and a gentleman should be" (p. 98). After this stimulating summer, Johnson returned to the preparatory division of Atlanta University, where he finished high school and started college with an old ambition "clarified, strengthened and brought into some shape—the ambition to write" (p. 99).

Atlanta University was also a powerful shaping force on Johnson. Modeled after Yale, which most of its white faculty had attended, Atlanta provided black youths like Johnson with a classical education and a strong sense of responsibility for public service. The issue of being "of service to the race" was an ethical question under constant discussion at the university, and Johnson was an active participant in debates on "the future of the Negro." He taught one summer in a backwoods Georgia school; he sang with a touring group that attempted to raise funds for the college by offering concerts of spirituals in northern cities. At the same time, the private life of the writer was being born. The

James Weldon Johnson Memorial Collection at Yale contains papers dating back to his college days, when he recorded essay topics, story plots, and play scenarios that reflected both his public interest in the issues of race and democracy and his imaginative interest in irony, melodrama, and tragedy. At this point in his life, Johnson had not yet found the connection between the public life, a life of service to the community, and the inner, imaginative life.

Upon graduation in May 1894, Johnson was appointed principal of the Stanton School in Jacksonville, choosing a situation where his actions would have an immediate impact. Putting into action his belief that individuals could advance the race, Johnson established the first high school for blacks in the state of Florida, offering the students an education very similar to the one he had received in Atlanta. In May 1895 Johnson began publishing the Jacksonville *Daily American*, the country's first daily black newspaper, which he produced almost singlehandedly for about eight months, until its financial collapse in the spring of 1896. Johnson turned next to the study of law and became the first black to be admitted to the Florida bar. He formed a partnership with an old college friend but found the kind of legal work available to him unsatisfying. For several years Johnson ran the Stanton School and managed to practice law for eight or nine months of the year, spending the summer months in New York City with his brother, John Rosamond, writing songs for the musical theater. It was the age of ragtime; popular culture, especially Broadway and its popular music, were having a love affair with images of the "plantation Negro," the "black dandy," the "dusky belle," and other outgrowths of minstrelry and post-Reconstruction southern writing.

Working with his brother and Bob Cole, a leading black performer and lyricist, Johnson produced highly successful songs for a variety of Broadway shows and tours, including a tour through Europe. Between 1900 and 1905 the Johnson brothers' songs were written almost exclusively in Negro dialect and were concerned with the theatrical stereotypes of "Negro" emotion or behavior. Johnson struggled to generalize these conventions; after his earliest efforts he avoided using the racist vocabulary of "coons" and "niggers" that white performers expected. Cole and Johnson Brothers' best work, such as "The Congo Love Song" and "Under the Bamboo Tree," while not avoiding plantation or jungle dialect, connect in their simplicity and playfulness to the audience's sense of the universal elements of affection:

If you lak-a-me, I lak-a-you;
    And we lak-a-both the same,
I lak-a-say, this very day,
I lak-a-change your name;
'Cause I love-a-you and love-a-true
and if you-alove-a-me,
One live as two, two live as one,
Under the bamboo tree.
       ("Under the Bamboo Tree,"
       quoted in Levy, p. 90)

Johnson and his partners consciously worked to transform the conventions of stereotype into a more universally appealing set of verbal and musical images. Bob Cole and J. Rosamond Johnson both wished to retain the ethnic distinctiveness of Negro music while at the same time developing and sophisticating a ragtime that they and James saw as ragtag and ephemeral. Perhaps because of their overexposure to European-American cultural standards—Rosamond had attended the New England Conservatory of Music—and correlative underexposure to indigenous black musical expression, the Johnson brothers conceived of the ethnic element as a raw material in need of refinement. None of them recognized the creative greatness under the racial signs of "primitive" and "inferior" that surrounded them in the work of Scott Joplin, Artie Matthews, James Scott, and other black composers of ragtime music.

Johnson had not yet drawn on his knowledge of the language of literature and his understanding of the languages of the African American folk for whom he wished to speak. Johnson's poetic efforts in the first twenty years of his creative life resisted the energy of the vernacular forms of the folk, or denatured that energy

James Weldon Johnson

through refinement. Even the successes are illustrative. One of Johnson's earliest collaborations with his brother was a song written not for Broadway or Tin Pan Alley but for a celebration of Abraham Lincoln's birthday in 1900. Johnson notes in *Along This Way* that "Lift Every Voice and Sing" was composed in the "poet's ecstasy," from a "sense of serene joy—which makes artistic creation the most complete of all human experiences." A poem that had come to take such an important place in the African American imagination—later adopted as the official song of the NAACP—was an odd mixture of sublime creation and profanely practical collaboration. The poem is effective in its musical setting, oddly but perhaps appropriately old-fashioned in its sentiments, which valorize the common ground of an oppressive history and confidence in the future founded on religious faith.

Lift every voice and sing
Till earth and heaven ring,

Ring with the harmonies of liberty;
Let our rejoicing rise
High as the listening skies,
Let it resound loud as the rolling sea.
Sing a song full of the faith that the dark
    past has taught us,
Sing a song full of the hope that the present
    has brought us.
Facing the rising sun of our new day begun,
Let us march on till victory is won.

(in *Saint Peter Relates an Incident*)

"Lift Every Voice and Sing" is nearly as much a manipulation of poetic conventions as Johnson's theater lyrics.

Other early literary work shows similar qualities of divided interest. Johnson's dialect poems, drawing on a genre abounding with a broad range of racial stereotypes, worked to undercut the racist presuppositions about black character while accepting the reality of dialect as authentic black language. From "Since You Went Away," first published in *Century* magazine in 1900, to the "Jingles and Croons" section in his collection *Fifty Years and Other Poems* (1917), Johnson, like his friend and literary mentor Paul Laurence Dunbar, tried to wrest the reader's attention away from the exotic sound of black English and toward the classic emotions and themes of lost love, parental exasperation, courtship, the death of a child. A few of these dialect poems—and there are no more than twenty of them in the 1917 collection—suggest that Johnson may have been working from experience or memory rather than from the model of Dunbar. The lyric simplicity of "Since You Went Away" and the comic exuberance of "Brer Rabbit, You's de Cutes' Of 'm All" are exemplary, as is "An Explanation":

Look heah 'Splain to me de reason
Why you said to Squire Lee,
Der wuz twelve ole chicken thieves
In dis heah town, includin' me.
Ef he tole you dat, my brudder,
He said sump'n dat warn't true;
W'at I said wuz dis, dat der wuz
Twelve, *widout* includin' you.
Oh. . . . !

There is greater appreciation for the verbal skills of the black folk here than in almost all the rest of Johnson's dialect verse. He would not draw so close to the natural expression of the folk again until *God's Trombones* (1927).

From 1902 Johnson lived in New York City as part of the black theater and music community. Because he was not a performer, he found himself with a great deal of free time, part of which he filled by taking literature courses at Columbia University with Brander Matthews. Matthews was a theater critic, the author of realist sketches of urban life, a progressive friend of Teddy Roosevelt, and an open-minded observer of the current theater scene, including the kind of black musical comedy that Johnson was then doing. Like Dr. Summers, Matthews took Johnson seriously, calling on Johnson's fluent Spanish in discussion of classic Spanish drama as well as his first-hand knowledge of the New York theater world. Johnson, for his part, shared with Matthews his new project, a novel, and sought his advice on its development. Matthews's encouragement of Johnson's literary interests helped Johnson to make his next career decision, for novel writing required greater free time and concentration than his work in the theater provided. In deciding to leave the partnership with his brother and Bob Cole, Johnson chose to mine a deeper vein of artistic ore, one that lay as much within himself as in the public world.

While working on his novel Johnson maintained himself financially by engaging in a career of public service: he secured an appointment as United States consul in Puerto Cabello, Venezuela, and took up his post there in the summer of 1906. Although his new employment would mean a reduction in annual income by two-thirds, he did not view his departure from New York as a sacrifice, but rather as an escape. A State Department career meant a chance to think about how he would make his mark in the world; he was "getting away, if only for a while, from the feverish flutter of life to seek a little stillness of the spirit" (*Along This Way*, p. 223). During his stay in Venezuela, Johnson spent his leisure time writing; in 1909 he was transferred and became consul in Corinto, Nicaragua, bringing with him his wife, Grace Nail. Johnson spent nearly four years in Nicaragua, witnessing revolutions and developing a sympathy for Latin Americans.

The novel he completed during his first two years of service to the State Department—*The Autobiography of an Ex-Colored Man*—is his only work of fiction. He published it anonymously in 1912 and did not acknowledge it until its republication in 1927 during the Harlem Renaissance. It is mentioned, but not discussed, in *Along This Way.* Despite these indications, Johnson was not indifferent to this novel. On the contrary, Johnson was deeply engaged with the story he told in *The Autobiography of an Ex-Colored Man*; writing it permitted him to challenge and defeat his own doubts about the value and validity of his ambitions and activities.

The nameless protagonist of *The Autobiography*, a light-skinned black man who also serves as the story's narrator, shares with his creator the marginal condition of the educated man of color. The narrator, however, is socially invisible; to all appearances he is merely another white person. Johnson did not share this physical ambiguity, but modeled his character on his old friend Judson Douglas Wetmore, with whom he had shared a law partnership in Jacksonville. In *Along This Way*, Wetmore's presence contrasts with and highlights Johnson's reticence: Wetmore is brash, daring, opportunistic, bold with women, materialistic, rebellious—and able to pass for white. Johnson both admired him and, characteristically, distanced himself from him, as he did when Wetmore moved to New York shortly before Johnson decided to enter the consular service. Wetmore was a kind of alter ego, the opposite of the socially committed artist/leader that Johnson imagined he wanted to become. While Johnson was becoming a man of the theater, Wetmore was becoming a man of substance. The need to choose between raceless personal comfort and race-conscious service is one of the themes of Johnson's novel. In the symbolic form of the narrator, Johnson struggles with his desire for public service and the temptation to achieve private comfort, as he thought Wetmore had done.

Johnson connects his own story to that of the "tragic mulatto," a literary convention that had, like the minstrel tradition he had struggled with in his songwriting, trapped and trammeled writers who wanted to describe black experience. Fairly recent literary efforts—such as William Dean Howells's *An Imperative Duty* (1892) and Mark Twain's *Tragedy of Pudd'n-head Wilson* (1894)—had broken with the long-standing image of the mixed-race American as either feckless victim (generally female) or frustrated and enraged sociopath (generally male). Charles Chesnutt's first novel, *The House Behind the Cedars* (1900), like Johnson's novel, has as its main character a young mulatto who chooses, with fatal consequences, to pass as a white because of his doubts about the future of the Negro. From this long-standing tradition, Johnson accepts the tragic situation of the mulatto. He shares his privileged narrator's middle-class tastes and desire to enjoy a citizenship not foreshortened by racial prejudice. The narrator is the illegimate son of a wealthy white southerner and his nearly-white black mistress. Raised in the North, the narrator remains ignorant of his black identity until it is imposed upon him at school by a teacher. From this point on, the narrator's struggle is to become a figure of achievement and thus to transcend the black stereotypes that both limit and shame him.

Johnson models his story on an autobiographical narrative, making his protagonist a subject instead of objectifying him in the manner of Howells, Twain, or Chesnutt. In this way the reader is not tempted to view the narrator as either frustrated madman or pathetic victim. Johnson improves on the tradition of the tragic mulatto by allowing his hero to indulge in self-analysis, as evident in the novel's opening page:

I know that in writing the following pages I am divulging the great secret of my life, the secret which for some years I have guarded far more carefully than any of my earthly possessions; and it is a curious study to me to analyze the motives which prompt me to do it.

But Johnson's invention cuts even deeper. His narrator presents himself in that opening paragraph as a self-assured and reliable analyst of his own feelings, but what makes the novel a truly effective work is the irony of his unreliability. The narrator reveals more about himself than he imagines, and the reader arrives at quite a different assessment of him than his narrative intends.

From his earliest childhood days, the narrator does whatever is required to protect himself from emotional discomfort. Though he resolves to be "a great colored man" when his Negro identity is thrust upon him at school, in every situation that calls for him to assert that identity (or accept responsibility for not doing so) he takes a cowardly, self-protective line of retreat.

After his mother dies, the narrator decides to attend Atlanta University. When his money is stolen at a boarding house he is so filled with shame and embarrassment that he does not register for classes but goes to Jacksonville, where he finds work making cigars. He lives there for three years, learning about the relationship between race, social class, and white power. His learning is, however, incomplete and selfish:

> I can realize more fully than I could years ago that the position of the advanced element of the colored race is often very trying. They are the ones among the blacks who carry the entire weight of the race question; it worries the others very little. (p. 60)

When the cigar factory suddenly closes, the narrator moves to New York City, where he is no longer part of a respectable society that includes membership in the literary society and Sunday carriage rides. In New York he is drawn into a bohemian world of nightlife, drinking, gambling, ragtime music, interracial sexuality, and, ultimately, violence. Fascinated by these pleasures of the city, the narrator soon learns to gamble and then to play ragtime piano for a living; he is befriended by a cultured gentleman, a millionaire, who functions in the narrative like a demon tempter, helping the narrator by hiring him as a piano player for private parties, a situation that automatizes and oppresses him:

> During such moments this man sitting there so mysteriously silent, almost hid in a cloud of heavy-scented smoke, filled me with a sort of unearthly terror. He seemed to be some grim, mute but relentless tyrant, possessing over me a supernatural power which he used to drive me on mercilessly to exhaustion. (p. 88)

Ignoring the occasional feelings of terror, the narrator comes to admire his millionaire patron, much as Johnson had come to admire Dr. Summers: "I looked upon him at that time as about all a man could wish to be." The narrator's relations with the millionaire climax with a trip to Europe during which the narrator decides that he should use his musical talents to transform black music—spirituals and ragtime—into classical European forms. The millionaire, marshaling the language of Victorian racial discourse and social Darwinism, attempts to dissuade him:

> This idea you have of making a Negro out of yourself is nothing more than a sentiment. . . . What kind of a Negro would you make now, especially in the South? . . . I can imagine no more dissatisfied human being than an educated, cultured, and refined colored man in the United States. . . . Perhaps some day, through study and observation, you will come to see that evil is a force, and, like the physical and chemical forces, one cannot annihilate it; we may only change its form. (p. 106)

The narrator rejects the millionaire's temptations, recognizing the selfishness in the proposal that he remain in Europe to study music. But he also finds sense in the assertion that he is throwing his life away "amidst the poverty and ignorance, the hopeless struggle, of the black people of the United States." In a curious compromise, the narrator returns to America, reasoning that he could attract greater attention as a colored composer than as a white one.

Bob Cole, James Weldon Johnson, and his brother Rosamond Johnson.

Thus, spiritually compromised, he undertakes his journey to the South in search of musical material, failing to reveal his racial identity.

The final collapse of the narrator's dream—of becoming a great colored man by recomposing in classic European forms the music of the black folk—comes when he witnesses a lynching in the Georgia woods. Shaken by the ferociousness and brutality of the whites and the impotence of the blacks, the narrator flees the South, abandoning his career plan, and protecting himself from psychological pain.

> All the while I understood that it was not discouragement or fear or search for a larger field of action that was driving me out of the Negro race. I knew it was shame, unbearable shame. Shame at being identified with a people that could with impunity be treated worse than animals. (p. 139)

Upon returning to New York, the narrator chooses to follow the white path of business and property rather than the black path of musical art and expression. In passing for white, he takes advantage of a special opportunity, but he must sacrifice his artistic self to do so. He mar-ries a white woman who keeps his secret from everyone, including their children. When she dies, the narrator realizes that his actions have negated his cultural identity, once inextricably connected to black art.

Though the narrator announces at the beginning of *The Autobiography* his intention of turning the telling of "the little tragedies of my life" into "a practical joke on society," it is clear by the story's end that the unintentional revelation of his moral inadequacy in the face of every racial challenge turns the joke on him, and this irony creates a solid artistic achievement.

Writing *The Autobiography of an Ex-Colored Man* allowed Johnson to exorcise his own temptations to seek the "wine of the world" rather than the life of service for which his education had prepared him. In November of 1908, the novel completed, Johnson wrote to Brander Matthews that he was contemplating a return to his old work in New York because, although he had found himself during his stay in Venezuela and felt [his] "power to do better [literary] work than before," he also felt "no incentive" to write. Johnson was expressing the exhaustion and emptiness that often comes with the completion of a struggle, even when the day is won.

By 1912 he had become more than a bon vivant songwriter. Although the *Autobiography of An Ex-Colored Man* had been published anonymously, Johnson's intimates knew that he was the author. His poem "Fifty Years," celebrating the Emancipation Proclamation of 1863, was published in the *New York Times* on 1 January 1913. About this time Johnson changed his middle name to Weldon, writing an old college friend that "Jim Bill Johnson will not do for a man who pretends to write poetry or anything else." Despite the playful self-deprecation, Johnson now saw himself as a man of letters accomplished enough to deserve his own trademark.

Within a few years, Johnson's careers as a spokesman for blacks and as a man of letters came together. In 1914 he began to write editorials for the New York *Age*, a black weekly newspaper. In 1915 he translated the libretto of Enrique Granados's new opera, *Goyescas,* for its Metropolitan Opera production. In 1916 he was hired by the National Association for the Advancement of Colored People as field secretary (or organizer). In 1917 his collection *Fifty Years and Other Poems* was published.

It was Johnson's commitment to "race improvement" as expressed in his New York *Age* columns that brought him to the attention of the NAACP. Though many in the organization viewed him as excessively conservative, the NAACP officers, including W. E. B. Du Bois, valued Johnson's breadth of knowledge, social skills, and refinement without snobbery, as well as his capacity for planning and sustained hard work. The *Age* columns demonstrated not only his didactic side, urging black readers toward self-improvement, but also his political understanding of race relations.

As field secretary of the NAACP, Johnson's duties included the organization of local chapters and the investigation of racially motivated incidents such as lynchings. In both capacities he traveled widely, especially in the South, often into dangerous situations. He was superbly effective, increasing NAACP membership in

two years from ten thousand to forty-four thousand. He reassured uncertain blacks that the NAACP, though less than ten years old, was a powerful and protective umbrella for their local branch's activities. Johnson, who was often able to bring together jealous, rival community factions in the name of racial justice, urged black professionals—teachers, doctors, ministers, lawyers—to serve as leaders. Although Johnson was able to organize the sympathy and will of professionals on behalf of the masses, he was not a grass-roots organizer, and many branches collapsed after the first enthusiastic year of activity or were incapable of dealing with local incidents. Nevertheless, after four years Johnson was promoted to the post of Secretary, the chief executive officer of the NAACP, a position in which he served with distinction until his retirement in 1930.

Fifty Years and Other Poems contains poems Johnson had written as far back as his Atlanta University days in the 1890s, others written as part of his work in the theater from 1900 to 1905, poems written between 1906 and 1912 in Venezuela and Nicaragua, and those written in New York between 1913 and 1916. It thus represents about twenty-five years of work as a poet.

Johnson's poetry can be easily categorized. First, there are a number of poems belonging to the tradition of nineteenth century post-romantic verse, such as the sonnet "Mother Night," which sounds a characteristic note of satisfaction in escape or withdrawal. The conventional subjects of sentimental verse—lost love, untimely death, courage—are sounded without weight or consequence. Nor are the lighter poems much better. "The Ghost of Deacon Brown," for example, turns a comic twist around the ghost-story ballad tradition, with a touch of E. A. Robinson or Edgar Lee Masters, but ends flatly. However fine an ironist, Johnson was not much of a comedian.

A second group of poems is on racial themes. Here, in the best poems in the book, Johnson's choices of forms often bolster rather than inhibit his themes. In "The White Witch," for example, he offers a warning on the dangers of sexual attraction between white women and his "brothers" in the form of a ghost ballad. The allegory of the narrative is sustained, and the antique diction is made appropriate by the choice of the ballad form. In "Brothers" he constructs dramatic dialogue between a brutal black "degenerate; the monstrous offspring of the monster, Sin" and an equally brutal white leader of a lynch mob. Johnson's irony is effective here; the victim has a spiritual and historical consciousness entirely lacking in the white leader, who enthusiastically describes the victim's death in the lynching fire and the subsequent division of trophies:

Stop! to each man no more than one man's
share.
You take that bone, and you this tooth; the
chain—
Let us divide its links; this skull, of course,
In fair division, to the leader comes.

"O Black and Unknown Bards" celebrates the artistic creativity of the black folk. The poet asks how the anonymous slave bards were able to create the transcendent beauty of "Steal Away to Jesus" and "Go Down, Moses."

There is a wide, wide wonder in it all,
That from degraded rest and servile toil
The fiery spirit of the seer should call
These simple children of the sun and soil.
O black slave singers, gone, forgot,
unfamed,
You—you alone, of all the long, long line
Of those who've sung untaught, unknown,
unnamed
Have stretched out upward seeking the
divine.

Written in 1908, during the composition of *The Autobiography of An Ex-Colored Man*, this lyric echoes the scene in the novel in which the narrator hears spirituals in a rural church and comes to appreciate the wonder of their production. The poem rejects the embarrassment many middle-class blacks felt about the music of slavery by focusing attention on the transcendent emotional power of the spirituals that "sang a race from wood and stone to Christ."

The implication here is large—that black Christianity is the creation of black art, that the spirituals mediated between African religion ("wood and stone") and Christianity, easing the painful transition from one form of culture to another. It is Johnson's deepest reading of the folk culture he was slowly coming to understand and appreciate. "O Black and Unknown Bards" stands alongside Johnson's novel as a document of his development of the limits of assimilation to white society with which he had, earlier in his life, been very comfortable. The particulars of black culture, such as the spirituals named in the poem, had taken on rich and unexpectedly strong meaning for him.

The third group of poems in the volume are dialect poems. Most make use of the dramatic monologue technique that Paul Laurence Dunbar had favored in his dialect verse, though none have the energy of Dunbar's best work in that genre.

The 1920s were James Weldon Johnson's most productive period. Throughout the decade, he served his people and his nation as Secretary of the NAACP. The NAACP led the battle for a federal anti-lynching law, and Johnson's skills as an attorney, public speaker, and power broker were marshalled in the lobbying effort, which nevertheless failed to persuade the Senate to act. During the decade Johnson was also extraordinarily active as a writer, editor, and proponent of black culture.

As an experienced and published writer, Johnson quickly became a moderate, senior spokesman for some of the ideas associated with the Harlem Renaissance. For twenty years Johnson had been a cosmopolitan and intellectual middle-class black who was comfortable with the kind of white liberals who were promoting black theater, art, music, and writing. Between his theater work and his work with the NAACP, he had met a great many of New York's influential publishers, producers, and patrons. Johnson was thus well placed to serve as a broker for the new artistic and cultural developments.

One of the ways Johnson performed this role was as an editor. In 1922 he published *The Book of American Negro Poetry*, an anthology of poetry by black Americans beginning with Dunbar (who had died in 1906), with a long historical and critical preface by Johnson. In 1931 he published a revised edition of this anthology, now enlarged to include Langston Hughes, Sterling Brown, and several other Harlem Renaissance writers whose work came to prominence after 1922.

Johnson's preface to the 1922 edition of this anthology yokes his public interest in racial advancement and his private interest in the universal pleasures of poetry and art. Johnson contends that "the final measure of the greatness of all peoples is the amount and standard of the literature and art they have produced." He goes on to say that the world's judgment of the American Negro as "distinctly inferior" would be dispersed by "a demonstration of intellectual parity by the Negro through the production of art and literature." In fact, Johnson argues, the Negro has already proven the possession of superior artistic capability—"the power of creating that which has universal appeal and influence." He points to the influence of black Americans on American dance, to ragtime music, to the folk stories of Uncle Remus, and to the spirituals as artistic products "universally acknowledged as distinctive American products." Like the narrator of his novel of a decade earlier, Johnson sees these products as folk art and considers them crude but powerful. Though he wants to consider the spirituals "a mass of noble music," he praises them for their melody, while finding their poetic content "often very trite." Moreover, as folk songs they "constitute a vast mine of material" for American musicians.

The characteristically conservative overview of the relations between art making and social change precedes Johnson's discussion of the history of African American poetry. His sketch of that history is an early statement of some of the issues about literature that others later expanded upon: race consciousness, comparability to the European or European-American tradition, professionalism, politics, and language, especially dialect.

In reviewing black American poetry from Wheatley to Dunbar in his preface to *The Book*

of American Negro Poetry, Johnson clarifies for himself as much as for his readers the connection between the folk and the artist that dialect represented. He notes that "it would be a disaway this quaint and musical folk speech as a medium of expression." He offers a literary prescription:

What the colored poet in the United States needs to do is something like what Synge did for the Irish; he needs to find a form that will express the racial spirit by symbols from within rather than by symbols from without, such as the mere mutilation of English spelling and pronunciation. . . . He needs a form that is freer and larger than dialect, . . . a form expressing the imagery, the idioms, the peculiar terms of thought and distinctive humor and pathos, too, of the Negro.

In his own poetic work of this period, following the publication of *Fifty Years and Other Poems,* Johnson followed his own prescription.

Although he did not collect and publish them until 1927, Johnson began composing a series of folk sermons in verse in 1917 and 1918. One of them, "The Creation," was completed and published in 1918, while several others already begun before the publication of *The Book of American Negro Poetry,* were laid aside temporarily because of the heavy load of NAACP work. In these poems Johnson represents the rhetoric of the black folk preacher without dialect. Instead, he presents characteristic figures of speech, a free verse rather than lock-step metered representation of speech rhythms, and an accurately observed vision of evangelical black Christian sentiments and customs.

Collected finally in *God's Trombones: Seven Negro Sermons in Verse* (1927), Johnson's finest poetic achievement consists of seven free-verse poems that capture the creativity of the oral tradition of the black folk poet/preacher in startling metaphors that yoke the Bible world and the daily world of the preacher's audience.

Young man—
Young man—
Your arm's too short to box with God

is the most famous example of Johnson's skill in evoking the folk preacher as word-magician. But the concept of youthful *hubris* is reprised later in "The Prodigal Son" when the preacher asserts that someday

> You'll have a hand-to-hand struggle with
> bony Death.
> And Death is bound to win.

Johnson also enriches the sermons by quotations from and allusions to familiar hymns and spirituals. For example, "The Crucifixion" ends by incorporating a line from "Were You There When They Crucified My Lord?":

> Oh, I tremble, yes, I tremble,
> It causes me to tremble, tremble,
> When I think how Jesus died;
> Died on the steeps of Calvary,
> How Jesus died for sinners,
> Sinners like you and me.

Johnson's earlier work on black poets and his collecting and editing of black spirituals is made manifest in the sermons and their relation between African American life and imagination and American social reality. Johnson's preacher's most detailed sermon is a rhetorical expansion of the spiritual "Go Down, Moses"—one of Johnson's favorites—in which the line "Let my people go" or some variant of it figures almost like a refrain. The identification between "the children of Israel" and the preacher's audience of "people" in "Let My People Go" is reinforced in the homiletic closing:

> Listen!—Listen!
> All you sons of Pharoah.
> Who do you think can hold God's people
> When the Lord God himself has said,
> Let my people go?

In *God's Trombones* and in the two volumes of American Negro spirituals that Johnson edited with his brother in 1925 and 1926, he shows that the voice of the folk was an adequate instrument of artistic expression.

In the preface to *The Book of American Negro Spirituals,* Johnson offers an extensive argument for the African origins of the spirituals, developing a theory of the process of folk composition based on his own observations of songleaders that synthesizes the role of creative individuals and that of the community (or congregation). Johnson discusses melody, rhythm, harmony, and performance practice of the spirituals in a social context before moving on to an evaluation of the form and language of the texts. The preface is scholarly in tone and intention; the preface to *The Second Book of Negro Spirituals,* however, is significantly more political. In it Johnson develops the relationship between the spirituals and the other artistic contributions blacks have made to American life. Johnson argues that the impact of the spirituals on American consciousness has been "more in sociology than in art." The music, he argues, has been "the main force" in changing the image of the Negro from that of "a beggar at the gate of the nation" to a potent creative force. In the preface to the 1926 volume, Johnson expressed as an artistic limitation the amalgamation, integration, and assimilation he had long sought in his public career and expressed in his early, raceless poetry. Johnson had learned something, perhaps from his younger Harlem writer-colleagues, about the range of black experience that was available to the writer who was "not afraid of the truth." As the senior member of the community of black writers in New York, Johnson found himself a spokesperson or mediator between black artists and their audience of readers, critics, and patrons. A measure of his position came in the form of a request that he write an entry on Negro poetry for the fourteenth edition of the *Encyclopaedia Britannica* (1929). In other essays written in the 1920s, Johnson capitalized on his name to bring together the literary moment and the social struggle.

In "Race Prejudice and the Negro Artist," published in *Harper's* in 1928, Johnson summarized black achievement in poetry, drama, fiction, and the essay, as well as the creative achievements of black singers and actors. He argued that black artists were changing America's stereotypical perceptions of the race in the nation's newspapers by replacing stories of black criminals with stories of black singers, actors, and writers. In this way, he added, writers and artists exercise a social power beyond their artistic success.

"The Dilemma of the Negro Author" (1928) demonstrates Johnson's understanding of the delicate relationship between black American writers and their audiences. The essay explores the pattern of "the divided audience" and a writer's conscious response to the potential white audience—the struggle with white preconceptions of black personality and social behavior—and a conscious response to a black audience, which involved dealing with the black community's pressure against the written expression of Negro "faults, foibles and vices." Although Johnson recognizes these powerful pressures, his model writer would push against the walls of white stereotype and black taboo with equal energy, thereby creating "a common audience."

In "Negro Authors and White Publishers," published in 1929 in the NAACP's journal, *Crisis*, Johnson argued that opportunities existed for the publication of the work of young black writers. Other black intellectuals—including W. E. B. Du Bois, the editor of the *Crisis*—believed that too many of the characters in the new black fiction focused on "the lower types" of Negroes to the exclusion of characters representative of a more wholesome, middle-class, and professional background. Johnson's essay stands against divisive complaining among the artists, but it is also perhaps naively overconfident in the ability of the individual text to overcome the stereotypical expectations of the market and its brokers, the publishers.

Toward the end of the 1920s, Johnson wrote a history of New York City from his own perspective as a black literary man. *Black Manhattan* (1930) is by Johnson's own admission in the preface "not . . . in any strict sense a history." Though thoroughly researched, it is neither documented like a historical study, nor balanced like one. *Black Manhattan* begins by telling the story of black New York from the Dutch landing in 1626 to the black theater mi-

lieu of the early 1900s. Most of the book from this point forward is a kind of memoir, a history of New York as experienced by James Weldon Johnson, a young man from the South entranced by both the theater and the city. Johnson develops two topics: the history of black writers, actors, and singers in the New York theater from the turn of the century until 1930; and the development of Harlem as a demonstration of "the Negro metropolis." While more pages are devoted to theater history and literary criticism than to social analysis, *Black Manhattan* is concerned with the relation between social development and literary and artistic achievement. In his concluding chapter, Johnson reiterates his notion that black artists are "going far towards smashing the stereotype" and "reshaping public sentiment and opinion." Though *Black Manhattan* pays scant attention to the Harlem poor and the job situation for blacks in New York City, it is the most extended discussion of Johnson's ideas about how individuals—artists, but also social leaders like W. E. B. Du Bois and businessmen like Philip A. Payton—can affect the development of the race.

After resigning from the NAACP and accepting a teaching position at Fisk University in Nashville, Johnson turned to writing his autobiography, *Along This Way*, which is impersonal and unemotional. Johnson presents himself, probably with little distortion, as a man without moments of rage, anger, or ill-chosen words. At least in his telling of it, his life was an event of which he was always in control. His biographer, Eugene Levy, notes that Johnson suppresses a few episodes of his life in *Along This Way:* his ties to Booker T. Washington that helped him get a consular appointment; his job pushing wheeled tourist chairs at the Chicago World's Fair; his adoption of a fanciful "literary" middle name; and his support for the American occupation of Haiti in 1915.

While teaching at Fisk, Johnson supplemented his modest income by lecturing to college and university students and civic groups in the North. After a few years of this peripatetic program, he worked out a schedule that permitted him to live during the fall in New York, lecturing at New York University's School of Education, teaching in the spring at Fisk, and spending the summer months in Great Barrington, Massachusetts. From 1934 until his death, this was Johnson's academic schedule, a full one for a man in his sixties.

In the fall of 1934 Johnson published a long essay titled *Negro Americans, What Now?* Addressed directly and unequivocally to black readers, Johnson's little book sets out to analyze the situation within which black people must choose a direction; it evaluates their institutional "forces and resources"; and it points out their most effective strategies for the near future.

The first section examines the choices available to black Americans—exodus, physical force, revolution, isolation, or integration. Johnson presents the failed history of emigration schemes and rejects that choice; he rejects force as an option, based on the history of slave insurrections and the further oppression they brought. Johnson also rejects communism as a solution, and he views isolation or separatism, a product of frustration, as an equally unacceptable path for black people. He acknowledges that individuals such as W. E. B. Du Bois are attracted to the idea of "making the race into a self-contained economic, social, and cultural unit" but argues against the possibility of duplicating "the economic and social machinery of the country" (p. 12). Black Americans, according to Johnson, are thus left with integration as the only viable solution to the problem of their relationship to America. Johnson is reaffirming his own life-long position in the racial struggle, but the attractiveness of alternative views had grown during the Depression. Communism had drawn some young writers, like Langston Hughes and Richard Wright, and Du Bois, who was disgusted with the pace of integration politics, was discovering both communism and separatism.

Johnson's essay inventories the strengths of black America: the churches, the black press, and fraternal organizations. He sees the NAACP as the leader of these racial organizations, mediating between them and the white world of political and social power.

Johnson's program for the advancement of black freedom, outlined in the third part of *Negro Americans, What Now?*, puts great emphasis on education, both formal and informal. Black Americans must seek formal education and provide informal education to whites. Lacking confidence in the ability of the white educational system to change students' prejudices, Johnson proposes that blacks engage directly in letting individual whites in on a truer picture of black values and achievements.

A lifelong Republican, Johnson had lost his zeal for the GOP during his work for the antilynching law in the 1920s. In *Negro Americans, What Now?* he urges black Americans toward political action whenever possible, but notes that local politics are often more important to black life than national politics, and warns any party from counting on the Negro vote.

Johnson proceeds to examine the question of labor and business. He proposes that blacks negotiate with unions that resist accepting black members, using the threat of boycotts or scab labor to persuade them. He approves the development of black businesses, a major plank in the platform of the isolationists like Du Bois, but notes that "race pride" is no substitute for good business sense. Though Johnson understood that racial solidarity was the necessary foundation for black business enterprise, he urged black Americans in business to look beyond the racial horizon and deal with all potential customers and associates. His confidence in the value of an open and basically integrated posture is again reasserted.

After urging his black readers to support black writers and artists in their efforts to destroy the old racial stereotypes and thereby give white Americans a more accurate picture of Negroes, Johnson turns from analysis to inspiration. He had ended *Along This Way* with a series of speculations on the future of race relations. At the end of *Negro Americans, What Now?* he urges his readers never to sacrifice their spiritual integrity. He then reads, but without egotism, from his own life's lesson:

I WILL NOT ALLOW ONE PREJUDICED PERSON OR ONE MILLION OR ONE

HUNDRED MILLION TO BLIGHT MY LIFE. I WILL NOT LET PREJUDICE OR ANY OF ITS ATTENDANT HUMILIA-TIONS AND INJUSTICES BEAR ME DOWN TO SPIRITUAL DEFEAT. MY INNER LIFE IS MINE, AND I SHALL DEFEND AND MAINTAIN ITS INTEGRITY AGAINST ALL THE POWERS OF HELL.   (p. 103).

At age sixty-three Johnson capped his best advice to the generations ahead with an unmediated appeal to an inner strength in which he had supreme confidence.

He had little more to say. In 1935 Johnson published *St. Peter Relates an Incident: Selected Poems.* The book consists of "St. Peter Relates an Incident of the Resurrection Day," a long, satirical poem that Johnson had written and published alone in 1930, and a selection of other poems, almost all of them reprinted from *Fifty Years.* The Byronic verse of "St. Peter Relates an Incident" is among Johnson's most clever and amusing; the failed, flat ending of the poem, however, draws our attention away from Johnson's effort to join the mock-heroic, a bit of urban black folklore (about the color of the Unknown Soldier in Arlington National Cemetery), and an old-fashioned folk-fantasy of heaven. None of the other new poems in the book is even as interesting as this one.

A week after his sixty-seventh birthday in 1938, Johnson's car was struck by a train at a railroad crossing in Maine, where he and his wife Grace were vacationing. Johnson was killed almost instantly. His funeral in Harlem was attended by over two thousand mourners from the literary, political, and theater communities. James Weldon Johnson was buried in Greenwood Cemetery in Brooklyn, where so many distinguished New Yorkers have been laid to rest.

Johnson's work as a writer not only advanced the social interests of black Americans by subverting the conventions of literary discourse about race, it also connected black art and artists to the currents of literary and cultural change that were so vitally important in the period from 1900 to 1930. Although he began his

life of leadership thinking of writing as an activity engaged in for its own sake, he ended it with a clear sense of a strong, modernist black writing in the service of both private pleasure and public principle.

Selected Bibliography

PRIMARY WORKS

FICTION

The Autobiography of an Ex-Colored Man. With an introduction by Brander Matthews. Boston: Sherman, French, 1912. With an introduction by Carl Van Vechten. New York: Knopf, 1927, 1966, 1989. With an introduction by Arna Bontemps. New York: Hill and Wang, 1960. With an introduction by Henry Louis Gates Jr. New York: Vintage, 1989. With an introduction by William L. Andrews. New York: Penguin, 1990.

POETRY

Fifty Years and Other Poems. With an introduction by Brander Matthews. Boston: Cornhill, 1917.
God's Trombones: Seven Negro Sermons in Verse. New York: Viking, 1927, 1969. New York: Penguin, 1990.
"Futility." *Harper's* 159:699 (1929). Uncollected poem.
St. Peter Relates an Incident of the Resurrection Day. New York: Viking, 1930. Limited edition of 200 copies, privately distributed. Reprinted as *St. Peter Relates an Incident: Selected Poems.* New York: Viking, 1935. With a preface by Sondra Kathryn Wilson. New York: Penguin, 1993.

NONFICTION

Black Manhattan. New York: Knopf, 1930.
Along This Way: The Autobiography of James Weldon Johnson. New York: Viking, 1930, 1968. Reprinted with an introduction by Sondra Kathryn Wilson. New York: Viking/Penguin, 1990.
Negro Americans, What Now? New York: Viking, 1934.

BOOKS EDITED BY JOHNSON

The Book of American Negro Poetry. Edited and with a preface by James Weldon Johnson. New York: Harcourt, Brace, 1922; Rev. ed. 1931.
The Book of American Negro Spirituals. Arranged by J. Rosamond Johnson. New York: Viking, 1925.
The Second Book of American Negro Spirituals. New York: Viking, 1926.

SELECTED PROSE

"Should the Negro Be Given an Education Different from That Given to Whites?" In *Twentieth Century Negro Literature; or, A Cyclopedia of Thought on the Vital Topics Relating to the American Negro, by One*

Hundred of America's Greatest Negroes. Edited by Daniel W. Culp. Napierville, Ill., 1902. Pp. 71–74; Miami, Fla.: Mnemosyne Publishing Co., 1969.

The Changing Status of Negro Labor. New York: National Council of Social Work, 1918. Pamphlet.

Africa in the World Democracy. With Horace Kallen. New York, 1919. Textbook.

"Self-Determining Haiti." *The Nation* 111:236–38, 265–67, 295–97, 345–47 (1920).

"The Truth About Haiti." *Crisis* 20:217–224 (1920).

"Lynching: America's National Disgrace." *Current History* 19:596–601 (1924).

"The Making of Harlem." *Survey Graphic* 6:635–39 (1925).

"Our Democracy and the Ballot." *Negro Orators and Their Orations.* Edited by Carter G. Woodson. Washington, D.C.: The Associated Publishers, Inc., 1925. Pp. 663–70.

"The Dilemma of the Negro Author." *American Mercury* 15:477–81 (1928).

"Race, Prejudice and the Negro Artist." *Harper's* 157:769–76 (1928).

"Negro Authors and White Publishers." *Crisis* 36:228–29 (1929).

"Negro Poetry." In *Encyclopaedia Britannica.* 14th ed. New York: Encyclopaedia Britannica, Inc., 1929.

"The Creative Negro." In *America as Americans See It.* Edited by Frederick Julius Ringel. New York: Harcourt, Brace, 1932. Pp. 161–65.

"The American Negro," "The Negro and Racial Conflict," and "Contribution of the Negro." In *Our Racial and National Minorities: Their History, Contributions, and Present Problems.* Edited by Francis J. Brown and Joseph C. Roucek. New York: Prentice-Hall, 1937. Pp 56–66; 549–60; 739–48.

The Selected Writings of James Weldon Johnson. Vol. 1, *The New York Age Editorials (1914–1927).* Edited and with an introduction by Sondra Kathryn Wilson. New York: Oxford University Press, 1995.

The Selected Writings of James Weldon Johnson. Vol. 2, *Social, Political, and Literary Essays.* Edited and with an introduction by Sondra Kathryn Wilson. New York: Oxford University Press, 1995.

MANUSCRIPTS AND PAPERS

The James Weldon Johnson Papers are in the James Weldon Johnson Collection of Negro Literature and Art, American Literature Collection, Beinecke Rare Book and Manuscript Library, Yale University.

SECONDARY WORKS

BIOGRAPHICAL AND CRITICAL STUDIES

Baker, Houston A., Jr. "A Forgotten Prototype: *The Autobiography of an Ex-Colored Man* and *Invisible Man.*" *Virginia Quarterly Review* 49, no. 3:433–449 (1973). Reprinted in his *Singers of Daybreak: Studies in Black American Literature.* Washington, D.C.: Howard University Press, 1974.

Bell, Bernard W. *The Afro-American Novel and Its Tra-*
dition. Amherst: University of Massachusetts Press, 1987.

Bone, Robert A. "Novels of the Talented Tenth." In *The Negro Novel in America.* New Haven, Conn.: Yale University Press, 1958. Rev. ed. New Haven and London: Yale, 1965. Pp. 45–49.

Bronz, Stephen H. *Roots of Negro Racial Consciousness; the 1920s: Three Harlem Renaissance Authors.* New York: Libra, 1964.

Carroll, Richard A. "Black Racial Spirit: An Analysis of James Weldon Johnson's Critical Perspective." *Phylon* 32:344–64 (1971).

Collier, Eugenia W. "The Endless Journey of an Ex-Colored Man." *Phylon* 32:365–73 (1971).

Fleming, Robert E. "Irony as a Key to Johnson's *The Autobiography of an Ex-Colored Man.*" *American Literature* 43, no. 1:83–96 (1971).

Fleming, Robert E. "The Composition of James Weldon Johnson's 'Fifty Years.'" *American Poetry* 4, no. 2:51–56 (1987).

———. *James Weldon Johnson.* Boston: Twayne, 1987.

Garrett, Marvin P. "Early Recollections and Structural Irony in *The Autobiography of an Ex-Coloured Man.*" *Critique: Studies in Modern Fiction* 13, no. 2:5–14 (1971).

Gloster, Hugh Morris. "James Weldon Johnson." In *Negro Voices in American Fiction.* Chapel Hill: University of North Carolina Press, 1948. Pp. 74–83. Reprint, New York: Russell & Russell, 1965.

Jackson, Miles M., Jr. "Letters to a Friend: Correspondence from James Weldon Johnson to George A. Towns." *Phylon* 29:182–98 (1968).

Levy, Eugene D. "Ragtime and Race: The Career of James Weldon Johnson." *Journal of Popular Culture* 1, no. 4:357–70 (1968).

———. *James Weldon Johnson: Black Leader, Black Voice.* Chicago: University of Chicago Press, 1973.

Long, Richard A. "A Weapon of My Song: The Poetry of James Weldon Johnson." *Phylon* 32, no. 4:374–82 (1971).

Rogal, Samuel J. "The Homiletic and Hymnodic Elements in the Poetry of James Weldon Johnson." *Marjorie Kinnan Rawlings Journal of Florida Literature* 7:113–31 (1996).

Skerrett, Joseph T., Jr. "Irony and Symbolic Action in James Weldon Johnson's *The Autobiography of an Ex-Coloured Man.*" *American Quarterly* 32:540–58 (1980).

Stepto, Robert B. *From Behind the Veil: A Study of Afro-American Narrative.* Urbana: University of Illinois Press, 1979. Pp. 95–127.

Thomas, Ruth Marie. "Author, Diplomat, and Public Servant: A Study of James Weldon Johnson's Writings." *Southwestern Journal* 5:58–72 (1949).

Vauthier, Simone. "The Interplay of Narrative Modes in James Weldon Johnson's *Autobiography of an Ex-Coloured Man.*" *Jahrbuch für Amerikastudien* 18:173–81 (1973).

Wagner, Jean. "James Weldon Johnson." In *Black Poets of the United States: From Paul Laurence Dunbar to*

Langston Hughes. Translated by Kenneth Douglas. Urbana: University of Illinois Press, 1973. Pp. 351–84. Originally published as *Les Poètes Nègres des Etats-Unis.* Paris: Librairie Istra, 1962. Sorbonne diss., 1963.

BIBLIOGRAPHY

Fleming, Robert E., ed. *James Weldon Johnson and Arna Wendell Bontemps: A Reference Guide.* New York: G. K. Hall, 1978.

GAYL JONES
(1949–)

CYNTHIA J. SMITH

GAYL JONES HAS always been fascinated with "language as heard" rather than with "language as written." As a child she learned as much from listening to people talk as she learned from written texts. She and her brother Franklin Jr. were never sent out of the room when grown-ups talked, and thus spoken texts— adult stories of love, joy, trouble, and triumph—were among her earliest influences.

Born in Lexington, Kentucky, on November 23, 1949, to Franklin Jones, a cook, and Lucille Jones, a housewife and aspiring writer, Gayl Jones spent her childhood in a speech community that she cites as one of her richest resources. Although she emphasizes the spoken texts of everyday community life in tracing her artistic roots, written texts were also an important part of her childhood. Her grandmother wrote plays that were produced at church, and her mother wrote fairy tales and stories of rural life in Warthumtown, Kentucky. Those written stories were meant to be read aloud—to be heard by an audience. Jones's mother and grandmother not only provided her with role models but also helped her to see that the oral traditions of storytelling could be inscribed successfully in writing.

Life

Jones began writing stories in the second or third grade, and by the time she was sixteen, she had what she calls a romantic conception of what a writer is. In her story "The Guitar," the central character "was a writer and all her friends were writers and they were someplace like Spain, sitting around at tables in one of those outdoor cafés and none of them ever had any money." She saw herself growing up to be "this independent woman . . . and I was always traveling, particularly to Spanish-speaking places, and I was a writer." Although she may have had a romantic notion of what it means to be a writer, success as a writer came early for Jones, much of it at Connecticut College and at Brown University.

As an undergraduate at Connecticut College, Jones earned an award for the best original poem written in the academic year 1969–1970, and she was one of four undergraduate poets chosen to tour the Connecticut poetry circuit. After earning a Bachelor of Arts degree at Connecticut College in 1971, she enrolled at Brown University, where she earned a Master of Arts (1973) and a Doctor of Arts (1975) in creative writing. It was perhaps fortuitous that Jones arrived at Brown when she did. The doctorate in arts program was then staffed by such notable figures as John Hawkes and Verlin Cassill in fiction, George Bass in theater, and Michael Harper (who became her mentor) in poetry. As a whole the program provided an atmosphere in which her talent could flourish. Jones was still a student at

Brown when she received national recognition with the publication of *Corregidora* (1975), her first novel, which Michael Harper had brought to the attention of Toni Morrison, who was a senior editor at Random House. *Corregidora* was preceded, however, by a great deal of exploration and experimentation with the themes and formal techniques that she has refined and developed throughout the body of her work.

Early Work

Jones thinks of herself as a storyteller rather than as a poet, dramatist, or fiction writer. Her early experience of stories as "things that were heard . . . That you listened to . . . That someone spoke" is directly translated into her early short fiction, poetry, and drama. It is the storyteller who makes the connections between oral traditions and written documentation while maintaining the integrity of the oral traditions. Jones attempts to accomplish the latter by assuming the storyteller's voice and writing in the first person. In an interview with Charles Rowell, she describes her early use of first-person narration in such short stories as "The Welfare Check" (1970), "The Roundhouse" (1971), and "The Return: A Fantasy" (1971) as "subconscious" and intuitive: "I didn't think out the fact that my early stories were written in first person as if an audience were being *spoken to* and that this sense of speaking to people rather than writing to them was important to me." By the time she was ready to write *Corregidora*, she understood the "specific connections between Afro-American oral traditions and literary forms."

Writing in the first person has allowed Jones to minimize authorial intrusion and to achieve the directness of the storyteller's relationship to her audience. In an interview with Claudia Tate, Jones has said that she aims for a perspective that is "up-close," where there is "no separation between the storyteller and the hearer," so that she removes most traces of authorial judgment:

When I write in the first person, I like to have the sense it's just the character who's there.

Judgments don't enter unless they're made by a particular character. And oftentimes that character's responses may not be what mine would be in the same situation. Also, I like to have that character as the storyteller without involving myself.

Jones has risked and received critical censure for her choice of narrative technique. She is very much aware of readers' tendency to equate the characters' preoccupations with those of the author—indeed, to assume that the characters and the author are the same. This tendency is especially problematic given the thematic emphases in her work: madness, sexuality, and violence.

But Jones also writes about transcendence and regeneration, and when she does so, she often makes use of the form and content of the blues. In 1973, *Chile Woman*, Jones's first play, was produced at Brown University by Rites and Reason, a university–community arts project. The work, directed by George Bass, won the new play award in the 1974 New England regional competition for the National American College Theater Festival. The theme of the play is that black people as a group have been broken and crushed by experiences that have left fragments rather than "wholeselves." The play seeks to recover those "wholeselves" through remembering and celebrating the fragments. As the play opens, a blues singer sings "Broken Soul Blues":

> You took your love away
> Then you know just how it feel
> When you got the broken soul blues
> I'm crying now
> But still I feel somehow
> I be laughing, baby,
> When you got the broken soul blues.

The blues singer sings a song well known as part of "Ma" Rainey's repertoire, but the other characters "sing" the texts of their own lives and the painful history in which those lives are embedded. Jones uses blues as the means by which the characters finger the jagged grain of their experience. Blues becomes a way of voicing the themes of the play and structuring its content.

In *Chile Woman* Jones explores the idea that slavery, with all of its terrible consequences for black men and women, must be remembered but must not be allowed to bind and destroy the present or the future. The troubled relationship between the man and woman in the "Broken Soul Blues" is part of a larger pattern of anguish and loss that had its origin in slavery. In *Corregidora,* Jones unites some of the thematic concerns explored in *Chile Woman* with the formal techniques discovered in her early fiction.

Corregidora

Corregidora was hailed as a first novel by a promising young black woman. It was also condemned for its raw language and its preoccupation with sex and violence. At the center of the novel is the haunting figure of Simon Corregidora, a Portuguese slave breeder and whoremonger who sired the grandmother and mother of the protagonist, Ursa. Both her mother and her grandmother have imposed upon Ursa the obligation to "make generations" as a way to preserve the evidence of the cruelty and exploitation of slavery. Although some readers might be repelled by the lurid details of this story, they should see that the abuse and exploitation of the master-slave relationship provide metaphors for the relationship between Ursa and her husband, Mutt.

In a fit of unwarranted jealousy, Mutt pushes Ursa down a flight of stairs as she leaves her job as a nightclub singer. Her work as a singer subjects her to the gaze of other men who "possess" her with their eyes. Mutt's jealousy stems from his desire for total and exclusive ownership of the singer and her song; he claims the right as her husband to exploit her sexuality, femininity, and talent exclusively for his own benefit in much the same way that Corregidora owned, exploited, and violated the bodies of his female slaves. But readers are not allowed to cast Mutt entirely in the role of villain, since it is he who inadvertently frees Ursa from a family ritual that in its celebration of past sins and evils threatens to perpetuate bondage among couples who cannot free themselves from the tensions and abuse that remain present in memories of the past.

Ursa's fall causes her to lose the child she is carrying and her womb as well. Unable to produce children, Ursa must redefine her relationship to the past and present. In order to do so, she must try to understand how the obligation to preserve the evidence of slavery destroyed her parents' marriage and threatens her own relationships with men, including Mutt. Even if she had not lost her womb, she is no longer sure of her own need to continue to hate Simon Corregidora. When she considers what she knows of her grandmother and great-grandmother, she wonders how much of their feeling was hatred and how much of it was love. This new understanding of her matrilineage and its impact on her own life expresses itself in the new voice with which she sings the blues.

Singing the blues is not only the means by which Ursa achieves a kind of transcendence; it is also a device that structures and organizes the novel. On the level of language, the pattern of the three-line blues song often shapes dialogue, as in the following exchange between Ursa and a friend:

"If that nigger loved me he wouldn't've thrown me down the steps," I called.
"What?" She came to the door.
"I said if that nigger loved me he wouldn't've throwed me down the steps."
"I know niggers love you do worse than that," she said.

Blues songs in the three-line pattern have two repeated lines followed by a resolution or answer in the third line. This pattern of repetition and resolution is also evident in the lives of the four generations of Corregidora women. Ursa's great-grandmother is debased by slavery and by the incestuous amorality of Corregidora. Rather than allow his memory to die, she instructs her daughter to preserve the evidence of her mother's debasement in the form of her own child. That daughter (Ursa's grandmother), who is sired by Corregidora and later impregnated by him, repeats the injunction to "make generations." When Ursa's grandmother learns that her daughter is pregnant, she convinces Martin, the child's father, to marry her. Martin deserts his wife because he resents the role of male breeder and resents the obsession his wife has with promulgating her hatred of Corregidora. Three generations repeat the pattern of sexual and psychic bondage, and it remains for Ursa to find the resolution or answer that will break her out of the pattern.

As in the blues, love and hate, pleasure and pain can coexist in the same situation. Within Corregidora's cruelty and exploitation as a slaveholder there is something akin to love as well, something intense enough to provoke rage and a desire to kill. Ursa learns what the something is in her own relationship with Mutt:

> It had to be sexual, I was thinking, it had to be something sexual that Great Gram did to Corregidora. I knew it had to be sexual: "What is it a woman can do to a man that make him hate her so bad he wont to kill her one minute and keep thinking about her and can't get her out of his mind the next?" In a split second I knew what it was, in a split second of hate and love I knew what it was, and I think he might have known too. A moment of pleasure and excruciating pain at the same time, a moment of broken skin but not sexlessness, a moment just before sexlessness, a moment that stops before it breaks the skin: "I could kill you."

When Ursa first meets Mutt, her songs about a train tunnel and a bird woman evoke the destructive power inherent in sexual passion:

> About this train going in the tunnel, but it didn't seem like they was no end to the tunnel, and nobody knew when the train would get out, and then the tunnel tightened around the train like a fist. Then I sang about this bird woman, whose eyes were deep wells. How she would take a man on a long journey, but never return him.

As the obviously phallic symbolism of this passages suggests, Ursa fantasizes about destruction, about inflicting psychic and sexual pain.

After being divorced and meeting again after not seeing one another for twenty-two years, Ursa and Mutt are ready with a new song that they sing together:

> "I don't want a kind of woman that hurt you," he said.
> "Then you don't want me."
> "I don't want a kind of woman that hurt you."
> "Then you don't want me."
> "I don't want a kind of woman that hurt you."
> "Then you don't want me."
> He shook me till I fell against him crying. "I don't want a kind of man that'll hurt me neither," I said.
> He held me tight.

The "song" that provides the novel's resolution creates a new pattern; instead of two repeated lines, there are three: one for each generation before Ursa, who in the resolution is able to renounce the old pattern of bondage and pain. And instead of a single voice bearing witness to anguish and pain, there are two in an exchange that brings about healing and reconciliation.

Eva's Man

If *Corregidora* is written as a blues song, *Eva's Man* (1976), Jones's second novel, plays the tune back in reverse. Whereas Ursa Corregidora is able to free herself from the bondage of the past, for Eva Medina Canada there is no regeneration when myths about race and gender turn into terrible realities. As the novel opens, Eva is imprisoned in a hospital for the criminally insane for having poisoned her lover, Davis Carter, and having castrated him with her teeth. Her literal bondage, however, is but a concrete manifestation of her imprisonment within the perceptions of others. Early in her childhood she learns that men think of her as a sexual object. Freddy Smoot, a neighbor boy, wants to play doctor with a dirty Popsicle stick; she is propositioned and importuned by Mr. Logan, caretaker of the building in which she lives, and by her cousin Alphonse.

Eva eventually comes to believe that men see her as a whore, that her destiny is prefigured by the problem of perception that affects the life of her parents. She describes her mother's involvement with a musician called Tyrone, a constant visitor while her father is at work. Although Eva never sees any evidence of a sexual relationship, her father, when he learns of the relationship, assumes that it is a sexual one and decides that violence is the appropriate response:

> Then it was like I could hear her clothes ripping. . . . But now he was tearing that blouse off and those underthings. I didn't hear nothing from her the whole time. I didn't hear a thing from her.
> "Act like a whore, I'm gonna fuck you like a whore. You act like a whore, I'm gonna fuck you like a whore."
> He kept saying that over and over. I was so scared. I kept feeling that after he tore all her clothes off, and there wasn't anymore to tear, he'd start tearing her flesh.

Eva's father acts on the belief that sexual promiscuity is an essential part of a woman's character. Because he perceives Eva's mother as guilty, he punishes her as though she were in fact the whore he believes her to be. Although Eva only overhears this scene between her parents, its violence is a first lesson in the consequence of female sexuality.

As she grows older, Eva becomes increasingly entrapped in the misperceptions of others. In a bar Moses Tripp offers her five dollars for her sexual favors, though she has done nothing to encourage his attention and is merely waiting for her cousin. Where her mother had responded with silence and passivity, Eva responds by stabbing Tripp, later refusing to explain her actions to the police or to her parents.

At age seventeen Eva marries a man three times her age, but discovers that he, too, thinks women are promiscuous by nature. When she and her husband, James, move to another town and Eva goes to school, James refuses to allow her to have a telephone because he does not want other men to call her. The scene between her mother and father is reenacted when a male classmate visits her to discuss an assignment and James makes the same assumptions about Eva that her father had made about her mother. Sexual violence is again the result.

Eva learns from her mother that passivity is one response to sexual violence, but Jones proposes other responses through the image of the Medusa and the story of the Queen Bee. Medusa is first invoked as an image through Jones's repeated references to Eva's uncombed and wild-looking hair. Eva's lover Davis introduces the word "Medusa" into the text by confusing Medina, Eva's last name, with Medusa. Davis's slip of the tongue reveals his repressed fear of being castrated and devoured by a dangerous and threatening femininity. There is attraction, however, as well as repulsion, for Eva describes herself as turning "their dicks to stone" in a symbolic erection. Jones uses Eva's murder of Davis Carter to mark the limits of phallocentric power and to reveal the power inherent in femininity. One manifestation of that power is the fact that Eva menstruates throughout the entire time she is involved with Davis. Her loss of body fluids calls attention to the death and renewal of her body and to her ability to create new life. Even though Davis is poisoned, it is his castration that marks his death as a masculine being.

The stabbing of Moses Tripp foreshadows Eva's use of sexual violence against Davis. The Queen Bee, introduced quite early in Eva's narrative, at first appears to be a harmless, unhappy woman whose lovers always die. But Jones activates the power in the analogy with the insect world in which the Queen Bee makes use of male drones and kills them when she is finished with them. Eva only succeeds in wounding Moses Tripp; the knife—suggestive of a phallus—is ineffective in her hands. Eva is successful against those who would exploit her and imprison her in their perceptions when the mouth displaces the genitalia as the site of castration. The text seems to suggest that Eva murders Davis in order to destroy male sexual dominance at its symbolic source. This reasoning is so subversive, however, that Jones chooses to present it as the product of a deranged mind, calling attention to Eva's unreliability as a narrator who takes readers into a world where norms seem unacceptable.

White Rat

Written and published between 1970 and 1977, the stories collected in *White Rat* (1977) reveal Jones's experimentation with the themes and fictional techniques she brings to fruition in her novels. Ten of the twelve stories in this collection are written in the first person. Jones is more interested in creating inner landscapes than in explaining the motivation of her characters. She attempts to enter the characters; she assumes their voices and lets them tell their stories in their own way. "The Roundhouse," the earliest of the twelve stories, is loosely based on the lives of her grandparents. The setting is a roundhouse (the place where trains come in to be polished) in Garrett, Indiana. The narrator meets her future husband when he begins work at the roundhouse where she already works. He seems to have no family or friends. When he becomes ill, she takes care of him and even risks losing her job to do so. Later, when layoffs at the roundhouse reduce the narrator's hours until she can barely make a living, a mysterious someone begins to pay her grocery and coal bills. Later she discovers that the man she had taken care of had returned to take care of her. The narrator's inner landscape is one of hard work and self-sacrifice. However, the story has even greater impact as a tale of love and courtship precisely because the language of romance is never used by the narrator.

"The Return: A Fantasy" is perhaps the most ambitious of the early stories in *White Rat*. The story contains general allusions to the life and work of Franz Kafka, but it seems to be rather specifically modeled on Kafka's story "The Metamorphosis." Joseph Corey, the main character in "The Return," is an avid reader of Kafka. For him the line between fantasy and reality blurs, then disappears. He explains to his wife, Dora, the narrator of the story: "The man became a bug. . . . Men can become bugs. There's no *as if*. You don't conduct your life *as if* you were Christ. You become Christ." Joseph's need to "become Christ" is motivated by conflict with his father over the treatment of his mother. Joseph's mother is accused by her husband of being a lewd woman. When he divorces her and takes away their child, she becomes the streetwalker he had believed her to be.

The story contains the germ of an idea Jones develops later in *Eva's Man*, in which, as we have seen, she presents Eva as having no essential reality of her own, existing only as a "fiction" in the minds of others. The fiction Joseph's father creates is so powerful and so painful that Joseph, as he imagines Kafka did, has to "resort to a world of fantasy." He transforms himself, becoming "both the doctor and the patient, the curer and the ill." He makes himself into a priest, borrowing elements from Christianity, Islam, and shamanism in order to work out his own salvation.

In "White Rat" (1975), the title story of the collection, Jones offers a variation on the tragic mulatto literature that was prevalent during the nineteenth and early twentieth centuries in both American and African American writing. Nicknamed White Rat, the central character has blond hair and white skin that would allow him to pass for white. Rat, however, insists on his identity as a black person. He has been taught by his father to hate whites simply on the basis of their appearance. But Rat recognizes the fundamental absurdity of this attitude, thereby failing to live up to his father's standard. The retribution he believes he deserves is visited upon his infant son, who is born with a club foot. "White Rat" suggests that race itself is surrounded with social "fictions" that can be passed on from generation to generation, an idea that Jones develops at greater length in *Corregidora*.

The sexual violation of black women during slavery is the historical backdrop for *Corregidora*. In *Eva's Man* psychic as well as physical violation becomes a part of contemporary institutions, and madness becomes a kind of refuge. In Jones's short story "Asylum" (1977), the narrator has been committed to a mental hospital for deliberately urinating in the living room during a visit by her nephew's teacher. Her use of the slop jar in the presence of the teacher shows lack of respect for the purposes and consequences of "formal education." Indeed, at the "asylum" the narrator thinks of herself as being "in school" since the therapy prescribed for her involves talking to the doctor and writing things down every day. The parallel between physical and psychic violation is suggested by the narrator's resistance to an examination of her genital area and by her refusal to open her thoughts to the doctor's examination as well:

> *"What does this word make you feel?"*
> *"Nothing."*
> *"You should tell me what you are*
> *   thinking."*
> *"Is that the only way I can be freed?"*

Although lesbian relationships appear frequently in her novels and short stories, Jones uses them for artistic rather than ideological purposes. Ursa Corregidora violently rejects the lesbian advances made to her after her hysterectomy, but the vehemence of her reaction indicates her vulnerability and fear of the loss of her femininity rather than a rejection of the women who express an interest in her. *Eva's Man* ends with Eva's seduction by her cellmate, Elvira Moody; however, the act of cunnilingus with which the novel culminates serves as a metaphor for the self-imprisonment of narcissism. The narrator of Jones's story "The Women" (1977) is a child who is aware even at a very early age of her mother's affairs with other women. The story charts the growth of her sexual knowledge and culminates in the narrator's first sexual experience with a boy. The fact that the narrator insists on taking her boyfriend to her mother's bed suggests that her decision is an important act of self-definition and a rite of passage from adolescence to adulthood rather than a condemnation of lesbianism. When she

writes about lesbianism, Jones neither vindicates nor condemns it. She writes about it simply because it exists.

"Version II," the last of the stories collected in *White Rat*, reveals how much Jones learned about her craft between 1971 and 1977. "Version II" is a revision of "The Return: A Fantasy." In it she focuses on the notion that metamorphosis is a process that can be captured in fiction. She replaces Dora with Joseph as the first-person narrator, a change that makes Joseph's movement in and out of other voices and personalities more fluid and resulting in a more convincing representation of madness.

Poetry

Jones has described her work as improvisational, by which she means that the form of a work is generated in the process of its creation. *Corregidora* went through a number of revisions, and *Eva's Man* began as a novella that she rewrote as a short story and then as a novel. The volume-length poem entitled *Song for Anninho* (1981) draws from the 1975 and 1979 published excerpts of the novel *Almeyda* and from the unpublished novel "Palmares," to which she has referred in interviews.

Song for Anninho offers a counterpoint to Jones's treatment of the blues relationships in her novels. Although both *Corregidora* and *Eva's Man* emphasize brutality, transcendence is unavailable to the characters in *Eva's Man*, whereas *Corregidora* sets the stage for an understanding of what it takes for tenderness—the alternative to brutality—to survive and grow. *Song* proposes that "Tenderness is a deeper thing / than cruelty." In the poem the central characters ask:

> *How we could sustain our love*
> *at a time of cruelty.*
> *How we could keep loving*
> *at such a time. How we could*
> *look at each other with tenderness.*
> *And keep it, even with everything.*

To reconstruct that "time of cruelty," Jones returns to seventeenth-century Brazil as a setting, painting a landscape not of the Brazilian rain forests but of imagination, dream, and memory.

In *Song,* Jones makes use of an actual historical event but centers the story on invented characters. The poem opens after a successful attack by the Portuguese on Palmares, a settlement founded by African slaves who had escaped from their Portuguese masters. The settlement, located in the forests of northeastern Brazil, had thrived for more than sixty years with its own government headed by a king who commanded great loyalty. Although there is a great opportunity to make this poem a protest against slavery and to make the Portuguese capture and reenslavement of the African fugitives the poem's significant event, Jones chooses to focus on the love affair between her central characters, Almeyda and Anninho. Almeyda's breasts have been cut off by a Portuguese soldier and thrown, with her, into the river. Zibatra, a wizard woman who "speaks in tongues" rescues her and takes her to her mountain home to recuperate. The wizard woman is

> . . . capable of transformations,
> as if there were no boundaries
> to the world—as if there were
> no impossibilities in it.

Yet she cannot bring Anninho back or change the events that have destroyed the pastoral serenity of life in Palmares. The transformation Almeyda seeks can be wrought not through magic but through art. As "singer" or poet, Almeyda can enact that transformation even though she and Anninho cannot be reunited. She creates a song that affirms the love between her and Anninho and places it where it cannot be touched by time or outside circumstances.

Although *Song* is different in its emphasis on spiritual transformation, it repeats patterns of imagery and meaning present in earlier works, and continues to argue that black women and men are much more than the bodies and body parts to which slavery and postslavery perceptions often reduced them. The stories the Corregidora women tell about slavery emphasize that "the Portuguese who bought slaves paid attention only to the genitals." The womb be-

came the means of production and capital formation. Yet both of the novels and *Song* involve some loss of some part of body, for instance, Ursa's womb and Almeyda's breasts.

When Ursa can no longer "make generations," this breaking of the chain of matrilineal descent allows us to hear her own voice, a voice that has both the authority of the blues artist and the authority that comes from her command of her own subjectivity. Although Almeyda loses her breasts through no fault of her own, her hopefulness serves as a strong contrast to the outlook of the self-mutilated woman, a minor character in the poem, who inflicts violence against her own sex organs "before she knew there was a future." Almeyda wants her womb to grow deep for Anninho, to bear his children. Regeneration is not to be achieved through reproduction alone, however, for the poem ends with the image of making roads, of engendering communication and spiritual oneness.

In a later volume of poems, *Xarque and Other Poems* (1985), the future presented in the title poem is not very promising. The lovers in *Song for Anninho* are not reunited, and there is no indication that there is to be a child. The narrative of *Xarque,* however, centers on Almeyda's descendants. Bonifacia, the daughter of Almeyda, describes herself as "an ordinary woman" unlike her mother, who

> could hear things
> that others couldn't
> and see things
> that were invisible to others.

The central character is Bonifacia's daughter, Euclida (Almeyda's granddaughter), who works in a *xarque* (dried meat) factory in Recife, Brazil. A loosely woven series of portraits, *Xarque* lacks both the passion of Almeyda's search for Anninho and the narrative unity of *Song,* in which the personal story of the lovers is joined to historical and nationalistic themes through Jones's repeated references to King Zumbi, his execution, and the united African resistance to Portuguese oppression even after his death. The resistance celebrated in *Song* is disempowered here by intertribal disharmony and disunity. The narrator comments,

> so much
> prejudices among African races
> I couldn't get the Sudanese
> and Angolans to get along.

Although there are scattered references to plans for massacres and uprisings, "the Sudanese and the Bantus / couldn't decide who would lead." When placed next to *Song, Xarque* comments on the dissipation of the spiritual energy that had once united an African people against oppression.

In her poetry as well as in her prose, Jones resembles a musician who, rejoicing in her technical virtuosity, plays endless variations on a given set of themes. With only one exception all of the poems grouped in *The Hermit-Woman* (1983), published between *Song* and *Xarque*, seem to make use of explorers and mapmakers as figures who chart unknown territory. Sometimes that territory is the self explored by a female narrator, but Jones also describes male figures for whom woman is the unknown and the unfamiliar. "Stranger" depicts the return of an explorer to a woman who, like the people the explorer has discovered, "makes poetry out of ordinary things." It celebrates the male explorer's understanding of otherness, an understanding that makes their love possible as they plant an evergreen tree as the symbol of that love.

The speaker in the title poem, "The Hermit-Woman," is an explorer who stays in one place. Others come to her, seeking wisdom and revelation, but what she has to offer is civility and hospitality. As a hermit she seeks to know and to transform only herself; the lovers who come to seek her out must answer their own questions. The speaker in "Wild Figs and Secret Places" creates herself through language, referring to a male explorer as "a foreigner here":

> clawing the edge of a shadow
> and I am in my own country
> made out of the words
> I toss at your ears.

The speaker *is* the unknown country that the explorer wishes to chart. But there are secret places, parts of the map, that she cannot reveal because in the explorer's country penalties against otherness, against those who "journey to secret places," are so severe.

The Healing

Many black writers have deliberately avoided the terrain of violence, sexuality, and madness, fearing to reinforce or to create negative stereotypes. Jones is one of an important handful of black women writers who have dared to enter that forbidden territory. But with the 1998 publication of *The Healing*—Jones's first English language novel in twenty-two years (she published *Die Vogelfangerin* [The birdcatcher] during the 1980s while in Germany, where she and her husband Bob Higgins relocated to escape his possible conviction for having threatened activists at a gay rights demonstration in Michigan)—Jones made a decided break from her former themes. Indeed, Jones has said in an interview with Veronica chambers that she intended *The Healing* as a rejection of *Corregidora* and *Eva's Man;* those novels, she argues, "emphasized the narrowest range of subject matter—the man-done-her-wrong-type blues." Such an emphasis, Jones suggests, ultimately belies the nature of the blues itself, for the latter "has more possibility and range" than she felt she allowed.

Although a repudiation of her earlier work, *The Healing* is nevertheless Jones's continued celebration of and investment in "language as heard." As is the case with *Corregidora* and *Eva's Man,* for example, Jones's new novel is told from the perspective of the "I"—in this case, Harlan Jane Eagleton, a former beautician turned rock star business manager turned faith healer. It is the latter Harlan that we first encounter, on a bus heading for yet another "tank town"—"I think they call 'em tank towns," Harlan explains, "on account of them water tanks, you know them water tanks, where the trains stop to take on water. And that water tank is always higher than all them little buildings in them towns"—where she will, as her skeptical hosts like to signify, "perform" one of her healings.

Harlan is like the irritatingly talkative passenger everyone dreads sitting next to on a long bus ride, who tells her story whether the listeners want to hear it or not. But her "confabulatory" tale proves so colorful and engaging that soon her audience is enraptured. Harlan indeed knows how to hook a listener in; while she reports that she became a healer once she found she could heal herself, Harlan doesn't say until the end of her tale how that happened. She also doesn't explain the nature of her particular hurt. *That* story comes only after the listener suffers her countless digressions and analyses about her bluesy relationship (which echoes the painful and complicated relationships Jones created in her former novels) with "Savage Joan the Darling Bitch," the rock star Harlan manages; her sometimes lover Josef Ehelich von Fremd, a rich and paranoid Afro-German, thoroughbred horse owner who hires former Central Intelligence Agency personnel and other shady figures to protect him and guard his Kentucky ranch; Norvelle, Harlan's former husband, who is a medical anthropologist conducting research in Africa; and Joan's former husband, with whom Harlan has a brief affair. She also spins out stories about her interactions with a host of other characters, including Harlan's mother and her grandmother Jaboti. Jaboti's confabulatory tale is that she had once been a Turtle Woman for a carnival, but she fell in love with a handsome young man, whom she followed until she turned into a human being. The listeners hear of Harlan's travels around the world and her assessment of the different peoples and cultures she encounters. Harlan is a far cry from Jones's earlier characters; her "problem" (if it can be called that) is not that she is unable to speak, but that she talks so much.

Through this "giddy outpouring of language" (as Valerie Sayers describes it), Gayl Jones puts to practice what she believes has been the trajectory of African American literature from the early twentieth century (beginning with Paul Laurence Dunbar): to free the African American voice from "the restrictive forms (inheritors of self-doubt, self-repudiation, and the minstrel tradition)" that are the consequence of Western culture's privileging of the written text over orality; in her 1991 volume of literary criticism, *Liberating Voices*, Jones argues that black writers have come to embrace their oral traditions and, in so doing, have come to create—precisely *through* the vernacular—whole, authentic, complex characters. "Oral tradition," Jones writes, "offers continuity of voice as well as its liberation."

Jones's critique of her earlier novels suggests that she did not go far enough to liberate the African American voice, that her choice of blues form, while certainly innovative and rich in its rendering of African American vernacular, nevertheless did not allow for the creation of whole, complex characters. And this lack, for Jones, has everything to do with the "range of subject matter." Thus, in *The Healing*, it is precisely the stuff of which Harlan converses that most clearly marks the novel's departure from Jones's earlier work. Without missing the beat of her storytelling, Harlan speaks with authority on topics ranging from Madonna to Pushkin; from "them neo-Fascists over there in Europe" to *National Geographic*; from flamenco to globalization:

> Sometimes the names of the towns themselves are painted on them tanks, you know, or the chief industry in the town sometimes uses them to advertise theyselves. The chief industry might be wine making or cigar making or coal mining or tractor manufacturing or maybe it's a cannery town, then the name of the town's leading employer is on that tank. Maybe that's free advertising for that employer, so's that employer'll stay in that little tank town and not take his business to Mexico or Korea.

In her rather maddening discussion of tanktowns, Harlan manages not only to critique the power many industries wield in small towns by virtue of their being the only source of employment for the people who live there: she also suggests industries' control of the labor force

438

GAYL JONES

through the threat of relocation to the cheaper Third World labor markets. Harlan is asserting, in other words, that the tank town is The Company's town, its residents The Company's oppressed subjects. Hence, the tanks bearing The Company's name are "always higher than all them little buildings in them towns"—including, we can surmise, the towns' government edifices.

Harlan, moreover, peppers her monologue with words and phrases from other languages, which include German, Spanish, and even Chinese:

"Joan say something to [the waiter] in Chinese and then order shrimp and fried rice in Chinese. I know that *ni hao*, that the only Chinese I know. And what's the other Chinese I picked up from Joan? *Ni shi neiguo ren*? That mean, Where do you come from? Seem like everybody need to know that in everybody language. And to ask them what they name? *Ni jiao shenmo minzi*?

Although Harlan claims that *ni hao* is the "only Chinese" she knows, she nevertheless goes on to recount other phrases, revealing that her knowledge of Chinese is perhaps more extensive than she lets on. And while one might be tempted to read Harlan as simply mimicking Joan (and Harlan certainly encourages us to make this assumption), the fact is that she *picked up* some Chinese from Joan and thus took command (though to a limited extent) of it herself. Indeed, it has become a part of *her* voice, her language.

Such is the case also with Standard English. That is, although Harlan does not talk in Standard English, she handles it easily, as we can see in her recollection of her initial encounter with Josef (whom she ventriloquizes):

During the war, the Second World War, being non-Aryans, we left Germany and settled in Zurich, in Switzerland. After the war, we returned to Berlin. I was born after the war and don't know all of that history, but I know we were exiles. But now we're treated like auslanders again, like foreigners, so that's why I

decided to come to America. . . . When I told some of my friends in Alexandria that I was coming to America, they all said that was their dream. My name is Josef Ehelich von Fremd. That sounds like a German name. Alexandria, ain't that in Morocco?

Harlan returns to the vernacular (signaled by the word "ain't") when she begins to speak in "her" own voice. But notice also how completely she renders Josef's story in Standard English, which not only gives us a sense of who Josef is and how he represents himself; but also reveals both Harlan's command of that form and her *preference* for the vernacular. The latter is, we must infer, her more authentic tongue, the one that conveys fully Harlan's sense of self as well as her worldview.

This play with Standard English is a critical move on Jones's part, for, as she argues in *Liberating Voices*, the vernacular has always been in Western literature "framed" by Standard English and thus presented as less serious, less artistic, as lacking "ingenuity or complex range." Orality, Jones writes, has been made to seem "more lightweight, a toy, rather than immediately valuable, an intricate jewel." Thus, in *The Healing*, Jones makes the vernacular the frame for Standard English, and in ways that not only call into question the latter's hegemony in written texts, but also reveal the vernacular as a powerful artistic form in its own right.

Some critics of *The Healing* have suggested that accepting Harlan as a credible and realistic character requires a suspension of belief on the part of the reader, or at least requires an assessment of Harlan as simply a good sponge who has absorbed fully the information given to her by others (namely Joan, who in addition to being a rock star is also a well-educated woman). After all, these critics seem to be asking, can we really attribute such intellectual and linguistic virtuosity to a beautician/rock star business manager/faith healer?

At the heart of this critique, of course, are not only good old-fashioned bourgeois assumptions about the working class, but also an unstated belief that, on the one hand, those who speak in the vernacular are necessarily intellec-

439

tually limited, and, on the other hand, that the vernacular is itself the language of intellectual lightweights. Jones ridicules this mindset, and precisely *because* a homegirl can be just as comfortable with the *National Enquirer* as she is with Nietzsche (Harlan had at one point audited a course on the philosopher). To think otherwise is to buy too easily into dominant cultural thinking about who qualifies as educated and intelligent and even about whose knowledge really matters.

Just as significantly, Jones also challenges the presumption that black people cannot speak with authority on any issues other than those considered "black"—a presumption that perhaps underlies some critics' skepticism about Harlan's authenticity. That she dares form an opinion about and speak of, for example, the rise of neofascism in Europe or Mexican *corridos* necessarily confronts widely held beliefs about what constitutes appropriate black political, social, and cultural discourse.

Mosquito

Jones drives these points home even further in her 1999 novel, *Mosquito*. In this work, Jones presents us with another character (Mosquito) whose intellectual and linguistic virtuosity is just as stunning—and ultimately as subversive—as Harlan's.

Harlan had actually introduced us to Mosquito early in her own story, at the moment when she musingly examines the front cover of a bus passenger's book. To Harlan, the cover seems to have on it a picture of "some kind of insect, a mosquito or something like that." And then she digresses: "I know about them African mosquitos. And them Caribbean mosquitos. I got me a friend nicknamed Mosquito, though she ain't named after none of them African or Caribbean mosquitos. Her real name Nadine. I don't call her Mosquito myself, I call her Nadine."

In fact, Mosquito's real name is Sojourner Jane Nadine Johnson, and she is an independent truck driver who gets involved in what she calls the modern-day Underground Railroad: the movement to provide a safe passage for illegal immigrants seeking sanctuary in the United States. Mosquito is virtually indistinguishable from Harlan; not only does she also discourse on everything from romance novels to Aztecs (since Mosquito's trucking route is the southwestern United States, she speaks often of Mexican and Native American culture and history), but she also slips in and out of different voices and languages. Moreover, she often uses the same turns of phrase, as, for example, when she peppers her sentences—like Harlan does—with the phrase "and shit": "They's [the border patrol] caught some of them smugglers, mostly Mexicans, which ain't to say it's only Mexicans doing that smuggling, ain't just smuggling people and drugs neither, but some of them's smuggling parrots and even cactus and shit." Like Harlan, Mosquito digresses interminably. In the instance just given, for example, Mosquito vacates the subject of the border patrol and begins a discourse on the different "exotic animals and plants and shit that's peculiar to Mexico. Delgadina roasted me some of them Mexican cactus. Taste pretty good with that salsa. Don't know if she roasted me one of them rare and exotic cactus, though, probably one of them ordinary cactus."

Delgadina, a Chicana bartender whose critiques of culture and politics Mosquito frequently asserts, is for all intents and purposes Mosquito's Joan the Darling Bitch. That is, just as Joan is a critical source of knowledge for Harlan, so also is Delgadina for Mosquito:

We's just a cosmic race. 'Cept nobody wants to identify with the African in the cosmos. That's how I read that multiracialism myself. Delgadina say them whites that's all for multiracialism just want to use the multirace as a buffer, you know. 'Cause somebody told them that in the next millennium the white people be the minority, so they wants as many people as they can to identify with them, rather than the other colored peoples. So now they's modifying they racial purity myth, 'cause it's in they best interest, so's they can coopt the multiracialists to play white. I ain't thought all that till after Delgadina start talking about it.

As frequently as Mosquito references Delgadina's viewpoints, however, she, like Harlan often does with Joan, undercuts any impulse we might have to read her as Delgadina's mimic:

> Delgadina she always be talking about that colonialism stuff and be calling us colonized and shit, be saying that women of color is colonized as women and people of color, where the gringa is only colonized as a woman.... Most of the time she be talking colonized I be colonizing me one of them Bud Lights or some of them pretzels or some of that salsa. *I know all about that colonization myself.* But Delgadina she see the world like that: who be colonizing whom. And she even talk about the colonized colonizers.... Of course when I said I'm gonna colonize one of them Bud Lights she be saying I don't understand that colonization, and I be saying she don't understand signification. (emphasis added)

Mosquito critiques Delgadina as one who, while knowledgeable, has a limited perception of the world, one that does not make room for a more complex and nuanced understanding of power. This understanding Mosquito subtly claims for herself; unlike Delgadina, she suggests, she attends to those shades of gray.

If there is any real difference between Jones's characterization of Harlan and Mosquito, it is that she makes the latter even more of a talker. *Mosquito* is 616 pages of the main character's unrelenting digressions and critiques, all of which effectively relegate "the story"—Mosquito's participation in the sanctuary movement—to the background. One could argue that the real story *is* Mosquito's telling of it. In other words, what matters, ultimately, is not so much what happens in the story, but what Mosquito says and how she conveys her opinions. What matters is the voice liberated, and our ability, as listeners, to recognize that this is precisely the work that orality can accomplish.

In *Liberating Voices*, Jones says of Miguel de Cervantes Saavedra, author of *Don Quijote*, that by "admitting Sancho as a main character speaking in his own voice," Cervantes is able to "admit experiences, free imagination, add new perceptions, and tell a whole story"—to do things, in other words, that are otherwise denied by the "rules" of "literary purists" and, indeed, the Western literary tradition. "Toward the end of the book," Jones writes, "when Don Quijote and Sancho exchange voices, reality and language, like the magical knight himself, become enchanted." By seeking to liberate the voice, by making orality the foundation of her art, Jones creates work that challenges and enchants us all at once.

Selected Bibliography

PRIMARY WORKS

FICTION

Corregidora. New York: Random House, 1975.
Eva's Man. New York: Random House, 1976.
White Rat: Short Stories. New York: Random House, 1977.
The Healing. Boston: Beacon Press, 1998.
Mosquito. Boston: Beacon Press, 1999.

DRAMA

"The Ancestor: A Street Play." *B(lacks) o(n) P(aper)*, no. 1:46–55 (1974).
Chile Woman. Shubert Playbook series, vol. 2, no. 5. New York: Shubert Foundation, 1974.
"Beyond Yourself (The Midnight Confession)—for Brother Ahh." *B(lacks) o(n) P(aper)*, no. 3:79–92 (1975).

POETRY

Song for Anninho. Detroit: Lotus Press, 1981.
The Hermit-Woman. Detroit: Lotus Press, 1983.
Xarque and Other Poems. Detroit: Lotus Press, 1985.

NONFICTION

"About My Work." In *Black Women Writers (1950–1980): A Critical Evaluation.* Edited by Mari Evans. Garden City, N.Y.: Anchor, 1984.
Liberating Voices: Oral Tradition in African American Literature. Cambridge, Mass.: Harvard University Press, 1991.

SECONDARY WORKS

BIOGRAPHICAL AND CRITICAL STUDIES

Athey, Stephanie. "Poisonous Roots and the New World Blues: Rereading Seventies Narration and Nation in

Alex Haley and Gayl Jones." *Narrative* 7, no. 2:169 (May 1999).

Basu, Biman. "Public and Private Discourses and the Black Female Subject: Gayl Jones' Eva's Man." *Callaloo* 19, no. 1:193–208 (Winter 1996).

Bell, Bernard W. "The Liberating Literary and African American Vernacular Voices of Gayl Jones." *Comparative Literature Studies* 36:247–58.

Byerman, Keith. "Black Vortex: The Gothic Structure of *Eva's Man.*" *MELUS* 7, no. 4:93–101 (1980).

———. "Intense Behaviors: The Use of the Grotesque in *The Bluest Eye* and *Eva's Man.*" *CLA Journal* 25:447–57 (1982).

Chambers, Veronica. "The Invisible Woman Reappears—Sort of." *Newsweek* February 16, 1998, p. 68.

Coser, Stelamaris. *Bridging the Americas: The Literature of Paule Marshall, Toni Morrison, and Gayl Jones.* Philadelphia: Temple University Press, 1995.

Dixon, Melvin. "Singing a Deep Song: Language as Evidence in the Novels of Gayl Jones." In *Black Women Writers (1950–1980): A Critical Evaluation.* Edited by Mari Evans. Garden City, N.Y.: Anchor, 1984.

Dubey, Madhu. "Gayl Jones and the Matrilineal Metaphor of Tradition." *Signs* 20, no. 2:245–67 (Winter 1995).

Gottfried, Amy S. "Angry Arts: Silence, Speech, and Song in Gayl Jones's *Corregidora.*" *African American Review* 28, no. 4:559–70 (Winter 1994).

Harris, Trudier. "A Spiritual Journey: Gayl Jones's *Song for Anninho.*" *Callaloo* 5:105–11 (October 1982).

Johnson, E. Patrick. "Wild Women Don't Get the Blues: A Blues Analysis of Gayl Jones' Eva's Man." *Obsidian II* 9, no. 1:26–46 (Spring 1994).

McDowell, Deborah. "The Whole Story." *Women's Review of Books* 16:10 (March 1999).

Pettis, Joyce. " 'She Sung Back in Return': Literary (Re)vision and Transformation in Gayl Jones's *Corregidora.*" *College English* 52, no. 7:787 (November 1990).

Sayers, Valerie. "Faith Healer." *New York Times Book Review,* May 19, 1998, p. 28.

Tate, Claudia C. "*Corregidora:* Ursa's Blues Medley." *Black American Literature Forum* 13:139–41 (1979).

Ward, Jerry W., Jr. "Escape from Trublem: The Fiction of Gayl Jones." *Callaloo* 5:95–04 (October 1982).

Wideman, John. "Frame and Dialect: The Evolution of the Black Voice in American Literature." *American Poetry Review* 5:34–37 (September–October 1976). (See pp. 35, 36.)

———. "Defining the Black Voice in Fiction." *Black American Literature Forum* 11:79–82 (1977).

Wilentz, Gay. "Gayl Jones's Oraliterary Explorations." *African American Review* 28, no. 1:141–45 (1994).

BIBLIOGRAPHIES

Weixlmann, Joe. "A Gayl Jones Bibliography." *Callaloo* 7:119–31 (Winter 1984).

Wilcox, Janelle. "The Reception and Reappraisal of Gayl Jones's Novels: An Annotated Bibliography of Reviews and Criticism." *Bulletin of Bibliography* 52, no. 2:113–20 (June 1995).

INTERVIEWS

Bell, Roseann P. "Gayl Jones Takes a Look at *Corregidora*—An Interview." In *Sturdy Black Bridges: Visions of Black Women in Literature.* Edited by Roseann P. Bell, Bettye J. Parker, and Beverly Guy-Sheftall. Garden City, N.Y.: Anchor, 1979.

Harper, Michael S. "Gayl Jones: An Interview." *Massachusetts Review* 18:692–715 (1977).

Rowell, Charles H. "An Interview with Gayl Jones." *Callaloo* 5:32–53 (October 1982).

Tate, Claudia C. "An Interview with Gayl Jones." *Black American Literature Forum* 13:142–148 (1979). Abridged version repr. in *Black Women Writers at Work* (New York: Continuum, 1983).

—The essay and bibliography have been revised for this edition by Alycee Lane.